Reading
and Learning from
Text

READING
AND LEARNING FROM
TEXT

Harry Singer
Dan Donlan

UNIVERSITY OF CALIFORNIA,
RIVERSIDE

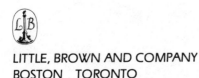

LITTLE, BROWN AND COMPANY
BOSTON   TORONTO

We dedicate this book to

Harriet, Deborah, and Abraham
and Carol, Kathleen, Ellen, and Michael

Library of Congress Catalog Card No. 79-92802

First Printing

*Published simultaneously in Canada
by Little, Brown & Company (Canada) Limited*

Printed in the United States of America

Preface

Today's secondary schools enroll students of widely varied attitudes, values, and abilities. Some students are active, independent learners; others are passive, dependent, even rebellious. Between the two extremes lies a range of individual differences that makes the classroom a challenge for teacher and administrator alike. A major part of the challenge is in meeting the range of ability and achievement in reading and learning from text. Our purpose in writing *Reading and Learning from Text* is to show teachers, administrators, and reading specialists how to develop and use strategies that will enable all students to read and learn in the content areas without stigmatizing any student.

Although we emphasize strategies at the high school level, teachers at the junior high school, and even at lower grade levels, could also apply these strategies. Indeed, this book is appropriate for teachers of any grade who want to teach their students how to read and learn from text.

Our text can be divided into four parts. The first part, chapters 1–3, explains the changing role of the school and the need for teachers and schools to shift from directing instruction at college-bound students to teaching subject-matter to all students.

The second part, chapters 4–9, describes single-text strategies that meet the wide range of individual differences in reading and learning from text. Since most schools have only one text available for content area classes, we focus first on strategies that will enable students to learn from single texts. We assume teachers will be applying these strategies as they learn them. Then, while teachers are having their students use single-text strategies, we present methods of teaching students to discuss in groups and to report to the class in a variety of ways, including in writing. These classroom processes prepare the way for multiple-text strategies.

The third part, chapters 10–14, starts with an explication of a blueprint for instruction used in both single- and multiple-text strategies. The blueprint explains how the teacher phases out and the students phase in in any strategy in reading and learning from text. Although the blueprint works out a year-long schedule, the phase-out/phase-in procedure can apply to any strategy over varying periods of time. We then explain the multiple-text strategies and apply them in a phase-out/phase-in sequence to the content areas of English, social studies, science, and mathematics. The strategies and the phase-out/phase-in are, of course, appropriate for any content area of the curriculum, including vocational subjects.

The fourth part, chapters 15 and 16, focuses on the complementary role of the reading and learning-from-text specialist as a member of the faculty. Chapter 15 explains how to classify and diagnose students with problems in reading and learning from text. Then we describe the types of reading laboratories or centers currently in operation in American education. We have provided enough detail for each of these types so that a school could use the description of each type to set up a duplicate, if it wanted to do so. We also provide a critique that questions the validity of each type. We recommend what we believe to be a better plan in Chapter 16, "The Future: A Schoolwide Program." This chapter details the roles of a reading and learning-from-text specialist in working in three types of programs in a school: (1) directing or teaching reading-acquisition classes using content-area materials; (2) cooperating with content-area teachers in developing introductory classes in reading and learning from text; and (3) advising content-area teachers on instruction in reading and learning from text. We have also provided competency-based outlines for these programs and an explanation of learning to read and learning from text.

Many people have participated in bringing this book into reality. We welcome the opportunity to express to them our appreciation. These teachers allowed us to observe in their classrooms and explained all aspects of their classes to us: Debbie Braden Merrill and Mary Bruce, Alessandro Junior High School, Moreno Valley, California; Ann Glaser, DeAnza Junior High School, Ontario, California; Caroline Ball, Kathleen Hall, and Fred Fleck, Ontario High School, Ontario, California; Alan Rhodes, Upland High School, Chaffey Union School District; Elaine Margaret Albert, Frisbee Junior High School, Colton, California. Rosie Russell and Betty Medved squired the text through our office. We are most grateful to Nancy Richards who with great equanimity deciphered our writing and transformed it all into a beautifully typed manuscript. We warmly thank the students and teachers in our classes at the University of California, who gave us valuable comments and enormous encouragement as they developed teaching units based on the ideas and strategies contained in this text. We also acknowledge the contributions to our text that resulted from the critical comments and kind commendations of our reviewers: James W. Beers, College of William and Mary; Mary M. Dupuis, The Pennsylvania State University; Allen Berger, University of Pittsburgh; and Karl D. Hesse, University of Oregon.

Finally, we owe a debt of gratitude to Mylan Jaixen, whose earnest, thoughtful, genial, and patient manner helped bring this text to fruition.

Harry Singer and Dan Donlan

Contents

4 | Single-Text Strategies 49

11 | English   259

12 | Social Studies   281

13 | Science   315

1 | Reading in the High School

CHAPTER OVERVIEW

Many students in today's classrooms cannot function because they can't seem to learn from the materials the teachers assign. Even students who have been "pulled out" for special reading instruction return to their content classes unable to understand their textbooks. These students may know the fundamentals of reading, but they can't apply their reading skills to gain information from their classroom texts. In others words, they have *learned to read*, but they can't quite *read to learn*. By the time you have finished this chapter you will (1) have a clearer understanding of the two phases of reading instruction — learning to read and learning from text, (2) learn how the high schools have traditionally handled reading instruction, and (3) discover the problems schools must solve in order to produce students who are independent readers and learners.

TECHNICAL VOCABULARY

Note: You will come across these words as you read the chapter. The words are defined in the glossary at the back of this book. They are also defined in context within this chapter.

text, texts
learning to read (reading acquisition)
reading to learn (learning from text)
developmental reading
deficiency

defect
disruption
difference
social promotion policy
convoy method

1

READING TO LEARN

Three Case Studies

Joe, Jo-Ann, and Jerry have a lot in common. First, they are products of a high school education. Second, they are venturing into the big world of college or work. Third, they are frustrated by their inability to function. Fourth, presumably literate, they are hampered by inadequate reading and learning skills. These three teenagers are not unlike many others who have "learned to read" yet can't make their reading work for them. In addition, large numbers of students can't function even in the classroom itself, let alone outside the classroom. Is the high school, then, failing those students it is dedicated to educate?

JOE. Joe graduated from high school with honors. His high grade point average earned him a scholarship to a local university. Once enrolled in classes, Joe became frustrated. The reading assignments were frequent and lengthy. The lectures supplemented rather than repeated the assigned reading material. Joe, accustomed to As and Bs, continually received Cs and Ds. No matter how long he labored over the books, his grades remained low. After his first semester, the university placed him on probation and his counselor recommended a remedial reading program or some tutorial assistance that would help Joe to comprehend college textbooks.

JO-ANN. Between her eleventh and senior year, Jo-Ann decided to seek a summer job. A newly opened department store was hiring part-time salesclerks. At the store's personnel office Jo-Ann was handed several forms to fill out in advance of an interview. The forms confused her. First of all, there were words she didn't understand: *residence, employment history, references, title of position, verification*. Second, she wasn't always sure whether she should be writing above or below the lines. Third, she filled in areas of the application form reserved for the interviewer. Fourth, when asked to describe her strengths and weaknesses she didn't know what to write. In frustration, she tore up the forms and left the store without an interview.

JERRY. Jerry had a part-time job at his uncle's gas station. He wanted to work into a full-time position after high school graduation. Only one aspect of the job bothered Jerry: he found using the parts catalogs tremendously difficult. Occasionally, Jerry's uncle, working on an engine, would send Jerry to a catalog to get information on parts. Jerry could never find anything. Finally, the uncle told Jerry that if he wanted a full-time job at the station he would have to learn how to use the catalogs.

Phases of Reading Development

High schools have long been providing instruction in the first phase of reading development: learning how to read (Smith, 1965a; Hill, 1971). But high schools have not been systematically teaching students to improve in the second phase of reading development: reading and learning from texts or textbooks in content areas.[1] Learning how to read is mastered by most students prior to the eighth grade, but reading to learn from text or any printed material of any length is an ability that continues to develop throughout a person's lifetime (Bloom, 1971; Cronbach, 1971).[2] Teachers in such content areas as English, social studies, science, and math contribute to both phases of reading development, but mostly to the second. They teach technical vocabulary and concepts, background information, patterns of writing, unique symbols, particular literary devices (allusions, similes, metaphors, personifications), and specialized modes of inquiry characteristic of their content areas (Russell and Fea, 1963; Smith, 1964a,b; Moore, 1969; Singer, 1973b; Robinson, 1975).

PREPARATION AND PROBLEMS OF CONTENT AREA TEACHERS

Most content area teachers have not been prepared by their education and training to know and apply instructional strategies designed to foster students' development in reading and learning from texts. The reason for this gap in professional preparation is that even now only nine states require prospective high school teachers to have had a course in reading instruction (Estes and Piercey, 1973). Consequently, not only beginning but also experienced teachers still have to acquire strategies for teaching the second phase of reading development in high school (Singer, 1973a).

In this book we stress classroom instructional strategies for content area teachers and an instructional blueprint for their use in each content area. This blueprint emphasizes a systematic progression from student dependence on teachers to independence in reading and learning from texts.

READING AND AMERICAN HIGH SCHOOLS: A BRIEF HISTORY

Past Solutions to the Range of Individual Differences in Reading

The wide range of individual differences in reading achievement among high school students is a major problem confronting all content area teachers who want to teach their students to read and learn from texts. In the past, four school practices were used to reduce this range: (1) Up to 1950 when the "100 percent" or *social promotion policy* went into effect

---

[1] The word *text* in the singular refers to any printed material of any length; the word *texts* in the plural refers specifically to text books.

[2] Complete references are located at the back of this book, beginning on page 00.

(Caswell and Foshay, 1950), students who did not achieve up to grade level often failed to be promoted to high school or dropped out of school. (2) Until recently when courts began to question the legality of tracking (see chapter 15), students who went on to high school were sectioned or tracked into low, average, and high ability or achievement groups. (3) Some reduction in the range of individual differences in reading achievement continues to occur in such academic subjects as foreign language, mathematics, science, and advanced English because students who are low in reading achievement avoid these subjects or are counseled not to enroll in these and other courses which have heavy and difficult reading assignments. (4) Some teachers still resist using teaching strategies that are appropriate to the different levels of reading abilities in their classes; they adopt a *convoy method* of classroom instruction which means they operate the class according to the level and rate of progress of their slowest or lowest achievers, students who are nonreaders. Instead of using a textbook, these teachers lecture or read to the entire class and do not give any reading assignments to the lower half of the class. Although these four strategies either reduce the range of reading achievement or avoid the problem, they do not produce homogeneous classes nor do they provide for equality of educational opportunity (Balow, 1962, 1964).

Moreover, reductionistic strategies tend to create additional problems: (1) Students who are not confronted with the problem of reading and learning from texts in content areas are less likely to improve in the specific content area or in general reading ability. (2) Sectioning or tracking students also creates another problem, perhaps more serious than the original problem. Students placed in the low track or in nonacademic programs tend to feel stigmatized and alienated from school. As these students have grown in number over the years, they have become increasingly difficult to manage. Indeed, alienation has been cited as a cause for violence and vandalism in schools. Although low reading achievement alone is not necessarily a cause of student rebelliousness, the school's way of responding to it could be a cause for alienation and its consequences.

At the other extreme of individual differences, students who are not challenged or who are paced too slowly are likely to become bored and react negatively; or, if put under too much competitive stress, they may withdraw or develop school anxiety.

Although the causes and effects of school strategies on student behavior are not easily discerned, there is little doubt that providing for individual differences and attainment of equality of educational opportunity have been growing problems in American schools.

Evolution of the American High School

The American high school has evolved dramatically in the last century from a selective institution with a narrow curriculum to an inclusive institution with broad, comprehensive curricula and a more heterogeneous student body. In 1880 fewer than 10 percent of the population in the age group from 14 to 17 were enrolled in high school. In 1980 close to 85 percent of that age group were enrolled. In 1880, students took a prescribed course of study with few electives; in 1980, students could select from numerous courses of study with a plethora of optional offerings. In 1880, the principal mode of instruction was lecture and the principal mode of learning was rote memory. In 1980, the teacher could supplement lectures with films, records, newspapers, magazines, transparencies, commercially prepared kits and packets; students could facilitate their own learning by engaging in discussion, problem solving, inquiry, and individualized, programmed instruction.

From 1880 to 1980, the high schools have been involved at various times in progressive education; life adjustment education, team teaching; flexible scheduling; differentiated staffing; a Great Depression (plus several small ones); two World Wars that were ''hot'' as well as many other conflicts classified as police actions or cold wars; the Civil Rights Movement; and the general social turmoil of the 1960s and 1970s. In effect, today's high school is the product of nearly a century of societal change.

As the schools evolved, so did reading instruction. Reading instruction in high school began during World War I in reaction to the high number of draftees who couldn't pass literacy tests (Hill, 1971). Classes in reading acquisition (learning how to read) have continued to be a permanent part of the high school program. By the 1940s and 1950s, the reading acquisition program in high schools was joined by *developmental reading,* a program that emphasized continuing instruction in reading from elementary school through high school for all students. From this movement grew the debatable notion that ''every teacher is a teacher of reading.''

In the 1960s federal funds subsidized countless high school reading labs to help build the so-called Great Society. In a survey of high school reading programs made between 1958 and 1968, most of the instruction was found to be focused on reading acquisition, not on learning from text (Early, 1969). But exceptional students who were mainstreamed, that is, returned to their regular classes after lab instruction, still could not read the textbooks assigned in content classes. Today, enlightened high schools are beginning to employ reading consultants for in-service education of faculty rather than solely as teachers of reading courses for students. All high school teachers are not teachers of reading; instead, they are content specialists who can help students to learn from texts.

PROSPECTS FOR THE FUTURE

Many high schools throughout the country have undergone a series of changes in the past three decades. The main difficulty is that the curriculum has remained fairly traditional whereas the student population for whom that curriculum was intended may no longer exist.

Components of the Curriculum

Generally, high schools, and many junior high schools, are departmentalized into areas of content — history, mathematics, English, and so on. Each content area is divided into segments and assigned to certain grade levels. The teacher's perceived function is, understandably, to make sure the content is absorbed by the student. When students come to class knowing how to read, write, and speak, the teacher's task is relatively easy. The teacher can become frustrated when students lack these skills: they may not be able to read the textbook independently, may not be able to discuss the course content in class, and may not be able to write reports or take examinations. As a result, students are labeled "deficient." In effect, these students enter class as predetermined failures.

The role of the teacher as dispenser of knowledge or content worked well while the population was more homogeneous, while not all students went to high school, and while the knowledge explosion and mass media had not yet threatened education. However, the current times demand that teachers do more than teach content, especially now since Public Law 94-142 requires that many exceptional children be mainstreamed, that is, returned to regular classrooms. Understandably, teachers feel pressured to cover the curriculum, even at the expense of student comprehension, but perhaps, as Alvin Toffler suggests in *Future Shock* (1970), students need to be taught processes for learning the expanding content and remembering it, rather than just remembering the content itself.

Need for a Focus

Solutions to the many problems facing today's high school will not come easily. Some problems with which education is expected to deal often lie outside the school's sphere — *de facto* segregation, busing, inflation, recession, unemployment, and intolerance. By graduation, a young person may have salable skills, read well, and communicate clearly in speech and writing, but still be unemployable because of social and economic conditions outside the school's control. In other words, Jerry could learn to use the parts catalogs but his uncle might not have the money to hire him. However, if education has taught Jerry to be an independent learner, he will at least be able to cope intelligently with the outside world. He will be able to learn new skills readily and convince prospective employers that he has something valuable to offer. Perhaps teaching students to be independent learners should be the focus of the school's curriculum so that students can adapt to a continually changing world (Buswell, 1956).

The Student as an Independent Learner

Whether you argue that school is preparation for life or a part of life, you might agree that educated people are independent: they can adjust, they can adapt, they can accommodate, they can cope, they can control their lives. The independent person, in effect, is always learning and altering behavior as a result of what is learned.

English teachers can teach students how to use language effectively and how to appreciate literature. Social studies teachers can show them how knowledge of the past helps individuals deal with the future. Mathematics teachers can demonstrate how people can cope with the world of measures and economics. Science teachers can explain the order of the universe and arouse curiosity to find out more. Physical education teachers indicate how people can be healthy. And the list goes on. Teachers use content as a means to develop independence. If students cannot comprehend the content or learn how to use it, they will not function independently. Hopefully, Joe, Jo-Ann, and Jerry can become independent learners.

Teaching Independence

All teachers want their students to be independent learners. What teacher, for example, would reject a class of students who complete every homework reading assignment and come prepared to discuss it the next day? The problem often is that teachers *expect* students to be independent learners before instruction begins. This assumption results in the students "covering" content without understanding it. In addition, many students function independently in one area of content, but not in another. For example, students who can read a novel or build an engine by reading a set of instructions can be deemed by science teachers to be nonreaders.

Every secondary school teacher is a content specialist. As a content specialist, the teacher is most knowledgeable in the thinking processes related to that content and the types of discussion and writing that students must perform to function well in that content area. No reading specialist can know mathematics, science, industrial arts, and history well enough to teach any student to read independently in all of those areas. No English teacher should be expected to teach students how to write science reports and social studies term papers. Likewise, no content teacher has time or experience enough to teach students reading acquisition skills or the basic fundamentals of sentence and paragraph construction. As a result, since 95 percent of the high school students can read, talk, and write minimally, the content teacher's responsibility is to show the student how to read specific content, how to talk about that content, and how to write about it. If students can process information independently, it matters less that they "cover the text."

Many schools have attempted to retrain their teachers to teach process as well as content. Institutions of teacher education offer preservice courses in content area reading. Articles in professional journals such as *Language Arts, English Journal, The Reading Teacher,* and *Journal of Reading* deal with the teaching of reading in different content areas. Professional organizations plan conferences that focus on the problems of teaching from text materials. School workshops train teachers in the use of specific strategies, such as DRA (Directed Reading Activity), SQ3R (survey, question, read, recite, review), and in the development of reading guides. Many times these efforts pay off with increased student motivation and performance. But too often, strategies are employed without a system, either a classroom system or a school-wide system.

The Need for a Structured Program

If schools decide to deal with the task of trying to teach all students to be independent learners, they must develop a comprehensive program. If a school's goal is student independence, then each teacher's classroom goal must be to promote student independence. Teachers must not relegate the responsibility of teaching textual reading to the reading teacher. Nor must teachers expect students to come to class fluent readers, proficient speakers, and competent writers. Furthermore, teachers must not expect all students to perform at the same level. Instead, teachers must be willing to offer guidance where needed, to individualize class assignments, and to know when to withdraw aid. In effect, an organized program for handling individual differences in the ability to read and learn from text must integrate a student's determination to learn independently, the teacher's instructional framework, and the administration's willingness to support this teacher-student effort.

The 4 Ds in Reading and Learning from Text

Actually, high schools need different strategies or programs for dealing with four types of difficulties that make up the range of individual differences in ability to read and learn from text. Special classes or reading laboratories for learning to read are necessary for some high school students. But these classes are not sufficient for meeting the instructional needs of high school students who have one of these types of difficulty in reading and learning from text: (1) Some of these students have a *deficiency* in reading; they are still unable to pronounce many of the words, general as well as technical, in their texts. The percentage of these students varies from school to school. Some schools, particularly schools with a large number of bilingual students, have a much higher percentage of students who are still in the acquisition phase of reading development. (2) A small percentage of these students may have physical or physiological *defects*, such as visual or auditory handicaps, which may interfere with ability to read. (3) A third group of these students, also relatively small, may experience *disruptions*, such as social or emotional disturbances, that adversely affect their ability to concentrate on reading and learning from text. (4) Most of these students are beyond the reading acquisition stage of development; they do not have any defects or any serious emotional disturbances; yet they may still have difficulties in reading and learning from texts in the content areas because their assigned texts do not match their ability. Some students read at the eighth-grade level but their texts are at the tenth-grade level in difficulty or higher. Or their reading abilities may be at the same level as the general difficulty level of the text but the students lack the specific ability to learn from the text in a particular content area; they may not have the specific skills for interpreting graphs or charts in social studies, comprehending symbols and manipulating them in chemistry, understanding irony and satire in English, or transforming and applying formulae in mathematics. These students do not have deficiencies, or defects, or disruptions; they have a *difference*, a mismatch between their abilities and the demands of their assigned texts (Wiener and Cromer, 1967; Samuels, 1970).

These four types of difficulties can be labeled the 4 Ds of reading difficulties. They cover the entire range of difficulties in reading and learning from text at the high school level. These difficulties with definitions, examples, suggested remedies, and high school programs for ameliorating them are summarized in table 1.1.

The classroom teacher's responsibility is to refer students with three of the four types of difficulties listed in table 1.1 to a reading specialist or a school counselor. The reading specialist should be called upon to diagnose students with deficiencies in reading, the first type, and to provide improvement programs for them that will help them read materials in their content area classes. (See chapter 16 for teaching reading acquisition using content area materials.) While the content area teachers will use strategies in the classroom that will help students with deficiencies (see chapter 4, "Single Text Strategies" and chapter 9, "Multiple Text Strategies"), these students need additional and more concentrated instruction in learning how to read than can be offered in a content area course.

Students with defects, the second type of difficulty, should also be referred to the reading specialist for screening and perhaps medical referral. But content area teachers and classmates can also help some of these students. Those who have hearing problems can be seated in the center of the room so they are equidistant from all sources of sounds and hence more likely to hear their classmates' recitations as well as their teacher's oral instruction. In the case of students with severe hearing difficulties, including deafness, classmates may volunteer to be buddies. The task of the buddy is to communicate missed information by repeating it orally during or after class, by providing the information in writing, or by shar-

TABLE 1.1. Four Types of Difficulties
in Reading and Learning from Texts

Type of Difficulty	Definition	Example	Remedy	Program
1. Deficiency	Inadequacy in skill development.	Inability to identify printed words.	Teach word recognition skills.	Reading acquisition classes.
2. Defect	Physical or physiological difficulty.	Visual difficulty, such as astigmatism.	Medical screening and referral to appropriate specialist or agency for correction.	Individual diagnosis and referral.
3. Disruption	Emotional interference in reading and learning.	Anxiety over inability to achieve in school.	Eliminate cause for disruption.	Individual diagnosis and referral to guidance or counseling staff.
4. Difference	Mismatch between instruction and student capability or mode of learning.	Texts in content area that are too difficult for some or most students.	Adjust instruction to individual students.	Classroom instruction strategies for handling individual differences.

ing notes; some buddies may even want to learn to communicate through sign language.

Students with the third type of difficulty, persistent emotional interferences in learning, should be referred to counselors for diagnosis and intervention. Concomitantly, classroom teachers (in consultation with the school counselor) can make appropriate classroom adjustments in order to relieve classroom stress upon these students.

For the fourth type of difficulty, differences, the classroom teacher has the main responsibility. The emphasis in this book is on helping the classroom teacher handle this type of difficulty by providing strategies that the classroom teacher can use to teach all students to read and learn from texts in the content areas.

We perceive that the differences difficulty is the greatest problem confronting classroom teachers at all grade levels and in all content areas. The magnitude of the problem is described and analyzed in chapter 3. However, solutions to the four types of difficulties listed in table 1.1 are not solely the responsibility of the classroom teacher; the entire high school staff has to be involved. To resolve the difficulties, the entire staff will need to have answers to the questions in the following section.

PROBLEMS TO SOLVE

To undertake a comprehensive program to teach reading and learning from texts, a high school staff will need to deal with specific problems:

1. What are the conflicting attitudes of content area teachers toward teaching students to learn from text?
2. How can teachers assess individual differences in achievement levels in the classroom?
3. What strategies are useful in teaching students to learn from text in each content area?
4. How might teachers use discussion and writing activities to facilitate students' response to text?
5. What sort of instructional framework can teachers develop to encourage students to become independent learners?
6. What particular instructional problems arise in individual content areas, and how must teachers deal with these problems?
7. How do schools currently teach students who are referred because of defects, deficiencies, disruptions, and low reading achievement?
8. How can students with deficiencies learn how to read in ways consistent with their content area courses?
9. How can administrators encourage development and maintenance of an all-school reading program?

The purpose of this book is to show teachers and administrators how to find answers to these questions. Chapters in this book deal with the nine problems in sequence.

Therefore, this book has value for the student teacher who will soon be joining a faculty, as well as for the seasoned teacher, reading specialist, department chairperson, or principal. In the book, we focus on explaining to teachers how to provide for equality of educational opportunity without stigmatizing students and how to encourage and educate secondary school students to become independent learners.

SUMMARY

Many of today's students are unable to learn from text, even though they have learned to read. Part of this problem is caused by the evolving nature of the school system and its curriculum. In effect, students are staying in school longer and are taking courses from a continually expanding curriculum. The result is that today's students have wider differences in ability and achievement than ever before. Schools need, then, to be sensitive to the problems students have in learning from their textbooks, specifically those problems caused by (1) deficiency, (2) defects, (3) disruption, and (4) differences. Teaching students to be independent learners is a school-wide responsibility. The process begins with changing attitudes.

ACTIVITIES

1. If possible, make a visit to the high school from which you graduated. Describe any changes you observe, focusing on:
   a. course offerings
   b. makeup of student body
   c. the physical plant
   d. special programs
   What do you attribute these changes to?
2. Interview a teacher who has taught at a high school for over twenty years. What changes have occurred at this school, as the teacher perceives them? How is the school dealing with these changes?

2 | Teachers' Attitudes

CHAPTER OVERVIEW

If a high school is to make a comprehensive attack on reading and learning problems, it must first focus on the attitudes that its teachers have concerning the teaching of reading and learning from texts. Many secondary school teachers, trained as content specialists, are hesitant to teach those reading and learning skills that help students comprehend their textbooks. In this chapter, you will examine the attitudes of certain teachers on the Monroe High School faculty. You will then see how these attitudes evolved, by studying a brief history of Monroe High's development. (As you read, compare Monroe High School with the high school you attended.) Finally, you will examine one specific method of measuring teachers' attitudes concerning teaching reading and learning from texts.

TECHNICAL VOCABULARY

attitude
reliable
mainstreaming

assumptive teaching
prescriptive teaching

TEACHERS' ATTITUDES IN ACTION

Why teach students to learn from texts? Perhaps the best way to answer this question is to let you observe a classroom and faculty lounge in action. This observation has been written in the form of a script for a play, entitled, "Making the Scene." Use your imagination to set the scene and then follow the dialogue.

Making the Scene
SCENE ONE. *An English classroom at Monroe High School. It is two minutes before the tardy bell rings. Mr. Inglish, the teacher, is standing nervously at the front of the room, watching the students enter the classroom, most of them in rather disorderly fashion — some pushing and shoving, some slinking, a few dropping books and papers at the doorway, some shouting to other students across the room and down the hall. As the tardy bell rings, Mr. Inglish finds himself answering questions from groups of students clustered around his desk: "I was absent yesterday. What was the homework assignment?" "I thought you wanted us to read Carl Sandburg. Joe said you assigned Walt Whitman. I couldn't find him in our textbook." "I couldn't understand the assignment. I thought it was dumb. Do we have to do it?" Mr. Inglish is desperately trying to free himself from the students clustered around his desk so that he can begin class. Finally, he nervously orders the students to their seats. He notes occasional gliders and wads of papers being passed and thrown around the room. He begins.*

Mr. Inglish: All right, I want you to quiet down. (*The students don't seem to hear him because it is too noisy.*) I said, I want you to quiet down. I am going to give you a quiz on last night's reading assignment. So will you please take out a sheet of paper, write your name in the right-hand corner, and number from one to ten down the red margin.
Joe: I didn't understand the homework assignment.
Jerry: Do I have to take this quiz? I wasn't here yesterday.
Mary: None of us were.
Phil: Do I get an F on this if I don't take it?
Chuck: Shut up, you guys. Mr. Inglish is getting mad.
Mr. Inglish: I believe I made last night's reading assignment very clear. Right before you left the classroom to go to third period, I said, "Read the poems of Carl Sandburg in your textbook."
Jo-Ann: Yes, but where do you find the poems? They're not all in the same place.
Jim: Yeah, who is this Carl Hamburg?
Phil: Sandburg, you dummy!
Mr. Inglish: First question! (*Groans from the class*) What does it mean to be a hog butcher of the world?
Mary: Hog butcher? What's that? What poem was that in?
Mr. Inglish: Quickly now, so that we can get on to the next question.
Joe: Would you repeat the question?
Mr. Inglish: Second question! What is the city that Sandburg writes most about?

(Time passes as the questions are read; the students groan. Finally, Mr. Inglish collects the papers and begins a discussion on the homework assignment.)

Mr. Inglish: You will notice that the assignment I gave you was to test your ingenuity in finding the poetry. As Jo-Ann noted, the poems are not in the same place. There were exactly four Sandburg poems in the book. One of them was on page 54, one of them on page 89, one on page 107, and the last one on page 143.

Barry: Why are we reading about Sandburg?

Ellen: That's what I want to know. He's so boring.

Mr. Inglish: He's one of this country's most distinguished poets.

Joe: Mr. Inglish, I found the poems by thumbing through the book, but I couldn't understand them when I tried to read them.

Jo-Ann: I used the index, but I still didn't like them. What do they mean?

Mr. Inglish: It seems to me that you need a little background, first on the nature of poetry, and second on the life of Carl Sandburg. Take out your notebooks. Please take notes while I talk to you about how to read a poem and how to understand the poetry of a man who has made an invaluable contribution to American literature.

(For the next twenty minutes, Mr. Inglish talks to the class about the nature of poetry and how a student should approach a poem differently from a short story. Then he starts a brief biography of Carl Sandburg and quotes lines from the four poems in the textbooks. Phil is yawning and drumming the desk as if he has heard the lecture before. Joe is doodling in his notebook. Jerry is squinting as if he is trying to understand. Jo-Ann is writing a letter to her boyfriend, who is in the navy. Other members of the class look as if they are taking notes. But one thing all the students have in common: their eyes are glazed and lifeless.)

Now that you have this background information, let's discuss the first poem "Chicago." Has anyone here been to Chicago? *(No students raise their hands.)* It's a beautiful city — lots of tall buildings. There's nothing in this town to equal it. I had a very scary experience one time when I flew to Chicago and the plane lost power over the airport. *(A few students begin to show signs of interest.)* But I don't want to get into that here. There's a picture of Chicago somewhere in the book. You might want to look at it after class. Is there anyone here who would like to read the poem aloud? Joe, why don't you? *(Joe begins to read and it is obvious that his problems with English prevent him from reading aloud effectively. Several students laugh, Mr. Inglish gets angry, and Joe becomes embarrassed but finishes the poem.)*

Ellen: I still don't understand the poem. Let's do some grammar.

Jim: Let's do English for a change. I'm tired of all this literature and stuff.

Mr. Inglish: (pained but persevering) For tonight's homework, I want you to reread all of Sandburg's poetry for a *test,* not a quiz, tomorrow. In addition, I'd like you to read all of the poetry of Emily Dickinson. Try to profit from last night's problems. There will be a quiz on her poetry tomorrow also. Now, you have one minute before the bell rings. Open your books and start reading. *(When Mr. Inglish said Emily Dickinson, one student said "She's neat." Mr. Inglish's pleasure was dimmed when he discovered that the "she" referred to a movie actress, not to Emily Dickinson.)*

(Curtain.)

SCENE TWO. *It is lunch time at Monroe High School. Mr. Inglish has just finished eating in the cafeteria and is proceeding in the direction of the faculty lounge. He enters, goes to the corner to draw a cup of coffee from the large urn.*

Mr. Harris: Well, how'd it go today, Inglish?

Mr. Inglish: Don't ask! I may just have had the worst morning of my professional life.

Ms. Stewart: What else is new?

Mr. Phelps: I never knew English teachers had any problems. You're supposed to be different from the rest of us.

Mr. Inglish: I gave those kids a homework assignment to read last night and you'd think by the response today that they don't know how to read.

Ms. Stewart: They don't, and that's because you guys in the English department don't teach them.

Mr. Inglish: Don't lay that on us. We have to teach them how to write and speak.

Mr. Phelps: Yeah, that's not fair. It's those elementary school teachers that don't teach them anything. They can't even locate the correct page numbers in their lab manuals.

Ms. Jones: Why should they? What's relevant about a lab manual?

Mr. Phelps: Social studies is relevant?

Ms. Jones: It's a matter of motivation. My kids can't read, so I tape all the chapters and have then listen to the tapes as they read.

Ms. Stewart: That may work for you, but what about algebra for my ninth graders? How can I tape math problems?

Mr. Inglish: I read aloud to them a lot. When I mentioned Carl Sandburg, one jerk said "Who's Carl Hamburg?" I'm sure those few bright kids in the class are really frustrated by the dummies — I mean, those kids who can learn but don't want to. I feel sorry for those kids who actually don't know how to read. Why have them all in the same class?

Ms. Stewart: Don't you remember, three years ago we made a push to return to ability grouping, but the young radicals on our campus claimed that would be stigmatizing kids, isn't that so, Ms. Jones?

Ms. Jones: You're darned right it's stigmatizing them. How would you like to be grouped in Building C with a group of low ability teachers?

Ms. Stewart: I'm grouped that way now!

(raucous laughter)

Mr. Phelps: It's just a simple matter. Don't let them out of elementary school until they can pass a reading test at the sixth-grade level.

Mr. Inglish: What if they can't? Do we hold them back? Do we continue to read to them? Do we kick them out? Do we show movies and play records five hours a day?

Mr. Harris: If our budget wasn't so overextended as it is, I would say to use different texts for different kids.

Mr. Phelps: That would be jolly! I've got all I can handle teaching out of one text, let alone thirty.

Ms. Jones: I still say it's motivation. Why should these kids learn to read? What's in it for them when they graduate?

Mr. Inglish: Are you saying that you can judge which kids will need reading and which ones won't? I'm glad I'm not in your classes.

Ms. Stewart: Well, we're not going to solve this problem, at least not today or even in my lifetime.

Mr. Inglish: So what do we do in the meantime?

(Curtain.)

Mr. Inglish has his own approach and attitudes towards instruction. Attitudes toward teaching vary considerably. Among members of a faculty, a range of attitudes towards any subject and instructional procedure is to be expected. Attitudes toward teaching have evolved as the high school itself has evolved.

Monroe High School is over one hundred years old. Mr. Inglish has been on the faculty for fifteen years; Ms. Stewart has been at Monroe for thirty-seven years; Ms. Jones for four years. Read now a brief history of Monroe High School to see how its development may have affected the attitudes of its teachers. As you read, compare Monroe with the high school from which you graduated or with a high school you've visited or are teaching at.

Monroe High School's Past

Monroe High School, located in the older section of Monroe, California, has a student population of 2156 students. The students represent a cross section of the city's population. Approximately 10 percent of the students are bused into school from the outlying rural areas. They are children of prominent ranchers and farmers who have owned land for several generations. Another 10 percent are black and walk or drive to school from a *de facto* segregated neighborhood that lies on the northwest corner of the high school's attendance area. From another *de facto* segregated neighborhood come first- and second-generation Mexican Americans, some bilingual, some speaking only Spanish, some speaking only barrio English. This group comprises about 15 percent of the school's population. Approximately 65 percent of the students are middle- and lower-middle-class white children. A few are children of professionals — doctors, lawyers, teachers — but most are the children of blue-collar workers or small business owners. Twenty-five percent of the students attending Monroe qualify for the free lunch program.

Time has brought many changes to Monroe High School. It was founded in 1875, shortly after the city had become incorporated. At that time, Monroe was a "one main street" community made up of small businessmen and a few professionals, but mainly farmers and ranchers. The community grew slowly. In 1925, the citizens of Monroe felt that a larger, more modern high school was in order; so one was built, farther away from the downtown area, closer to the pleasant tree-lined residential neighborhoods.

Monroe, California, underwent three dramatic growth spurts. World War II brought defense-supported industry to the quiet community. From 1941 to 1945, the population increased by 30 percent. Two new wings were added to Monroe High. More teachers were hired and more businesses opened. Old-timers soon discovered they didn't know everyone in town by first or even second names. Banks became less friendly about loans. PTA meetings became more formal. Vested interests saw the town's land developers and farmers taking sides in many conflicts. The ethnic nature began to change as black families, Mexican-American families, and, after the war, Japanese families moved into what were formerly all white neighborhoods, each group forming its own cultural community. In addition, scores of middle-westerners, sometimes crudely referred to as Okies, found employment in the once sleepy, rural town.

In 1946, Monroe High established its first reading class, remedial reading, taught by a junior member of the English department with no prior training in reading. In 1947, so many students were referred to this teacher that additional classes were created to satisfy the demand. In 1948, a course in speed reading was added. By 1950, Room 9 was designated "the reading lab" where five classes in "reading" were taught. Though the demand increased, no additional resources were added until 1968 when a grant of federal funds under Title I enabled the school to construct a building housing a reading communications center.

In 1953, two prominent packing houses opened up canneries to take advantage of the rich harvests in the area. More people moved to Monroe. A second high school was built to serve the outlying middle-class and upper-middle-class suburban neighborhoods that were expanding. Rivalries developed between the two high schools, both friendly and not so friendly. Teachers at Monroe were somewhat bitter over losing the "better" students to the other high school; yet they coped. Although Monroe sent fewer students to college than did the other high school, Monroe's students scored higher on entrance examinations and made higher grades once enrolled. This was due in part to an intricate tracking system that had been developed in the late 1940s. Students with IQs over 110 were placed in the A-track (college preparation). Those with IQ scores between 90 and 110 were placed into a B-track (community college). Students with scores between 70 and 89 were placed in a C-track (terminal education). The B-track was a watered down A-track, with a lower proportion of students taking algebra and chemistry and a higher proportion taking homemaking and industrial arts. C-track students were taught the so-called basic skills and enrolled in shop and home arts courses. If they didn't drop out of school, they graduated, married, went to work, or joined the military.

By 1964, a space industry located in Monroe, bringing with it increased opportunities for employment. Again the population increased sharply — a third high school was built and later a fourth. Government money was lavished on the schools in the early post-Sputnik years to improve the quality of scholarship in mathematics, science, and foreign languages and, in the late 1960s, to improve the learning environments for the disadvantaged. As a result of shifting population and urban sprawl, Monroe found itself with a majority of the town's disadvantaged students and received huge sums to build a reading and language lab for these students.

In April 1970, with inflation, public antipathy, and economic recession, Monroe experienced its first student demonstration. Fifty A-track students formed a picket line in front of the school's entrance to protest the dress and hair code. In May, the black students joined with the Mexican-American students to protest the discrimination of the tracking systems. The following October, a postgame dance was interrupted by a racial incident. In November, vandals entered the Title I reading lab and did damage amounting to $50,000. The faculty, confronted with confusion and strife, argued over whether the school's situation was a result of too much student freedom or too little. During the 1972–1973 school year, Monroe almost lost its accreditation because of its tracking system, its "insensitivity" to student needs, and its inability to deal properly with segments of the community that were demanding reform.

By fall of 1975, Monroe, in its centennial year, had abolished the tracking system and returned to open enrollment. Monroe's handful of university-bound students were bused across town for Latin, physics, and trigonometry. As one teacher commented: "In the thirty years I've been here at Monroe the quality of students has declined. There's no more respect for us or the school. They don't want to learn. Many *can't* learn. Why must we deal with them?" Echoing this teacher's sentiments is a Monroe High student: "I don't know what's happening around here. My father went to this school and got a great education. So did my aunt and uncle. Even my older brother got by here. But I'm not getting anything. The courses are aimed for the slow learners; many of these kids can't speak English. There's no discipline. How am I expected to get an education in this circus?" Another student comments: "The teachers, they don't care whether you learn anything or not. I can't read the books. They're dull. Even if I graduate, what do I know to make a living?" A school administrator offers an explanation: "The school, like the town, has undergone destructive changes. The town grew without a master plan. Schools were built with little concern for balancing the school population. For instance, the fourth high school we built has a student mean IQ of 109. Monroe's is 95. And even then we have widespread differences. Many of our students want to attend a two-year or four-year college or a university; yet while we are forced to structure watered-down college courses, the courses themselves aren't watered-down enough for most of the students in the classes. Our teachers often get the feeling that we're just putting in our time.''

On February 8, 1977, after a heated faculty meeting, a group of teachers, all department chairpeople, went to the principal with a proposal for an in-depth study of the school's problems: the curriculum; the attitudes of students, faculty, administrators, and community toward the school; and the school's physical and emotional environment. The principal approved the study, school-wide committees were formed, and the study was implemented. The results, presented at the May 1978 faculty meeting, showed the following: (1) the basic curriculum had not substantially changed since 1965; (2) students generally perceived school as not meeting their needs; (3) teachers were frustrated by lack of success; (4) administrators were alarmed at low student and faculty morale; (5) many students were graduating without knowing how to read, write, or perform mathematical operations.

Monroe High School's Future

Monroe High School is facing perhaps the worst crisis in its century-long history. How the administration, faculty, and students handle the crisis will affect the future of Monroe High School. If shortsighted, expedient solutions are sought, the school will undoubtedly remain in chaos and confusion. If, however, a comprehensive program of reform is implemented, the school's future will be brighter. Such a program might well begin with an examination of the varying attitudes of its teachers toward students and learning. Why, for instance, does Ms. Stewart distrust the "young radicals" on the faculty? Why does Ms. Jones value "relevance"? Why does Mr. Inglish continue to lecture about poetry appreciation? By examining differences in values and attitudes, a school may better understand itself and what it is trying to accomplish.

The principal of Monroe High School might want to begin attitude assessment with an instrument that focuses on reading instruction, since reading is at the core of the school's problems. The following section presents such an assessment instrument.

ASSESSING ATTITUDES TOWARD TEACHING READING

To prepare for reading this section, you can begin by determining your own *attitude* toward teaching reading. Follow the directions given in box 2.1 to complete the "Attitude Inventory Toward Teaching Reading in the

Content Areas'' (Otto and Smith, 1969). The items in the attitude inventory and results, based on this inventory, will be discussed in the subsequent sections of this chapter. By taking the attitude inventory yourself, you will not only become aware of your own attitudes, you will also be able to compare your attitudes with other teachers' responses.

BOX 2.1. Attitude Inventory Toward Teaching Reading
in the Content Area

Directions: Read the statement on the left. Then decide whether you strongly agree, agree, are undecided, disagree, or strongly disagree with the statement. Indicate your response by circling the number on the right under the appropriate column. (If you do not want to write in your book, number 1 to 14 on a separate piece of paper. Then copy down the number you would have circled. Thus, if you strongly disagree with the first statement, you would copy down "5" after the first statement because that is the number you would have circled. The numbers change. So look and copy down the correct number.)

	SA	A	U	D	SD
1. In the secondary school, the teaching of reading should be the responsibility of reading teachers only.	1	2	3	4	5
2. Secondary school teachers can teach reading effectively without special university courses in methods of teaching reading.	5	4	3	2	1
3. The teaching of reading skills can be incorporated into content area courses without interfering with the major objectives of these courses.	5	4	3	2	1
4. Any secondary school teacher who assigns reading should teach his or her students how to read what is assigned.	5	4	3	2	1
5. With rare exceptions, students should know what there is to know about reading before they are permitted to leave the elementary school.	1	2	3	4	5
6. Only remedial reading should be necessary in the secondary school and that should be done by remedial reading teachers in special classes.	1	2	3	4	5

7. Teaching reading is a technical process that secondary school teachers generally know nothing about.	1	2	3	4	5
8. Secondary school teachers cannot teach reading without special materials designed for that purpose.	1	2	3	4	5
9. Teaching reading is a necessary and legitimate part of teaching any content course in secondary school.	5	4	3	2	1
10. Teaching reading takes all the fun out of teaching at the secondary school level.	1	2	3	4	5
11. Every secondary school teacher should be a teacher of reading.	5	4	3	2	1
12. At the secondary school level students want to learn content, not how to read.	1	2	3	4	5
13. Integrating the teaching of reading with the teaching of specific content can be as exciting for the content teacher as teaching content only.	5	4	3	2	1
14. Content area teachers in the secondary school are probably more competent to teach the reading skills needed for their subjects than special reading teachers.	5	4	3	2	1

Key: SA — strongly agree; A — agree; U — undecided; D — disagree; SD — strongly disagree.

Scoring Your Attitude Inventory

To find your score on the attitude inventory, simply add the numbers you circled. The total is your score. Your score can be interpreted by comparing it with the scores derived from a sample of junior and senior high school teachers shown in table 2.1.

Otto and Smith, who obtained the scores from the junior and senior high school teachers, computed reliability coefficients of .80 for the junior high and .92 for the high school teachers on this inventory. These coefficients are high enough for groups at the junior high level and *reliable* enough for individuals at the high school level. These reliabilities indicate teachers are consistent in their attitudes on this scale. In short, if you filled out the scale again, you would probably circle the same numbers. Since the scale is reliable, it is worthwhile comparing your scores with the sample and interpreting your responses.

TABLE 2.1. Results of the Attitude Scale
for Teaching Reading in the Content Areas

	Junior High	*High School*
Size of sample	38	48
Range of scores	22 to 65	19 to 54
Average score	42	45

Interpreting Your Attitude Inventory

If you responded to each statement and followed the scoring directions correctly, you can compare your results with the sample of junior and senior high school teachers. You can ask yourself whether your score is within the range of scores of junior and senior high teachers and whether your score is above or below the average score. If you have a high score, your attitude is highly favorable toward teaching reading in content areas. If you have an intermediate score, you may agree that reading should be taught in junior and senior high school, but you yourself are not the person to do it. If you have a low score, then you think not only that you should not teach reading but also that reading should not be taught at all after elementary school. If you have an extremely low score, you may even resent the idea of students not being prepared well for junior or senior high school reading by teachers in lower grades. How do you think Mr. Inglish, Ms. Jones, and Ms. Stewart would score?

In general, junior high and senior high school teachers agreed on their responses to the scale. However, fewer junior high school teachers believed elementary students should know all there was to know about reading before they left elementary school (item 5) and more junior high teachers believed every teacher should be a teacher of reading (item 11). Apparently junior high teachers, perhaps because they are closer to elementary school, are more willing to be responsible for teaching students to read.

Look at the remaining items. On items 1, 6, 9, and 11, teachers generally disagreed that reading should be the responsibility of reading teachers only. But on item 2, teachers also generally disagreed that secondary teachers could teach reading effectively without further training. Apparently secondary teachers would like to teach reading, but believe special training is necessary to do so.

Secondary teachers think they can teach both reading and the content of the course without interfering with instructional objectives (item 3). Moreover, they agree a teacher who assigns reading should teach students how to read the assigned material (item 4). In addition, they believe that they know something about the teaching of reading (item 7), that they can teach reading without special materials (item 8), that teaching reading would not take the fun out of teaching content (items 10 and 13).

Despite their favorable and agreeable attitudes towards teaching reading, teachers are divided in their attitudes about whether students want both content and reading (item 12); and they believe the special reading teacher is more qualified than they are to teach reading in the content area even though the special reading teacher does not have competence in the content area (item 14).

ASSESSING ATTITUDES TOWARD LEARNING FROM TEXT

Now take the attitude inventory in box 2.2. This inventory is similar to the previous scale you took, but it does have an essential difference. Read each item carefully and record your response. Then, we will interpret your score.

BOX 2.2. Attitude Inventory Toward Teaching Students to Learn from Texts in the Content Areas

Directions: Read the statement on the left. Then decide whether you strongly agree, agree, are undecided, disagree, or strongly disagree with the statement. Indicate your response by circling the number on the right under the appropriate column.

	SA	A	U	D	SD
1. In the secondary school, teaching students to learn from texts should be the responsibility of reading teachers only.	1	2	3	4	5
2. Secondary school teachers can teach students to learn from texts effectively without special university courses in methods of teaching reading.	5	4	3	2	1
3. Teaching skills in learning from texts can be incorporated into content area courses without interfering with the major objectives of these courses.	5	4	3	2	1
4. Any secondary school teacher who assigns chapters in texts for students	5	4	3	2	1

should teach the students how to acquire information from these chapters.

5. With rare exceptions, students should know what there is to know about learning from texts before they are permitted to leave the elementary school.	1	2	3	4	5
6. Only remedial reading should be necessary in the secondary school and that should be done by remedial reading teachers in special classes.	1	2	3	4	5
7. Teaching students to learn from texts is a technical process that secondary school teachers generally know nothing about.	1	2	3	4	5
8. Secondary school teachers cannot teach students how to gain information from texts without special materials designed for that purpose.	1	2	3	4	5
9. Teaching students how to learn from texts is a necessary and legitimate part of teaching any content course in secondary school.	5	4	3	2	1
10. Teaching students how to gain information from texts takes all the fun out of teaching at the secondary school level.	1	2	3	4	5
11. Every secondary school teacher should teach students how to learn from texts.	5	4	3	2	1
12. At the secondary school level students want to learn content, not how to gain information from texts.	1	2	3	4	5
13. Integrating the teaching of learning from texts with the teaching of specific content can be as exciting for the content area teacher as teaching content only.	5	4	3	2	1
14. Content area teachers in the secondary school are probably more competent to teach the learning-from-text skills needed for their subjects than special reading teachers.	5	4	3	2	1

Key: SA — strongly agree; A — agree; U — undecided; D — disagree; SD — strongly disagree.

TABLE 2.2. Results of Attitude Scales for Teaching Students (a) Reading vs. (b) Learning from Text in the Content Areas

	Sample Size	Mean or Avg. Score
Elementary		
(a) Reading	24	48
(b) Learning from text	21	50
Secondary		
(a) Reading	50	44
(b) Learning from text	57	53

Scoring and Interpreting Your Attitude Inventory

Add up the circled numbers. If you are an elementary teacher, you are likely to find your score on this scale higher than your score on the previous scale; and if you are a secondary teacher, you are likely to have an even higher score. Is your score higher? Compare your score with the mean or average scores shown in table 2.2. If you are an elementary teacher and your score is above 50 or if you are a secondary teacher and your score is above 53, then you have a more favorable attitude towards teaching students to *learn from text* than the average elementary or secondary teacher.

Comparing Responses on Reading and Learning from Text Attitude Scales

To know what items teachers respond to more favorably, we can compare the distribution of responses to our two scales: (a) Reading and (b) Learning from Texts in the Content Areas. We shall compare our secondary teachers' results on each item by a statistical technique known as chi-square. This technique will indicate whether the teachers who filled out our attitude scales responded in significantly different ways to the items on the two scales. Look at the results in table 2.3. The items for each scale are listed in the table. (The underlined phrase in each item appeared in the scale in box 2.1. The phrase in parentheses in each item appeared in the scale in box 2.2.) The percent of responses to each item on each scale (Rdg = reading; LFT = learning from text) is shown next to each item.

The first item for the scale in table 2.3 is: "In the secondary school *the teaching of reading* should be the responsibility of reading teachers only." The line of figures next to item 1 that starts with *Rdg* shows that, of the secondary teachers who responded to this item, 2 percent strongly

TABLE 2.3. Attitudes of Secondary Teachers Toward Teaching Reading vs. Learning from Text, Tested by Chi-Square for Significance of Difference

		SA	A	U	D	SD	Significance
1. In the secondary school, *the teaching of reading* (teaching students to learn from text) should be the responsibility of reading teachers only.	Rdg:	2.0	10.0	14.0	28.0	44.0	ns
	LFT:	0.0	5.3	8.8	43.9	40.4	
2. Secondary teachers can teach *reading* (students to learn from text) effectively without special university courses in methods of teaching reading.	Rdg:	2.0	10.0	22.0	44.0	22.0	s
	LFT:	0.0	28.1	31.6	35.1	5.3	
3. *The teaching of reading skills* (teaching skills in learning from texts) can be incorporated into content area courses without interfering with the major objectives of these courses.	Rdg:	26.0	42.0	10.0	14.0	6.0	s
	LFT:	35.1	45.6	17.5	1.8	0.0	
4. Any secondary teacher who assigns *reading* (chapters in texts) should teach his or her students how to acquire information from this assignment.	Rdg:	22.0	48.0	8.0	14.0	8.0	s
	LFT:	59.6	21.1	10.5	8.8	0.0	
5. With rare exceptions, students should know what there is to know about *reading* (learning from texts) before they are permitted to leave the elementary school.	Rdg:	30.0	30.0	14.0	12.0	12.0	s
	LFT:	10.5	28.1	21.1	33.3	7.0	
6. Only remedial reading should be necessary in the secondary school and that should be done by remedial reading teachers and special teachers.	Rdg:	4.0	20.0	14.0	28.0	34.0	ns
	LFT:	1.8	14.0	19.3	36.8	28.1	
7. Teaching *reading* (students to learn from texts) is a technical process that secondary school teachers generally know nothing about.	Rdg:	8.0	26.0	34.0	26.0	6.0	ns
	LFT:	1.8	22.8	26.3	28.1	21.1	
8. Secondary school teachers cannot teach *reading* (students how to gain information from texts) without special materials designed for that purpose.	Rdg:	8.0	16.0	20.0	38.0	14.0	ns
	LFT:	0.0	10.5	15.8	50.9	22.8	

9. Teaching *reading* (how to learn from texts) is a necessary and legitimate part of teaching any content course in secondary school.

	SA	A	U	D	SD	
Rdg:	26.0	32.0	20.0	14.0	6.0	*s*
LFT:	45.6	45.6	1.8	7.0	0.0	

10. Teaching *reading* (students how to gain information from texts) takes all the fun out of teaching at the secondary school level.

	SA	A	U	D	SD	
Rdg:	0.0	6.0	22.0	36.0	34.0	*s*
LFT:	1.8	1.8	5.3	47.4	43.9	

11. Every secondary teacher should *be a teacher of reading* (teach students how to learn from texts).

	SA	A	U	D	SD	
Rdg:	12.0	22.0	20.0	22.0	22.0	*s*
LFT:	38.6	33.3	10.5	14.0	3.5	

12. At the secondary school level students want to learn content, not how to *read* (learn from texts).

	SA	A	U	D	SD	
Rdg:	6.0	26.0	18.0	40.0	4.0	*s*
LFT:	1.8	8.8	19.3	50.9	19.3	

13. Integrating the teaching of *reading* (learning from texts) with the teaching of specific content can be as exciting for the content area teacher as teaching content only.

	SA	A	U	D	SD	
Rdg:	18.0	30.0	32.0	10.0	4.0	ns
LFT:	28.1	40.4	28.1	1.8	0.0	

14. Content area teachers in the secondary school are probably more competent to teach the *reading* (learning from text) skills needed for their subjects than special reading teachers.

	SA	A	U	D	SD	
Rdg:	6.0	20.0	20.0	36.0	14.0	*s*
LFT:	12.3	38.6	28.1	19.3	1.8	

Key: SA—strongly agree, A—agree, U—undecided, D—disagree, SD—strongly disagree. Total percentages may be less than 100 because nonresponse percentages are not shown.

Source: Harry Singer, "Attitudes towards Reading and Learning from Text." In M. L. Kamil and A. J. Moe, eds., *Reading Research: Studies and Applications,* 28th Yearbook of the National Reading Conference. West Lafayette, Indiana: The National Reading Conference, 1979. Reprinted by permission.

agreed, 10 percent agreed, 14 percent were undecided, and 28 percent disagreed. What was your response to item 1 in the scale in box 2.1?

The first item's alternative states: "In the secondary school, *teaching students to learn from text* should be the responsibility of reading teachers only." As shown on the line next to item 1 starting with *LFT*, no secondary teacher who responded to this item strongly agreed, 5.3 percent agreed, 8.8 percent were undecided, 43.9 percent disagreed, and 40.4 percent strongly disagreed. What was your response to this item in the scale in box 2.2? Were you more or less favorable to this item when it used the term "learning from text" instead of "reading"?

On the extreme right side of table 2.3 a column is labeled "significance." Two symbols occur in this column. The symbol "ns" (nonsignificant) indicates only a chance difference occurred when responses on the two scales were compared. For example, the "ns" on item 1 indicates that this item, whether it included the words *the teaching of reading* or *teaching students to learn from text,* would not cause teachers to respond differently. In other words, we wouldn't expect teachers to change their attitudes on this item much when we shifted from *reading* to *learning from text.* Thus, on the issue of *responsibility* in item 1, secondary teachers do not differ, whether the wording is *reading* or *learning from text.* But on both scales they disagree with statements that such instruction should be the responsibility of reading teachers only.

Now, if you look down the "significance" column, you will find the symbol *s* beside item 2. An item with an *s* in the last column means that this item elicited significantly different responses when the word *reading* was replaced by the phrase *learning from text.*

On the second item, which focuses on *preparation,* secondary teachers tend to disagree that they can teach reading without special university courses. However, they tend to shift toward agreement that they are prepared to teach students to learn from text. But, even though a significant shift in attitude occurs, a high percent are still undecided or disagree that they can teach students to learn from text without having a special university course to prepare them for doing so.

The third item focuses on a *conflict in objectives:* teaching content *vs.* teaching skills for learning content. Secondary teachers would have less conflict in integrating skills involved with learning from text in content area classes than they would in incorporating the teaching of reading skills.

The fourth item, *assignment,* indicates that secondary teachers tend to agree that they assign *chapters in text* more than they do reading and that, although they should help students learn how to gain information from either assignment, significantly more of them agree that they should teach students how to gain information from assigned chapters in texts.

The fifth item is on *proficiency standards.* Significantly more secondary teachers agree that students should have mastered reading before being allowed to graduate from elementary school, but they disagree that students should know what they need to know about learning from text when they graduate from elementary school. Apparently, secondary teachers recognize that it is normal for high school students to have to acquire skills they need to learn from texts.

Item 6 concerns *remedial reading.* Both scales had the identical statements. The difference in responses on the two scales, as expected, was not significantly different. Secondary teachers disagree that only remedial reading should be necessary in high school and that it should be the responsibility of remedial reading teachers.

Item 7 emphasizes that teaching reading or learning from text is a *technical process.* Although teachers do not differ on this item, they tend to disagree more that they know nothing about teaching students to learn from text than they do about teaching reading.

Item 8 deals with *materials* for teaching. Although the difference is noι significant, secondary teachers disagree more that they need special materials for teaching students to learn from text than they do for teaching reading.

On *legitimacy*, item 9, both scales elicit a favorable reaction, but significantly more teachers agree that teaching students to learn from text is a necessary part of teaching any content course in secondary school.

On *enjoyment* in teaching, item 10, teachers disagree that teaching reading or learning from text takes all the fun out of teaching.

On *slogan*, item 11, secondary teachers agree that every secondary teacher should teach students to learn from text, but disagree that they should be teachers of reading.

On *student objectives*, item 12, secondary teachers indicate their feelings about students wanting to learn content rather than reading skills or skills to gain information from text. But more teachers disagree with the statement that students want to learn content rather than how to gain information from text.

On *integration* of skills, teaching (reading or learning from text) with content, item 13, teachers agree that this integration can be as exciting for the content teacher as teaching content alone.

On Item 14, *competence* in teaching reading or learning from text: secondary teachers feel they are significantly more competent than special reading teachers to teach students skills for learning from text (as contrasted with teaching reading skills) for their subjects.

Thus, the phrase *learning from text* elicits a significantly more favorable attitude on nine of the fourteen items. On the other five, the difference is not statistically significant when *learning from text* is used in place of *reading*, but all five of these items on both scales elicit favorable responses toward teaching the skills of learning from text or reading (Singer, 1978b).

Why do we get more favorable attitudes when we substitute the phrase *learning from text* for *reading* in these scales? The answer comes from the definition of the term *reading*. Secondary teachers define *reading* as "learning how to read," something that is taught in the primary grades. They do not see such instruction as their main task. What they do perceive is that their task is to teach students how to learn from text. Hence, they respond much more favorably to this idea. Indeed, in preservice and in-service courses, as well as throughout this text, we shall emphasize the second phase of reading, "learning from text." We shall also show how such instruction can be accomplished in heterogeneous groups of students, which have recently been made even more heterogeneous with the passage of PL 94-142, the Education for All Handicapped Children Act. This act has led to the return of some handicapped children, including low-achieving students, from special education to regular education classes for at least part of the day. This procedure is known among teachers as "mainstreaming."

BASIS FOR TEACHER ATTITUDES

Because elementary teachers prepare to teach all subjects, including reading, they experience no conflict between their preparation, expectations, and attitudes towards instructional requirements in elementary school. Indeed, elementary teachers enjoy teaching students how to read and observing their development in reading throughout the elementary grades. First graders are highly specific in their abilities in reading. Mostly they know only those words and skills they have been taught. But gradually elementary students generalize and integrate their abilities and skills, achieving some convergence by grade three (Guthrie, 1973). By that time, if they do well on one skill such as word recognition, they tend to perform about as well in another skill such as use of syntax or semantics for anticipating words. They are also able to pronounce words that have not been directly taught (Gates, 1961) because they can apply their skills in use of syntax and semantics plus skills in word recognition to identify new words. By the sixth grade, most students have integrated their language abilities (syntactic, semantic, and phonological) with their well-developed responses to graphic stimuli. At this point in their reading development, they are adding more words to their vocabulary from reading than from listening (Armstrong, 1953). But they still need help in pronouncing words, particularly in placing accent or stress and in identifying words borrowed from other languages. For example, without help in pronunciation some students might erroneously say ep′ ə tōm for i pit′ ə mē when they read the word *epitome*.

While elementary teachers succeed in teaching most students how to read, they do not prepare students well for the reading and study skill requirements of junior high school (Spache and Spache, 1969). Indeed, in the intermediate grades, teachers may still teach some students how to read, but they usually do not give instruction on reading in the content areas. That is, they usually do not teach students how to learn from texts in social studies, science, mathematics, literature, and other content areas. If students know how to read, teachers in the intermediate grades as well as those in junior high and high school presume students can read in all content areas. Hence, *assumptive* rather than *prescriptive* teaching becomes the rule in reading assignments for students. That is, as students progress through the grades, they are assigned chapters or books to read without any instruction on how to read the chapters or books (Herber, 1970).

Teachers may engage in assumptive teaching because they have not been taught how to teach reading in content areas nor how to teach students to learn from texts. Consequently, it is possible to observe a class in the intermediate grades during the reading period reading books that are appropriate to their widely divergent reading levels; but during social studies, science, or math period, the students are all reading out of the *same* text without any instruction in how to read or learn from the text. As in junior or senior high school, intermediate grade teachers tend to focus only on the content of the text.

When confronted with the discrepancy between what they know about the range of individual differences in the reading abilities of their students and the reading difficulty of assigned texts, intermediate grade teachers defensively complain they have only one text for teaching a particular subject. But when materials became available for teaching reading in the content areas, such as *The Harper and Row Basic Reading Program: How to Read in the Subject Matter Areas, Strand II* (O'Donnell and Cooper, 1963), and even when these materials are state-adopted and present in the classroom, teachers do not use them, perhaps for the reason cited by junior high and high school teachers: they have not been trained in how to use such materials. Thus, intermediate grade teachers, as well as junior and senior high school teachers, have to learn how to teach students to learn from texts and how to use various strategies for meeting the wide range of individual differences in reading ability.

Teachers in junior and senior high schools largely prepare to teach the subject matter of their major field. In fact, in 1973 only nine states required prospective secondary school teachers to take a course in reading (Estes and Piercey, 1973; Freed, 1973), even though organized reading instruction began in high schools as early as the 1920s when the public became aware of reading deficiencies in World War I recruits. Since junior or senior high school teachers do not prepare to teach reading, they do not identify with the processes of instruction involved in reading, do not feel competent to teach reading, and believe that reading instruction, although necessary, should be taught by a reading specialist, even in their own content areas!

Thus, Otto and Smith's findings from use of the attitude inventories are not surprising. But experts, including Otto and Smith, formerly believed secondary teachers had to be persuaded to take responsibility for teaching reading in their content areas. Perhaps the experts were talking about beginning rather than experienced teachers. If the attitudes found by Otto and Smith can be generalized, then secondary teachers appear to be somewhat willing to add reading instruction to their teaching skills, particularly after they have had experience in teaching in high school and have become familiar with problems of teaching, especially with the problem posed by the wide range of individual differences in reading achievement.

However, as we have explained using the results reported in table 2.3, secondary teachers are more confident teaching students to *learn from text* and are more willing to provide such instruction. We think that, when they acquire the single- and multiple-text strategies presented in this text, they will be even more confident and more willing.

CONCLUSION

Whether your high school is like or unlike Monroe High, one fact is clear: high schools are pressured to change as society changes. Today, more students receive a high school education than ever before. As a result, student bodies are more widely varied than ever (in ability, achievement, and culture), as we will see in the next chapter. Yet schools often fail to deal with these increasing differences. As a result, both teachers and students become dissatisfied, even frustrated. Since the ultimate goal of education is to produce independent learners, it is each teacher's responsibility to train students to comprehend the text material assigned in class. However, some teachers don't perceive teaching comprehension as their responsibility; other teachers feel inadequate to handle the task. Consequently, high school teachers desiring change must first deal with the disparate attitudes of other faculty members. They can start by investigating and revealing to the faculty the range of individual differences in general reading achievement that exists within each class. In the next chapter, we will explain how large this range is and how it can be measured.

SUMMARY

Two scales for assessing teacher's attitudes were used to show that junior and senior high school teachers have a more favorable attitude towards teaching students to *learn from text* than towards teaching students to *read*. The reason for this discrepancy is that teaching *reading* can be defined as an instructional procedure for elementary school while teaching students to *learn from text* is consistent with high school instruction. Consequently, when the phrase *learning from text* or *teaching students to learn from text* is used as an aspect of a teacher's role, teachers are likely to respond more favorably. They are also more likely to (1) determine the range of individual differences in their students' abilities to learn from text and (2) acquire the strategies and skills for teaching students to learn from texts in the content areas.

ACTIVITIES

1. Compare your scores on the two attitude scales in this chapter with the scores of other students in your class. Discuss the reasons for any differences on each item.
2. Interview an experienced teacher to find out how this teacher responds to the items on the attitude scales.

3 | Individual Differences Among Students

CHAPTER OVERVIEW

Within a given classroom, differences in learning abilities among students are large. Even before Public Law 94-142 mandated mainstreaming certain exceptional children into "regular" classrooms, a teacher could expect an ability span equal to two-thirds the average chronological age of the students enrolled in a class. In a tenth grade history class, for example, where the average chronological age is 15 years, there will be at least a ten-year span of achievement, perhaps from fifth grade to college level. After you read this chapter, you will see why a teacher cannot assume all students are alike.

TECHNICAL VOCABULARY

individual differences
reading acquisition
learning from text
reading age
standardized test

reading range
expected reading range
mastery level
survey test

A TENTH-GRADE HISTORY CLASS AT MONROE HIGH

Ms. Jones wasn't looking forward to teaching her third period tenth-grade, world history class. From her experience, she realized that fifteen-year-olds tend to be difficult to motivate. First of all, there would be a wide range of individual differences in ability. In last year's class there were students who were reading five years below grade level as well as students reading four years above grade level. This year's class would include several mainstreamed students, increasing last year's ability span. Second, the adopted textbook was written at the eleventh-grade level, so many of the students in class would not be able to comprehend the textbook. During the first week of class, Ms. Jones received scores on reading tests from the counseling office. The data that Ms. Jones received are compiled in table 3.1. Ms. Jones used the data to construct the histogram shown in figure 3.1.

TABLE 3.1. Reading Achievement Scores for Ms. Jones's Class

Student	Reading Grade-Equivalent Scores
Adams, Jane	8.3
Anderson, Bob	12.7
Baker, Fred	5.1
Blotski, Barb	7.2
Carrington, Iris	4.1
Clutzton, Dan	9.3
Davis, Roy	6.4
Dixon, Tabby	13.9
Ebbing, Sasha	9.0
Farthing, Ray	14.5
Fremont, Tony	10.2
Groutinski, Lou	7.1
Hirostad, Myra	11.4
Ibert, Margie	8.0
Jackson, Phil	10.3
Kato, Umeko	11.8
Logan, Mary	2.9
Lysert, Roger	7.3
Mathens, Carter	16.9
Morgan, Rose	9.8
Parker, Joe	9.4
Quodas, Xlicis	—
Romero, Marta	11.3
Smith, Sammy	10.1
Thomas, Tommie	12.3
Victa, Lota	3.3
Young, Iola	8.9

FIGURE 3.1. Histogram of Reading Grade-Equivalent Scores in Ms. Jones's Class.

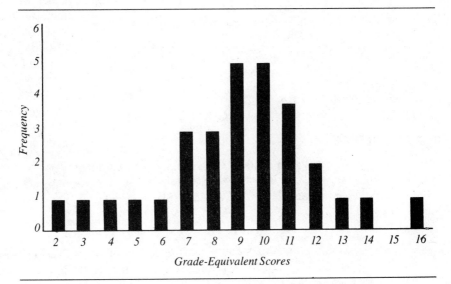

Note that in tallying grade-equivalent scores, Ms. Jones dropped the decimal point; for example, she counted 8.9 as 8. She then constructed a bar graph to indicate the number of students who had scores at the same grade-equivalent levels. She could then answer the following questions by simply looking at her bar graph:

1. What is the range of reading achievement in this class? (*Answer:* Grade-equivalent 2 to 16, a total of 14 grades.)
2. What are the two most frequently occurring reading grade equivalent scores? (*Answer:* Grades 9 and 10.)
3. If Ms. Jones has an opportunity to adopt a new text for her class, what grade level of reading difficulty should the text have? (*Answer:* If the text has a reading grade difficulty of 9 to 10, then Ms. Jones would have the least difficulty in adapting the text to all the students in her class. Do you agree with this answer?)
4. If Ms. Jones uses the text with the eleventh-grade reading level, but did not adapt it to the students in the class, which students do you think would give Ms. Jones the most problems in the areas of (1) discipline, (2) attitude, and (3) achievement. Why? What can Ms. Jones do to eliminate or reduce the problems?

Ms. Jones should be aware that there are two overlapping phases of reading development: (1) the *reading acquisition* phase (learning how to read) and (2) the *learning-from-text* phase. Her students at the low end of the range are in the reading acquisition phase while those at the upper end are in the learning-from-text phase. Students in the middle range are in-between, with some who are on the verge of mastering the first phase and others who have recently achieved the *mastery level*. The next section explains these two phases of reading development.

INDIVIDUAL DIFFERENCES IN LEARNING TO READ AND LEARNING FROM TEXT

Learning to Read

1. Learning to read consists of an integration of two processes. The first process is use of language abilities, such as syntax and semantics, for anticipating words. Consider this sentence:

The car raced down the _____.

Syntax leads to the expectation of a noun after the noun determiner *the*. The context of the sentence suggests that the noun will be a word such as *hill, highway, street, road, freeway, avenue, track*.

2. The second process consists of the acquisition and application of letter-to-sound relationships. Students have to learn to relate letters, letter combinations, and words to the sounds they stand for. Hence, if the reader can use language abilities for anticipating words and can relate letters or groups of letters to the sounds they represent, the combination can drastically delimit choices in word identification and can facilitate the process of reading. For example, when the initial consonant is added to the following sentence, the choices for the missing word are limited to one or two words that begin with the sound of *h:*

The car raced down the h_____.

Readers already have well-developed language abilities when they enter school. They do not have to learn oral language; but they do have to learn how to use their language abilities in reading. Of course, if they do not speak the language used in the school, special arrangements will have to be made for them. The acquisition of print-to-sound relationships takes time because these relationships are complex. However, the number of print-to-sound relationships that have to be learned is finite or limited.

About 95 percent of students can learn to read (Bloom, 1971); indeed, many students master the process of reading before they reach the sixth, seventh, or eighth grades. Learning how to read is the first phase of reading development. The range of individual differences in this phase of reading decreases as a group of students progress through school and master the processes involved in learning how to read.

Learning from Text

The second phase of reading development overlaps the first phase and involves the ability to comprehend, or learn from text. Readers learn from text by using their general information, their knowledge of sequences of events, their semantic and conceptual abilities, and their reasoning capacities to interact with information gleaned from the text (Winograd, 1972; Rumelhart, 1976; Schank and Abelson, 1977; Singer, 1977; Anderson et al., 1977). For example, a reader sees the sentence: "The cigarette caused the forest fire" (Kintsch, 1974). The text of the sentence provides some information while the reader brings to the text other information: the meanings of the words, general knowledge, and especially the sequence of events that probably occurred (the cigarette had been lit and then, perhaps, thrown on dry tinder). Indeed, the reader can even construct a scenario of imagined events that depict a cigarette causing a forest fire. Thus, a reader and a text interact to produce new knowledge that may get stored in the reader's long-term memory. We refer to this entire process as *learning from text*. The processes and contents of thinking which underlie a person's ability to learn from text develop most rapidly while a person is in school. Moreover, the contents of thinking (including semantic and conceptual, as well as knowledge about the world) continue to increase throughout a person's lifetime. Hence, the ability to learn from text improves as a person matures. Since the processes and contents of thinking are part of a person's general mental ability, then the capacity to learn from text increases at a rate that correlates with the development of general mental ability (Singer, 1974, 1977).

Thus, reading development consists of two overlapping phases: (1) learning to read and (2) learning from text. Learning to read is mastered by most students prior to eighth grade. However, learning from text is an open-ended process that is never mastered, but continues to develop throughout life as a person gains new information, vocabulary, concepts, and general knowledge of the world in various content areas.

Since increases in general reading achievement or ability to learn from text are correlated with general mental ability, and since the range of individual differences in general mental ability increases as a group of students progress through school, we can expect that the range of general reading achievement will increase from grade to grade. Indeed the range of individual differences in a class does increase as students progress through the grades.

INCREASE IN RANGE OF READING ACHIEVEMENT ACROSS THE GRADES

Students vary in reading achievement as early as the first grade. Durkin (1964) found that one percent of beginning first graders are already able to read at a grade equivalent of 2.3 (second grade, third month). At the other extreme are children who, when tested on a reading readiness test, did not know the names of any letters of the alphabet. In lessons taught as part of a reading readiness test, these same children did not learn sounds for any letters. Nor could they learn even one of the ten sight words taught as part of the same reading readiness test (Murphy and Durrell, 1965).

If we follow the same group of students through school, we will find that the junior high school teacher reports a wider range of reading achievement than the elementary teacher reported for the same class. The high school teacher confronts an even greater *reading range* in this class. For evidence of this rate of increase, look at the graph in figure 3.2. It shows the actual reading comprehension scores of students in grades 2 through 8. The scores are reported in age-equivalent terms. If a student has an age-equivalent score of 10, it means that the student, regardless of his or her *actual* age or grade, has a reading comprehension score equal to the score earned by an average 10-year-old student. In other words, the student has a *reading age* of 10.

Find *Grade 2* on the left side of the graph. You will see the reading ages range from a reading comprehension age of 5.5 to 10.0, a difference of 4.5 years. Notice, as you go up the grades, that the range increases. At grade 5, the range is from 8.0 to 15.5, a difference of 7.5 years. At grade 8, the difference has increased to 10 years. In other words, at the eighth-grade level, the lowest achieving student has a reading comprehension age equal to that of an average nine-year-old (a fourth-grade student) while the highest reading achiever in the eighth grade comprehends as well as the average nineteen-year-old — the reading achievement score of an average student one year after graduation from high school! Thus, the range of reading achievement in any class is very wide, at least as wide as the mental-age range of the group.

Shown below is a formula for computing the *expected reading range* in a class where student IQs range from 67 to 133.

Expected reading age range = ⅔ × average chronological age of the group

The range in reading achievement for a tenth-grade class, which includes all, or a representative sample of, the students in the tenth grade and which has an average chronological age of 15, is shown below.

Expected reading age range = ⅔ × 15 = 10 years

Since the average reading age in the tenth grade is 15, the reading range would vary from 10 to 20 years. Half of the 10 year range would be added to the average of 15 and half would be subtracted from this average age.

Knowing the expected range of reading achievement in their classes, teachers are not likely to believe that all students should be reading up to grade level or that they should try to keep any student from going beyond

FIGURE 3.2. Measured Range of Reading Comprehension Ages in Grades 2 Through 8

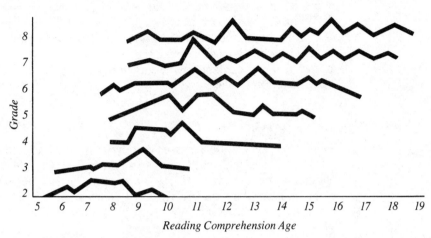

Reprinted from E.F. Lindquist, ed., *Educational Measurement* (Washington, D.C.: American Council on Education, 1951), p. 13. Used by permission.

grade level in achievement. Instead the ideal goal for teachers at successive grade levels would be to increase the range of reading achievement. Why? Because the mental-age range for a group increases each year, and we assume that students should be attaining reading-achievement levels equal to their mental-age levels. Nor should junior high or high school teachers complain that elementary teachers should have done a better job of teaching reading, if in fact the group fits the expected range in reading achievement. Teachers at each level have to accept the fact that the range in reading achievement increases as students progress through the grades and learn to teach all students within this normal, expected range. Even if students are divided into ability levels, or into achievement groups, or placed into tracks, there would still be a range of reading achievement in each group (Cook, 1951; Balow, 1962) and this range is even likely to increase as a result of downward and upward adaptations of the curriculum (Balow, 1964). Since homogeneous groups, in which all students are alike do not exist, teachers can expect classes made up of students with a wide range of individual differences in reading achievement. Each teacher should determine the range of reading achievement in his or her class.

DETERMINING THE RANGE OF INDIVIDUAL DIFFERENCES
IN GENERAL READING ABILITY

To determine a class or a school's range of individual differences in general reading ability, teachers can administer a *survey test*. An annotated list of survey tests is given in box 3.1. Survey tests usually assess reading comprehension, speed, and vocabulary. The Gates-MacGinitie Reading Tests are typical. We shall use the Gates-MacGinitie as an example of a survey test and explain how it can be employed for determining range of individual differences.

Comprehension

The Gates-MacGinitie assesses comprehension by a multiple-choice type of cloze test.[1] Each paragraph has two key words omitted. Below the paragraph are two rows of five words, one row of choices for each key word omitted. The student reads the paragraph and underlines the one word in each row to indicate his or her choice of one of the missing key words in the paragraph. See the sample paragraph in box 3.2.

BOX 3.1. Some Widely Used Survey Tests
of Reading Achievement in Junior and Senior High School

Gates-MacGinitie Reading Tests, Surveys E, Grades 7–9, and F, Grades 10–12.
 Published by Teachers College Press, Columbia University, 1970. The test has
 three subscales: speed and accuracy, vocabulary, and comprehension. Test time:
 46 minutes. A reliable and well-constructed test. Uses a multiple choice type of
 technique for assessing comprehension.
Metropolitan Reading Achievement Test, Advanced Form, Grades 7–9. Published
 by Harcourt Brace Jovanovich, 1970. Measures vocabulary and comprehension.
 Test time: 46 minutes. Well-constructed test.
Nelson-Denny Reading Test, Grades 9–16. Published by Houghton Mifflin, 1973.

---

[1] The cloze type of comprehension test deletes words from a passage that is usually about 250 words long. In the traditional form of the test, every fifth word is deleted. A reader then tries to infer from the meaning and the syntax of the passage what the missing words are and retrieve them from their vocabulary storage. See chapter 10 ("Determining Reading and Readability Levels") for an example of a cloze test. The Gates-MacGinitie modifies the task by deleting only key words in a short paragraph and providing readers with a multiple choice of words for the necessary key words.

Comprehension can also be assessed in other ways. See Gibson and Levin (1975) and Singer and Rhodes (1976). At the high school level, the intercorrelations among these various ways of assessing comprehension are high.

Tests rate vocabulary and comprehension. Test time: 40 minutes. Mostly suitable for college prep students.

Nelson Reading Test, Grades 3–9. Published by Houghton Mifflin, 1962. Measures vocabulary and comprehension. Test time: 30 minutes. Inadequate data on reliability and test construction.

Sequential Tests of Education Progress (STEP), *Series II: Reading, Grades 4–14.* Published by Educational Testing Service, 1969. Measures only comprehension. Contents include a wide range of material: directions, announcements, newspapers and magazine articles, letters, stories, poetry, and plays.

Stanford Achievement Tests, Grades 7–12. Published by Harcourt Brace Jovanovich, 1966. Measures mostly literal and factual comprehension. Reliable and well-constructed test.

For a comprehensive review of tests, see O. K. Buros *The Seventh Mental Measurements Yearbook, Volume II.* (Highland Park, New Jersey: Gryphon Press, 1972). For a summary of tests, see Nancy A. Mavrogenes, Carol K. Winkley, Earl Hanson, and Richard T. Vacca, "Concise guide to standardized secondary and college reading tests." *Journal of Reading,* vol. 18, no. 1, October 1974, pp. 12–22.

BOX 3.2. Sample Comprehension Paragraph
from the Gates-MacGinitie Reading Test

Directions: Draw a line under the best word in Rows C1 and C2 for each of the blanks.

The Weather Bureau gives each hurricane a girl's name. Each year the first ____C1____ is given a name that begins with A, such as ____C2____

C1. month   hurricane   name   Bureau   start

C2. Mary   Betsy   Linda   Susan   Alice

The comprehension paragraphs are arrayed from easy to difficult. As students progress through the test, they find that they have more and more difficulty in filling in the missing blanks. Eventually, the students stop because they realize they have reached their limit in reading achievement or else they run out of time. Some students may find that the entire test is too difficult and do not answer any of the items correctly. Others guess at answers and get only a chance score.   ↑PROBLEMS w/

The Gates-MacGinitie Reading Test, like any survey test, ~~spans a wide~~ TEST; ~~range of reading achievement. Yet a test standardized for a particular grade level may be too difficult for some students and too easy for others.~~

Students who score at the "bottom" of the test (zero or close to zero items correct) should be retested on a test standardized for a lower grade level, while those students who score at the "top" of the test (all or almost all items correct) should be retested on a *standardized test* for the next higher grade level.

Another problem with survey tests is that students who are slow readers may nevertheless be powerful readers. These students may, in fact, be superior in reading comprehension, but time limits on the test prevent them from obtaining a high score in comprehension. Two criteria can be used to detect this type of reader: (1) All or almost all items attempted on the comprehension test are correct, and usually at least 50 percent of the items have been attempted. (2) On a speed of reading test, this type of reader may score in the bottom half of the group. Consequently, a speed of reading test has an important function in diagnosing reading.

Speed of Reading

Students have a variety of reading rates, depending on their purpose in reading and the difficulty of the material (Holmes and Singer, 1966). Hence, the speed of reading assessed by the Gates-MacGinitie Reading Test is only one type of speed of reading.

The Gates-MacGinitie determines speed of reading by having the student read relatively easy paragraphs of uniform difficulty. After each paragraph, students answer a simple question. Hence, this speed of reading subtest might be called a rate of comprehension test for relatively easy material. See the sample paragraph in box 3.3.

BOX 3.3. Sample Paragraph from Speed of Reading Subtest of Gates-MacGinitie Reading Tests, Form F

Directions: Read the paragraph. Under the paragraph are four words. Draw a line under one of the four words that best answers the question asked in the paragraph.

In the far north, a frozen river winds between two high mountains. It does not melt even in summer. A river like this is found only in places that are

mild   hot   cold   sunny

Students who have mastered the first phase of reading development can get all the paragraphs correct on the speed of reading subtest, if given enough time. But time for reading and responding to the thirty-six paragraphs in the test is drastically limited to only 4 minutes. Indeed, the time limit was set low so that no student would be able to read and respond to all the paragraphs. Consequently, results on the test will show the range of individual differences in speed of reading.

The results on both the speed and comprehension subtests may indicate that a student is a slow but powerful reader or that the student is a slow reader who has not yet mastered the initial phase of reading. The vocabulary subtest of the Gates-MacGinitie Reading Test helps to differentiate these two types of readers.

Vocabulary

The vocabulary subtest consists of items in which a key word is followed by a multiple choice of five words. The student's task is to select the synonym closest in meaning to the key word. The list of fifty items of the vocabulary subtest starts with relatively easy, commonly used words; gradually the words become less common and more difficult. See the sample item from the vocabulary subtest in box 3.4.

BOX 3.4. Sample Item from Vocabulary Subtest
of Gates-MacGinitie Reading Tests, Form F

Directions: Read the first word, "rush." Then draw a line under one of the five words that means most nearly the same.

> *rush*
>
> back
> grab
> grow
> hurry
> spend

Copyright © 1969 Teachers College, Columbia University. Reprinted by permission of Houghton Mifflin Co.

Interpreting the Results

If a student gets a relatively high score in vocabulary and a low score in comprehension and speed of reading, the student is a slow reader, but he or she may be a powerful reader if given adequate time to read. However, a student who scores low on all three tests is likely to be in the initial phase of reading development, that is, still learning how to read.

The distribution of survey test scores reveals the magnitude of the class's range of individual differences. The teacher's task, if he or she is to provide for equality of educational opportunity, is to adopt strategies that will handle this range of individual differences. Ideally, this will be done without stigmatizing students, yet all students will have the opportunity to develop towards their level of capability and towards independence in reading and learning from texts. Strategies in the next chapter and throughout this text are aimed at helping teachers achieve these objectives, not only in general reading ability, but also in learning from texts in each content area.

SUMMARY

Reading development consists of two overlapping phases: (1) learning how to read and (2) learning from text.

Learning how to read (reading acquisition) can be mastered by most students. Indeed, many students master the process of learning how to read prior to eighth grade. Individual differences in this first phase of reading development consequently *decrease* as a group of students progresses through the grades. But, even though students have mastered the process of reading, they will still have to learn how to pronounce and read technical terms, symbols, and other features of text peculiar to each content area.

Learning from text is a process that is highly correlated with general mental ability. In progressing through school, students increase their ability to learn from text as they acquire new information, vocabulary, and concepts; as they improve in their reasoning abilities; and as they learn modes of thinking that are characteristic of each content area. This improvement is related not only to learning and instruction in the content areas, but also to mental age which increases from grade to grade. Therefore, ability to learn from text, as indicated by a survey test of general comprehension, also *increases* as students progress through school. Hence, the major task of teachers shifts from teaching students how to read towards teaching them how to learn from texts in the content areas.

This chapter also explained how a teacher can determine the range of individual differences in general reading achievement. Three parts of a survey test, the Gates-MacGinitie, were described and a sample item from each part of the test was provided, along with some directions for administering and interpreting the results of the test.

Knowledge of the range of general reading achievement (an index of ability to learn from text) will make a teacher appreciate the necessity of developing strategies to meet this wide range of individual differences in his or her class. The next chapter will describe these strategies.

ACTIVITIES

1. If you are teaching or assisting in a classroom, construct a frequency distribution of the results of a reading achievement test. To do so, use the graph in figure 3.3. Simply write all the test scores on the horizontal axis. Then, in the box below each test score, write the number of students who earned that score. Next, draw bars above the scores to show the frequency (the number of students) who earned a particular score. Compare the results with the data shown in the graphs in figures 3.1, and 3.2. Does your class show more or less variability than is shown on these two graphs?

2. If you teach a public school class, give a norm-referenced test for your grade at the beginning of the year. At the end of the year, give the same test to all students. Analyze results for: (1) the total class and (2) only those students who scored between the 25th and the 75th percentile at the beginning of the year, and (3) those students who scored above the 75th percentile and below the 25th percentile. Plot the percentile gains for individual students and for the class means. Which students have gained? Which students have not? What would you recommend for students in either category?

FIGURE 3.3. Frequency Distribution Graph for Results of a Reading Achievement Test

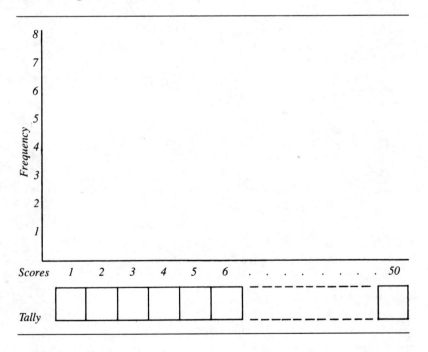

4 | Single-Text Strategies

CHAPTER OVERVIEW

Most secondary school classrooms are populated by students with a wide range of individual differences. A tenth-grade history class may be expected to have a ten-year range in learning ability. Yet these same students may have to learn history from the same textbook. This chapter will discuss ways of teaching students of varying abilities to learn from the same text. After you read this chapter, you should understand and be able to apply four specific *single-text* strategies.

TECHNICAL VOCABULARY

strategy
directed reading activity (DRA)
unstructured assignment
glosses
guides
reading guides
overview guide
vocabulary guide

processes-of-reading guide
learning-from-text guide
SQ3R
active comprehension
preposed questions
postposed questions
adjunct questions
cross-ability teaching

MISMATCH BETWEEN LEVELS OF STUDENT
ABILITY AND TEXT DIFFICULTY

If you recall Mr. Inglish's ill-fated discussion of Carl Sandburg's poetry in chapter 2, you will remember that most of the students were having a problem reading and understanding the text. Although some high school students suffer from a defect, deficiency, or disruption that interferes with their ability to read and learn from text, the major problem at the high school level is the difference between content area texts and the wide range in reading achievement. Even if a text fits the average reader in a class, a mismatch occurs between the text and at least half of the students in the class.

To prevent this mismatch, or at least reduce its interference with student achievement, teachers can effectively employ single-text *strategies* that are suitable for the normal range of ten to twelve years in reading achievement levels that exist in high school classes. A single-text strategy consists of modifying or supplementing a text or teaching students ways of processing information that will enable them to read and learn from a particular textbook. Although some teachers are fortunate to have multiple texts at their disposal (multiple-text strategies will be discussed in chapter 9), most teachers face the problem of making one text appropriate for students with wide-ranging abilities. In this chapter, four single-text strategies will be defined and explained with clear examples of classroom materials: DRA (directed reading activity), glosses, reading guides, and SQ3R.

1. DIRECTED READING ACTIVITY (DRA)

A basic technique for teaching a class how to read and learn from text is the directed reading activity (DRA). This technique involves an instructional dialogue between teacher and students as they read a selection together. We shall start our explanation of the technique by illustrating what may occur when a teacher gives an *unstructured assignment.* ("Read this passage and get the ideas from it. Tomorrow we will discuss the ideas.") Then we will contrast this kind of assignment with a highly structured dialogue between instructor and students in which the students are not only taught to comprehend a passage thoroughly, but are also led from teacher-directed to self-directed thinking by switching from answering teacher-formulated questions to asking their own questions and then reading to answer them.

In discussing both unstructured and structured assignments we shall use the same relatively easy sixth-grade level passage. In the unstructured exercise in box 4.1 the students are to count the ideas in the passage as an indication of how many they are likely to remember if they were given an assignment to read and remember the ideas in the selection for a discussion later.

BOX 4.1.

Unstructured Exercise in Reading a Paragraph. Read this paragraph and count the number of ideas in it. Write down the number as soon as you finish counting.

My husband and I wanted to make a moving picture of savages, and Martin finally decided on Malekula, second largest of the New Hebrides Islands in the Southwest Pacific. We left Sydney, Australia, on a small ship. Soon a storm of warning broke around us.

Osa Johnson, "Filming a Cannibal Chief." In *Reading Skill Builder, Level VI, Part I,* edited by Guy Wagner, Gladys Person, and Lillian Wilcox. Pleasantville, N.Y.: Readers' Digest, 1950.

When given to a large group of students, the number of ideas counted in the paragraph usually ranges from three to more than fifteen. Those students who count only three ideas cannot understand how some students can get more than fifteen out of this paragraph; while the students who get more than fifteen cannot understand how the other students could have overlooked so many ideas. The reason in both cases is that the term *idea* was not defined. Left up to the students, *idea* is defined broadly by some and narrowly by others. The result is that the broad definers end up with few ideas and the narrow definers get many ideas.

This unstructured exercise is tantamount to what may occur when students are told merely to read a chapter and be prepared to discuss it the next day. Without being told how to read the chapter, some students merely skim it, getting the general idea; others may get the central thought of the chapter with some supporting details; a few students may read the chapter analytically, as though they were going to be examined in detail on the entire chapter; and some students won't even take the book home! The result is that when the teacher conducts a discussion the next day, student contributions vary considerably. This range of variation reflects the way in which students defined for themselves how they were to read the chapter.

In marked contrast to the unstructured assignment is the directed reading activity (Herber, 1970; Burmeister, 1974). Instead of merely assigning the chapter and presuming students will know how to read it or will read it in the way the teacher would want it read, the teacher takes students through the chapter and teaches them how to read it, as shown in the steps below. After using this method with several chapters, the teacher can determine whether students have learned how to use it by asking them to read the next chapter in the same way. After various reading strategies have been taught to students, the teacher can then be more precise and, in assigning a chapter, specify whether it is to be skimmed (read only for the central idea and supporting evidence) or analyzed in detail. Observation of student participation after the chapter has been read will give the teacher some evidence of whether students have learned how a chapter should be read.

Steps in the Directed Reading Activity

STEP 1: DETERMINING BACKGROUND. Students frequently have experiences they can relate to the chapter. The teacher can elicit these experiences and have them communicated during vocabulary instruction. This information will augment the meaning of the vocabulary and provide the basis for formulations of questions.

STEP 2: BUILDING BACKGROUND. The teacher explains the technical terms in the chapter. To identify them, the teacher either skims through the chapter or searches the index to find them. If the teacher has reordered the entire index by page number, then the technical terms could be organized and grouped by chapters. Thus, they would be readily available for vocabulary instruction.

Teachers frequently assume students, particularly bright students, do not need vocabulary development. Although it is true that brighter students are further advanced in vocabulary than average or less-than-average students, they still need to develop their vocabulary, especially their technical vocabulary. Indeed, all students need to learn technical vocabulary in each content area. If they do, their comprehension in content area is likely to improve. In fact, research evidence indicates that vocabulary is the single best predictor of reading comprehension at all grade levels (Holmes and Singer, 1966; Singer, 1964).

STEP 3: PREQUESTIONING AND READING. Teacher-formulated questions can stimulate and direct student thinking and serve as a model of the kinds of questions that are appropriate for the content and processes involved in a particular content area.

As students learn to ask appropriate questions in a given content area, teachers can gradually stop asking questions and begin eliciting student-formulated questions. Students can then read to answer their own questions. Teachers will thus be taking students from dependent and teacher-directed thinking to independent and self-directed thinking in reading. This process, which we refer to as *active comprehension*, consists of asking questions throughout the chapter or text, not only at the beginning. In general, it is a kind of dialogue between the student and the text, with the student asking questions and the text "answering" them.

One way to get students to formulate their own questions is to ask a question which gets a question in return. After students have read the title and first paragraph of a chapter, the teacher can ask, "What would you like to know about this chapter?" As the class progresses through the chapter, the teacher can ask such questions as, "What would you like to know next?" Or the teacher can call attention to subheadings and ask students to formulate questions about these subheadings. Then students can read *actively* to answer their own questions. In this way, students will learn a *process of reading* as they progress through the chapter.

STEP 4: REVIEW ACTIVELY. At the end of the chapter, the class can review, not just by recalling the contents of the chapter, but by going over questions they themselves asked during their reading of the chapter. Then they can test themselves by trying to answer these questions again. If necessary, they can reread the chapter to resolve disputed issues. Or they can consult other reference works and texts to find answers to questions not answered in the chapter.

STEP 5: EXTENSION. After students have reviewed the chapter, they may do further reading or engage in individual or group projects related to what they've read.

A Sample DRA

A highly structured example for teaching the DRA technique with active comprehension (DRA-AC) is presented below. It is based on the same passage used to illustrate the unstructured assignment. Only part of the DRA-AC steps are used in the example.

Filming a Cannibal Chief

My husband and I wanted to make a moving picture of savages, and Martin finally decided on Malekula, second largest of the New Hebrides Islands in the Southwest Pacific. We started from Sydney, Australia, on a small ship. Soon a storm of warning broke around us.[1]

STEPS 1 AND 2 COMBINED. In using the DRA-AC strategy the teacher might do this: Ask students to skim the paragraph to find words they cannot pronounce or define. Usually they ask for the pronunciation of *Malekula* and *New Hebrides*. The teacher can then invite anyone who knows anything about the islands to present the information to the class.

The teacher-student dialogue continues, as shown below. Note that the teacher asks questions which get student *questions*, not answers, as responses. However, the teacher could switch to a question that gets an

[1] Osa Johnson, "Filming a Cannibal Chief." In *Reading Skill Builder, Level VI, Part I*, edited by Guy Wagner, Gladys Person, and Lillian Wilcox. Pleasantville, N.Y.: Readers' Digest, 1950.

answer as a response. We have shown this switch in the dialogue below as a *teacher response* that reflects questions back to the group. Thus, the teacher can lead students to ask and answer their own questions.

> *Teacher question:* What does the size of the ship make you wonder about the trip?
>
> *Student questions:* Why were they going in a small ship? How small was the small ship? Why didn't the author describe the ship?
>
> *Teacher response:* Who wants to give an answer to this question? (*Teacher calls on several students, in turn, to answer.*)
>
> *Teacher question:* Look at the last sentence. What questions pop into your mind as you read that sentence?
>
> *Student questions:* What is a storm of warning? What kind of danger are they about to encounter? Will they survive? What was the warning? Did they still go ahead with the trip?
>
> *Teacher response:* Read on to get answers to your own questions.

STEP 3. Motivated by their own questions, students could go ahead on their own, rapidly reading the story to answer their own questions. In the process, they also answer other questions. As they reach answers to their questions, they have a positive feeling, tantamount to saying, "That's an answer to my question!"

STEP 4. When the class finishes reading the entire story from which the example was taken, the students can review their questions and answers. Through this process, students can learn to be active readers and apply the process to all of their reading, not just to the opening paragraph, as in the above example. This process contrasts with alternative processes — the initial survey of the SQ3R technique (Robinson, 1961) and turning titles, headings, and subheadings into questions (Smith, 1973). Although Robinson's and Smith's processes are helpful for learning from text, they are static because they teach students to ask questions only at the beginning of a passage or only at the beginning of a section. In contrast, *active comprehension* is dynamic because it is a *continuous* question-and-answer dialogue between the reader and the text (Singer, 1973b, 1978a).

What effect do questions have upon student achievement? Although extensive research has been conducted on teacher questions, only recently has some evidence been developed on student-formulated questions.

Research on the Effect of Questioning

Questions inserted into the text are called *adjunct questions*. Questions placed *before* a passage are called *preposed questions;* questions placed *after* a passage are called *postposed questions*. Preposed questions enable students to learn and retain answers to the specific questions asked before or during the passage (Rothkopf, 1966). However, postposed questions help students learn and retain not only answers to the postposed questions but also additional information (Rothkopf, 1966; Frase, 1967, 1968a, 1969b). Rothkopf and Bisbiscos (1967) believe that questions placed at the end of a section in a passage lead students to be more attentive and to read more carefully the materials following the questions. But Watts and Anderson (1971) think that the postposed questions lead to review of the passage; that is, when students come to the questions at the end of a section in a passage they mentally review what they have read. In the process, they answer not only the questions that have been asked but also recall additional information. The process of recalling the information helps students learn and retain the target information — the information that answers postposed questions — as well as the additional information, even though the additional information is not used to answer any postposed questions.

Caution has to be exercised in use of adjunct questions. They tend to narrow students' focus of attention, particularly when only preposed questions are given. Even postposed questions can narrow students' attention if students are given time to review. For then they read the questions at the end of an assignment and use these questions in reviewing the assignment as though they were preposed questions; they reread only to answer the questions (Heller, 1974).

In summary, preposed questions help students select and retain answers to the specific questions asked. Hence, the teacher who wants students to gain only specific information from a reading assignment should provide students with questions related to this specific information *before* students read the assignment. If teachers want students to learn and retain more than question-specific information, they should not give students questions until after they have read the assigned material. Then the students are likely to read and review all the information in the assigned reading, just as they do when they are preparing for an examination.

However, questions at different levels of difficulty have different effects on low- and high-ability students. Higher-level questions help low-ability students while they seem to hinder high-ability students who have their own strategies for learning (Shavelson, Berliner, Ravitch, and Loeding, 1974). The implication is that the teacher should differentiate assignments, giving only low-ability students high level preposed questions to guide their study, then providing both the low- and high-ability students with postposed questions at various levels of difficulty to use in review for an examination.

Students can learn to imitate the teacher's questions and formulate their own questions (Rosenthal, Zimmerman, and Durning, 1970). If they do so as they are reading, they will have the benefits of both preposed and postposed questions. Not knowing what questions the teacher will ask on an examination, the students are also likely to review broadly for the examination, benefiting from both adjunct questions and broad review. Thus, student use of active comprehension, or self-formulation of questions, as they read is likely to be a very effective strategy for learning from text. Of course, teachers must pose questions initially to demonstrate to students what kinds of questions they should ask about the material they are reading. Gradually, students can be taught to ask their own questions.

A general kind of question teachers can pose and students can learn to ask themselves is: Is this material which is presented as factual really true? This questioning of factual material can teach students to be critical of data as well as to go to other sources to check on its validity. Teachers can teach students to be critical by posing critical questions as part of a marginal gloss.

MARGINAL GLOSSES

Glossing is an old technique. Although it had ceased to be used for quite a long while, it is gaining renewed popularity, particularly in social studies and science textbooks. *Glosses* are notes written in the margins of texts. The notes may serve any content or process purpose. In teaching students to learn from texts, marginal glosses can be used to explain technical terms, to prepose questions that will direct reader attention to certain material, to rewrite a passage of text so that it is more readily understood, or just to emphasize a point in the text. Essentially, the gloss is like a teacher accompanying a student through a text. The teacher must anticipate what students will need to know as they read their texts. But in writing glosses, teachers will have to be careful to use simpler definitions and explanations than the text uses and to be terse lest students avoid the glosses because they are burdensome and provide more information than is needed or wanted. To use marginal glosses, teachers can take the following steps:

1. Read through the text, identifying vocabulary or other material to emphasize or clarify.
2. Write marginal glosses on ditto master with page numbers and line numbers indicated on the left-hand side of the ditto master.
3. Give dittoed glosses to students who insert them in their texts and refer to them as they read.

Constructing a Marginal Gloss

A series of examples will illustrate the glossing strategy. Example 1, below, is a passage without the gloss. Box 4.2 is the same passage with a gloss. Note the difference in your reading and learning from the two examples.

EXAMPLE 1. Imagine that you are a ninth-grade English student. Your teacher has assigned Edgar Allan Poe's "The Tell-Tale Heart" to read for homework. About nine o'clock in the evening you settle in a chair to begin your reading. You are immediately confronted with the opening paragraph from the story:

> True! — nervous — very, very dreadfully nervous I had been and am; but why *will* you say that I am mad? The disease had sharpened my senses — not destroyed — not dulled them. Above all was the sense of hearing acute. I heard all things in the heaven and in the earth. I heard many things in hell. How, then, am I mad? Harken! and observe how healthily — how calmly I can tell you the whole story.

As a typical ninth-grade student you might have some problems getting into this story, perhaps because of vocabulary, perhaps because of inverted sentence structure; the first-person narration may also have caused you difficulty.

EXAMPLE 2. If the text you brought home looked like the one in box 4.2, what problems might have been eliminated?

BOX 4.2. Glossed Passage from "The Tell-Tale Heart"

Restated: "I have been nervous and still am." See if you can rephrase other sentences in plain language.

True! — nervous — very, very dread-
(a)
fully nervous I had been and am;

but why *will* (you) say that I am mad?

The (disease) had sharpened my senses — not destroyed — not dulled them.

physical or mental? See (a), (b), and (c).

You, the reader, or someone else in the story? You may find this out later.

Above all was the sense of hearing
(b)
acute. [I heard all things in the heaven
(c)
and in the earth.] [I heard many things in hell.] How, then, am I mad? Harken! and observe how healthily — how [calmly I can tell you the whole story.]

In light of (a), (b), and (c), would you want to be the narrator's close friend? What might his "story" be?

acute: sharp, keen

Harken: listen

The glossing technique in example 2 was used to facilitate reading the Poe story. Notice that several kinds of notes were used: definitions of difficult words, clarifications of difficult sentence structure, and guiding questions concerning the paragraph's internal organization. This first paragraph from "The Tell-Tale Heart" is important because it establishes the insanity of the narrator. If the student-reader fails to understand that the storyteller's credibility is suspect, the power of the suspense in this classic will be lost. (*Note:* A good dramatic oral reading of this Poe story can dispel an amazing number of reading problems.)

EXAMPLE 3. Here is another paragraph from "The Tell-Tale Heart." Try your hand at glossing it:

> But even yet I refrained and kept still. I scarcely breathed. I held the lantern motionless. I tried how steadily I could maintain the ray upon the eye. Meantime the hellish tattoo of the heart increased. It grew quicker and quicker and louder and louder every instant. The old man's terror *must* have been extreme! It grew louder, I say, louder every moment! — do you mark me well? I have told you that I am nervous; so I am. And now at the dread hour of the night, amid the dreadful silence of that old house, so strange a noise as this excited me to uncontrollable terror. Yet, for some minutes longer I refrained and stood still. But the beating grew louder, louder! I thought the heart must burst. And now a new anxiety seized me — the sound would be heard by a neighbor! The old man's hour had come! With a loud yell, I threw open the lantern and leaped into the room. . . .

EXAMPLE 4. As you glossed, you took into consideration vocabulary, sentence structure, and the writer's organization. Your gloss might look something like box 4.3.

BOX 4.3. Glossed Passage from "The Tell-Tale Heart"

refrained: held back	But even yet I <u>refrained</u> and kept still. I scarcely breathed. I held the lantern motionless. I tried how steadily I could maintain the ray upon the eye. } "I tried to see how . . ."
tattoo: beat	Meantime the hellish <u>tattoo</u> of the heart increased. It grew quicker and quicker and louder and louder every instant. The old man's terror *must* have been extreme! It grew louder, I say, louder } As the beat gets faster and louder, what is happening to "I"? To the victim?
	every moment! — do you mark me

well? I have told you that I am nervous; so I am. And now at the dread hour of the night, amid the dreadful silence of that old house, so strange a noise as this excited me to uncontrollable terror. Yet, for some minutes longer I refrained and stood still. [But the beating grew louder, louder! I thought the heart must burst. And now a new anxiety seized me — the sound would be heard by a neighbor!] The old man's hour had come! [With a loud yell, I threw open the lantern and leaped into the room. . . .]

anxiety: worry, uneasiness

What does this tell you about the narrator's state of mind?

Why did "I" leap at this moment? Read the previous two sentences.

Research on Glossing

What evidence is there that glosses are beneficial? School districts have experimented with and evaluated the glossing technique. For instance, in 1972, Tolleson Union High School (Tolleson, 1973), located in Tolleson, Arizona, experimented with vocabulary glossing, a technique requiring teachers to do the following:

1. Read each day's lesson and underline difficult vocabulary and idiomatic phrases.
2. List these items on a stencil and define them in easy English.
3. Use only definitions consistent with the context.
4. Provide each student with the glossary.
5. Spend five to ten minutes going over the glossary before the lesson.
6. Use grade level material rather than simplified material.

At the end of the first year results of reading growth were reported as shown in table 4.1. The grade-equivalent reading levels were determined through use of the Gates-MacGinitie Reading Tests (EM 1, 2, 3).

We do not know whether the improved scores at Tolleson Union were due to the glossing procedure or to some other cause or causes since the school did not have a control group of students for comparison. A control group is equal to the experimental group when the experiment begins, and has the same content but does not have the same experimental treatment (in this experiment, glossing the vocabulary). If the school wanted to determine whether the glossing was valid (the cause of the improved

TABLE 4.1. Tolleson Union High School's Average Reading Level After One Year of Glossing Vocabulary

Date	Average Reading Grade-Equivalent Level
September, 1972	6.2
May, 1973	9.4

scores), half the students should have been assigned randomly to the experimental group and the other half to a control group. The procedure for random assignment can be as simple as putting all the students' names into a box, drawing them out one at a time, and putting one name into the experimental group and the next name into the control group. This procedure would continue until all the names have been drawn and placed into the two groups.

Marginal glosses can be replaced by a more able student who acts as a tutor. The tutor can carry out the functions of a teacher and a marginal gloss, enhancing a student's reading and learning from text not only by giving out information in advance but also by answering questions as they arise. Through this tutorial process, known as *cross-ability teaching,* a student-teacher can help another student match up with a text.

Although marginal glosses can help students with those aspects of the text that the teacher decides to emphasize or clarify, they do not stress and interrelate in a systematic way the factual, inferential, interpretive, and evaluative thinking processes needed to understand information in a text. These thinking processes can be incorporated systematically in reading guides and learning-from-text guides.

READING AND LEARNING-FROM-TEXT GUIDES

Textbooks can be made appropriate for a heterogeneous group of readers by using *guides.* Guides generally take the form of mimeographed or dittoed sheets that engage the students in identifying and classifying information in the text, and in discussion or writing activities aimed at helping them comprehend the textbook. Two basic types of guides are *reading guides,* which focus on reading skills, and *learning-from-text guides,* which focus on thinking processes. We shall look first at several types of reading guides: *overview guides, vocabulary guides,* and *processes-of-reading guides.* Then we shall examine learning-from-text guides.

Reading guides :

Overview Guides

Overviews of the content may take the form of a précis (a brief summary of the content) as in the overviews that precede each of the chapters in this text. The example below is an overview guide for a physics text section on Boyle's Laws.

> This section explains the relationships among the variables of pressure, temperature, and volume of a gas. To understand the relationships among them, keep one variable constant, vary a second, and observe its effect on a third. More specifically, (a) with temperature constant, increase pressure and observe volume decrease, (b) with pressure constant, as temperature increases, volume increases. These relationships occur in the cylinders of an automobile engine. As shown in figure 4.1 the piston goes up, decreasing through compression the volume of gas, as in example A. Then, as shown in B, an increase in temperature through a firing of the spark-plug ignites gas, increases the volume, and pushes the piston down, making the automobile engine revolve.

An overview guide can also be constructed from technical vocabulary used in a chapter. To determine technical vocabulary, a book's index can be reorganized numerically according to page numbers where the vocabulary is introduced. This reorganization can be accomplished by putting

FIGURE 4.1. Automobile Engine Cylinder Exemplifying Boyle's Laws.

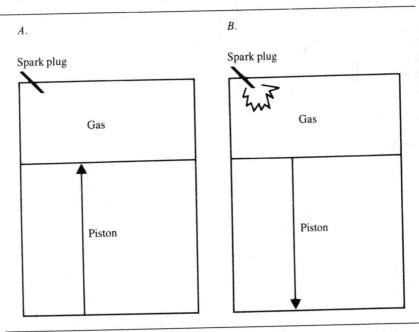

FIGURE 4.2. Overview Guide of a Mathematics Text.

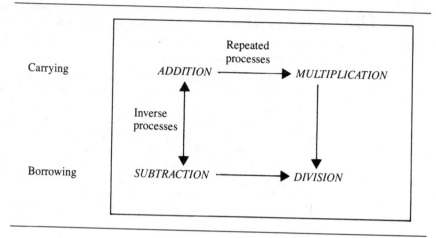

each concept and its page number on a file card, then arranging the file cards by page number.

An example of an overview guide, depicting the concepts and interrelationships of a mathematics text, appears in figure 4.2. This overview guide shows interrelationships among addition, multiplication, subtraction and division. Multiplication and division are repeated processes of addition and subtraction, respectively. Carrying is used in addition and multiplication while borrowing is used in subtraction and division. Addition and subtraction are inverse processes of each other, as are multiplication and division.

EFFECTIVENESS OF OVERVIEW GUIDES

Are overview guides more effective than other organizational techniques in enhancing reading and learning from text? Estes, Mills, and Barron (1969) compared structured overviews with advance organizers and preposed questions. The overview they used was a diagram showing the relationships among technical terms in a biology lesson. Advance organizers are generalizations or technical terms under which subsequent information in a text can be grouped. For example, under the term *nutrition*, we would place information on *food, vitamins, fruit, vegetables, oranges, apples,* and so forth. Preposed questions are both general and specific questions given to students before they read a passage. In contrast to advance organizers and preposed questions, the investigators argued that their overview diagram not only provided the technical terms but also showed their interrelationships. They thought the overview diagram would be superior to both advance organizers and preposed questions for enhancing learning and retention of the passage. However on a multiple-choice biology posttest, the group that used the structured overview did no better than the group that used the advance organizers but scored significantly higher than the group using preposed questions.

Earle (1969) also found that a group which had a structured overview on mathematical relationships learned the mathematical relationships better than a control group. Both groups, of course, read texts containing the technical terms.

The results of both these experiments indicate that either structured overviews or advance organizers to teach technical terms and the relationships among these terms leads to superior comprehension. Moreover, both strategies are better than not giving students any previous instruction or just giving them questions before they read.

2. Vocabulary Guides

Students often need help with understanding new and difficult words, especially technical terms. A vocabulary guide can provide this help. To construct this kind of guide, go through a text or chapter to select technical terms and any difficult general terms. (We have done this and placed a list of such terms at the beginning of each chapter.) Or, if the text's index has been reorganized numerically according to page number, select technical terms from the chapter from the reorganized index. (Students in the class may be given the task of reorganizing the index. Give each student a pack of 3" x 5" cards with instructions to copy a column of terms in the index, putting each term on a card along with its page number. Then organize the cards by page number.)

Technical vocabulary can be taught directly, employing the approach used in dictionary entries. Each entry should contain the following information:

> **word** (syllabified and marked for pronunciation or unmarked with the understanding that the teacher will pronounce it for the students); the meaning(s) of the word; and the location of the word in the text or its context.

After they have been given these specifications, students can complete a vocabulary guide.

An example of a vocabulary guide is shown in box 4.4. The purpose of the directions is to have students apply meanings of the technical terms in their reading and to learn the terms' meanings as determined by context.

BOX 4.4. Vocabulary as Part of a Reading Guide

Directions: Some difficult words may give you problems. Read the following words, their syllabication, and definitions. I will pronounce the words for you. Page numbers where these words occur in this anthology selection have been included. Your task is to locate the word in the passage on the page indicated and write in the space provided the sentence in which the word occurs.

Word	Definition	Word occurs on page	Locate and write the sentence in which the word occurs.
scan-dal-ous	offending the sense of what is right and wrong; causing offense or shame	577	
com-mis-er-at-ing	feeling or expressing sympathy or pity	578	
so-lil-o-quize	to talk to oneself; to deliver a monologue	578	
op-por-tune	well-timed; reasonable; suitable	580	
tart-ly	sharply; severely	582	
ex-on-er-at-ed	freed from blame, as of a charge or accusation	584	

This guide was prepared as part of a unit by Karen Skoog in our course "Reading in the Content Areas."

---

3. Processes-of-Reading Guides

Processes of reading can also be taught by a reading guide: paragraph structure can be taught as a means of showing students how to locate main ideas. In a *processes-of-reading guide*, students would be given the information shown in box 4.5.

BOX 4.5. Reading Guide for Paragraph Structure

A paragraph is a group of sentences, all related to a main idea. Usually the main idea is explicit, stated as a sentence. Occasionally, the main idea is implicit, not stated as a sentence. Then the reader has to infer the main idea from the information given in the sentences in the paragraph. Five types of paragraph structure can be identified according to location of the main idea, indicated below as a longer line in the diagram of paragraph structure.

Location of Main Idea	*Diagram of Paragraph Structure*
1. Beginning of the paragraph.	1. ———————————— ———————— ———————— ————————
2. Middle of the paragraph.	2. ———————— ———————— ———————————— ————————
3. End of the paragraph.	3. ———————— ———————— ———————— ———————— ————————————
4. No main idea: inferential type.	4. ———————— ———————— ———————— ———————— ————————
5. Split type: main idea is divided into two parts; each part is clarified by other sentences in the paragraph.	5. ———— or or —— —— —— —— —— — —— —— —— ———— —— ———— ——

Examples of each of the five types of paragraph structure listed in box 4.5 can be given with a note of humor. The teacher can illustrate all three types of paragraph structure simply by reorganizing the sentences in the following paragraph:

> John wanted a raise in salary. So he went to see his boss. He told his boss he had not had a raise in years. All during this time the company had high profits. Inflation was on the increase. His wife was going to have a sixth child.

The main idea, stated in the first sentence, can be shifted to the end of the paragraph. Start the paragraph then with the sentence: "John went to see his boss." Keep the rest of the sentences in order and end with the first sentence. Notice that some sentences will be changed slightly.

> John went to see his boss. He told him he had not had a raise in years. All during this time the company had high profits. Inflation was on the increase. His wife was going to have a baby. John wanted a raise in salary.

To put the main idea in the middle of the paragraph, start with the sentence: "John went to see his boss." Keep the next three sentences in order. Then state the main idea ("So John wanted a raise in salary."). Finally, add the last sentence: "Moreover, his wife was going to have a sixth child."

> John went to see his boss. He told him he had not had a raise in years. All during this time the company had high profits. Inflation was on the increase. So John wanted a raise in salary. Moreover, his wife was going to have a baby.

To provide an example of a paragraph in which the main idea must be inferred, completely omit the second-last sentence in the above paragraph. Start the paragraph with the sentence: "John went to see his boss." Then give the remaining sentences. Finally, add this sentence: "John waited for his boss to reply."

> John went to see his boss. He told him he had not had a raise in years. All during this time the company had high profits. Inflation was on the increase. His wife was going to have a baby. Then John waited for his boss to reply.

For a paragraph of the split type, add another element to the main idea: "John wanted a raise in salary *and a more responsible position*." Then state the main idea in two sentences. The first would be: "John wanted a raise in salary." Sentences two to six then support this idea. The second part of the split idea can be stated at the end of the paragraph with or without additional sentences supporting it, as shown below. The structure of this paragraph would be a split main idea, with a sentence stating the first part at the beginning and a sentence stating the second part at the end of the paragraph.[2]

---

[2] Additional reading processes and skills are discussed in chapter 16, "The Future: A Schoolwide Program."

John wanted a raise in salary. So he went to see his boss. He told him he had not had a raise in years. All during this time the company had high profits. Inflation was on the increase. His wife was going to have a sixth child. Moreover, John asserted that he could handle a more responsible position in the company.

After this explanation of the main idea and the structure of paragraphs, students are ready for a guide on reading for main ideas, as shown in box 4.6.

BOX 4.6. Reading Guide for Main Ideas

STUDENT GUIDE FIVE

Introduction to the Medieval Romances of Charlemagne
   Reading Skills: Reading for Main Ideas
                  Active Comprehension

Before You Read

   In reading for main ideas, you must read the whole of each paragraph in the article or story. The main idea of the paragraph is the *meaning* of the paragraph — its heart and core. Without it there is no point to the paragraph at all.

   The main idea of a paragraph is usually located in one sentence. This is the sentence to which all the other sentences are related. Most often, this key or topic sentence can be found at the beginning of the paragraph. It may also appear at the end or somewhere in the middle. Sometimes, a paragraph may contain no *direct* statement of main idea although it may be implied. However, more often than not, one topic sentence occurs in a paragraph.

   Use these guidelines when reading for main ideas:
1. Read each paragraph carefully.
2. Look for the sentence in each paragraph that expresses the meaning of the *whole* paragraph. This will be the topic sentence which contains the main idea.
3. Be sure that the other sentences of the paragraph relate to this key sentence.
   An example:

   Malory speaks of the Round Table in two senses. First, he refers to it when he means the fellowship that bound King Arthur and his knights. Secondly, he refers to the Round Table when he means the actual table, seating one hundred and fifty knights, that could be transported from Camelot to another of Arthur's courts.

   The main idea of the above paragraph is: The Round Table has two meanings. It occurs in the first sentence — the topic sentence. The other two sentences relate directly to this key sentence.

While You Read

Read the introduction to "Charlemagne and Elegast." Do the following:
1. Determine the main idea of each paragraph and write it down in the space

provided below. There are three of them. (Skip paragraph one as it is only one sentence long.)

2. Determine which sentence is the topic sentence. Write it down in the space provided below.

Introduction to "Charlemagne and Elegast"
Translated by Lubertus Bakker

The medieval romances that were written about Charlemagne during the height of the Middle Ages were inspired by the historical figure who actually had ruled most of western Europe in his lifetime.

Charlemagne, or Charles the Great (742?–814 A.D.), became King of the Franks in 768. The Franks were a Germanic people who originally lived near the North Sea in the valley of the Rhine River. They invaded France in the fifth century. By the time Charlemagne inherited the throne, the Frankish kingdom was the most powerful in western Europe. Its territories included France, Belgium, and most of Germany. Charlemagne brought even greater glory to the Frankish kingdom. He expanded his territories through military conquest, subdued his pagan enemies and did his utmost to spread the teachings of Christianity. He became a close ally of Pope Leo III, who crowned him Emperor of the Romans in 800. According to many historians, Charlemagne's coronation marks the beginning of the Holy Roman Empire.

It was not surprising that a king and emperor of such power and prestige would soon be exalted in story and song. As his life was embroidered with fiction, Charlemagne passed into legend. He acquired a legendary birth and a group of twelve chivalric knights, or paladins, to share his legendary adventures. He became, moreover, the man chosen by God to defend the Christian faith.

In about the eleventh century, French minstrels claimed Charlemagne as their national hero and sang many *chansons de geste* ("songs of heroic deeds") about him and his paladins. The most famous of these is the *Song of Roland,* which is based upon one of Charlemagne's campaigns in Spain. The Frankish kingdom had long been threatened by the Moors, who conquered Spain early in the eighth century. In 778 Charlemagne led his army across the Pyrenees to establish a neutral zone between France and Spain. While returning to French territory, the rear guard of his army was attacked by natives of the mountains. The *Song of Roland* describes this disastrous attack upon the rear guard, which is commanded by Roland, one of Charlemagne's legendary paladins. Roland, facing certain annihilation, can summon Charlemagne's help if he will sound his horn. He repeatedly refuses to do so. When he finally relents, it is too late for Charlemagne to reach him. French verse epics, like the *Song of Roland,* were the major source of the many medieval romances about Charlemagne and his paladins.

Remember, the main idea of a paragraph is the *central point* of the paragraph. It may appear in the first sentence, the last sentence, or somewhere in the middle (or it may be implicit). It may also be stated more than once. Follow the guidelines given in the *Before You Read* portion of the guide and you should have no trouble.

Paragraph 1: Skip
Paragraph 2: Main idea_____

                    Topic sentence_____
          _____
          _____
Paragraph 3: Main idea _____
              Topic sentence_____
          _____
          _____
Paragraph 4: Main idea _____
              Topic sentence_____
          _____
          _____

Key: Topic sentences — last sentence in paragraph 2 and first sentence in paragraphs 3 and 4. Selection is from *Exploring Life Through Literature,* by Robert C. Pooley, et al. Copyright 1951, © 1957, 1964, 1968 by Scott, Foresman and Company. Reprinted by permission.

Following one or more reading guides, students can read a chapter with greater ease and understanding. They can also be helped through the chapter with a learning-from-text guide. To explain this type of guide, we shall begin by reviewing a taxonomy (or classification) of reading objectives.

B. LEARNING-FROM-TEXT GUIDES

Objectives

A modified organization of reading comprehension objectives based on the taxonomy formulated by Barrett (1968) is shown in figure 4.3. An assumption underlying this taxonomy is that mastery of an objective at a level lower in the taxonomy is a prerequisite for mastering an objective at a higher level. Inspection of the objectives indicates that this assumption is logical.

The objectives are divided into two dimensions. The cognitive dimension precedes the affective dimension. In the cognitive dimension, students recognize (read) literal statements and store them in memory. They can use the information they recognize (or recall from memory) for inferential comprehension and for reorganization of information. In the affective dimension, students can make judgments about the information based on external criteria or standards that the individual brings to reading. The standards can be either intellectual or valuational. Students can also respond emotionally to content through reactions to language (connotative and denotative properties of words); to imagery evoked by content; to characters in the story (identification); or to the structure, style, and form used. These judgments and emotional responses make up the affective dimension of reading comprehension.

FIGURE 4.3. Cognitive and Affective Dimensions of Reading Comprehension.

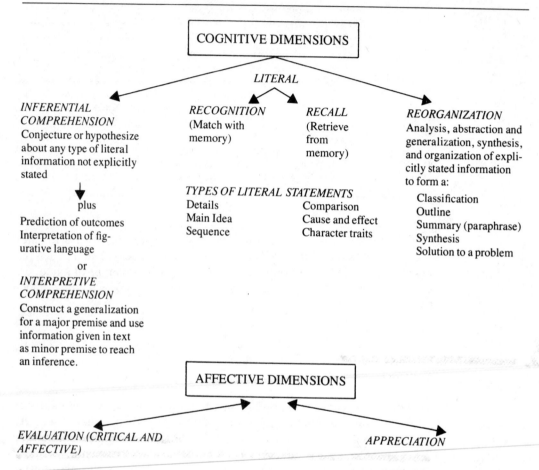

COGNITIVE DIMENSIONS

LITERAL

INFERENTIAL COMPREHENSION
Conjecture or hypothesize about any type of literal information not explicitly stated

plus

Prediction of outcomes
Interpretation of figurative language

or

INTERPRETIVE COMPREHENSION
Construct a generalization for a major premise and use information given in text as minor premise to reach an inference.

RECOGNITION
(Match with memory)

RECALL
(Retrieve from memory)

TYPES OF LITERAL STATEMENTS
Details   Comparison
Main Idea   Cause and effect
Sequence   Character traits

REORGANIZATION
Analysis, abstraction and generalization, synthesis, and organization of explicitly stated information to form a:

Classification
Outline
Summary (paraphrase)
Synthesis
Solution to a problem

AFFECTIVE DIMENSIONS

EVALUATION (CRITICAL AND AFFECTIVE)

Judgment based on:
  Personal standards or values
  External Criteria
  Reality vs. Fantasy
  Fact vs. Opinion
  Adequacy and Validity
  Appropriateness
  Worth, Desirability, Acceptability

APPRECIATION

Knowledge of and emotional responses to literature:

Literary techniques, form, style, and structure.

Emotional response to content, centered on identification of the characters.

Reactions to use of language or imagery.

Thomas E. Barrett, "The Barrett Taxonomy: Cognitive and Affective Dimensions of Reading Comprehension," in H. M. Robinson (ed.), *Sixty-Seventh Yearbook of the National Society for the Study of Education,* Part II. Chicago, Ill.: University of Chicago Press, 1968, pp. 19–23. Adapted with permission.

The reading comprehension objectives can be put into learning-from-text guides and used to teach students to comprehend their texts. The next section explains how to construct this type of guide.

Constructing a Learning-from-Text Guide

To make a learning-from-text guide, follow this procedure.

STEP 1. Read through a chapter of assigned reading material to determine which content is relevant. The assumption in this step is that students do not need to learn all the content in a chapter. Some chapter content may be irrelevant to the teacher's objectives.

STEP 2. Analyze relevant content and categorize it as follows for use in the three levels of the guide:

a. *Information, explicit or directly stated* (for use in the informational level): This information is given in the words of the text; for example, a detail, inference, interpretation, or evaluation given by the author.
b. *Relationships, inferences, or interpretations* (for use in the inferential and interpretive level): A *relationship* consists of an integration or synthesis of facts or information stated in the text. *Inferences* are deductions from major and minor premises stated in the text. *Interpretations* are inferred by constructing a major generalization and using a stated detail as a minor premise.
c. *Generalizations and evaluations* (for use in the generalized and evaluative levels): The teacher selects a generalization from the text: All great civilizations rise and fall. Students can then debate whether the information in the text supports this generalization. Or the teacher may construct a generalization that goes beyond, but assumes, information and generalizations contained in the text; that is, the central ideas of the text can be grouped under the extended generalization. For example, this quotation from Robert Browning's poem "Andrea del Sarto" can be debated by members of a group as being applicable or not applicable to Einstein's life as presented in a given biography:

Ah, but a man's reach should exceed
    his grasp,
Or what's a heaven for?

The teacher can also select or formulate evaluative statements. These statements may refer to the truth or validity of information or conclusions in the text or to the desirability or worth of the information or conclusions. An example of an evaluation statement is given in box 4.7.

In constructing the guide, work backwards: start with the generalized or evaluative statements; then select the inferences and interpretations which support them; and finally list the factual level of information which supports the inferences, interpretations, and generalizations.

STEP 3. Construct the factual, informational, or explicit, level of the guide by listing significant statements made in the text and interspersing among them statements not made in the text. The students' task is to read these statements and determine which statements were made in the text and which were not. Students may justify their identifications by locating and writing down, next to the statement, the page in the text where the informational or explicit statement was made.

The purpose of the informational, or explicit, level of the guide is twofold: (1) to indicate which information in the text is important for students to know and (2) to form the basis for inferences, interpretations, generalizations, and evaluations. All students who are striving to do well and who are beyond the reading acquisition stage can usually get all the informational items correct. Some students who have not gotten many items correct on previous class exercises or on standardized tests are delighted to get so many explicit items correct on learning-from-text guides. Since informational statements are more numerous than the other types of statements in the guide, the score of items correct can be quite high for all the members of the class. Note: Included in the informational level are all statements explicitly made in the text, even though some of them are inferences, generalizations, and evaluations *made by the author.*

STEP 4. Construct the inferential and interpretive level of the guide. This level goes beyond recognition or recall of explicitly stated information. The processes of thinking required at this level of the guides are (1) inference and (2) construction of generalizations that can be used along with factual or explicitly stated information for making interpretations. The classic example of an inference is shown in figure 4.3. The missing word in the conclusion is, of course, *mortal.* Socrates is in the class *all men,* and what is true of all men is therefore true of Socrates.

This inference is also shown in the Euler circles in figure 4.4. Euler circles are used to represent sets (collections of objects) and their relationships. The larger circle represents the set *all men who are mortal.* The smaller circle represents Socrates, a man, and consequently a member of the set *all men who are mortal.* Therefore, the conclusion must be that Socrates is mortal because the smaller circle is entirely within the larger circle and what is true for what the larger circle represents is also true for what the smaller circle represents.

In a story, the major and minor premises are usually not stated or not stated succinctly. The reader has to perceive the relationships among

FIGURE 4.4. Classic Example of an Inference Shown in Two Forms.

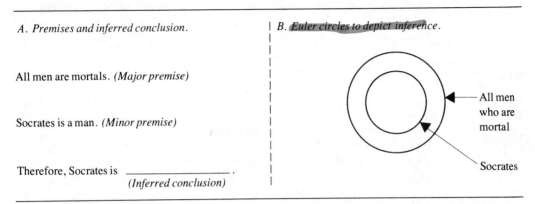

A. *Premises and inferred conclusion.*

All men are mortals. (*Major premise*)

Socrates is a man. (*Minor premise*)

Therefore, Socrates is _____.
                        (*Inferred conclusion*)

B. *Euler circles to depict inference.*

All men who are mortal

Socrates

---

sentences and infer or interpret in order to arrive at a conclusion. For example, this sentence occurs in a short story:

> My husband and I wanted to make a moving picture of savages, and Martin finally decided on Malekula. . . .

Perception of relationships in the sentence will provide a reasonable inference of an answer to the question, "Who is Martin?" The answer is "the writer's husband." How do you know? To explain, you would point to the proximity of the phrase "my husband and I" to the name "Martin," which suggests that Martin is the husband. But you would have to add that this inference is only a plausible hypothesis, to be confirmed or refuted by subsequent passages in the story. This process of hypothesizing and confirming is fundamental to the ability to learn from text.

Another example of constructing a generalization and using explicitly stated details to arrive at an inference occurs in answer to this question about the sentences below — How did the son feel?

> An explorer, about to sail off on a voyage, says goodbye to his nine-year-old son at the dock, boards his ship, and sails off. His son, waving goodbye, remains on the dock until the ship is out of sight.

The passage itself does not answer this question. A major premise, such as the following, has to be constructed:

> When fathers go off on exciting adventures and leave their sons at home, their sons are unhappy.

With this major premise and a minor premise that states the son was left at home, the reader can infer that the son was unhappy.

STEP 5. Construct the generalized and evaluative levels of the guide. A generalization or application consists of statements that encompass literal or interpretive information, but go beyond the passage. In the passage about the father leaving his son behind, the generalization might be:

> Adventurous jobs make for unhappy family life.
>
> *or*
>
> Absence makes the heart grow fonder.

These generalizations can be debated. To conduct a debate, set a time limit. Divide the class into pairs or small groups so that students can express their opinions to each other and become aware of their own systems of values. This grouping also permits many students to talk at the same time. Thus, maximum participation is attained with minimal use of class time.

The truth or falseness of a generalization can also be debated, perhaps leading to reference reading to buttress a position. After reading about the history of Egypt, Greece, Rome, or Great Britain, a generalization that may be made is: *All great civilizations rise and fall.* This statement can be debated. In an advanced history class, students might do supplementary reading to get evidence on the applicability of the generalization. Or, they might draw upon their previous reading to gather evidence for a debate.

An Example

An example of a learning-from-text guide is shown in box 4.7. After reading "Seagull Story," individual students can complete the guide on their own or under the teacher's direction; or the students can be grouped to (1) complete the guide, (2) compare their answers and try to resolve discrepancies, and (3) discuss their justifications for selection of the statement that *best* represents ideas in the passage read. Later, questions on these three levels can replace statements (see the questions used in the guide in box 5.15, p. 104).

After completing the three levels of the guide, the students' affective and critical responses to a selection can be elicited by *evaluation activities*. Critical and affective responses should be based upon external criteria or personal standards and values (Russell and Fea, 1963). Kinds of questions that will elicit evaluative responses follow: How did you feel about . . . ? Was it right or wrong for the main character to . . . ? Is the author's statement true? After writing brief sentences to crystallize their affective reactions, students can form groups and communicate and discuss their reactions with each other.

BOX 4.7. A Learning-from-Text Guide

Directions: Read the story below. Then respond to the items in the informational and inferential sections by checking "yes" or "no." If the response is "yes," indicate the line or lines in the story on which you base your response. You can also respond to the Generalized and Evaluative Level items with a "yes" or "no." It would be helpful to explain, discuss, and justify your responses, especially those for the last level, in a class or group discussion.

SEAGULL STORY

   For years millions of hungry seagulls have flown inland and seriously damaged Swedish crops and gardens. Experts at first tried to reduce the number of gulls by destroying their eggs but found that the gulls merely laid more eggs.
   Now armed with saucepans and cooking stoves, the experts boil the eggs and carefully replace them in the nests. The gulls, not knowing the eggs will never hatch, sit on them hopefully until it is too late to try again.

READING GUIDE

Informational Level (What the Author Said)	Yes	No	Line
1. Seagulls are seriously damaging Swedish crops and gardens so attempts are being made to reduce the number of gulls.	――	――	――
2. A way to keep seagulls from multiplying is to make it impossible for their eggs to hatch.	――	――	――
3. Seagulls actually help farmers.	――	――	――

Inferential Level (What the Author Means;
Relationships Among Statements)

4. Seagulls outwitted the experts.	――	――	――
5. Seagulls don't recognize hard-boiled eggs even when they are sitting on them.	――	――	――
6. The Swedes have found a way to control the seagull plague.	――	――	――

Generalized and Evaluative Levels
(Broader Idea; Discussion: Explicate Values)

7. Man's ingenuity insures his survival.	――	――	――
8. If at first you don't succeed, try, try, and try again.	――	――	――

   Harold L. Herber, *Teaching Reading in Content Areas,* © 1970, p. 63. Reprinted by permission of Prentice-Hall, Inc., Englewood Cliffs, New Jersey.

   An example of an evaluation activity is shown in box 4.8. This one, designed for a unit on ecology, presents the pros and cons of an issue.

Students can use this guide by selecting a position on the issue and debating their views in groups.

BOX 4.8. An Evaluation Activity in Ecology

Students first read a selection which gives the following information:

> The Colorado River was dammed up to create Glen Canyon Dam. The river's water backed up behind the dam to form Lake Powell. Hundreds of miles of scenic canyons now lie buried beneath the lake; while water released from the dam runs down to turn turbines and drive generators producing millions of watts of electricity. Swiftly and quietly the electricity is transported to distant cities to provide energy for people and machines who are unaware of changes wrought in nature to create their power.

The evaluation guide consists of the following statements:

1. Man's need for electrical power is more important than protection of scenic areas.
2. Scenic areas are legacies for our children. We should protect and preserve these areas at all costs.

To enhance the process of debating their views on the issue presented in box 4.8, students can use the *Reader's Guide to Periodical Literature* to locate newspaper and magazine articles written before, during, and after Glen Canyon Dam was built. The students would then have more information to buttress their points of view. Although the issues may not be resolved, students participating in the debate would, in the process, tend to achieve the objective of using external criteria explicitly or formulating and stating their own standards and values for evaluating this and similar social issues.

Research on Guides

Guides that are similar to our learning-from-text guides have been found to be effective in helping students comprehend text that is difficult relative to their levels of reading achievement (Herber and Sanders, 1969; Herber and Barron, 1973). Although Estes (1973) found these guides were not superior to preposed questions (teacher questions given to students before they read a passage), the guides did significantly enhance the posttest performance of low reading achievers. However, guides for highly interpretive material are helpful to all students (Berget, 1973).

TEACHING STUDENTS TO USE GUIDES OR ANY NEW TECHNIQUE

Phase-In Technique

A three-phase process can be used for teaching students any new technique, such as how to use a guide. In the first phase, the teacher takes the class through a guide, acting as a chairperson for the entire class. The teacher uses the discussion processes explained in chapter 6 for taking a group through the various levels of comprehension. In the second phase, the teacher divides the class into groups and assigns chairpersons and reporters for each group. Then each group goes through the process of using a guide. During the process the teacher acts as a consultant to the groups. By the third phase, individuals should be able to fill out their own guides. (For a more detailed explanation of this phase-in technique, see chapter 10, "An Instructional Blueprint for Learning from Text.")

The process of constructing guides is time-consuming for a teacher. But the teacher's task is to develop the students towards independence in reading and learning from texts, and the guide is a means towards this end. To help with this time-consuming task, the teacher can have the class construct its own guide.

Class-Constructed Guides

Students can learn how to construct their own guides after going through several teacher-prepared guides. A phase-in technique can be used for teaching them to construct their own guides. Students in groups construct guides for (1) explicitly or directly stated information; then the groups construct (2) directly stated and inferential or interpretive guides; next, they develop (3) directly stated, inferential or interpretive, and generalized or evaluative guides. At each step, the groups can try their guides out on each other.

After a class has become adept in constructing guides, each group can take a chapter of a text and construct guides for it. Thus, a teacher can have an entire set of guides for a text. This procedure should answer the often-asked question, "Where do I find time to construct a guide?" It also benefits the class because the process of constructing guides is a way of having the class acquire content and practice the processes involved in learning from texts.

SQ3R — A STRATEGY FOR DEVELOPING INDEPENDENT LEARNERS

The last of the single text strategies to be discussed is *SQ3R* — survey, question, read, recite, and review. Consider a chapter from a sewing textbook. First, the students *survey* the contents of the chapter, focusing on such parts as (1) an overview, (2) a summary, (3) pictures of sewing patterns or products, (4) marginal gloss, (5) headings and subheadings, (6) highlighted vocabulary. Second, since this survey suggests to the students what the chapter is about, the students pose *questions* that they will try to answer by reading the text: "What kinds of clothing will this chapter teach me how to make?" "What materials will I learn to use?" "How can I make certain kinds of stitches?" Third, having posed these questions, students then actively *read* to find answers to their questions. Fourth, having read, students can *recite* the material, by putting the chapter contents into their own words, either in writing or in discussion. Last, students could *review* the information, perhaps by making a garment according to the guidelines set down in the chapter. Once the students learn to use SQ3R, they are on the road to becoming independent readers.

SQ3R, formulated by Robinson (1961), is the oldest strategy for developing independent learners. He based the strategy on implications drawn from basic research in human learning. However, to be effective in using it, students have to learn what questions are appropriate to each content area. We demonstrate how SQ3R can be applied to each content area in chapters 11–14.

SUPPLEMENTARY TECHNIQUES

Two techniques that can be used to supplement the preceding strategies are (1) cross-ability teaching and (2) using visual aids. These techniques can also be used by themselves to make texts more intelligible to students with a wide range of abilities.

Cross-Ability Teaching

Cross-ability teaching involves an able person teaching a less able one. According to this definition, cross-ability teaching is what teachers have been doing all along. However, in its technical meaning, the term is more restricted. *Cross-ability teaching* usually refers to more able *students* teaching less able *students*.

Within a class, cross-ability teaching occurs naturally in group situations when members of the group are discussing controversial issues or trying to solve problems or answer questions through reference reading. In this group situation, cross-ability teaching consists of one member of the group explaining something or trying to convince another member of the group. Frequently, cross-ability teaching means pairing two individuals from the same class or from two different classes. To avoid resentment in both tutor and tutee, pairing is best done on a voluntary basis.

Frequently tutors benefit more than tutees, particularly when tutors need further practice in what is being taught. If instruction consists of content or processes the tutor has already mastered, the tutor will experience no gain. However, the tutee may still benefit considerably from the instruction. At the other extreme, if the tutor does not understand what is being taught, neither tutor nor tutee is likely to benefit. The optimum condition is somewhere in the middle, a situation in which the tutor is more advanced than the tutee in knowledge or ability, but has not yet mastered the content or processes involved. The tutor, for example, may know the Bill of Rights, but not without some hesitation; after teaching them to another student, the tutor is likely to have progressed towards mastery of them.

Is cross-age tutoring effective? Cross-age tutoring has been found frequently to help tutors more than tutees. However, this benefit does not necessarily occur when tutors are not very capable. For example, high school seniors in a low-ability class volunteered to teach low-ability seventh and eighth graders for a year. They attended weekly seminars on tutoring before and after one-hour weekly tutoring sessions. Despite weekly training and teaching sessions, these tutors did not gain significantly over a control group (Dillner, 1971).

Tutoring can have a significant effect on tutees, especially when the tutors are competent. For example, students in grades 4, 7, and 10 were randomly assigned to adult tutors, ages 21 to 55, who were recruited by newspaper advertisement. The tutors passed *Sequential Tests of Educational Progress*[3] and an interview. The results showed that, with intelligence controlled on the *California Test of Mental Maturity*,[4] students tutored by these adults were significantly higher than a control group in reading achievement and received better grade-point averages in math, social studies, and English.

From these research studies, we can draw conclusions about what kind of tutor is likely to be effective. Tutors may benefit from the instruction they give if they need to practice processes already acquired in the content area and if they have the capabilities and the maturity for doing so. If they already have some knowledge and some skill in processes of reading and learning from texts in a content area, they may use their skills to acquire additional content in that area as they tutor. In doing so, tutors can demonstrate and teach tutees processes of reading and learning from text. Tutors must know either content or processes of reading and learning from texts in a content area and know how to communicate them effectively if the tutees, or the tutors themselves, are to benefit from the instruction.

[3] Educational Testing Service, Princeton, New Jersey, 1969.
[4] California Test Bureau, Division of McGraw-Hill Book Co., Del Monte Research Park, Monterey, California.

Visual Aids

Visual aids can be used in all the preceding strategies. Use of such aids is, in itself, a strategy for handling individual differences in modes of processing stimuli: some students can learn and recall relationships better in pictured form than they can in verbal form. Hence, whenever possible, teachers should use visual aids and teach students to transform verbal statements into pictorial relationships. See chapter 14, box 14.10 — "Mathematics," for examples of this type of transformation.

EVALUATION OF SINGLE-TEXT STRATEGIES

In this chapter we have presented four single-text strategies. Although we have reviewed research that supports the effectiveness of some of them for handling individual differences in the classroom, teachers should also make their own evaluations of the effectiveness of these strategies in their own classrooms with their own students. In this section of the chapter we shall present several ways in which teachers can evaluate use of single-text strategies in their own classrooms.

To evaluate any of the single-text strategies, divide a class into two groups. A simple way to do this is to rank the class according to students' reading ability. Then begin to assign students alternately to Group 1 and Group 2. This procedure is likely to produce two groups of equal ability in reading. Then have one group use one of the four strategies to accompany its reading of a passage while the other group simply reads the same passage. Both groups should be told that their comprehension will be tested at the end of the passage. After administering the comprehension test, find the average scores of both groups. Did the group that used the strategy have a higher average score than the other group?

Also obtain the affective reactions of the two groups. At the end of the comprehension test, ask both groups the following questions:

1. How do you rate the difficulty of this passage? Indicate your responses by circling one of the following choices: 1. Very easy, 2. Easy, 3. Average, 4. Difficult, 5. Very difficult.
2. How interesting was this assignment? 1. Very interesting, 2. Interesting, 3. Average, 4. Uninteresting, 5. Very uninteresting.

Average the choices circled for each group and compare. See if the group that used one of the strategies in this chapter found that the passage was easier and/or more interesting.

You can compare the effectiveness of the strategy for the low-achieving readers (lower half of the class) and high-achieving readers (upper half of class) in each group by writing the average, first on the comprehension test and then on the affective questions, for each group in each box in

FIGURE 4.5. Comparison of Average Comprehension Test Scores
of High- and Low-Reading Achievers
Who Used a Strategy vs. Those Who Did Not.

		Teaching technique		
		Did not use strategy	Used strategy	Sum
Reading achievers	High (upper half of class)	A. Nine students Avg. = 85	B. Nine students Avg. = 87	172
	Low (lower half of class)	C. Nine students Avg. = 68	D. Nine students Avg. = 73	141
	Sum	153	160	313

figure 4.5. For example, the average comprehension test score earned by the high reading achievers who did not employ the strategy goes in box A of figure 4.5.

Figure 4.5 will help you determine whether the strategy was effective, regardless of general reading achievement, by adding B + D, then A + C. By comparing the two sums, you can determine whether the strategy made a difference. If B + D is much greater than A + C, the strategy probably was effective.[5] Since figure 4.4 shows that those who used the strategy scored 160 compared with 153 for those who did not use the strategy, we can conclude that the strategy, in this class, was probably effective in raising the comprehension test scores. You can also determine whether high-reading achievers still attained more than low-reading achievers, regardless of the strategy, by comparing the sum A + B with the sum of C + D. Since the sum of A + B (172) is much greater than the sum of C + D (141), then high-reading achievers probably attained more despite the strategy.

You can also find out whether there is an interaction between level of reading achievement and use of the strategy by determining whether the differences between B and D are less than the differences between A and C. Here B − D (87 − 73 = 14) is less than A − C (85 − 68 = 17). Any interaction can be perceived by plotting the results as shown in figure 4.6. The converging lines in the figure indicate one kind of interaction between strategy and level of reading achievement: the low group benefits from the strategy more than the high group.

---

[5] For a statistical test of significance of differences such as analysis of variance, see an introductory statistics text.

FIGURE 4.6. Average Scores of Groups Who Used a Strategy vs. Those Who Did Not.

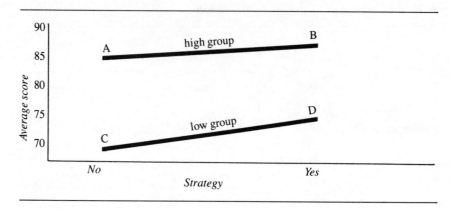

The following are additional ways to evaluate the effectiveness of the strategies:

1. Observe whether students are more attentive to reading and learning from text with a strategy than without one.
2. After students have participated in one of the strategies, rate whether they concentrate on the assignment more, whether they are more independent of the teacher, whether they participate more in class discussion, or whether their reports are more germane and contain more technical vocabulary and higher level responses. In

FIGURE 4.7. Tally Table for Rating Each Student's Reaction to an Assignment.

| | | *Strategy* | | | |
| | | No | | Yes | |
		High	Low	High	Low
Concentration or independence or participation or quality of reports	Upper half of group				
	Lower half of group				

figure 4.7, fill out the two by two tally table for each of your students. Rate each one's reaction as either high or low and classify the rating according to whether the student had used a strategy or not and was in a high or low reading-achievement group.

3. Observe whether students of high and low ability levels are able to learn from the assignment. If so, you would expect an equal number of high and low ability members in each "No" and "Yes" column in the above figure.

4. Interview a sample of your students and use their reactions to put them into one or another category in your table. Ask, for instance, "How did you like this assignment?" "Did the assignment help you?" "Would you like more assignments like this one?"

The evaluation procedures can be applied not only to the single-text strategies but also to the multiple-text strategies to be presented in chapter 9 of the text.

SUMMARY

Single-text strategies that enable students varying widely in ability to read and learn from a text without stigmatizing any of them were defined in this chapter. Although a teacher may use a textbook that fits the average reading level of a class, she or he needs to employ one or more strategies to make the text more appropriate to the class's range of ability to read and learn from the textbook. These strategies involve the use of DRA-AC (directed reading activity with emphasis on active comprehension), glosses, guides, and SQ3R. All of the single-text strategies are also useful in so-called homogeneous classes and in college preparatory classes because even these classes include students with varying ability.

Although the single-text strategies were described separately in this chapter, they can be used in varying combinations. In the next chapter, we shall demonstrate how the single-text strategies can be combined to teach students how to read and learn from a textbook currently being used in a junior high school social studies class and a senior high school woodshop class.

Of course, single-text strategies, such as guides for reading and learning from text, require preparation time. Mostly the materials can be perceived as part of a teacher's plans for teaching lessons or for helping students with their reading assignments. However, resourceful teachers who have mastered the strategies will think of ways of having students, teaching aides, or community volunteers assist with preparation of materials under their direction. Some suggestions for doing this are given in subsequent chapters.

ACTIVITIES

1. Select a poem by Carl Sandburg, or any poet. Develop a single-text strategy for teaching high school students to read that poem. Suggestions: (1) Follow the steps in DRA. (2) Develop a reading process guide that focuses on the reading of poetry. (3) Develop a learning from text guide that takes the students through the four levels of comprehension.
2. Select a chapter in any content area textbook of your choice and prepare a lesson on it, using the five steps of the DRA.
3. Explain in detail how you would attempt to teach students to use SQ3R in comprehending a science text.
4. Explain how you would test the *relative* effectiveness of two different types of reading guides used in a hypothetical class.

5 | Teaching Students to Learn from a Chapter

CHAPTER OVERVIEW

In the last chapter, you learned about strategies for teaching students to learn from a single text. In this chapter, you will learn how to apply some of these strategies to specific textbook chapters. Chapters will be taken from two textbooks: the first, a junior high school social studies text; the second, a high school woodshop text.

TECHNICAL VOCABULARY

entry level test
behavioral objectives
task analysis

Until improved textbook organization occurs, and perhaps even afterwards, teachers will have to continue to teach students how to learn from texts. In the last chapter, you learned that DRA (directed reading activity), glosses, reading and learning from text guides, and SQ3R are four strategies for helping students to learn from a single text. In this chapter, we will combine some of these strategies to show you how to teach a complete chapter from a junior high school social studies text.[1]

In demonstrating the strategies, we will introduce you to several supporting techniques as we go along. In the second part of this chapter, you will examine some reading and learning-from-text guides for teaching a chapter from a woodshop textbook. Thus, we will demonstrate that single-text strategies are equally applicable to both academic and vocational texts.

TEACHING A CHAPTER FROM A SOCIAL STUDIES TEXTBOOK

Before You Teach a Chapter

Before you present a chapter for class study, you should make sure the students have the background to read it. One way of doing this is to administer an *entry level test*. An entry level test assesses what information the students have retained from prior reading that will be useful in forthcoming reading. Examine box 5.1. Notice that the entry level test contains test items on vocabulary, factual recall, inferences, and generalizations from the previous chapter. The teacher who prepared this test selected information from *Quest for Liberty*, chapter 2, that students would need to know to understand chapter 3. The objective nature of the test makes it easy to score, thus less time-consuming. Simply going over the answers in class might be enough to prepare the students for chapter 3.

Not only is the entry level test easy for the teacher to score, it is also easy for the student to take. All the student has to do is read each item and respond to it, either with an X or with no mark. If the items were written so as to demand short answers, the student would have to rely on expressive language, which for some students would be difficult. Chapter 7 will show you how to teach students to write answers to study questions.

---

[1] Throughout this chapter, the social studies text chapter referred to is chapter 3, "The Colonies Fight for Independence," in *Quest for Liberty* by Chapin, Mettugh, and Gross (San Francisco: Field Educational Publications, 1971).

BOX 5.1. Entry Level Test

CHAPTER 3: "THE COLONIES FIGHT
FOR INDEPENDENCE"

Part 1. Vocabulary. Match the terms on the left with their meanings on the right.

    ____ 1. colony   A. a labor contract
    ____ 2. dissent   B. doing what the group does
    ____ 3. indenture   C. mother country getting raw
    ____ 4. mercantilism   materials from colony
    ____ 5. representation   D. a source of supply
    ____ 6. resource   E. to disagree with a majority
    ____ 7. conformity   F. democracy
                              G. people choose others to act for them
                              H. totalitarianism
                              I. a territory ruled by people in
                                 another land

Part 2. Put an X by all factual statements about the colonial period that are true.

    ____ 1. Prior to 1790, English, Irish, and Negroes made up the largest proportion of immigrants.
    ____ 2. The Southern colonies, unlike New England and the Middle colonies, were primarily agricultural.
    ____ 3. Catholicism was the main religion in the New England colonies.
    ____ 4. Puritans, unlike other colonists, tended to be sober and serious people who wore dark clothing.

Part 3. Put an X by all conclusions that you can make about colonial life.

    ____ 1. Opposition to slavery in the colonies was based on good business rather than on high ideals.
    ____ 2. Religious intolerance was transplanted from England and Europe to the colonies.
    ____ 3. Religion influenced the economic and cultural lives of the colonists.
    ____ 4. The colonies, from the start, lacked unity; to form them into a United States would be an almost impossible task.

Part 4. Put an X by all general sentences that apply to life today.

    ____ 1. The present conflicts between the North and the South developed right before the Civil War in the 1850s.
    ____ 2. Religion still has an influence on political life in the United States.

BOX 5.2. Overview Guide

CHAPTER 3: "THE COLONIES FIGHT
FOR INDEPENDENCE"

Part 1. Background of the
American Revolution (pp. 75–84).
a. What is a revolution? (p. 76)
b. What happened when the colonies
   started to govern themselves? (pp.
   76–77)
c. What happened when England
   started to crack down? (pp. 78–79)
d. How did the colonies react to
   England's crackdown? (pp. 79–81)
e. How did England go too far? (pp.
   82–84)

Events *1* (b–e)
caused the
Declaration of
Independence
to be developed.

Part 2. The Declaration of
Independence (pp. 84–88).
a. How is the *Declaration* organized?
   (pp. 84–87)
b. What can we tell about the people
   who signed the *Declaration*? (pp.
   87–88)
c. Why was it dangerous to sign the
   Declaration of Independence?

2 (a–b)
resulted in war.

Part 3. The Revolutionary War
(pp. 88–103).
a. Who fought in the war? (pp. 88–89)
b. What was it like to fight in the war?
   (pp. 89–94)
c. How were the Americans able to
   win the war? (pp. 94–101)
d. What happened when peace finally
   came? (pp. 102–103)

Parts 1–3. Overview (pp. 75–103).
a. It would have been impossible for
   the British to have won the War for
   American independence. Attack and
   defend that statement in one
   paragraph.
b. In what ways were the colonists
   ready to handle independence?

Pages referred to are from *Quest for Liberty.*

In introducing the chapter to the students, a teacher might want to give the students an *overview guide* of the chapter. In box 5.2 you can see that one social studies teacher prepared an overview guide by dividing the chapter into three logical sections, asking major questions, and indicating where the students could find answers to those questions.

Accompanying the overview guide is a list of *behavioral objectives* (goals written in terms of student activity) which are subdivided by step-by-step enabling activities. Notice the detail that one social studies teacher used in preparing the objectives list in box 5.3.

BOX 5.3. Behavioral Objectives

CHAPTER 3: "THE COLONIES FIGHT
FOR INDEPENDENCE"

Goal. After reading chapter 3, "The Colonies Fight for Independence," you will understand the causes for and the effects of the American Revolution.

Objective. In studying the background for the American Revolution, you will be able to explain how freedom in the colonies caused England to create controls which, in turn, caused the colonists to rebel.

Enabling Objectives:
a. You will look over *Part 1* of the *Overview Guide* to see what kinds of questions the text material on pp. 75–84 will answer.
b. You will write the exercises in the *Process Guide* (see box 5.6) on cause and effect.
c. You will read pp. 75–84 and answer questions 1:a–e in the *Overview Guide.*

Objective. In studying the *Declaration of Independence* you will be able to describe its organization and draw conclusions about the signers.

Enabling Objectives:
a. You will look over *Part 2* of the *Overview Guide,* which covers pp. 84–88 of the text.
b. You will read pp. 84–88 of the text and answer questions 2:a–c of the *Overview Guide.*

Objective. In studying the American Revolutionary War, you will be able (1) to list and identify the participants, (2) to describe battle conditions, and (3) to demonstrate how the Americans were able to win.

Enabling Objectives:
a. You will look over *Part 3* of the *Overview Guide,* which covers pp. 88–103 of the text.
b. You will read pp. 88–103 of the text and answer questions 3:a–d of the *Overview Guide.*

Ways of Teaching a Chapter

The techniques discussed so far — the entry level test, the overview guide, and the behavioral objectives — have been preteaching activities. Now, a number of ways in which a teacher actually teaches students to learn from a textbook chapter will be discussed.

A chapter can be taught in various ways. For instance, the teacher can expand the list of behavioral objectives into a teacher *task analysis*. If you look at box 5.4, you can see one social studies teacher's task analysis for chapter 3 of *Quest for Liberty*. Notice how this teacher has, for each objective, listed (1) the content the student must know to fulfill the objective and (2) the reading and thinking processes the student must have to master the content. In order for a student to describe the organization of *The Declaration of Independence* and draw conclusions about the signers, the student must know the relationship of main idea to subordinate idea and be able to draw inferences from facts. This task analysis focuses the teacher's attention on important areas of instruction and provides guidance for developing techniques and strategies. For instance, it looks like some teaching of the cause and effect thinking process is in order.

BOX 5.4. Teacher's Task Analysis

CHAPTER 3: "THE COLONIES FIGHT
FOR INDEPENDENCE"

Goal and Objectives	Content	Process
Students will understand causes and effects of the American Revolution by —		
1. explaining how freedom in the colonies caused England to create controls which, in turn, caused the colonists to rebel	definition of term *revolution* colonies' self-government England's pressure colonists' reaction to pressure	cause and effect
2. describing the organization of *The Declaration of Independence* and drawing conclusions about the signers	the main idea of the Declaration supporting ideas backgrounds of the signers	main idea/ subordinate idea drawing inferences from facts

3. listing and identifying the war's participants, describing battle conditions, and demonstrating how the Americans were able to win	who fought in the war
	  Colonists
	  Indians
	  British
	  French
	the battles
	  sequence
	  outcomes
	  conditions
	superior strategy of colonists
	  use of surprise
	  guerrilla warfare
	conditions of peace
		reading for details
		reading for chronological order
		drawing inferences from facts

Combining DRA with Other Approaches

After preparing the task analysis, the teacher might decide to teach a chapter with the directed reading activity (DRA) approach, first by providing background information. After providing this background, the teacher would introduce the chapter vocabulary, possibly through use of a reading guide that focuses on vocabulary. In box 5.5 you can see how one social studies teacher prepared a vocabulary guide for chapter 3, *Quest for Liberty*.

BOX 5.5. Vocabulary Guide

CHAPTER 3: "THE COLONIES FIGHT
FOR INDEPENDENCE"

Hard Words. Below are some difficult words you will run across in this chapter. I will pronounce them for you. Study the meaning of the word and the sentences from the chapter that use the word. Some of this information can be found in the textbook glossary (pp. 660–663).

Word	Meaning	Sentence from Text
compromise	the process of settling a conflict in which each side gives in on some points	The two sides were unable to *compromise.* (p. 83)
nationalism	love of your country to the point that you support it at the expense of other countries	Demands for independence are usually related to a growth in *nationalism.* (p. 104)

Word	Meaning	Sentence from Text
neutral	not a part of either side of a conflict	Historians used to think that about only one-third of the colonists actively supported the war, and that another third were *neutral* . . . (p. 88)
patriots	those who are extremely loyal to their country	The British soldiers met the American *patriots* on the village green . . . and shooting broke out. (p. 83)
rebellion	organized opposition to and defiance of a government or someone in authority	The *rebellion* against England became a practical possibility because the British had allowed some free institutions to flourish in the colonies. (p. 76)
revolution	a rapid and far-reaching change, especially the overthrow and replacement of a government	The desire for independence often leads to a *revolution*. (p. 76)
treason	an attempt to overthrow one's government	Some in the middle colonies were reluctant to commit "treason" and break permanently with England. (p. 84)

Having reviewed the vocabulary, the students could profitably reexamine the overview guide (box 5.2) for questions to guide their reading. Perhaps, the students could even add questions of their own. At this point, the teacher might want to insert a *processes-of-reading guide*. As you see in box 5.6, the teacher, concerned that students might have difficulty with cause and effect, prepared a processes-of-reading guide that took the students step-by-step into the text material. Good practice suggests that the teacher do the first half of the guide orally with the class as a whole and gradually ease the students into working on their own as they read the chapter.

BOX 5.6. Processes-of-Reading Guide: Cause and Effect

CHAPTER 3: "THE COLONIES FIGHT
FOR INDEPENDENCE"

Cause and Effect

Just knowing the order in which events happen is not enough. In reading and understanding history it is important to know the CAUSES and the EFFECTS of the events. Below are some everyday events. Try to figure out what caused these events to happen, and what the effects of the events were:

Example:
Event: The milk in the refrigerator is sour and lumpy looking.
Cause: It was either bad when it was bought or it was left too long in the refrigerator.
Effect: Someone will have to go to the store for more milk or go without.

Event	*Cause*	*Effect*
1. All the lights at home suddenly go out.		
2. You reach into your pocket for money to pay for a Coke; the pocket is empty.		
3. Your younger brother hits you with a toy truck.		
4. War protesters refuse to fight in Viet Nam.		

Now, relate cause and effect to history.

Pages 85–104. As you read, jot down the *causes* for the following events:
1. The Continental Congress was moved and stirred to demand official independence from England.
2. Not all colonists supported the Revolution.
3. Colonists massed for attack at Breed's Hill and Bunker Hill.

Pages 90–104. As you read, jot down the *effects* of the following events.
1. General Gage won the battle at Bunker Hill and Breed's Hill.
2. Washington surprises the Hessian troops on Christmas Eve at Trenton.
3. Fighting conditions were unhealthful and unsanitary.
4. American colonists employ guerrilla warfare.

In addition to a processes-of-reading guide, the teacher might also wish to *gloss* some sections of the chapter. Look at box 5.7 to see how one teacher, who felt The Declaration of Independence was hard reading, glossed it for the students.

BOX 5.7. Gloss

CHAPTER 3: "THE COLONIES FIGHT
FOR INDEPENDENCE"

Instructions: The main ideas are underlined. Read those first, then read the entire selection. The words in italics are technical terms for which synonyms appear in the margins.

The Declaration of Independence

Even when the war with England had been going on for more than a year, many colonists still hoped for a peaceful settlement. Some in the middle colonies were reluctant to commit "treason" and break permanently from England. On the other hand, in the Continental Congress the delegates from Virginia and New England *favored* an official declaration of independence.

wanted

Then, in January, 1776, Thomas Paine, a newly arrived immigrant from England, published his famous article *Common Sense,* in favor of independence. Within several months, 120,000 copies were printed. The piece was widely discussed by the colonists. Paine's brilliant arguments pointed out for the first time the disadvantages of living under a king and the ability of Americans to rule themselves better. This article helped *stir* the Continental Congress to demand official independence from England.

move

In June, 1776, the Continental Congress (*proposed*) that independence be ~ strongly urged ~ considered for the colonies and that the ties with England be finally cut. The Continental Congress chose a committee of five to write a statement of the official reasons for the separation of the colonies from England. Young Thomas Jefferson was the principal author of this Declaration of Independence. The other committee members were Benjamin Franklin, John Adams, Roger Sherman, and Robert R. Livingston.

changed   The Congress (*modified*) some of the documents prepared by the committee. One part, blaming the king for promoting the slave trade, was (*omitted*) because of objections from slaveholders as well as New England delegates. Why would (*the latter group*) have objected? On July 4, 1776, Congress formally adopted the Declaration of Independence.

left out

the New England delegates

Analysis of the Declaration

The document is divided into three main parts: (1) the first two paragraphs, outlining the basic rights of man; (2) a very long, detailed list of (*grievances*) ~ strong complaints ~ that were directed against King George III, although Parliament had officially passed the laws; and (3) additional reasons that forced the colonists to separate from England.

The Declaration of Independence was truly a (*revolutionary*) document. In ~ It contained shockingly new ideas. ~ an age when most European nations

were ruled by kings, the idea of rebel-
ling against the king was considered
dangerous and radical. Certainly, if the
independence movement failed, its
leaders and the signers of the Declaration of Independence would be risking
their lives, their fortunes, and their sa-
cred honor. Benjamin Franklin was
right when he told the signers, "We
must indeed all hang together, or, most
(assuredly,) we shall hang separately."   definitely

Passage from *Quest for Liberty* by June R. Chapin, Raymond J. McHugh, Richard E. Gross. Copyright © 1971, 1974 Field Educational Publications, Inc. Reprinted by permission of Addison-Wesley Publishing Company, Inc.

Having read the chapter, the students are now ready for discussion and writing. The teacher could construct this discussion around a *learning-from-text guide,* aimed at assessing four levels of comprehension: (1) directly stated or informational, (2) inferential, (3) generalized, and (4) evaluative. Box 5.8 presents such a learning-from-text guide based on chapter 3, *Quest for Liberty*.

Having discussed and written about the chapter, the students can extend their learning to another situation. Box 5.9 contains a list of problems that junior high school students might enjoy working on after they have read chapter 3.

BOX 5.8. *Learning-from-Text Guide*

CHAPTER 3: "THE COLONIES FIGHT
FOR INDEPENDENCE"

Part 1: Informational Level

Instructions: Answer the following questions while you are reading chapter 3, "The Colonies Fight for Independence." The page and paragraph numbers will help you find the answers.

1. Name three things the colonists did to show they were capable of governing themselves. (page 77)

   a. (page 77, paragraph 3)_____

   _____

   _____

   b. (page 77, paragraph 4)_____

   _____

   _____

   c. (page 77, paragraph 5)_____

   _____

   _____

2. What did England do to regain control? (page 79, paragraph 2)

   _____

   _____

3. In what ways did the colonists protest? (pages 79–81 or chart on top of page 79)

   a. England did: _____

   The Colonists did:_____

   b. England did: _____

   The Colonists did:_____

   c. England did: _____

   The Colonists did:_____

4. What act by parliament was "the last straw," as far as the colonists were concerned? (page 82, paragraph 3)

   _____

   _____

5. What are the three main divisions of The Declaration of Independence? (page 84, paragraph 6–page 85, paragraph 1)

   _____

   _____

6. What battle gives you the clearest picture of what it was like to fight in the Revolutionary War? (page 85, paragraph 2)

   _____

   _____

7. Name three things the Americans did to win the war. (pages 94–101)

a. (94)_____

_____

b. (97)_____

_____

c. (99)_____

_____

Part 2: Inferential Level

Instructions: Match the historic fact, on the left, with the conclusion you could draw, on the right.

_____ 1. Fifty to seventy-five percent of white colonial males could vote for their own representatives.

_____ 2. New England and the Middle colonies start to manufacture their own products.

_____ 3. British troops fight French and Indians on American soil.

_____ 4. The British tax tea.

_____ 5. American soldiers use guerrilla warfare.

A. England could easily be frightened by competition.

B. England is in sore need for money.

C. People do what is natural to them.

D. Democracy was flourishing before the Revolutionary War.

E. The British want to "control the action."

Part 3: Generalized and Evaluative Level

Instructions: Reread "Bringing issues up to the present" (page 104 of the text) and answer the following questions. Then, in small groups, compare your answers and try to resolve your disagreements.

1. Do you feel that America feels the same today as it did in 1776 about these issues:
   a. colonialism
   b. mercantilism
   c. slavery
   d. taxation
   e. freedom

2. If there have been changes in attitude since 1776, have these changes been good or bad? Give reasons for your opinions.

3. Is it good or bad that today conflicts exist between states, specifically, the North and the South? In answering this question, cite current events that will support your beliefs.

BOX 5.9. Problems

CHAPTER 3: "THE COLONIES FIGHT
FOR INDEPENDENCE"

Instructions: Select one of the following problems to write up. Use classroom sources and/or go to the library.

1. You are a movie director who is working on a high-budget movie about the Revolutionary War. For your producer, the man who gives you the money, prepare a list or what you'll need for one scene: *The Battle of Bunker Hill.* What would you need in the way of (1) scenery, (2) equipment and props, (3) actors, (4) animals, (5) cameramen to shoot from different angles? Since your producer will prepare a budget, be specific as to how many of each item you want.
2. Assume you are a British subject visiting the colonies. One night you take a stroll down to the harbor and find that you are an eyewitness to the Boston Tea Party. Write home to a friend, describing in detail what you saw.
3. Assume you are a British General in the midst of the Revolutionary War. Draw a battle map of Boston, showing how you would surround the city and force the colonists to surrender.
4. Pretend you are a judge. Get one person to be trial lawyer for the crown and another to be trial lawyer for the colonies. What would the judge want to know about the following:
   a. Who started the war?
   b. What were the claims on each side?
   c. Were the claims justified?
   d. What other questions would be asked?
   Have the trial lawyers argue the merits of the case. Let the class be the jury.

TEACHING A CHAPTER
FROM A WOODSHOP TEXTBOOK

You have learned in detail how to teach a social studies chapter. This section will describe, in much less detail, how to help woodshop students understand the text *Wood Materials and Processes.*[2] Boxes 5.10–15 will show you a teacher task analysis, sample reading guides, and learning-from-text guides.

Our purpose in showing you how to teach from the social studies and the woodshop texts is to demonstrate that (1) the reading and learning-

[2] John L. Feirer, *Wood Materials and Processes* (Peoria, Ill.: Charles A. Bennett, 1975).

from-text guides can be applied to all content areas and that (2) the specific characteristics of each content area result in variations in the guides. For example, social studies has verbal and pictorial materials (charts, maps, and graphs), whereas woodworking has verbal and pictorial materials (blueprints), *plus* measurement, computational, and motor activities. These additional activities in woodshop overlap with mathematical and science content where measurement and computation are the main activities. Hence, woodshop students require separate sections on measurement and computation in their reading and learning-from-text guides. (See chapters 13 and 14 for science and math guides.)

BOX 5.10. Teacher Task Analysis

SECTION IV

"Making Pieces of Curved or Irregular Designs," pp. 164–180

Unit	Content	Process
18 D R A W	Identification and description of tools a divider a pencil compass trammel points Procedures for laying out and transferring designs circles rounded corners octagons hexagons ellipse Procedures for enlarging designs	Relating verbal description to diagram and picture Reading definitions Following directions a. verbally b. from diagrams and pictures
19 C U T	Identification and description of tools coping saw saw bracket vise compass saw Procedures for cutting curves adjusting blades turning handles	ditto

20	S M O O T H	Identification and description of tools spokeshave drawknife file rasp surform tool solid-router drills Procedures for forming and smoothing curves	ditto

BOX 5.11. Overview Guide

SECTION IV

"Making Pieces of Curved or Irregular Designs," pp. 164–180

When you finish reading Section IV, you should know how to do the following things:

Draw Designs *(Unit 18, pp. 165–170)*	*Cut Designs (Unit 19,* *pp. 170–174)*	*Smooth Designs* *(Unit 20, pp. 175–180)*

You will learn how to put curves and irregular designs on wood before you cut it.
 	
I. Tools you will need
  a. a divider
  b. a pencil compass
  c. trammel points
II. Designs you can make with these tools
  a. circles
  b. rounded corners
  c. an octagon
  d. a hexagon
  e. an ellipse
III. Enlargements of irregular designs that you can make
	You will learn how to cut curved patterns.
	  I. Tools you will need
	    a. a coping saw
	    b. a compass saw
	  II. Methods of cutting with these tools
	    a. with the work supported on a saw bracket
	    b. with the work held in a vise
	    c. proper turning of the handle by sawing
		You will learn how to form and smooth the curves you have cut.
		  I. Tools you will need
		    a. spokeshave
		    b. drawknife
		    c. file and rasp
		    d. surform tool
		    e. solid-router drills
		  II. Things you can do
		    a. cut concave and convex edges
		    b. Remove large amounts of stock quickly
		    c. scrape wood
		    d. smooth and form wood

1 **DRAW** —→	**2** **CUT** —→	**3** **SMOOTH**

BOX 5.12. Vocabulary Guide

SECTION IV

"Making Pieces of Curved
or Irregular Designs," pp. 164–180

Instructions: Below are some of the hard words you will find in Unit 20. Look over the definitions and the sentences from the textbook that contain them.

Word	Page	Definition	Sentence from Text
convex	175	a curve that bends outward	A spokeshave is used to plane *convex* (dome-shaped) and *concave* (cup-shaped) edges.
concave	175	a curve that bends inward	
exposed	176	open, in plain sight, not hidden	The long, *exposed* blade can be dangerous.
bevel	176	slant	Hold the tool in both hands, with the blade firmly against the wood and the *bevel* side down.

Pages referred to are from *Wood Materials and Processes.*

BOX 5.13. Processes-of-Reading Guide
FOLLOWING PRINTED INSTRUCTIONS

Activity 1. Look at each one of the houses below. What is wrong with each house?

  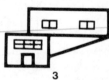

        1   2   3

Activity 2. Each of those houses was built poorly because instructions were not followed. What sorts of instructions were not followed in each case?

Case 1: _____

_____

Case 2: _____

_____

Case 3: _____

_____

Activity 3. Test your own ability at following written instructions by drawing pictures as you are directed to do.

1. Draw six parallel lines.

2. Draw circle with a one-inch diameter.

3. Draw a circle with a one-inch radius.

4. Draw a three-inch line. Divide it into three equal parts. Starting on your left, erase the first part. Darken the second part. Draw an X through the third part.

Activity 4. Read these instructions before you begin. Write your name in the top right hand corner of the paper. Draw a line connecting "Activity 4" with your name. On this line list the names of three tools you have used in woodshop this past week. After you write your name, don't do anything else.

BOX 5.14. *Learning-from-Text Guide*

SECTION IV: UNIT 18

Instructions: Read each of the following statements. If the statement is true put an X in the space provided.

Informational Comprehension
_____ 1. A divider, like sandpaper, is useful for smoothing out a piece of wood you have cut.
_____ 2. Trammel points come in handy when you are drawing circles.
_____ 3. When laying out a rounded corner, a try square and a divider are more useful than trammel points and a ruler.
_____ 4. Unlike an ellipse, you can draw a hexagon without a pencil compass or divider.

Inferential Comprehension
_____ 1. When drawing a circle, if your lines don't meet the problem might be with the thumbscrew.
_____ 2. John and Mark are both making table tops — one a hexagon, one an octagon. If they start drawing plans at the same time, Mark will be finished before John.

Generalized Comprehension

_____ 1. George has found some plans in a magazine for building an American Eagle wall plaque. However, the plans are ⅟₁₆ the size of the actual plaque when built. The drawing is 8″ by 8″. George cannot hang his finished eagle over the fireplace.

Evaluative Level

_____ 1. The chapter was well written and the pictures and diagrams were clear to me.
_____ 2. The information in this chapter got me more interested in woodworking than I was before.

BOX 5.15. Learning-from-Text Guide

SECTION IV: UNIT 19

Questions for Informational (or Directly Stated) Comprehension
1. What does the frame of a coping saw look like? (page 170, column 1, paragraph 4)
2. If you are going to cut a hole in the middle of a piece of wood, what would you need to do to your coping saw? (page 171, column 1, paragraph 1)
3. If cutting with the coping saw gets hard, what can you put on the blade to help? (page 171, column 2, paragraph 1)
4. Describe the shape of the compass saw. (page 173, column 1, paragraph 2)
5. How do you handle the compass saw in such a way so as to allow you to cut curves? (page 173, column 1, paragraph 4)

Questions for Inferential Comprehension
1. Contrast the designs of the coping and the compass saw. What sorts of tasks would be better done with a coping saw rather than a compass saw?
2. Why is the direction of the saw's teeth, with respect to the handle, important when using a saw bracket?

Question for Generalized Comprehension
Explain how you would go about cutting the letters of your first name.

Questions for Evaluative Comprehension
1. What items in this unit were particularly well presented?
2. What items were not clearly presented? How might the unit have been better presented?

Pages referred to are from *Wood Materials and Processes.*

SUMMARY

You have studied many techniques for teaching a chapter. We provided you with examples from social studies and industrial education. Using a chapter in social studies, we showed you how to construct such preteaching devices as (1) an entry level test, (2) an overview guide, (3) behavioral objectives, and a (4) teacher's task analysis. These techniques would help prepare your students for reading. Techniques to help your students while they are in the process of reading and learning from text are (1) a vocabulary guide, (2) a processes-of-reading guide, (3) a gloss, and (4) a learning-from-text guide. After students have read, you can present them with problems related to the chapter. We also showed you a variety of techniques that could be used in teaching a chapter from a woodshop text.

As you can see, to teach students to read and learn from a textbook chapter requires a large amount of your time and effort. Since you do not have the time to use *all* the strategies on *all* the chapters you teach, select a few, try them, reuse them, select others. Over a few years, you will have a fine collection of instructional materials. You will also have become experienced in the use of these strategies.

ACTIVITIES

1. Select a section of text from your own content area and prepare instructional materials for three parts of a lesson: one to be used by students before reading, one to be used while they are reading, one to be used after they have finished reading. If you have two sections of students taking the same course, use all three sets of instructional materials with one group but use none with the other. Simply assign the second group the chapter to read. Give the two groups a comprehension test based on the chapter. Is there a significant difference in the scores of the two groups?
2. Teach one of the strategies in this chapter, such as the use of a learning-from-text guide, to a group made up of your classmates (preservice teachers). Select content for your guide from any textbook. Tape the lesson for analysis and evaluation of your teaching.

6 | Letting the Students Do the Talking

CHAPTER OVERVIEW

As you recall from reading the last two chapters, teaching students to learn from textbooks involves planning discussion activities so that you can see what they know. Unfortunately, not all students come to class willing and/or able to participate in classroom discussions. This chapter focuses on three concepts: (1) teacher and student behaviors and attitudes that ensure a successful classroom discussion, (2) the types of discussion that stimulate student interaction, (3) procedures for grouping students for discussion and related work.

TECHNICAL VOCABULARY

discussion clusters
LTD method
Taba's levels of thinking
controlled discussion

free discussion
semicontrolled discussion
discussion

Learning through discussion   *9. sequential levels*

STUDENTS TELL WHAT THEY KNOW

To evaluate a student's ability at swimming, a coach usually has the student swim. To evaluate a student's ability at painting, a teacher has the student paint. The same is true of music, writing, and speaking. It is ironic that teachers usually evaluate a student's ability at reading and learning from text by asking the student to speak or write. Perhaps the most common classroom devices used to evaluate student ability at reading and learning from text are (1) classroom discussions and (2) written assignments. This chapter will focus on discussion; the next chapter, on writing.

THREE "DISCUSSIONS" AT WORK

Suppose that you, the reader, could be transported immediately to Monroe High where, at this moment, three science teachers are carrying on "discussions" with their students. Standing outside their respective rooms, you might hear the conversations that follow.

Classroom A

Mr. Phelps: All right, class, as you know, you were asked to read chapter 2 last night. As you recall, the chapter dealt with fresh water communities. Certain plants and animals can get along in some types of fresh water environments and some cannot. For instance — I hope you plan to take notes on this, especially in light of the test we're having next Friday — in sluggish water, such as that which you find in ponds, you will find algae, perhaps even fungi, that couldn't survive in the more rapid streams of the mountains. Ducks live beautifully on ponds, but I doubt that you'd find them paddling around the treacherous rapids of the Merced River, for example. Examine the long sleek appearance of the trout, and I dare any of you to find a better environment for the trout other than the swiftly running stream. How long do you think a goldfish could survive in a tank of chemically softened water? Not very long I tell you. It's nature's way to have the environment interact with the life forms that exist in it. Are there any questions you have on our discussion? Yes, Jim?

Jim: What does the word *environment* mean?

Mr. Phelps: Look it up in the dictionary! Any other questions for discussion? Good. Now for tonight, read the next chapter and we'll discuss it tomorrow.

Classroom B

Ms. Carley: Class, last night for homework you read chapter 2. Would you open your books to page 41? And let's talk about the chapter. First of all, what is an alga? *(No response.)* You might be familiar with it by its plural form, *algae.* Yes, Jim.

Jim: Isn't it a plant that grows in the water?

Ms. Carley: Lots of plants grow in the water! Could you be more specific? Yes, Mary.

Mary: It's a scum?

Ms. Carley: What do you mean by *scum?*

Mary: Slimy?

Ms. Carley: We're still not making it. Refer to the glossary at the back of your book. Would anyone care to read the definition for *alga* out loud? Yes, Pete?

Pete: "One of the group called *algae*"?

Ms. Carley: That does us a lot of good. What are algae?

Pete: Do you want me to read that definition?

Ms. Carley: Please.

Pete: "A group of water plants that produce their own food. They often take the form of scum on rocks."

Mary: That's what I said.

Jim: Me, too.

Ms. Carley: Yes, that's true, but your definition was not as precise as it might have been. Now, let's take that definition and look at the pictures on page 45. How does the definition fit the pictures? Yes, Tom?

Tom: Can I sharpen my pencil?

Classroom C

Mr. Spont: Open your books to page 43. I want you to study the picture there. Now how many of you would want to go swimming in that body of water? I don't see any hands. Don't you like to swim?

Jim: I like to swim, but not in that junk!

Mr. Spont: What do you mean "junk"?

Mary: Look at all that slimy stuff that's on the water. Look at the ducks.

Pete: What if you swallowed some of that stuff?

Mr. Spont: Where would you rather swim?

Joe: In a pool.

Mary: A lake.

Pete: A river, the ocean. But not in that stuff. It's like a swamp.

Mr. Spont: Why do you think the ducks like it?

Mary: They're probably used to it. They get their food from the pond.

Mr. Spont: What do they eat?

Pete: Bugs, worms. I guess.

Mr. Spont: What do the bugs and worms eat?

Jim: Littler bugs and worms, maybe. Plants.

Mr. Spont: What do the plants eat?

Mary: They get their food from the water.

Mr. Spont: What does this all mean?

Pete: That animals and plants depend upon each other.

Mr. Spont: Can you think of any other situations in which plants and animals depend upon each other?

WHAT IS DISCUSSION?

You can see, from the three examples above (and any experience you may have had in the classroom) discussion is not the easiest strategy to develop. If you asked all three teachers what they were doing they would probably all say they were attempting to carry on a discussion. Nevertheless, even a casual observer would note the dramatic differences in the three teaching styles.

In classroom A, Mr. Phelps is lecturing — that is, imparting to the students information which they are to assimilate. Even though the teacher asks for questions, it soon becomes clear to the students that he would consider any contribution they might make to be at best minor.

In classroom B, Ms. Carley is making some attempt at interaction, that is, asking questions about the text material which, it is hoped, the students can answer. However, students perceive that the teacher wants specific, almost preconceived answers, and after a minute or so, the casual observer is aware that this "discussion" will be short-lived, collapsing from lack of interest.

In classroom C, Mr. Spont is stimulating student response to text by posing an offbeat question or problem which the students solve by using text material. Unlike Mr. Phelps and Ms. Carley, Mr. Spont neither transmits information nor asks narrow questions, but rather encourages active responding by refusing to pass value judgments on the responses and by giving shape to student responses in the form of new questions. Even in classroom C, however, discussion is not functioning at the optimum level because only four students are participating. What are the other twenty or thirty students doing? Listening? Taking notes? Daydreaming? Doodling?

This chapter will focus on ways to stimulate total participation as students respond to text material. The first parts of the chapter are concerned with the nature of discussion and the relationship between discussion and critical thinking. The second part of the chapter will deal with grouping strategies that can be used to help a teacher ensure better discussion.

A popular school dictionary (Thorndike & Barnhart, 1971) defines *discussion* as the process of "considering [an issue] from different points of view . . . talk." Discussion can range from perfunctory chatter about the weather to the awesome deliberations of the United Nations. Somewhere between these two extremes is classroom discussion — more formal than over-the-fence gossip, less formal than summit conferences. If one accepts that a classroom of students is a social structure, the importance of that discussion is obvious.

TYPES OF DISCUSSION

Effective classroom discussion varies with the instructional purpose. Four general types of discussion, however, make differing demands on teachers: *free discussion, semicontrolled discussion, controlled discussion* (Hill, 1969; Taba, 1965, 1967), and *discussion clusters*.

Free Discussion

Free discussion is relatively unstructured and demands a minimum of teacher control. It allows students to (1) react emotionally to a text selection, (2) speak randomly on an issue, (3) let off steam, or (4) raise an issue for future consideration. Read the following excerpt from a free discussion in Ms. Jones's tenth-grade world history class.

> *Ms. Jones:* What did you learn about the ancient Egyptians last night?
> *Joe:* I didn't like them.
> *Mary:* I didn't either.
> *Ms. Jones:* Why not?
> *Joe:* They were mean — the way they made their slaves do everything.
> *Carlo:* I couldn't see why they're so important.
> *Mark:* I couldn't pronounce half the names.
> *Jo-Anne:* The book shows you how to pronounce them.
> *Chris:* The chapter was too long. . . .
> *Gloria:* Too many facts. . . .
> *Ms. Jones:* Didn't any of you like anything about the Egyptians?
> *Sally:* They built pyramids.
> *Sam:* What's so good about that?
> *George:* Hey, man, that's great architecture. . . .

Notice that, in the previous discussion, the teacher's focusing question was general, open-ended, allowing students to expound freely on what they liked or didn't like about content in their world history chapter.

Although free discussions are occasionally beneficial, even therapeutic, they should be balanced with discussions that get somewhere, that reach a conclusion, such as the semicontrolled and the controlled discussions.

Semicontrolled Discussion

Semicontrolled discussion occurs when students exchange and integrate information for some future instructional purpose. Generally, this strategy is used when students have different, but related, textbook assignments. In Mr. Inglish's twelfth-grade literature class one group had been assigned the poetry and prose of John Milton; another group the Cavalier poets; another group selected readings from John Dryden, Izaak Walton, and Samuel Butler; and a fourth group the plays of William Congreve. After the class had done most of the reading, Mr. Inglish brought them together to discuss social problems in seventeenth-century England as reflected in the literature, in preparation for a research paper assignment. An excerpt from that discussion follows:

> *Mr. Inglish:* What social problems did the seventeenth-century British writers write about, either directly or indirectly?
>
> *José:* Religion was one.
>
> *Margo:* There was so much religious confusion.
>
> *Mr. Inglish:* Who wrote about that?
>
> *Margo:* Milton. I don't think Roman Catholics or Anglicans cared too much for his view of God in *Paradise Lost.*
>
> *Mr. Inglish:* Before we get into that, what other problems were there?
>
> *George:* Milton also wrote about censorship, in *Areopagitica.*
>
> *Jo-Anne:* Some writers didn't deal with social problems.
>
> *Jim:* Izaak Walton — fishing.
>
> *Mary:* What about all those poets?
>
> *Marcella:* They *were* a social problem. . . .
>
> *Jim:* Now watch that stuff, Marcy.
>
> *Marcella:* You know what I meant.
>
> *Mr. Inglish:* We'll need to list a few more. Then we'll go back one by one, starting with religion, and see what research paper topics we can come up with.

Like free discussion, semicontrolled discussion begins with a fairly broad focusing question: What social problems did the seventeenth-century British writers write about, either directly or indirectly? Also, students are encouraged to contribute with little control from the teacher. Note, however, that students are contributing information which will be used later in the discussion — they are not merely talking freely — and that the teacher is starting to shape the direction the discussion will follow.

Controlled Discussion

Controlled discussion occurs when students contribute to a carefully planned, articulated, and sequenced hierarchy of questions, generally starting with those meant to elicit lower-order cognitive processes and going on to those calling for higher-order reasoning. Unlike free discussion, the teacher controls the flow of discussion to ensure the maintenance of sequence. Two models of controlled discussion provide direction for teaching discussion of text: the Learning Through Discussion (LTD) method (Hill, 1969) and Hilda Taba's levels of thinking and method of discussion (Taba, 1965, 1967).

LEARNING THROUGH DISCUSSION (LTD)

Mr. Spont teaches an ecology course. One chapter in the textbook focused on how industry has altered the physical environment. One student remarked that the book's treatment was unfair to industry. Another student claimed the book was objective. To settle the argument to the class's satisfaction, Mr. Spont decided to use the *learning through discussion method (LTD), which is a method for effective problem-solving*. The topic the class discussed was whether the chapter was biased or objective. Mr. Spont led them through the nine steps of LTD in sequence. See box 6.1.

BOX 6.1. The Learning-Through-Discussion Method

1. Definition of terms to be used in solving the problem the readings pose is first rendered by the participating students.
2. One or more students state in general terms the author's message.
3. The principal themes are established.
4. Time is allocated for the discussion and its sub-parts.
5. Major themes of the text are discussed.
6. Ideas are integrated.
7. Ideas are applied to another situation.
8. The author's message is evaluated.
9. The discussion process itself is evaluated.

Whereas LTD may be too formal and academic for many teachers' tastes, *Taba's levels of thinking* is more acceptable.

LEVELS OF THINKING AND METHOD OF DISCUSSION

This method of controlled discussion, developed by Taba (1965, 1967), proceeds in nine sequential levels grouped in three major divisions, as shown in box 6.2.

BOX 6.2. Taba's Levels of Thinking
and Method of Discussion

Note: The levels are arranged from the beginning of the discussion at the bottom of the table and proceed upwards.

Level	Activity	Major Divisions
9	Verifying Predictions	III. Application
8	Explaining/Supporting Predictions	of Principles
7	Predicting Consequences	
6	Making Inferences	II. Interpreting
5	Explaining Identified Points	Inferring
4	Identifying Points	Generalizing
3	Labeling/Categorizing	I. Concept
2	Grouping	Formation
1	Enumerating and Listing	

To direct a discussion that gets somewhere, that is, leads to a conclusion, the teacher will have to pose a series of questions that will move the discussion sequentially from recall of factual information to construction of a generalization. As discussion proceeds the teacher must be in control to prevent students moving too quickly to higher levels of thinking or staying too long at one level.

In the role of discussion leader, the teacher must be able to (1) set the focus for discussion; (2) refocus on the discussion topic as student contributions wander from the topic; (3) change the focus of discussion when such a shift is needed; (4) clarify confusing points; (5) offer support (broaden patterns of thinking); (6) initiate exploration of new dimensions; (7) recap and summarize; and (8) lift the discussion to higher levels by having students abstract from literal levels and then asking them to generalize and/or evaluate a conclusion.

In box 6.3 are excerpts from a high school class discussion that follows the Taba method. Left marginal glosses indicate the roles the teacher is assuming in the discussion. Right marginal glosses indicate the levels of thinking being used.

BOX 6.3. Excerpt from a Taba Levels-of-Thinking
Discussion in a High School English Class

Focus ———→ *Mr. Inglish:* What would the plots of Shakespeare's tragedies be like if Shakespeare were writing today?

Mary: They'd be about today's problems.

George: No, they would be about the past. Shakespeare didn't write about his own times.

Refocus ⟶

Mr. Inglish: Now before we go off in all directions, it's important that we think this topic through carefully. What sort of things do we know about Shakespeare? As you say these items, I will list them on the board.

I. Concept Formation

Jo-Anne: He wrote plays and poems.

Sam: He was popular. Everyone liked his stuff.

A. Enumerating and Listing (Level 1)

Margo: He wrote quickly and much.

Sally: He said things that are still quoted today.

Mary: He wrote different types of plays: comedies, tragedies, and histories.

Refocus ⟶

Mr. Inglish: We may want to use that information later, but right now we want to concentrate on the tragedies.

Phil: This may also be off the track, but weren't very few of his plays original? Didn't he borrow his plots from other sources?

Support ⟶

Mr. Inglish: Yes he did, and we'll use that.

George: He wrote in verse.

Mary: And, as you pointed out, the same lines could mean different things to different people. For instance, with *Macbeth* some of the audience actually believed in witches, so the weird sisters were truly frightening to them. To other people in the audience, witches were only symbols.

José: You can never tell what Shakespeare's true feelings are.

David: You don't know which character to side with. There don't seem to be villains — I mean there are villains but you tend to like them.

Clarification ⟶

Mr. Inglish: Shakespeare makes all his characters human — is that what you're saying?

David: Yes, they are all complicated people.

Martha: I couldn't stand *Hamlet*.

Initiating a new
dimension ⟶

Mr. Inglish: Maybe we should take a look at our list now and see where we are. Do any of the items on the board group themselves with other items?

B. Grouping
(Level 2)

George: "Plays and poems" seems to go with "he wrote in verse."

Phil: "Popular" goes with "lines with different meanings for different people."

Margo: "Wrote quickly and much" goes with "borrowing plots." That's probably why he wrote so fast.

Initiating a new
dimension ⟶

Mr. Inglish: Do these groups have titles — that is, can we give names to these groups?

C. Labeling/
Categorizing
(Level 3)

Dan: We seem to have two categories up there: items about plays themselves and items that deal with the way people react to reading or seeing the plays.

Clarification and
recap ⟶

Mr. Inglish: In other words, you are saying the items group themselves like this: *(Teacher puts the following chart on board).*

The Plays Themselves
1. He wrote plays and poems.
2. He wrote in verse.
3. He wrote quickly and much.
4. He borrowed his plots.
5. His characters were three-dimensional, complicated.

How People Reacted to Plays
1. The plays were popular.
2. They had something for everyone.
3. You can't figure out Shakespeare's attitudes and beliefs.
4. People today still quote lines from Shakespeare.

Mr. Inglish: Is there anything else that could be added in either category?

Tom: If people quote lines from Shakespeare, doesn't that mean they would have to read or see the plays more than once.

Broadening
patterns of
thinking ⟶

Mr. Inglish: We'll add that point. What bothers me about this list is that these statements could hold for all plays. Is there anything we could say about tragedies?

Dan: I thought we had said the villains were likeable. That would be a specific comment about tragedies.

Refocus, clarification ⟶

Mr. Inglish: We could list that, I guess. But there were villains in comedies, too.

Mary: Evil always tends to be punished.

Margo: The leading characters usually destroy themselves through some sort of weakness in their personalities.

Phil: A lot of times they get caught up in their own plots.

José: Another thing I have noticed is that, even though they lose out in the end, you sort of feel that they could have made it if they'd tried harder.

Recap ⟶

Mr. Inglish: I think we've got enough to start with here. Let's see, we've listed some characteristics about the plays themselves and another group of items that deal with how people have reacted to the tragedies. Now our next concern is to see how this

Initiating a new dimension ⟶

information can help us see what Shakespeare's tragedies would be like today. Let's start with the category of facts under people's reactions. Were the people in Shakespeare's time different in tastes than the people today?

II. Interpreting, inferring, and generalizing

José: It depended on the social class you were from, but generally, as far as our book said, the chief competition for the theater was bear-baiting. That's bloody. So the people wanted something sensational, exciting.

Identifying point #1

Mr. Inglish: Is that different from people today?

Mary: No, look at the attendance at football games, basketball games, boxing matches. People like the sight of blood.

Explaining point #1

José: Yes, but are Shakespeare's tragedies as bloody as a boxing match?

Mary: Bloodier. The blood's real, not make-believe.

Clarification ⟶ *Mr. Inglish:* What you seem to be saying, is that Elizabethan audiences liked real blood and make-believe blood about the same, but that you're not sure about modern audiences.

David: Modern audiences like make-believe blood more. More people watch crime shows on television than go to boxing matches — or even better, more people watch sporting events on TV than in person.

Refocus ⟶ *Mr. Inglish:* Hold the discussion of TV for later. So we've identified violence as one common characteristic of today's and Elizabethan audi-

Broadening patterns of thinking ⟶ ence. What other common characteristics are there? *(Waits, but there are no other contributions.)* Well, are there points of contrast?

Jack: Behavior at plays was different then than it is today. People sat all over the place, ate food, even yelled back to the players. It was more like being at a sporting event. Theaters today are more stuffy and who can afford them. My Dad paid twenty-five dollars for two tickets to a play.

Identifying point #2

Explaining point #2

Clarification ⟶ *Mr. Inglish:* What you seem to be saying is that the theater has become more middle-class and upper-middle-class.

Margo: People today like television and movies more. That's where the entertainment is focused. TV and movies have something for everyone; theater doesn't.

José: Just as we said people saw Shakespeare plays over and over, today we see movies over and over. My aunt claims she saw *Gone With the Wind* twelve times.

Mary: And everyone knows lines from *Casablanca.*

George: In fact, I think if Shakespeare were living today, he'd be writing not for the theater, but for television or the movies.

Inference drawn from discussing points #1 and #2

Initiating a new → dimension

Mr. Inglish: How do the rest of you react to that? *(General agreement.)* All right, let's say that Shakespeare would be a television or movie writer. Would he be able to write tragedies that have the characteristics we've talked about?

Margo: I don't think people would dig verse, even if it were in modern language.

Identifying point #3

John: There have been some modern plays in verse, like some of Maxwell Anderson's.

Explaining point #3

Clarification →

Mr. Inglish: But, remember, John, we're talking about movies and television.

John: I saw the movie *Winterset,* but I can't remember if that was in verse.

David: I saw something on television several years ago — a story about men in space, and it was in blank verse.

Clarification → *Mr. Inglish:* But was it popularly received?

Margo: How many in here heard of it? *(No hands.)*

Recap → *Mr. Inglish:* It seems, then, that Shakespeare's tragedies could not be in verse, if he were to write for movies and television and be popular.

Inference drawn from point #3

John: Television writers write a lot — and fast too. So do movie writers. Shakespeare would fit in well here.

Identifying/ explaining point #4

Support
Broadening patterns of thinking

Mr. Inglish: No disagreement here, John. What about borrowing plots? Would that go on television?

Identifying point #5

Jim: There are only so many plot lines. Practically everything you see on television is a rehash of something else.

Explaining point #5

Clarification →

Mr. Inglish: That may be true, but Shakespeare's borrowings were more than a rehash. He got the ideas from other literary works or historical sources and then modeled suc-

Refocus ———→	cessful literary works from them. Now the question is what comparable sources would be available to today's Shakespeare?	
	Mary: Newspaper stories, magazine articles.	
	Phil: Novels. That's done all the time.	
	George: Television writers even rewrite old Broadway plays or even older movie scripts.	
Recap ————→ Broadening patterns of ———→ thinking	*Mr. Inglish:* So today's Shakespeare could still borrow and convert satisfactorily. What about complicated characters?	Inference drawn from point #5 Identifying point #6
	Sally: That's hard to deal with. Most people like heroes and villains and don't want to think.	Explaining point #6
	José: But Shakespeare, I think we said, entertained on all levels. He could have complicated characters but present them in such a way that people who were simple could still enjoy the play.	
	Jo-Anne: How could that be done?	
	José: By making the plot interesting, having lots of action, humor, even slapstick. Look at some of those funny scenes in *Hamlet*.	
Clarification and recap ———→	*Mr. Inglish:* So, then, you feel that today's Bard could have complicated characters without alienating the audience. *(General agreement.)*	Inference drawn from point #6
	(The discussion proceeds through other characteristics of Shakespearean tragedy.)	
Recap	*Mr. Inglish:* So far we have determined that Shakespeare today would probably be writing for movies or television, that he could successfully portray complicated characters, in borrowed plots, and that these plots could have downbeat, or unhappy, endings without alienating the audience. Now, can we predict some specific plot lines that Shakespeare might write successfully?	III. Application of principles
Initiating a new dimension ———→		
	José: How about a love story set in the midst of the Civil War, in which a	A. Prediction of consequences

young Yankee soldier falls in love with a Southern Belle — and all the problems they get into.

Margo: What about a ruthless businessman whose ambition drives him to commit murder and later pay the consequences with a guilty conscience.

Sally: How about a young college student returning home from a year of study, only to find his widowed mother remarried to his uncle, who he thinks killed his father.

Initiating a new → dimension

Mr. Inglish: What makes you think that these would be Shakespeare's plots, other than the fact that you borrowed these ideas from his plays? Let's start with José's plot.

B. Explaining/ supporting predictions

George: Stories about the Civil War make good viewing. Look at *Gone With the Wind, The Red Badge of Courage, Raintree County* — all movie scripts borrowed from other sources.

Judy: Plus the fact that many people were killed in the Civil War. We think of it a lot. It makes us sad.

Mary: And the characters could seem modern. The boy could look and act like a high school senior today. The girl could act like a cheerleader or something like that. Shakespeare's characters were all Elizabethan, regardless of where the play was supposed to take place.

(The class moves through the other two plot lines.)

Initiating a → new dimension

Mr. Inglish: Now that we have established three probable plot lines for today's Shakespeare, how can we verify that our predictions are correct?

C. Verifying predictions

Jim: One way is to get the television ratings and box office statistics for movies and programs that have comparable plot lines. We could see what the popular appeal will be.

Mary: Well, you know right now that

crime, violence, and sex are the entertainment world's staple products.

Jerry: Another way is to research the lives of prominent movie and television writers to see how they write, what attitudes about human beings they have, and where they got their ideas.

Support ⟶ *Mr. Inglish:* These are all good ideas. Since time is running out, I would like to summarize what we've done. By examining the nature of Shakespeare's tragedies and the people who attended them, we felt that today's Shakespeare would write for television and/or the movies. His tragedies would have lots of action,

Recap ⟶ be based on novels, plays, magazine articles, or any other available source; they would also have complicated characters and unhappy endings. We predicted the content of three such tragedies, supported our predictions by comparisons to Shakespeare's existing works as projected into a twentieth-century medium, and were able, potentially, to verify our plot predictions by television ratings and box office sta-

Support ⟶ tistics. I'd say you did a good day's work today. Class dismissed.

So far you have seen examples of teacher-led discussion. In teaching your students to be independent learners you should instruct them to apply LTD and Taba's levels of thinking to their own student-conducted discussions. The best device for applying these two is the discussion cluster, which can be led by students.

Discussion Clusters

Discussion clusters, or groups, can be used in panel discussions. The teacher may pose a specific problem, divide the class into five or six clusters to discuss a problem and come up with solutions. Under ideal circumstances, the chairperson of each cluster then forms a staged panel discussion to deal with the various solutions. Ms. Stewart's mathematics class became involved in a heated discussion about the relative merits of new mathematics and old mathematics. During the discussion Ms. Stewart listed these five points on the board:

1. Inability to get help at home
2. Elaborateness of the textbook explanations
3. The questionable need to know how mathematics concepts are developed
4. The mixing of areas of mathematics — mixing algebra with geometry
5. Teacher education

Since time didn't permit a detailed discussion of each one of these points, the teacher divided the class into five clusters, and assigned one problem to each. Every cluster was to (1) select a leader to moderate discussion and a recorder to take notes, (2) determine how serious the problem was, (3) pose solutions to the problem, and (4) have the recorder write down the cluster's findings. The students were given five minutes to discuss the question and each cluster leader was given one minute to report to the rest of the class. From the first to the last shuffling of chairs, the entire discussion took less than fifteen minutes, but Ms. Stewart felt it covered an amazing amount of material.

When first using clusters, the teacher should keep the tasks simple. When the clusters return to the total class setting, the teacher should have the students discuss how they performed as cluster members.

GROUPING STUDENTS FOR DISCUSSION

So far in this chapter, you have read examples of successful and unsuccessful classroom discussions. You have noted that, although free discussion has its place in the classroom, controlled discussion that gets somewhere requires students to develop and use multiple thought processes. In teaching students to discuss what they've read from text, you must be a model discussion leader, and you must transmit discussion skills to the students so they can function independently in small group discussions. Consequently, you will need to understand (1) the nature of grouping, (2) how to group successfully, and (3) how to teach discussion skills to students.

The Nature of a Group

Several definitions of *group* provide insights into the nature of clustering students for discussion of text or related work. Lee (1968) defines a group as "those children who at that time have common specific concerns, needs, interests, or plans [p. 198].'' Evans (1966) gives a definition that is psychologically oriented. It differentiates between *group* and *togetherness*. The group is goal-directed. *Togetherness* implies no particular goal other than social interaction. Another definition of *group* (Barrington and Rogers, 1968) stresses student self-selection and self-direction. All these definitions include (1) united effort and (2) orientation toward a task.

How to Group Successfully

According to Flanders (1954), successful grouping procedures are difficult to achieve for five reasons:

1. Some teachers have misguided notions about grouping.
2. Some teachers have not developed the skills necessary to handle small groups.
3. Successful groups cannot be formed randomly or haphazardly.
4. Developing leadership in each group is a challenge to any teacher.
5. Students must be indoctrinated as to their roles as group members.

Suggestions on how to avoid each of these difficulties are given as prerequisites 1–5.

PREREQUISITE 1. AVOID ACCEPTING MYTHS ABOUT GROUP WORK. Teachers hear many myths about small group work. The first myth is that a group can learn. In reality, only individuals within a group can learn (Allen, 1968). As a result, a teacher cannot assume that success in a group project necessarily means that all group members participated equally and learned the same amount. A second myth is that group success occurs automatically when students of similar achievement and intelligence levels are bound together in a united effort. It is wrong to assume that achievement and intelligence are the only bases for grouping; it is equally wrong to assume that students will automatically be self-directed once they are placed in groups. A third myth is that grouping requires the teacher to prepare an endless number of questions for the group to answer. Although a teacher-prepared discussion guide containing questions is useful, students in a group need to generate their own questions and problems. (See chapter 4 for procedure on teaching students to ask their own questions.)

PREREQUISITE 2. ACQUIRE THE SKILLS NECESSARY TO HANDLE SMALL GROUPS. Success in handling small groups requires certain qualities in the teacher. Flanders (1954) suggests nine teacher qualities necessary for successful small group procedures. These qualities are:

1. Alertness and readiness to share responsibility of selecting particular students to be in a group
2. Knowledge of the subject matter used in groups
3. Sensitivity to pupil readiness for group work
4. Evaluative skill
5. Tolerance of noise and confusion
6. Calmness
7. Willingness to foster independence in students
8. Sensitivity toward differences in group pace
9. Willingness to share ideas with the principal and the rest of the faculty

Now, turn to the three discussions on pages 108–109 of this chapter. Which of the above qualities did the teachers in Classrooms A, B, and C exhibit? Which of the above qualities might the teachers in Classrooms A, B, and C have the potential to exhibit, given the appropriate classroom circumstances?

PREREQUISITE 3. KNOW HOW GROUPS ARE BEST FORMED. Knowing how to form a group is, in a sense, the most difficult problem for a classroom teacher. Teachers can group students geographically, that is, by where they sit in the classroom. In just a few seconds, students can move their chairs around to form small clusters. One teacher staged practice drills in which students were timed to see how quickly they could move into groups. Teachers can also group students randomly by assigning numbers (1, 2, 3, 4, 5, 6) to six students and repeating for another six students, and so forth. (If the division is not even, assign any leftover students to the groups being formed.) Then all the 1s will form one group, the 2s will form another group, and so forth.

Another way to form a group is by interest. The teacher circulates a list of discussion topics. Students sign up for the topics that interest them. Then they form groups with others who signed up for the same topics.

No matter which grouping technique is used, teachers should pay attention to group size and balance of topics. One recommendation for group size is a minimum of *three* and a maximum of *eight* (Barrington and Rogers, 1968). With less than three, group process is impossible. With more than eight, it is improbable. Also crucial is the list of topics: all topics should be equally attractive. Avoid situations in which there is oversubscription to one topic on the one hand and universal rejection of another topic on the other hand.

We shall illustrate successful grouping by means of the case study presented in box 6.4. In this case study a teacher employed group discussion techniques and experienced several problems.

BOX 6.4. Case Study: Reading of a Short Story
Followed by Group Discussion

Introduction: Stephen Crane's short story, "The Open Boat," can be difficult reading, even for seniors enrolled in "Modern Literature," a course designed for students planning to attend community colleges. The students, generally speaking, didn't do their homework; as a result, the teacher scheduled time in class for quiet reading. After introducing the story, reviewing reading and language problems the students might have with it, the teacher allowed thirty minutes of class time for the students to read "The Open Boat"; they were asked to finish the story for homework.

By the next day, the teacher had prepared a small group discussion guide to facilitate understanding of the story. At the beginning of the period, she had the students count off by 4 and had them form groups based on their numbers. Each group was asked to select (1) a chairperson who would direct discussion, (2) a recorder to take notes and report the group's findings to the rest of the class in a symposium with the other recorders, and (3) a topic from the discussion guide — topic I, II, III, or IV. What follows is a copy of the discussion guide. The parenthetical comments were made by the teacher observing the discussions.

"THE OPEN BOAT"

A Discussion Guide with Parenthetical Comments
by the Teacher on Students' Discussion

I. *Characterization. (This was a popular topic that three of the four groups selected. It seemed to be easier than the other three. Problems arose in the symposium because three of the four recorders said about the same thing. It would have been better if I had advised two of the three groups to change topics.)*
   A. The cook
      1. What impressions does Crane give us about the cook in the second paragraph of the story? *(Students found the word* impressions *difficult to deal with. I had to explain to each of the three groups what I meant.)*
      2. How do his manner of speech and his appearance fit together?
      3. What verbs in this paragraph are particularly effective in describing the cook?
      4. What additional character traits does the cook reveal as the story progresses?
   B. The oiler
      1. In what ways is the oiler prepared for his struggle with the sea?
      2. How does he differ from the cook? List several specific ways.
   C. The correspondent
      1. How does the correspondent differ from the cook and the oiler? *(Students complained that these questions were repetitive and uninteresting.)*
      2. Crane says that the correspondent "wondered why he was there." What is the significance of that line? *(I should have written* importance *rather than* significance.*)* In other words, what does the line reveal about the

correspondent's character and personality? *(I'm glad I added this enabling rephrasing of the previous question.)*
D. The injured captain
 1. What is the author's general attitude toward the captain? *(Students copied sentences from the book, I feel, without understanding what they meant. Recorders tended to read the copied sentences rather than paraphrase them.)*

II. Plot *(One group picked this topic.)*
 A. Conflict
  1. What are the two forces pitted one against another, creating a vital conflict situation? *(I had to rephrase this question for the group.)*
  2. Are the forces evenly matched? Explain. *(There occurred much giggling in the group because students started talking about matches and cigarettes.)*
  3. Does the conflict of the men in the boat bring out the strengths and weaknesses of their characters? Explain, using specific examples and direct quotations from the story. *(I overheard the chairperson ask a conscientious student to get the right answers, write them out, and give them to him to read. The student obliged.)*
 B. Artistic Structure *(I should have written "Plot Structure.")*
  1. At what point in the story does the suspense reach the highest point — the turning point in the story? *(The students couldn't agree on the turning point; they insisted on finding the "right" answer.)*
  2. This turning point is called the climax or crisis. What are the events preceding the crisis that would make up the rising action? *(Students wanted to know what I wanted from them.)*
  3. What events following the crisis would make up the falling action?

III. Theme *(No group took this section.)*
 A. Is "The Open Boat" merely a story about a group of men who battle the sea or is there a deeper significance to the story? Explain.
 B. What are the attitudes of the characters toward the sea? Indicate their specific actions that reveal these attitudes.
 C. What do you think is the author's attitude toward nature? What poignant phrases does he use to reveal this attitude?
 D. Of what significance is the fact that the oiler, the most fit to survive, is the one to drown?
 E. Why hasn't Crane given his characters specific names?
 F. Do the four occupants of the boat make up a cross section of society? Explain. Look up the word *microcosm* in the dictionary. How does that word apply to the story "The Open Boat"?

IV. Style *(No group took this section.)*
 A. How would you characterize Crane's use of language: simple or complicated? Take into consideration such factors as the words he uses, the formality or informality of his sentences. Why does he use this particular style of language?
 B. One critic has said that Crane has caught the rhythm of the sea by varying his sentence length so that, in a given paragraph, a short sentence is followed by a longer sentence and then by a still longer sentence, then a shorter

sentence, then a short sentence. Select several paragraphs, and by counting the number of *syllables* in each of the paragraphs, determine if the critic was correct.

C. Crane is a master at mood. He can prejudice the reader by the words he uses. How does Crane prejudice the reader against the forces of nature? Select several of his most vivid passages for examples.

Now that you have reviewed the discussion guide with the teacher's parenthetical comments, ask yourself these questions:

1. Was the teacher unduly critical of the discussion guide or was he justified?
2. Refer to Flanders' nine teacher qualities on page 125. How many of these qualities were present in the preparation of the discussion guide?
3. How might the grouping of the students, the distribution of topics, and the questions themselves been handled more thoughtfully? Refer to the discussions of LTD and Taba's levels of thinking on pages 113–114.

PREREQUISITE 4. TRAIN STUDENTS TO BE LEADERS. The concept of group leadership is complex. To be effective, each small group should function with a student leader, selected either by the group (internal authority) or by the teacher (external authority). Evans (1966) sees the type of leadership role as dependent upon (1) the source of the leader's authority and (2) the source of the task, whether an external source (the teacher), the leader of the group, or the group itself. His chart on the possible leadership situations is in table 6.1.

Barrington and Rogers (1968) describe, in more general terms, three types of leadership. The *authoritarian* leader maps out a plan of action which the group members accept and follow. This type of leadership is desirable when the goal is a high-quality *product* or result. However, when the goal does not emphasize the product, nor the process, nor the means to a goal, then *democratic* leadership, where there is group agreement on division of labor through preliminary discussion, is best. *Laissez-faire* leadership, where each member marks out a particular aspect of work for himself or herself and then proceeds with it, can end in chaos.

Since many students lack knowledge and skill in leading a group, training for leadership skills should become an important part of the curriculum. Have training sessions for your discussion leaders in which you communicate to them the LTD and Taba methods. The leaders could function as a small group with rotating leaders. See the Quest procedure in chapter 13 (page 00) and review the sections on LTD and Taba on pages 113–114 of this chapter for discussion procedures.

TABLE 6.1. Possible Leadership Situations

Leader	Source of Authority	Source of Task
I. outsider	external	external
outsider	external	leader
outsider	external	group
II. outsider	internal	external
outsider	internal	leader
outsider	internal	group
III. group member	external	external
group member	external	leader
group member	external	group
IV. group member	internal	external
group member	internal	leader
group member	internal	group
V. no leader		external
		group
		no task

Source: K. M. Evans, "Group Methods," *Education Research* 9 (1966): 44–50. Reprinted by permission.

~~PREREQUISITE 5. TEACH STUDENTS TO ASSUME ROLES IN GROUPS.~~ In training students to become leaders, a broader consideration of the possible roles a student can assume in a discussion group is helpful. As shown in box 6.5, there can be as many as eighteen. Students can learn to assume maintenance and task roles. They can also learn to avoid self-serving roles by frequently evaluating themselves and others in group situations.

BOX 6.5. Student Roles in a Discussion Group

I. Maintenance roles
  A. Encouraging
  B. Expressing group feelings
  C. Harmonizing
  D. Compromising
  E. Gatekeeping (keeping communications channels open)
  F. Setting standards

II. Task roles
  A. Initiating
  B. Information or opinion seeking

     C. Information or opinion giving
     D. Clarifying or elaborating
     E. Summarizing
     F. Consensus taking
III. Self-serving Roles
     A. Dominating
     B. Blocking
     C. Deserting
     D. Quarreling
     E. Recognition seeking
     F. Goofing off

PHASING OUT THE TEACHER

By teaching students discussion techniques, group process, and leadership, a teacher can train students to be independent in discussions. This training occurs in phases:

Phase 1: the teacher is a model discussion leader, exhibiting in classroom discourse ideal leadership traits.

Phase 2: students become aware of these traits and on a gradual trial and error basis, with teacher evaluation, attempt to model them in small group discussions.

Phase 3: students gain so much facility in discussion that they rely on teacher direction less and less.

SUMMARY

Discussion can be a rewarding way for a student to respond to text. However, the discussion process must be taught actively and learned. This instructional activity means that the teacher must know how to lead a discussion that reaches a conclusion. In turn, students must learn to be discussion leaders and develop skills as participants in a discussion group. Some types of discussion a teacher can use include free discussion, semicontrolled, and controlled discussions. Procedures for conducting these types of discussion are Learning Through Discussion (LTD) and the Taba methods. Through imitation and a phase-out strategy, students can eventually learn to function independently in small discussion groups.

In addition to discussion, another way to respond to text is through writing. Our next chapter presents types and ways to teach writing.

ACTIVITIES

1. Review the three discussions presented on pages 108–109 of this chapter. Select a discussion conducted by one teacher — Mr. Phelps, Ms. Carley, or Mr. Spont — and write a critique of the discussion, using the five prerequisites of good discussion as a basis for your critique. See how your critique agrees or disagrees with another student's critique. Discuss the reasons for the differences. Are your perspectives and values on education different from that student's in any way?

2. Plan a discussion activity in your content area that requires discussion clusters. Remember to pose a general problem which is to be solved by dividing it into subproblems for small group discussion. Try your plan out in two classes. In one class, give the groups only the main problem. In the other class, give the groups each a subproblem. Note which class discusses the problem at greater length and depth. Why?

7 Letting the Students Do the Writing

CHAPTER OVERVIEW

In the last chapter, you learned how students can be taught to discuss what they read. In this chapter, you will see how students can learn to write clearly about what they have read. Although the teaching of writing is primarily the responsibility of the English teacher, other teachers who give writing assignments need to help their students learn how to do them. This chapter will demonstrate how to teach such writing techniques as paraphrasing, reporting procedures, exposition, narration, argumentation, and answering essay questions. In addition, you will learn how to prepare *model papers* for students to emulate, how to evaluate papers, and how to grade them. At the conclusion of this chapter, you will be taken, step by step, through a specific writing assignment involving reference reading.

TECHNICAL VOCABULARY

composing *vs.* copying
paraphrasing
reflexive writing
extensive writing
reporting

exposition
narration
argumentation
holistic evaluation techniques

Like discussion, writing in the classroom is an important means for student response to text. Like discussion, writing can take many forms. Like discussion, writing is often taken for granted: it is assigned but not taught. As a consequence, student writing can result in bitter disappointment for teacher and student alike. Ms. Jones gave this essay question to her history class: "Who do you think was the most important figure in the Revolutionary War?" Consider her chagrin when she read the answer below.

> I think the Gorge Washinton the most impartat figure in the Revaltionary War. He new how to get long well with is men and the respect him. Tack for insense, the surprise attack at Vally forge. The British wernt expect him, so he cam down on knight and suprized them his men follow him the hole way. Thats why Washington most importat of alother peopel in this war.

Then consider how the chagrin deepened when Ms. Jones subsequently received this library report, done at home, by the same student:

> WASHINGTON, GEORGE (1732–1799), won a lasting place in American history as the "Father of his country." For nearly 20 years, he guided his country much as a father cares for a growing child.
> In three important ways, Washington helped shape the beginning of the United States. First, he commanded the Continental Army that won American independence from Great Britain in the Revolutionary War. . . .[1]

Student writing does have its lighter moments. Examine the following samples from Mr. Inglish's literature class:

1. "Bewick Finzer" was indeed a sadist; he was always going around feeling sorry for himself.
2. The bus pulled to the curb, stopped, and got off.
3. The dark figure crept up behind her and stabbed her between the nose.

The extreme difficulties of students' learning to write clearly can be vividly seen in the H*Y*M*A*N K*A*P*L*A*N stories by Leonard Q. Ross (Leo Rosten). Hyman Kaplan is an exuberant, undaunted immigrant who is taking night-school English to gain citizenship. He is not unlike the students at Monroe High for whom English is a second language. In one of the stories, Hyman Kaplan writes on the front board the composition below for class analysis.

My Job A Cotter in Dress Faktory
Comp. by H*Y*M*A*N K*A*P*L*A*N
Shakspere is saying what fulls man is and I am feeling just the same way when I am thinking about mine job a cotter in Dress Faktory on 38 st. by 7 av. For why should we slafing in dark place by laktric lights and all kinds

---

[1] *The World Book Encyclopedia*, 1972, s.v. "Washington."

hot for $30 or maybe $36 with overtime, for Boss who is fat and driving in fency automobil? I ask! Because we are the deprassed workers of world. And are being exployted. By Bosses. In mine shop is no difference. Oh how bad is laktric light, o how is all kinds hot. And when I am telling Foreman should be better conditions he hollers, Kaplan you radical!! . . . So I keep still and work by bad light and always hot. But somday will workers making Bosses to work! And then Kaplan will give to them bad laktric and positively no windows for the air should come in! So they can know what it means to slafe! Kaplan will make Foreman a cotter like he is. And give the most bad dezigns to cot out. Justice.

Mine job is cotting Dress dezigns.

T-H-E E-N-D[2]

You may not have a Hyman Kaplan in your classroom, but you will have a range of individual differences in writing as evident as the range in reading. In one class, you might have students who have severe spelling problems and who can barely form complete, coherent sentences. In the same class, you might have students who write maturely with ease and fluency. Although this chapter describes in depth techniques for improving the writing of students who vary widely in ability, a few general techniques might be mentioned now. To improve spelling, have students keep individual lists of words they have misspelled and supply them with a list of "spelling demons" in your content area. To improve sentence accuracy and coherence, have students read their papers aloud either to themselves or to other students, to catch errors.

Students can learn to write. In this chapter we will present ways of solving the problem of how to get students to write clearly and effectively in response to text material. The first section will explain basic issues with respect to teaching writing. The second section discusses teaching writing through direct instruction. The third section will examine writing and describe different types of writing as a reflection of thinking in various content areas. A fourth section deals with the paragraph, a basic unit of writing. The last section will suggest methods for evaluating writing.

BASIC ISSUES IN WRITING

English Teacher vs. All-School Responsibility

In many ways reading and writing are beset with the same pedagogical problems. Almost everyone agrees that teaching students to read and write is important, but few teachers seem to perceive teaching them as their individual responsibility. Consider the secondary school situation.

---

[2] From Leonard Q. Ross (Leo Rosten), *The Education of H*Y*M*A*N K*A*P*L*A*N*, copyright © 1937 by Harcourt, Brace and World, Inc. Reprinted by permission of Harcourt Brace Jovanovich, Inc., and Constable & Company Limited.

The reading teacher has the primary responsibility for teaching students *how to read*. But the reading teacher cannot ensure that students will make appropriate application of skills to reading in every content area. Application and instruction in how to learn from the particular textbook or textbooks used in the classroom are the responsibility of the content area teacher. Likewise, the English teacher has the primary responsibility for teaching students *how to write*. However, since the English teacher teaches a content of literature and language and subsequently asks students to write about that content, the English teacher cannot ensure that students will make appropriate transfer of skills to writing in every other content area. In effect, just as teaching students to read is an all-faculty responsibility, so is teaching students to write.

Composing vs. Copying

Having read the answer to the essay question and the library report on George Washington earlier in this chapter, you probably noted the startling differences that can exist between composing and copying. Composing is a creative act; copying isn't. Composing demands that the writer translate his or her thoughts into special, idiosyncratic language; copying doesn't. In effect, composing at its best can be an exhilarating experience; copying at its best is only degrading. Consider the joy of a second-grader after writing a first poem, the pride of a student on a short story just finished, the glory of a valedictorian's graduation speech. No doubt these young writers feel as stimulated as did the great novelist Virginia Woolf when she wrote in her diary:

> . . . Determination not to give in, and the sense of an impending shape keep one at [writing] more than anything. I'm a little anxious. How am I to bring off this conception? Directly one gets to work one is like a person walking, who has seen the country stretching out before. I want to write nothing in this book that I don't enjoy writing. Yet writing is always difficult.[3]

Each teacher is responsible for teaching students the difference between composing and copying, especially when assigning library reports. Three techniques can be invaluable in assigning library reports. First, base the assignment on more than one source so that the student will have to assimilate the material. Second, control the sources; that is, limit the references to only a few that every student has access to. If necessary, duplicate the sources for the entire class. Third, conduct brief *paraphrasing* exercises in class in which students synthesize two sentences relating identical or similar content into one original sentence.

Ms. Jones might teach students to paraphrase by following the three steps in box 7.1.

---

[3] Janet Emig, *The Composing Processes of Twelfth Graders*. Urbana, Ill.: National Council of Teachers of English, 1971, p. 11.

BOX 7.1. Steps in Teaching Paraphrasing

Step 1: Present the student with a textual passage together with its paraphrase. Ask the student to discuss differences in language.

Text	*Paraphrase*
After teen-aged George Washington gave up hopes of becoming a sailor, he became interested in exploring the frontier. Becoming a surveyor and marking out new farms in the wilderness would give him a chance to leave home to seek adventure.	When George Washington was a teenager, he realized he would rather be a surveyor than a sailor. Surveying would permit him to lead a more adventuresome life away from home.

Step 2: Have the student paraphrase short passages from text, supplying guide questions as hints.

Text	*Hints for Paraphrasing*
Braddock assembled his forces at Fort Cumberland, Md., about 90 miles southeast of Fort Duquesne.	1. What phrase would sound less bookish than "assembled his forces"? 2. Locate Fort Cumberland on a map and see if you can write an alternative location, other than 90 miles southeast of Fort Duquesne. 3. Can the 15 word passage be rewritten in fewer words?

Step 3: Provide the students with a longer piece of text to paraphrase. Eliminate or reduce the number of hints.

Text

At the age of 26, Washington turned to seek happiness as a country gentleman and to build a fortune. During the next 16 years, he became known as a skilled farmer, an intelligent businessman, a popular legislator, a conscientious warden of a Church of England and a wise county court judge.

All *Text* copy is from *The World Book Encyclopedia,* 1972, s.v. "Washington."

Instructing students in paraphrasing is only one aspect in the teaching of writing.

Teaching vs. Assigning Writing

The maxim "Most writing is assigned, not taught" is all too true. The five-hundred word composition or the ten-page library report, assigned on Monday and collected on Friday without any intervening instruction in how to write a composition or prepare a library report, has unfortunately secured a fast place in American education. The by-products of such a system include confused students, blatant plagiarism, unimaginative writing, and disappointed teachers. Fortunately, some educators have devised methods of teaching writing. Within the last decade, James Moffett, Dan Kirby, Tom Liner, Frank O'Hare, Janet Emig, and James Britton — to name only a few — have made significant contributions to the teaching of writing through direct instruction.

TEACHING WRITING THROUGH DIRECT INSTRUCTION

Composition as Transaction

James Moffett (1968) isolated and described types of writing he referred to as "Writing up," "Writing down," "Writing out." These include stories, jokes, riddles, puns, sensory recording, dialog recording, memory writing, fiction, idea writing, dramatic dialog, Socratic dialog, journals, diaries, reportage, research, and reflection. Writing of any type, Moffett believes, should flow naturally from classroom discussion and from reading literature. Students should meet frequently in small groups to react to and critique each other's writing. Moffett believes that students learn best by learning from each other's critiques. Box 7.2 contains a lesson outline inspired by Moffett's philosophy.

BOX 7.2. Lesson Outline for Writing

A CHILD'S CHRISTMAS IN WALES

by Dylan Thomas

[*Synopsis:* The great Welsh poet recalls fondly, with rich sensory detail, how Christmas was celebrated in his home town when he was a child.]

1. *Before Reading*
   a. *Writing:* Students are asked to recall a favorite Christmas or comparable holiday and write down random memories as they come to mind.
   b. *Discussion:* Students talk together in small groups about what they have written.
2. *While reading* "A Child's Christmas in Wales" students add more details to their lists.

3. *After Reading*
   a. *Discussion:* Students in small groups discuss their personal reactions to "A Child's Christmas in Wales," using their own experiences as a basis.
   b. *Writing:* Students compose their own memory writings, based upon previous discussion and writing.
   c. *Discussion:* Students meet in small groups to react to each other's first drafts.
   d. *Writing:* Students compose second drafts based upon comments from fellow students. The second drafts are submitted to the teacher.

In the example in box 7.2, students respond to text while writing about their own feelings, beliefs, and ideas. Notice that their responses to the ideas presented in the text may change as they react to each other's drafts. This change in ideas is referred to as *transaction*.

Now that you have some information on direct instruction in writing, you might be able to answer this question. How would the students have responded if Ms. Jones, the history teacher, had given the following writing assignment without any writing instruction? "Now that you've read the chapter on the Revolutionary War, assume that you are George Washington. Write a letter home to your wife Martha recounting the hardships of Valley Forge; yet show your determination to overcome the enemy."

Composition as Personal Growth

Emig (1971) has suggested that students put more effort into *reflexive* writing than *extensive* writing. Motivation to write is stronger when it comes from a personal desire to communicate than from a determination to meet the demands of the teacher's assignment. For example, a fourteen-year-old girl will spend twice as much time and precision composing a letter to her best friend than writing answers to end-of-chapter study questions. Since most students easily engage in some form of personal writing, teachers should try to make effective use of personal writing in their classrooms.

One of the best vehicles for personal writing is the journal, or what Kirby and Liner (1980) refer to as "the J." Kirby and Liner believe journal writing increases students' fluency and self-awareness. First, the journal is private; so students feel free to explore, with their own language, their feelings and ideas. Second, journal writing is fairly unstructured and thus inviting. Third, since the journal is private and unstructured, students tend to express themselves more honestly and powerfully. Fourth, since students write journals to themselves, they may be more critical of what they write. Contrast, for instance, these two passages written by a thirteen-year-old Ellen Mary. The first is a response to a teacher's assignment; the second is an entry in her personal journal:

The poetry of Walt Whitman was patently revolutionary for its time. Critics entertained it with hostility and derision. One reason for this deluge of criticism was Whitman's employment of free verse, a form then considered barbaric.

The street is quiet. Too quiet. To the people who live on the street the silence is deafening. No birds singing, no dogs barking, no radio playing, and no cars rumbling. No one speaks or even breathes too loudly. Through the silence a baby screams. No one goes to it and it soon quiets.

The first passage, written in response to an end-of-chapter question, is bookish, perhaps copied. The second passage, an unassigned journal entry, shows the student's use of personal, and powerful language. Though appearing extreme, these two examples dramatize the differences between assigned and personal writing.

Kirby and Liner suggest four types of journals that students can keep: (1) the writer's notebook, (2) the class journal, (3) the project journal, and (4) the diary. The *writer's notebook* is a type of journal in which students systematically make personal notes about their observations. The notebook may contain interesting words and phrases the student has collected, as well as ideas, insights, and reactions. These data may become the basis for a writing assignment. Some teachers encourage students to observe human behavior and speech patterns before composing short narratives. Students, keeping these observations in writers' notebooks, may use or adapt them for the short story assignment.

The *class journal* is used for in-class personal writing. Teachers use class journals in various ways. Some teachers allow students five to ten minutes each period to make free or spontaneous entries. Other teachers supply a focus for the entries, for instance, a film, guest speaker, class discussions, or textbook reading assignments. Teachers find the class journals useful in determining how students are responding to class activities.

Students use *project journals* for keeping track of their progress while preparing a long-term individual or small group project, such as a research or library paper, a dramatic presentation, or a demonstration. Entries could consist of notes on pertinent readings, lists of possible sources, minutes of group planning sessions, deadlines, or lists of things to do. Project journals help students plan their time on long-term assignments, precluding the "night before rush job."

The *diary* functions as an emotional outlet for students. Students frequently use diaries to record intimate feelings and beliefs. Some teachers choose never to read these; other teachers collect them, read them, and, on occasion, respond with personal notes to the student. Most sensitive teachers avoid responses that are preachy and moralizing. Many teachers, however, feel uncomfortable with the diary, and never use it.

Journal writing is widely practiced in English language arts classrooms.

TABLE 7.1. Overview of Suggested Journal Uses, by Type and by Content Area

JOURNAL TYPE	English	Social Studies	Science	Math	Industrial & Home Arts
Writer's Notebook	Recording observations of people in preparation for a short story	Personal reaction to propaganda on television and radio	Logs of growing plants; record of climatic changes	Record of humorous experiences with counting of money or change	Personal opinions of new fashions in clothing and automobiles
Class Journal	Writing short stories or poems to music as it is playing	Reacting to a teacher-selected or student-selected current event	Recording of observations during a demonstration or experiment	Recounting problems experienced in completing math homework	Log of successful and unsuccessful experiences in operating equipment
Project Journal	Plans and procedures for preparing an 8mm film on poetry of nature	Progress on research paper sources, notes on readings, rough drafts, outlines	Progress notes on a science fair project: experiments, observations	Materials, measurements, procedures for building a geodesic dome	Daily progress entries on problems and procedures in building a chest of drawers
Diary	Student records personal and intimate ideas, beliefs, attitudes, and values.				

Source: Dan Kirby and Tom Liner, *Inside Out: Developmental Strategies for Teaching Writing.* Rochelle Park, N.J.: Hayden, 1980.

Teachers in other content areas, too, might find journals useful classroom activities. Table 7.1 shows how the four types of journals can be used in various content areas.

Composition as Language Structure

In reviewing over fifty years of research in composition, Richard Braddock and others (1963) came to the conclusion that the formal study of grammar had little or no effect upon writing proficiency. This conclusion came as a blow to staunch supporters who had consistently defended the applicability of grammar to speech and writing.

Subsequent to Braddock's review, a series of studies attempted to show that practice with sentence building effected maturity in student

~~writing~~. The most recent of these studies is that of O'Hare (1973) who improved seventh graders' writing by having them perform exercises in sentence combining. Although students manipulated many different grammatical structures, they did so without being exposed to the complex terminology of grammar. A sentence-combining exercise might proceed in the sequence shown in box 7.3.

BOX 7.3. Sentence-Combining Exercise

Instructions: Combine each of the following groups of sentences into one sentence, using THAT or THE FACT THAT.

1. Julio should admit SOMETHING. He was there.
   Answer: Julio should admit *that* he was there.
2. Peter notices SOMETHING. There were nine golf balls in the river.
   Answer: (You supply.)
3. SOMETHING is certain. Human beings will survive.
   Answer: (You supply.)

These are only simple exercises. Try your hand at combining the following series of sentences in one short sentence:

The gas station attendant stumbled out of his shack.
He was *an emaciated looking fellow.*
He had *white hair and skin the color of an old saddle.* (WITH)
He *stood scowling at us.* (AND)
His chin was *thrust forward.* (WITH)
His eyes were *blazing.*

Here is what you might have come up with:

The gas station attendant, an emaciated looking fellow with white hair and skin the color of an old saddle, stumbled out of his shack and stood scowling at us, with his chin thrust forward, his eyes blazing.

Ms. Jones might have helped her students with their writing assignment by having them do the exercises in sentence combining similar to the two which follow.

Combine these three sentences in one:

1. George Washington was a general in the Revolutionary War.
2. He suffered many hardships at Valley Forge.
3. He was a courageous soldier.

Combine these three sentences in one:

1. American colonists were clever soldiers.

2. They acted like today's guerrillas.
3. They always outsmarted the British.

Composition as Process

Very little is known about the processes students use in writing. Emig (1971), studying how eight twelfth-grade students wrote, found that they spent more time composing and revising in response to their own thoughts and feelings *(reflexive writing)* than in response to classroom experiences *(extensive writing)*. Echoing Emig's findings, Britton and others (1975), in an assessment of thousands of papers written by British school children, found that when they were writing for the teacher, children produced stilted, uncreative language. In effect, when a writing assignment demands that a student report facts, the teacher assumes the role of *examiner*. According to Britton, this role makes student writers uncomfortable and constrained. Nevertheless, content area teachers, assessing what students have learned from text, are functioning as examiners. If they occasionally modify their role of "examiner" to "helper" (or as Britton puts it, "trusted adult") students might feel freer to express their thoughts and feelings at greater depth. Ms. Jones might have had better luck with her students had she asked them to write on this topic: "Which of your closest friends is most like George Washington (or any other figure in the Revolutionary War) and why?" On giving the assignment, Ms. Jones could make it clear that she would read and respond to it in writing, but would not grade or discuss it in class.

Summary of Writing Through Direct Instruction

In stressing direct instruction of writing, not merely assigning it, five specialists in English language education have aided English teachers and their students. Their ideas for direct instruction can also be used by teachers in other content areas. Box 7.4 summarizes these ideas.

BOX 7.4. Summary of Ideas for
Direct Instruction of Writing

Specialist	*Contribution*

1. Moffett	1. *Classroom organization*
	   a. Small groups for reading, discussing, and writing.
	   b. Writing as a natural outgrowth of classroom reading and discussion.

2. Kirby and Liner

c. Student reacting to the writing of their peers.
d. Prewriting activities and revision techniques.

2. *Composition as data about the writer*
   a. Use of student journals and diaries.
   b. Drawing inferences about students based upon what they write.
   c. Planning additional reading and writing based on cues from student writing.

3. O'Hare

3. *Improving student writing style*
   a. Sentence-combining exercises.
   b. Drawing sentences from individual content areas: e.g., George Washington led his country in war and peace. He was called the father of his country.

4. Emig and Britton

4. *Composition as Process*
   How students act when they are in the process of writing — in class and at home — both for the teacher as examiner and as trusted adult.

It is primarily the English teacher's responsibility to teach students how to write, using the ideas of specialists prominent in the field of composition. Since teachers in other content areas assign writing, they too should know the ideas of these specialists. In addition, all teachers should be familiar with the four basic types of writing that can be assigned.

TYPES OF WRITING APPLIED TO CONTENT AREAS

On the following pages four types of writing will be defined and specific examples of them will be supplied: *reporting, exposition, narration,* and *argumentation.*

Reporting

Written reporting can be defined as the relaying of information in response to a question or an assignment. Frequently, the teacher gives the student a set of *study questions* for which the student is to supply answers; the answers may vary in length from one sentence to several paragraphs. In this activity, a teacher assumes the role of a *helper*. In addition to study questions, teachers give written examinations, in which students relay information ranging from answers of one sentence or phrase to whole paragraphs. In this role, a teacher functions as an *examiner* and *evaluator*. As an evaluator, the teacher's task is to apply explicit criteria to students' writing. Another form of reporting is the library report in which students demonstrate that they have retrieved and organized the relevant information on a given topic. Here the teacher may function as an interested adult reader, an evaluator, or both.

Reporting and other forms of writing can be differentiated by the creative demands they make on the student. Reporting is simply information retrieval and relay; it requires factual recall and paraphrasing. Consider this assignment: "Report on the contributions of Pythagoras to modern geometry." It merely asks the student to tell what the contributions are, not apply them, analyze them, synthesize them, or evaluate them.

STUDY QUESTIONS

Generally, as students use reading and learning-from-text guides, they are directed to write answers to questions that facilitate the reading of the chapter. In devising study questions, the teacher must make it clear to students whether they are to write a sentence or phrase, a short paragraph, or a more extended answer. In boxes 7.5, 7.6, and 7.7 are guide questions and these different types of answers by students.

BOX 7.5. Guide Questions and Short Answers
(Phrases or Sentences)

SCIENCE

What causes the green color you see on a pond? (page 4, column 1, paragraph 2)

pond scum or algae

The green color you see on a pond is caused by *pond scum* or *algae*. (Some teachers believe students should answer questions in complete sentences.)

SOCIAL STUDIES

What was the purpose of the Boston Tea Party?

to protest the tax on tea

ENGLISH

Why did "I" in Edgar Allan Poe's "Tell-Tale Heart" want to kill the old man?

"I" wanted to get rid of the old man's eye.

Sometimes study questions demand more response than a sentence or sentence fragment. Read the question and answer in box 7.6.

BOX 7.6. Guide Questions and Paragraph Answers

SCIENCE

Briefly describe the environment of a pond.

> A pond's water is slow moving or still. Because of this, a scummy growth called algae can be seen on the top and under the water. Ducks and other waterbirds like ponds because of the gentle water and the bugs that live there.

Box 7.7 contains study questions that require short answers, paragraphs, and more extended answers. Decide what kind of answer each question calls for.

BOX 7.7. Study Questions for Report Type Answers

MATHEMATICS

Explain the meaning of this equation: $3 \sqrt{56} < 15 \times 4$.

SOCIAL STUDIES

Why were the Hessians surprised at Valley Forge?

ENGLISH

What preparations had Pepe made for his trip to the mountains in Steinbeck's "Flight"?

SCIENCE

Describe the environment of a mountain lake.

INDUSTRIAL EDUCATION

What equipment would be necessary for you to repair a Model-T Ford?

WRITTEN EXAMINATIONS

Just as study questions demand report type of responses ranging in length from a single sentence or sentence fragment to one paragraph or more, so do written examinations. In fact, some teachers use study questions to "dry run" written examinations. Consequently, much of what was said on the preceding pages about study questions holds for written examinations.

Many students have difficulty writing longer examinations — essay examinations — principally because they do not understand what is expected of them. It is possible that a high school history student might answer each of the four questions below in the same way:

1. What were the causes and effects of the Spanish-American War?
2. What was the principal significance of the Spanish-American War?
3. What were the principal events in the Spanish-American War?
4. Describe the principal outcomes of the Spanish-American War.

Question 1 asks for two sets of data: what phenomena led to the war and what changes in American society resulted after the war's conclusion. Some students may not understand the difference in the definitions of *cause* and *effect* and, as a result, may merely summarize the war without differentiating between the two sets of data. In addition, the term *what* does not clearly indicate how much the student is to say about each cause and each effect. Specifically, is the student to list, to describe, to evaluate — or WHAT?

Question 2 does not request specific information about the war. It asks the student to recall what the textbook mentioned was the long-range, retrospect importance of the Spanish-American War. But the question is not specific because it doesn't say "significance to what." Significance to American foreign policy? Significance to American culture? Significance to America's economy?

Question 3 merely asks the student to recall the major happenings of the war. Again the student might not know the meaning of *events*. Does *events* refer to battles, legislation, political strategies, speeches?

Question 4 may appear to be similar to part of Question 1; however, *outcomes* suggests more immediate results than does *effects*. Whereas *effects* might concern changes in foreign alliance, legislative acts, changes in attitudes, *outcomes* might concern deaths and casualties, victories and defeats, fiscal gains and deficits.

As a result of analyzing these four essay questions on the Spanish-American War, it becomes apparent that teachers must learn to write clear essay questions and teach the students to read them carefully and analyze them.

WRITING EFFECTIVE ESSAY QUESTIONS

A well-written essay question contains three elements: (1) a *performance verb*, that is a verb that tells the student how to answer the question; (2) an indication of the *content* of the response; and (3) *enabling suggestions* for how to proceed in organizing the answer. Box 7.8 contrasts a set of poorly-written essay questions with the same essay questions in well-written form.

BOX 7.8. Poorly-written and Well-written Essay Questions

1. What were the causes and effects of the Spanish-American War?

performance verb —(List) the [causes and effects of the   content Spanish-American War.] Include the causes in one paragraph and the effects }enabling in a second paragraph. Then write a suggestions third paragraph describing your own feelings about whether the war was worth the effort.

2. What is a pond's environment like?

performance verb —(Describe)[what a pond looks like, including such information as (1) the appearance of the water, (2) the types of }content plant and animal life in the pond, and (3) how the plants and animals depend on one another.] Devote several sen- }enabling tences to each of the three points listed. suggestions

3. How would you repair a Model-T Ford?

How would you [repair a Model-T Ford's transmission after the gears had }content been stripped?] (1) (List) each piece of performance verbs equipment you would use and why you }enabling would use it. (2) (List) the steps you suggestions

> would take in fixing the transmission. Write one paragraph for (1) and one paragraph for (2).

Writing essay questions in this way facilitates evaluation by establishing the following criteria for a good answer: *a mode of response* (list, compare, contrast, describe), *content of response* (causes, effects, outcomes, important features) and *organization of response* (three sentences, two paragraphs). But it is not enough to write good essay questions. You have to teach students to comprehend those questions.

TEACHING STUDENTS TO COMPREHEND ESSAY QUESTIONS

The first step in teaching students to comprehend essay questions is to explain the various performance verbs and the modes of response they suggest. Table 7.2 contains some of the most commonly used performance verbs in well-written essay questions, their definitions, and the modes of response they evoke.

The second step in teaching students to comprehend essay exam questions is to have them articulate what is expected of them in given essay questions. A class discussion on a given essay question might focus on questions like 1–3 in Box 7.9.

BOX 7.9. Class Discussion of Essay Questions

What difficulties would you have answering this essay question:

List the causes and effects of the Stamp Act.

1. What would you be expected to do in a list?
   a. What form would the list take?
   b. How much detail would you have to supply for each cause and effect?
2. What are causes and effects?
   a. Are causes the same as effects — or different?
   b. Is there an effect for every cause?
3. Which of the following pieces of information would not be appropriate in writing the essay?
   a. Principal politicians responsible for the Stamp Act.
   b. The history of taxation patterns in the colonies.
   c. Armed resistance to the British army.
   d. The Boston Massacre.
   e. The Boston Tea Party.

TABLE 7.2. Performance Verbs Commonly Used in Well-written Essay Questions and Modes of Response to Them

Verb	Definition	Suggested Mode of Response
1. to list	to compile a series of related items	Student enumerates the requested items *with little or no further explanation*. List may be in outline, numbered sequence, or sentence form.
2. to identify	to describe the most significant features	Using one or more sentences, the student describes *only the most important* aspects of a person (what he or she did that was noteworthy), a place (what happened there, why it is unique), an idea (what makes this idea different from all others), and an event (What happened? Why is it important?).
3. to describe	to write about major and minor features	Using one or more paragraphs, the student will write about all of the features of a person, place, idea, or event—not merely the most important ones.
4. to compare	to show the similarities and dissimilarities of two or more phenomena	The student will show how two phenomena are alike in one paragraph and different in a second paragraph.
5. to contrast	to show only the dissimilarities of two or more phenomena	The student will show how two phenomena are different by selecting several key aspects and devoting a paragraph to each aspect.
6. to illustrate or amplify	to give examples	The student will supply examples to clarify a point, devoting a sentence or two for each example.
7. to justify	to give reasons for	The students will supply reasons to defend or argue a point, devoting a sentence or two for each reason.
8. to discuss	to talk over	Students consider a topic from various points of view.
9. to define	to make clear the meaning of a term or concept	Students explain what is meant by a term, supplying an example.
10. to explain	to define or otherwise make clear	Students clarify an idea, process, concept, event.
11. to outline	to list major points and minor subpoints	Using letters and numbers, students arrange a sequence of major and minor ideas.

In addition to understanding the meaning of the performance verbs, deciding what mode of response is appropriate, and discussing the meaning of given essay questions, students must follow the enabling suggestions on organization. When the enabling suggestions in an essay question say "write one paragraph on *causes* and one paragraph on *effects*," the student ought to check the answer to be sure it contains information on the *causes* and *effects* in order to satisfy the requirements of the question.

SAMPLES OF WELL-WRITTEN ANSWERS TO ESSAY QUESTIONS

Boxes 7.10–7.12 show three samples of student writing in response to essay questions from three content areas: social studies, science, and English. Each of the samples contains the topic, the teacher's enabling suggestions, and marginal glosses explaining what the student did to meet the criteria of the assignment.

BOX 7.10. Social Studies

1. Topic: *What were the causes and effects of the Spanish-American War?*

List the causes and effects of the Spanish-American War. Put the causes in one paragraph and the effects in a second paragraph. Then write a third paragraph describing your own feelings about whether the war was worth the effort. — Teacher's enabling suggestions

Was It Worth It? — Catchy title

Introduction — It seems as if the United States has always found it difficult to stay out of armed conflicts. The Spanish-American War is no exception. The Spanish-American War was caused by several factors. — Topic sentence

Enumeration transition — First, the Americans were displeased over Spanish tyranny in Cuba. Uprisings against the Spanish were powerful enough to unsettle Spanish rule but not overthrow it. Second, William Randolph Hearst and other journalists exaggerated the conditions in — Three causes

Transition

Cuba and got the Americans interested
in intervening. (Third,) the battleship *Transition*
Maine, sent to Cuba to protect Americans from pro-Spanish rioters, myste-
riously exploded, killing 260 people on
board. The situation was ripe for war. *Clincher statement*

Topic sentence   As with most wars, there was disagreement as to the positive value of
Transition   the effects. (In the first place,) Cuba
was granted freedom, and the United
States acquired Guam, Puerto Rico,
Contrast transition   and the Philippines. (In addition, however,) strong anti-imperialist feelings *Three effects*
grew in the United States, questioning
Contrast transition   the goodness of foreign policy. (Nevertheless,) the urge, now, to connect the
Caribbean Sea and the Pacific Ocean
led to the building of the Panama
Canal.

I have mixed feelings about the *Topic sentence*
Transition   Spanish-American War. (On the positive side,) America became less isola-
tionist and began to grow as a world
power. Our commerce and industry
grew as a result of our expanded inter- *Positive and*
Contrast transition   national interests. (On the negative side,) *negative reactions*
our territorial claims outside the conti-
nental United States have made us tar-
gets of criticism. How much we help
the territories and how much we ex-
ploit them has been a never-ending discussion. Eventually, we will be forced
to choose between granting total freedom to our territories or continually
justifying what appears to be an impe-
rialist foreign policy.

BOX 7.11. Science

2. Topic: *What is a pond's environment like?*

> Describe what a pond looks like, in- ⎤
> cluding such information as (1) the ap- ⎟
> pearance of the water, (2) the types of ⎟ Teacher's
> plant and animal life in the pond, and ⎬ enabling
> (3) how the plants and animals depend ⎟ suggestions
> on one another. Devote several sen- ⎟
> tences to each of the three points listed. ⎟
> Confine your writing to one paragraph. ⎦

The Pond

Topic sentence	A pond is fairly easy to recognize.
	(First of all,) unlike rivers and streams, — Enumeration transition
Appearance of water	the water has a still surface. Unlike a
	lake's, the pond's surface is spotted
	with plant life. (Second,) much of this — Enumeration transition
	plant life consists of algae and scum.
	These and other forms of pond growth,
	such as rushes, stimulate an active in-
Plant and animal life	sect community. The stillness of the
	water, which fosters the growth of
	these plants, also makes for attractive
	living quarters for water birds, particu-
	larly ducks. (Third,) water, plants, and — Enumeration transition
	animals live together effectively. As
	small fish and insects feed on plants,
	larger fish and birds feed on the insects.
Dependence	Animals give CO_2 to the plants. You
	can always find nature's balance at — Clincher sentence
	work in a pond.

BOX 7.12. English

3. Topic: ~~Compare and constrast~~ the ways in which Holden Caulfield and Gene Forrester coped with the world around them.

Define "coping" in an introductory paragraph that gives an overview of your composition. In a second paragraph, point out similarities that exist between Holden and Gene. In a third paragraph, point out dissimilarities between the two boys. Illustrate general statements with specific information from the novels *A Catcher in the Rye* and *A Separate Peace*. In a concluding paragraph, attempt to judge which boy "copes" better.

Enabling suggestions

To Cope: An Adolescent Problem

Offbeat opening

A recent successful Broadway musical has focused on the increasing inabilities people have in learning to cope with life around them. "To cope" means to adjust to life's pressures and "make the best of it." Two adolescent fictional heroes — Holden Caulfield from *A Catcher in the Rye* and Gene Forrester from *A Separate Peace* — try to cope with life, but with varying degrees of success.

Main idea for composition

Both Holden and Gene have the brains to deal with life, if they want to. Both boys are incisive about human nature, particularly the ability to see through sham. For instance, just as Holden detects the detachment and lack of interest shown by his teachers

Two points of similarity

Example transition

at Pency, so does Gene sense the irrelevance of the teachers at Devon. (However,) despite this incisiveness, both boys escape when life makes demands. (For example,) Holden runs away from school, and home, before his parents are notified of his expulsion. In a more subtle way, Gene escapes learning about himself by submitting to Devon's many questionable rituals. (In effect,) opposing forces — intelligence versus fear — in both boys make "coping" a difficult task.

— Contrast transition

Example transition

— Conclusion transition

Topic sentence

Holden and Gene have marked contrasts in personality that affect their respective abilities to cope. Holden takes a light-hearted, almost glib, look at the world's shortcomings, criticizes them, and consciously sets himself apart. In reality, Holden is guilty of the same types of sham he lampoons in others. His patronizing attitude toward the nun and his pseudo-sophistication with the prostitute are only two examples of his lack of self-awareness. Gene, (on the other hand,) less glib, less willing to attack or lampoon, makes a more conscious attempt to act consistently with his values. He recognizes the seriousness of what he has done to Finny and broods over it. (In addition) to being more self-aware, Gene is more willing to accept society's norms and live within them — to compromise; Holden cannot compromise.

Topic sentence

Two points of dissimilarity

Contrast transition

Extension transition

> In conclusion, <u>one can argue that</u>
> <u>Gene copes with life better than Hol-</u>   Topic sentence
> <u>den</u>. The reader is allowed to see Gene,
> a mature man, having come to peace
> with himself. Although we are not al-
> lowed to see Holden as a mature man,
> <u>the final chapter of the book suggests</u>
> <u>that he may always have problems</u>   Clincher sentence
> <u>dealing with those aspects of life he</u>
> <u>can't accept.</u>

LIBRARY RESEARCH

Students frequently engage in reference reading for their English, social science, and science classes. In reference reading, they have to find the answer to a question by locating and reading relevant materials in the library. This presumes that the students know how to locate information in the library and judge its relevancy. These skills will be taken up in chapter 15, "The Current Scene: Centers for Reading and Learning from Text."

Let's suppose for now the student has located the references needed to answer the question. The student still has to judge which parts of the references are relevant. To teach the student to judge relevancy, the teacher can take the entire class through the two exercises below. In the first, a question is stated, discussed, and broken up into its implicit subquestions. References should be available to answer each subquestion.

Main Question: How do mass media attempt to control the ways in which people act?

Subquestions: How are people influenced by advertising? How can newspapers try to control how people think? What devices do politicians use to influence people?

Then the teacher takes the class through an exercise like that in box 7.13 for judging the relevancy of a reference passage for answering a question or subquestion.

BOX 7.13. Exercise for Judging Relevancy

Question: How are people influenced by advertising?
Passage: Generally speaking, color photographs, rather than black and white, appeal to slick magazine readers. The sight of a freckled child grinning over a bowl of steaming tomato soup can stir the gastric juices.
Teacher: Does this passage contain any information for answering our question?

The teacher takes the class through a reference a passage at a time, asking the students to judge whether or not each passage is relevant to a given question. If so, the essential information is put on cards.

To teach the students to get the most relevant material, start with the broadest relevant topics and proceed to the narrower topics. Looking under the broad topic "government," students could eventually find the steps in the passage of a bill through the legislature; but the process would be slow. It would be better to teach students, first, to use an index to search for the specific category. If this search fails, they can switch to the broad-to-narrow search strategy.

Research on reference reading (Gans, 1940) suggests that (1) if students are frustrated in their search, they modify the question to such an extent that the answer obtained is the answer to an entirely different question; (2) students do not appear to improve from fourth grade to college in reference reading; and (3) reference reading results in more achievement than reading a single textbook, perhaps because students can select books they can comprehend (Barrilleaux, 1967).

The probable reason for lack of development in reference reading is that it is not taught systematically through the grades. Teachers tend to assume students know how to read reference literature in each content area. Not until students get to the college level do they have courses, such as historiography, in which they learn how to do library research.

To teach reference reading, teachers should admonish students to keep their questions in mind; use an index; search from broad to narrow categories; judge relevancy; and, as a follow up, they should check to make sure students answered the questions as they were posed, not as they may have modified them.

WRITING REPORTS

After the information has been collected, the next step is to organize it to use in a written report. The teacher asks the class to organize cards into groups that contain similar information. These groups are then placed under their related subquestions. Now the information can be organized in paragraphs for a report.

The first step in writing paragraphs is to decide on a writing pattern for a particular group of cards. See table 7.3 for types of writing patterns. Of course, the same information can be written into different types of paragraphs as shown in box 7.14. After paragraphs have been written for each group of cards, decide on the type of organization for the entire report — expository, chronological, problem-solution, question-answer — and arrange the paragraphs to fit this organization. Then write an introductory paragraph and transitional sentences. The result is a completed report. Essentially, the process is the reverse of reading and then outlining a passage.

BOX 7.14. The Same Information in Two Writing Patterns

1. People tend to be influenced by the colors they see in magazine advertisements. Red makes them excited. Blue and green are soothing. Yellow produces a warming sensation.
2. The fiery red of a lipstick ad would not be appropriate for use in a coffee ad. Yellow would be ineffective in selling cigarettes. People are affected by the colors they see in magazines.

After teaching the whole class to write reports, the next step is to give the same set of information to different groups and have each group organize and write a report. The last step is to assign each individual to organize and write a report based on given information on a question. Through this sequence, the teacher phases out from maximum to minimum direction. Each member of the class should now be ready to engage in reference reading and writing. To evaluate their ability, the teacher might give each student a question to research in the library. Every student does the library work (locates and abstracts relevant material) and writes a report with the resulting information. (Preferably the library assignment and the report will be short.) Students then read their reports in groups for initial critical evaluation, editing and polishing, and final group evaluation. With successful completion of this assignment, the teacher will know the members of the class are ready for reference reading and report writing.

Reporting is only one of the four types of writing. The second type of writing is called *exposition*.

Exposition

Exposition is the type of writing that deals with explanation — explanation of a process, explanation of a point of view, explanation of a work of literature, explanation of an idea, explanation of a philosophy, and so forth. This type of writing is more demanding than reporting because, rather than merely recalling and relating information, the writer interprets the information, analyzes the information, or reacts to the information. In box 7.15 are some writing topics that demand exposition, not mere reporting. These topics can be used for in-class or out-of-class writing assignments.

BOX 7.15. Topics for Expository Writing

SCIENCE

1. Which one of the following scientists made the most significant contribution to physical science: Lavoisier, Newton, Priestley, Galileo? Explain the significance of this contribution. (Contrast this topic with "Report on the contributions of Lavoisier, Newton, Priestley, and Galileo to physical science.")
2. What erroneous assumptions about the universe did Copernicus make? Why did he make them? (Contrast this topic with "Describe Copernicus' view of the universe.")

SOCIAL STUDIES

3. Do you think that Benedict Arnold was truly a traitor? Explain your thinking.

ENGLISH

4. How does the horror in Nathaniel Hawthorne's "Dr. Heideggar's Experiment" differ from the horror in Poe's "The Cask of Amontillado"?
5. Do you think Holden Caulfield acts immaturely? Explain your answer.

MATHEMATICS

6. Explain why the intersection of two planes makes a *straight* line and why the intersection of a plane and a sphere forms a *curved* line.

HOMEMAKING

7. Explain what you would have to do differently in preparing a dinner for two and a dinner for eight hundred that would be equally satisfying to all the diners.

As with reporting, students find it difficult to organize their ideas for expository writing. For writing exposition, there is no better advice than: "Tell 'em what you're gonna tell 'em; tell 'em; and tell 'em you told 'em." In other words, you need a beginning, a middle, and an end. In the technical vocabulary of the writer, you need an introduction, a body, and a conclusion.

An *introduction* can do several things. First, it can contain eye-catching, highly motivating material that arouses the reader's interest. Second, it can pose a provocative question. Third, it can state the main idea of the composition. Fourth, it can provide information on what will appear in subsequent paragraphs. Here is the opening paragraph of a student composition entitled "How to Conduct a Scientific Experiment":

> It wasn't a large explosion — merely a hiss as the piece of magnesium I had dipped in bromide water flew away after I lighted it on the Bunsen burner. Had I done wrong by experimenting? Wasn't this how all great discoveries were made — through trial and error? I have now learned that scientific experimentation is more than mere trial and error. In the following paragraphs, I will (1) review the basic steps in conducting any scientific experiment, (2) describe an experiment, using the basic steps, and (3) contrast this experiment with one in which I had used trial and error.

Certainly, every introductory paragraph doesn't need to be so elaborate. In fact, many teachers might prefer a simpler, more direct introduction:

> In this paper, I am going to contrast trial-and-error experimentation with the scientific method.

or

> That scientific method and trial-and-error experimentation are in sharp contrast will be demonstrated in this paper in three stages. First, I will review the basic steps in scientific inquiry. Second, I will describe an experiment, using the basic steps. Third, I will contrast this experiment with one using trial and error.

The *body* of a piece of expository writing usually contains two or more paragraphs, each focusing on one aspect of the paper's main idea. In a paper with the topic above, one paragraph might focus on reviewing the steps of scientific inquiry. A second paragraph would focus on the properly conducted experiment. A third paragraph would contrast the scientific experiment with another experiment using the trial-and-error method.

A *conclusion* summarizes the paper briefly and leaves the reader with a sense of completeness:

> In this paper I have attempted to demonstrate the differences between scientific method and trial-and-error experimentation. By citing actual experiments, I hope I have made the contrasts more vivid.

A sequence of brief activities which will help you to *teach* expository writing is given in box 7.16.

BOX 7.16. Sequence of Activities
for Teaching Expository Writing

Select one of the seven topics listed in box 7.15. Briefly describe how you would help students to organize a four or five paragraph composition focusing on the topic. Be sure to:

1. help the student plan a main idea (indicate what this main idea might be).
2. offer suggestions for body paragraphs that would function as subpoints to the main idea.
3. offer suggestions for writing an introduction.
4. offer suggestions for writing a conclusion.

After students gain experience at writing library reports and expository compositions (preferably using resources that you can control), they may be ready to begin elementary forms of research. Systems that can help in the teaching of term paper and research paper writing are available to teachers. Such systems generally include methods for writing bibliography cards and note cards, outlining, writing footnotes and bibliographies, and so forth.[4] With the ubiquitous nature of such materials, it would be repetitious to dwell on research writing, other than to say that it is frequently assigned.

The values of the long research paper for high school students has been debated often. Many teachers maintain that the experience of writing a term paper will assist students who plan to attend college. Other teachers maintain that the time demanded to teach the term paper is excessive in relation to the quality of work that high school students are capable of doing. Still other teachers have their students do the research but write a short paper or abstract.

Most teachers require students to give credit for ideas that are not original. This crediting of sources is called *documentation*. There are two types of documentation, formal and informal. Formal documentation requires footnotes for direct quotations, indirect quotations, and any other references to ideas that are not original to the writer of the research paper. Box 7.17 contains an example of formal documentation.

---

[4] For examples of these methods see the following: Dorothea M. Berry and Gordon P. Martin, *Guide to Writing Research Papers*. New York: McGraw-Hill, 1971; Kate L. Turabian, *A Manual for Writers of Term Papers, Theses, and Dissertations*, 4th ed. Chicago: University of Chicago Press, 1973; The University of Chicago Press, *A Manual of Style*, 12th ed., rev. Chicago: University of Chicago Press, 1969.

BOX 7.17. Example of Formal Documentation

. . . . That Washington was the greatest military leader in American history has been disputed by prominent historians.[4] One in particular wrote, "The fact of the matter is that whereas George Washington was a brilliant strategist, there were many of his colleagues equally qualified."[5] Indeed, Jon Best believes that Benedict Arnold had superior qualities of military leadership.[6]

[4] Philip Bowson, "What Leading Historians Say about George Washington." *History Journal,* vol. 34 (April 1956), p. 36.

[5] Beaudreau McDorf, *George Washington: Leader of Men.* (New York: Bragwick Publishing, 1965), p. 467.

[6] Jon Best, "Not Now, Traitor," *Timely History,* vol. 76 (June 1948), pp. 33–45.

With informal documentation the writer merely cites the author and work within the context of a paragraph as shown below.

. . . . That Washington was the greatest military leader in American history has been disputed by prominent historians. In his article "What Historians Say about George Washington," appearing in the April 1956 issue of *History Journal,* Philip Bowson refers to at least twenty historians who cite Washington as being of lesser military ability than contemporary American generals . . . .

Whether teachers assign short research papers or long ones, students, particularly those in upper grades, should be taught methods of careful documentation. If students cannot discriminate their own ideas from those of other writers, the experience of research writing will be hollow for them.

Narration

Simply stated, *narration* is storytelling. It usually involves a series of events (often chronologically arranged) and sometimes dialogue. Some of the more common forms of narration assigned to students are jokes, anecdotes, tall tales, vignettes, short short stories, and short stories. One of the most difficult problems in narration is writing dialogue. In box 7.18 is an example of correctly written story dialogue, glossed so you can see the number of conventions in form.

BOX 7.18. Story Dialogue Illustrating Conventions in Form

The two men faced each other un-
believingly.

The taller man spoke. "Don't I   Note sequence of
know you from somewhere?"   punctuation

Explainer   "Yes," the shorter man said. "Your
bank refused my loan application."

No explainer   "Yes, I remember now. You didn't
needed   have enough collateral."

"Now I have less." He stared in-   Explainer
tently at the taller man with almost   continues thread
frightening ferocity.   of story

Argumentation

The last type of writing to be discussed is *argumentation*. Unlike exposition, which explains an idea from an *objective* viewpoint, argumentation is *subjective*. The writer's purpose is to persuade the reader to accept a point of view. Among several types of argumentation are these:

1. defending a social, political, religious, or cultural ideology
2. taking a stand on a current event
3. attacking or defending an individual

The following paragraph is an excerpt from a high school composition, an argument, entitled "What School Rule Needs Changing Most"? The intended audience was to be a group of the school's administrators and counselors:

Another reason the campus should close is student morale. As it is now, students are allowed to come and go as they please. Sometimes there's more going than coming — with a harmful result: students feel teachers don't care if they come to class or not. We used to think freedom on campus was a good thing. But kids can't handle too much freedom — they mistake freedom for indifference . . . .

Summary of Writing Types

The basic types of writing are (1) reporting, (2) exposition, (3) narration and (4) argumentation. As you have read, these types have basic differences. Table 7.3 summarizes these differences.

TABLE 7.3. Characteristics of Four Basic Writing Types

Writing Type	Purpose	What Is Required of the Student	Sample Assignment
Reporting	Organize and relay information	Gather information and organize it according to questions or other directions	1. Answers to study questions 2. Answers to essay questions 3. Library research
Exposition	Explain	Interpret, analyze, and react to information	1. Solve a problem 2. Tell how to do something
Narration	Entertain	Retell fictional events in chronological order; use dialogue	1. Anecdotes 2. Vignettes 3. Short stories
Argumentation	Persuade	Defend a point of view by supplying only the evidence that supports it	1. Taking a stand on a current event 2. Attacking an individual 3. Defending a political belief

Although students may use four different types of writing in responding to text, they will organize their writing around one basic unit — the paragraph.

A BASIC UNIT OF WRITING: THE PARAGRAPH

Writing and reading are intimately related. What an author writes, someone is likely to read. When an author writes in simple, straightforward language, the reader has few problems comprehending the text. When an author writes in difficult, convoluted language, the reader has many problems comprehending the text. For example, which of the two passages below is harder to read?

> *High School Leaders Flunk Out!*
> You'll find it is hard to lead an active extracurricular life and keep up your grades. Last year, for example, four cheerleaders failed English. Next, five varsity players had only C averages. Then, twelve members of the marching band had to drop math or science classes because they couldn't keep up. So, you can see that extracurricular activity and study don't mix too well.
>
> — Sammy Smith, Grade 10 for *Monroe High Currier*

Failure Among High-potential Students

Involvement in extracurricular activity frequently precludes effective scholarship. Last year's grade average statistics verify the above assertion. Students directly and indirectly affiliated with varsity sports were frequently unable to make high grades or to carry appropriate academic course loads. That scholarship and peripheral school-sponsored activities do not mix is patently obvious.

— George Phelps, in response to
Monroe High School Accreditation Inquiry

Both passages say approximately the same thing. Sammy, a tenth grader, wrote in his own straightforward style for the school newspaper. Those who read Sammy's article should have few problems comprehending it. George Phelps, a science teacher, wrote in his own technical style for a school accreditation team. Those team members who read Phelps's article should have few problems comprehending it. The problem arises when Sammy tries to write like Mr. Phelps or when Monroe High students try to comprehend what Mr. Phelps has written. However, with instruction, you can teach students to read paragraphs such as that written by Mr. Phelps, and later to write such paragraphs. In other words, instruction in learning from text and instruction in writing are closely connected. Therefore, content area teachers might profitably spend some time showing students how to read and write paragraphs, since the paragraph is the basic organizational unit of writing.

Table 7.4 contains a list of paragraph types and the purposes they serve in communication (Robinson, 1975; Shepherd, 1978). Each type has some signal words that indicate the writer's intent and prepares the reader for what is coming. Students should become knowledgeable about the paragraph types and the signal words to help them in writing and in reading. In the last column of the table are listed teaching strategies to help the student become familiar with paragraph types through writing or reading exercises. A general strategy, not listed in the box, is to have students do a paragraph-by-paragraph analysis of a text: Students are likely to discern that the text follows a pattern of writing, as a sequence of paragraph types begins to repeat itself on successive topics in the text. This knowledge will help the students understand writing style and facilitate their reading and learning from text as well as their own writing in response to text.

EVALUATING WRITING

The concept of evaluating writing is simple: you make a judgment on how well the student has met the criteria of the assignment. If you haven't established the criteria or goals for the student to attain, you have no basis for evaluation. If you ask students to write a ten-page report on rocks, you have expressed only two criteria: length and subject. Whereas

TABLE 7.4. Paragraph Types

Paragraph Type and Purpose	Example	Signal or Transition Words	Teaching Strategy
1. Introductory overview, establish purpose (sometimes written in narrative style)	"In this chapter we shall explain three ideas."	this chapter describes; let's examine; here we will study . . . (questions)	State major points of section or chapter
2. Narrative (who, what, where, when, how) tell a story, integrate ideas and feelings in concrete situations, form visual image	"John is going through three steps now."	the scene is	Answer *wh* questions
3. Descriptive set the scene, visualize	"Picture this scene . . ."	describe; imagine; picture	Draw a picture or diagram
4. Definitional (may overlap with expository) clarifies meaning of word, phrase, or clause	"Rubella is a virus."	called; for example; means; that is (aids: parentheses, comparison or contrast, synonym, appositional phrase)	1. Tell what something is or means. 2. What is something like? 3. What is another word for?
5. Expository or Explanatory explain and inform	steps in process; chronology; directions; relate cause-effect; problem-solution; question-answer	first, next, after, then, to make, to do, since, because	1. Outline steps or events. 2. Answer question on cause for effect or solution for problem or answer to question.
6. Summary and Conclusion restate essential ideas	To summarize the two main points covered: (1)____ and (2)____.	thus: to briefly review; consequently; hence; you can see; in summary; to conclude we found . . . ; from the evidence; therefore; as a result . . .	State major points of section or chapter.

| 7. *Transitional* (hybrids, mixture of two or more types) relate what proceeded to what follows (may be in question form) | ''Now that we have covered our first two points, let's go on to our third point.'' | Now we shall consider . . . ; What do these reports tell us? however; on the other hand; yet; meanwhile; although; conversely; nevertheless; otherwise | Separate preceding from forward pointing ideas |

many students would have no problem meeting your requirements, some students might mistakenly believe they were meeting the assignment by copying the entire report from reference books.

Establishing Criteria

The first step in establishing criteria is to decide upon the *manuscript form* you wish the students to use and distribute a copy of it at the beginning of the course; thus, you will avoid having to repeat the conventions each time you give the assignment. In box 7.19 are directions for manuscript form that you may want a student to follow throughout the course.

BOX 7.19. Directions for Manuscript Form

Please follow these directions for each manuscript you turn in during this course.
1. Write on one side of each page. Use pen or typewriter (double space).
2. Number all pages in the right-hand corner beginning with the second page.
3. Fold paper in half lengthwise and endorse on the outside flap in the following way:

LAST NAME, First name
Class name, period
Date
Assignment Title

The second step in establishing criteria is to decide *how much spelling, punctuation, capitalization, and usage will count, if at all*. Students in English classes are used to being evaluated in terms of the ''correctness'' of their writing, but they seldom expect it in other classes unless the teacher announces it ahead of time.

The third step in establishing criteria is to *decide what the paper's content is to be and how the student should organize the content*.

Using Holistic Rating Strategies

English teachers spend many hours evaluating student papers — writing in margins; supplying introductory and terminal comments; correcting spelling, punctuation, and usage; and perhaps even rewriting passages. Although this has proved to be most useful in helping students to improve their writing, other content area teachers shy away from such an onerous task, and perhaps they should. To avoid lengthy and time-consuming evaluation of student papers, teachers may use two rating techniques that are not only quick but also *holistic*, that is, they evaluate all aspects of a paper (Braddock and others, 1963; Cooper and Odell, 1977). The first of these holistic *evaluation* techniques is the *general impression method*. The teacher reviews each paper quickly and assigns a grade based on a general impression. The general impression is formed by the criteria that the teacher has established for the assignment. Box 7.20 contains an example.

BOX 7.20. Assignment with Enabling Suggestions and Holistic Criteria for Evaluating Written Responses

ASSIGNMENT

Student Instructions: Select a Civil War battle that you feel accomplished little or nothing for either the North or the South. In an introductory paragraph describe the battle briefly. In a second paragraph explain how the battle accomplished nothing for the North. In a third paragraph explain how the battle accomplished nothing for the South. Remember to use specific names of people, places, and events; in other words, give good, clear examples. Attach a brief summary paragraph.

CRITERIA

Rating	Description
6	A **6** paper will be *outstanding* in all aspects. The selected battle will be summarized *briefly, yet fully*. The writer will *clearly* show, by concrete example, how both the North and South gained little or nothing from the battle. The four-paragraph structure will be *strictly maintained as required by the assignment*. The paper will show *excellent style* and be *accurately written* with regard to spelling, punctuation, usage, sentence structure.

5   A **5** paper will be *strong* in all aspects. The selected battle will be summarized *briefly*, yet *fairly completely*. The writer will *tend to show* by concrete example, how both the North and South gained little or nothing from the battle. The four-paragraph structure will be *reasonably maintained as required by the assignment*. The paper will show a *sense of style* and be, *for the most part*, accurately written with regard to spelling, punctuation, usage, sentence structure.

4   A **4** paper will be *adequate* in all aspects. The selected battle will be summarized *briefly*, but the *writer may forget one or two important events in the battle*. The writer will *occasionally* show, by concrete example, how both the North and South gained little or nothing from the battle. The four-paragraph structure will *occasionally be disregarded*. A sense of style *may be absent*. The paper will show *occasional* errors in spelling, punctuation, usage, sentence structure.

3   A **3** paper will be *flawed* in one or two aspects. The selected battle will be summarized in *unneeded length* or the writer may *forget many important events*. The writer will *tend to avoid* concrete examples, although he or she may include one or two. The essay will either be in *one complete paragraph or in many small paragraphs. No attempt at style will be made.* The paper has *frequent* errors in spelling, punctuation, usage, sentence structure.

2   A **2** paper will be *seriously* flawed. The selected battle will be badly and inaccurately summarized. There will be *no concrete examples*. The paragraph structure will be random and chaotic, totally disorganized. The paper has *so many errors that it is virtually unreadable.*

1   A **1** paper fails to respond to the assignment.

Another holistic rating strategy is the *analytical evaluation*, whereby a reader assigns points to various aspects of the writing, adds up the points, and arrives at a final score. In box 7.21 is a writing assignment, together with the rating scale for its analytical evaluation.

BOX 7.21. Writing Assignment with Analytical Rating Scale for Evaluating Responses

ASSIGNMENT

Using three library sources, write a report describing the Mojave desert environment. Include such information as (1) the appearance of the desert, (2) the types of plant and animal life that coexist in the desert, and (3) the damage modern technological society is doing to the desert environment. The report should be written in five paragraphs: an introduction, one paragraph each for (1), (2), (3), above, and a conclusion. Attach a bibliography at the back of the report. Synthesize the information; do not copy. Concentrate on correct usage, variety in sentence length and structure, and accurate use of technical vocabulary.

RATING SCALE

Organization	40 points
introduction	5 points
paragraph on appearance	10 points
paragraph on life	10 points
paragraph on damage	10 points
conclusion	5 points
Documentation	30 points
synthesis of information	10 points
use of three sources	10 points
bibliography	10 points
Style	30 points
correctness of language and convention	10 points
sentence variety: length and structure	10 points
appropriate use of vocabulary	5 points
manuscript appearance	5 points

SUMMARY

This chapter has focused on the teaching of writing, not just assigning it. In doing so, it has emphasized that the general characteristics of writing can be taught in English classes, but that content teachers have to supplement this instruction by teaching students the writing requirements emphasized in their content areas, including spelling of technical words, correct word choice, and ways of organizing information in written responses. Four types of writing were explained: reporting, exposition, narration, and argumentation. The special case of essay writing, particularly on examinations, was discussed with emphasis on well-written questions as a prerequisite for well-written answers. The seven types of paragraphs were defined and illustrated. Throughout we gave suggestions for teaching students to write, including how to write a report on reference reading. We concluded with a section on two holistic ways of evaluating writing: general impression and analytical.

When students can respond to texts with fairly fluent discussions and writing, they are ready to move into multiple-text situations. But, first, you will have to know ways of determining reading and readability levels. Then you will be able to select an appropriate range of textbooks. We shall explain how to determine reading and readability levels in the next chapter.

ACTIVITIES

1. Select a textbook in a content area you want to teach. Develop two writing assignments you would give in (a) narration and (b) argumentation that would show what the students learned from the text. Compare the results, noting how different types of writing led to different emphases of information in the text.
2. Compose directions for a writing assignment in your content area. Include all the criteria you wish to evaluate. Then develop both a general impression and an analytical rating scale for evaluating it. Which one is more useful for diagnosis? Which is easier to construct and score?
3. Examine two textbooks in your content area. Do they suggest writing assignments, other than particular study questions? Do they give the students enough help in writing these assignments? Are the criteria for evaluation clearly stated?
4. Rewrite the following vague essay questions. In rewriting, (1) supply performance verbs that suggest the mode of student response; (2) limit the content of the response; and (3) make enabling suggestions as to the organization of the response.
   a. Discuss the differences between tropical and subtropical climates.
   b. How was Billy Buck a friend to Jody in *The Red Pony*?
   c. How do the "new mathematics" and the "old mathematics" differ?
   d. Discuss Priestley's experiment using mercurous oxide.
   e. Describe a well-equipped auto shop.
   f. Why are soufflés difficult to make?

8 | Determining Reading and Readability Levels

CHAPTER OVERVIEW

If you teach a ninth-grade science class, a strong possibility exists that half of your students will not be able to comprehend the textbook, even if the book has a ninth-grade readability level. This important chapter focuses on the readability of textbooks. First, you will learn several methods for computing or otherwise determining the reading difficulty of the textbooks you use. Second, you will be shown strategies for predicting how well your students will be able to comprehend their textbooks. Finally, you will see results from surveys and research studies that indicate how well people have to read to survive in school, to function well on the job, and to engage in pleasure reading.

TECHNICAL VOCABULARY

readability
fluency level
instructional level
frustration level
Reading Ease Formula
cloze technique
Personal Reading Inventory (PRI)

Informal Reading Inventory (IRI)
recreational reading level
functional reading level
reading frequency
readability formula
SEER technique

Teachers make a single textbook appropriate to the range of individual differences in a class by using the single-text strategies, described in Chapter 4, in two ways: (1) they use directed reading activities (DRA), reading and learning-from-text guides, and the SQ3R method to adapt the text to individual differences among students; and (2) they teach students to use these strategies for reading and learning from text on their own (see chapter 10, "A Blueprint for Instruction," for procedures on developing students towards independence in reading and learning from text).

Another way the teacher makes the single text fit the needs of all students is to use some procedure for determining the *readability* of the text for a group of students. If the teacher can select a textbook that is about average in difficulty for the class, the text will be easier to adapt to the entire range of abilities in the class than a text that is closer to the low or high achievers.

If textbook selection is made during the summer when students are not present, the teacher has to rely only upon the characteristics of the text itself and personal judgment to determine whether the text would be appropriate for the class. For this purpose, the teacher can use either a *readability formula* or a technique for estimating readability. The formulas that we shall explain in some detail in this chapter are the Flesch Reading Ease Formula and the Fry Readability Graph. The technique for estimating readability is the SEER technique.

However, if the students are available, then the teacher does not have to use a formula that *predicts* reading difficulty or a procedure for *estimating* readability. Instead, the teacher can actually try the material out with the students and find out how difficult *in fact* the text is for them. The "try out" types of readability testing are the cloze technique and the personal or informal reading inventories. These ways of determining readability require considerable student and teacher time but provide the best way of determining readability for a particular group of students.

Determination of readability and reading difficulty fits into four categories: (a) computational formulas, (b) a noncomputational technique, (c) the cloze technique, and (d) reading inventories. We shall first briefly describe each of these techniques and then explain in greater detail how to use or construct them.

DESCRIPTION OF FORMULAS AND PROCEDURES FOR ESTIMATING READABILITY

Readability formulas of the computational type have been available for the past forty years (Klare, 1963; Singer, 1975). All of them use some variation of sentence complexity and word difficulty (Klare, 1974–1975). Three of the standard formulas in wide use are appropriate for somewhat different segments of the grade level continuum. The Spache formula

(1953) was designed for grades 1–3, the Dale-Chall (1948) for grades 4–8, and the Flesch (1949) formula for grades 4 to college graduation. Although readability formulas have helped determine what makes reading easy or difficult, much is still unknown about reading difficulty (Klare, 1974–1975).

The computational formulas are time-consuming and tedious to use. They require the user to count syllables, words, or sentences. Consequently, some researchers have developed procedures for reducing the time and tedium in computing readability levels of materials (Fry, 1968; McLaughlin, 1969). A noncomputational procedure has achieved the greatest reduction in time for estimating readability level. This procedure consists of matching unknown material to a standard scale. Although this third approach to determining readability level is somewhat subjective, it is nevertheless as accurate as some computational procedures (Singer, 1975).

The *cloze technique* uses a totally different way of determining reading difficulty level. To employ this technique in the original way, as defined by its inventor, Taylor (1953), simply delete or omit every fifth word from a passage of approximately 250 words. Leave a sentence before and after each passage intact. A total of 50 words will be deleted from the passage. The reader's task is to infer from the remaining context what the missing words are, retrieve the exact words from vocabulary stored in his or her memory, and insert them into the passage. When you score only the exact original word as correct, you prevent disputes from arising on whether a word is a synonym for the missing word or not. The cloze technique places a premium upon the reader's ability to infer the missing words from the semantics and syntax of the remaining words in the passage and upon the reader's vocabulary repertoire and ability to retrieve words from storage in memory. Since the reader also has to identify printed words in order to infer the missing words, the reader performing on the cloze test has to use semantics, syntax, graphophonemics, graphomorphemics (Goodman, 1976; Ruddell, 1976), and reasoning processes (Davis, 1968; Fredericksen, 1972). Look at this sentence: *After locating his flock, the shepherd gathered the sh_____.* The *semantics,* or accumulated meanings of the sentence, suggest what the shepherd gathered. The *syntax,* or the order in which words in English must occur, signals the type of word that should be coming next or at least soon in a sentence. In the sentence above, the noun determiner *the* indicates a noun belongs in the next slot in the sentence, the slot for the missing word. *Graphophonemics* is the ability to give sounds to individual letters or to letter groups which function as single units, such as *sh. Graphomorphemics* is a two-part process. In one process, the student recognizes boundaries between meaningful units in words, such as *shep-herd.* Knowledge of words and word structures in English enable the reader to recognize and correctly segment words at their structural boundaries. Then the reader can apply graphophonemics to relate the units of print to sounds. The reader also has to use *reasoning processes,* such as inference, to try to determine the word that has been deleted. Hence the cloze technique is a way of assessing all of these systems and their operation in the process of reading (Singer, 1975). Of course, other factors also enter into replacing missing words, such as knowledge of an author's style.

A fourth way of estimating readability of content area materials is through a reading inventory based upon graded material drawn from a specific content area. In this procedure, an individual reads and answers questions on successively more difficult, graded paragraphs. As the reader progresses through the paragraphs, more errors in answering comprehension questions occur, provided the questions that the teacher constructs are relevant and appropriately difficult for the grade level of the paragraphs. Later in this chapter we shall present information on how to construct these questions. The resulting score determines the reader's fluency, instructional, and frustration levels. These levels use arbitrary criteria that teachers find useful. The *fluency level* is the grade level of a passage at which the reader can correctly answer 90 percent or more of the comprehension questions. The *instructional level* is the grade level of a passage at which the reader attains 70 to 90 percent comprehension. The *frustration level* is the grade level of a passage at which the reader's comprehension drops below 70 percent.[1] How readers respond to their difficulties in reading is also dependent on other factors, especially their interest in the material and their desire to read it.

Now that we have had an overview of the various ways of determining readability and reading difficulty, we shall go into each way in greater detail.

COMPUTING READING DIFFICULTY LEVEL

The Flesch Reading Ease Formula

The Flesch Reading Ease Formula for computing readability level uses two criteria: number of syllables per hundred words and average number of words per sentence in a 100 word sample. The number of syllables in a

---

[1] In an arbitrary set of criteria devised by Betts (1947), in widespread use at the elementary school level, word recognition errors are also counted in determining reading levels: five or more errors per hundred words with less than 70 percent comprehension define the frustration level, while more than 90 percent comprehension and one or few word recognition errors indicate a fluency level. The instructional level lies in between the frustration and the fluency levels. However, other factors, such as motivation and interest, may also determine whether a student is likely to read and comprehend reading material despite a high degree of word recognition difficulty.

See Powell (1971) for a critique and modification of the formula, but note that the Powell formula is also arbitrary.

word is an index of the difficulty of the word because longer words are usually more difficult. The words per sentence is an index of sentence complexity. Usually longer sentences are syntactically more complex and hence more difficult.

To use the Reading Ease Formula, count the syllables in a passage that has approximately 100 words. Remember that a word has as many syllables as it has vowels or vowel-like sounds. Simply say each word and count the number of vowel sounds you hear. Examples of common syllables are shown in table 8.1.

For words per sentence, count the number of words and then divide by the number of sentences in the passage. The scales in figure 8.1 will allow you to determine the Reading Ease Score without further computation. Just locate the words per sentence on the left scale and syllables per hundred words on the right scale. Then connect the points on the two scales with a ruler. The point where the ruler intersects the middle scale indicates the Reading Ease Score of the passage. See the example on page 179.

TABLE 8.1. Basic Syllables and Combinations of Basic Syllables

Word(Basic Syllables)	Number of Syllables
oak	1
bet-ter	2
on-ly	2
a-ble	2
nick-el	2
ea-gle	2
work-er	2

Word (Combinations of Basic Syllables)	Number of Syllables
un-a-ble	3
ad-van-tage	3
au-to-mo-bile	4
op-por-tu-ni-ty	5
un-a-li-en-a-ble	6

The division of syllables follows *Webster's Third New International Dictionary,* which, unlike the *Second,* switched from phonetic division to printer's division of syllables. For example, *i-de-a* is divided in the latest edition as two syllables, *i-dea,* because a printer would not put a hyphen after *e* and carry a syllable over to the next line if *idea* came at the end of a line and space allowed for only two syllables on the line.

FIGURE 8.1. "How Easy?" Chart

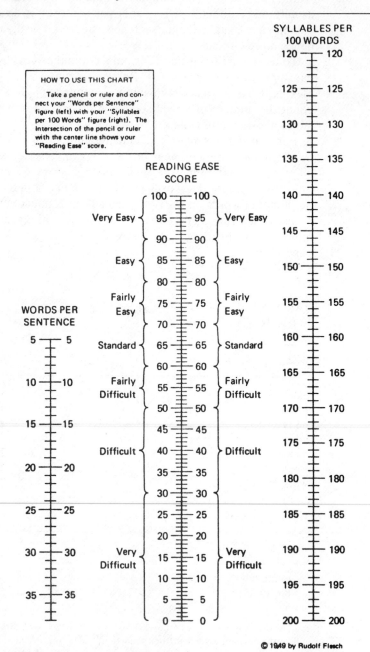

© 1949 by Rudolf Flesch

From *The Art of Readable Writing*, rev. ed. by Rudolph Flesch. Copyright 1949, © 1974 by Rudolph Flesch. Reprinted by permission of Harper & Row, Publishers, Inc.

Words per sentence = 15
Syllables per 100 words = 160
Intersection point = 57

The score of 57 indicates the passage is fairly difficult.

Now look at table 8.2 to see the grade level of the passage and the kind of publication that usually contains passages this difficult. Table 8.2 indicates that a Reading Ease Score of 57 is equivalent to passages found in such magazines as *Harper's* and *Atlantic*. Also, the grade level of the passage is equivalent to the difficulty of printed materials in grades 10–12 (high school).

TABLE 8.2. Meaning of Reading Ease Scores

Reading Ease Score	Style	Grade	Typical Magazine
90 to 100	Very Easy	5	Comic books
80 to 89	Easy	6	Pulp fiction, such as *Western Magazine*
70 to 79	Fairly Easy	7	Slick fiction, such as *True Stories; California Driver's Handbook*
60 to 69	Standard	8–9	*Reader's Digest, Time* magazine
50 to 59	Fairly Difficult	10–12 (high school)	Some high school texts; journals, such as *Language Arts;* magazines, such as *Harper's* and *Atlantic*
30 to 49	Difficult	13–16 (college)	Academic—college texts
0 to 29	Very Difficult	17+ (graduate school)	Scientific, such as *American Medical Association Journal;* graduate school texts, such as *Theoretical Models and Processes of Reading*

Source: Adaptation of pp. 177 and 178 from *The Art of Readable Writing*, rev. ed. by Rudolph Flesch. Copyright 1949, © 1974 by Rudolph Flesch. Reprinted by permission of Harper & Row, Publishers, Inc.

BOX 8.1. Computing the Reading Ease Score of a Passage

Find the Reading Ease Score of the passage in box 8.1. If you follow steps 1–6 correctly, you should obtain the results shown in box 8.2.

THE NEGATIVE IMAGE OF WOMEN
IN CHILDREN'S LITERATURE

> In considering select nursery rhymes and folk tales, one can see that women are portrayed somewhat negatively, either as ineffectual creatures who need to be dominated by men or as aggressive monsters who must be destroyed by men. One can assume that these folk materials were born in and perpetuated by societies that maintained the "natural inferiority of women." However, today, when women are seeking liberation and equality, a young child's image of what is read to him may be in sharp contrast to what he sees. On the other hand, liberated women may unwittingly be perpetuating the "monster" image; after all, one of the liberation organizations was called W.I.T.C.H.

1. Number of words_____
2. Number of sentences_____
3. Number of words per sentence (divide 2 into 1)_____
4. Number of syllables per 100 words_____
5. To obtain the Reading Ease Score on figure 8.1, use a ruler or pencil to connect the words per sentence figure and the syllables per hundred words figure. Read the score where the pencil or ruler intersects the middle scale and enter it here:_____
6. Find the Reading Ease Score on table 8.2 and write the grade equivalent here:_____

Quoted passage is from Dan Donlan, "The Negative Image of Women in Children's Literature," *Elementary English* (April 1972): 604–11.

BOX 8.2. Sample Computation of a Reading Ease Score

In considering select nursery rhymes and folk tales, one can see that women are portrayed somewhat negatively, either as ineffectual creatures who need to be dominated by men or as aggressive monsters who must be destroyed by men. One can assume that these folk materials were born in and perpetuated by societies that maintained the "natural inferiority of women." However, today, when women are seeking liberation and equality, a young child's image of what is read to him may be in sharp contrast to what he sees. On the other hand, liberated women may unwit-

$\overset{1}{\text{tingly}}$ be perpetuating the $\overset{5}{\text{"monster"}}$ $\overset{1}{\text{image}}$ $\overset{2}{}$ $\overset{2}{}$ (100 words in passage to this point); after all, one of the liberation organizations was called W.I.T.C.H. (110 words in total passage)

1. Number of words __110__
2. Number of sentences __4__
3. Number of words per sentence (divide 2 into 1) __27.5__
4. Number of syllables per 100 words __171__ (Note: Syllables are marked in the passage.)
5. Reading Ease Score at intersection of straight line formed by placing pencil or ruler between words per sentence of __27.5__ and syllables per 100 words of __171__ is: __34__.
6. Table 8.2 indicates that a Reading Ease Score of *34* is equivalent to passages usually found in *academic and scholarly* magazines or in reading material used at grade levels 13–16 (college).

If the answer you computed in box 8.1 agrees with the answer in box 8.2, then you have learned how to use the Flesch Reading Ease Formula. However, the Reading Ease Formula does not provide grade equivalent scores. Another formula, which does, and is also easy to use is the Fry Readability Graph.

The Fry Readability Graph

The Fry Readability Graph appears in figure 8.2. This figure also contains directions on how to compute readability with an example. In the Fry technique, you find the average number of syllables and the number of sentences in three samples of a hundred words. Then you use these figures as coordinates and determine where they intersect on the graph in figure 8.2. The large number between the lines on the graph which is closest to the point of intersection indicates the approximate grade level of the passage.

The example in figure 8.2 is for three hundred-word samples from a text with an average of 141 syllables and an average sentence length of 6.3. To use the graph to determine readability level, locate 141 on the top of the graph and put the finger of your right hand at this point. Then locate 6.3 on the left side of the graph and put a finger of your left hand on this number. Now move your right finger down and your left finger across the graph. Where they intersect you'll find a dot between two lines. The number between these two lines stands for grade 7. Since the dot is close to, but not on line 7, you then estimate the readability of the passage is about grade level 6.9.

FIGURE 8.2. Graph for Computing Readability

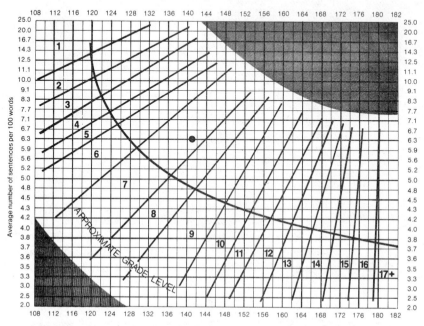

GRAPH FOR ESTIMATING READABILITY — EXTENDED

Average number of syllables per 100 words

DIRECTIONS: Randomly select 3 one hundred word passages from a book or an article. Plot average number of syllables and average number of sentences per 100 words on graph to determine the grade level of the material. Choose more passages per book if great variability is observed and conclude that the book has uneven readability. Few books will fall in gray area but when they do grade level scores are invalid.

Count proper nouns, numerals and initializations as words. Count a syllable for each symbol. For example, "1945" is 1 word and 4 syllables and "IRA" is 1 word and 3 syllables.

EXAMPLE:

	SYLLABLES	SENTENCES
1st Hundred Words	124	6.6
2nd Hundred Words	141	5.5
3rd Hundred Words	158	6.8
AVERAGE	141	6.3

READABILITY 7th GRADE (see dot plotted on graph)

For further information and validity data, see Edward Fry, "Fry's Readability Graph: Clarifications, Validity, and Extension to Level 17," *Journal of Reading* (December 1977).

A procedure that does not compute readability, but simply judges it by comparison with a standard is the SEER technique.

The SEER Technique for Estimating Readability Level

SEER is an acronym for "Singer Eyeball Estimate of Readability" (Singer, 1975). It is a judgmental technique that involves taking a passage, usually a paragraph of about 100 words from materials of unknown readability level, and matching it to a paragraph in a set of scaled paragraphs whose reading levels have been computed and are indicated next to the paragraphs. The directions for using the SEER Scale tell the teacher to take a paragraph whose readability is to be estimated, move the paragraph up and down the scaled paragraphs until a judgment is made that the unknown paragraph is about equal in difficulty to a paragraph on the scale. In making a judgment, the teacher is likely to use such criteria as sentence length, word difficulty, writing style, and concept level. Then the teacher notes the readability level of the paragraph on the scale which matches the paragraph whose readability level is being judged. If the difficulty of unknown paragraph lies between two of the scaled paragraphs, assign the grade level readability between the two paragraphs. The graded paragraphs on science content in table 8.3 can be used in the SEER technique, particularly for estimating the difficulty of science content.

The SEER technique is more accurate when the textual material for matching and the scaled paragraphs are in the same content area. The estimated reading level of a matching paragraph will be accurate, plus or minus one grade level, in two out of three cases. This technique of estimating readability is easier than the Fry technique's tedious and time-consuming computations (Singer, 1975). If the content of the scaled paragraphs and the paragraphs for matching do differ, the reading level estimation is likely to be off by about plus or minus 1.5 grade levels for two out of three comparisons (Carver, 1974). That means that the readability of a passage estimated to be at a grade 10 level of difficulty might be somewhere between grades 8.5 and 11.5. This measurement variability applies to all computational formulas. However, this degree of accuracy is still useful for practical purposes.

To select passages for constructing a set of scaled paragraphs in a particular content area, such as history, biology, mathematics, literature, use the school library catalogs. Note that only the elementary school catalogs (chapter 9, table 9.2) provide readability grade levels. Readability grade levels of 7–9 are implied by listing books in the junior high catalog, and readability grade levels of 10–12 are implicit in books listed in the high school catalog. If a book is not listed in the catalogs, the teacher can use the SEER technique.

Another estimation formula determines the probable range of reading ability of a heterogeneous group of students. Although we have already presented this formula in chapter 3, we shall simply repeat it here, and refer you to chapter 3 for further discussion of it:

Expected range of reading level = ⅔ × average chronological age of the group.

Thus, a tenth-grade class with an average age of 15 will have a ten-year reading range, from grade equivalent 5 to grade equivalent 15.

The Flesch Reading Ease Formula and the Fry Readability Graph compute and predict the grade level of reading material from characteristics of the printed material alone. The SEER technique *estimates* grade-level difficulty. Unlike any of these, the cloze technique requires that a sample of the printed material must be tried out on the individual or group of students who are actually going to read the material. Thus, the cloze technique determines the difficulty of the material relative to the reading ability of the students who are actually going to read the material.

The Cloze Technique

In the cloze technique every fifth word from a 250 word passage is deleted, but the sentence before and after the passage is left intact. A modification calls for the deletion of every tenth word from a 500 word passage. The technique implicitly requires the reader to rely upon the syntax and semantics of the passage plus such aspects as writing style to infer what the missing words are and then to retrieve these words from his or her vocabulary repertoire. In scoring, only the exact, original word is counted as correct. The original technique did not score synonyms as correct. Such a scoring procedure is not practical because it is difficult to determine the boundary lines for synonyms, that is, where a word stops being a synonym for another word and becomes a word whose meaning is different for the passage.

To use the cloze procedure, simply select graded material from a content area. Lists of these graded materials can be found in library catalogs for the three school levels. (See chapter 9, ''Multiple Text Strategies,'' table 9.2, for glossed directions on how to read the library catalogs.) Once suitable materials have been found, follow the steps below:

1. After selecting a book at each grade level from a particular content area, take a passage of about 125 words from each book. Then delete every fifth word from each passage, but leave the first and last sentences intact. (If you want to make this task less difficult, take 250-word passages and delete every tenth word.) You can then combine results on successive passages to obtain the required 250-word passage length.
2. Have the students read the passages, starting at the lowest level, and ask them to insert the missing words. Count the number of exactly correct inserted words. The formula for determining the percent of correct words is:

$$\text{percent correct} = \frac{\text{words correct x 100}}{\substack{\text{total words deleted} \\ \text{from passage}}}$$

3. The instructional level is the level at which the student begins to obtain a score of 44 percent correct insertions in the passage. A score below 44 percent means the material is frustrating for the student; and a score above 58 percent means the material is too easy or at an "independent study" level for the student (Bormuth, 1968). The "supervised" instructional level is between 44 and 57 percent.
4. The cloze test results will indicate the range of reading achievement of the class in the content area books selected. The teacher can use this knowledge to select an appropriate range of reading materials for the class.

Box 8.3 contains an example of a series of graded passages in the content area of general science. A teacher selected these passages from books in the school library catalogs, and made them into a cloze test by simply deleting every fifth word.

You can use the cloze technique in other ways. You can assess knowledge of technical vocabulary in a content area text by simply deleting the technical words in a passage. You can also provide students with multiple choices for the deleted words, just as the Gates-MacGinitie Survey Test does (see chapter 3 for examples of the Gates-MacGinitie Test). Unlike the traditional way of using the cloze technique, these other ways have no rules for determining what scores mean. However, the information can be useful in making teaching plans: the test on technical words can provide information on how familiar the technical terms are and which terms need to be stressed.

You can administer a cloze test before and after instruction. If the scores on the pretest are low and those on the posttest are high, a teacher can reasonably infer that students have learned the content during the course.

A limitation of the cloze technique is that it tends to work best only when the passages are near the reader's difficulty level. If the passages are too easy for students, the students are likely to insert many synonyms. These synonyms are then scored as errors. Consequently, easy passages lead to an underestimation of students' actual reading levels (Smith, 1972–1973). At the other extreme, if the passages selected are too difficult, readers also obtain a low score for different reasons: they do not have the missing word in their vocabulary, cannot retrieve it from their memory, cannot use syntax or semantics from which to infer the missing word, lack motivation to search for it, or some combination of these reasons. Hence, the cloze technique should be used cautiously. If readers' scores are low, get higher, and then become lower as they progress through graded passages, the passages which yielded the higher scores should be used for obtaining students' readability levels.

Counting only exact words correct simplifies the task of scoring the cloze test because it eliminates pondering over what is a synonym and what is not. If you do decide to accept synonyms in scoring, allow students to judge which synonyms are acceptable; this will save you a classroom hassle. However, the meanings of the scores given in the list on page 187 are not appropriate when synonyms are accepted. Indeed, researchers have not devised any scoring method applicable to the use of synonyms.

The cloze technique has advantages over other readability techniques because teachers can construct test passages easily and do not have to write comprehension questions, as they do when using the personal or informal reading inventory technique which is discussed next.

BOX 8.3. Applying the Cloze Technique to Science Passages

Directions: In the following passages, we have deleted every fifth word. Your task is to insert the missing words. Then compare your answer with the key provided at the end of the box. The point where your cumulative score drops below 44 percent, indicates when the material has reached your frustration level of reading. Above 44 percent you are at the instructional level and above 57 percent at the fluency level in this type of reading material.

PASSAGE 1

Grades 1–3

Passage length: 122 words

What Things Will Stick __1__ Magnets?
 Touch a tack __2__ the end of your __3__ .
 What happens?
 The tack __4__ to the magnet!
 Now __5__ a nail and a __6__ and see if they __7__ to the magnet.
 Touch __8__ toothpick, a penny, a __9__ band with the magnet.
 __10__ happens now?
 They do __11__ stick to the magnet.
 __12__ around your house and __13__ a pencil, a book, __14__ bobby pin, a glass, __15__ eraser, a nail, a __16__ of scissors, a toy.
 __17__ you think any of __18__ will stick to your __19__?
 Try each one.
 If __20__ things you touch have __21__ in them, they will __22__.
 If they do not __23__ iron in them, they __24__ not stick.

PASSAGE 2

Grades 2–4

Passage length: 132 words

Look around you. You __1__ see many things made __2__ metal. Perhaps you see __3__ metal doorknob, a key, __4__ pair of scissors, or __5__ shiny band around one __6__ of your pencil. All __7__ things are made of __8__. Any of them made __9__ iron will be pulled __10__ by a magnet. In __11__, you can use a __12__ to help you find __13__ that are made with __14__.

The space around a __15__ where its pulling power __16__ found is called a __17__ field. A magnetic field __18__ away from a magnet __19__ all directions.

You cannot __20__ a magnetic field, but __21__ can outline its shape. __22__ a heavy piece of __23__ on top of a __24__. Sprinkle some iron filings __25__ the paper. Tap the __26__ edge gently.

PASSAGE 3

Grade 5

Passage length: 134 words

The first kind of __1__ known to man was __2__ natural magnet. Natural magnets __3__ found in the ground. __4__ look like dark-colored rocks __5__ stones and are rough __6__ irregular rather than round __7__ smooth. These natural magnets __8__ made up of an __9__ ore called magnetite and __10__ called lodestones.

Sailors learned __11__ ago that when they __12__ a thin piece of __13__ on a string and __14__ the magnetite to swing __15__ it would point to __16__ north. This helped the __17__ to find their way __18__ night when they could __19__ see land. It helped __20__ to find their way __21__ it was cloudy and __22__ could not see the __23__. The magnetite would always __24__ them on the right __25__. The sailors called the __26__ of magnetite "leading stones."

PASSAGE 4

Grade 7

Passage length: 139 words

Long before the birth __1__ Christ, Chinese philosophers found __2__ second magnetical quality in __3__ magnet-stone. They placed it __4__ a wooden raft floating __5__ a bowl of water. __6__ stone on its raft __7__ turned slowly until it __8__ pointing north-and-south.

The Chinese __9__ it showed where south __10__. Their floating magnet-stone was __11__ tchi-nan, the chariot of __12__ south. This was apparently __13__ first compass, and it __14__ said to have guided __15__ caravans across the endless __16__ of Tatary in Asia.

__17__ hundreds of years passed __18__ men on the opposite __19__ of the world also __20__ that the magnet-stone could __21__ more than "drawe yron __22__ it selfe." They chose __23__ think of the magnet-stone __24__ pointing north. They sometimes __25__ the stone, and sometimes __26__ suspended it by a __27__. The stone spun slowly.

PASSAGE 5

Grade 9

Passage length: 126 words

Magnetism in the Atom. __1__ things are made of __2__ units called molecules (MOLL-uh-kyouls). Each __3__ is made up of __4__ units called atoms. Scientists __5__ formed a picture of __6__ atom that explains how __7__ behave. The picture of __8__ atom shows that every __9__ is a small magnet. __10__ is the reason why:

__11__ atom is made of __12__ small lump called a __13__ (NEW-klee-uhs) surrounded by electrons. The __14__ has an electrical charge __15__ the kind called positive. __16__ electron has an electrical __17__ of the kind called __18__.

The electrons in an __19__ are moving in two __20__ ways: 1) The electrons revolve in __21__ around the nucleus the __22__ the earth revolves around __23__ sun; 2) each electron spins __24__ an axis like a __25__.

PASSAGE 6

Grade 11

Passage length: 153 words

There is yet another __1__ source of understanding about __2__ nature and phenomena of __3__ upper atmosphere and the __4__ beyond. This is the __5__ of the variations of __6__ earth's magnetic field. The __7__ may at first seem __8__, because the earth's magnetism __9__ a property of the __10__ earth. Its cause is __11__ yet fully understood, but __12__ believed to be a __13__ of electrical currents flowing __14__ the inner liquid core __15__ the earth. Unless continuously __16__, such currents would die __17__, owing to electrical resistance. __18__ period of decay might __19__ reckoned in many thousands __20__ years, but is certainly __21__ brief compared with the __22__ of the earth (a __23__ billion years). Hence the __24__ currents are believed to __25__ maintained by a process __26__ similar to that of __27__ self-exciting dynamo: the dynamo __28__ electric currents by motion __29__ some of its parts __30__ the magnetic field generated __31__ these same currents.

KEY

Passage (Grade Level)	Deleted Words
1 (1–3)	1. to, 2. with, 3. magnet, 4. sticks, 5. touch, 6. clip, 7. stick, 8. a, 9. rubber, 10. what, 11. not, 12. look, 13. find, 14. a, 15. an, 16. pair, 17. do, 18, these, 19. magnet, 20. the, 21. iron, 22. stick, 23. have, 24. will.
2 (2–4)	1. can, 2. of, 3. a, 4. a, 5. the, 6. end, 7. these, 8. metal, 9. with, 10. on, 11. fact, 12. magnet, 13. things, 14. iron,

15. magnet, 16. is, 17. magnetic, 18. stretches, 19. in, 20. see, 21. you, 22. place, 23. paper, 24. magnet, 25. on, 26. paper.

3 (5)

1. magnet, 2. a, 3. were, 4. they, 5. or, 6. and, 7. and, 8. are, 9. iron, 10. are, 11. long, 12. hung, 13. magnetite, 14. allowed, 15. freely, 16. the, 17. sailors, 18. at, 19. not, 20. them, 21. when, 22. they, 23. stars, 24. keep, 25. course, 26. pieces.

4 (7)

1. of, 2. a, 3. the, 4. on, 5. in, 6. the, 7. always, 8. was, 9. said, 10. is, 11. called, 12. the, 13. man's, 14. is, 15. great, 16. grasslands, 17. many, 18. before, 19. side, 20. discovered, 21. do, 22. to, 24. as, 25. floated, 26. they, 27. thread.

5 (9)

1. all, 2. tiny, 3. molecule, 4. smaller, 5. have, 6. the, 7. atoms, 8. the, 9. atom, 10. here, 11. every, 12. a, 13. nucleus, 14. nucleus, 15. of, 16. each, 17. charge, 18. negative, 19. atom, 20. different, 21. orbits, 22. way, 23. the, 24. around, 25. top.

6 (11)

1. important, 2. the, 3. the, 4. space, 5. study, 6. the, 7. fact, 8. surprising, 9. is, 10. massive, 11. not, 12. is, 13. system, 14. in, 15. of, 16. maintained, 17. away, 18. their, 19. be, 20. of, 21. very, 22. age, 23. few, 24. electrical, 25. be, 26. essentially, 27. a, 28. produces, 29. of, 30. through, 31. by.

Passage 1 from Tillie S. Pine and Joseph Levine, *Magnets and How to Use Them* (New York: McGraw-Hill, 1958), pp. 10–11. Passage 2 from Raymond Sacks, *Magnets* (New York: Coward-McCann, 1967), pp. 18–21. Passage 3 from Edward Victor, *Exploring and Understanding Magnets and Electromagnets* (Westchester, Ill.: Benefic Press, 1967), p. 8. Passage 4 from E. G. Valens, *Magnet* (New York: World Publishing Co., 1964), pp. 4–5. Passage 5 from Irving and Ruth Adler, *Magnets* (New York: John Day, 1966), pp. 25–26. Passage 6 from Sydney Chapman, *I.G.Y.: Year of Discovery* (Ann Arbor: University of Michigan Press, 1959), p. 76.

The Personal Reading Inventory (PRI) or Informal Reading Inventory (IRI)

The Personal Reading Inventory or Informal Reading Inventory — both names appear in journals — are tests that teachers construct. The inventory uses graded passages and comprehension questions after each passage to assess reading level. To use this technique, follow the steps below.

1. Simply take a set of graded passages in a content area. See the graded passages in box 8.3. The passages should be at least 100 words long.

2. As a rule of thumb, write three or four comprehension questions for each passage. In general, ask one or two questions at the literal level (what the passage stated explicitly, including technical vocabulary defined in context), one or two at the interpretive or inferential levels (what the passage means), and one or two at the generalization level. (See the headings ''Directed Reading Activities'' and ''Reading and Learning-from-Text Guides'' in chapters 11–13 for questions in four content areas; chapter 13, table 13.1, for information on constructing a table of specifications and using it for diagnostic purposes; chapter 13, Box 13.4 for seven types of questions.)

3. Have a student start at a level about one grade below your estimate of his or her reading level. After each passage, students try to answer the questions on the passage they have just read. Multiple-choice answers will make the scoring objective and easy.

4. Determine student's reading level according to the following rule-of-thumb criteria:

Fluency Level: 90% or higher comprehension
Instruction Level: 70–89% comprehension
Frustration Level: 69% and lower in comprehension

As students progress upwards, from easy to more difficult passages, their comprehension scores should decrease. If the drop is not progressive, then you will have to modify the comprehension questions. Note that the type of questions in box 8.4 appear in parentheses next to each question. The types form a gradient in difficulty. The questions in the lower grades are literal and shift to paraphrase in the middle grades, and end up in the upper grades as inferential, interpretive, and generalization types of questions.

You can test out the passages and questions on students who are at grade level for a passage. For example, give the passage and questions at grade 7 level to seventh graders, the passage and questions at grade 8 level to eighth graders, and so on. If the students at each level on the average get about 50 percent of the questions on a passage correct, you know you have a well-graded set of questions. Using this criterion, we would probably have to modify the questions in box 8.4 which we constructed only as a classroom exercise.

BOX 8.4. Reading Inventory on General Science Content

The teacher has a student begin the inventory at a passage that is at least one grade level below the student's estimated reading level and lets him or her continue until the comprehension level drops below 70%. In this inventory, we have only two or three questions per paragraph. We therefore use this rule-of-thumb: stop when a student answers two successive questions incorrectly.

Directions: Read each passage, starting with a passage that is easy for you. Then answer the questions for the passage. The key for checking your answers is at the end of the reading inventory. Continue on to more difficult passages. Stop when you miss two successive questions. Your reading level is the grade level just before these two questions.

PASSAGE 1

Grades 1–3

Passage length: 162 words

A bird seems to float like a feather and be blown like a leaf; climb up on the wind; slide down on a breeze; play tag through the trees.

Why can't you?

A bird can fly because its wings are big compared to its small, light body. Even a tiny bird has wings enough to move the air, big enough to hold it up. Air moves under and over a bird's wings.

You have no wings. You have arms. Your arms are smaller than your body. Your arms can't catch the air and move it under and over you. That's why you can't fly.

BUT a bird has no hands on its wings! Think of all the things you can do with your hands. You can catch a ball and write your name, hold a book, pick a flower, and button your coat. Wouldn't you rather have hands than wings? You can always fly in airplanes and in dreams.

Comprehension Questions (and Types)

1. What can birds do that you can't do? (Contrast)
   (a) fly
   (b) eat
   (c) play
   (d) climb
2. A bird can fly because (Literal)
   (a) the wind blows it
   (b) it has wings bigger than its body
   (c) it has feathers all over
   (d) it wanted to and learned how to fly
3. A bird has no (Literal)
   (a) wings
   (b) feathers
   (c) hands
   (d) feet

PASSAGE 2

Grade 5

Passage length: 150 words

From Reservoir to You. People can get a drink of water in lots of ways. They can scoop water up from a brook, a handful at a time; they can haul it up from the well, a bucketful at a time; they can pump it up, a splash at a time.

But in your wonderful house, all you need to do is turn a faucet. The water will keep coming, as long as you want it to. It won't stop until you shut it off. You don't have to scoop it up, or haul it up, or pump it up. What makes the water keep coming up from the cellar, through the pipes into your faucet?

All the water that's not in pipes goes down. Rain falls down, rivers and brooks flow down. But the water in your house flows up from the cellar, no matter how high up you live.

Comprehension Questions (and Types)
1. All a person has to do to get water in a modern house is   (Literal)
   (a) pump it up
   (b) scoop it up from a brook
   (c) turn on a faucet
   (d) haul it from a well
2. Water in rivers and brooks
   (a) flows down only   (Literal)
   (b) flows up only
   (c) flows up and down
   (d) flows only down in pipes

PASSAGE 3

Grade 7

Passage length: 169 words

No matter where or when you walk you are always completely surrounded by a great variety of noises. Strangely enough, most of the time you do not hear them unless you make a definite attempt to do so.

You have trained yourself from childhood not to listen to most of the customary sounds. But now, in order to make your scientific walking jaunts more exciting, you should try to analyze or track down some of these sounds. It can be fun to find the origin of a strange sound by making it into a game or treasure hunt. Call it a "sound-hunt."

If you stop for a few minutes and listen carefully to every sound, you will be surprised to find that in the "silence" around you there are many noises indeed. First and foremost today are the sounds of automobiles starting, stopping, popping, squealing, or hissing. Then there are airplane noises, bird calls, church bells chiming, and electric tools whining. You may even hear the rustling of leaves!

Comprehension Questions (and Types)
1. Wherever you walk you can always hear   (Inference)
   (a) trees

(b) autos
(c) noises
(d) people

2. The reason you do not hear many noises most of the time is because you   (Paraphrase)
   (a) learned not to hear them
   (b) are more interested in looking
   (c) do not have good hearing ability
   (d) do not listen to unusual sounds

3. The noises you usually do not listen to occur   (Paraphrase)
   (a) rarely
   (b) only at night
   (c) frequently
   (d) only when you are walking

PASSAGE 4

Grade 9

Passage length: 137 words

There are three most prominent kinds of "citizens" in the world within the atom. They are the protons, the neutrons, and the electrons. The number of these particles within the atom determines the weight and chemical character of the atom. Two of the particles, the protons and neutrons, are found only in the nucleus, the very tiny, very heavy central core of the atom. They both have about the same weight. To determine the relative weight of different atoms, which are much too light to be actually weighed, the protons and neutrons are considered one unit of atomic weight each. Thus the oxygen atom, with eight protons and eight neutrons in its nucleus, has an atomic weight of sixteen. And the uranium atom, with 92 protons and 146 neutrons, has an atomic weight of 238.

Comprehension Questions (and Types)

1. Electrons are   (Inference)
   (a) found in the nucleus of atoms
   (b) without any weight
   (c) determiners of atomic weight
   (d) not part of an atom's nucleus

2. In determining the weight of an atom, scientists   (Paraphrase)
   (a) weigh its particles
   (b) add together its protons and neutrons
   (c) do not attempt to do so
   (d) use oxygen atoms as a unit of atomic measurement

3. The particles outside the central core of the atom are   (Inference)
   (a) heavy protons
   (b) light electrons
   (c) light protons
   (d) heavy electrons

PASSAGE 5

Grade 11

Passage length: 157 words

Almost in the beginning was curiosity.

Curiosity, the overwhelming desire to know, is not characteristic of some forms of living organism, which, for that very reason, we can scarcely bring ourselves to consider alive.

A tree does not display curiosity about its environment in any way we can recognize; nor does a sponge or an oyster. The wind, the rain, the ocean currents bring them what is needful, and from it they take what they can. If the chance of events is such as to bring them fire, poison, predators, or parasites, they die as stoically and as undemonstratively as they lived.

Early in the scheme of life, however, independent motion was developed by some organisms. It meant a tremendous advance in their control of the environment. A moving organism no longer had to wait in stolid rigidity for food to come its way; it went out after it.

Comprehension Questions (and Types)

1. Curiosity is a characteristic of   (Generalization)
   (a) all things that live
   (b) the beginning of living things
   (c) all organisms with locomotion
   (d) all organisms that ingest food
2. Trees and other organisms such as sponges and oysters   (Interpretation)
   (a) control their own environment
   (b) like all living creatures, are curious, but only in unusual ways
   (c) search constantly for water and nourishment
   (d) are victims of noxious environmental elements

Key: Passage 1 (1–3) 1a, 2b, 3c. Passage 2 (5) 1c, 2a. Passage 3 (7) 1c, 2a, 3c. Passage 4 (9) 1d, 2b, 3b. Passage 5 (11) 1c, 2d. Passage 1 from Jeanne Bendick, *Why Can't I?* (New York: McGraw-Hill, 1969), pp. 12–17. Passage 2 from Herman Schneider and Nina Schneider, *Let's Look Inside Your House* (New York: William R. Scott, Inc., 1948), p. 5. Passage 3 from George Barr, *Young Scientist Takes a Walk* (New York: McGraw-Hill, 1959), pp. 22–23. Passage 4 from Melvin Berger, *Triumphs of Modern Science* (New York: McGraw-Hill, 1964), pp. 110–111. Passage 5 from Isaac Asimov, *The New Intelligent Man's Guide to Science* (New York: Basic Books, 1965), p. 1.

A variation on the PRI is the "Open Textbook Reading Assessment" (Shepherd, 1973). In this variation, the instructor writes comprehension questions at all three levels (literal, inferential, and generalized) on three sample passages taken from the textbook that is to be used in the class. Those students scoring below 70% get further, individual testing. First, they read the passages orally so that the teacher can determine whether their relatively low comprehension scores reflect word recognition difficulties. If not, they take a test on the technical vocabulary terms from the specific text passages to determine whether low vocabulary ability is the causal factor for their low comprehension scores.

CRITIQUE OF READING DIFFICULTY FORMULAS

The reading difficulty of a text can be determined apart from any particular reader, as the Fry and Flesch formulas do. In addition to the criteria these formulas use for arriving at readability levels, we may also consider other features of the text. For example, a text may be relatively difficult because it has a high density of ideas and a high degree of interrelatedness or coherence among the ideas. But, whether these characteristics of a text are difficult or not also depends upon the reader's prior knowledge, vocabulary ability, reasoning processes, purposes, and goals in reading the text. For example, if a text is densely packed with ideas but the reader's purpose is only to get the general idea of the text, the reader is likely to find the text easier than if his or her purpose was to comprehend the text fully. Hence, we recognize that the difficulty level of a text as computed by the Fry and Flesch formulas and as estimated by the SEER technique is only the *average* or *general* level of difficulty of a text.

To determine the difficulty of a text for a particular reader, for example, a student who was having difficulty in reading and learning from a text, we would examine factors not only within that text but also within the reader. In short, *reading difficulty for a particular individual depends upon an interaction between the text and the individual.*[2]

APPLICATIONS OF KNOWLEDGE ABOUT READABILITY

Making Reading Materials Easier or More Difficult

Although teachers do not usually have time to modify teaching materials or write them, they sometimes find themselves working on summer projects to prepare materials for teaching. Sometimes a school district may even provide time for preparation of materials. Occasionally teachers take a course or participate in a workshop where they write materials for teaching. Then they can use their knowledge of readability criteria to modify or construct reading materials so as to make them easier or more difficult. Two variables that can be manipulated for this purpose are sentence length and word difficulty.

---

[2] The cloze technique and the informal reading inventory come closest to a practical procedure for assessing this interaction between text and reader. Kintsch (1978) has devised a more complex formula for assessing this interaction, but his formula is more appropriate for researchers than for practitioners.

Longer sentences are usually more syntactically complex and may have one or more embedded sentences, or subordinate clauses. (See chapter 7, box 7.3 for sentence combining exercises.) Hence, combining sentences, especially where subordination results, is likely to increase the difficulty of the sentence, but not always (Pearson, 1974–1975). Although it may at first appear more difficult, the longer sentence in 2, below, is easier than the three shorter ones in 1 because the reader does not have to infer the inter-sentence relationships:

1. In the lab, Kimber mixed oxygen and hydrogen. He got water. (He also got an explosion.)
2. In the lab, Kimber mixed oxygen and hydrogen to get water (plus an explosion).

Researchers have not discovered much about intersentence syntax and intersentence difficulties (Bormuth et al., 1970) or about syntactic difficulties in different types of sentences and paragraphs. However, they have found out that students are more likely to comprehend written passages in which the syntax is the same as the syntax they use in their own oral language (Ruddell, 1965).

Word difficulty is another variable to use for manipulating the difficulty of reading material. You can substitute synonyms of higher frequency to make the material easier and, conversely, synonyms of lower frequency to make the material more difficult. Armed with a Thesaurus and Carroll, Davies and Richman's (1971) word frequency book, a teacher or writer can modify the difficulty level of textual materials. But the teacher has to exercise judgment because word frequency counts do not encompass all indices of word difficulty. They do not account for difficulty of word identification in context or for the difficulty of the contextual meaning of words. Students might understand *run* as a verb form but have more difficulty in comprehending it as a noun form, or as part of an idiom (a *run* on a bank or a *run* in a stocking).

Although materials that the teacher has simplified may enable more students to comprehend the content of the materials, such simplification represents downward adaptation of the curriculum. Another tack to take is to *stimulate* the development of students by teaching them to comprehend more complex material. For example, teach students to analyze complex sentences and make them simpler. Also teach them to comprehend the meaning of affixes (prefixes and suffixes) and roots so that they can analyze the meanings of complex words by breaking them into their constituent parts. Wolfe (1974) has reported considerable success in improving high school students' reading by having them learn affixes and roots and then using them in analyzing content area technical terms.

To help students develop towards greater maturity in reading and learning from text, follow a sequence like this: simplify material at first;

then teach students to comprehend more complex words and syntactical relationships within and between sentences (McCullough, 1971). Table 7.4 in chapter 7 contains a list of sentence and paragraph cues that will help. For this sequential instruction, use textbooks you have selected from school catalogs that are graded in difficulty. (See an example of such graded materials in box 8.3.)

Applications of Reading Difficulty Formulas

How well do students have to read? To answer this question, we would have to respond rhetorically by asking another question: how well do students have to read *for what purpose?* How well do students have to be able to do recreational reading at various levels of difficulty, or to do the practical reading required in everyday life (newspapers, job applications, receipts, recipes, directions, and so forth), or to comprehend job-required reading materials, or to learn from texts in various content areas? Researchers have used reading difficulty formulas to determine reading levels in each of these areas.

Recreational Reading Levels

Flesch (1949) applied his Reading Ease Formula to various types of *recreational reading material*. As shown in table 8.2, a fifth-grade level of reading ability is necessary for comprehending print in comic books. *Time* magazine has an eighth-to-ninth-grade level of reading difficulty and *Atlantic* magazine a tenth-to-twelfth-grade level of reading difficulty.

Functional Reading Requirements

The army coined the term *functional reading* in World War II. Then, the term meant ''the ability to understand written instructions for carrying out basic military tasks.'' A serviceman was functionally literate if he could read at least at the fifth-grade level (Sharon, 1973–1974).

Today, a higher reading level would probably be necessary for the attainment of functional literacy. (See table 8.4, ''Readability Levels of Texts in Vocational Courses,'' and the information under the heading ''What Are Job-Related Reading Requirements?'' on page 200.) However, neither university researchers nor public school officials have reached any agreement on a definition of functional literacy. Perhaps we can define functional literacy only in relation to a person's purpose, the requirements of the situation (reading government forms, textbooks, and so forth), and the school's expectation for successful accomplishment in reading and learning from text. For a cook in the army it would be one level; for a college student, another level; and so on. Hence, we could not

TABLE 8.3. Time per Day That Adults Spend Reading

	Percent of adults	Time spent on reading (in minutes)
1. Traveling and commuting	70	3
2. Recreation	54	7
3. Working around house	46	7
4. Meals	42	3
5. Shopping	33	7
6. Work	33	61
7. Club or church work	10	16
8. School	5	68
9. Theater, other events	4	7

state that functional literacy is at a fifth-grade, ninth-grade, or any specific grade level.[3]

One way to determine *functional reading level* is to determine what adults actually read and how much time they spend on reading. Sharon (1973–1974) conducted a cross-sectional survey of a national sample of 5,067 adults. The results indicated that the average adult reads for about 2 hours on a typical day, frequently while pursuing such daily activities as working, shopping, attending school or church or theater, traveling or commuting, as well as during free time.

The survey indicated that adults read the materials listed below.

1. Newspapers: 70 percent of adults read newspapers for an average of 35 minutes a day.
2. Mail: 53 percent read mail for five minutes a day, but 96 percent receive mail every day.
3. Magazines: 40 percent read magazines for 35 minutes a day.
4. Books: 33 percent read books about 47 minutes a day.

When do adults do their reading? The answer is in table 8.3. According to the survey, the higher an individual's socioeconomic status, the more reading he or she did. But 5 percent of all adults interviewed were unable to read (defined as unable to read newspaper headlines) including 2.3 percent who were visually handicapped, 1.6 percent who were foreign language readers, and 1.1 percent who were illiterates (those adults who never learned to read in any language and did not have visual difficulties).

[3] See chapter 15 for a functional reading test that twelfth-grade students have to pass in order to receive a diploma upon graduation from Los Angeles high schools.

The members of this nonreading group were also members of an extremely low socioeconomic group. They had to depend on others to read to them.

How Well Do Adults Comprehend Functional Reading Tasks?

The National Reading Council, appointed by President Nixon, commissioned Louis Harris and Associates (1970) to measure the literacy rate in the nation, using a representative sample of 1,685 persons, ages 16 and up. The study measured the "survival" literacy rate for functional, or practical, reading skills. These reading skills consist of the ability to read such application forms as required for obtaining a Social Security number, a personal bank loan, public assistance, medicaid, and a driver's license. Those who answered three questions incorrectly (30 percent of the items on the forms) were considered illiterate. The percentage ranged from 3 percent (public assistance form) to 34 percent (medicaid form). On the average, one out of eight adults (or, at that time, 18.5 million Americans) would have had difficulty in obtaining government assistance because they could not read well enough to fill out the application forms.

The lowest age group in the Harris survey (age 16–24) had the lowest illiteracy rate (range 1 to 9 percent). The lowest illiteracy rate in the nation was found in the West and the highest was in the South.

The remedy for inability to read application forms and other functional reading tasks is twofold: (1) simplify the language used in the forms, use larger print accompanied by pictured directions, and provide cassette tapes for auditory explanations; (2) seek to improve literacy, starting with high school students still in the functionally illiterate category, and reducing the relatively low rate of this group even further; then go on to older illiterates.

What Are the Reading Demands of Texts in Vocational Courses?

Using a modified Dale-Chall readability formula, Sticht and McFann (1975) found that the texts used in secondary school and community college vocational programs had the readability levels shown in table 8.4. The two researchers then gave a general reading test to students enrolled in these courses. They found that the average reading ability of students was *below* the average difficulty of the texts they used — about 0.6 of a year below in food services, 1.0 years below in auto mechanics, 1.7 years below in building trades, 3.5 years below in welding, and 4.0 years below in radio and T.V. repair! The instructors of these courses corroborated the findings. They reported that over half the students in their courses could not comprehend their texts without the instructor's help.

TABLE 8.4. Readability Levels of Texts
in Vocational Courses

Course	Readability Grade Level of Text
Radio and TV Repair	14.0
Welding	12.0
Appliance Repair	12.0
Medical Office	11.2
Clothing Services	10.5
Building Trades	10.2
Auto Mechanics	10.0
Food Services	9.2

What Are Job-Related Reading Requirements?

Sticht and McFann (1975) used a specially constructed set of tasks based on *actual* reading done in various army occupations. As a criterion they used the percent in comprehension scored by enlisted men with various levels of reading ability. Cooks, mechanics, and supply clerks whose general reading level was about 6.5 scored only 50 percent in comprehension, and students reading at grade level 12.8 got 90 percent. With a 70 percent comprehension score as the criterion, the reading level required to be a successful cook would be the seventh-grade level, for mechanics the ninth-grade level, and for supply clerks the tenth-grade level.

What Are the Reading Demands of Texts in Academic Courses?

High school texts vary considerably in difficulty level even in the same content areas. Belden and Lee (1961) found that four of five biology texts had average readability levels higher than the average reading levels of students in six Oklahoma high schools; only one text had a readability level suitable for 50 percent of the students who used it.

Mallinson, Sturm, and Mallinson (1952), using the Flesch formula, found that 11 of 16 high school physics texts had ninth-grade readability levels; these texts were suitable for all students enrolled in physics classes. Three texts scored between ninth- and tenth-grade reading levels; they were appropriate only for average and better physics students. But, two texts were too difficult even for superior students!

These studies indicate that the teacher of content area classes should be aware that there is a range of texts from which to choose for content

~~area instruction.~~ If limited to one text, the teacher can probably select a text that is appropriate for at least half the class. But if more than one text is available, knowledge of the readability levels of texts and reading abilities of students would enable the teacher to select texts appropriate to the entire class.

To give the reader a concrete idea of the difficulty level of content area reading materials, we selected some texts used in some high schools in southern California. We took samples from them and computed their Flesch Reading Ease scores. See the results in box 8.5.

BOX 8.5. Flesch Reading Ease Scores
for Sample High School Textbooks

CHEMISTRY

One of the activities of science is the search for regularity. Regularities that directly correlate experimental results are generally called rules or laws. A more abstract regularity, expressing a hidden likeness, is generally called a model, theory, or principle. Thus, the behavior of oxygen gas summarized in the equation $P \times V = a \; constant$ is called a law. The explanation of this same regular gas behavior in terms of the motion of particles is called a theory. It is a greater abstraction to connect the PV product with the mathematical equations that describe rebounding billiard balls. Nevertheless, rules, laws, models, theories, and principles all have a common air — they all systematize our experimental knowledge. They all state regularities among known facts.
Words in sample = 118
Average sentence length = 15
Syllables per 100 words = 198
Reading Ease score = 26
Evaluation = very difficult: college level material

PHYSICS

Radiation damage can be prevented. Radioactive isotopes, x-ray machines, and nuclear reactors must be shielded so that dangerous radiation does not reach the people who operate them. Alpha and beta rays can be stopped by thin shields, but x-rays, gamma rays, and neutrons are more penetrating. Neutrons from a reactor are controlled by reflecting them back into the reactor, often by a layer of graphite. The ability of a shield to stop x-rays and gamma rays depends on its thickness and its density. The more mass there is between a person and a reactor, the better he is protected.
Words in sample = 98
Average sentence length = 16
Syllables per 100 words = 162
Reading Ease score = 56
Evaluation = fairly difficult: high school grades 10–12.

HISTORY

American relations with the nations of the Western Hemisphere have undergone a noticeable change in recent decades. A spirit of cooperation and partnership has gradually supplanted an attitude of paternalism. Whereas in the past this nation's sister republics in Latin America both envied and feared American political power and economic wealth, they no longer seem so frustrated by the "Colossus of the North" in their search for national identity and importance.

Past American policy regarding hemispheric problems had caused conflict and resentment. Much of this can perhaps be attributed to the fact that Americans have attempted to understand very different cultures on the basis of American values and beliefs.

Words in sample = 108
Average sentence length = 20
Syllables per 100 words = 190
Reading Ease score = 27
Evaluation = very difficult: college-level material

ALGEBRA

The set of all points associated with ordered pairs of numbers in the solution set of an open sentence in two variables is called the graph of the solution set, or simply, the graph of the open sentence. The graph of every equation equivalent to one of the form $Ax + By = C$, where A, B, and C are constants such that not both A and B equal 0, is a straight line. Notice that in any linear equation, $Ax + By = C$, each term is either a constant or a monomial of degree 1. Hence, $2x + 3y = 27$ is a linear equation; but $y = x^2$ and $xy = 5$ are not, and their graphs are not straight lines.

Words in sample = 124
Average sentence length = 31
Syllables per 100 words = 150
Reading Ease score = 47
Evaluation = fairly difficult: material for high school grades 10–12

ENGLISH

The novel is a comparatively new form of writing in the English language. About three hundred years old, it came into being after a major political and social revolution that took place in England in the seventeenth century. During that revolution the English monarchy in the person of King Charles I was overthrown by the followers of Oliver Cromwell, who sought a more democratic form of government than that offered by the crown. As a result of this revolution, a new social class — the middle class of merchants, bankers, and shopkeepers — started its rise to power, firmly establishing itself by the eighteenth century.

Words in sample = 102
Average sentence length = 25
Syllables per 100 words = 166
Reading Ease score = 42
Evaluation = Fairly difficult: material for high school grades 10–12

Chemistry passage from George E. Pimentel, ed., *Chemistry: An Experimental Science* (San Francisco: W. H. Freeman, 1963), p. 17. Physics passage from Robert Stallberg and Faith Fitch

Hall, *Physics: Fundamentals and Frontiers* (Boston: Houghton Mifflin, 1965), p. 140. History passage from Robert F. Madgic, et al., *The American Experience* (Menlo Park, Calif.: Addison-Wesley, 1971), p. 335. Algebra passage from Mary P. Dolciani, Simon L. Berman, and William Wooton, *Modern Algebra and Trigonometry: Structure and Method, Book Two* (Boston: Houghton Mifflin, 1965), p. 82. English passage from V. S. Pritchett, "The Novel," in *Adventures in Appreciation* (New York: Harcourt, Brace and World, 1968), p. 585.

These texts ranged from fairly difficult (requiring some high school grades completed) to difficult (high school and some college work completed) to very difficult (college completed). Only the fairly difficult levels would be appropriate for even advanced high school students!

Of course, the passages in these texts do not represent the range of difficulty within each text. More difficult and easier passages could be found in each text. That is why an average based on at least three samples from three different parts of a text is necessary in establishing the reading level of the text.

Readability formulas have other limitations. They do not take into account the conceptual level nor the information density of the material. The algebra sample is equal in difficulty to the English sample, but the algebra vocabulary appears to be much more difficult than the English vocabulary. Hence, in addition to using a formula for assessing readability, teachers should analyze the content of a text to determine its semantic difficulty, information density, conceptual level, and style of writing. Unfortunately, scales for assessing semantic difficulty, or for conceptual levels, or for density of concepts or information, or for relating writing styles to difficulty of reading are not available. Consequently, teachers can make only subjective appraisals of these aspects of reading difficulty.

How Well Do College Students Have to Read?

At the college level (as well as at any other level) the question has to be: how well should a student have to read what kind of material and for what degree of comprehension? As Sticht and McFann (1975) pointed out, above, readers can have varying degrees of comprehension. Furthermore, required reading materials in college (as in other levels of education) vary in readability level; and the average and range of reading ability of college students also vary. The University of California, which has nine campuses (Berkeley, UCLA, Riverside, and so forth), by law can accept only the top 12.5 percent of high school graduates who have taken a particular program of academic courses. Hence, freshman classes consist of students from the upper 12.5 percent of their high school classes.

To compete effectively in this freshman environment, a student should have reading comprehension abilities at least equal to those of the top 12.5 percent of high school seniors. However, the California State University and College System (San Francisco, San Diego, Fullerton, Humboldt, San Bernardino) which is a separate system from the University of California, can accept the top one-third of high school graduates. Students with reading abilities at least within the range of the 67th to the 99th percentile of high school seniors are likely to be able to compete with varying degrees of success in the State University and College System. The community colleges in California can accept any high school graduate. Consequently, a wider range of reading abilities occurs among the junior college population. Similar variation exists among institutions of higher education throughout the country.

Since teachers tend to normalize instruction, that is, teach towards the average student, the reading demands and criteria for successful academic accomplishment are likely to reflect the capacities and skills of the average student. In short, to decide what level of reading achievement a student needs to be successful at the college level, teachers have to know (1) a student's capacities (particularly the skills of reading and learning from text) and aspirations for achievement as well as (2) the demands of the institution and the average level of ability of students in the institution.

Speed of reading, a factor that is important at any level, becomes increasingly significant as students progress through the grades and becomes crucial at the college level because of the heavy load of reading.

To determine why speed of reading is crucial at the college level, let's look at the reading requirements at college and compute the time required to do the assigned reading and complete the texts. D. W. Gilbert (1955) estimates that a college student at the University of California has 16,000 pages of reference reading to do each semester. The average college freshman reads relatively easy (sixth-grade level) material at a rate of 250 words per minute. Van Wagenen (1953) determined this speed in his rate of comprehension test. (See box 8.6 for speed of reading data.)

BOX 8.6. Description and Norms for
Rate of Comprehension

TYPICAL RATE OF COMPREHENSION PARAGRAPH

Directions: Cross out the word that does not fit in with the meaning of the rest of the paragraph.

Jane needed a spool of silk thread to finish her new dress. But when she went to the store for her mother she forgot to get the buttons she needed.

Reading Ease Score: fairly easy, sixth-grade level

Answer: You should have crossed out the word "buttons."

The scale has 56 paragraphs similar in difficulty to the sample paragraph. In grades 4 to 9, only 5 minutes, and in grades 10–12, only 4 minutes are allowed for working on the scale. In this type of reading task and with these time limitations, the following norms or average scores are attained:

Words per minute	Grade Level	Age Level
237	13.0	18-2
220	12.0	17-2
207	11.0	16-2
188	10.0	15-2
170	9.0	14-2
157	8.0	13-2
134	7.0	12-2
117	6.0	11-2
93	5.0	10-2
63	4.0	9-2
50	3.0	8-2

Quoted passage is from *Rate of Comprehension Scale, Form A.* Minneapolis, Minn.: M. J. Van Wagenen, 1953.

We recognize that an individual has different rates of reading that vary with his or her purpose and the demands of the material (Holmes and Singer, 1966); by thinking of 250 words per minute as a kind of average rate of reading, estimating 500 words per page, and assuming a forty-hour week of reading, we can compute the number of weeks required to read through 16,000 pages as follows:

$$\frac{16,000 \text{ pages} \times 500 \text{ words per page}}{250 \text{ words per minute}}$$

Computation gives 32,000 minutes or 533 hours—about 13.5 forty-hour weeks![4] Since a semester is usually 18 weeks long, the student who reads at this average rate has to spend most of the semester reading assigned

---

[4] When reading and learning from more difficult texts, particularly when the purpose is to prepare for an examination, the rate is, of course, likely to be much slower. Consequently, 250 words per minute is probably an overestimate of a high school or college student's reading rate for typical textbook material. Therefore, at a lower speed of reading, a student will take longer than the 13.5 weeks to read 16,000 pages of material.

material in order to survive academically. Hence, students have to learn to be extremely efficient in reading and to develop effective strategies for reading and learning from text.

Instead of waiting until students reach high school or college, we need to start at earlier levels to teach them efficient and effective strategies they can acquire cumulatively as they progress through school. In chapters 15 and 16 we explain roles content area teachers and reading specialists can play in working towards the goal of improving the ability of all students to read and learn from texts efficiently and effectively.

Prior to this chapter, we provided knowledge, strategies, techniques, and tools for teaching students with a wide range of individual differences to read and learn from a *single* text. We are now ready to explain ways of handling individual differences through strategies for reading and learning from multiple texts.

SUMMARY

We can determine readability of written materials and reading levels of students in several ways. Two types of techniques for arriving at the readability or reading difficulty-level of materials are (1) computational procedures: the Flesch Reading Ease Formula and the Fry Readability Graph; and (2) a noncomputational, estimation procedure: the SEER technique. We can use standardized tests to measure the reading levels of students. (For a description of standardized tests, see chapter 3.) Or we can compute student reading levels on samples of materials that are to be read in class by using the cloze technique and the personal reading inventory (PRI) or the informal reading inventory (IRI). Because the cloze technique and the inventory assess students on samples of actual classroom materials, these procedures have content and curricular validity; they also assess more closely the difficulty level of the interaction between the text and the reader.

Comparison of reading levels of students with readability of materials demonstrates the usefulness of these procedures in revealing the reading demands that various types of written material (recreational and functional materials, vocational texts, job-related materials, and academic texts) place upon the reader.

Recreational reading of magazines demands reading levels varying from a fifth-grade level for comic books to advanced high school level for the *Atlantic* magazine. The average American adult reads newspapers, magazines, mail, and books for a total of about two hours per day, doing most reading at work or at school. But five percent of the population cannot read at all in English. However, only 1.1 percent of American adults are illiterate, that is, they cannot read in any language. These adults speak English, and they are not visually handicapped. Yet, 12.5 percent of the adults in this nation have difficulty in reading and filling out various application forms.

Vocational texts can vary in difficulty from a ninth-grade level for food services to the fourteenth-grade level for radio and television repair manuals. Students in these vocational courses have reading abilities that, on the average, are below the readability levels of the texts: from 0.6 of a year in food services to 4.0 years in radio and television repair courses. To read materials needed on the job with a 70 percent level of comprehension, an army cook would have to read at a seventh-grade level, mechanics at a ninth-grade level, and supply clerks at a tenth-grade level.

Academic texts also vary in difficulty. Although high school texts in any academic subject can be below or at the average level of reading ability of the students who use them, most texts are appropriate only for advanced high school students or for college students. The implication is that teachers can adopt single texts appropriate to the average reading ability of their students or they can select multiple texts to suit the entire range of reading abilities in their classes.

College students have to be effective *and* efficient readers because of the difficulty of their texts and the abundance of reading required each semester. Many beginning college students read at least at the thirteenth-grade level and with a speed of 250 words per minute when reading fairly easy (sixth-grade level) material. However, the average reading ability of college students varies from one college or university to another as a function of student selection and institutional admission policies. Since college and university professors, as well as classroom teachers, tend to normalize instructional demands, that is, teach towards the average student, and use texts appropriate to this level, competition for a student with a particular level of reading ability can be less in one institution and greater in another. Of course, successful achievement is also dependent on a student's level of aspiration. For example, a B average may mean success to one student and failure to another, even though both may have the same reading ability.

Although procedures for determining student reading levels and text readability levels have their limitations, they are nevertheless useful for estimating difficulty of reading tasks, for selecting material appropriate to the range of a class's reading abilities, and for understanding problems in teaching and reading and learning from text. We can conclude from information on these problems that ability to read and learn from texts is not only dependent upon a student's reading level and motivation but also upon the difficulty of a text and the instructional demands that are made by the teacher.

ACTIVITIES

1. Select a passage from this text or from a content area textbook. Determine its readability using the Flesch, Fry, and SEER techniques. Compare the results. How do you account for differences? Compare your explanation with that of another student.
2. Administer a cloze test on a passage from a content area textbook to (a) one or more of your colleagues in your content area and (b) one or more colleagues out of your content area. Compare the results and explain differences, if any.

9 | Multiple-Text Strategies

CHAPTER OVERVIEW

In the last four chapters, you have learned (1) how to teach students to learn from a single text, (2) how to teach discussion and writing, and (3) how to determine the readability of textbooks. This information can now be applied to multiple-text strategies as students start to become more independent readers. Three multiple-text strategies will be discussed in this chapter. Since these strategies frequently require group work, the chapter will also cover various ways in which groups can report to the rest of the class.

TECHNICAL VOCABULARY

inquiry
concept technique
project approach
symposium

panel discussion
debate
colloquy

TEACHING FROM
MORE THAN ONE TEXT

In Chapter 4, you read about strategies to use when teaching a single textbook to an entire class. These strategies are crucial to teaching all students to learn from text, without holding some students back and stigmatizing other students as slow. The single-text strategies accomplish this goal because they take a text, which has a particular level of reading difficulty, and make it fit better the wide range of ability to read and learn from text that is present in a class. In other words, single text strategies enable more students to read and learn at their own levels from the class's single textbook.

Moreover, single text strategies develop some skills that are required for use with multiple-text strategies. The Directed Reading Activity (DRA) with emphasis on active comprehension and SQ3R strategies teaches students to formulate their own questions. The reading and learning-from-text guides give students opportunities to learn to conduct and participate in group discussion and to report to the class. Discussion and writing are necessary skills for multiple-text strategies. We devoted separate chapters to each of these skills so that teachers can demonstrate and teach them to their students. On the assumption that teachers have done so while using the single-text strategies, we are now ready to go on to multiple-text strategies. The first is the inquiry method. To introduce this technique, we shall start with a scenario that dramatizes the need for inquiry.

INQUIRY

Scenario

One day after school, Ms. Jones was chatting with one of her students, Iris Carrington. Iris was angry because she felt she'd been ''ripped off'' by a cosmetics company that sold her a preparation ''guaranteed to free the buyer of any complexion problems.'' Iris had sent the company a money order for ten dollars and had received back a small bottle of what looked and smelled like ocean water. When she applied it to her face, her skin became increasingly irritated. In consoling her, Ms. Jones pointed out that she was an innocent victim of propaganda. Iris stared at her blankly as if to ask, ''What's *propaganda?*''

Ms. Jones reflected on the hundreds of teenagers who are victims of false and misleading advertising, on the thousands of adults who are prey to political speeches, inflammatory editorials, and malicious gossip. Ms. Jones thought of how many people react to things they read and hear emotionally rather than analytically: why did Iris think that a cosmetics company, unknown to her and hundreds of miles away, could solve her complexion problems?

It was then that Ms. Jones decided to teach her students *inquiry* — the technique of solving problems by careful examination, interpretation, and evaluation of evidence. The students, having been instructed in single-text strategies, were developing good critical reading habits. It might, she felt, be a good opportunity to see if they could apply what they had learned to multiple-text situations.

Types of Inquiry

Ms. Jones was aware that there are different types of inquiry, so she tried to decide which one would be the best for the purposes of students in her classroom. Three types of inquiry she studied about were (1) open inquiry, (2) guided inquiry, and (3) text-based inquiry.

OPEN INQUIRY. In open inquiry, a teacher poses a problem and the students have to solve it, using any means they have. One time, Mr. Inglish had given his class a series of ethnic jokes that had been generated by one culture about another culture. The jokes had been edited to eliminate specific references that might cue the students to the true identity of either culture; what remained was humor. The problem was to determine the characteristics of (1) the culture that produced the creator of the jokes and (2) the culture that the jokes were about. In solving the problem, the students used material in the jokes, their own experience, other examples of ethnic humor, and materials they had read inside and outside of class. Mr. Inglish's objective was to see if the students could apply critical reading skills to solve a problem. Mr. Inglish consulted with students upon request but didn't direct them through a series of problem-solving steps.

GUIDED INQUIRY. In guided inquiry, a teacher poses a problem and the students have to solve it using a specified sequence of steps. These steps usually include (1) identifying and gathering data, (2) interpreting data, (3) analyzing data, (4) judging data, (5) hypothesizing from data, and (6) testing hypotheses. Examples of this type of inquiry will be discussed in chapters 11 and 12.

TEXT-BASED INQUIRY. In light of what had happened to Iris, Ms. Jones felt that text-based inquiry might be valuable for her students. Text-based inquiry is a process of determining whether a so-called factual statement in a text is true. Ryan and Wheeler (1974) point out that information presented as fact in a textbook, or for that matter in any written material, may not be true. Their example is taken from a social science text which stated that Admiral Byrd was the first person to fly over the North Pole. They raised this question: "How do we know this statement is true?" Their next question was: "How can we find out whether it's true?"

If the class is not familiar with inquiry procedures, the teacher must first instruct the students in means for obtaining evidence, including newspaper stories and especially reports by observers at the events the news reports describe. The class Ryan and Wheeler worked with was led by the *Readers' Guide to Periodical Literature*[1] away from a single text toward other texts, including newspaper reports written at the time of Byrd's flight by reporters located at Byrd's base camp. The class discovered one newspaper report that charged Admiral Byrd merely faked a flight over the Pole. The class got additional information from other sources. The students then had to weigh the evidence pro and con. They selected a jury to hear the evidence presented by students who were for as well as those who were against Byrd. The jury concluded that the evidence presented by the former students supported the claim that Admiral Byrd was the first person to fly over the North Pole.

Information in any text may be disputed. In challenging information in a text, students can learn to be critical, to search for evidence, and to arrive at their own conclusions. In doing so, they can learn to ask two basic questions of any content area: (1) What does the author mean? and (2) How does the author know?

In answering these questions, students will engage in library activities similar to those suggested for use in the project approach discussed later in this chapter. If the library has a variety of references at different levels of difficulty, then students can select materials appropriate to their levels and contribute whatever information they have located. If students are working in groups or teams, they can help each other locate information and evaluate it.

The teacher's task is to help students formulate standards or determine criteria for evaluating any controversial material they might read. Ms. Jones did just that.

Iris Carrington had, in effect, believed the statement "guaranteed to free the buyer of any complexion problems" to be a fact when it obviously wasn't. Ms. Jones collected a series of statements from advertising and political campaigns and built a lesson around teaching the students to detect the difference between fact and opinion. Her lesson sheet appears in box 9.1.

[1] *Readers' Guide to Periodical Literature.* New York: H. W. Wilson Company, 1900– .

BOX 9.1. Ms. Jones's Lesson Sheet for Teaching
Fact vs. Opinion

Activity A. Below are seven statements. If the statement is a fact, put a *check mark* in the box provided. If the statement is not a fact, put a *zero* in the box.

☐ 1. All Democrats believe in heavy taxation.
☐ 2. Presweetened cereals are most harmful to your digestive system.
☐ 3. Most human hands contain five fingers.
☐ 4. Ninety-nine percent of people dying of cancer each year have eaten a pickle at least once in their lifetime.
☐ 5. Labor unions keep the economy rolling.
☐ 6. Compact cars are the wave of the future.
☐ 7. Bankers are stingy people.

Comment: Only one item in activity A is a *fact,* that is, a statement that you can verify by observation. The rest of the items may read like facts but actually are not; they are statements that try to persuade you to think a certain way. These statements are called *opinions*. In other words, your past experience verifies that most human hands have five fingers, but you would have a hard time verifying that all Democrats believe in heavy taxation. Yet many people would accept both statements as being equally true. To prove that Democrats believe in heavy taxation you would have to survey a representative sample of the Democrats in the United States. Do you think they would all believe the same way?

Activity B. Explain what you would have to do to prove statements 2, 4, 5, 6, and 7 in activity A are true.

Comment: As you probably discovered in activity B, to prove whether a statement is fact or opinion requires a lot of effort. The library might help you determine fact from opinion since it has many sources of information.

Activity C. Read each of the following statements. What sources of information in the library would help you determine whether these are statements of *fact* or *opinion?*
1. Babe Ruth was the greatest hitter in baseball history.
2. Cigarette smoke causes lung cancer.
3. Classical music is greater than pop rock.
4. Big cities breed crime.
5. Senior citizens are healthier today than they were twenty years ago, but less happy.

Comment: As you continue to use the library you will probably add more sources to your list.

After the students had completed Activity C, Ms. Jones gave them a problem that needed to be solved by checking sources of information in the library. The problem is stated in box 9.2.

BOX 9.2. Inquiry Problem for Ms. Jones's Students to Solve at the Library

Instructions: Read the following three news releases concerning the Operator's Union Strike at the Rapid Transit Company. When you are through, answer the questions at the end of the lesson by using library sources.

NEWS RELEASES

News Report (Factual)

   The strike between the Operator's Union and the Rapid Transit Company is now entering its 30th day. The operators are demanding a 25-cent-per-hour wage increase and the company has countered with an offer of a 10-cent-an-hour increase. No settlement is in progress.

The Same Report Slanted Toward the Operators (Opinion)

   The good citizen interested in fair play is watching the dispute between the Operator's Union and the Rapid Transit Company with a mixture of admiration and alarm. He knows the average operator is trying to maintain a decent home for his wife and children, and that living costs have skyrocketed to the highest point in history. Even when the operator is working (to make management richer) he can scarcely make ends meet. While the Company officials sit out the strike complacently in plush offices and smoke 50-cent cigars to pass the time, the carman is worrying about shoes to carry his children back to school and milk for their lunch pails. The solid citizen takes off his hat to the patient courage of the operator, but he, too, is wondering what will happen to the innocent youngsters.

The Same Report Slanted Toward the Company (Opinion)

   In some circles, the sympathy in any strike goes to the worker. But what are the facts in the current hold-up by the Operator's Union for wage increases? Despite miracles of economy in operation, rising costs have forced R. T. Co. to operate at a loss for the past two years. In the interest of public service, no dividends have been declared and top management agreed to sharp cuts in personal salaries. Meantime the workers have asked and received three separate wage boosts, so that they are now better paid than the police and the teachers. But still they can't live on their wages. Caviar and Cadillacs come high this year.

   Fortunately the Company does not need to be concerned about the public reaction. The people are too smart to be duped by gangster tactics. With the facts on the table it becomes entirely clear that the operators are not striking for groceries but for glory. Labor has its eye on the national scene.

QUESTIONS FOR LIBRARY INQUIRY

1. The "news report" came from the November 15, 1977 issue of the *Monroe Herald*. Check similar news reports in the *Monroe Eagle* and the *Monroe Times*. Do the three newspapers agree on (a) the duration of the strike, (b) the amount of the wage increase and (c) the amount of the counter offer? If they don't agree, how would you determine what the truth is?

2. What opinions expressed in the report favoring the operators would the operators accept as fact? Select one opinion and try to check it against library resources to see if it is true, e.g.: "Even when the operator is working (to make management richer) he can scarcely make ends meet."

3. What opinions expressed in the company report would management accept as fact? Select one opinion and try to check it against library resources to see if it is true.

4. Below are descriptions of seven propaganda techniques. See how these techniques are used in the two slanted reports.

   a. *Card stacking.* In this technique, facts are provided, but not *all* the facts, only those favorable to one side of the argument. Beware when the trial lawyer says, "Ladies and gentlemen of the jury, I shall now summarize the facts of this case. Since you are intelligent people, I know you will use these facts to arrive at correct conclusions." The lawyer then provides only facts favorable to one side of the case, omitting those that are unfavorable. The lawyer has also used flattery to get the audience to arrive at conclusions favorable to his or her side of the case.

   b. *Authority.* An expert may testify. The idea is to have the expert's testimony be accepted because of his or her reputation as an expert. The assumption is that experts really know, but that assumption is not always true. The expert may have a conflict of interest and therefore be biased, or the expert may not be as expert as someone else who comes to a different conclusion. Hence, experts are cross-examined carefully by trial lawyers, or other experts are brought in to dispute their testimony. Internal consistency in presentation of a viewpoint and ability to resolve discrepancies are two criteria for determining which person is more objective and more expert.

   c. *Transfer.* A well-known, popular, or admired person is associated with something or someone. The characteristics of the admired figure are carried over to the new object or person. For example, advertisers use sports figures in their commercials so that the viewing public can associate the admired sports figures with shaving lotion or shaving cream. The idea is that if you use it, you will also be admired.

   d. *Name calling.* Name calling may be used to discredit someone or something. The process may be blatant or subtle. For example, a union may be striking for higher wages. Management then reports how much *some* workers are being paid per hour, what kind of cars they drive, what kind of homes they own (card stacking). The implication is that the workers are well paid, but they are still not satisfied. They want more, more than their share. The implication is that workers are hogs.

   The workers' propaganda retaliates by describing the "cigar-smoking, Cadillac-driving, coupon-clipping officers of the company who are getting rich off workers' labor." They are really Simon Legrees, whipping the poor workers and benefitting from the workers' hard labor.

e. *Bandwagon.* The idea of this technique is that the trend of events is going in a particular direction, and if you want to be on the side of a winner, you should jump aboard the wagon. At one time bandwagons were actually used in political campaigns. People who sided with particular candidates jumped upon their bandwagons.

If opinion polls are favorable to them, political candidates will cite the results. If the polls are not favorable, they'll try to ignore or discredit them, sometimes using name calling and implying that the pollsters are dishonest.

Stock market reports that stocks are going up create a bandwagon effect. The propaganda is that if you want to make money, you should buy stocks now and make money as you see the price of the stock go up. Of course, if stock prices go down, it is rationalized or explained away as "only an adjustment," or "profit-taking," or some *temporary* downward turn. The desired effect of propaganda from the viewpoint of the companies involved is that you should not get on the downward bandwagon and sell. Instead, you should, "Wait, the stocks will go up again."

f. *American values.* Motherhood, family, God, and patriotism are some things Americans value highly. These values are being used when political candidates introduce their mothers, display their wives and children, hire bands to play patriotic music, and let everybody know they attend church regularly. For example, reports are regularly issued about the president's churchgoing activities, whether he is in the White House, on vacation, or on a ship out at sea.

g. *Glittering generalities.* Sweeping phrases that sound good, but do not specify what is meant, may appeal to you. For example, the president said, "What this country needs is solid progress." But he did not specify what solid progress is nor what he would do to bring it about.

5. Apply these propaganda techniques to the speeches of two candidates for public office who are debating an issue.

News releases are from Doris Wilcox Gilbert, *Power and Speed in Reading.* Englewood Cliffs, N.J.: Prentice-Hall, Inc., 1956, p. 150. Reprinted by permission of D. W. Gilbert and Prentice-Hall, Inc.

CONCEPT TECHNIQUE

After using inquiry, students can function more independently in the concept technique. The *concept technique* consists of using a group of materials all related to one particular concept. By definition, a *concept* is an "idea of something formed by mentally combining all its characteristics and particulars" (Stein, 1973).

In literature, the idea might be *courage;* in social studies, *revolution;* in science, *power,* and in mathematics, *calculators.* Another unique feature of the technique is a three-stage process that allows students to have greater self-selection, independence, and responsibility. The first stage consists of teacher-conducted lessons that explain the various facets of the idea. The second stage allows those students interested in a particular facet to form a group for further investigation of it. The third stage permits individual self-selection of a facet and materials to pursue an independent investigation.

Teachers could choose their own concepts and select materials to develop them by using the *Children's Catalog* (Shor and Fidel, 1972), the *Junior High School Catalog* (Fidel and Bogart, 1970), and the *Standard Catalog for High School Libraries* (Fidel and Berger, 1972). Glossed examples from these catalogs are shown in box 9.3. Teachers could select books on a particular concept from these three catalogs. The annotation for each book in the catalogs would help in the selection. If time does not permit the construction of a conceptual organization of books, but money is available for buying materials, a commercially produced series that could fit into a school's literature curriculum are the Scholastic Literature Units (Scholastic Units, 1970).

BOX 9.3. Glossed Directions for Reading Three Catalogs

CHILDREN'S CATALOG

920.03 Biography — Dictionaries, encyclopedias → Dewey Decimal subject designation

Author ← **Ward, Martha E.**
Authors of books for young people. 2d ed. by Martha E. Ward and Dorothy A. Marquardt. Scarecrow 1971 579 p $15 920.03 → Bibliographic information on Ward's book

Subject heading ←
1 Authors — Encyclopedias
2 Children's literature — History and criticism
ISBN 0-8108-0404-2 → International identification number

Summary of book's contents, including source of review
Containing 2161 brief biographies, this volume incorporates all those included in the first edition (1964) and the 1967 supplement, both entered in the main catalog, ''as well as new material with revisions and updating. . . . All recipients of the Caldecott and Newbery medals through 1970 are included. . . . The new edition also identifies publisher and year of publication for

each title listed, and provides cross references for pseudonyms.'' Publisher's note

JUNIOR HIGH SCHOOL CATALOG

(970.1 American Indians) ——————→ Dewey Decimal subject designation

Author ←——————— **Jones, Jayne Clark**

The American Indian in America. Lerner Publications 1973 2v illus maps (The In America ser) lib. bdg. ea $3.95   970.1 } Bibliographic information on Jones's book

Subject heading ← { 1 Indians of North America — History

Summary of book's contents { Contents: v 1 Prehistory to the end of the 18th century (ISBN 0-8225-0224- →International 0); v 2 Early 18th century to the present   identification (ISBN 0-8225-0227-5) ——————→number

The author describes the origin and culture of the American Indian, the impact of white civilization on Indian societies, life on the reservations, the reawakening of Indian pride in recent times, and the contributions made by American Indians in various fields

''Ms. Jones has attempted to write a corrective to the numerous tales of daring-do depicting heroic cavalry charges and sly savage natives that dominate juvenile histories of the American Indians. . . . Rather than a history, the two volumes are more a bill of particulars in an indictment against white treatment of the American Indian.'' Science Bks } Direct quotation from book review, with source.

STANDARD CATALOG FOR HIGH SCHOOL LIBRARIES

(812 American drama) ——————→ Dewey Decimal subject designation

Author ←——————— **Baldwin, James**

One day, when I was lost; a scenario based on Alex Haley's ''The autobiography of Malcom X.'' Dial Press 1973 (c1972) 280p illus $7.50   812 } Bibliographic information

Subject heading ←————1 Malcolm X — Drama

Background on ←————First published 1972 in England
book   "This film script outlines the facts ⎤ Direct quotations
                      of Malcolm's life. The first part, using ⎟ from book
                      flashbacks, describes his early life. Part ⎟ reviews, with
                      two, beginning with his conversion to ⎟ sources
                      Islam traces his career and closes with ⎟
                      his assassination in 1956." Book Rev ⎟
                      Digest ⎟
                      "An extremely moving reading ex- ⎟
                      perience recommended for mature ⎟
                      young adults, whether they have read ⎟
                      the original or not." Booklist ⎦

Author ←————**Simon, Neil**
                      The comedy of Neil Simon; with an ⎤ Bibliographical
                      introduction by Neil Simon. Random ⎬ information
                      House 1971 657p $12.95   812 ⎦

International ←————ISBN 0-391-47364-7
identification
number   "A bright wit warmed with honest ⎤ Direct quotation
                      compassion and a clear understanding ⎬ from book review,
                      of the foibles of men and women ⎟ with source.
                      characterize Simon's plays brought ⎟
                      together here. . . . Simon adds a ⎟
                      humorous biographical introduction ⎟
                      titled Portrait of the writer as a schizo- ⎟
                      phrenic." Booklist ⎦

Scholastic Literature Units

Eleven Scholastic Literature Units, for grades 6 to 10, are available. All the units are listed in table 9.1

Each unit is divided into three phases: (1) an anthology for classwide reading, (2) books for group reading, and (3) books for individual reading. Each student receives a Student Log containing directions for required and optional activities for independent work. A Teacher's Notebook consists of lesson plans for teaching and writing, reproductions of the Student

TABLE 9.1. Scholastic Literature Units Series 5100: Themes in Literature

Grade Range	Unit Title	Literary Focus
6-7-8	*Animals*	Short story
	Adventure and Suspense	
	Small World	
	Family	Family biography
7-8-9	*Courage*	Novel
	Decisions	Biography, Vocational literature
	Frontiers	Novel, Personal narrative
8-9-10	*Mirrors*	Drama
	Survival	Novel of adventure, Personal narrative
	Personal Values	Autobiography
9-10	*Tomorrow: Science Fiction and the Future*	

Source: Dwight L. Burton, Stephen Dunning, and Terrence D. Mosher, *Scholastic Literature Units: Courage.* Copyright © 1972 by Scholastic Magazines, Inc. Reprinted by permission of Scholastic Book Services, a division of Scholastic Magazines, Inc.

Log activities, procedures for managing the program, guides and quizzes for each book, and a final test. Also, posters depicting the theme accompany the unit.

A Teacher's Guide accompanies each story in the unit. An example of the guide for *The Red Badge of Courage* is shown in box 9.4. The guide consists of a synopsis, a critical discussion, incidents illustrative of the central concept, and a list of difficult vocabulary in the story. At the end of the guide is a Check Quiz.

Designed to cover six weeks of instruction, the unit is divided into three two-week phases. Because the units are identical in organization, we shall explain the three phases in more detail for only one of them, Burton, Dunning, and Mosher's unit, *Courage:*

PHASE I: CLASS READING, DISCUSSION, AND WRITTEN WORK. Students read the anthology *Courage.* Lesson plans contain procedures for discussing articles in the anthology.

PHASE II: GROUP READING, DISCUSSION, AND ORAL PRESENTATION. After reading and reporting as a class, students group themselves through

TABLE 9.2. Phase II Books

Least Difficult	Average Readers	Sophisticated Students
A Man Called Horse, Dorothy Johnson *The Contender,* Robert Lipsyte	*The Endless Steppe,* Esther Hautzig *No Easy Answers,* C. G. Hart	*Fahrenheit 451,* Ray Bradbury *The Old Man and the Sea,* Ernest Hemingway

Source: Dwight L. Burton, Stephen Dunning, and Terrence D. Mosher, *Scholastic Literature Units: Courage.* Copyright © 1972 by Scholastic Magazines, Inc. Reprinted by permission of Scholastic Book Services, a division of Scholastic Magazines, Inc.

self-selection of Phase II books (table 9.2). Students who select the same book form a group. Each group reads its Phase II book, uses Group Discussion and Program Suggestion Sheets for guidance in sharing ideas, and completes activities in the Student Log. Finally, each group prepares and presents group programs.

PHASE III: INDIVIDUAL READING AND REPORTING. Eight titles related to the theme of the unit *Courage* are used in this phase. The books range in difficulty and conceptual sophistication from Stephen Crane's *Red Badge of Courage* to easier books such as Leon Phillips's *Split Bamboo.* The titles for this phase are shown in table 9.3.

TABLE 9.3. Phase III Books

The Red Badge of Courage, Stephen Crane
My Enemy, My Brother, James Forman
Love of Life, Jack London
Split Bamboo, Leon Phillips
The Soul Brothers and Sister Lou, Kristin Hunter
Patton, Ira Peck
Profiles in Courage, John F. Kennedy
Megan, Iris Noble

Source: Dwight L. Burton, Stephen Dunning, and Terrence D. Mosher, *Scholastic Literature Units: Courage.* Copyright © 1972 by Scholastic Magazines, Inc. Reprinted by permission of Scholastic Book Services, a division of Scholastic Magazines, Inc.

BOX 9.4. Teacher's Guide

THE RED BADGE OF COURAGE

by Stephen Crane

Synopsis: Farm boy Henry Fleming enlists in the Union Army to take part in the Civil War. After weeks of monotonous drilling and fatiguing marching — a far cry from the excitement he had expected — Fleming comes finally to the scene of battle. The vast confusion of commanding, shooting, and shouting horrifies him, and when the enemy charges his regiment, Henry drops his rifle and runs. He wanders about the rear area in a lonely nightmare of confusion and conscience, and finally returns to his regiment at night. Ironically, he is welcomed as a semihero, for his companions mistake the wound on his head, which he received from the gun butt of a fleeing Union soldier, for a graze by a Confederate bullet. His problem now is to live up to his "red badge of courage," which he does in a succession of battles and brief respites. In the purposeless horror of war, "he had been to touch the great death and found that, after all, it was but the great death. He was a man. . . . He had rid himself of the red sickness of battle. The sultry nightmare was in the past. . . . He turned now with a lover's thirst to images of tranquil skies, fresh meadows, cool brooks — an existence of soft and eternal peace."

Point at Which Conflict or Problem Appears in Story: Henry enlists in the Union Army, p. 5.

Critique: This short novel has been hailed as one of the masterpieces of American fiction, and it furnishes an appropriate challenge to the superior reader. Its greatness lies in its power of style and its insight into the psychology of men in battle. Crane's mastery of words and description makes this a compelling story in which the reader moves through the nightmarish confusion of battle with a young Everyman, referred to in the novel as "the youth." It does not matter that this war is the Civil War. This is a universal situation of men in battle and of callow youth's inevitable rendezvous with evil, a painful initiation that is nevertheless essential to growth and maturity. This is a tribute to the courage demanded by circumstance; that is, the courage through which men who are suddenly faced with nightmarish conditions of violence and horror somehow find it possible to remain rational and perform their duties. It is through this courage of circumstance that Henry earns his red badge.

Courage Focus: A badly wounded soldier is bearing up unbelievably, making conversation with Henry, and praising the courage and fighting ability of his comrades (pp. 60–61); Henry's badly wounded friend finds the strength to go on his own; he seems ashamed to accept help even at this time (p. 64); in the midst of battle, Henry and another soldier rescue the colors from the hands of the dying Color Sergeant (pp. 125–126).

About the Author: Stephen Crane was born in 1871, the son of a New Jersey minister. He attended Claverack College, Lafayette College, and Syracuse University, although he graduated from none of them. For four years after he left school, he struggled to support himself, occasionally reporting for New York and New Jersey newspapers. In the last years of his life, he traveled as a correspondent to Mexico, Greece, and Cuba. He didn't see actual combat until his visit to Greece in 1897 — although *The Red Badge of Courage* was published three years before. Stephen Crane died in 1900. (See also pages iii–vi of *The Red Badge of Courage*.)

Vocabulary

word	page	word	page
purled	1	annihilated	44
twoscore	2	pommeling	47
oblique	3	resplendent	53
prowess	4	redoubtable	54
effaced	4	abject	54
impregnable	5	maniacal	57
clangoring	5	trepidation	62
adieu	7	doggerel	68
vivacious	8	spectral	72
martial	8	reiterated	73
secular	8	ague	77
dexterously	11	philippic	78
altercation	13	contortion	78
unscrupulous	16	sinuous	84
ominous	18	malediction	85
orbs	18	altercation	95
vindication	20	gamin	90
felicitating	20	audacity	110
blithe	20	lugubrious	114
pilfer	20	fracas	119
satanic	21	temerity	125
pontoon	26	accouterments	139
extricate	26	stoic	141
ponderous	27	gyrated	144
aggregations	27	epithets	149
perambulating	27	tableau	153
harangue	31	portals	155
demeanor	32	perturbation	155
reconnoitering	34	portentous	165
viands	34	expletives	165
crescendo	35	paroxysm	168
prophetic	36	catapultian	170
facetious	39	ghouls	172

Check Quiz

1. _____ Before he enlisted in the army, Henry lived (a) in the South; (b) on a farm; (c) in a large city; (d) in the Far West.

2. _____ Before his first battle, Henry was most worried that he would (a) be killed; (b) be wounded; (c) run from battle; (d) not be able to fire his gun.

3._____ During his flight through the forest after the second battle, Henry came upon (a) a wounded enemy soldier; (b) a young girl; (c) a dead soldier; (d) a dying horse.

4._____ Henry fled from the tattered soldier (a) because he wanted to know where Henry had been wounded; (b) because he threatened to report Henry as a deserter; (c) because he was a Confederate; (d) for no reason at all.

5._____ The title *The Red Badge of Courage* refers to (a) a flag; (b) a medal; (c) an armband; (d) a wound.

6._____ Henry was wounded by (a) an enemy bullet; (b) a blow from a retreating Union soldier's rifle; (c) his best friend Wilson; (d) a bad fall.

7._____ Henry overheard an officer say his regiment, the 304th, fought like (a) lions; (b) heroes; (c) children; (d) mule drivers.

8._____ Henry and his friend first earned the respect of their fellow soldiers and their commanders by (a) rescuing the Union flag when its bearer was shot; (b) holding the enemy off singlehanded; (c) discovering the enemy's hiding place; (d) taking a very important message to the President.

9._____ During the final battle, Henry and his friend captured (a) the enemy's flag; (b) an enemy soldier; (c) an enemy tank; (d) enemy ammunition.

10._____ At the end of the story, Henry Fleming felt that he was a (a) a farmer; (b) a man; (c) a true Confederate; (d) still a boy.

In Phase III, as in Phase II, students select their own books. Since all books are related to the theme of the unit, all students can enter into a discussion, contributing examples and critical incidents on the concept of courage from their own books. As a consequence, students develop a rich and differentiated conception of courage. Thus, the thematic or concept technique provides a way of solving the problem of individual differences in reading ability without stigmatizing students.

Preparing Your Own Unit

An advantage of the Scholastic Units for teaching is their completeness. They come with lesson plans, tests, titles organized around a theme, a management system, and paperbacks of each title for the entire class. However, teachers can prepare their own units, provided they have a library with materials already on hand or a fund for purchasing paperbacks, and, of course, the necessary time.

Using the *Children's Catalog* (Shor and Fidel, 1972), *Junior High*

FIGURE 9.1. Strategy for Teaching a Class with Varying Reading Levels

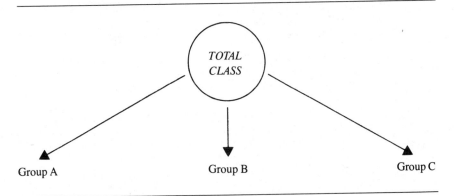

School Catalog (Fidel and Bogart, 1970), and the *Standard Catalog for High School Libraries* (Fidel and Berger, 1972) examples of which are shown in box 9.2, and the *Reader's Guide to Periodical Literature,* a group of teachers participating in a master's degree program constructed units and reading guides to accompany them.[2] Students selected a concept, such as the American Dream, conflict, courage, greatness, human evolution, pollution, power. Essays, short stories, incidents from novels, and newspaper articles of different levels of reading difficulty were selected, all related to the same concept. The chosen materials were then reproduced and stapled in booklet form. The class read some materials together and then subgroups were formed, based on self-selections of materials students chose to read. Each subgroup read and discussed the selection and completed the reading guide accompanying the selection. Class discussions were conducted in which all members participated by adding information to the discussion gleaned from materials they had selected. All individual differences in reading were accommodated by this self-selection strategy, and no group could dominate the discussion because each group read materials on the same concept at a suitable reading level. A schematic design of this organization is shown in figure 9.1. Note that the entire class reads some materials as a class. Then the class is subdivided into discussion groups A, B, C, according to materials selected. Each group contributes ideas gleaned from the material read in a general class discussion on the same concept. A condensation of the unit on the American Dream is presented in box 9.5.

---

[2] Teachers enrolled in a master's degree program at the University of California, Riverside, constructed these units under the direction of Dr. Robin McKeown. The teachers were Sylvia Andreatta, Anthony Bechtold, Jane Davenport, Chris Gutierrez, Vaughn Hudson, David Kahl, Dale Johnson, Jean Fruehan, Patsy Miller, Margaret Minor, Bonnie Parmenter, and Richard Zimmerman, and the supervisor was Elizabeth Arnold.

BOX 9.5. Teacher-constructed Unit
on Multi-ethnic Literature

THE AMERICAN DREAM — A DREAM DEFERRED?

by Anthony Bechtold and Dale Johnson

Focus: Racial and ethnic intolerance in contemporary America

Central Questions: Why is there racial and ethnic intolerance? How is it expressed? What are the apparent reasons for it? What are unique aspects of intolerance experienced by some group? What is integration? Separation? Pluralism?

Level: Junior and Senior High; reading range: grades 4–8.

Objectives of the American Dream: Liberty and justice for all. More specifically: What is most important is the drawing out of students' personal responses to the readings. The unit assumes that fear, ignorance, or threat to one's established security leads to inequality of liberty and justice. It assumes further that (1) the expression of one's own fears, (2) the confrontation of one's own ignorance, and (3) the discussion of the threat to one's own security will lead to a recognition of the essential humanity of others, regardless of racial or ethnic background. Although it is hoped that the unit will increase student sensitivity to the consequences of intolerance, the unit cannot guarantee that students will become more tolerant as a matter of fact. It must be recognized that increased polarization of student emotion may be the result.

Procedure
1. Unit is taught in ten 50 minute class periods.
2. Period 1. Orientation: taped recording of Langston Hughes's "One Friday Morning." Discussion topic: Why racial intolerance? Explain unit: self-selection of readings grouped within a topic, followed by discussion within groups, and then between groups in class discussion on how tolerance is expressed in each selection and its probable causes.
3. Period 2. Focus on definition of issue and terms. Students get reading lists, make selections from the lists, form into groups to complete guide.
4. Periods 3–6. Complete reading guides based on students' reading selections and then discuss each section of the guides.
5. Period 7. Present hypotheses on causes of intolerance.
6. Periods 8–9. Test hypotheses again, new selections.
7. Period 10. Complete unit by selecting a way of expressing conclusions: writing, art, music, and so forth.

Annotated Topic for the Unit
   Reading #5. "After You, My Dear Alphonse" by Shirley Jackson. In *Small World,* edited by R. Smith, J. Sprague, and J. Dunning. (New York: Scholastic Book Services, 1964), pp. 136–141. Short story, 4½ pages, Dale-Chall score 4.5.
   This story was chosen because it reveals, in a very subtle manner, some of the stereotyped ideas about Blacks that are still widely accepted in American society. It is the story of Mrs. Wilson's patronizing attitude toward a Black friend of her son,

and her injured sensibilities as she slowly learns the reality of his average, middle-class background. As the boys are in their early teens, many of her prejudicial comments are lost on them because of their innocence. Although the story is very easy to read in the decoding sense, these subtleties may have to be drawn out in the discussion. One question which might prove fruitful in this respect is: "How are prejudices passed on from one generation to another?"

Direction to Teacher: This is the reading guide for the selection. Students are to complete the guide by finding the page and the paragraph on which the True-False statements occur. They are to discuss Section B. The passages on which Section B is based are shown on the key. Section C goes beyond the selection to generalizations which students can discuss and articulate their own beliefs.

Anthony Bechtold and Dale Johnson earned their M.A. degrees in Education at the University of California, Riverside. Mr. Bechtold is a reading consultant in Poway, California, Unified School District and Mr. Johnson is a high school teacher in the Oceanside, California, Unified School District. This unit is reprinted with their permission.

In case you want to teach this unit on multi-ethnic literature, the selections are listed in box 9.6. They should be available in almost any large library. Read and annotate them and prepare your own reading and learning-from-text guides.

After they have used a few guides you have prepared, some students in your class may become so sophisticated with guides that they can construct their own and thus help you prepare guides for the entire unit. (See the sections on reading and learning-from-text guides in chapter 4, pp. 60–69 and the boxes in chapter 5, pp. 91–104.)

Remember that students are to be given a choice of titles within a group of selections, regardless of the reading level of the student or the selection. Students who choose the same selection read the selection and meet to complete the guide based on the selection. The size of the group may be limited by the number of copies available. Indeed, the size of the group should be limited so that all students in a group can have an opportunity to participate in discussion.

BOX 9.6. Readings for the Unit
"The American Dream — A Dream Deferred"

BLACK

"One Friday Morning" by Langston Hughes in *American Negro Short Stories,* John Henrik Clarke, ed. (New York: Hill and Wang, 1968), pp. 114–123. Short story, 9 pages, Dale-Chall score 8.0.

From *Native Son* by Richard Wright (New York: Harper and Row, 1968), pp. 18–25. Conversation from a novel, 7 pages, Dale-Chall score 7.6.

"The Revolt of the Evil Fairies" by Ted Posten in *The Best Short Stories by Negro Writers,* Langston Hughes, ed. (Boston: Little Brown, 1967), pp. 86–90. Short story, 4 pages, Dale-Chall score 7.5.

From *Soul on Ice* by Eldridge Cleaver (New York: Dell, 1968), pp. 173–175. Conversation from chapter, 2 pages, Dale-Chall score 5.8.

"After You, My Dear Alphonse" by Shirley Jackson in *Small World,* Smith, Sprague, and Dunning, eds. (New York: Scholastic, 1969), pp. 136–141. Short story, 4½ pages, Dale-Chall score 4.5.

MEXICAN-AMERICAN

"Ramon Lopez — Between Two Worlds" by Ramon Lopez in *Scholastic Scope,* 10:10 (April 11, 1969), pp. 4–9. Autobiography, 2½ pages, Dale-Chall Score 4.9.

"Court Vindicates Farm Workers' Dead Hero," by Gene Blake, Los Angeles *Times* Morning Edition (February 3, 1970), pp. 1, 22. Newspaper report, 1 page, Dale-Chall score 8.7.

From "Enemy Territory" by William M. Kelly in *Sight Lines,* Charlotte Brooks, general editor (New York: Holt, Rinehart and Winston, 1969), pp. 197–202. Narrative, 5 pages, Dale-Chall score 6.0.

From "The Land of Room Enough" by E. P. Maxwell in *Search for America,* Charlotte Brooks, general editor (New York: Holt, Rinehart and Winston, 1969), pp. 169–171. Incident from a short story, 3 pages, Dale-Chall score 6.0.

NATIVE AMERICAN

"To Catch a Never Dream" by Bruce King in *Scholastic Scope,* 11:2 (September 22, 1969), pp. 10–13, 25, 28, 30. Play, 5 pages, Dale-Chall score 4.5.

"The Returning" by Daniel de Paola in *Conflict,* Charlotte Brooks, general editor (New York: Holt, Rinehart and Winston, 1969), pp. 72–85. Short story, 12 pages, Dale-Chall score 6.4.

"Fire" by Lawrence E. Stotz in *Small World,* Smith, Sprague and Dunning, eds. (New York: Scholastic, 1964), pp. 17–21. Short story, 4½ pages, Dale-Chall score 8.5.

ORIENTAL-AMERICAN

"An American-Born Japanese In America" in *Orientals and Their Cultural Adjustment,* Social Science Source Documents #4 (Nashville, Tennessee: Social Science Institute, 1964), pp. 95–100. Autobiographical account, 5 pages, Dale-Chall score 8.4.

"A High School Japanese Student's Opinion on the Race Problem" in *Orientals and Their Cultural Adjustment,* Social Science Source Documents #4 (Nashville, Tennessee: Social Science Institute, 1964), pp. 105–106. Autobiographical account, 2 pages, Dale-Chall score 8.3.

"Born in Los Angeles — Reared in Oriental Fashion" in *Orientals and Their Cultural Adjustment,* Social Science Source Documents #4 (Nashville, Tennessee: Social Science Institute, 1946), pp. 24–26. Autobiographical account, 2½ pages, Dale-Chall score 8.3.

WHITE

"Tracke" in *Manhattan Transfer* by John Dos Passos (Boston: Houghton Mifflin Company, 1953), pp. 101–103. Incident from section of a novel, 3 pages, Dale-Chall score 5.5.

"Yes, Your Honesty" by George and Helen Papashvily in *Small World,* Smith, Sprague, and Dunning, eds. (New York: Scholastic, 1969), pp. 39–47. Autobiographical account, 8 pages, Dale-Chall score 5.4.

"Strong Contrast Between Elsinore Today and City of Hate" by Will Thorne, Riverside *Press-Enterprise* (February 15, 1970), Section B, p. 5. Newspaper article, 3 pages, Dale-Chall score 11.5.

From "Prelude" by Albert Halper in *Search for America,* Charlotte Brooks, general editor (New York: Holt, Rinehart and Winston, 1969), pp. 120, 121, 130–133. Short story, 5 pages, Dale-Chall score 4.4.

"Konnichi Wa" by Barbara L. Reynolds in *Small World,* Smith, Sprague, and Dunning, eds. (New York: Scholastic, 1969), pp. 10–16. An incident from a short story, 2 pages, Dale-Chall score 6.7.

"A Man Called Horse" by Dorothy M. Johnson in *Sight Lines,* Charlotte Brooks, general editor (New York: Holt, Rinehart and Winston, 1969), pp. 161–182. Biographical account, 17½ pages, Dale-Chall score 8.0.

CONCLUDING READINGS

"A Word of Warning" by Tom Galt in *Small World,* Smith, Sprague, and Dunning, eds. (New York: Scholastic, 1969), pp. 1–2. Short story, 2 pages; Dale-Chall score 5.6.

"Which Way Toward 'Liberty and Justice For All'?" in *Scholastic Scope,* 10:8 (March 21, 1969), pp. 6–14. Essay, 9 pages, Dale-Chall score 7.7.

PROJECT METHOD — INDEPENDENT FORMULATION OF QUESTIONS

The *project approach* is the most complex of the strategies because it gives students a greater range of choices in questions, places the most responsibility upon students, and gives them the greatest independence in reading and learning from text. Unlike the inquiry strategy which focuses on a narrow range of questions or the concept strategy which is organized about a single idea, the project approach covers an entire unit of study, such as the Westward Movement, and allows students to formulate and investigate any question on the unit which interests them. However, the inquiry strategy is like the project approach in that it allows students to select their own materials to answer their questions; also, as in both the inquiry and concept strategies, students using the project approach discuss issues in groups and report as a group to the entire class. But the reports are complementary and eventually form a complete unit as the information gathered by the various groups is combined. After the group process, students work on individual units and report to the class. Because the project approach utilizes all the features of the other strategies — including formulation of questions, selection of library materials for reference reading, participation in discussion groups, writing reports, and communicating results to the class — the project approach is the most complex and therefore last of our strategies. All the rest of the strategies lead up to it. Yet, this approach has some steps that are unique.

The project approach starts not with a text but with (1) arousing student curiosity, (2) encouraging student formulation of questions, (3) grouping of students who have questions in common, (4) providing for student self-selection of books or reference reading to get information for answering their own questions, and (5) advising students on novel and creative ways of reporting answers to their questions.

Steps in the Project Method

1. Create an atmosphere for arousing student curiosity by using posters, newspaper clippings, dramatizations, movies, prominent speakers, or discussions of local events. Any one or a combination of these ways of introducing a topic could arouse students' curiosity; of course, the introduction has to be relevant to the subject. For example, a unit on United States history might begin with discussion of a local building or geographic site related to the particular era in the history unit.

2. Conduct discussions of curiosity-arousing episodes. (See chapter 4 on discussion strategies and techniques.) Perhaps you could empanel a board of inquiry. To end this step, have students formulate their own questions to pursue in studying the unit. In a curiosity-arousing environment, students are likely to formulate their own questions eagerly, unless they have little rapport with the teacher or are completely jaded by previous negative experience in school. The teacher may simply ask students what they would like to know about the topic in such an environment. Try to obtain at least one question about the topic from each student. Use your imagination for eliciting questions. A ninth-grade English teacher injected competition into question-formulation by pitting one side of the room against the other side. Students wrote questions formulated by their side on the board. Each side tried to list more questions than the other side.

3. Group students. First lead students to group questions in categories. Simply ask students to group together the questions that have something in common. In a history unit, all the questions on government would form one category, military events would be

another category, economics would be a third, and so on. Then students whose questions are in the same category should form a group to search out answers to their questions. Since all members of the group have responsibility for answering all questions in the category, members of the group can help each other. Consequently, cross-ability tutoring (page 78) is likely to occur and an atmosphere of cooperation is fostered within the group.

4. To answer their questions, the group must have access to books containing information to answer the questions asked by the group. For each question or topic, the books should also vary in reading difficulty so that all students can locate materials on their own level. Some students may choose books at a relatively easy level, while other students may select books above their reading levels. The criterion is to get a book that will help to answer a question or questions. The teacher may aid students in selecting books, but should refrain from assigning them so that no stigma is likely to be attached to students for using easy books.

5. Allow time for students to engage in reading references. The key to success in reference reading is (a) to formulate and keep a question or questions in mind, (b) to judge whether the reading material is relevant while searching for information, and (c) to select only the relevant material. Relevancy is, of course, a matter of degree. (See further discussion on library or reference reading on pages 158–159.)

6. Encourage all members of a group to discuss answers to their questions. This verbalization will enable students to perform well in the next step, writing answers to their questions.

7. Use procedures similar to those suggested in chapter 7 for teaching students to write answers to their questions.

8. Act as a consultant to the groups; encourage members of a group to cooperate; get them to agree on a chairperson and a recorder; help the group locate materials; make sure the group tests whether questions are being maintained and relevancy judgments are made; and help the group decide on an interesting way to report findings to the class.

9. Suggest methods for reporting. Findings can be reported in writing, or in novel, more creative ways. For example, groups can give dramatized reports, weaving information into the drama or they can turn out a newspaper reporting answers to questions as though they were current events.

10. Leave time for evaluation. The class can evaluate each report to determine whether the questions have been answered. Then the class can relate answers to each other and perhaps formulate higher-order generalizations. (See chapter 6, pp. 112–122, for dis-

cussion procedures and for techniques to elicit generalizations from a group discussion.)

Example of the Project Method

A ninth-grade teacher used the project method to teach a biography unit (Zimmerman, 1973).[3] He gave students their choices of any of the paperback biographies provided. Students could select a biography of a particular person at an elementary, junior high, senior high, or college level of reading difficulty. A wide selection of biographies was available to meet the varying interests of students.

Students formulated questions on what they wanted to know about people in general and about the subjects of their biographies in particular. These questions supplemented the questions on literary purposes the teacher had posed for the biography unit. Students who were interested in the same biography formed a group. Altogether, the teacher had six groups.

Students in each group discussed the general and specific questions about their biographies. Then each group gave its report to the class. One group gave a typical report, a written one read by a member of the group. But another group gave a very creative report: they presented a play they had written containing all the information they had found. Another group communicated the information on the subject of its biography in a series of murals with tape-recorded explanations of each mural.

Reports can be given in a variety of ways. In the next section, we discuss various ways in which groups can report back to the class orally.

REPORTING BACK

Since multiple-textbook strategies involve the use of small groups of students (Donlan, 1976), you should teach your students techniques of reporting information back to the entire class. However, junior and senior high school students might know how to give individual oral reports to the class. These reports may take the form of informal talks, book reviews, or some other kind of *individual* student oral account. Reports of this kind are common. What is not common is having *groups* of students report. We shall present four types of group reporting that you can teach to your students.

---

[3] Richard Zimmerman was one of ten teachers enrolled in the senior author's federally funded training project for preparing content reading specialists for the junior high school (Singer, 1973).

The Symposium: A Staged Series of Reports

A *symposium* involves a group of two or more students reporting together, each on separate aspects of a problem or topic. Often mislabeled a *panel discussion*, a symposium has limited, or no, interaction among the participating members (Donlan, 1974). For this reason, the symposium is the easiest group-reporting technique for students to learn. It is usually staged before the class and, for the most part, operates free of questions from the teacher. Generally, the symposium chairperson introduces each speaker separately and makes transition statements between speakers. A symposium on famous mathematicians and their contributions would have each group member either (1) reporting on a different mathematician, or (2) reporting on a different concept and incidentally discussing how various mathematicians contributed to the concept. Following the symposium, the students or the teacher may decide to have a *forum,* or question period, during which members of the class ask questions of the participating members of the symposium. The following paragraph describes how a symposium can develop.

Assume that you are teaching a unit on the Revolutionary War. You notice that several students have shown more than average interest in the topic, as evidenced by their willingness to participate in class discussions, and that the same students appear to read the text material with little difficulty. You might encourage these students to form a group that would present a symposium on "Heroes of the American Revolution: The Human Interest Angle" or some other topic that either you or the group select. You could free these students from regular classroom participation, and have them use class time for library research and planning sessions. In the presentation (an enrichment experience for the rest of the class) the chairperson of the symposium has a dominant role from start to finish. The chairperson introduces the topic and presents an overview of what each participant will be talking about. Then the chairperson introduces each speaker. Their topics might be: (1) George Washington's medical problems; (2) the strange disappearance of Thomas Paine's remains, and (3) the many talents of Thomas Jefferson. After each speaker, the chairperson makes a transition statement to the next speaker. At the end, the chairperson summarizes and concludes, then solicits questions from the audience and directs them to the appropriate speakers.

Panel Discussion

Very similar to the symposium is the *panel discussion*. It consists of a group of three or more students staging a problem-solving situation before the class. The group members, working from a common outline of main points, interact with one another under the guidance of a strong chairperson who regulates the discussion so that each member participates. All members of a panel, unlike members of a *symposium*, are equally conversant with all aspects of the problem.

Teaching students to stage discussions may be difficult. One successful teacher would randomly select five or six students to sit at the front of the room and "talk about" a highly charged emotional issue: *Should students be allowed to smoke on campus? Should juvenile crime be punished more severely than it is now? Should the minimum driving and drinking age be the same?* After several sessions, the students realized they could stage lively discussions that were as engrossing as informal out-of-school discussions.

With the principal obstacle to staged discussion eliminated — stagefright — students could be taught more controlled staged discussion. Such discussion demands that students (1) realize the various roles discussants can assume (chapter 6); (2) work together in cooperative problem-solving; (3) explore the ramifications of a problem; and (4) pose alternative solutions.

Consider the topic *Should juvenile crime be punished more severely than it is now?* The group might decide to rephrase the topic as a problem: *How should juvenile crime be punished in a fair and equitable manner?* Next, the group might prepare a discussion outline like the one that is given below.

I. Problem: How should juvenile crime be punished in a fair and equitable manner?
II. Background
   A. Statistics on recent juvenile crime
   B. Notorious news stories involving juvenile crime
   C. Published pleas for reform in juvenile justice
III. Should juvenile justice be reviewed and revised?
   A. Arguments in favor
   B. Arguments opposed
IV. What specific changes in juvenile justice should be made?
   A. Proposed change #1
   B. Proposed change #2
   C. Proposed change #3
V. If changes are made, what might be the effects of these changes?
VI. Conclusion

After planning the outline, the members of the group would do outside reading on one or more of the subtopics and meet frequently to pool notes. The staged discussion would, then, involve all of the members talking about their combined information under the direction of a chairperson who moderates.

Debate: A Staged Argument

A more difficult form of group report is the *debate*. Debate involves the presentation of two opposing views. Rules for formal debating require affirmative and negative deliveries followed by rebuttal and cross-examination. Informal debates may be carried on in a variety of ways. Unlike a panel discussion, there is no attempt in a debate at compromise or problem-solving. Speakers hold firmly to their positions, and the class may vote on which side made the most convincing presentation. Cross-examination may take the form of a forum, or questions from the students.

The first prerequisite for a successful debate is an issue (preferably controversial) to whet the divided opinions of the students: *single* versus *multiple interpretations of a poem; biblical* versus *scientific theories of the origin of humanity; new mathematics* versus *old mathematics; states' rights* versus *federal control;* and so forth.

After the issue is established, you should present it in the form of a question:

1. Does a poem have only one meaning?
2. Is the biblical interpretation of the origin of humanity the most valid?
3. Is the new mathematics superior to the old mathematics?
4. Do states' rights have precedence over federal control?

Unless you present the issue in question form, it will not be clear what the affirmative and negative sides will be.

Next, select students (preferably verbal, resourceful students) to debate the two sides. Some teachers ask students to debate the side they agree with; other teachers feel emotional involvement with an issue precludes effective argumentation. At any rate, debaters should be able to present their points of view articulately. Articulateness can occur only if the students (1) organize their points in an outline and (2) document their statements with authoritative sources — newspapers, magazines, books, editorial writers, news commentators. Unless students are well organized and prepared, debate is rather pointless. Consequently, debate is not for all students.

After the student debaters have been given time to prepare their points of view, speaking order and time allotments should be determined. Debate teams usually consist of two speakers per side, but one or three per team can be used. More than three on a side produces repetition and decreases sharpness of presentation. Normally, the affirmative speaker is first. Here are some possible speaking orders:

A. Initial Argument
   1. Affirmative Speaker 1

    2. Negative Speaker 1
    3. Affirmative Speaker 2
    4. Negative Speaker 2
  B. Rebuttal
    1. Negative Speaker 2
    2. Affirmative Speaker 2
    3. Negative Speaker 1
    4. Affirmative Speaker 1
  C. Cross-examination
    1. Affirmative Speaker 1
    2. Cross-Examination from Negative Speakers
    3. Negative Speaker 1
    4. Cross-Examination from Affirmative Speakers
    5. Affirmative Speaker 2
    6. Cross-Examination from Negative Speakers
    7. Negative Speaker 2
    8. Cross-Examination from Affirmative Speakers

After the speaking order has been determined, it is vital to set time limits, for the entire debate as well as for each speaker. Consider, first, the length of the class period; do not hold the debate on a day when a school assembly shortens the class period. In some formal debates, speakers are allowed 8 minutes each for an initial argument and 4 minutes each for a rebuttal or cross-examination — a 48 minute presentation. A teacher may wish to scale down the time allotments — with equity. Members of the class (the audience) should refrain from participating with questions or comments until the debate is concluded.

The audience may vote on which team gave a better presentation, but the voting should be based on debating skill, not on the merits of one or the other side of the issue.

Colloquy: A Panel of Experts

Colloquy occurs when a "panel of experts" is available for further information, clarification, or settlement of dilemmas. For instance, if a group of high school students is presenting a symposium or debate, perhaps even a panel discussion, on the works of John Steinbeck, the colloquy might include English professors from neighboring colleges. Ideally, the colloquy makes no formal presentation but merely serves to advise.

Summary of Reporting Back Techniques

As you use multiple-text strategies with your students, you will need to show them how to report back. Some techniques of reporting back are more difficult than others, so you should teach the techniques sequentially. Begin with the *symposium*. Although it is *staged*, members of a symposium do not have to interact, merely report. After the students have gained experience reporting in a staged situation, introduce the *panel discussion*. Students will feel easier if you suggest that a panel discussion is like a staged discussion cluster. Because of the argumentative nature of *debate*, students will participate in debate more readily if they've had experience participating in symposiums and panel discussions where weighing of evidence and problem-solving are practiced. Last, and most difficult, is the *colloquy*. Students have to make arrangements for bringing outside experts to the classroom. They have to make sure that these experts function only in a consultant capacity. In other words, students must integrate the contributions of experts into their own well-organized and staged symposium, panel discussion, or debate.[4]

SUMMARY

In this chapter you have learned three ways to teach through multiple-text strategies. With *inquiry*, the students investigate assertions made in their textbooks by doing additional reading. When *concept technique* is used, students select books on varying levels of difficulty but related to the same *concept*, such as "survival" or "courage." The *project approach* focuses on students formulating their own questions and engaging in reference reading to answer these questions. In addition to multiple-text strategies, you have studied four ways in which groups of students can report back to the class on what they have learned: the symposium, the panel discussion, the debate, and the colloquy. Having learned about single- and multiple-text strategies, you will discover in chapter 10 how to put these strategies into an instructional blueprint.

ACTIVITY

Drawing upon a topic from your own content area, develop a multiple-text strategy, using either inquiry or the concept technique.

---

[4] Other reporting activities are role-playing, improvisational dramatics, news broadcasts, murals or collages, class newspapers or magazines, and slide-tape presentations.

10 | An
Instructional
Blueprint

CHAPTER OVERVIEW

Many well-seasoned, experienced teachers are able to plan learning experiences for their students that extend from September to June. So far this text has provided you with numerous strategies for teaching students how to read and learn from content area textbooks. Now, you may ask: how does it all fit together? Chapter 10 will present you with a blueprint for combining these strategies in an instructional framework. While you are reading this chapter, keep this question in mind: *Should a teacher instruct a class the same way in June as in September?*

Successful teachers tend to build a repertoire of classroom activities that work. This repertoire is the result of continual experimentation and revision. Occasionally, teachers discover that sound educational theory and research support what they've been doing instinctively in the classroom. Both authors of this book have had considerable teaching experience. In both cases, their repertoire included the phase-in/phase-out technique as part of their teaching style long before they wrote this book. The primary assumptions of the phase-in/phase-out technique are (1) that the purpose of education is to produce independent learners and (2) that teaching means showing students how to teach themselves. However, the class usually starts with activities done under close teacher-direction and may gradually lead to independent learning. One of the authors recalls, for instance, the trauma of facing 40 hostile seniors in an English class that was required for graduation. For self-preservation, he had to plan each class period tightly, with four or five activities, to provide the necessary structure for gaining control of a class. Subsequently, as his discipline problems began to dissolve, he needed fewer teacher-directed activities and found that the class could progress to student-centered activities — discussion clusters, panel discussions, trips to the library, projects, even improvisational dramatics. Without the structure at the start of the school year, students might never have been able to function in the more independent situations.

As you read this chapter, keep in mind that the instructional blueprint we advocate in this chapter isn't a pipe-dream; the philosophy of progressing from a teacher-centered to a student-centered classroom and from dependent to independent learners is in reality just good sense.

PURPOSES OF THE BLUEPRINT

So far in this book, you have learned that today's high school has evolved in the last century from a selective institution with a narrow curriculum to an all-inclusive institution with seemingly unlimited educational offerings. Concurrent with growth, increasing problems of high school students have complicated the teacher's job. For instance, in a given "average" tenth-grade class, a ten-year range in student achievement precludes much success if the teacher chooses to move all students from instructional level A to level Z at the same time with *identical* instruction. At the other extreme, *individual instruction* is unmanageable. With wide-ranging differences in reading achievement in a class, you must teach *some* students how to read and *all* of the students how to learn from text, specifically how to get meaning from interacting with the text and how to talk and write about what they have read. Our single- and multiple-text teaching strategies facilitate students' learning how to learn from text. Yet, the random and unsystematized use of these strategies will not be effective in teaching students how to learn. What is needed is a blueprint for instruction in which all the strategies are integrated.

An instructional blueprint insures purposive teaching and learning. Such a blueprint has three dimensions: (1) teachers should plan instructional time in such a way that students progress from dependent to independent learning; (2) the teacher has to use a variety of teaching techniques to prepare the students for learning from text, to guide them while they are reading, to assess their responses to what they have read, and to decide upon the next teaching step; (3) the teacher should teach students how to discuss and how to write so that they can express their responses to text in varied and articulate ways. We have organized these three dimensions into an instructional blueprint.

DIMENSION ONE: PHASING OUT THE TEACHER AND PHASING IN THE STUDENT

A psychological definition of *learning* would point out that it involves initiation of behavior or change in a learner which is relatively permanent and which occurs as a result of reacting to a situation and obtaining knowledge of results (Hilgard and Bower, 1975). Teaching is one way to produce such an initiation of behavior or change in the learner. The change is from dependent to independent learners. The teacher's goal is to guide learners toward independence (Herber, 1970). Parents "teach" their children to talk and walk with the hope that independent communication and movement will result. Swimming instructors teach children to survive in water on their own. Primary school teachers want their students to read books at home and to solve day-to-day arithmetic problems in their lives. In effect, good teachers phase themselves out by teaching their students how to perform alone. If students and teachers realize this objective, students will be more capable of directing their own learning at the end of a course than they were at the beginning of the course. However, if students are still dependent upon the teacher to provide "the right answers" at the end of the course, they will not have become independent learners. The teacher and the students will have failed to attain a basic objective of education.

Teachers, then, need to be teaching differently in September and October than they were teaching in May and June. Specifically, in September, the teacher will initiate most of the student activity; in June students should be able to initiate and independently carry out similar activities. In September a teacher would direct class discussion of a text chapter by posing questions and problems; by June, the students should be directing discussion around questions and problems they have posed for themselves. If this happens, the teacher will have trained students to become more independent learners (Rosenthal, *et al.*, 1970).

What the Teacher Does Between September and June

Many teachers who assign reading, discussion, and writing complain about the low level of student performance without realizing that it is the continued dependence of students on the teachers that contributes to this low-level performance. Such teachers continue to give assignments without instructing students in how to read and learn from text and how to express themselves through discussion or writing. A swimming instructor who taught this way would support students in deep water until the end of the course. Then, when the student went on to another course where the water was even deeper, the students would have to learn to swim alone or sink. Although some students learn to survive this kind of instruction, learning can occur more readily with the proper kind of teaching. Even though many students might prefer to take the path of least effort and remain dependent, the job of teachers is to have students overcome this inertia and become independent.

A teacher who wants to phase out by June plans a careful and gradual turnover of learning to the students who accept responsibility for their own learning. The teacher phase-out process can occur through use of a specific teaching plan.

Three Stages to Independence

A three-stage teaching plan will take students from dependence to independence as they learn how to use a particular strategy. It will phase in the students as the teacher phases out.

FIRST STAGE. The teacher introduces a strategy to students and directs the entire class through all steps in the strategy. Suppose, for example, that a teacher initiates the use of a reading and learning-from-text guide. (See an example of this type of guide in chapter 5.) Under teacher direction, students read the text and then as a group complete the guide, perhaps volunteering information on facts and main ideas, interpretations and inferences, and then discussing generalizations, central ideas, or evaluating the material (the section, chapter, or story) covered. This stage of the teaching plan may cover more than one class period, perhaps an entire week.

SECOND STAGE. The teacher, serving as leader of a group made up of the entire class, demonstrates how to operate as a group. All students learn the roles of members of the group and, at least some, learn through imitation to serve as leaders of a group. The teacher then divides the class into groups of about six students each, including a chairperson and a reporter. The task of every group is to complete a reading and learning-from-text guide.

At this stage, the teacher has to establish "ground rules" for group chairpersons and members and for giving reports (Evans, 1966). The chairperson will: keep members of the group on task (Donlan, 1973), have each member participate in completing the guide, allow members to justify their responses to the guide, and make sure individuals listen to each other, particularly when the group discusses controversial issues or makes evaluations. The chairperson should realize, particularly when the group is making *affective* evaluations, that various values can emerge from a group; consequently, the chairperson, at this second stage, has to decide whether the group members can converge to a consensus or whether the group will end up with a plurality of affective evaluations. Each member's role is to participate, contribute, listen to others, and help the others to think through their own ideas. The reporter's task is to take notes on what the group has done, fill in the guide, and when the class reconvenes, to relate what the group accomplished. Thus, in stage two, the group applies not only skills in gaining information from text but also skills in discussion and writing.

An advantage of the group process is that more students are likely to formulate and express their ideas than would have done so in a whole-class situation. Since the act of expression requires people to create ideas and to organize and direct their thinking processes, more individuals would have the opportunity to do so in a small group than in a large class situation. Through the give-and-take process in small groups, students teach each other and learn through experience the validity of the frequently made observation: "If you want to learn something, teach it."

THIRD STAGE. Having learned from teacher guidance of the whole class and from group interaction, students are now able to complete guides individually. At least they fully understand what they are to do. The guides the students complete on their own can be used as a means of evaluating their skills and abilities in applying reading, thinking, and learning processes to the content areas.

What the Students Do Between September and June

THE STUDENT IS A GROUP MEMBER

Figure 10.1 shows in schematic form, the three stages in learning a strategy. In *stage I*, students function as members of a class. The teacher is the leader of the class. In this stage, the teacher teaches the class as a whole, and therefore each student in the class, and models what the chairperson of a group does and what is expected of each member of the group. The teacher can also appoint a reporter at this stage and have a member of the class demonstrate this role.

In *stage II*, the students function as members of smaller groups. The teacher relates to each group as a consultant and moves from group to

FIGURE 10.1. Scheme of Three Stages in Teaching a Strategy

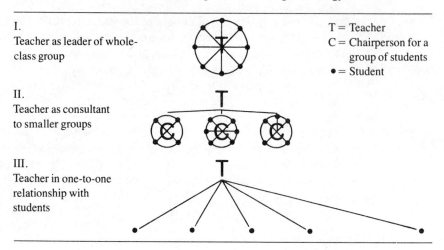

I.
Teacher as leader of whole-class group

II.
Teacher as consultant to smaller groups

III.
Teacher in one-to-one relationship with students

T = Teacher
C = Chairperson for a group of students
• = Student

group. At each group, the teacher-as-consultant observes, defines, and receives problems, and helps the group develop its group processes and solve its problems.

The *C* at the center of each group represents the chairperson. The role of this person is similar to the role modeled by the teacher in stage I. Presumably the chairperson's role is learned by imitation and by experience in the role.

For the first attempts, the teacher can appoint chairpersons, reporters, and group members. Ideally, each group ought to be heterogeneous in ability and knowledge in the particular subject area so that cross-ability teaching can occur. Although the more knowledgeable students will probably benefit more from this relationship, all students will have to learn the strategy, if not in stage II, then in stage III. The chairpersons at first may be highly respected members of the class, but subsequently the position ought to rotate. Likewise for the reporter.

At first, the task of the group should be relatively short, perhaps covering only a section or a page, and accomplishable in less than a class period. After 20 to 30 minutes of group activity, the teacher can call for reports and have each group evaluate its understanding of the strategy and how it functioned as a group. Subsequently, as groups demonstrate their knowledge of the learning strategy and their ability to function as groups, they should be given longer assignments and required to report periodically.

In *Stage III*, individuals complete their own guides and, through them, communicate directly with the teacher. The teacher can use the individually completed guides to evaluate student progress and to diagnose reading, learning, and thinking skills and processes. For this purpose, the teacher should confer with individual students and obtain explanations of how and why they gave the responses they did.

THE STUDENTS CONSTRUCT THEIR OWN GUIDES

The next step in guiding students towards independence is to teach them to *construct* their own guides. The teacher can do this in the same three stages used in teaching the class to *use* a guide. The aim for both single- and multiple-text strategies is to have students eventually internalize a process of thinking while learning from text. The means for attaining this goal of learning how to learn and inquire in each content area is to have the class first learn to *use* a particular strategy in three stages. Then the class members should learn how to construct and self-administer the strategy. Finally, the students should know the strategy so well that they can apply it automatically to gaining and communicating information in each content area. In all strategies used in any content area, students are to learn to formulate and answer their own questions, at first by observing and answering the kinds of questions formulated by teachers and then, by imitation, formulating their own questions (Rosenthal *et al.*, 1970).

The teacher's objective, then, is to get students to the point where they can pose their own questions and use this ability not only before reading in content areas but throughout the entire study of the content (Singer, 1978a, 1979). The process is analogous to a question-and-answer dialogue with single texts or with multiple texts. Hence, successful teaching means that students begin to think like content area specialists who know not only the content of their subject area but also its mode of inquiry, whether the content be industrial arts, English, science, or social science. Thus, evaluation of students is also a self-evaluation for teachers. The question is whether students have become independent learners in a particular content area. If so, the teacher has been successful.

A Teacher's Blueprint

One teacher's blueprint for developing student independence in using reading and learning-from-text guides over the academic year appears in table 10.1.

Notice that teacher input is heavy in September-October but light in January-February when students have learned to *use* a strategy. In March-April teacher input is again heavy as a new process begins: teaching students to make guides. Notice also that the reverse is true for student input. The planned phase-out of the teacher might be diagrammed, as shown in figure 10.2.

TABLE 10.1. One Teacher's Blueprint for Developing Student Independence

Month	Instructional Goal
September October	Teacher leads the class through chapters 1–4 with guides; conducts class discussion.
November December	Teacher groups students for chapters 5–8; students work with guides and learn independent small group discussion.
January February	Students select guides they need for chapters 9–12. They form their own groups for discussion.
March April	Teacher shows students how to make guides for chapters 13–16 for their own use.
May	Students prepare their own guides for chapters 17–18.
June	Students learn from chapters 19–20 without preparing guides.

FIGURE 10.2. Teacher Phase Out, Student Phase In for Two Strategies

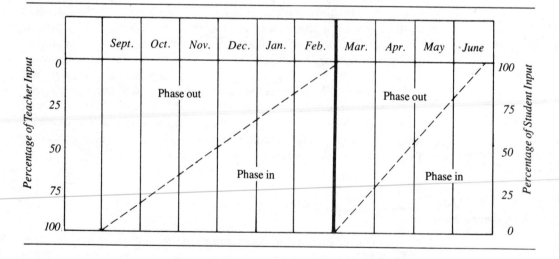

DIMENSION TWO: CLASSROOM TEACHING STRATEGIES

The best way to guide students to become independent learners, then, is to teach them to do for themselves what many teachers ordinarily do for them. Before you can do this, you have to know what the strategies are and how to use them.

Single-Textbook Strategy

In the traditional high-school learning situation, the entire class works from a single textbook (Herber, 1970). Since the students represent a wide range of achievement, many will not learn from one text readily, but fortunately a variety of teaching strategies and techniques can be used for meeting the wide range of individual differences in reading and learning from single texts.

How Should You Prepare Students to Learn from a Single Text?

Before students begin to read the text you can provide certain classroom activities to facilitate their learning.

DO A TASK ANALYSIS

Before assigning a chapter from a textbook, make a brief outline of the main concepts you want to stress and a companion outline of the processes the students will need to know to master the content. In chapter 5 (box 5.4), you saw an example of a task analysis for a chapter in a history text. Notice that it stressed "main concepts" rather than an accumulation of more or less related facts. Ineffective learners tend to approach all ideas with little differentiation. As a result, you will have to identify the essential main ideas (or the main ideas you want to teach) and relate the rest of the detail to these ideas. In addition, you will have to teach the students the thought processes the textbook authors used. Notice that the task analysis for the American history chapter includes *cause and effect* as a thought process students would need to know before reading the chapter. Table 10.2 gives an overview of concepts and processes in specific content areas. Table 10.3 gives a detailed task analysis for a series of related concepts in science. *Once you make a task analysis, show it to your students and tell them how you prepared it.* Later in the school year, you may want them to compose their own task analyses.

GIVE YOUR STUDENTS AN ENTRY LEVEL TEST

To ascertain what your students need in order to read a chapter, plan a test to evaluate how adequate the students' backgrounds actually are for learning the chapter (Glaser, 1962). The test could be no more than a brief quiz, containing true-false, multiple-choice, short-answer, or matching items. Prerequisite content might be found in the previous chapter of the text you are using; thus, a final examination for chapter *D* might be used as an entry level test for chapter *E*. Prerequisite processes could be evaluated by simple classroom exercises. One test item, for instance, might

TABLE 10.2. General Task Analyses
for Specific Content Areas

	Concept	Prerequisite Process
English/ Language Arts	Poetry	Understanding figurative language
		Reading with rhyme/meter
		Drawing inferences
	Reading nonfiction	Main idea/supporting details
		Chronological order
Social Studies	The American Revolution	Cause and effect
		Chronological order
		Reading maps
	Declaration of Independence	Main idea/supporting details
		Using context clues
Science	The ecology of water	Drawing inferences from pictures and charts
		Cause and effect
	Conducting lab experiments	Following printed directions
		Using formulas
		Interpreting diagrams
		Drawing inferences
Mathematics	Percentage/interest	Reading word problems
		Translating symbols
	Solving algebraic equations	Reading math ''sentences''
		Interpreting symbols
		Moving numbers

be a scrambled list of events that is to be unscrambled. This test item
might assess a student's knowledge of events and ability to perceive
chronological order. *Show your students how to make entry level tests
and let them participate with you in composing these tests.*

WRITE CLASSROOM OBJECTIVES

A task analysis and entry level test can help you to write classroom
objectives or revise existing objectives (Gagné, 1962). After the task analysis, you might write objectives on how you want students to perform
after they've read the chapter. These objectives would be *ideal* performances. Results from the entry level test might cause you to revise, scale
down, or expand your original objectives. Differentiated performance on
the entry level test might suggest individualization of objectives; that is,

TABLE 10.3. Task Analysis for a Science Unit
on the Ecology of Water

Concept	Prerequisite Process
Water environments affect plant and animal life	Drawing inferences from pictures Cause and effect
Fresh water communities differ from salt water communities	Comparison/contrast Reading diagrams
Life in ponds, lakes, and rivers varies as a result of the water conditions	Cause and effect Technical terminology Context clues
Water changes as chemicals are added	Following directions Drawing inferences from visual data Understanding sequence

the entry level test might determine what individual students need to know to benefit from the next chapter. Individual "contracts" indicate what objective(s) each student agrees that he or she must achieve. Consider figure 10.3. Sarah DeJong agrees that she needs to accomplish objectives 1, 2, and 3; but Margaret Amato sees that she needs to accomplish all 14 objectives. Figure 10.3 also shows that Joseph Adams, who contracted for all 14 objectives, completed only 6. Mike Borjus, on the other hand, has to date completed 3 out of the 4 objectives he contracted to achieve.

Show your students how to write performance objectives and give them practice at composing their own (Mager, 1962). Box 10.1 shows several types of performance objectives, glossed with explanation.

BOX 10.1. Types of Performance Objectives

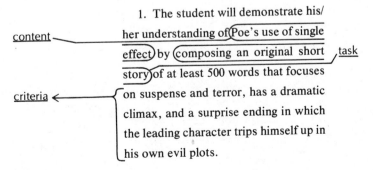

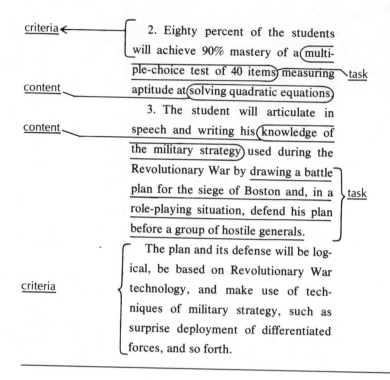

criteria → 2. Eighty percent of the students will achieve 90% mastery of a multiple-choice test of 40 items measuring ⟨task⟩ aptitude at solving quadratic equations ⟨content⟩

content 3. The student will articulate in speech and writing his knowledge of the military strategy used during the Revolutionary War by drawing a battle plan for the siege of Boston and, in a role-playing situation, defend his plan before a group of hostile generals. ⟨task⟩

criteria The plan and its defense will be logical, be based on Revolutionary War technology, and make use of techniques of military strategy, such as surprise deployment of differentiated forces, and so forth.

GIVE THE CLASS A CHAPTER OVERVIEW

Before students read a chapter, tell them what they should expect to find (Ausubel, 1964). An overview activity might consist of reviewing the items on your task analysis. It could also be an outline of the chapter's content, based on the author's organizational principles. It could be a series of page references with a brief statement about what the student will find on each page. You can give the overview orally, offering explanations as the students thumb through the chapter; or you can use a dittoed handout that you could take the class through. *Show the students various methods of preparing overview activities and, later in the year, have them prepare their own overviews.*

REVIEW DIFFICULT VOCABULARY

In addition to understanding the author's thought processes, students need help with vocabulary, technical terms and other difficult words. By going over vocabulary before the students read, you can facilitate their learning the concepts of the chapter. First, present the students with a list of words, pronounce them for the students, give the page numbers where

FIGURE 10.3. Teacher's Record of Contracted and Completed Objectives

Key
* = contracted objectives
✔ = completed objectives

STUDENT	1. Knows water affects life	2. Drew inferences from pictures	3. Explained cause/effect	4. Fresh water/salt water differ	5. Made comparison/contrast	6. Read/understood diagrams	7. Ponds, lakes, rivers differ	8. Showed cause/effect	9. Knew technical terms	10. Used context clues	11. Conducted lab experiment	12. Followed directions	13. Inferred from visual data	14. Understood sequence
Adams, Joseph	* ✔	* ✔	* ✔	* ✔	* ✔	* ✔	*	*	*	*	*	*	*	*
Amato, Margaret	* ✔	* ✔	* ✔	* ✔	* ✔	* ✔	* ✔	* ✔	* ✔	* ✔	*	*	*	*
Blake, Sam	* ✔	* ✔	* ✔	* ✔	* ✔	* ✔	* ✔	*	*	*				
Borjus, Mike											* ✔	* ✔	* ✔	*
Carter, Louise	* ✔	* ✔	* ✔	*	*	*								
Donato, Manuel	* ✔	* ✔	* ✔	* ✔	* ✔	* ✔	* ✔	* ✔	* ✔	* ✔	* ✔	* ✔	* ✔	*
DeJong, Sarah	* ✔	* ✔	*											

the words occur, define the words in simple language, and provide a context for each word in a sentence from the textbook. Second, you can present merely the context sentence and work with the students in trying to infer meaning. Third, you can present the vocabulary in a demonstration apart from the text. Many shop teachers label tools and shop areas with signs and take the students on a tour prior to reading a chapter of text. *Teach your students the various means of learning the definitions of words and have them construct their own vocabulary lists.*

TEACH THE STUDENTS NEEDED THOUGHT PROCESSES

Your task analysis indicated certain thought processes the students would need to develop in order to comprehend the content of a chapter. You will have to teach the students how to engage in these processes: you will have to help them develop their thought processes. In chapters 4 and 5 (specifically, in box 5.6), you saw an outline for a processes of reading guide that attempts to teach students how to engage in cause and effect thinking. The best way to teach a thought process is to begin with a practical, everyday problem and then have the students explain how they would solve the problem. Consider teaching students the logical order of directions. First, supply the students with a list of *scrambled* steps one must take to make something — for instance, a peanut butter and jelly sandwich. Second, as the students unscramble these steps, have them take note of the clues they are using to obtain the proper order. Third, see if they can apply what they have learned to another situation, for instance, unscrambling the events in a recent film. Fourth, see if they can now apply what they have learned to a textbook situation — unscrambling events in a chapter. *Teach your students to teach themselves to think by having them prepare their own processes of reading guides. (See chapters 4 and 5.)*

How Should You Guide the Students While They Are Reading?

So far you have been concerned with preparing students for reading by using task analyses, entry level tests, writing and revising objectives; by leading overview activities, learning-to-read activities, processes-of-thinking activities; and, most of all, by showing them how you teach. Preparation, however, is not enough by itself. You have to provide guidance while the students are reading and, more important, show them how to guide themselves.

PROVIDE THEM WITH LEARNING-FROM-TEXT GUIDES

You can provide the student with a set of preposed questions for which they will find answers while they are reading. You might even supply the page numbers where the student may find the basis for answers. If the students review the questions prior to reading, they will search for answers as they read. The questions will lead them to focus on what your preposed questions have, in effect, emphasized. Later in the year, you can have the students pose their own questions. *Show students how to write questions* that ask for information, that ask for inferences, and that ask for evaluation and application of what they have learned. In box 10.2 is an example of a learning-from-text guide.

BOX 10.2. Learning-from-Text Guide

LIFE: ITS FORMS AND CHANGES

Chapter 1, pp. 4–23

A. *Factual Level*
   1. What causes the green color that you see on a pond? (page 4, column 1, paragraph 2)
   2. What are *algae* and how do they help out in a pond? (pages 4, 2, 1)
   3. List the names of two algae that have similar shapes. (pages 5 and 6)
   4. List two other types of plants that live in the pond. (page 7)
   5. List four types of animals that eat the plants of the pond. (pages 10 and 11)
   6. Who are the producers of the pond and who are the consumers? (pages 18, 19, 23)
B. *Inferential and Interpretive Level*
   1. If there were no producers in the pond what would happen to the consumers?
   2. Of what use is the microscope to people who want to study life in a pond?
   3. Are producers always plants and are the consumers always animals?
C. *Generalization and Evaluative Level*
   1. If you wanted to build a giant glass aquarium for people to examine pond life, what would you have to fill it with to keep everything from dying?
   2. What problems do managers of public aquariums face every day?

While early in the year it is important for you to pose the questions in a learning-from-text guide, you can gradually teach students to write questions on different levels, and eventually they will be able to ask their own questions and direct their own learning (Rosenthal, et al., 1970).

IF POSSIBLE, GLOSS A CHAPTER

Glossing is a helpful learning device. As you recall, glossing is the use of marginal notes to facilitate learning. Glossing may take the form of word definitions, paraphrasing, and the posing of questions. Many textbooks use glossing, but even if you use such textbooks you may wish to add your own touches. Since you cannot collect the students' textbooks every night and write marginal notes for all your students, you'll have to resort to expedient measures. First, you can dictate glosses to the students for them to write in the margins of their own books (or in their notebooks if writing in books is not allowed). Second, if your "textbook" consists of dittoed handouts, you can write the gloss directly on the ditto masters. Third (a fairly complicated measure), you can duplicate glosses aligned with the textbook margins on facing ditto pages that can be slipped between the textbook pages. *Eventually, you can educate students to write their own glosses, based on what they perceive as their own learning problems.*

How Do You Assess Student Learning After Reading?

After students have read, you will want to assess what they have read by getting them to *react* to the text and *evaluate* it.

PLAN REACTION ACTIVITIES

You will want to plan activities that allow students to react to what they've read. At a simple level, one such activity could be a discussion of answers to the questions posed in the learning-from-text guide. At a more complex level, students could engage in individual and group projects in which they apply what they have learned. Science students, after reading a chapter on osmosis, might devise an experiment showing the process of osmosis, demonstrate the experiment before class, and relate the experiment to content in the text chapter. Reaction activities can involve symposia, panel discussions, debates, dramatic improvisations, student-written plays and stories, demonstrations or research projects, as well as answering questions that show the students' abilities at making inferences, analyzing ideas in a text, and problem solving. *As with other strategies, you can show students how to plan reaction activities and later get them to plan, implement, and evaluate their own activities.*

PLAN EVALUATIVE EXPERIENCES

Too often, students are not given the opportunity to evaluate the textbooks they are reading nor the ideas within the textbooks. Students have ideas and feelings that are well worth exploring. Permit them the opportunity to pass judgment on a textbook, but require that they substantiate their judgments. Evaluation activities could include a range of experiences from direct responses to cognitive judgments (Is the material correct? How do you know?) to subjective questions (What did you like least about this chapter? Why?) to role-playing situations. (A group of students could function as an editorial board in a publishing house responding to the content and style of the class text.)

Multiple-Text Strategy

An increasingly popular learning approach in high school is the use of multiple texts within the same classroom. Three multiple text approaches indicate the need for deft planning: the use of multilevel texts, the use of multiple textbooks with core readings, and the use of multiple textbooks without core readings.

MULTILEVEL TEXTBOOKS

As the name suggests, in a multilevel textbook approach, two or more textbooks at varying levels of readability and parallel organization serve as the basis for grouping students for instruction. Consider a tenth-grade science class with a ten-year range of reading achievement. The entire class could be studying photosynthesis, but each student could select one of three texts best suited to her or his ability and use it to search for answers to questions. All three texts would include content on photosynthesis. Consequently, all the students could participate in discussion and other class activities even though they had used different texts that varied in difficulty level. Since students could select their own texts, no stigmatization is likely to occur. In a situation like this, you would use single-text strategies where needed for each of the three books. You would assume that high-achieving tenth-graders would experience problems with a text they selected just as low-achieving students would have problems with a text. In effect, the type of teaching you would be doing in a single-text situation would not be very different from the type you would be doing in a multilevel text situation. You would just be doing it several times. For example, in a situation where you had three levels of text and were using a Directed Reading Activity (DRA) strategy, you would construct lesson plans for each text. In the same way, if you had a marginal gloss strategy, you would prepare a gloss for each text. You would also prepare three learning-from-text guides.

MULTIPLE TEXT WITH CORE READINGS

More common than the approach involving multilevel texts is the multiple-text approach that involves supplementary core readings (Ryan, 1963). Using this approach, you would employ single-text teaching strategies to have the entire class engage in the common reading of a single anthology or a science text. Following the reading of the one text, you would allow students to choose, individually or in groups, additional reading on their own and report back to the class. Independent and group projects, generated from core readings, can provide you with additional opportunities to assess student learning. In addition, these projects allow students opportunities to try their wings in independent work. If you plan ingeniously by continually alternating core reading experiences with group and individual projects, students can learn, developmentally, to learn on their own.

MULTIPLE TEXTBOOKS WITHOUT CORE READINGS

In using this approach, in which students share no common reading experience, you will have to build other classroom activities to bring students together, particularly overview activities. In such activities, you and the students define and pose problems and schedule reporting sessions in which students can share what they have learned.

DIMENSION THREE:
TEACHING DISCUSSION AND WRITING

In order for you to evaluate how well your students are learning from text, they must respond in ways that can be assessed. A student in sewing class demonstrates proficiency by sewing. A swimmer demonstrates proficiency by swimming, a pianist, by playing music. A reader cannot demonstrate proficiency by reading only. The reader must make his or her reading and learning from text audible or visible if you are to assess it. Therefore, to demonstrate what he or she has learned, a reader must speak or write for a teacher or student audience. Discussion and writing are vital activities in assessing reading and learning from text. However, if you expect students to speak and write effectively, you must teach them how to do so. To meet this challenge, teachers should devote time, especially at the beginning of the school year, to showing students how to participate in a discussion and how to prepare writing assignments. For specific suggestions on teaching discussion and writing, see chapters 6 and 7.

SUMMARY

Teachers in today's classrooms must provide for a wide range of individual differences in ability to read and learn from text. Single- and multiple-text strategies for teaching students to read and learn from text are effective in dealing with this range of individual differences; and they are even more effective when organized into a blueprint for instruction.

A blueprint for instruction has three dimensions. First, it provides for phasing out the teacher and phasing in the student in a three-stage process:

1. The teacher introduces a strategy and directs the entire class through it.
2. The teacher has the students work through the strategy in small groups. In this stage, the teacher functions as a consultant.
3. The students learn to apply the strategy independently.

Second, the instructional blueprint provides for a sequence of classroom teaching strategies, beginning with single-text strategies and shifting to multiple-text strategies. Third, the instructional blueprint insures that the teacher will teach students various ways of discussing and writing about the text. The teaching goal implicit in the instructional blueprint is to change students from dependent to independent learners.

ACTIVITIES

1. Review the three stages of the phase-out/phase-in procedure. Develop three separate lesson plans that incorporate discussion, using topics from your own content area. The first discussion should be teacher directed, with the entire class participating. The second discussion should be planned for small groups of students, using topics generated by you. The third discussion should be planned for either the entire class or for small groups of students, where students generate their own topics for discussion.
2. Explain by example how, in May, you would teach technical vocabulary to students in your content area differently than you did in October. If you wish, use the form suggested for vocabulary guides in chapter 5.

11 | English

English is one of the most complex subjects in the curriculum. Not only does it integrate three intellectual disciplines — literature, linguistics, and rhetoric — but it also includes the basic communicative processes — reading, writing, speaking, and listening. This chapter will focus upon teaching students to learn from literature texts. The beginning sections of the chapter deal with the structure of the study of literature and the processes students use in responding to literary text. The bulk of the chapter, however, presents a series of single- and multiple-text strategies teachers can use to help their students learn from reading literature.

TECHNICAL VOCABULARY

literary criticism
schools of criticism
aesthetic criticism
literary genres
historical/biographical criticism
humanistic criticism
topics, themes
valuing in literature
alliteration
processes of literature
characterization

description
foreshadowing
discrimination
nonfiction
relation
rhyme
interpretation
symbol
generalization, in literature
evaluation of literature
creation in literature

THE LITERATURE CURRICULUM

You could argue that English is the most important subject in the curriculum because it includes instruction in basic communicative processes — reading, writing, speaking, and listening. Students use these skills in most of the other content fields. However, most English teachers will argue that their subject involves much more than preparing students for other content areas. They will point out that English has its own *content:* literature. Consequently, they will say, their curriculum consists of literature, language, and composition. Although some of these teachers may use three texts — a literature text, a language text, and a composition text — and achieve some degree of integration of these texts, English teachers spend the majority of their teaching time on literature. Therefore, this chapter will focus on how teachers can enable students to comprehend literature.

To gain a consensus on a definition of *literature* is difficult. Nineteenth-century critic Matthew Arnold referred to literature as the best that has been thought and said in the world. A high school student once defined it as "anything you read." We will define *literature* as "those writings of a country or from a period of time that are known for their beauty and universal appeal." G. Robert Carlsen (1967) attempted to bridge the two viewpoints by separating literature from what he termed *subliterature:* comic books, juvenile and adult romance, westerns, and other adventure yarns. Subliterature tends to use formula plots, stereotyped characters, and it tends to present a false picture of life. Although many teachers shun subliterature, other teachers use it in the classroom to motivate students to read serious literature. Regardless of definition, selection of literature for any program is the reflection of teacher taste, student need, instructional purpose, and school or district guidelines.

How Is the Study of Literature Organized?

Literary criticism, written by scholars who analyze and evaluate works of literature, has influenced the teaching of literature to generations of students. When critics agree about the salient aspects of literature, their views form ways of thinking, or *schools of criticism.*

Some critics in the school of *aesthetic criticism* see the greatness of a poem, for example, as emerging from the poet's skill at blending elements of meter, sound, imagery, and message. Aesthetic critics have influenced teachers to use the *literary genre,* or type, approach to teaching literature. Consequently, we find that units, courses, and minicourses in today's classrooms focus on genres such as the short story, the novel, poetry, and drama. The advantage to the students of studying literature by type is that they can learn more readily the form and style inherent in a genre. Frequently, the genre approach includes a collateral creative writing element, allowing students the opportunity to apply literary principles to their own writing.

Some critics stress authors' lives and times. These critics attempt to gain insight into literature by studying how an author's personality and environment affected his or her writing. Some critics, for example, have examined the impact of Edgar Allan Poe's personality on the content and quality of his writing. Other critics have focused on how history shaped the writing of given authors. They have examined the works of Mark Twain and Bret Harte, for example, as products of the Westward Movement. Their views form the school of *historical/biographical criticism* and have influenced teachers to use the historical approach to teaching literature. Consider high school courses you may have taken in American literature (Washington Irving to Ray Bradbury), British literature (*Beowulf* to Harold Pinter), or more recently, ethnic literature — black literature, native American literature, Mexican-American literature, Jewish-American literature and so forth. Your teachers tended to organize these courses historically or biographically. The advantage to students of studying literature historically and biographically is that they can view literature not only as art but also as a result of interacting social, economic, and political forces.

Critics in the school of *humanistic criticism* tend to stress the human values implicit in literature. They become concerned with how well women and men in literature meet the challenges of life. They believe that human beings should be portrayed as having the potential for nobility, greatness. These humanistic critics have influenced teachers to use topical or thematic approaches to teaching literature.

In a topical approach, literary selections of various types and from various historical periods are clustered in *topics: survival, courage, man and nature, self-fulfillment*. Thematic units, like topical units, cluster literary selections around ideas, rather than around genres or historical periods. Unlike topics, *themes* are propositional statements:

Topics	*Themes*
1. Survival	1. The survival of the human race depends upon its knowledge of scientific laws.
2. Courage	2. Courage is born from stubbornness.
3. Man and Nature	3. Man eventually loses his struggle against nature.
4. Self-fulfillment	4. Self-fulfillment is a by-product of hard work and frustration.

Themes are narrower than topics. The principal difficulty, and disadvantage, to topical and thematic teaching of literature, is the artificiality of "pigeon-holing" diverse selections and perhaps imposing relationships among selections that might not exist; we could classify *The Catcher in the Rye, Don Quixote,* and *The Diary of Anne Frank* under each of the above topics or themes, but the classification would not be appropriate. The principal advantage of a thematic and topical approach, and perhaps the reasons for its immense popularity, is that it deemphasizes traditional aesthetic and historical academic approaches in favor of issues and ideas.

In effect, an English teacher's mode of organization tends to reflect a set of values. It is hoped that the teacher will base these values upon reasonable assumptions about how students learn effectively.

What Are the Processes of Literature?

In addition to being aware of the various schools of literary criticism, teachers of literature are concerned about how students *respond* to literature. They sometimes refer to the modes of response that students use as the *processes of literature.* Charles Cooper and Alan Purves (1973) have isolated and defined eight such processes:

1. *Description:* The students can talk or write about what they read in their own words.
2. *Discrimination:* The students can discriminate among pieces of writing; for instance, they can identify them by type, author, or main ideas.
3. *Relation:* The students can relate several elements of a piece of literature to each other and to the entire piece.
4. *Interpretation:* The students can figure out what they think an author is saying and defend their interpretations.
5. *Generalization:* The students can apply what they have learned about one piece of literature to the reading of another selection.
6. *Evaluation:* The students can evaluate the worth of a piece of literature using specific criteria.
7. *Valuing:* The student can indicate the importance of literature to their own lives.
8. *Creation:* The students can respond to literature by creating an art-media project, a musical medley, original prose or poetry, pantomime or dance.

An effective teacher of literature will attempt to build classroom activities that will allow students to engage in as many of these processes as possible.

TEACHING STUDENTS TO LEARN FROM LITERATURE TEXT

In teaching students to understand literature, Mr. Inglish, the English teacher at Monroe High School, faced a wide range of individual student differences. Some of his students came to class never having read a book voluntarily in their entire lives. Other students were voracious readers. Under the headings below are descriptions of Mr. Inglish's classroom strategies designed for effective teaching of literature to mixed-ability classes. The activities are in a developmental sequence; that is, they are arranged in the order in which Mr. Inglish used them during a school year. Toward the beginning of the year he made heavier use of *Directed Reading Activities* (DRAs) and *glosses;* toward the end of the year he made heavier use of *inquiry* and the *project method.*

To present the strategies in a unified and coherent way, we shall demonstrate their use in a hypothetical topical unit, *Moments of Choice,* that Inglish devised. As the unit develops, Mr. Inglish moves through the progressing from single-text strategies — DRA, glossing, reading learning-from-text guides, and SQ3R — to multiple-text strategies concept, inquiry, and project methods. In this hypothetical unit, Mr. goes through the seven strategies in four to eight weeks. In reality, would take a school year to go through this sequence. Some of the strategies given in boxes will be glossed with literary terms you might want to teach directly or indirectly to your students.

Single-Text Strategies

It is probably wise to begin the school year by having all of the students read the same text assignment. First of all, it facilitates planning. Second, it provides an opportunity to observe individual differences in ability to read and learn from text.

DIRECTED READING ACTIVITY

In teaching students to comprehend literature, you will want, at first, to provide them with much guidance. Before they read a selection, you will want to *prepare* them for what they are about to read. This involves (1) exploring their background to see what personal experiences they are approaching the selection with and (2) building any background you feel they will need to comprehend the selection. While the students are reading, you may want to guide them with preposed questions. After the students read, you will want to engage the students in discussion and other follow-up activities that will *extend* their understanding of the literature.

In box 11.1 is a DRA lesson on Nelson Algren's fast-moving story "He Swung and He Missed" (1965). If you were teaching the unit *Moments of Choice,* you might want to make "He Swung and He Missed" one of the opening selections, just as Mr. Inglish did. As you read through the lesson, try to imagine yourself teaching these activities to a high school English class.

BOX 11.1. Unit: Moments of Choice (DRA)

"HE SWUNG AND HE MISSED"

by Nelson Algren

Synopsis: Rocco grew up the hard way, by fighting. Unfortunately, he was never a winner. When offered money to throw a fight he refused, lost the fight anyway, but found himself.

I. Mr. Inglish explores his students' background.
  A. Mr. Inglish asks the students if they have read the books *Rocky* or *Sylvester Stallone's Official Rocky Scrapbook,* and if so, what they liked about the books. Other questions might be:
    1. What was there about Rocky, the man, that you particularly liked or disliked?
    2. Was Rocky a winner or a loser?
  B. Mr. Inglish asks students to place items 1–6 on a values continuum:
    1. Watching prize fighting on TV
    2. Watching boxing in person
    3. Watching movies about boxing
    4. Collecting autographs of boxers
    5. Boxing
    6. Teaching boxing

Values Continuum

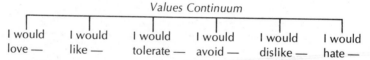

| I would love — | I would like — | I would tolerate — | I would avoid — | I would dislike — | I would hate — |

II. Mr. Inglish builds students' background.
  A. Mr. Inglish explains difficult words from "He Swung and He Missed":
    1. nurtured
    2. languidly
    3. impassive
    4. feinted
    5. decapitated
  B. Mr. Inglish reviews boxing jargon used in "He Swung and He Missed":
    1. catch weight
    2. purse
    3. middleweights
    4. light-heavies
    5. took a dive
    6. set up
    7. soft touch
    8. comer
    9. duke
    10. put down for ten
  C. Mr. Inglish gives the students a few preposed questions to guide their reading:
    1. What sort of person is Rocco?
    2. What important decision does he make?
    3. Would you want Rocco as a friend?

III. The students read the selection in class or for homework.

IV. Mr. Inglish has the students discuss the selection:
   A. Informational, or Directly-Stated, Level
       1. How did Rocco's earlier matches turn out?
       2. What people did Rocco particularly like?
       3. Before his "moment of choice" what deal did he make?
       4. After he married, what was his career like?
       5. Did he live up to his bargain?
       6. What was the surprise ending?
   B. Inferential Level
       1. What do you learn about Rocco's character from the following lines?
          a. "Friends came, friends left, money came in, was lost, was saved. . . ."
          b. "He gave Lili every dime of that [prize] money."
          c. "He'd end like he started, as a fighting man."
          d. "Miss Donahue would have been proud."

               Making inferences about characterization through dialogue

       2. In what ways had Algren prepared you, the reader, to accept Rocco's quick switch in the ring?

               → (1) Foreshadowing
                   (2) Motivation

   C. Generalized Level
       1. Does Rocco fit a stereotyped image of prize fighters? Explain.
       2. We are all "tested" sometime during our lives, usually by having to make crucial decisions. How was Rocco tested? Did he "pass the test"? Explain.
V. Mr. Inglish has the students participate in activities that extend their understanding of "He Swung and He Missed."
   A. Dramatics
       1. Suppose Rocco had won the fight. Reenact the final scene between Rocco and Lili.
       2. Enact a spontaneous scene in which Rocco is being interviewed by a well-known sports writer prior to the fight. In the dialogue make use of prize-fight jargon.
   B. Writing
       1. Describe a tense moment during an athletic event. Create tension by using powerful verbs that denote action.
       2. Rewrite from memory the fight between Rocco and Kid Class. Compare your version with the original.
       3. Describe a situation which "tested" you because you had to make an important decision. Why did you make the decision you did?

"He Swung and He Missed" first appeared in Algren's collection, *Neon Wilderness* (New York: Hill & Wang, 1960). It has been widely anthologized, and appears in Robert C. Pooley et al., eds., *Accent USA* (New York: Scott, Foresman and Company, 1965). Both Julia Sorel's *Rocky* (1977) and *Sylvester Stallone's Official Rocky Scrapbook* (also 1977) are available in paperback, *Rocky* from Ballantine and the *Scrapbook* from Ace Books.

GLOSS

In addition to using the Directed Reading Activity, you might also gloss several reading selections to help your students learn to understand literature. The process of *glossing,* you remember, includes providing *marginal aids* to comprehension, such as defining difficult words, clarifying difficult concepts, asking thought questions. Glossing poetry is often necessary because the intensity of meaning contained in terse and concise language can make comprehension of poetry very difficult. Fortunately, poems tend to be short and therefore require little time to gloss. When students have poems or other difficult materials to read as homework assignments, the gloss becomes the "guardian angel," the "teacher" away from school. To determine what you want to gloss, ask yourself what questions students might have to ask you as they read at home or quietly in your classroom; answer those questions with the gloss.

In box 11.2 is Mr. Inglish's gloss of a fairly difficult poem "We Wear the Mask," by Paul Laurence Dunbar. Read through the poem and see if the gloss helps you understand its meaning:

BOX 11.2. Moments of Choice (Gloss)

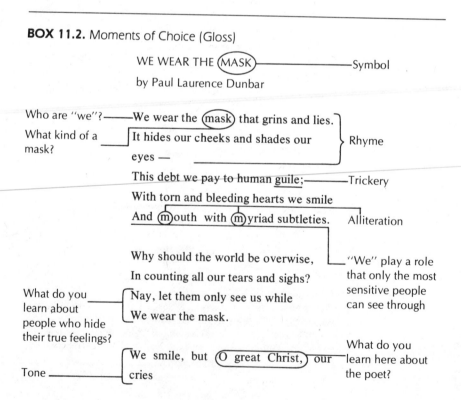

To thee from tortured souls arise.

We sing, but oh, the clay is <u>vile</u>————Most unpleasant

Beneath our feet, and long the mile: ⌐How does the

But let the world dream otherwise,——⌐ outside world

Is this by choice?——<u>We wear the mask.</u> treat the mask-
wearers?

The poet is black. Does that change the meaning of the poem? Could "we" be of any color?

"We Wear the Mask" reprinted by permission of Dodd, Mead and Company, Inc. from *The Complete Poems of Paul Laurence Dunbar.*

READING AND LEARNING-FROM-TEXT GUIDES

The strategies used thus far (DRA and glossing) progress from teacher dependence toward student independence. The next step in this progression is the use of reading and learning-from-text guides. We shall see how these guides apply to teaching a novel.

Fahrenheit 451, by Ray Bradbury, a novel that Mr. Inglish taught in the unit *Moments of Choice,* contains difficult language and difficult concepts. Even some independent readers have problems interpreting what Bradbury is trying to say. To deal with the difficult language, you might want to prepare a processes-of-reading guide. In box 11.3 is a processes of reading guide for *Fahrenheit 451.*

BOX 11.3. Processes of Reading Guide

FAHRENHEIT 451

by Ray Bradbury

MAKING INFERENCES ABOUT CHARACTER

Instructions: It is human nature to make judgments about other people on the basis of what these people say and do. If you see a small child lying on the floor of a supermarket crying and kicking, you might conclude that the child is *spoiled.* If you see a young woman pick up a package that an elderly man has dropped, you assume that this woman is *thoughtful.* These judgments that you make about people's character are called *inferences.* Generally, people reveal their character through what they say and through what they do.

Activity I. Below are statements that people have made. What inferences about their character can you make?

A. Young man, don't you dare talk to me like that again!

B. If I were you, I'd wear something a little nicer and more expensive looking.

C. Now, as your best friend, I think you should know that people are talking about you behind your back.

Activity II. Below are descriptions of what people have done. What inferences about their character can you make?

A. A fourth-grader sticks his tongue out at his teacher when the teacher's back is turned.

B. An elderly woman fills her purse with food she hasn't eaten at a restaurant.

C. A man fixing a clock seizes the clock and throws it against the wall.

Activity III. The book you are about to read, *Fahrenheit 451,* contains interesting and complicated characters. It is important for you to know how to make inferences about their character by judging what they say and do. Below are statements by and about characters from *Fahrenheit 451.* Even though you haven't started to read the book, see if you can make inferences about the characters:

A. Clarisse

   1. "I like to watch people. Sometimes I ride the subway all day and look at them and listen to them."
   2. Clarisse attends amusement parks and likes to ride in the jet cars.
   3. Clarisse eavesdrops on conversations in soda fountains.

B. Beatty

   1. "You must understand that our civilization is so vast that we can't have our minorities upset and stirred."
   2. "That's what we live for, isn't it? For pleasure, for titillation?"
   3. Beatty believes that books should be burned in order to keep people happy with life.

C. Montag

   1. "You ever seen a burned house? It smolders for days. Well, this fire'll last me the rest of my life."
   2. Though a fireman, Montag doesn't like the idea of burning books.

Passages quoted in this box are taken from Ray Bradbury, *Fahrenheit 451* (New York: Ballantine, 1953).

SQ3R

The purpose of sequencing DRA, glosses, and reading and learning-from-text guides is to change the students from dependent learners to independent learners. SQ3R is another step towards the goal of student independence in learning. It teaches by having students formulate and find answers to their own questions. SQ3R is not an effective technique for reading fiction. It works much better for nonfiction essays or articles.

In box 11.4 is Mr. Inglish's lesson on the essay ''Sport's Worst Tragedy,'' by Joseph P. Blank, an illustration of how to teach students the SQ3R technique.

BOX 11.4. Unit: Moments of Choice (SQ3R)

''SPORT'S WORST TRAGEDY''

by Joseph P. Blank ────────────────────────────────→ nonfiction

Synopsis: This essay is a terrifying account of a riot during a soccer match in Lima, Peru. The essay shows how people react in the face of panic.

I. Mr. Inglish has the students *survey* the essay by asking questions like these:
   a. When you see the title ''Sport's Worst Tragedy,'' what do you think about? In other words, what sort of tragedy might it be?
   b. Read the first paragraph of the essay. Notice that Maria Rodriguez wonders how it was possible for her son to be killed at a *futbol* game. Examine these passages:
      1. ''The crowd carried me halfway down the tunnel without my feet touching the concrete floor.''
      2. ''My wife and five children are dead. All dead! My God!''
      3. ''Only spectators like St. Dongo in the North section witnessed the horror that seethed in the stands and erupted in the tunnels.''

II. Mr. Inglish has the students ask themselves *questions* they want to find answers for. These questions could emerge from their survey of the essay:
   a. What caused the crowd to react in horror, to seethe?
   b. Did eyewitnesses shed any light on how the tragedy occurred?
   c. What caused people to be killed during a *futbol* game?
   d. Could this sort of tragedy happen in the United States today?

III. Mr. Inglish instructs the students to *read* the essay to find answers to their questions. (If the teacher wishes, students can write the answers to the questions when they finish reading.)

IV. Mr. Inglish then has the students *recite* their answers to questions in a variety of ways. Students can submit written answers or share differing questions and answers with classmates in total class or small group discussion.

V. The students might engage in ''review-by-doing'' projects such as these:
   a. Doing outside reading in popular psychology magazines on the subject of mass hysteria and crowd behavior.
   b. Researching another disaster involving group panic: the *Hindenburg* explosion, the sinking of the *Andrea Doria*.
   c. Rereading the essay to come up with further insights.

Passages quoted in this box are from Joseph P. Blank, ''Sport's Worst Tragedy,'' *Kiwanis Magazine* 30:3 (March 1965), pp. 34–36, 45–47. This article is reprinted in its entirety in Jay Cline, Ken Williams, and Dan Donlan, eds., *Voices in Literature, Language, and Composition 2* (Boston: Ginn and Company, 1969).

Multiple-Text Strategies

So far, you have been teaching your students to comprehend literature independently. For this purpose, you have used DRA, glosses, guides, and SQ3R in *single-text situations*. Now you are ready to have your students try out multiple-text situations. We will explain and apply three multiple-text strategies: the concept method, inquiry, and the project method.

CONCEPT TECHNIQUE

Despite continuing attention to training independent learners, you may still find wide differences in your students' ability to learn from text on their own. You want to use a strategy that will allow students to read and learn from texts that are appropriate to their abilities, but you do not want to stigmatize any student. You also want your students to read texts on the same topic or theme so that they can all engage in a class discussion and enrich their understanding by learning from each other. One of the best ways to provide for individual differences without stigmatizing students is to have the students self-select what they will read and, more or less, group themselves. You might, for instance, choose five or so reading selections that vary in difficulty, introduce the selections to the class as a whole, and permit the students to make the choices (Ryan, 1963). This technique should be introduced with short selections and later followed with longer ones. Accordingly, we will describe two of Mr. Inglish's self-selection activities in box 11.5, one for short stories, the other for novels.

BOX 11.5. Unit: Moments of Choice
(Concept Technique)

SHORT STORIES

Mr. Inglish: So far the entire class has been reading the same literature. Now you are going to select one particular story from a group of five that deal with the unit's theme *Moments of Choice*. Before you decide which story you want to read, you will probably want to have a "teaser" on each story. Textbook page references are on the blackboard. Copy them down for your handout in case you want to glance through the story before making your choice. You will receive a handout that lists the story "teasers." Later, a sign-up sheet will be passed around; indicate your choice of story on this sheet by signing your name in the appropriate section. You will later participate in a group of students who chose the story you selected. Your group will discuss and plan a presentation for the rest of the class.

Handout: Story "Teasers"

1. "Flowers for Algernon," by Daniel Keyes: Is it possible for a mentally retarded adult suddenly to become a genius? Do scientists have the right to decide whom they will experiment upon? Charly, a retarded adult, and Algernon, a rat, share common experiences.
2. "An Occurrence at Owl Creek Bridge," by Ambrose Bierce: A man is about to be executed. He suddenly discovers he has an opportunity to escape. What should he do? What will be the consequences of his decision?
3. "The Most Dangerous Game," by Richard Connell: Rainsford finds himself staying in the luxurious home of a strange retired army officer. Suddenly, the comfortable experience becomes a nightmare and Rainsford finds he has to choose a method of survival.
4. "Four Eyes," by Joseph Petracca: Joseph Esposito finds out he can't read the blackboard at school. His teacher wants him to get glasses, but Joey's father won't allow it. Some hysterically funny situations arise as Joey finds himself caught in the middle.
5. "Beauty Is Truth," by Anna Guest: Jeanie is told by her creative writing teacher to write about real-life experiences. Poignantly, she describes her life in Harlem. Her classmates find it a memorable experience.

Sign-Up Sheet

Instructions: After you have selected one of the five stories, sign your name under its title below. You and other classmates who select the story will (1) discuss the story in small groups; the discussion will be on answers to questions your group has proposed; (2) plan a discussion, debate, dramatization, or media presentation; and (3) present your project to the rest of the class.

1. "Flowers for Algernon"
   a. _____
   b. _____
   c. _____
   d. _____
   e. _____
   f. _____
2. "An Occurrence at Owl Creek Bridge"
   a. _____
   b. _____
   c. _____
   d. _____
   e. _____
   f. _____
3. "The Most Dangerous Game"
   a. _____
   b. _____
   c. _____
   d. _____
   e. _____
   f. _____

4. "Four Eyes"
   a. _____
   b. _____
   c. _____
   d. _____
   e. _____
   f. _____
5. "Beauty Is Truth"
   a. _____
   b. _____
   c. _____
   d. _____
   e. _____
   f. _____

NOVELS

Mr. Inglish: Now that you have had experience working in small group projects on a fairly short-term basis, you are now about to embark on small group projects that may take three or four weeks to complete. Although you will have class time for the project, you will have to do most of this work on your own time. Some groups may find they will have to meet outside of class after school or on weekends to complete the work. For this project, you will select a novel from a group of five that deal with the unit's theme *Moments of Choice.* As I did before, I will give you a handout that provides an overview of each of the five novels. Later, you will sign up for a particular novel and be responsible for a series of group activities related to it.

Handout: Novel Overviews

1. *Dinky Hocker Shoots Smack,* by M. E. Kerr. Dinky is not a narcotics addict. She is, however, overweight — and self-conscious about it. Unhappy, she decides to take revenge on the world.
2. *The Catcher in the Rye,* by J. D. Salinger. Holden Caulfield decides to quit school and have a fling in New York City. He learns a lot about himself, almost too late.
3. *A Separate Peace,* by John Knowles. Gene and Finny are close friends; nevertheless Gene feels a sense of rivalry, an uneasiness about their friendship. Perhaps unconsciously, he triggers an unfortunate chain of events that bring near tragedy to himself.
4. *Native Son,* by Richard Wright. The setting is Chicago during the depression of the 1930s. Bigger Thomas, a black chauffeur for a wealthy white family, is confused by the contradictions in the white world that he feels shapes his life. He strikes out, with tragic consequences.
5. *Cress Delahanty,* by Jessamyn West. A teenage girl discovers the excitement of life, growing up in Orange County, California, as it was twenty-five years ago. Her family doesn't always approve of her antics, but you will find many of the book's situations funny, enjoyable.

Sign-up Sheet: Novels
1. *Dinky Hocker Shoots Smack*
   a. _____
   b. _____
   c. _____
   d. _____
   e. _____
   f. _____
2. *The Catcher in the Rye*
   a. _____
   b. _____
   c. _____
   d. _____
   e. _____
   f. _____
3. *A Separate Peace*
   a. _____
   b. _____
   c. _____
   d. _____
   e. _____
   f. _____
4. *Native Son*
   a. _____
   b. _____
   c. _____
   d. _____
   e. _____
   f. _____
5. *Cress Delahanty*
   a. _____
   b. _____
   c. _____
   d. _____
   e. _____
   f. _____

Group Instructions
1. Meet in class in small groups to survey the novel and pose questions to which you want answers. Allow one week to complete the book. (You will have some class time each day for reading.) Plan to devote three half-hour meetings to organize the oral presentation based on your reading of the novel; these three meetings will be during class time. The remainder of the meeting time will be on your own time.
2. Decide the form your class presentation will take: symposium, panel discussion, debate, role-playing, improvisational dramatics, media.

3. Assign individual responsibilities with specific deadlines for task completion. Some deadlines could coincide with each of your three scheduled meetings.
4. In planning your group project, try to deal with these questions:
    a. How does your novel relate to the unit topic *Moments of Choice?* }————Theme
    b. How is your novel like or unlike other selections read in this unit?
    c. Keep logs of your feelings and reactions to your novel. The entries in your log may provide you with ideas for the group project: How was I affected by the book?

The short stories discussed in this box are widely anthologized. Many of them can be found in the series, *Voices in Literature, Language, and Composition* (Boston: Ginn and Company, 1969). The Keyes and Bierce stories can be found in volume 4, edited by Jay Cline, Ken Williams, Barbara Mahoney, and Kay Dzuik. The Petracca story appears in volume 1, edited by Jay Cline, Ken Williams, and Dan Donlan. The Guest story appears in volume 3, edited by Jay Cline and Ken Williams. Richard Connell's story can be found in *Adventures in American Literature,* edited by Rawley Bell Inglis, et al. (New York: Harcourt Brace and World, 1953). All of the novels discussed are available in inexpensive paperback editions: *Dinky Hocker Shoots Smack* (first published in 1972) from Dell, *The Catcher in the Rye* (1951) and *A Separate Peace* (1960) from Bantam, *Native Son* (1940) from Harper & Row, and *Cress Delahanty* (1954) from Avon.

INQUIRY

Inquiry, unlike expository teaching, engages the students actively in problem-solving (Clark and Starr, 1976, pp. 224–225). Recognition of a problem occurs after a certain amount of exploration. Students define the problem, state a hypothesis, test the hypothesis, and come to some sort of conclusion. Inquiry is more commonly used in social studies and science, but we can adapt it to the study of literature.

In the unit *Moments of Choice,* students have read literature selections where characters have had to make important decisions. What isn't always clear is the *why* or the *what* of the decisions. In this particular lesson (box 11.6), Mr. Inglish uses Kohlberg's (1968) stages in moral reasoning from which to draw hypotheses and asks students to determine whether these hypotheses explain why characters in the literature selections made the decisions they did. The teacher (1) reviews the problem posed in the literature selections the students have read; (2) introduces the Kohlberg stages; (3) tests the stages by having the students collect data from the literature selections; (4) has the students form an hypothesis about a character's level of moral reasoning; and (5) has the students test the hypothesis with more examples from the character's moral reasoning. In addition, students can interview people they know and test their levels of moral reasoning. Such an activity is appropriate as a culmination to a unit on decision-making.

BOX 11.6. Unit: Moments of Choice
(Inquiry)

Mr. Inglish: The characters in the literature we have been reading so far in this unit have all been tested; that is, they have
had to make important choices. It has been hard to determine specifically what made them choose as they did; their ⎤——— Motivation
reasons are not always clear. ⎦

Lawrence Kohlberg, a psychologist, believes that people make important
moral decisions for a variety of reasons: (1) they act out of fear of punishment, or
out of anticipation of reward; (2) they act to help someone with the idea that they
will be helped in return; (3) they want to be known as "good boys" or "nice
girls"; (4) they act out of a respect for law and order; (5) they act out of respect
for their fellow human beings; (6) they act out of a noble and high sense of what
is right. Kohlberg claims that these six reasons are levels or stages that people
move through as they get older. For instance, a small child would tend to act
more out of fear of punishment than out of respect for fellow human beings.
Imagine a five-year-old boy who decides not to pull his sister's hair because he
suddenly discovers his mother watching, not because such a physical assault will
hurt his sister. An adult, on the other hand, would tend to act out of respect for
fellow human beings rather than out of fear of punishment: one would hope that
a husband brings his wife candy and flowers to make her happy, not to atone for
staying out late the night before.

We are going to examine the leading characters of the literature we've been
reading in this unit to see if there is a correlation between age and level of moral
choice.

*(At this point the teacher takes the class through filling out the data collection
sheet in table 1.)*

Mr. Inglish: We've now documented the age (or approximate age) of each of the
leading characters of the literature we've read in this unit. We also have the levels
of moral choice they were operating from. Now can we hypothesize that there is
a correlation between the age of the person and a higher level of moral choice
being used?

*(Suggestion: Arrange the characters chronologically by age, from young to
old. Next to their names list their ages and levels of choice. Divide the list in half
at the middle. You now have two populations: younger and older. Determine the
average level of choice with the younger group and compare it with that of the
older group. If the score is higher in the older group, then the hypothesis is
correct. If the score is lower in the older group then the hypothesis is incorrect.)*

Mr. Inglish: We began with the idea that as people get older the reasons for making
moral choices tend to be on a higher level. Now the result of our examination of
literature shows some older people are more able to reason at higher moral levels
than younger people, but the evidence isn't conclusive. On the basis of this, do
we wish to form a new hypothesis? If so what would it be? *(Writes on blackboard:
New Hypothesis:_____.)* Now, how would we go about testing this hypothesis?

(Suggestions: (1) Students could compile a revised data chart based on the

TABLE 1. Data Sheet

Selection	Character	Age	Docu-mentation (page)	Moment of choice (describe)	Docu-mentation (page)	Choice (describe)	Level of choice: 1,2,3,4,5,6 (explain)
"He Swung and He Missed"	Rocco						
"We Wear the Mask"	(unnamed)						
"Fahrenheit 451"	Montag						
"Sport's Worst Tragedy"	any character						
"Flowers for Algernon"	Dr.Strauss						
"An Occurrence at Owl Creek Bridge"	Peyton Farquahr						
"The Most Dangerous Game"	Rainsford						
"Four Eyes"	Joseph						
"Beauty Is Truth"	Jeanie						
Dinky Hocker Shoots Smack	Dinky						
The Cat-cher in the Rye	Holden						
A Separate Peace	Gene						
Native Son	Bigger						
Cress Delahanty	Cress						

new hypothesis and examine five or ten additional selections of literature, filling in the sheets as they go. Perhaps the selections could be ones read prior to the unit. (2) Students could compose a moral dilemma with six possible solutions. They could then field-test the situation by asking 25 or 30 people of various ages to select one of the choices. Students could then correlate the level of choice with the age of the respondent.)

Suggested Moral Dilemma

You are a member of a poor family. Your mother has a high fever and may die if she doesn't get more of a drug prescribed by the family doctor. It is two in the morning. The drug stores are closed and the doctor cannot be reached. No one can help. The corner drugstore contains the needed drug and you know exactly where it's kept. Would you break into the drugstore to get the medicine? Why? Why not?

Suggested Data Collection Sheet

	Respondent	Decision	Reason for Decision	Implied Level of Decision
(Ages 10–12)	1.			
	2.			
	3.			
	4.			
	5.			
(Ages 12–15)	1.			
	2.			
	3.			
	4.			
	5.			
(Ages 16–18)	1.			
	2.			
	3.			
	4.			
	5.			
(Ages 19–25)	1.			
	2.			
	3.			
	4.			
	5.			
(Ages 26–40)	1.			
	2.			
	3.			
	4.			
	5.			

PROJECT METHOD

Once students have learned inquiry techniques they are ready to branch out into more independent learning. The project method stimulates students to perform independent reading to answer a question or solve a problem. Box 11.7 has a project activity, drawn from the unit *Moments of Choice*, which shows how students can actively engage in reading to find answers to questions and solve a teacher-posed problem.

BOX 11.7. Unit: Moments of Choice
(Project Method)

Background: Assume that you are the chairperson of a board of directors of a major manufacturing company. The president of the corporation has just died of a sudden heart attack. The board has decided to hire *outside* the firm. Five finalists have been selected for the position:

Holden, from *The Catcher in the Rye*
Joseph, from "Four Eyes"
Miss Kinnian, from "Flowers for Algernon"
Montag, from *Fahrenheit 451*
Jeanie, from "Beauty Is Truth"

Your Assignment: Select a new president for your corporation.

Assume:
1. All five candidates are 35 years of age.
2. All five candidates have had successful corporate training and experience.
3. You are bound by fair decision-making procedures, including the consideration of Affirmative Action guidelines — that is, equal treatment to women and members of ethnic minorities.

Your president must have:
1. High intelligence
2. Adaptability
3. Rationality when acting under pressure
4. Ability to make competent decisions

You must:
1. Compose a series of questions you would ask in an interview to all five characters above.
2. Compose an imaginary interview with each of the five, indicating how each would respond to your questions. Be sure the characters act consistently with the way they act in the literature you have read about them.
3. On the basis of the interviews and your job criteria, make a choice of a president and defend it.

SUMMARY

Although English integrates the studies of language composition and literature, this chapter focused only on literature. Teachers organize the content of literature by literary type, literary period, or literary theme. The processes of comprehending literature are both cognitive (interpreting, evaluating) and affective (valuing, creating). In illustrating how students learn from literary text, we selected a topical unit — *Moments of Choice* — around which we built single-text strategies (DRA, glosses, reading and learning-from-text guides, and SQ3R) and multiple-text strategies (concept technique, inquiry, and project method). In the next two chapters, you will see how these seven strategies apply to social studies and science. Since students in literature classes read much nonfiction and technical writing, English teachers might want to read chapters 12 and 13.

ACTIVITIES

1. Using the DRA lesson in this chapter as a model, construct a directed reading activity for a short story that might be added to the unit *Moments of Choice*. Teach the lesson to a small group of English students or to an entire class. List the ways in which you perceive the lesson helps the students.
2. Would SQ3R work if you were teaching students to comprehend detective stories? Give reasons for your answer.
3. Select a poem that you feel would be hard for students to comprehend, and gloss it. To determine the effectiveness of the gloss, have two groups of students read the poem, but only one group use the gloss. Then administer a brief comprehension test for both groups and compare the results.

12 Social Studies

CHAPTER OVERVIEW

Like English, social studies is an integrated subject. The individual academic disciplines comprising social studies range from history, which can be considered part of the humanities, to psychology, which is a behavioral science. Two conflicting theories on teaching social studies maintain that the content should be taught (1) in integrated fashion, using the "problem" approach, or (2) as a series of discrete academic disciplines. Both theories may be operating even within the same high school department. This disparity of approach, combined with the incredible range of textual materials used in social studies classes, makes teaching the subject a challenge. By reading this chapter, you will get a clearer understanding of how the subject social studies is organized. In addition, you will learn various single-text and multiple-text strategies that will help you to teach your students to become independent learners in the social studies.

TECHNICAL VOCABULARY

academic discipline

issue

fact

concept

generalization, in social studies

hypothesizing from data

theory

valuing in social studies

A social studies student is sitting in a classroom, listening to a discussion of the "Teapot Dome scandal." The day has been long, and he is tired. Looking out the window he notices that the steel plant a block away is belching smoke. He has thought about the benefits of having many factories in his home town — he is the son of a foundry worker — but the disadvantages of heavy industry are obvious to him, too. He begins asking himself questions about industry's relationship to the environment, its use of human and natural resources, and its demands on society for governmental services. It occurs to him that he isn't sure how much and what kinds of industry are good for society.[1]

Shive dramatizes, in the above passage, the natural curiosity young people have concerning social problems. Occasionally, curiosity leads to taking sides, and arguments highlight the complexity of the problems. Social studies is that area of the curriculum where students are taught to deal with complex social problems. According to Kenworthy, social studies "is wide as the world and as long as the history of man, yet it can be defined with one word. That word is *people*." [2] And since, to paraphrase the words of poet Alexander Pope, the proper study of people is people, what other area of the curriculum deals more directly with the reality of life!

WHAT IS SOCIAL STUDIES?

To answer the question "What is social studies?" you must determine, first, the content of the social studies curriculum and, second, the processes students use to deal with the content.

Social Studies as Content

Ehman, Mehlinger, and Patrick (1974) have compiled data that dramatize the lack of consensus regarding the nature of social studies content. They interviewed students who saw social studies as the study of revolutions, wars, and depressions, and felt the focus should be on issues. Kenworthy (1973) notes that teachers often disagree on the content of social studies. On one end of the continuum, he suggests, is the teacher who isolates history from geography, teaching them as separate disciplines. On the other end of the continuum is the teacher who believes "that anything which helps children to become wholesome, worthwhile, contributing

---

[1] Jerrald R. Shive, *Social Studies as Controversy*. Pacific Palisades, California: Goodyear, 1973, p. xi.

[2] Leonard S. Kenworthy, *Social Studies for the Seventies*. Lexington, Mass.: Xerox Publishing Company, 1973, p. 5.

members of various groups is a part of the social studies." [3] Ehman and others (1974) quote six leading authorities on social studies education, each with varying definitions of content.

Social Studies and Academic Disciplines

Social studies encompasses many *academic disciplines*. Fraenkel (1973), for instance, includes under social studies history and social science disciplines — anthropology, geography, economics, political science, psychology, and sociology.

HISTORY

According to Clark, history is the study of facts seen through the eyes of a historian, a "humanistic study of things past." [4] Since, as Wesley and Wronski point out, the past cannot be observed directly, the historian relies upon "those observations, clues, or traces that are left behind." [5] These historical sources include *records* and *remains*. Clark includes, under *records*, three types of tradition — written, oral, and pictorial. Written tradition includes documents and reports. Oral traditions are in national and local legends and folk tales. Pictorial traditions are in maps, diagrams, sculptures, and pictures. Unlike records, which purposively are intentional, *remains* such as artifacts and relics tend to be, in Clark's words, "accidental survivals of the past." [6] By critically examining these sources, the historian can reconstruct the story of human life.

Fraenkel (1973) suggests that the teaching of history can be organized according to generalizations, or major ideas. One such idea is: *Historical events can rarely, if ever, be explained in terms of a single cause.* Using this idea, the teacher trains students to examine historical text as a complex framework of cause and effect. Wesley and Wronski (1973) suggest another major idea: *The past can help us to deal with the present and the future.* Using this idea, the teacher trains students to examine historical text as a data source to solve present problems. Crucial to this approach is student skill at comparison and contrast. For instance, to determine whether Washington's advice to stay out of entangling alliances would work today, students would need to compare the social, economic, and political situation today with that in eighteenth-century America.

---

[3] Kenworthy, p. 3.

[4] Leonard H. Clark, *Teaching Social Studies in the Secondary Schools: A Handbook.* New York: Macmillan, 1973, p. 177.

[5] Edgar B. Wesley and Stanley P. Wronski, *Teaching Secondary Social Studies in a World Society.* Lexington, Mass.: D. C. Heath, 1973, p. 153.

[6] Clark, p. 178.

ANTHROPOLOGY

"Anthropology has one foot in the field of science and the other in the domain of the social sciences." [7] As a science, anthropology focuses on the physical features of human beings. As a social science, anthropology is concerned with culture, that is, how societies live. Anthropologists gather data from fieldwork, personal observation, surveys, censuses, and psychological tests. Experts in social studies (Clark, 1973; Fraenkel, 1973) agree that anthropology deals with certain major ideas, such as *man has needs; man's needs are satisfied within a social structure; the social structure itself has needs which must be satisfied if it is to persist.*

GEOGRAPHY

Like anthropology, geography is not exclusively a social science. Clark (1973) notes that geography contains elements from natural and biological science as well as from social science. Geography is concerned with *spatial relationships*. Fraenkel lists certain major ideas shaping the teaching of geography, such as: "The similarities among different areas have been brought about through different combinations of physical, biotic, and societal forces" and "Uniform and modal regions are often related to each other through gravitation to the same central place." [8] Wesley and Wronski (1973) stress two major concepts in teaching geography — *accessibility* (how easy it is to get from one place to another) and *centrality* (how far away in terms of time and distance one place is from another). Village A may be only three miles away from village B (centrality) but a treacherous river and an impassable mountain separate the two (accessibility).

For students to understand geography, they must be able to read maps, charts, and graphs. Environmental issues related to geography demand that students engage in critical thinking so they can answer questions such as these:

1. How is population related to the standard of living?
2. Should governments exercise population control?
3. How does overcrowding affect the personality of individuals?
4. What relation exists between population pressures and war? [9]

[7] Kenworthy, p. 20.
[8] Jack R. Fraenkel, *Helping Students Think and Value*. Englewood Cliffs, N.J.: Prentice-Hall, 1973, p. 117.
[9] Wesley and Wronski, p. 188.

FIGURE 12.1. A Circular Flow Model of the American Economy

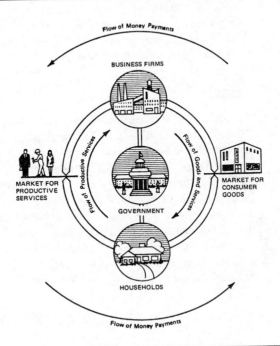

ECONOMICS

Economics is the study of "the ways in which we manage our productive human and natural resources and the goods that result from the employment and use of those resources.[10] Basically, economics is concerned with supply and demand, or,

1. What shall we produce with our limited resources?
2. How much can we produce and how fast can our economy grow?
3. Who shall get the goods and services produced?[11]

Wesley and Wronski (1973) claim that the economist's tools are statistical data, models, and logic. *Statistics* comprises much of the raw data that students deal with. Students must understand and interpret the data. Pictorial and diagrammatic *models* can sometimes explain complicated economic concepts. In figure 12.1 is one such model.

[10] Clark, p. 229.
[11] Kenworthy, p. 22.

Since most students have limited backgrounds in economics, they may often engage in fallacious thinking: One such fallacy "leads many to look upon government fiscal operations as being subject to the same conditions that govern finance."[12] For example, we have the fallacious statement that "if the federal government spends more than it takes in, it will go bankrupt."

POLITICAL SCIENCE

According to Wesley and Wronski, political science is concerned with "the institutionalized and informal patterns of power functions in the polity and the behavior of people with respect to these formal and informal patterns."[13] Political science consists of nine fundamental ideas: e.g., "As the people's wants enter the political system for satisfaction, they become demands. These demands are screened."[14] Clark (1973) maintains that students of political science need to learn (1) how to gather data, (2) how to use political science and methods, and (3) to think critically about political issues. Students of political science gather data from a continuum of sources, from civic documents to novels that deal with political behavior (Wesley and Wronski, 1973).

PSYCHOLOGY AND SOCIOLOGY CONTRASTED

Psychology and sociology are alike in the sense that they both focus on human behavior. Whereas psychology is concerned with the behavior of individuals *per se,* sociology stresses behavior of individuals as members of groups. Wesley and Wronski (1973), admitting that psychology is a relatively new subject in secondary school curriculum, describe several lessons where students deal with psychology content to analyze the nature of *rebellion.* Students begin by reading a technical article that attempts to relate adolescent behavior to social pressure. Students examine two case studies of adolescents and then have to decide, using information in the article, which of the two students is more likely to rebel against the system.

Sociology, like psychology, can deal with problems of great concern to adolescents, especially when you consider how important belonging to groups is to most teenagers. Fraenkel (1973) maintains that sociology deals with three major ideas:

1. Values and norms are the main sources of energy to individuals and society.

[12] Wesley and Wronski, p. 222.
[13] Wesley and Wronski, p. 197.
[14] Fraenkel, p. 112.

2. Society's values and norms shape social institutions, which are embodied in organizations and groups, where people occupy positions and roles.
3. People's positions and roles affect their attitudes toward society's values and norms, and result either in support of the existing values and norms, or in demands for modification of them, and the circle starts again.

Students of sociology study or originate questionnaires, interviews, cases, and experiments in addition to performing logical analysis, historical analysis, and content analysis (Clark, 1973).

Relationships Among the Social Studies

In figure 12.2 is a simple diagram that presents the content of the social studies curriculum. It shows that social studies comprise three areas: humanities, physical science, and social science. Each of these areas has its own subfields. Humanities subsumes history. The physical sciences and social studies overlap in geography and anthropology. The social sciences subsumes economics, political science, psychology and sociology.

Social Studies and Issues

Whereas some teachers believe that they should teach the individual academic disciplines of social studies separately, many other teachers believe that they must integrate the disciplines in order to analyze social *issues* and solve problems. Consider the issue we presented at the open-

FIGURE 12.2. The Subfields in the Social Studies Curriculum.

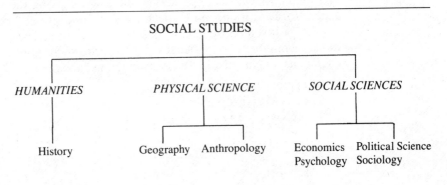

ing of this chapter: *How much industry is good for society?* Such a complex issue involves more than the *economics* of supply and demand. It also includes knowledge of the effect of industry on the physical environment (geography) and the effects of heavy industry upon the personalities of urban dwellers (psychology). How management and labor view expanding industry is the subject of sociology. How government policy regulating industry is influenced and implemented is a concern of political science. According to Shive, "There are no economic, political, social, or anthropological issues. There are only issues with economic, political, social, and anthropological dimensions."[15]

Social Studies and Levels of Thought

Social studies content has four levels of knowledge: facts, concepts, generalizations, and theories (Fraenkel, 1973).

Facts, according to Fraenkel:

> . . . are what logicians refer to as contingent statements or testable propositions. Their proof is contingent upon the presence or absence of empirical evidence with which any disinterested or nonpartial observer would agree.[16]

Here are some examples of social studies facts:

1. Columbus discovered America in 1492. (history)
2. The distance from Modesto, California, to San Francisco is 93 miles. (geography)
3. In 1941, a loaf of bread cost about 12 cents. (economics)

All higher learning in social studies is based on factual knowledge. However, when teachers make students "learn the facts," the teachers should have a clear idea as to what the students are expected to do with them.

Factual learning by itself has limited value. Facts have to be organized into some type of framework; otherwise the universe will appear chaotic and random. A *concept* becomes our way of giving the universe some type of organization. More specifically, "Concepts . . . are mental constructions invented by man to describe the characteristics that are common to a number of experiences."[17] Here are social studies concepts that encompass, respectively, the facts in the list above:

1. exploration (history)
2. centrality (geography)
3. prewar prices (economics)

[15] Shive, p. 16.
[16] Fraenkel, p. 93.
[17] Fraenkel, p. 95.

The attention that social studies teachers give to the teaching of technical vocabulary reflects their interest in concept development. In learning about government, students soon realize that *democracy, referendum, congress,* and *propaganda* are basic ideas, not merely hard words to look up in the dictionary.

When concepts are in some valid relationship, they form a *generalization.* Even more than concepts do, generalizations provide a structure for data. Consider these generalizations:

1. During the Renaissance, European rulers sought to extend their influence by exploring new continents. (history)
2. Modern highway construction has eliminated many geographical barriers to direct travel. (geography)
3. The expenses of World War II caused much worldwide inflation during the middle and late 1940s. (economics)

Just as a generalization represents a set of interrelated concepts, a *theory* represents sets of interrelated generalizations. Social studies theories might include:

1. Given social, political, and economic conditions at home are prerequisite for a country's colonial ambitions. (history)
2. As geographical barriers are eliminated, rapid communication among disparate cultures ensues. (geography)
3. When a country engages in war, it begins to destroy its economy. (economics)

In summary, the diagram in figure 12.3 represents the relationships that exist among the four levels of thought:

FIGURE 12.3. Relationships Among Four Levels of Thought.

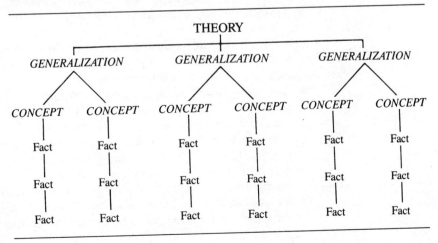

Social Studies as Process

Whether teachers present social studies as separate academic disciplines, as issues, or as levels of ideas, students have to *process* the content, both cognitively and affectively.

COGNITIVE PROCESSES

Here are some steps in processing social studies content:

1. *Identifying and Gathering Data:* Students first need to get the facts. Facts are in a plethora of sources: newspapers, textbooks, maps, charts, reports, court transcripts, television and radio broadcasts, graphs, films, records, biographies.

2. *Interpreting Data:* Students need to deal with two questions. First: What are the data? Second: What do the data mean? For instance, a graph might indicate that the rate of growth for Company A is higher than Company B. But what if Company A is a local corporation, employing 45 and Company B is an international firm, employing three million. Data *say* A is faster growing than B. However, the data *mean* that it is easier for a smaller company to grow at a *faster rate* than it is for a larger company. The data *do not mean* that A is necessarily on sounder economic ground.

3. *Analyzing Data:* After students make inferences about what the data say and mean, they can move to more intense examination. For instance, in a political speech, a senatorial candidate asserts that he is a proponent of Civil Rights. Students wishing to test the truth of the assertion will look for substantial evidence in the text of the candidate's speech and check that evidence against previous speeches the candidate has made, possible voting records, news stories and editorials about the candidate. In effect, analyzing data involves collecting evidence to substantiate truth or falsity of the data.

4. *Judging Data:* After students have gathered, interpreted, and analyzed data, they need to judge the worth of them. For instance, assume students are looking for a worthy corporation to invest imaginary money in. Stock market data and company financial reports suggest that Blaylock Automobiles is a fast-rising corporation where investments can double in a short period of time. Two editorials in newspapers mention Blaylock by name. The first, written by a prominent economist, warns the public against speculative automobile investments, especially with government restrictions on fuel consumption. The second, written by a prominent investment broker, claims that the automobile industry is the surest investment for quick return on investments. The answer to the question "Is Blay-

lock a good investment?'' will become evident in time, but a shrewd student-investor will weigh the authority of the economist against that of the broker and make a choice.

5. *Hypothesizing from Data:* After judging data, students can develop informed opinions or generalizations about the data:

   a. Companies with less than 5000 employees tend to grow at a faster rate than do companies with more than 5000 employees.

   b. Political candidates who emphasize Civil Rights in their speeches sometimes mask their true feelings as documented by prior words and actions.

   c. In times when fuel shortages exist, automobile industries become poor investments for short-term speculators.

6. *Testing Hypotheses:* Perhaps the most exciting aspect of social studies is testing original hypotheses. After students develop informed opinions, they can test their opinions by repeating the process of identifying and gathering, interpreting, analyzing, and judging data, and perhaps even forming new hypotheses.

VALUING: AN AFFECTIVE PROCESS

Social studies is concerned with human behavior. When human beings interact, potential for controversy exists as stated in the old aphorism: *No two human beings are alike.* What makes people differ, primarily, is their value systems — what they like, dislike, stress, ignore, treasure, discard. The study of controversies on *valuing in social studies* can lead to these interesting questions:

1. Were the colonies justified in wanting independence from Britain?
2. In a democratic society, does a monopoly have a right to exist?
3. Does a democracy eventually legislate freedom away from the people?
4. Is public welfare in violation of the democratic spirit?

To facilitate the controversial handling of values in the classroom, students can engage in values-clarification activities (Simon, Howe, and Kirschenbaum, 1972). Such activities not only help to clarify for students what their own values are but also educate students in how to deal with values different from their own. One such exercise, *values whips,* has the teacher firing rapid, short-answer, values questions at students in the classroom. The questions may put students on the spot, but they make them aware of their values. Here are some examples: What is something you are proud of? What is something you really believe in strongly? What is some issue about which you have taken a public stand recently?

Students should reflect on their own values to see how valuing could affect the way they function in society.

LEARNING FROM SOCIAL STUDIES TEXT

Types of Text

What kinds of text are social studies students likely to use? The answer, of course, rests with the teacher. Some teachers use a single textbook, such as the one used in Chapter 5. Other teachers may draw on additional materials such as newspapers, magazines, novels, government reports, court transcripts, even the *Congressional Record*. These book and non-book texts impart information principally through prose and graphic aids.

PROSE

Most of the material that social studies students encounter is written in prose — descriptions of historic events, case studies, transcripts, explanations, comparisons and contrasts, and examples. Shepherd indicates that social studies students who have learned to read story type material and acquired literary concepts in the earlier grades will be "faced with factual prose jammed with data when they enter high school social studies class."[18] The principal problem the students will have with social studies, Shepherd claims, will be their lack of background to understand the concepts. In addition, students will find it difficult to deal with vocabulary, sentence structure, and ideational relationships within paragraphs in social studies texts.

Vocabulary is a three-level problem. First are those general words which are unfamiliar to the students, such as *constraint, ubiquitous, prerequisite*. Second are those words which have both general meanings and technical meanings, perhaps confusing the students, such as *revolution, principal, initiative*. Third are words that stand for abstract concepts, such as *democracy, propaganda, referendum*.

Sentence structure can present reading problems even to students who understand the vocabulary contained in the sentence. Consider these examples.

1. Not only was the general ill-advised in attacking the fort, he was also ignorant concerning battle conditions, including climate, with which he was excusably unfamiliar, and land forms, with which he was inexcusably unfamiliar.
2. Contrary to public opinion, Senator Clotz, long an opponent of public welfare programs, voted against the Welfare Reform Bill for reasons no one here, at least at the Capitol, can understand.

---

[18] David L. Shepherd, *Comprehensive High School Methods*, second edition. Columbus, Ohio: Merrill, 1978, p. 188.

As you can see, the two sentences given contain no particularly difficult vocabulary, but they do contain difficult grammatical structure. Note especially the internal phrases set off with commas, such as "with which he was excusably unfamiliar" and "at least at the Capitol." Had the two passages been written in simpler sentences, using the same vocabulary, students would no doubt comprehend the meaning more readily. For example, compare these paragraphs with originals.

1. The general was ill-advised in attacking the fort. He was also ignorant of battle conditions. For example, he was excusably unfamiliar with the climate, but he should have been more familiar with the land forms.
2. Senator Clotz has long been an opponent of public welfare programs. However, contrary to public opinion, he voted against the Welfare Reform Bill. No one at the Capitol seems to understand his reasons.

Students also have problems understanding *how ideas relate to one another* in a paragraph. Generally, when students understand the *structure of paragraphs,* they can also understand how ideas within that paragraph relate. Chapter 7, "Letting the Students Do the Writing," goes into great detail on the organization of paragraphs as well as how transition expressions (*first, second, on the other hand*) clarify for the reader how sentences within a paragraph relate.

Shepherd (1973) indicates that social studies texts have certain, recurring specific patterns of thinking and writing, such as *cause and effect, sequential events with dates, comparison/contrast, detailed statement-of-fact, propaganda, fact/opinion.* To understand these patterns, students need to (1) recognize main ideas, (2) draw inferences, (3) understand relationship of time, place, and events, (4) anticipate outcomes, and (5) make evaluations (Thomas and Robinson, 1972).

GRAPHIC AIDS

In addition to the prose in social studies texts, students must use maps, graphs, charts, pictures, and pictorial models to get information.

MAPS. According to Shepherd (1973), students may encounter as many as thirteen types of maps, ranging from street maps to weather maps. Each type of map presents a specific kind of information. General map skills students will need include: understanding north-south, east-west direction; comprehending longitude and latitude; using scales and keys; locating places; making inferences from symbolic and abstract representations.

GRAPHS. Graphs generally present information, usually numerical information, along vertical and horizontal axes. Students must be able to translate spatial and symbolic representations into verbal statements and then draw information from these. Later in this chapter, we will present a lesson on reading graphs.

CHARTS. Charts contain pictorial, verbal, and numerical information arranged in such a way that its mere visualization assists the reader in understanding the information. Look at the example in table 12.1.

PICTURES. All too frequently, students skip the pictures in texts, mainly because they assume the pictures are not relevant to the text. Teachers need to prepare students to use the pictures by making sure they understand the objects in the pictures and by asking questions that demand inference.

Learning-from-Text Strategies

So far, this chapter has discussed the content of social studies, the learning processes necessary to get students to interact in a meaningful way with social studies texts, and the specific learning skills students need to comprehend a wide variety of social studies text material. Now you will see how we can apply these single- and multiple-text strategies (DRA, glosses, reading guides, SQ3R, the concept technique, inquiry, and the project method) specifically to social studies text.

Chapter 5 has already provided you with an abundance of single-text strategies and multiple-text strategies for teaching social studies material. However, the focus was on teaching only *one chapter* out of *one partic-*

TABLE 12.1. Rutland Motors Sales Records
(In Millions of Dollars)

Year	Tractors	Trailers	Trucks
1930	90	10	70
1940	80	30	40
1950	65	50	20
1960	53	70	10
1970	21	90	0

ular history textbook. Here the focus will be on teaching a wide variety of social studies materials over the school year, using the phase-in/phase-out procedure dealt with in Chapter 10.

Single-Text Strategies

As we noted in chapter 11, "English," a teacher who has a classroom of students with a wide range of learning abilities ought to begin by having the students read from the same text at the same time with the help of single-text strategies. Early in the school year, the DRA and glosses provide specific and direct guidance. A little later in the year, the teacher might introduce reading guides — first for use by the entire class, second for small groups of students, and third for individuals. When the students can work on reading guides individually, they can begin to use SQ3R. We will now demonstrate how to use each of these single-text strategies in a sequence for teaching social studies.

DIRECTED READING ACTIVITY

DRA is an effective strategy to use when introducing the class to their first reading assignment in a textbook. As we noted before, students find social studies text material difficult because it is replete with factual data condensed into a few words. An entire battle of the Civil War can be "told" in five or six densely packed sentences. A complete chapter of this type of condensed writing can present many problems to less able students who look on all words, all sentences, all ideas as being of equal importance. With the DRA, the teacher (1) explores the students' backgrounds to see what personal experiences they are approaching the chapter with and (2) builds the background they need. While students are (3) reading the chapter, either in class or at home, the teacher can guide them with preposed questions. After the students have read the chapter, the teacher can engage the students in (4) discussion and (5) other follow-up activities that extend their understanding of the chapter.

In box 12.1 is Ms. Jones's DRA lesson on "Explorers of the Western Hemisphere," the first chapter in *Quest for Liberty*.[19] As you read through the lesson, try to imagine yourself teaching these activities to a junior high school history class.

[19] June R. Chapin, Raymond J. McHugh, and Richard E. Gross, *Quest for Liberty* (Palo Alto, California: Field Enterprises, 1971).

BOX 12.1. Class: American History (DRA)

"EXPLORERS OF THE WESTERN HEMISPHERE"

(pp. 10–39)

I. Ms. Jones explores students' backgrounds.
   A. She shows the students a series of pictures or slides depicting strange or exotic, deserted geographical locations (desert scenes, surface shots of the moon or Mars, tropical jungle). She then poses these questions:
      1. What do all of these pictures have in common? (They are out of the way, weird, scary, deserted, strange.)
      2. How would you feel if you, alone, suddenly found yourself in the middle of one of these places? What would you do?
      3. If you moved around in your surroundings, what might you expect to find in the way of (a) people, (b) animals, (c) buildings, (d) plants?
   B. *Ms. Jones:* What you have just described to me is called *exploration* — that is, moving around in strange surroundings trying to find out what's there. Today, there are very few areas on earth that are unexplored. But if you still wanted to be an explorer, where would you most likely go? (the ocean, outer space.) I would now like you to see this movie about the 1969 landing on the moon. As you know, Mr. Armstrong was the first human being, we believe, that put a foot on the moon. As you watch the film, try to put yourself in his place as he walks around in a totally strange atmosphere. What sorts of things might you have expected to find?" (Ms. Jones shows the film and then reposes the questions.)
II. Ms. Jones builds students' background.
   A. Ms. Jones summarizes the previous experience and introduces the chapter: "If you find your exploration of the moon frightening as well as thrilling, you are no different from the early explorers of the Western Hemisphere (pointing to the Western Hemisphere on a map). In olden days, people used to think the world was *flat* and that if you sailed too far you would drop off the edge of the world and into the clutches of monsters. You can imagine what courage it took the early explorers to sail into unknown lands, not knowing what danger awaited them. The chapter you are about to read talks about the early explorers of the Western Hemisphere and what they found.
   B. Ms. Jones next gives the students an overview of the chapter by having them read the summary on page 36 and by showing them the various old maps and pictures that form the chapter's abundant illustrations.
   C. Ms. Jones reviews with the students difficult vocabulary they will encounter — hard general words and the technical vocabulary which is clearly explained in context on the textbook pages indicated in parentheses below:

Hard General Words	Technical Vocabulary Explained in Context
1. debate (p. 12)	1. authentic (p. 12)
2. encounter (p. 13)	2. archeologists (p. 13)
3. influence (p. 15)	3. cultures (p. 15)

| | Technical Vocabulary |
Hard General Words	*Explained in Context*
4. flourished (p. 17)	4. data (p. 21)
5. smelted iron (p. 21)	5. primary sources (p. 21)
	6. secondary sources (p. 21)
	7. standards and values (p. 25)
	8. environment (p. 29)
	9. technology (p. 30)

   D. Ms. Jones gives the students a few preposed questions to guide their reading:
      1. How much of the Western Hemisphere was explored between 1450 and 1620?
      2. What types of good information sources do we have today to let us know what these early explorations were like?

III. The students read the chapter in class or at home, using any of the following strategies:
   A. The students can be assigned the entire chapter to read overnight at home.
   B. The teacher can assign the first part of the chapter for in-class reading, with the remainder to be completed for homework.
   C. The entire chapter can be read in class over one or more class periods.
   D. Since the chapter is long, the teacher can break the assignment into smaller units and intersperse discussion sessions.

IV. Ms. Jones has the students discuss the chapter.
   A. Informational Level Questions
      1. What explorations of the Western Hemisphere took place before the time of Christopher Columbus?
      2. What evidence is there to verify these earlier explorations?
      3. What explorations of the Western Hemisphere took place after the time of Christopher Columbus?
      4. What two kinds of sources do historians refer to when they attempt to reconstruct the past?
      5. What are the two kinds of environment that this chapter discusses with respect to the Western Hemisphere?
   B. Inferential Level Questions
      1. Why are historians referred to as detectives?
      2. Suppose that you want to find out why explorers voyaged to the Western Hemisphere. For which group of explorers would you be most likely to find more evidence — pre-Columbus explorers or post-Columbus explorers? Why?
      3. What arguments would you use against the statement: "All secondary sources are worthless?"
      4. If you were an archeologist, would you be more interested in the physical environment or the cultural environment? Why?
   C. Generalized Level Questions
      1. The year is 4000 A.D. You, as a historian, are given the task of determining how extensive the exploration of the moon was in the Twentieth Century. What primary sources would you use? What secondary sources?

2. Describe the physical environment of the town or city where you live. What sorts of things would you include in your description of the cultural environment of your community?

V. Ms. Jones has the students do activities that extend their understanding of the chapter.
  A. Discussion and dramatics
    1. Assume that Leif Ericson and Christopher Columbus had an argument over which of them actually *discovered* America. Dramatize this debate, using information from the textbook to support the claims of either explorer.
    2. Suppose that a time machine has moved you ahead three thousand years and has dropped you on a strange planet. Enact a skit in which you and several companions explore the unknown planet. Be sure to include elements of both physical and cultural environment that you might encounter.
  B. Writing, drawing, construction
    1. Construct a map of your town as you think it might have been 1000 years ago. Imagine a civilization living there and how their community might be laid out. Construct a diorama of this community using a shoe box.
    2. Create a primary source document that would question Columbus's claim to discovering America and support the claim of Sir Winston Pilgrim, a little-known English explorer of the Thirteenth Century.

GLOSSES

As with the directed reading activity, glosses provide students with guidance, but without teacher-student interaction. *Glossing* gives the students marginal aids to comprehension (defining difficult words, clarifying difficult concepts, asking provocative questions). Some teachers underline main ideas to help students skim or scan the text. The teacher can effectively gloss a chapter in different ways: (1) by having students write in the margins of their books (if the school district permits); (2) by preparing ditto guide sheets aligned with text margins that students can insert between text pages; (3) by listing the glosses on a separate study sheet, with appropriate cross references to text pages, columns, and paragraphs. It is much easier, though, to gloss shorter text items, such as newspaper clippings. In box 12.2 is a gloss of a newspaper clipping that (1) guides the student to the main points of the article, (2) provides definitions and clarification, and (3) shows the student the process of reading a newspaper article.

BOX 12.2. Text: News Story (Gloss)

PLANE WITH 156 HIJACKED IN INDIA ──────── Eye-Catcher

Flight Believed Seized by Japanese Leftists ──── Additional eye-catching material

From Reuters ──────── News service agency

Place from which ← Tokyo — A Japan Air Lines DC-8 was | story was released hijacked today shortly after takeoff from Bombay and the airline said (un-

A four-engine jetliner.

Rumored or unchecked — confirmed) reports indicated it had been seized by members of the radical Japanese Red Army guerrilla group.

Par. 1. *Lead* Who? What? Where? This sentence contains the key information.

How would you like to be on that plane? — The airline said the hijackers had ordered the aircraft, carrying 142 passengers and 14 crew members, to head toward its scheduled destination of

A city in Thailand — Bangkok. The flight originated in Paris with a final destination of Tokyo.

Par. 2. Further information but less important than the lead

Why do you think so much of this story contains unconfirmed facts? — The number of hijackers and their demands were not immediately known, but the airline quoted an unconfirmed report from a Bombay air traffic controller that they were members of the ultra-left Red Army. Airline spokesmen said the pilot had sent a signal

Par. 3. More information but less important than par. 2

For some reason, he didn't want to go into more detail. — about the hijacking, but declined to elaborate.

This must have confused the passengers. — The aircraft at one stage turned back toward Bombay but then changed course again for Bangkok.

From here on the information becomes less important.
Note: News story writers are trained to put the most important information at the beginning because editors trim the stories from the bottom.

The first report of the hijacking came in a brief radio message from the aircraft's pilot to the Bombay airport control tower.

Japanese airliners have been hijacked in the past by Red Army guerril-

This is not the first hijacking. Should this type of terrorist activity be dealt with severely? How? What can be done to discourage it?

las, but the most recent such incident was more than seven years ago, in March, 1971.

The extreme-left Red Army, which advocates "world simultaneous revolutions" through armed actions, has carried out several guerrilla operations in different parts of the world.

The most spectacular was the massacre at Israel's Lod airport in May, 1972, when three Red Army guerrillas killed 25 people and wounded more than 80 others. Two of the terrorists were killed.

Other operations included an abortive attack on an oil refinery in Singapore in 1974, an attack on the French Embassy in The Hague, Netherlands, later that year, and a raid on the U.S. Embassy in Kuala Lumpur, Malaysia, in 1975.

News stories must contain facts, not opinions, unless they are quoted from people whose names appear in the story.
Bad Journalism: The Red Army is a pack of gangsters.
Good Journalism: "The Red Army is a pack of gangsters," said Barry Philbein, an airlines ticket agent.

Article reprinted by permission of Reuters, from the *Los Angeles Times* (September 28, 1977), pp. 1, 14.

READING AND LEARNING-FROM-TEXT GUIDES

After you have used the DRA and glossing techniques, you could begin using reading and learning-from-text guides in the classroom, implementing a phase-in/phase-out procedure. Chapter 5 presents a number of guides which you can use in teaching a chapter from a history text. You might want to review that chapter before reading the remainder of this section.

Since graphic aids are a significant part of social studies text, this chapter will present *processes of reading guides* that teach students how to read and learn from graphs. In box 12.3 is a processes of reading guide that Ms. Jones used to teach students graph reading.

BOX 12.3. Subject: Business and Government (Learning guides)

THREE PROCESS GUIDES

for Learning to Read Graphs

Version A: Teacher presents guide to entire class.

Lesson Objective: The purpose of this lesson is to teach you how to read the graph in figure 1. To begin, you will learn to read some simple scales.

FIGURE 1. Comparative Sales Figures for Rutland Motors' Tractors
and Trailers over the Past Forty Years.

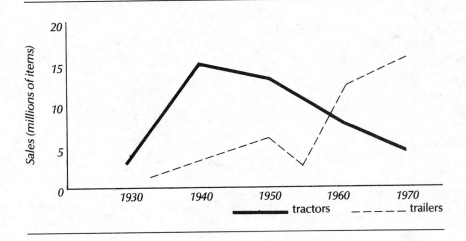

Activity 1: Learning how to read graphs is easy once you learn how to read scales. Look at each of the scales in figures 2 and 3. Then answer the questions that follow.

FIGURE 2. Scale on the Dashboard of an Automobile.

0	10	20	30	40	50	60	70	80	90	100	110

1. If you saw the scale in figure 2 on the dashboard of an automobile, what sort of scale do you think it would be?
2. The line which ends at 60 tells you what information?

FIGURE 3. Scale on the Outside of a Building.

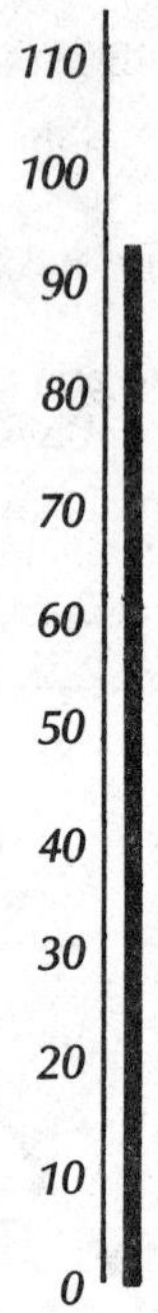

3. If you saw the scale in figure 3 on the outside of a building, what sort of scale would you think it would be?
4. The line which ends at 90 tells you what information?

Activity 2: In Activity 1, you learned that you can read information on scales going across, or *horizontally,* and up-and-down, or *vertically.* Dots, or other marks, on the scale give you specific information about that scale. The horizontal scale, or speedometer, in figure 2, showed you that the driver was going 60 miles an hour. The vertical scale, or thermometer, in figure 3 showed you that it was 90° F. Each of the scales in figure 4 has dots placed on them. See if you can read the information correctly.

Activity 3: So far you have learned to read scales, both horizontal and vertical. But a scale can give you only one type of information. What would happen if you put two scales together — one horizontal scale and one vertical scale?

Result: By putting the two scales together you make a *graph* like the one in figure 5. A *graph* has two lines of information — one horizontal and one vertical. When you put dots on graphs you show the *relationship* that exists between the information on the vertical scale and the information on the horizontal scale. Examine the graph in figure 5 and answer these questions:

FIGURE 4. Three Types of Scales.

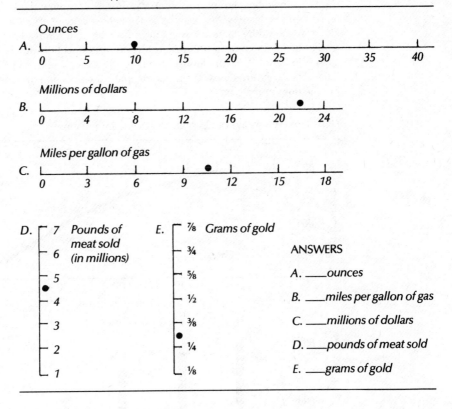

ANSWERS

A. ____ounces

B. ____miles per gallon of gas

C. ____millions of dollars

D. ____pounds of meat sold

E. ____grams of gold

FIGURE 5. Dots, Intersection Points, Alone on a Scale.

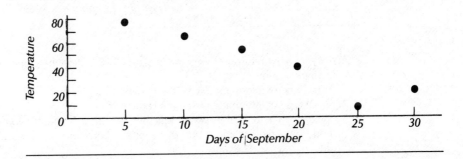

1. How hot was it on the fifth of September?
2. How hot was it on September 30?
3. As the month of September moved along, what was the general tendency of the temperature? What was the one exception to this tendency?

So, the preceding graph told you the relationship between *temperature* and *different days in September*. From this information (dots) you drew the inference that *with one exception, the weather became cooler between September 1 and September 30*. Figure 6 shows the same information in two different forms. Since dots on graphs tend to be hard to read, graphmakers tend to (a) connect the dots with straight lines, as in *A* in figure 6, or (b) highlight the dots with heavy bars, as in *B* in figure 6. *A* is a *line graph* and *B* is a *bar graph*. Sometimes, the dots do not appear on graphs — just the lines or the bars.

FIGURE 6. Two Ways of Graphing the Same Information.

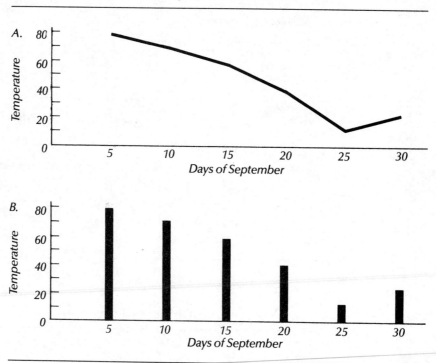

Activity 4: Now return to the graph in figure 1. Examine the graph and answer the following questions:
1. What type of information is on the horizontal scale?
2. What type of information is on the vertical scale?
3. When the two scales come together, as in this graph, you are trying to find out the relationship that exists between _____ and
   _____.
4. First look at the solid line on the graph that represents *tractors*.
   a. In what year did Rutland Motors make its *best* sales in tractors? How many were sold?
   b. Other than in 1930, in what year did Rutland Motors make its *worst* sales? How many tractors were sold?

    c. Between what years did the sale of Rutland's tractors *boom,* or sell best?

    d. What has been the trend in sales since 1940?

5. Now look at the broken line on the graph that represents *trailers.*

    a. In what year did Rutland Motors make its best sales in trailers? How many were sold?

    b. In what year did Rutland Motors make its worst sales in trailers? What could account for those low sales?

    c. Between what years did Rutland's trailers experience a strange sales pattern? What do you think happened then?

6. Suppose you were on the board of directors of Rutland Motors. What recommendations might you make concerning the manufacturing and sales of tractors? About the manufacturing and sales of trailers?

Activity 5: Select either the information about *tractors* or the information about *trailers* and convert it from its present form, a line graph, to a bar graph.

READING GRAPHIC AIDS

Students frequently do not pay attention to graphic aids in textbooks. First, students may not know how to read them and extract information from them. Second, students may think of graphic aids as pictures, rather than as abstractions of complex concepts and their relationships in the form of symbols, numbers, lines. These features of graphic aids need to be stated. Students have to identify the symbols, numbers, lines, and bars, and state the information they represent. Next they must interpret and infer relationships, and finally draw whatever general conclusions are appropriate from the data in the graphic aid. After all this, the student can make judgments and evaluations. Teachers frequently do not teach students to get information from graphic aids, perhaps because they assume that students already know how to read and learn from them.

The strategies for teaching a text can be applied to teaching graphs. Box 12.3 shows a processes-of-teaching guide on graph reading. The process of reading graphs and learning from any graphic aids can be taught in other ways. For example, a DRA technique or a learning from text guide could show students how to read a specific graphic aid located in the textbook. Regardless of strategy, you want the students to (1) know what the aid says (informational level of understanding), (2) know what the information in the aid means (inferential level of understanding), (3) generalize or apply knowledge about the aid to another situation (generalized level of understanding), and (4) evaluate the information and make judgments based upon the information, interpretation, and generalizations drawn from the aid. For example, let's focus on graphs:

Informational level. To know what a graph says, students must know how to read the horizontal and the vertical axes and translate this information into words. See how to teach the reading of graph axes and how to identify the information in the graph by examining box 12.3, *Activities 1 and 2.*

Inferential level. To know what a graph means, students must understand the relationships that exist between the horizontal and vertical axes and be able to express those relationships in words. See how to teach students to draw inferences from graphs in *Activities 3 and 4.*

Generalized level. After students learn to read axes and extract meaning from them, students can generalize about what they have learned from them.

Evaluative and judgmental levels. Next, students can evaluate the information from the graph and make judgments by applying the information to the solution of a problem. See *Activity 4, Item 6* and *Activity 5.*

Although we have concentrated on graphs, the same procedure of moving from informational level to inferential level to generalized level can be applied to pictures, charts, and maps.

SQ3R

The reason for sequencing DRA, glosses, and learning guides is to move the students from dependence to independence in learning. SQ3R requires students to become more independent. It teaches them to find answers to their own questions. In box 12.4 is Ms. Jones' lesson on "The Civil War and Reconstruction" [Chapter 10 of *Quest for Liberty* (Chapin, McHugh, and Gross, 1972)]. It demonstrates how to teach students the SQ3R technique.

BOX 12.4. Course: American History (SQ3R)

"THE CIVIL WAR AND RECONSTRUCTION"

1. Ms. Jones has the students *survey* the chapter, particularly the headings, by asking questions like these:
   A. When you see the chapter title "The Civil War and Reconstruction," what do you think is to be reconstructed? What had been destroyed?
   B. Look through the pictures of the chapter and note their captions. What impressions are you left with? What questions are raised in your mind about the Civil War and the Reconstruction period that followed?
2. Ms. Jones has the students ask themselves questions they want to find answers for. These questions might be some that emerge from their survey of the chapter headings and graphic aids.

    A. What were some of the harmful effects of the Civil War and Reconstruction on the South? On the North?

    B. What was the effect of Lincoln's assassination upon the politics of the South? Of the North?

3. Ms. Jones instructs the students to *read* the chapter to find answers to their questions. (If the teacher wishes, students can write the answers to their questions when they finish reading.)

4. Ms. Jones then has the students *recite* their answers to questions in a variety of ways. Students can submit their written answers or share differing questions and answers with classmates in total class or small group discussion.

5. Ms. Jones invites the students to engage in "review" projects such as these:

    A. Do additional outside reading on topics of particular interest: Lincoln's assassination, the KKK, Mitchell's *Gone With the Wind,* W. E. B. DuBois, Booker T. Washington.

    B. Reread the chapter to come up with further insights.

The chapter under discussion in this box is chapter 10 in Chapin, McHugh, and Gross, *The Quest for Liberty,* pp. 296–327.

Multiple-Text Strategies

So far, you have been educating your students in how to comprehend social studies text material independently. DRA, glosses, guides, and SQ3R have been used in single-text situations. Now your students should be ready to work independently in multiple-text situations. We will describe three strategies: the concept technique, inquiry, and the project method.

CONCEPT TECHNIQUE

Even though you have been teaching students to be independent learners, you may still find that they have wide differences in learning ability. In this case, your job is to allow all of your students the opportunity to engage in independent learning, but at differing levels of difficulty. A good method for providing for individual differences without stigmatizing students is by having each student select what he or she will read. Then all the students who have selected the same book will form discussion groups. You might provide four or more reading selections that vary in difficulty, introduce the four selections to the class as a whole, and permit each student to choose one of the four. In box 12.5 is Ms. Jones's self-selection/self-grouping strategy for social studies.

BOX 12.5. Unit: The Faces of War

Ms. Jones: So far the entire class has been reading the same sources. Now you are going to be asked to select one particular source from a group of four that deal with the unit's theme, *The Faces of War.* Before you decide which source you want to read, you will probably want to know what each one is about. You will receive a guide that gives you an overview of each source. Later, I will pass around a sign-up sheet. You will indicate your choice on this sheet by signing your name. You will later form groups according to the text-source you select. Your group will then plan a presentation for the rest of the class.

OVERVIEW GUIDE

Sources for *Faces of War* (World War II)

1. *Anne Frank: A Portrait in Courage,* by Ernst Schnabel. This is not the diary, but it is a sensitive description of the young girl who wrote the diary, then left it behind on her way from Amsterdam to a Nazi prison camp. Schnabel gives you a keen insight into the personal feelings of the teenage girl who was forced to live in hiding in an attic apartment for three years because she was Jewish. Although she died in March 1945 in the concentration camp at Bergen-Belsen, she lives today in the hearts of all who understand and appreciate courage.
2. *Hiroshima,* by John Hersey. An unforgettable account, nonfictional, of the horrible aftermath of the destruction of the Japanese city of Hiroshima in the closing months of World War II. Descriptions of pain and suffering are graphic. This book is not for the squeamish.
3. *Up Front,* by Bill Mauldin. Strangely enough, war can have its humorous side. Read of the hilarious misadventures of Willie and Joe, two soldiers in World War II who get themselves into ridiculous situations. You may have seen the movie made from this book.
4. *Brave Men,* by Ernie Pyle. Ernie Pyle was a war correspondent during World War II. He was killed before the war ended. However, he managed to set down memorable portraits of fighting men he knew. This book gives you a rare insight into what war is really about.

Sign-Up Sheet for *Faces of War* (World War II)

Instructions: Select one of the five sources below and sign your name under it. You and other classmates who select the source will be asked to (a) discuss the story in small groups, the discussion to be based on answers to questions your group has preposed; (b) plan a discussion, debate, dramatization, or media presentation; and (c) present your project to the rest of the class.

1. *Anne Frank, a Portrait in Courage*
    a. _____
    b. _____
    c. _____
    d. _____
    e. _____
    f. _____

2. *Hiroshima*
   a. _____
   b. _____
   c. _____
   d. _____
   e. _____
   f. _____
3. *Up Front*
   a. _____
   b. _____
   c. _____
   d. _____
   e. _____
   f. _____
4. *Brave Men*
   a. _____
   b. _____
   c. _____
   d. _____
   e. _____
   f. _____

Of the books discussed in this box, *Anne Frank* (first published in 1958) and *Hiroshima* (1946) are available in inexpensive paperback editions, Schnabel's book from Harcourt Brace Jovanovich and Hersey's from Bantam. *Up Front* (1945) was reissued in hardcover by Norton in 1968. *Brave Men* (1943) is out of print, but should be available in most libraries.

INQUIRY

As we noted in chapter 11, "English," inquiry is the direct opposite of expository teaching. With inquiry, students engage actively in problem-solving. Recognition of a problem occurs after a certain amount of exploration. Students define the problem, state a hypothesis, test the hypothesis, and come to some sort of conclusion. Look at Ms. Jones's inquiry lesson in box 12.6.

BOX 12.6. Unit: The Rights and Privileges
of Voting

INQUIRY

Ms. Jones: So far in this unit we have been reading and talking about what it means
   to be able to vote, the rights and privileges, one of which is the right to a secret

ballot. In line with this last right, here is a clipping from a recent newspaper in which this right has been challenged. Read the clipping and we'll discuss the questions that follow it:

Court may jail citizens who refuse to reveal how they voted

By THEODORE ILIFF

ANN ARBOR, Mich. (UPI) — Who is correct — the defeated mayoral candidate who says he has the right to know whether the 20 votes illegally cast were for him or against him? Or some of the 20 voters, who say they will go to jail rather than give up their right to a secret ballot?

That dilemma comes up in Circuit Court this week, and stands a good chance of winding up in the state Court of Appeals.

For the 20 voters, the dilemma is more than academic, because they are facing contempt of court citations that could put them in jail. One 21-year-old college woman already has spent 90 minutes in handcuffs for refusing to tell her vote.

The candidate, Louis Belcher, a Republican, lost by one vote to Democratic incumbent Albert Wheeler in last April's mayoral race. Belcher immediately went to court alleging voting irregularities.

In July, election officials admitted that 20 residents of unincorporated "township islands" were registered as legal city voters but actually were not entitled to vote. Officials emphasized it was the city's error, not the voters'.

But how can the 20 votes be thrown out if it isn't known what they were?

That's what Belcher is trying to find out in court and last week, Susan VanHattum, a 21-year-old University of Michigan junior, was asked in court how she voted. The question was based on a 1929 state court ruling that illegal voters could not keep their ballots secret.

When VanHattum refused to answer, Visiting Circuit Judge James Kelley cited her for contempt. She was handcuffed and confined in his chambers for 90 minutes. He then freed her, giving her until tomorrow to change her mind.

Diane Lazinsky, a UM research assistant, also balked at the same question. Although spared the handcuffs, she was given the same ultimatum. Three other witnesses revealed their votes.

Belcher, a 38-year-old management consultant, said he had a sinking feeling as VanHattum quietly insisted on her right to secrecy.

"I don't want to see anyone go to jail," Belcher said in an interview. "But now that it's out, I assume the judge will go through with this.

"Once the question was asked and (VanHattum) refused to reply, there was nothing I could do. It became a matter between the witness and the judge, and I felt kind of helpless."

Other than Belcher, few principals want to discuss the case. Kelley, Wheeler, and both of the women are avoiding publicity.

"I've caught a cold, I can't get any sleep and I've fallen behind in my school work," VanHattum said. "I'll do all my talking in court."

The American Civil Liberties Union said it would ask the state Court of Appeals today to take control of the case on grounds Kelley ignored the 1963 state constitution and later laws mandating ballot secrecy.

However, Belcher, while regretting the threat to witnesses, said he would not budge from his contention that the election was invalid.

He said the rights of legitimate city voters also were at stake in the case that already has cost him $13,000 in legal fees.

"The rightful electorate has a right to know how the ballots were cast," he said. "What rights of the 21,000 legal electorate are being violated? Right now there is no way of saying if the people of Ann Arbor have had their say on who is going to be mayor."

Questions

1. Before we consider the problem, let's deal with certain basic facts as presented in this newspaper article:
   a. What election is the focus of this problem?
   b. What was the final result of the election?
   c. Who challenged the results of the election?
   d. On what grounds did he challenge the election?
   e. What court did he go to for satisfaction?
   f. What did Judge Kelley insist that those who testified tell him?
   g. On what legal precedent did Judge Kelley act?
   h. Why did some of those who testified refuse to answer the judge's question?
   i. What happened to those who refused to answer?
   j. What was the reaction of the election officials?

    k. What was the reaction of the American Civil Liberties Union? What was their legal precedent?

2. Now that we understand the facts of the article, we can begin discussing the problem. The problem occurs because a number of individuals and groups are asserting what they believe to be their rights. Review the article again and finish the incomplete sentences below, in addition to citing any page references from your textbook and supplementary sources that support the individual's rights.

    a. *Louis Belcher* claims, "I have a right to know _____

_____ , because _____

         (what has he a right to know?)

_____ .

         (state what you think are his reasons)

Textbook pp. _____ support Belcher's rights. (Other

sources _____ .) Textbook pp. _____ do not support

Belcher's rights. (Other sources _____ .)

    b. Judge Kelley claims, "You voted illegally; therefore, you must tell

me _____ because _____

         (what does he want to know?)

_____ .

         (what are the judge's reasons?)

Textbook pp. _____ support the judge's right to information. (Other

sources _____ .)

Textbook pp. _____ do not support the judge's right to information.

(Other sources _____ .)

    c. Susan VanHattum and Diane Lazinsky claimed, "We don't have to tell

you _____ , because _____ ."

         (what information?)   (give their reasons.)

Textbook pp. _____ support the two women's rights.

(Other sources _____ .)

Textbook pp. _____ do not support the two women's rights. (Other

sources _____ .)

3. You now have (1) the facts of the case, (2) the issues involved, and (3) some legal grounds for making a court case. Suppose the case is moved to the state Court of Appeals. Also suppose that you are the judge that hears the case.

    a. Would you defend Judge Kelley's right to obtain ballot information from the

unqualified voters? _____ yes _____ no. Why? _____

_____

    b. Would you defend VanHattum's and Lazinsky's right to remain silent?

_____ yes _____ no. Why? _____

_____

Ms. Jones: Now that each one of you has "judged" the case, let's see how the class as a whole voted. How many of you favored Judge Kelley's right to obtain information? (Ms. Jones tabulates the vote.) How many of you favored the two women's right to keep silent? (Ms. Jones tabulates the vote.) What we have here is a ratio: the number who favor the judge as opposed to the number who favor the two women: (5 to 30 or 12 to 23 or 15 to 20). You are all high school government students who have voted on this case. Do you think other people, for instance, high school students who have not had a course in government, would vote in the same proportion? Why or why not?

(Ms. Jones engages the students in discussing why the other students might or might not vote in the same proportion. The following hypothesis is formed and Ms. Jones writes it on the board: "Given the information in the Belcher case, students not taking government will respond differently than students taking government.") How would we go about proving this? For instance, what does "respond differently" mean and how will we know if they do respond differently or not? Should we form more specific hypotheses? *(The class refines the first hypothesis into the following more workable hypotheses, which Ms. Jones writes on the board.)*

1. Given the information in the Belcher case and asked to support either the judge or the two women, nongovernment students will support the judge in a (greater, lesser) proportion than did government students.
2. Given the information in the Belcher case and asked to support either the judge or the two women, nongovernment students will support the two women in a (greater, lesser) proportion than did government students.
3. When asked to give reasons for their decision, nongovernment students will cite personal feelings and emotions rather than personal knowledge of law and government.

Ms. Jones: Now how shall we go about determining whether our hypotheses are correct? Here is a suggestion: Each student in the class can contact another student who has not had government, ask the other student to read the editorial, and decide either in favor of the judge or the two women, giving reasons. Then we can collect and tabulate the results in class.

Article reprinted by permission of United Press International, from the Riverside (California) *Enterprise* (October 10, 1977), p. A-3.

PROJECT METHOD

Once students know how to engage in inquiry, they are ready to branch out into more independent learning. The project method motivates students to perform independent reading to solve problems. In box 12.7 is Ms. Jones's project activity which shows how students can become actively engaged in reading for problem solution.

BOX 12.7. Unit: Industry and Ecology (Project)

Instructions: Assume that you are the president of Rutland Motors, a company that manufactures trailers and tractors. Business is going so well that you would like to recommend to the board of directors that a new plant be opened. The board agrees in principle, but requests that you prepare a report on each of three possible sites: Sacramento, California; Mobile, Alabama; and Detroit, Michigan. At the conclusion of the report, you are to rank the three sites according to the following criteria:
1. Potential for business opportunities in the area, particularly the lack of competition from similar industries, that is, other tractor or trailer companies.
2. Favorable environmental impact studies, that is, how civic organizations would react to having your plant in their area, with regard to pollution, noise, and use of the area's human and natural resources.
3. Accessibility to raw materials and effective transportation and shipping systems. Prepare such a report. Use textbooks, encyclopedias, maps, atlases of the area, information you can get from chambers of commerce. The final report should be about five pages that contain the necessary information the board wants to know.

SUMMARY

Social studies, like English, is an integrated subject. Two conflicting theories about teaching social studies advocate respectively (1) presenting the content as separate disciplines and (2) focusing on problems and issues. The processes students use in learning social studies are both cognitive (gathering data and so forth) and affective (valuing and so forth). In learning from social studies text, students encounter prose and graphic aids. Prose text includes textbooks, magazines, newspapers, and government documents. Graphic aids include maps, graphs, charts, and pictures. In teaching students to learn from text, teachers whose students have a single text may use DRA, glosses, guides, and SQ3R. If students have multiple texts, teachers may use the concept technique (self-selection/self-grouping), inquiry, and the project method.

ACTIVITIES

1. Using the DRA lesson in this chapter as a model, construct a directed reading activity for a social studies chapter. Teach the lesson to a small group of social studies students or to an entire class. List the ways in which you perceive the lesson as helpful to the students.
2. Select and gloss a newspaper article or editorial that you feel would be difficult for students to comprehend. To determine the effectiveness of the gloss, have

two groups of students read the article, but have only one group use the gloss. Administer a brief comprehension test for both groups and compare the results.

3. Construct a processes-of-reading guide that teaches students to learn from a graphic aid (map, chart, graph). Use the guide with a small group of social studies students, and describe the ways in which the guide helps the students learn from the graphic aid.

13 | Science

CHAPTER OVERVIEW

Most students have a natural curiosity about scientific principles — What keeps airplanes aloft? What makes trees grow? Why is the sky blue? What keeps the earth from disintegrating? Answers to these universal questions can be found in science texts. Unfortunately, the reading difficulty of most science materials (caused by condensed and technical language) prevents many students from satisfying their curiosity by reading and learning from science texts. This chapter demonstrates how teachers can make science textbooks more understandable to their students. After you read this chapter, you will understand a number of methods for helping your students learn from science texts.

TECHNICAL VOCABULARY

scientific method
observation
hypothesis
concepts
generalizations

theory
QUEST
Problem Demonstration Sequence
Table of Specifications

315

Although natural and life sciences are organized into three branches of knowledge — physics, chemistry, and biology — these branches are nevertheless interrelated. The interrelationship occurs in such courses as physical chemistry and biochemistry. Yet, even when divided up, year-long courses in physics, chemistry, and biology are still so broad that instructors and texts have to be selective in the topics they can cover. This selection is apparent in an examination of curricula developed for these subjects.

CONTENTS AND PROCESSES OF SCIENCE COURSES

Curricula

Box 13.1 summarizes three courses developed by scientists and teachers working together in a large-scale, federally funded project. These scientists and teachers cooperated to develop courses that would better prepare students at the high school level for future careers as scientists (Heath, 1964). The physics course was organized around the two theories of how light travels. The emphasis in the chemistry and biology courses was on methods of inquiry. All of these courses recognize that the role of scientists is to produce knowledge.

BOX 13.1. Outline of Natural and Life Sciences Curriculum Revisions Under the National Defense Education Act

I. *Physical Sciences Study Committee Curriculum (PSSC)*
   A. *Organizing Concepts*
      1. Two theories on how light travels (the wave and particle theories)
      2. Theory of the atom
   B. *Topics*
      1. Optics
      2. Wave theory
      3. Newton's Laws of Thermodynamics
      4. Electric forces
      5. Atom
   C. *Collateral Reading*
      1. Sound
      2. Electric circuitry
      3. Theory of relativity
II. *Chemical Education Material Study Curriculum (Chem Study)*
   A. *Organizing Concepts*

1. Experimental approach
   a. Perform experiments prior to reading about them in the text. Purpose: to emphasize discovery approach to learning; to collect and analyze data in order to answer questions to unknown problems; and to formulate data-based generalizations.
   b. Teach students to distinguish between observation and interpretation.
2. Arrange the series of forty-four experiments in hierarchical order with decreasing teacher direction and increasing student mobilization of cumulative knowledge and procedures gleaned from previous experiments. (Phase out teacher/phase in student.)

B. *Three Phases in the Organization of Text and Related Experiments*
   1. Phase I
      a. Atomic-molecular theory
      b. Chemical reactions
      c. Gas phase
      d. Kinetic theory
      e. Condensation phase
      f. Atom structure
      g. Periodic table
   2. Phase II
      a. Energy
      b. Rates
      c. Equilibrium
      d. Chemical calculations
      e. Atomic theory and structure
      f. Molecular structure
      g. Bonding
   3. Phase III: Application of principles developed in Phases I and II to chemistry of typical elements and their compounds.

III. *Biological Science Study Committee Curriculum (BSSC)*
   A. *Organizing Concepts*
      1. Topics
         a. Organic evolution
         b. Nature of racial and individual differences
         c. Sex and reproduction in the human species
         d. Population growth and control
      2. Emphasis on biology as experimental science with methods of inquiry
         a. Controlled experimentation
         b. Confirmable, accurate, and quantifiable observation
         c. Mathematical analysis of data
      3. Divided scope of biology into three courses
         a. *"Yellow" Course:* Initially: Genetic and developmental knowledge. After revision: Cellular approaches and integration of biochemical with biological processes.
         b. *"Blue" Course:* Initially: Biochemical and physiological topics. After revision: origin of life and its evolution, and nature of scientific inquiry presented like a detective investigation.

c. *"Green" Course:* Ecological and evolutionary approaches. (No revision.)

4. Themes included in courses
   a. Interdependence of structure and function
   b. Regulation and homeostasis
   c. Genetic continuity of life
   d. Evolution of life
   e. Diversity of type together with unity of pattern
   f. Biological roots of behavior
   g. Relation of organism to environment

5. Treatment of topics
   a. Levels of organization: molecular to ecosystem
   b. Stages of process: chemical reaction through ontogenetic growth and development to evolutionary changes.

6. Laboratory
   a. Demonstrations
   b. Use of microscope
   c. Dissection of plants and animals
   d. Labeling drawings and learning names

7. Use scientific method to investigate
   a. Growth of microbes
   b. Nutrition
   c. Interaction
   d. Amount of growth and development
   e. Interdependence of structure and function

8. Develop logic of scientific inquiry
   a. Observation, collection of data, hypothesis formulation, design and control experimentation to test hypothesis.
   b. Concepts of causality: factors, multiple causality, time sequences, negative causation, and feedback mechanisms.
   c. Quantitative relationships: linear and experimental, rate and rate of change, limits and constants.
   d. Function in biology: evidence of doubtfulness, argument from design, argument from adaptation.

Descriptions of curricula in this box were taken from Heath (1964). Congress passed the National Defense Education Act in reaction to Russia beating the United States in the race to outer space by launching Sputnik in 1957. The Act aimed to improve the education of future scientists, engineers, and mathematicians, in part by developing better high school courses. The development of these courses was extremely expensive: $6,000,000 to construct the physics course; another $6,000,000 to train teachers in how to teach the course!

Moreover, each of the three courses recognizes that as a result of conducting experiments students are likely to gain a better understanding of current scientific theories, laws, and concepts, and learn how to acquire and modify scientific knowledge. Perhaps the lab activities and the job of discovery, particularly when supplemented by encouragement from an enthusiastic instructor, will help students identify with the role of scientists and foster careers in science. Essentially, these federally funded science courses do not stress mastery of content, but use of content for learning how to learn principles and procedures that will generate knowledge. Although the three courses have unique problems, concepts, procedures, and instruments for laboratory investigations, they do have some features in common: (1) they all contain theories, generalizations, and concepts about ultimately observable events; and (2) they all rely upon the scientific method as a way of determining whether explanations are supportable or not.

In contrast, traditional science courses emphasize content. Some of these courses organize their content in accord with, for example, a definition of physics as a study of matter and energy and the transferability or conversion of energy into heat, electricity, light, sound, and mechanical forces. Topics in such a physics course would be matter, molecules, fluids, solids, gases, heat, sound, light, magnetism, electricity, electronics, and radiation. Texts for courses like this present these topics in a didactic way rather than promoting discovery. See *Elements of Physics* (Boylan, 1962) for an example.

Traditional courses and curriculum in science continued in many high schools during the great curriculum revision of science in the 1960s. Now those schools that tried the new courses have tended to return to traditional courses as funds became unavailable for purchasing lab equipment, films, and inservice training for teachers — all necessary features of the new courses.

Objectives

However, in either type of course, even though the emphases may differ, students must (1) learn definitions for technical terms and symbols; (2) become knowledgeable about the scientific method, measurement devices, and units and how to apply them (see box 13.2 for steps in the scientific method, the definitions of these steps, and their application to a particular problem); (3) develop familiarity with a selected set of theories, generalizations, and concepts; and (4) learn to use knowledge acquired to analyze, compute, interpret, and generalize from data frequently presented in the form of charts or graphs. (See chapter 12, and especially box 12.3, for procedures on teaching students to read and learn from charts and graphs.)

BOX 13.2. Steps in the Scientific Method

Observation: A can, without a cap, such as one that had contained duplicating fluid, is placed on a source of heat. After a few minutes, the cap is replaced, screwed down tightly, and the heat is removed from the can. Gradually, the can begins to crumple. Why?

Hypothesis (Explanation that is to be tested): Air pressure causes the can to crumple.

Design to test a hypothesis: The hypothesis or explanation can be tested by arranging conditions so that one variable can be changed (independent variable) while other variables are held constant, or controlled. Under these conditions, variation in the independent or antecedent variable can be related to its consequent, the dependent variable. Under this rule of the single variable, cause and effect can then be logically inferred.

 Design A: To test the effect of heat alone, use two identical cans with plastic window on one side, caps off, thermometers attached to their sides, one air pressure gauge inside each can, and one outside the cans; put only one over heat; place balloons over the caps; observe which balloons expand and which can crumples when the balloons are removed; the caps are replaced and the cans are removed from the heat.

 Design B: To test effect of heat and prevention of air from being sucked back in can, use two identical cans, place both over sources of heat, place balloons over cans, cap one, and remove both from heat. Observe which can crumples and which does not.

Observed measurements and Interpretation: The temperature in the cans went up, then down as the heat was removed. The air pressure in the heated can went up as the can was heated, then down below 14.7 lbs/sq inch as the capped can cooled. The can continued to crumple until the air pressure inside the can equalled the outside air pressure. The cans remained intact when the heat was not applied or when the heat was applied but the cap was removed during the cooling period, but they crumpled when the heat was applied and followed by replacement of the cap. Since it is known that heat causes a gas to expand and that air pressure is 14.7 lbs/sq inch, we can infer that heat caused the gas to expand and was forced outside the can, but could not return when the cap was replaced; then as the can cooled, the gas contracted, exerting less pressure inside the can. The greater outside air pressure then caused the can to crumple.

Conclusion: Objects, such as tin cans, do not crumple when the pressure inside and outside are equal. But, if the pressure inside is reduced, the atmospheric pressure will crush any such object whose walls cannot resist 14.7 lbs of pressure.

 Since concepts, generalizations, and theories are such important ideas in science, we shall define each of them and then explain a strategy for teaching students to formulate them in science classes.

Definition of Concepts, Generalizations, and Theories

A concept is a label for an abstraction and organization of properties that an idea or an object has in common with other ideas or objects. A concept may also be related to other concepts. The concept of an apple, for example, consists of such properties as color (which can vary in value from yellow to purple), size (from the size of a crabapple to that of a delicious apple), shape (round to heart-shaped), taste (sweet to sour), and so forth. Of course, *apple* can also refer to a particular apple, such as a Winesap, which consists of variations in these properties: color (purple), size (medium), and shape (round). But when we think of an apple in an abstract way, we have to think of what all apples have in common (their properties and variations in these properties). Likewise, concepts in science, such as *gravity* in physics, *atom* in chemistry, and *cell* in biology are abstractions from observed phenomena. Concepts can be developed by providing students with a range of objects that embody the attributes and variations in the attributes that make up a concept. Then, students can be taught to perceive what properties the objects have in common.

Generalizations are relations between or among concepts. The generalization *The volume of a gas is directly proportional to its temperature, keeping pressure constant,* consists of relationships among the concepts of volume, temperature, and pressure. (Of course, the generalization also contains other concepts, such as "proportional" and "constant.") This particular generalization holds up over such a wide range of variations that it qualifies as a *law* (Boyle's Law). A generalization can be taught by first developing the concepts involved in the generalization and then guiding students to perceive the relationship among the concepts. In Boyle's Law, for example, gas pressure can be observed to correlate with temperature (when temperature increases, so does pressure, if volume is kept constant).

A *theory* is an explanation that usually involves interrelationships among a set of generalizations. For example, molecular theory which consists, in part, of explanations and conditions which affect molecular movement, can be used to explain Boyle's Laws.

TEACHING SCIENCE

Now, notice that in progressing from concepts to generalizations to theories, we proceed from observation of particular objects or events to abstractions (or concepts), relationships among these abstractions (or generalizations) and on to theories (abstractions and the interrelationships among the generalizations). We can use this progression in teaching science. That is, a science lesson can start with observation or recall of objects or events in everyday life. From these observations, we can construct abstractions and then form these abstractions and the relationships between them into generalizations. A lesson in physics can start with an ordinary household candle. Students can observe that the candle changes from a solid to a liquid state, and from a liquid to a gaseous state as heat is applied. As we use similar examples, we can teach students to abstract from these examples and to form generalizations.

The purpose of using the candle example is to illustrate how a lesson can progress from concrete to abstract levels of thinking (Taba, 1965). This progression is one way that the teacher can try to cover the range of ability among students. Most, if not all, students can grasp the concrete stage of the lesson; some can go on to the more abstract levels; and some students may be able to progress to comprehension of the more abstract theoretical levels of thought, the quantification of relationships, and even express them in mathematical form. By starting with observable concrete objects and events and progressing in steps to more abstract levels, we can accommodate a greater range of individual differences in ability in a science lesson than if the lesson started at an abstract level of thought. Therefore, more students can learn science, at least the concrete aspects of it, if we start a lesson at the concrete level and then proceed to more abstract levels.

Question Sequence for Teaching Thinking (QUEST)

An instructional procedure for taking students from observation to conceptualization, and from conceptualization to generalization consists of a question sequence for teaching thinking (Taba, 1965). This *question sequence for teaching* thinking (acronym: *QUEST*) is a way a teacher can direct a discussion that does not meander, but goes somewhere, and through phase out of the teacher and phase in of students can teach them to direct their own thinking processes.

Development of teaching plans for Quest, as for any instructional procedure, begins with the formulation of an objective. In the example given in box 13.3, the objective is to develop the generalization: *Energy is neither created nor destroyed, only transformed.* Then the teacher works backwards to ask what concepts or interpretations or inferences this generalization rests upon. (concepts of electrical and mechanical energy) The answer to this question, then leads to the question: "What input observations, measurements, or data must these concepts rest upon?" (Measurement of energy input and energy output from such transformations as electrical to mechanical energy, as in an electric clock.) Then the teacher must provide for this input, either through direct experience (a laboratory investigation) or a vicarious experience (the use of films or texts). In short, lesson planning works backward from the teaching goal or objective, while actual instruction, such as the Quest procedure, works forward as demonstrated by the lesson in box 13.3.

BOX 13.3. Questioning Sequence for Teaching Thinking (QUEST) Applied to a Science Lesson

Type of Question	Purpose	Question
Focusing	Initiate discussion or focus on issue.	What types of energy conversion do we observe in a house? From electrical to mechanical (clock), to heat (broiler), to radiant energy (lamp); from mechanical to electrical (crystal in phonograph).
Controlling	Direct or dominate discussion.	Would you focus now only on the house?
Extending	Obtain more information at a particular level of discussion.	What other examples can we think of? Mechanical to kinetic (door opening); mechanical to potential (coiled door spring); chemical to heat (burning gas).
Ignoring or rejecting	Maintain current trend of discussion.	Would you bring that issue up later?
Raising	Move discussion from factual to interpretive, inferential, or abstraction and generalization level.	In all of these energy conversions, is energy created, destroyed, or only transformed? What can we say about all changes in energy? (Formulate the law of conservation of energy.)

The Quest procedure systematically develops a sequence of thinking. However, the progression from one level to another in this sequence is in marked contrast to what actually occurs in the classroom. Most of the questions teachers ask are at the literal level of comprehension (Guszak, 1967). They are the *how, what, who, where, when* type of questions. They aim at memory, or direct recall, of information. Of course, information at the literal level is necessary before teachers can ask higher-level questions, questions that lead to interpretations, inferences, generalizations, and evaluations. But some teachers are prone to stop their question-asking at the literal level instead of stimulating students' thinking at higher levels.

QUESTIONS AT VARIOUS LEVELS OF THOUGHT

Spache and Spache (1977) stress seven types of questions. In box 13.4 we define and apply them to science content.

BOX 13.4. Questions at Various Levels of Thinking
Applied to Science Content

1. *Memory:* Recognizing or recalling information.
   a. Who formulated the theory of relativity?
   b. What is meant by the formula $E = mc^2$?
2. *Translation:* Expressing ideas in different forms (words to pictures, pictures to words, numbers to graphs, etc.) or language (paraphrase).
   a. In your own words, explain the laws of genetic inheritance.
   b. Using the data in this temperature table, draw a graph to depict the average daily temperature over the last three months.
3. *Interpretation:* Constructing a generalization that can be used for inferring the meaning of an event.
   (Construction of generalization): After grass has been covered by a log for a week, the grass is yellowish. Why? (Sunlight is necessary for plants to produce chlorophyll which give their leaves green color.)
   (Observation): The log prevented the sun's light from reaching the grass.
   (Inference): Therefore, the grass's chlorophyll content was reduced, resulting in a yellowish color.
4. *Application:* Using a given generalization or concept to solve a problem.
   What use can be made of the knowledge that barium hydroxide (BaOH) combines with hydrochloric acid (HCh) to form an insoluble compound, barium chloride ($BaCl_2$)? (One application: use barium hydroxide to remove chlorine from water.)
5. *Analysis:* Dividing a problem into its several parts or following a procedure to separate a problem into its constituents.
   Which system is malfunctioning in the television set? (Observe first whether the picture, sound, or power system is not functioning. Then isolate the problem further within each of the three major components.
6. *Synthesis:* Combining elements to make a whole which has its own properties.
   How would you make table salt from the basic elements? (Combine sodium and chlorine.)
7. *Evaluation:* Making judgments by applying criteria.
   Which is more efficient, a steam or a gas engine? (Formulate criterion for efficiency: ratio of output/input. Then use this criterion on the two engines.)

The questions in box 13.4 elicit answers or *products* of thinking. Another set of questions can elicit not only answers but also *processes or procedures for arriving at the answers*. To get at these processes, we can ask students: (1) What steps would you follow in doing an experiment? (2) How would you determine that a child inherits an equal number of chromosomes from each parent? (3) What process converts radio waves into sound?

Questions — whether they are in a sequence as in Quest, or whether they are aimed at products of thought or processes — are useful ways of directing students' attention and getting them to think about the content and mode of inquiry within a course, either before or after they read. If we use a phase-out procedure in conjunction with these questioning strategies, then we phase students in to asking their own questions and using their own questions to guide their own thinking. The following is a procedure for transferring Quest to students. (We can use a similar procedure with the other types of questions.)

PHASE OUT/PHASE IN FOR QUEST

The teacher can initiate phase out in a lesson by dividing the class into groups, providing them with a Quest guide, and appointing discussion leaders who will take their groups through input, focusing, extending, raising, and higher-order questioning until the groups form a generalization. Eventually almost every student should be able to use a Quest guide alone.[1]

Questioning Strategies

Questioning strategies help solve the problem of individual differences in ability to learn content in science. Almost all students can make or recall observations and answer *wh*-type questions (those beginning with the words *who, what, when, where, how*). Fewer are able to follow higher levels of questioning. Even fewer can attain the more abstract, generalized levels of thought. But all students can participate to the limits of their capabilities, and the questioning strategies can stimulate the further development of their capabilities. Another way in which to make science understandable to a wider range of students is through use of what we call a Problem Demonstration Sequence.

Problem Demonstration Sequence

Frequently the authors of science texts present definitions, concepts, measurements, and principles in a chapter, then ask students to apply

[1] Of course, we can apply the steps in this phase-out/phase-in procedure to other materials, such as programmed instructional material for teaching science content or procedures for doing a laboratory investigation.

them to the solution of problems at the end of the chapter. However, they give no demonstration in the chapter of how to solve the problems. Often, the teacher places the burden of integrating and applying the chapter content to the solution of problems upon the student. Of course, we can agree that students who can solve these problems without assistance have passed a difficult test of their understanding of the chapter. But students who cannot do so experience frustration and unnecessary failure. Science texts, like mathematics texts, should demonstrate how to work a problem before students are asked to solve similar problems on their own. If they did, more students would be likely to have successful experiences with science and consequently develop a more favorable attitude toward the subject. If a science text does not demonstrate how to solve problems, the teacher can supply this missing instructional step. The following example is similar to one in a physics text (Boylan, 1962), which contains a "step-by-step" method for solving problems that we have augmented in the demonstration in box 13.5.

BOX 13.5. Problem Demonstration Sequence

Problem	Demonstration
A 300 pound block of granite weighs only 50 pounds when completely submerged in water. What is (a) its apparent loss of weight, (b) the weight of fluid displaced, and (c) the volume of the block?	a. The apparent loss of weight of the object is its weight in air minus its weight after submerging in water: $300 - 50 = 250$ pounds. The apparent loss of weight is equal to the weight of fluid displaced, which is the same as the buoyant force exerted by the fluid on the object.
	b. The weight of the fluid displaced is also 250 pounds, for according to Archimedes' law, an immersed body is buoyed up by a force equal to the weight of the fluid displaced by it.
	c. The volume of the block is the weight of the fluid displaced (250 lbs) divided by the weight of the fluid displaced by a one-cubic-foot (ft^3) object, which is 62.5 lbs. Therefore, 250/62.5 lbs. = 4 ft^3.

Even if a science text does demonstrate how to solve a problem, it may not provide instruction in (1) how to manipulate a formula to solve for one unknown, given the other variables, (2) how to transform the syntax so that the variables stated in the problem come in the same order as the variables in the formula, (3) means for recognizing synonyms (for example: *buoyancy* and *lifting force,* and (4) interrelationships among formulas that are necessary for solving multiple-step problems.

After awhile, a class will become familiar with the algebraic and linguistic manipulations in science problems. As they do, the instructor can phase out of doing these manipulations and phase in the students. After this instructional sequence, the instructor would know, not just assume, that the students could do the manipulations.

Box 13.6 presents an outline and an application of Problem Demonstration Sequence. The outline shows algebraic and linguistic manipulations, plus recall of unsupplied information necessary for solving the problems. The formulae used in box 13.6 are on buoyancy. Notice that we have stated terms of the formulae as variables which means that each term can vary in value and that the formulas are in a general form. (See chapter 14 for discussion of more abstract formulas.)

BOX 13.6. Problem Demonstration Sequence

1. List basic formulae

Variable A	Variable B	Variable C
Weight in air	− Weight submerged	= Apparent loss of weight *or* (synonymously) buoyant force exerted on the object.

2. Show how basic formula can be algebraically manipulated so that given any two variables, the third can be computed:
   a. Given A and B, find C: $A - B = C$
   b. Given A and C, find B: $A - C = B$
   c. Given B and C, find A: $B + C = A$

3. Show how linguistic manipulations can be made, that is, how synonyms and syntactic transformations can vary the way in which problems are stated. Demonstrate the reverse processes students must use so that they know what formula to apply. They can then do the necessary computation, which involves relatively simple arithmetic.

   Example: What is the "force by which an object is buoyed up?" (Recognize this means the same as "buoyant force exerted on the object.") Then, students know questions can be answered by solving for C (formula 2a, above).

4. Recall the physics principle which is necessary for solving the problem.

   Example: What volume of fluid is displaced? Students are to recall Archimedes' principle: "An immersed body is buoyed up by a force equal to the weight of fluid displaced by it." Consequently, students can recognize that in formula 2a, variable C will give them the weight in pounds of fluid displaced. But, the question asks for volume. Consequently, students must know how to transform from weight in pounds to cubic feet.

5. Teach transformation of measurement:
   a. Recall that 1 cubic foot of water = 62.5 lbs.

   b. Therefore, volume in cu ft (D) $= \dfrac{\text{pounds of fluid displaced (C)}}{62.5 \text{ lbs/ft}^3 \text{ (E)}}$

   c. Recognize algebraic restatement of above formula:

   $$D \times E = C, E = C/D$$

   d. Now, given C (pounds of fluid displaced), D (volume in cubic feet) can be found by substituting in above formula.

The Problem Demonstration Sequence may accompany other teaching strategies such as the directed reading activity (DRA), marginal gloss, and reading and learning-from-text guide.

TEACHING STUDENTS TO READ AND LEARN FROM SCIENCE TEXT

Introduction to a Science Text

Individual differences also occur in how students orient themselves to a text. Some students may familiarize themselves with a text and adopt appropriate strategies for using it. Other students may read only the assigned pages. To overcome this difference among students, the instructor may derive valuable pay-off by taking some time to introduce the text.

FEATURES OF A TEXT

Introduction to a text is useful for pointing out features students frequently overlook. First, explain the organization of the text. You can glean the organization from noting the sequence of topics in the table of contents and in the chapter headings and subheadings. Also, organizational information may be found in the preface to a text. (Often the preface contains ideas and suggestions on how to use the book.) Second, point out data in the appendices, such as tables that will be helpful in comprehending the text. Third, have students note other information in the appendices, including possibly a glossary of technical terms and an answer key for problems in the text. Fourth, demonstrate the value of the index for obtaining information located in diverse places in the text. To solve a problem in electronics, for example, students might need to get information on the theory from chapter II, on electrical circuits from chapter IX, and on electrical measuring devices from chapter X.

After this overview, the teacher should clarify certain science terms that occur frequently in science texts. We have defined a few such terms in box 13.7.

BOX 13.7. Some Science Terms and Their Definitions

Term	Definition
1. science	1. Knowledge obtained and tested through use of the scientific method.
2. scientific method	2. A procedure, such as a controlled experiment (see box 13.2), for confirmation or disconfirmation of an hypothesis whose terms can be operationally defined.
3. operational definition	3. A definition that is based upon identifiable and repeatable operations or observations. For example, electricity can be defined by voltmeter and ohmmeter measurements of an electrical circuit. These measurements then define electrical current as: $$I = \frac{E}{R}$$ where: I = current in amperes E = pressure in volts R = resistance in ohms
4. observation	4. A fact or phenomenon recognized directly through the senses or indirectly through measurements. For example, Darwin's observations about coral led him to suggest an hypothesis for the formation of atolls.
5. hypothesis	5. An explanation of some phenomenon, pending further evidence that may confirm, disprove, or modify the hypothesis.

6. theory

6. A theory is an explanation based on several hypotheses. For example, Einstein's famous theory on the relationship between energy and matter:

$$E = mc^2$$

where: E = energy
m = mass
c = velocity of light
(186,000 miles/second)

7. controlled experiment

7. A planned test of an hypothesis that involves a change in one factor or condition at a time. A scientist can then observe the results (effects) and with some degree of certainty relate them to the changed factor or condition. For example, see box 13.2. Repeated confirmation of this cause-and-effect relationship results in the formation of a scientific law.

8. law

8. An observed regularity of nature; a statement or formula of an order or relationship that so far as is known has been found to be invariable (unchanging) under the same conditions. For example, the law of gravitational pull is the product of the masses of two bodies divided by the square of the distance between them. The formula is:

$$\frac{m_1 \text{ times } m_2}{d^2}$$

where: g = gravitational pull
m = mass of each body
d = distance between the bodies

ORGANIZATION OF A TEXT

Texts usually have a plan for organizing and presenting information within chapters. An analysis of a text will reveal this plan. Pointing out the plan to the students should help them learn the content. One physics text uses this plan: after an introduction consisting of a few concepts drawn from observations or examples in everyday life, a major generalization is stated at the beginning of a chapter. Then the rest of the chapter explains the concepts, the generalization, and measurements that can be made. Thus, in a chapter entitled "Buoyancy" are examples like these: *Your body feels lighter in water. You float near the top of the water. As you lift objects out of water, they feel heavier.* Then the text sums up by stating a generalization: "Fluids buoy up all objects immersed in them." [2] The rest of the chapter explains this generalization by (1) experimental proof of the principle, (2) experiments on flotation, and (3) applications of the law of flotation. These explanations involve the use of appropriate measurements and formulas.

The chapter concludes with a summary, a list of words and laws presented in the chapter, discussion questions, and problems. A similar pattern is repeated in each chapter. (Patterns of textual organization vary, of course, from text to text. Consequently, instructors have to analyze each text and then communicate this organization.)

STYLE OF WRITING

Another pattern may be detected in the author's style of writing. The style may consist of a similar sequence of paragraph types in each chapter. The types of the paragraphs may be definition, enumeration, classification, comparison and contrast, generalization and proof, hypothesis and evidence, problem and solution, sequence of events (Smith, 1965b; Robinson, 1975). (See chapter 7 for further explanation of paragraph types.) In pointing out the style of writing, a teacher can facilitate students' reading and understanding of text.

GRAPHIC AIDS

Science writing differs from literary writing not only in use of a high density of technical terms and formulas but also in several other ways. Unlike English texts, which rarely include tabular graphic aids, science texts are replete with them. Students frequently skip over them when reading. We think they do so because they do not know how to read and interpret them. Consequently, we urge science instructors to use instructional procedures on teaching construction and interpretation of graphic aids, like those explained in chapter 12, to help their students read and learn from them as they occur in their texts. Such instruction will also develop students' ability to draw conclusions based on evidence, to evaluate interpretations and conclusions, and other reasoning abilities.

Semantic Hierarchies in Text

DEFINITION. Another type of organization is a semantic hierarchy. In a semantic hierarchy, the technical terms in a content area are arranged in

---

[2] Paul J. Boylan, *Elements of Physics*. Boston: Allyn and Bacon, Inc., 1962, p. 56.

such a way that exemplars underlie concepts, which in turn are placed under more abstract, superordinate concepts, and those concepts that have properties in common are placed closer to each other. An example of a semantic hierarchy for nutrition is shown in figure 13.1.

ASSESSMENT. A cloze pretest can determine whether a text is appropriate for a class. A text is appropriate if the class's average on the cloze test is between 41 and 60 percent correct insertions (Thelen, 1976). See chapter 8 for a more detailed explanation of the cloze technique.

Adapting Text to Students

What if a cloze pretest indicates that the difficulty of a science text exceeds the reading ability of the students? That is, what if the students get less than 40 percent of the insertions correct? Indeed, this is likely with any text because of the wide range of reading ability that exists in any class. One solution is to rewrite the text. Will rewriting help? Corey (1977) reported on the rewriting of ninth-grade biology materials to simplify the style of writing and vocabulary. The rewritten materials significantly enhanced an experimental group's comprehension on a 100 item test that had high reliability and content validity. Although the materials had been rewritten to benefit students whose reading ability was below grade level, the students who were reading above grade level also comprehended better. The technique of rewriting materials is similar to the marginal gloss strategy. Why does it work? We think rewriting passages or constructing marginal glosses are effective because they provide a semantic bridge between abstract ideas in the text and the students' knowledge hierarchy. In short, rewriting a text or providing a marginal gloss for it enables students to relate new ideas to concepts already within their repertoire.

We recognize that teachers have little time during the school year for rewriting, but we also know that some school districts are providing release time for preparation of materials and are supporting such activities during the summer time. Consequently, the suggestions in this section may be put to use at these times.

Adapting Students to Text

An alternate to rewriting is to develop students' semantic hierarchies to the point where the semantic level of technical terms in the text is close to the highest level of abstraction in the students' semantic hierarchies. Then, if a student reads a passage which contains technical terms that are new, the teacher can use directed reading activities, marginal glosses and reading and learning-from-text guides to relate these terms to subordinate concepts in the student's semantic hierarchy. A student may have a semantic hierarchy that goes up to *food,* but not to *nutrition.* Since *nutrition*

FIGURE 13.1. Semantic Hierarchy for Nutrition

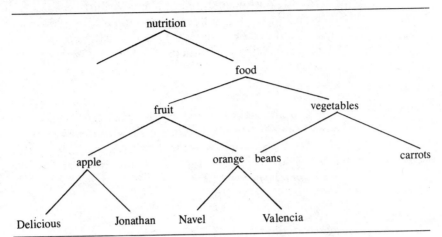

is semantically close in level of abstraction to *food,* the student is likely to make the connection when the relationship is pointed out.

A structured overview (Barron, 1969), which is a visual arrangement of technical terms in a text, depicts the semantic relationships among the technical terms. If students have this overview before reading a text, they can use it to perceive where technical terms fit into a semantic hierarchy as they encounter the terms. Of course, not all the technical terms in a science text could be put into an overview. An overview for technical terms in a particular chapter would be reasonable. As students progress through a text, the highest-level terms in one chapter can be related to equally abstract terms in subsequent chapters. Thus, students could accumulate a semantic hierarchy for the entire course as they progress through it.

TECHNICAL VS. GENERAL VOCABULARY

In developing students' semantic hierarchies, teachers should be aware that science vocabulary must be differentiated from general vocabulary. The word *field,* for example, is defined as a large, open expanse of land in general vocabulary and, of course, in the technical vocabulary of agriculture. But the technical term *field* in electricity refers to the invisible lines of force that emanate from magnets and electrical circuits. Students must also realize that a technical term in one content area may have a different meaning in another. The word *current* in physics means something different than *current* in social science.

Although the vocabulary load of science is high, the load decreases when you instruct students in the meanings of roots that occur in many words (*therm*al, iso*therm,* and *therm*ometer), and when you teach the meanings of affixes that appear in words in science text (therm*al* and *iso*therm). Fortunately, many scientific terms are constructed from combinations of Latin and Greek roots and affixes. Teaching the meanings of these word parts will facilitate the acquisition of technical science vocabulary. (See chapter 16 for a list of affixes and roots.)

RELATIONAL WORDS

You can also help students by teaching relational words that occur frequently in science texts. Among such words are those that imply cause and effect (*therefore, because*), time (*during, after, before*), comparisons (*like, different, than*), degree of importance (*essential, least*), and evaluation (*best, poorest*) (Shepherd, 1978). See chapter 7 for a list of these and other signal and transitional words.

TRANSLATING SYMBOLS AND FORMULAS

Students also have to relate technical terms to the symbols that represent them so they will be able to translate these symbols into words. If the symbols are in an equation, then the translation of symbols into words has to be expressed in sentences. Consider this formula:

$$g = \frac{m_1 m_2}{d^2}$$

where: g = gravitational pull
m = mass of a body
d = distance between the two bodies

Translated into words, the formula reads: *The gravitational pull between two bodies is equal to the product of their masses divided by the square of the distance between them.* This translation takes the abstract formula a step in the direction of a more concrete level of thinking. Students next have to use their semantic hierarchies for these terms in order to relate them to concrete events. These events in science are frequently observations of reactions made visible through the use of measuring devices and other apparatus. For example, the "Bubble Chamber" is a liquid medium for making visible the tracks of high energy particles passing through it.

Overlap Between Skills in Science and in Teaching Students to Read and Learn from Text

Skills in science and skills in reading and learning from text overlap. Carter and Simpson (1978) point out that designing investigations, collecting and interpreting data, communicating results, and formulating conclusions are analogous to processes used in general reading and study skills. Consequently, it is not surprising to find that instruction in science enhances reading achievement (Morgan, Rachelson, and Lloyd, 1977) and *vice versa*.

All of these similarities and differences between the study of science and the general ability to read and learn from text can be taught through the use of single- and multiple-text strategies. We believe that, if the single- and multiple-text strategies presented in this book are applied to any text, more students could successfully learn the content of physics, chemistry, and biology to the limits of their individual abilities. What teachers need to do to achieve this goal is to start with concrete, everyday activities and progress to abstract levels of thought. To do so, they can use (1) single-text strategies such as directed reading activities, marginal glosses, reading and learning from text guides (RLTs), SQ3R, and (2) multiple-text strategies, such as the concept technique, the inquiry approach, or the project method. Although these strategies are applicable to teaching any science content, we shall demonstrate how to apply all of them to reading and learning from text in a physics course.

Single-Text Strategies

DIRECTED READING ACTIVITY (DRA)

Science texts are dense with technical terms, examples, concepts, and generalizations. But students do not necessarily have to learn and remember all this content, at least not all the examples. The task of the teacher is to (1) decide which content to stress and point it out to students and (2) explore and build background, then use preposed questions to guide students while they are reading and learning from the chapter and use postposed questions afterwards to make sure students understand and remember the important points. Some texts try to incorporate these DRA components, but no text can carry out an interaction between an instructor and a class as DRA does.

In box 13.8 is Mr. Phelps's DRA for a chapter from *Elements of Physics* by Boylan.

BOX 13.8. Class: Physics (DRA)

"HOW MATTER BEHAVES,"

   I. Mr. Phelps explores the students' background.
     A. Mr. Phelps questions the class about their experiences with concepts to be developed in this chapter (properties of matter: inertia, elasticity, universal gravitation, and impenetrability).
       1. Have you been on a bus when it started or stopped suddenly?
       2. What happens when you squeeze a rubber ball or stretch a rubber band and then let go?

    3. If you jump up, how long do you stay up?

    4. When you get into a bathtub, what happens to the level of water?

  B. Mr. Phelps then explains the relationship between the students' background and the concepts in the chapter: "These questions are related to the four major concepts you are going to learn in this section. Look at the summary on page 22 of your physics text; this summary will give you an overview of this chapter."

II. Mr. Phelps builds the students' background.

  A. Mr. Phelps reviews with the students the technical vocabulary in this chapter. *Technical Vocabulary*

    1. Inertia (p. 13): Matter can neither start nor stop itself.

    2. Elastic (p. 14): Most matter upon which a force has acted, within certain limits, tends to return to its shape.

    3. Universal attraction (p. 15): Each particle of matter attracts every other particle.

    4. Impenetrable (p. 16): Matter cannot occupy space already occupied by other matter.

    5. Length (p. 17): the distance between two points

    6. Time (p. 17): the duration or interval between two events

    7. Mass (p. 17): the quantity of matter in a body

    8. Force (p. 20): a push or pull that tends to change a body's motion or shape (One pound force = change of velocity of 1 slug or <u>pounds</u> by one ft/sec/sec).

    9. Density (p. 21): mass per unit of volume of a substance: (space) ^{32} (mass/volume)

    10. Weight (p. 17): the force with which a body is attracted towards the earth

  B. Mr. Phelps gives some preposed questions to guide reading:

    1. What properties does matter have?

    2. What measurements in what units are used to measure energy changes?

    3. What is Hooke's law?

III. Students read chapter.

IV. Following the reading, the class engages in a discussion.

  A. Factual level

    1. Questions on definitions

    2. Preposed questions

    3. Process questions (How do you find volume? Mass?)

  B. Interpretation or Inferential level

    1. What property does plastic or glass lack that allows it to be broken when a force is applied?

    2. Why can a nail be driven into wood?

    3. The mass of a body never changes, but its weight does. Why?

  C. Generalized level (These questions require use of principles explained in the chapter. The teacher can demonstrate their application, then divide the class into groups to solve other problems.)

    1. If you watched two cars start from rest and wanted to know which had the better engine, what measurements would you take and what computations would you make?

2. How many pounds of force is required to steadily lift a shot put that has a mass of 16 pounds?

3. You want to know whether a crown is made of gold or silver. How would you find out if you know only that the density of gold is 1200?

V. Mr. Phelps involves students in extending their understanding of how matter behaves.

Discussion: How would matter, such as a 16-pound shot put or a 180-pound man, behave after it had been transported to the moon? Remember: the gravitational pull of the moon is one-sixth that of earth. Apply your discussion to each of the concepts listed in the technical vocabulary.

Examples in this box are adapted from *Elements of Physics,* revised by Paul J. Boylan, pp. 13–23. © Copyright 1962 by Allyn and Bacon, Inc. Reprinted by permission. Numbers in parentheses identify the pages in the Boylan text where the technical vocabulary is explained in context.

MARGINAL GLOSS

A marginal gloss is analogous to having the instructor accompany the student while he or she is reading a homework assignment. The marginal gloss may consist of paginated, dittoed notes handed out to students when homework is assigned. Students may use these notes as they do their assigned homework.

In the dittoed notes, the instructor may clarify a term in the text; explicate a passage; provide background information that is necessary for comprehension; concretize or relate an abstract idea to students' experiences; indicate what is significant and important to remember (some students may think everything is equally important and hence suffer from an information overload); and, most important, show students how to solve assigned problems (see Problem Demonstration Sequence, boxes 13.5 and 13.6). In short, the instructor provides whatever marginal notes are necessary for helping students read and learn from text. In some cases, the gloss may contain more words than the original text. In box 13.9 is a marginal gloss that Mr. Phelps provided for maximum clarification of a section in a chapter of a textbook. Italics have been added.

BOX 13.9. Gloss Examples

TEXT: "MOLECULES AND THEIR BEHAVIOR"

Gloss	*Text*
Ancients refers to those thinkers who lived in an early period of history before A.D. 476. Why could they not prove it?	The ancients had the idea that matter was made of small particles, but *they could not prove it.*

Definition of a molecule. Note two important points: (1) smallest particle of matter, (2) retains properties of the substance. For example, the properties of chalk are whiteness, softness, fine-grained, easily rubbed off.

. . . The molecule is the smallest particle of substance (chalk, iron, sugar, etc.) *which has the properties of the substance.*

This passage implies that molecules can only be further divided by chemical, not by physical, means. Chalk consists of the compound C_aCO_3. Divided chemically into atoms, it consists of atoms of calcium, carbon, and oxygen. How different are the properties of these atoms from C_aCO_3? Remember: The only important point in this section to remember is the definition of a molecule.

If you persuaded a chemist to break up the chalk molecule, by chemical, not physical means, you would have smaller units, called atoms, of which the chalk molecule is made, but which are different from the chalk.

Note contrast: *Cohesion* refers to attraction between *like* (same) molecules.

Adhesion refers to attraction between *unlike* (different) molecules.

. . . The name we apply to the attractive force between like molecules is cohesion. *. . . This attractive force between unlike molecules is called* adhesion.

The phrase, "it seems," implies that scientists are not sure, but only think that all molecules are in motion. Molecules exhibit two kinds of motion. Can you "dance" without changing your location?

It seems certain molecules of all substances are in a state of motion . . . real motion in which the molecule gets somewhere . . . or simple vibration in which a molecule dances around and ends up where it started.

Remember the definitions of *cohesion* and *adhesion* and the two types of molecular motion. Molecular motion will help you understand the next section on the three states of matter (solids, liquids, and gases).

In the remainder of the chapter learn the properties of solids, liquids, and gases, and why they have properties.

Text passages in this box are from *Elements of Physics*, revised by Paul J. Boylan, pp. 23–25. © Copyright 1962 by Allyn and Bacon, Inc. Reprinted by permission.

READING AND LEARNING-FROM-TEXT GUIDE

The reading and learning-from-text Guide (RLT) organizes information in a science text so that it progresses from observations or facts to concepts, inferences or interpretations, and then on to generalizations. The basic purpose of an RLT is to facilitate progression from concrete to abstract, and from particular events to generalizations that subsume these events.

The way to construct an RLT is to start with one or more generalizations students are to read, learn, and understand in a section or in an entire chapter of a text. Then work backwards to single out the concepts, interpretations, or inferences which support the generalization(s). (The author may have developed some of these concepts in a previous chapter. The concept of molecules and force occurred in the text prior to the passage we used for our RLT guide in box 13.9. We listed these and other concepts from our passage concepts in a section on definitions.) Next, list the concrete elements, the observations, facts, or literal statements underpinning the entire structure. In science, we also need a section in our RLT on measuring devices and units. These devices represent an application of the scientific principles explained in the passage.

To demonstrate how to construct an RLT, let's take another chapter from the science text we have been using.[3] The major generalization in this chapter is Pascal's law, which applies to all fluids, whether they are liquids or gases, and *at rest* (Note: the limiting condition, the law applies to fluids at rest.): *Pressure applied to an enclosed fluid is transmitted equally in all directions without loss, and acts with equal force on equal surfaces.* A basic concept in this law is *pressure*, which is defined as "force per unit area." Along with this concept, students must learn that pressure is measured in units of lb/in^2, lbs/ft^2, g/cm^2, $kilograms/cm^2$, $dynes/cm^2$. They also need to know that fluids transmit pressure in two ways: (1) pressure applied to the liquid from without or (2) gravity pressure from the liquid's own weight. Why do fluids transmit pressure? Because molecules which make up fluids are free to move, and they continue to move against each other and their container until the pressure is the same on each molecule and the wall of the container. Now, these concepts and Pascal's law rest upon observations that can be made in everyday life: (1) When a flat fire hose fills with water, the hose becomes round, indicating that the fluid is pushing at right angles. Puncture the hose and the water squirts out at right angles. (2) A skater on thin ice may break the ice, but the same skater lying down on a board on the ice might not, illustrating that the skater's weight per square inch (or pressure) on the ice is less when the skater is lying down on the board. (3) Press a water gun and you see the water squirt out — your finger transmits pressure to the water which increases the force per unit area at the narrower area of the nozzle. What are some practical applications of the principles of hydraulic pressure? The major ones are a hydraulic jack or hydraulic brakes.

Mr. Phelps put this information into an RLT (box 13.10) in such a way

[3] Boylan, "Pressure in Fluids," *Elements of Physics*. Boston: Allyn and Bacon, 1962, pp. 39–45.

that students became cognizant of the definitions, the relationships be-tween observations and generalizations or principles that explain them, and the applications of these principles to measuring devices and other uses.

BOX 13.10. Reading and Learning-from-Text Guide

"PRESSURE IN FLUIDS"

Definitions: Use your text to match these terms with their definitions. (If a term is not defined in this section, use the glossary at the end of the text.)

Terms	Definitions
1. fluid ( )	a. force per unit area
2. pressure ( )	b. stationary
3. static ( )	c. flow
4. force ( )	d. push or pull
5. millibar ( )	e. 1000 dynes/cm²

Facts or Observations: Indicate which of the following are true (+) or false (−) observations.
1. When a garden hose which is going full blast is punctured, the water at the puncture site dribbles out ( ) or squirts out at a right angle to the hose ( ).
2. Lifting a filled bucket by its handle with your hand is more difficult than with your finger ( ).
3. When you decrease the nozzle opening, the water from your hose squirts farther ( ).
4. A pressure gauge at the waterworks miles away from your home will indicate the same pressure as a gauge on the closed faucet at your home ( ).
5. Water in a pan on a level surface is stationary ( ).

Concepts, Interpretations, or Generalizations: Next to each statement below, fill in the number of the observation above that goes with it.
1. Two equal forces acting in opposite directions on an object result in no movement of the object.   ( )
2. When you *decrease* the area on which a force is being exerted, you *increase* the pressure.   ( )
3. A fluid always pushes at right angles against the wall that holds it.   ( )
4. Pressure is force per unit area.   ( )
5. Pressure applied to an enclosed fluid is (a) applied equally in all directions without loss of force and (b) acts equally on all equal surfaces.   ( )

Measurement: Fill in the missing word or numbers in these sentences from the choices given below.
1. A pressure gauge works because water pressure is exerted _____ and at _____ _____.

2. A 160-pound person standing on the ice exerts a _____ of 160 pounds on his or her shoes.
3. Pressure is force per unit area or Pressure $= \dfrac{\text{Force}}{\text{Area}}$. If the force is 160 lbs and the area is 32 cm², then the pressure is _____ per cm².
4. Pressure can also be measured in metric units of _____ per cm² or _____ cm² or _____ per cm².

Choices:

5 lbs	dynes
grams	kilograms
force	right angles
equally	

Applications (for group discussion):
1. Explain how a 200-pound person using a hydraulic jack can lift a car to change a tire on a 5000-pound car.
2. Your car has hydraulic brakes. Why does pressure on one brake pedal exert pressure on four brake surfaces with enough pressure to stop a car? Draw a diagram to illustrate your explanation.

Material in this box is adapted from *Elements of Physics,* revised by Paul J. Boylan, pp. 39–45. © Copyright 1962 by Allyn and Bacon, Inc. Reprinted by permission.

SQ3R

SQ3R is, in a sense, a self-instructional study procedure. The student learns to survey (S) the material, formulate questions (Q) to be answered while reading the material; then the student reads (R_1) the material, recites (R_2) the answers to the questions, and, finally, reviews (R_3) the material to check the answers.[4]

Preceding SQ3R with the other strategies (DRA, Gloss, and RLT) can help teach the student (through transfer of learning) what to observe in a survey of a section or chapter of a text and what kinds of questions are appropriate and valid to ask about a particular content area text. A phase-out/phase-in strategy applied directly to SQ3R may also directly develop this learning. In the phase-out/phase-in procedure, the instructor first demonstrates with one section or chapter for the entire class, then has groups each do an SQ3R on another section or chapter, and eventually has individual students use SQ3R on their own as a valid procedure for reading and learning from their text.

In using SQ3R, the students might (a) note the headings as they survey

[4] A variation on SQ3R is PQRST (Spache, 1963). The letters stand for **Preview** (skim selection), **Question** (develop questions to be used as purposes for reading), **Read** (to answer self-posed questions), **Summarize** (organize and write summary of information), **Test** (compare summary with information in passage).

the section, and transform them into *wh- questions* (who, where, what, when, how, why); (b) check to see if the text defines technical terms in bold-faced type or italics; (c) put these terms into *wh- question* form, (d) do likewise with generalizations, (e) observe whether the text provides generalizations in the form of formulae; (f) ask how they apply; (g) look for measuring devices and ask how they work; (h) check for questions at the end of the section; read the questions; use them as preposed questions for subsequent reading, reciting, and reviewing. See box 13.11.

BOX 13.11. SQ3R

"GRAVITY PRESSURE"

1. SURVEY AND QUESTION
   Heading: *Gravity Pressure*
   Question: How is gravity pressure different from external pressure?
   Heading: *Pressures due to Gravity*
   Question: What is pressure due to gravity? How great is this pressure?

   Note italics:
   Pressure depends upon vertical height of the liquid above the surface pressed upon and *pressure depends upon the density of the liquid.*

   Question: What does gravity pressure depend upon?
   Note formula: Pressure = height × density, or p = hd.
   Question: What is the formula for determining gravity pressure?
   Heading: *Size and Shape of Container*
   Question: How do the size and shape of the container affect gravity pressure?
   Heading: *Upward and Sideward Forces*
   Question: Are the upward and sideward forces the same as the force on the bottom?
   Heading: *Water Power*
   Question: How is water power developed and used?
   Heading: *Water Supply Systems*
   Question: How are water supply systems designed?
   Heading: *Manometers*
   Question: What is a manometer? How does it work? Why does it work this way?
   Heading: *Calculations of Pressure and Total Force*
   Question: How are pressure and total force computed? What units are used?

   Note at the end of the chapter: questions, summary, words to understand and learn, discussion questions, problems

2. READ AND RECITE: Read a section, using the questions posed for that section.
   Recite: test yourself on each question.

3. REVIEW: Reread section by section to check on the accuracy of your answers.

Headings in this box are from *Elements of Physics*, revised by Paul J. Boylan, pp. 45–55.
© Copyright 1962 by Allyn and Bacon, Inc. Reprinted by permission.

Multiple-Text Strategies

Although a science class usually has only one textbook to use, other science texts at different levels of difficulty are available. You can use these other science texts for group or individual reference projects. Moreover, you can identify books on various science topics in the school catalogs. (See chapter 11 for use of these catalogs.) A selection of these books can also be useful for group or individual projects.

INQUIRY

At the heart of a science course is a mode of inquiry, the scientific or experimental method. Consequently, science students learn not to accept information on the basis of the text's or the instructor's authority but to question and determine the validity of assertions made in the text or in the class. In short, science students learn to use the assertion as an hypothesis and then apply the scientific method to test the hypothesis. (See box 13.2 for the steps in this method.)

Suppose the students' text states: "Water rises to its own level." Is this statement true? How can it be tested experimentally? The class can proceed to investigate this question under teacher direction. If the class has already had some phase-out training in the use of the scientific method, the students can divide into groups. If you have already given students enough training in the experimental method, they can pursue the question on their own.

PROJECT METHOD

The Project Method consists of the students formulating questions about a chapter and getting answers through library research — first as a class, then as members of groups, and finally as individuals. (See chapter 9 for further explanation of the project method.)

You can investigate almost any topic in a chapter. Some topics, such as conversion of water energy to electricity, may require construction of a miniature hydroelectric system. Students might search the library for information on how to construct their own weather stations, radio receivers, television sets, or telescopes and use the information to actually build these instruments. The results can be displayed at science fairs.

Science fairs have featured projects at all school levels for many years; but, frequently, the projects have not been a part of regular classroom instruction. However, the sequence of strategies from DRA to the project method can take students progressively from dependence towards independence in reading and learning from text and can teach students how to get information to satisfy their own curiosity. The phase-out/phase-in sequence applied to each strategy will contribute to this progression towards independence. Through use of the project method, we think more students would do projects on their own. In doing projects, they would also gain greater understanding of and interest in science and its applications, not just as a school subject, but as an important part of their everyday lives.

Although teachers can observe whether students are learning to read and learn from text through classroom observation, student reports, and construction activities, they should also use a systematic way of evaluating student achievement. For this purpose, in the last section of this chapter, we explain the construction and use of a table of specifications. To illustrate this table we use content and processes from physics, but the table of specifications is a generic concept that works in any content area, with, of course, appropriate modifications in the table's content and processes.

A TABLE OF SPECIFICATIONS
FOR EVALUATING ACHIEVEMENT

Teacher-made tests should start with a *table of specifications* to determine whether evaluation is comprehensive and appropriate for the course. See an example of a table of specifications for an entire physics textbook in table 13.1. The table consists of content (major concepts) on one dimension, and processes (definitions, observations, concepts, interpretations, generalizations, measurement, and applications) on the other dimension. The cells of the table indicate the particular content for a particular process. The sums for each column and each row of the table show the number of items on the test for a particular content or process. The number of items in cells, rows, or columns thus indicates the emphases within the test. Ideally, the test emphases should match the instructional emphases.

Let's see how we would interpret a table of specifications. In table 13.1, the numbers in the cells refer to the items in box 13.10, which we can also use as an achievement test. Table 13.1 shows that our test was entirely on the content of a chapter section — pressure in fluids — and that we asked twenty-one questions on five of the seven processes. We did not question students on the processes of interpretation or generalization. We had about equal emphasis on four of the five processes. The least emphasis was on applications. Therefore, this test stressed retention of knowledge more than interpretation and generalization. (A test of a laboratory investigation might have the opposite emphasis.)

After we administer the test to a class, we can summarize the results on another table of specification. By inspection, we can then determine the cells in which the class did well or poorly. We can do likewise for an

TABLE 13.1. Table of Specifications for a Physics Text

PROCESSES

CONTENT	Definition	Facts or Observations	Concepts	Interpretations	Generalizations	Measurement	Applications	Subtotal
Matter								
Molecules								
Fluids	5	5	5			4	2	21
Solids								
Gases								
Heat								
Light								
Magnetism								
Electricity								
Electronics								
Radiation								
Subtotal	5	5	5			4	2	21

individual's test results. Then we would have to investigate whether the class did poorly on some items because of instructional inadequacies, learning and retention inadequacies, or both.

SUMMARY

Although science courses can vary in emphasis (from science as a body of knowledge to be mastered to science as an application of principles to produce new knowledge), they all contain an abundance of technical words, concepts, generalizations, theories, and, of course, procedures for discovering and verifying new knowledge.

The verbal density, particularly of high-level abstractions, places a heavy burden upon science teachers and students. But, if science lessons can progress from the factual or concrete to the abstract and theoretical aspects of science, more students could successfully learn science. For this purpose we advocate (1) use of a problem-solving sequence that not only demonstrates the steps in solving a problem but also explains the linguistic, algebraic, and recall processes that are necessary for solving a problem, particularly in physics, and (2) a questioning sequence (Quest) that will stimulate students to think in a systematic way from observation to generalization.

Following this emphasis on content vs. process and instructional procedures in teaching science, we then move on to teaching students how to use texts and strategies on how to read and learn from texts. The strategies are directed reading activities, glosses, reading and learning-from-text guides, SQ3R, inquiry, and the project method. These strategies help students to progress from dependence toward independence and from teacher-directed to self-directed learning.

In all of these strategies, students must learn technical terms and how to differentiate these terms from everyday vocabulary. The teacher's task is to help students make this differentiation and to be sure that a gap does not arise between the semantic and knowledge hierarchy students bring with them to science, on the one hand, and the level of meanings and technical knowledge required for reading and comprehending science texts on the other. Teachers can either select appropriate texts, rewrite or gloss passages, provide guides, or, in general, develop students' semantic and knowledge hierarchy through single- and multiple-text strategies, problem-solving, and Quest sequences so they can comprehend the specialized content and processes of scientific writing.

Scientific writing has some unique aspects to it, including not only technical concepts but also measurements, the scientific method, graphic and tabular data, and emphasis upon particular types of paragraph structures (enumeration, classification, comparison and contrast, generalization and proof, problem and solution, and sequence of events). Often authors adopt a style of writing in which they use these paragraphs in a sequence in each chapter of a textbook. If teachers point out this style of writing, they can facilitate the students' processing of a text.

Of course, the reading of science materials is similar to reading in other content areas. The skills necessary include detection of main ideas and the use of reasoning abilities — making inferences, interpreting, generalizing, and evaluating conclusions.

A table of specifications for a test of achievement can be used to determine whether the content and processes on the test reflect what the teacher has taught. If the teacher records the class's or an individual's test results in a table of specifications, the teacher can see where the class's or individual's strength and weaknesses are. This knowledge will be helpful in making subsequent plans for teaching students to read and learn from texts.

ACTIVITIES

1. Analyze the pattern of a physics text by identifying the sequence of paragraph types at the beginnings of successive chapters. (Use the paragraph types in chapter 7 to help you with this activity.) Is the sequence of paragraph types the same in both chapters?
2. Prepare a Problem Demonstration Sequence of a physics problem. (See box 13.6.) Follow it up with a lesson plan for a Quest sequence to develop observation of factual information, concepts, and relationships among concepts. (See box 13.3.)
3. Write out your plan for a directed reading activity (DRA) covering one section of a text. Anticipate in your plan student questions and your responses to them.

14 | Mathematics

CHAPTER OVERVIEW

So far in this book you have studied general methods of teaching students to learn from their textbooks. In addition, you have seen how these methods can be applied to the content areas of English, social studies, and science. The chapter you are about to read focuses on *mathematics*. As you read you will see how two conflicting theories of learning have influenced the teaching of mathematics in today's schools. You will also discover not only that mathematics is a language in itself but also that it shares with English many grammatical features. In addition to learning about four types of mathematics vocabulary, you will learn how to apply DRA, marginal gloss, RLT guides, SQ3R, the project method, and phase-in/phase-out to mathematics textbooks.

TECHNICAL VOCABULARY

layer curriculum
drill theory
gestalt
meaningful arithmetic
quantitative hierarchy
SMSG
spiral curriculum

story problems
commutative law
associative law
distributive law
metalanguage
language of mathematics
logograph

MATHEMATICS CURRICULUM

The mathematics curriculum has gone through two revolutions within the past two generations. The curricula that grew out of both are still in use. To understand the math curriculum today, it is necessary to understand both the old and the new.

Layer-by-Layer Curriculum

The old curriculum could be characterized as a layer-by-layer curriculum. In the *layer curriculum* topics were presented by grade levels, as shown in box 14.1.

BOX 14.1. Mathematics Topics in the Layer Curriculum

Primary Grades: arithmetic operations (addition, subtraction, multiplication, division)

Intermediate Grades: fractions, decimals

Junior High School: measurement, percent, introduction to algebra

High School: geometry, advanced algebra, trigonometry, introduction to calculus. (Calculus has moved back and forth from high school to college; it now is taught in some high schools and in all college math programs.)

Instruction in the layer curriculum, particularly in the elementary schools, was based on Thorndike's *drill theory* of arithmetic (Brownell, 1961). This theory of teaching arithmetic stemmed from Thorndike's stimulus-response theory of learning. Thorndike's theory stated that individuals learned when they responded to a stimulus and found the consequences satisfying, as when the teacher said, "Yes, that's a correct answer." According to the theory, a teacher would show a stimulus (3 + 5 =) and identify the correct response, 8, for a student. Then on subsequent trials whenever the student saw the stimulus "3 + 5" and responded with "8" the teacher would say, "Yes" (Stephens, 1956). Moreover, the connection between the stimulus (S) and the response (R) was strengthened through practice that had satisfying consequences. Hence, students not only gave the correct responses, but they also practiced them till they could make the correct response to the basic arithmetic fundamentals accurately and efficiently.

Thorndike assumed that understanding or insight was a consequence of building up a framework of connections. After students had learned the arithmetic fundamentals, they would then begin to perceive the inter-relationships within each operation and between the operations — that the columns and rows in an addition table consisted of increments of one; that subtraction is the inverse of addition; that multiplication is successive addition or combining into groups; that division is successive subtraction or separating into groups.

The drill theory was heavily criticized by *gestalt* psychologists because students were not given an opportunity to perceive relationships in arithmetic at the beginning of instruction. Under the drill theory concept, only after the students had learned to add by 1's, then 2's, then 3's, and so on through 10's were they allowed to perceive the complete addition table. The gestalt psychologists thought the sequence should be reversed. They would start learners off with the table, show them the interrelationships, and *then* have them learn the individual combinations.

Mechanical vs. Meaningful Learning

Brownell (1949) was also critical of the drill theory of arithmetic, which he called "mechanical learning." In its place, he advocated what he referred to as *"meaningful arithmetic."* In meaningful arithmetic, students were instructed to understand relationships rather than learn them on the basis of teacher authority and rote memorization. They were taught to think of 3 + 5 as 3 one's (111) added to 5 one's (11111). Hence, a student could get the answer by counting up the one's. Likewise, they were taught to see 7 × 6 as 7 sixes, which is different from 6 sevens. To determine whether students understood the relationships and the number system in general, Brownell would give a transfer test, that is, he would test the students to see if they could apply their arithmetic understanding to situations in which they had received no training. Students who had been trained to add 3 (ones) + 5 (ones), would be tested, for example, on adding 6 (ones) + 4 (ones). After testing, Brownell would interview students to determine whether they had learned merely by authority (rote memory) or in a meaningful way. He would challenge the validity of their responses and then see whether students had an alternate solution. For example, he would ask a student who had learned the multiplication tables, "What is 7 sixes?" If the students said, "42," Brownell would say the answer was wrong. If the student disagreed, Brownell would say, "Prove it." The student could do so by adding up a series of 7 sixes. Brownell would again challenge the answer, still saying it was wrong. The student would then have to go further and translate each six in the series to a group of six ones and add by ones,[1] as shown in box 14.2. After this step, Brownell would agree that the student had learned multiplication in

---

[1] This process can, of course, be taken one more step to actual objects, such as apples or oranges.

a meaningful way by developing a *quantitative hierarchy* of knowledge.
   Algebra extends this quantitative hierarchy to a higher level of abstraction; for example, let a equal each group of six ones in our arithmetic hierarchy. Then, 7 times $a = 42$, as shown in box 14.3.

BOX 14.2. A Quantitative Hierarchy for
the Multiplication of Seven Sixes

$$
\begin{array}{ccccc}
6 & & 6 & & 111111 \\
\underline{\times 7} & = & 6 & & 111111 \\
42 & & 6 & = & 111111 \\
& & 6 & & 111111 \\
& & 6 & & 111111 \\
& & 6 & & 111111 \\
& & \underline{+6} & & \underline{+111111} \\
& & 42 & & 42
\end{array}
$$

BOX 14.3. An Algebraic Equivalent for
the Multiplication of Seven Sixes

$$
\begin{array}{rl}
a & = 1111111 \\
a & = 1111111 \\
a & = 1111111 \\
a & = 1111111 \\
a & = 1111111 \\
a & = 1111111 \\
a & = \underline{1111111} \\
7a & = \quad 42
\end{array}
$$

The relationship can be made more abstract and more general: let b equal a multiplier that can represent any number, including 7. Then $ba = 42$. To make the equation completely general, let c equal the product, then $ba = c$. Thus, algebra makes relationships and equations among numbers abstract and general, and takes the quantitative hierarchy to a higher cognitive level.
   Through its laws, algebra also makes arithmetic operations abstract and general. In elementary arithmetic, students learn to add, subtract,

multiply, and divide. Algebra states general rules for these operations as shown in box 14.4.

BOX 14.4. Algebraic Rules for Arithmetic Equations

Arithmetic	*Algebra*
$2 + 3 = 5$	$a + b = c$
$5 - 2 = 3$	$c - a = b$
$3 \cdot 4 = 12$	$a \cdot b = c$
$\dfrac{12}{4} = 3$	$\dfrac{c}{b} = a$

In demonstrating the continuity between arithmetic and algebra, a teacher shows that the quantitative hierarchy progresses from the concrete to the abstract level. This demonstration hopefully enables students to develop a mental framework without any discontinuity in it. We suspect that some students who do not perceive the relationships between arithmetic and algebra get lost in algebra because they cannot move down the hierarchy whenever it is necessary to substitute numbers for algebraic letters. Hence, they cannot draw upon their arithmetic knowledge for understanding algebra and for solving algebraic problems.

The job of the teacher is to provide the bridges and fill in the gaps between arithmetic and algebra. We suggest that these bridges be built in an inductive fashion, using the Quest technique. (See chapter 12 for an explanation of Quest.) The teacher should thus construct (1) a number hierarchy that spans the range from numbers representing objects to letters for depicting general quantities and relationships and (2) functions of arithmetic that are subsumed by the fundamental laws of algebra — the *commutative law*, the *associative law*, and the *distributive law*. These laws represent arithmetic operations at a more abstract level, as shown in box 14.5.

BOX 14.5. Algebraic Laws That Represent
Arithmetic Operations

1. *Commutative Law*
   a. Addition: $a + b = b + a$, or $2 + 3 = 3 + 2$
   b. Multiplication: $a \cdot b = b \cdot a$, or $2 \cdot 3 = 3 \cdot 2$
2. *Associative Law*
   a. Addition: $x + (y + z) = (x + y) + z$, or
      $2 + (3 + 4) = (2 + 3) + 4$

b. Multiplication: $x \cdot (y \cdot z) = (x \cdot y) \cdot z$, or
$$2 \cdot (3 \cdot 4) = (2 \cdot 3) \cdot 4$$
3. *Distributive Law of Multiplication over Addition:*
$x \cdot (y + z) = xy + xz$, or
$2 \cdot (3 + 4) = 2 \cdot 3 + 2 \cdot 4 = 6 + 8 = 14$
or $2 \cdot (3 + 4) = 2 \cdot 7 = 14$

By building these hierarchies, students will perceive the continuity between arithmetic and algebra at the same time they are developing their mathematical hierarchy to a higher level of abstraction and generalization. They will then have a mental framework that will help them not only read but also comprehend algebra.[2]

Thorndike also used a social criterion for the curriculum. The only arithmetic topics to be included in the curriculum were those that adults actually used in their everyday lives. Hence, after conducting a survey on arithmetic adults used, Thorndike recommended elimination of such arithmetic instruction as finding the cube root of a number. Indeed, elimination of such rarely used algorithms was beneficial to the curriculum.

Spiral Curriculum

The meaningful approach to arithmetic instruction was followed by curriculum revision on a large scale in the 1950s and 1960s (Heath, 1964). One of the major groups involved in this curriculum revision was the School Mathematics Group (*SMSG*). This group, directed by E. G. Begle, was funded over a five-year period (1958–1963) for more than $5,000,000 by the National Science Foundation (Wooton, 1964). In this group, mathematicians, high school mathematics teachers, and representatives of science and technology banded together to write sample textbooks — first for grades 7 to 12 and subsequently for elementary school. They then tested these books in school settings, revised them, and made the revisions available for purchase. The content of the textbooks was not much different from the traditional curriculum, but concepts and mathematical structures were provided that gave meaning to the skills and facts stressed in the texts. Box 14.6 shows the content of SMSG.

---

[2] This mental hierarchy should also be extended to geometry, trigonometry, and to more advanced courses in mathematics. See Anderson *et al.* (1977) for a discussion of schema hierarchies in the acquisition of knowledge.

BOX 14.6. *Content of School Math Study Group*

Grade 7: numeration, number systems, plane geometry (intuitive); applications

Grade 8: graphs; plane, solid, and nonmetric geometry (intuitive); probability; additional work with number systems; applications

Grade 9: elementary algebra

Grade 10: Euclidean plane and solid geometry

Grade 11: algebra and trigonometry

Grade 12: elementary functions and matrix algebra

SMSG also decided to present mathematics for students in grades 7–12 in less formal fashion, using more concrete illustrations and a slow pace, so that the middle range of students could learn algebra and geometry. Moreover, some, but not all, of the content was related to physical models, such as topics found in physics texts.[3]

The elementary materials included concepts such as commutation (7 + 2 = 2 + 7) and some simple geometric ideas (points, lines, plane figures) which provide a bridge (number line) between geometric and numerical ideas. The elementary texts also introduced algebra concepts (N + 2 = 5) and taught arithmetic operations in bases other than 10 so that students could gain a better understanding of the number system. In short, elementary mathematics no longer consisted of a layer-by-layer curriculum but was characterized by a *spiral curriculum*. Assuming that any individual could learn anything at any age, provided it was presented in a thought form appropriate to the individual's stage of development (Bruner, 1963), topics from geometry and algebra were introduced in the primary grades at a concrete level of thinking. Later in the spiral curriculum, the same topics were tackled at a more abstract level, just as American history is taught in grades 5, 8, 11, and again at college at increasingly higher levels of abstraction.

Along with the revision of the curriculum, many teachers took in-service training courses, frequently in summer institutes funded under the National Defense Education Act. Some states, such as California, required all elementary teachers to have a course in mathematics taught by a math department. Many parents also took math courses so they could help their children. The teachers and parents were taught what was called the "new mathematics." Although the new math was new to most ele-

---

[3] Some mathematicians would emphasize the use of mathematics for the solution of physical problems and would present all mathematical concepts in physical or geometric terms (DeMott, 1964).

mentary teachers and parents, it had been known to mathematicians for hundreds of years.

Teachers placed great emphasis on having students understand the new math. While doing so, they tended to teach students to be accurate and effective, but not efficient, in doing fundamental arithmetic operations. Consequently, while students may have learned to understand math, their performance on tests which stressed computation (particularly when the testing time was short) was not as good as it should have been. As a result, some teachers and school districts dropped the new math and returned to the drill theory of teaching arithmetic. So today, mathematics instruction is a mixture of the old and the new arithmetic.

A more recent development occurred with the advent of inexpensive electronic calculators. They are now in wide use not only in math classes but also in physics classes where they have replaced the slide rule that was once part of every engineering student's basic school equipment. They are also being used in elementary schools. Calculators and miniature computers are now serving as cash registers and in almost all monetary operations. Indeed, clerks have hardly any arithmetical operations to perform; they only have to read prices, punch buttons correctly, recognize bills, and count out change.

This brief review of curriculum revision provides a background for our approach to teaching students to read and learn from math texts. We agree that accuracy, meaning, and efficiency in arithmetic operations, whether presented in a layer or spiral curriculum, are necessary prerequisites for computing and solving problems (particularly algebra problems) in high school mathematics. But we also believe that many students who know, understand, and can perform the fundamental operations of arithmetic, with or without a calculator, can become more effective in higher-level math courses (particularly algebra and trigonometry), if they are taught through strategies that can cope with a wide range of individual differences. These strategies do not assume that students already know what they are to be taught. Nor do they rest upon the discovery method of learning, teacher-posed questions, or text-posed problems given as homework after only a rule and a single problem has been worked in a text. Our strategies for teaching students to read and learn from text progress from maximum dependence on a teacher to maximum independence for the student through a phase-out of the teacher and a phase-in of the student. This phase-out and phase-in is used for each strategy. Thus, as students progress through such strategies as (1) directed reading activities, (2) marginal glosses, (3) reading and learning-from-text guides, (4) SQ3R, (5) the use of multiple texts, and (6) the project method, they become increasingly able to learn how to learn from text on their own. We shall show how these strategies apply to teaching mathematics after we have set the scene that will enable us to differentiate reading from comprehension in mathematics. The scene consists of a lesson in a junior high school text and a frequently heard complaint about students' inability to read story problems.

DIFFERENTIATION OF READING
FROM COMPREHENSION IN MATHEMATICS

Let's take a look at the interaction leading up to *story problems*. A typical instructional plan in an algebra text appears in box 14.7.

BOX 14.7. Plan for Teaching Students to Read a Formula
and Substitute Numbers in It

1. Computing interest is introduced with a statement that interest is the amount of money earned by a loan of money at a given rate.
2. Then a formula is stated:

$$\boxed{\text{Interest} = \text{Principal} \times \text{rate} \times \text{time}}$$

3. The third step is to apply this formula to a problem: $500 is loaned at six percent interest for one year. The interest is computed as follows:

   $I = P\,r\,t$
   $I = \$500 \times 6\% \times 1$
   $I = \$500 \times .06 \times 1$
   $I = \$30 \times 1$
   $I = \$30$

4. Then story problems are presented, usually for homework assignments. These problems are stated in various ways:
   a. A man gives a *sum* of money. . . .
   b. Two men make an *investment* in a company. . . .
   c. A person gets a *loan.* . . .

Notice that in none of these problems is the term *principal* used. Instead, synonyms are used: *sum, investment, loan.* If students do not know that these words are synonyms for *principal,* they have no way of doing the problems. What's the remedy? It is twofold:

1. State the first story problem using the same terms as in the formula. The teacher can then assess whether students understand the problem as presented.
2. Teach students synonyms for the technical terms in the formula. Almost all the other words in story problems are usually within students' reading abilities, particularly those students with reading abilities above the sixth-grade level.

Another problem students encounter is manipulation of syntax. The formula is presented in a given order, I = Prt. But in the story problem students might get the information for this formula in a variety of sequences: Prt, rPt, trP, tPr. To use the formula, students have to reorganize the sentence or else substitute information in the correct place in the formula without regard to the order in which the information is given. What can the teacher do? Again, the teacher can do two things:

1. Make sure that information in the first story problem is stated in the same language and order that the formula requires: I = Prt. If so, the initial problem will be relatively easy and will give students confidence that they understand how to do such problems.
2. Prepare students for changes in wording by teaching synonyms, and for changes in syntax either by presenting the information in the formula in various orders, by stating information in the problem in various ways and showing students how to substitute the information in the correct order in the formula, or both.

Assuming that students know the arithmetic involved, the probability is high that the students can then solve the problem. Thus, additional instructional steps will increase the ability of students to read story problems.

A third step the teacher could take would involve showing students not only how to *read* but also how to *comprehend* a formula. Consider the following formula for computing distance:

$$\text{distance} = \text{rate} \times \text{time}$$

To *read* this formula, the student must know how to identify the three words and the two symbols: *distance, rate, time,* and the symbols for equality and multiplication. Most students can read the words by the ninth grade. If not, it would not take much time in a math lesson to teach them how to do so.

Synonyms for the multiplication symbol also have to be taught. These synonyms are parentheses: (r)(t); a dot: $r \cdot t$; the times sign: $D = r \times t$; or nothing at all between rate and time: $D = rt$. If students can identify the terms and symbols they can *read* the formula.

Students must not only know word and symbol synonyms and syntactic manipulation of text, they must also be told that the time has to be measured in the same unit as the rate. If the rate is per annum, then the time must also be expressed in years. If a problem asks how much interest was earned in six months and the rate was expressed per annum, the time must be computed as a fraction of a year.

Moreover, the teacher should help students to comprehend a formula by mentally manipulating it or by transforming it. The students might be taught to comprehend, I = Prt, by asking themselves, "What happens to

I when P, r, or t increases?'' Also, students must be able to transform the formula to comprehend its relationships. Hence, they should be taught to ask, "What if you know P and t and I but not r? How can you determine what r is?" The answer:

$$r = \frac{I}{Pt}$$

Likewise, if they need to know what t is, given r and I and P:

$$t = \frac{I}{Pr}$$

These ways of thinking about the formula and these types of questions enable students to *comprehend* the formula. In essence, the reason why students do not know how to do story problems is that they are usually taught only how to *read* a formula, that is, only to identify its terms, and then substitute figures for the formula's variables. They also need to learn how to *comprehend* a formula by asking a series of questions about it. These questions concern two aspects of a formula: (1) treating terms as variables by asking what happens when a term increases or decreases and (2) determining relationships among the variables by transforming the formula and solving for each term in the formula. Consequently, when story problems are presented, students will have a greater probability of solving them because they have been taught not only how to *read* but also how to *comprehend* a formula. Eventually students will internalize the comprehension processes for a formula and ask their own comprehension questions. Of course, they might still have some difficulty with story problems, but the difficulties are not likely to be with the reading and comprehension of the formula or with the words and syntax of the story problem. Instead, they are likely to be mathematical difficulties.[4]

Summary

To teach students to read and comprehend a formula, teach them to identify the terms and symbols in the formula and to know their synonyms. Then teach them to manipulate the formula in answer to self-formulated questions. These manipulations should consist of treating the terms as variables and solving for each variable. In practice, the teacher may teach students to comprehend a formula this way by a series of lessons, with each step followed by application to a homogeneous set of problems. Of course, the number of problems necessary and the number

[4] Among the difficulties may be lack of realization that a problem involves two or even three steps that must be solved in order. Hence, problems should be organized in order of complexity and students shown how the problems can be solved through multiple-step procedures (Pribnow, 1969).

of steps that can be covered in a single lesson depend on a particular class's ability and how far along the class is in understanding how to comprehend formulas. By the end of a semester, students should know how, on their own, to read and comprehend new formulas. They will then more likely be able to answer the typical guiding questions for solving a story problem: "What is given?" and "What is asked for?"

If students know their basic arithmetic operations and can read and comprehend formulas, they are ready for instruction in algebra. This instruction can begin by making students aware that, in their everyday speech, they are using quantitative language involving the kind of quantitative thinking which occurs in arithmetic and algebra.

TWO OVERLAPPING LANGUAGE SYSTEMS: ENGLISH AND MATH

Quantification and arithmetical processes are implicit in English; indeed, it is almost impossible to construct a sentence in English in which quantification does not occur (Gleason, 1961). For example prearticles (*each one of, every one of, all, none of, any of, some of*) and articles (*the, a*) precede nouns or pronouns in such sentences as "One of the boys . . . ," "None of us. . . ." Cardinal and ordinal numbers occur in such a sentence as, "He took the first five volunteers." Comparisons, implying equality between two things, are expressed in such sentences as, "Harry ran as fast as Dan." Inequalities are communicated by such comparisons as, "Irving is taller than Harry," or "Harry is not as strong as Jay." Superlatives identify comparisons of an arrayed series of more than two items, such as "Hal is the tallest of the three men" (Knight and Hargis, 1977).

Arithmetic operations also enter into day-to-day language. For example, "Debbie joined the group" or "Abe left the team" or "Each member of the winning team gets an equal share of the prize money" or "He went to practice each day for the entire month."

Even the commutative, associative, and distributive laws of mathematics occur in everyday language: "Robert and Mary" will be recognized as equal to "Mary and Robert" — commutative law: $a + b = b + a$; "Robert and Mary were together with Ann" equals "Ann and Mary were together with Robert" — associative law: $a + (b + c) = (a + b) + c$ (Capps, 1970).

Although children as early as first grade use quantification and arithmetic operations in their natural language, students may have difficulty transforming the meanings of these terms from natural to mathematical language. Consequently, some practice in making these transformations is necessary and may enhance problem-solving ability. Box 14.8 contains some English sentences translated into mathematical language.

BOX 14.8. English Statements and Their
Mathematical Equivalents

English Statement	*Mathematical Equivalent*
Each one of the boys writes fast.	$1 + 1 + 1 \ldots$
Harry ran as fast as Dan.	In respect to running, Harry = Dan
Irving is taller than Harry.	In repect to tallness, Irving > Harry
Harry is not as strong as Jay.	In respect to strength, Harry < Jay
Hal is tallest of the three.	In respect to tallness, Hal > x and y; Hal = tallest. tallness
Debbie joined the group.	Group + 1
Abe left the team.	Team − 1
Each member of the winning team gets an equal share of the prize money.	$\dfrac{\text{Prize money}}{\text{number of members}} = \text{Equal share}$
He walked five miles each day, or 155 miles, during July.	5 miles × 31 days = 155 miles.

Students should realize that (1) although mathematics has its own language, it overlaps with English and (2) quantitative knowledge and processes underlie both languages. However, students also should realize that mathematical language is different from English.

THE LANGUAGE OF MATHEMATICS

Language is a system of organized symbols whose meanings are shared among members of a speech community (Ruddell, 1974). The three major components of a language system are sounds, syntax, and semantics.

Sounds

The sound system used for responding to English print and to mathematics is the same. When numbers are spelled out, the principles of English phonology are used; for example, in *seven*, each symbol (letter) corresponds to a sound. However, a *logograph*, *7*, can also be used; when it is, it can evoke different phonological responses, for example, *sieben* in German. Thus, the number system in its logographic form can be and is used as a symbol system for the sound systems of various languages. In this sense, the *language of mathematics* is truly international.

Syntax

In English, syntax can be transformed in various ways. In box 14.9 are four story problems that represent four major types of syntactic transformations in English.

BOX 14.9. Syntactic Transformations
of a Story Problem

1. *Active:* Harry earned five percent interest on the $500 he loaned to Irving for a year.
2. *Active, negative:* Harry did not earn any interest on the $500 he loaned to Irving for a year.
3. *Passive:* Five percent interest was earned by Harry on the $500 he loaned to Irving for a year.
4. *Passive, negative:* Five percent interest was not earned by Harry on the $500 he loaned to Irving for a year.

However, all of these transformations are still read in a left-to-right sequence following English convention. Although syntactic transformations also occur in mathematics (as demonstrated above in our section on "Differentiation of Reading from Comprehension in Mathematics") mathematics itself is not limited to a left-to-right sequence but can be read in a variety of directions: horizontally (left to right or right to left), vertically (top to bottom or bottom to top), diagonally, or a combination of these (Hater, Kayne, and Byrne, 1974). The same problem can be read in three directions: "What does 30 divided by 6 equal?" can be written and read as follows:

$$\frac{30}{6}, \; 30 \div 6, \; \text{or} \; 6\overline{)30}.$$

Graphs often require horizontal, vertical, and diagonal eye movements as the student reads the values on the ordinate (*y*-axis) and abscissa (*x*-axis) and then follows the graphed line; or the reverse sequence may occur, proceeding from the graphed line to the *x* or *y* axis. Because of such syntactic variations in mathematics, it is not surprising that training of seventh-graders in the use of syntax in mathematics improved their arithmetic achievement (Sax and Ottina, 1958).

Semantics

Both syntax and vocabulary may be sources of interference in problem-solving. When the difficulty level of the syntax and vocabulary of the same problem were varied, and both versions were presented to fourth graders, the problem with the easy syntax and easy vocabulary resulted in the best problem-solving (Lindille, 1970).

While the number of syntactic arrangements are relatively few, the vocabulary load is voluminous. Indeed, dictionaries of mathematical terms are available (James and James, 1959; Gundlach, 1961).[5] Moreover, the terms can be known at various levels of difficulty, including the concrete, the functional, and the abstract levels (Chase, 1960). Addition, for example, can mean any one of these levels of response:

1. Put one box on top of another (concrete)
2. When you see 2 + 1, you say 3 (functional)
3. You combine numbers to get a sum or total (abstract)

While a graded curriculum may teach the level of abstraction commensurate with the students' mental capabilities, students respond to mathematical terms at various levels of abstraction. Their response levels are moderately correlated with their mental capabilities (Chase, 1960); but perhaps their levels of responding are also related to whether and how they had been taught these terms. In either case, instruction can improve students' mathematical vocabulary ability. The techniques of direct study, including explanation by the teacher, class discussion, and use of a dictionary, improved the general mathematical vocabulary of fifth-graders significantly as assessed by the *Iowa Test of Basic Skills* (Vanderlinde, 1964).

Instruction and practice on mathematical vocabulary in isolation through test-like exercises (such as matching symbols with their verbal definitions, which is recommended by Hafner (1977) and which frequently occurs in math laboratory exercises) do not appear to transfer to math problem-solving ability (Johnson, 1944; Vanderlinde, 1964). Indeed, numerous studies have demonstrated that transfer is more likely to occur if teachers provide for it by having students practice in the actual situations

---

[5] Structured overviews depicting interrelationships among branches of mathematics and topics within particular branches have also been devised. The claim is that such overviews enable students to perceive relationships among the terms, including those that have been studied, those that are being learned, and those about to be learned. To prepare one, simply arrange the vocabulary in a tree-type diagram that depicts the relationships among the concepts (Earle, 1976).

TABLE 14.1 Some Symbols That Occur in Algebra

=	is equal to	$\stackrel{?}{=}$	is this statement true
≠	is not equal to	√	yes, statement is true
<	is less than	‖	absolute value
≮	is not less than	≥	is greater than or equal to
>	is greater than	≤	is less than or equal to
≯	is not more than	ℜ	(the real numbers, 1, 2, 3 . . .)
{}	set	%	percent
ε	is an element of	±	plus or minus, *or* positive or negative
∉	is not an element of	$\overline{AB}$	line segment A, B
φ	empty set	$\overrightarrow{AB}$	ray AB
•••	continues unendingly, *or* and so on through	∠A	angle A
		m∠A	measure of angle A
υ	union of sets	$\overrightarrow{AB}$	vector AB
∩	intersection of sets	#	number
⊂	is a subset of	△	triangle
≈	is approximately equal to		
∴	therefore		
○	circle		
⊖	radius		

Source: The list is from Mary P. Dolciani and William Wooton, *Modern Algebra: Structure and Method,* Book I, revised edition. Copyright © 1973 by Houghton Mifflin Company. Used by permission.

---

in which teachers want transfer to occur.[6] Hence, we think that vocabulary instruction should occur in context, that is, as an intrinsic part of classroom lessons in mathematics. Accordingly, we have done so in the five strategies we demonstrate in the last half of this chapter.

The vocabulary that has to be taught can be grouped into four categories.[7] One category consists of symbols. A partial list of symbols used in algebra is provided in table 14.1; the symbols consist of nouns, conjunctions, adjectives, and some verbs. Table 14.2 contains another set of symbols for arithmetic with their verbal representations; these symbols

[6] See Lewis Aiken's (1972) comprehensive review of language factors in learning mathematics. When Call and Wiggin (1966) participated in a controlled experiment in which vocabulary as well as other reading skills were taught by an *English teacher* in the context of teaching algebra, the group so taught performed significantly better on problem-solving in algebra than the control group taught by an algebra teacher!

[7] Of course, instances of several categories, such as verbal, numerical, and literal can exist in the same context (Earp, 1970). For example, Principal = $100 × r · t. In reading this equation, the reader shifts from alphabetic (Principal) to numerical (100), to symbolic ($, =, ×, ·), and finally to literal (r, t) responses.

TABLE 14.2. Symbols for Arithmetic Operations and Their Synonyms

+	and, plus, increased by, sum, add, together
−	less, minus, take away, decrease, subtract, diminish, reduce

$a \times b$ ⎫
$a \cdot b$ ⎬ times, multiplied by, product of (note that multiplication of a and b is
$a(b)$ ⎪ indicated by four symbols)
ab ⎭

$\div$ ⎫
$\overline{)\;}$ ⎬ three symbols that mean divide or find number of groups in a number
$/$ ⎭ $(8\,\overline{)32}$: finding number of groups of 8 in 32)

x^2	multiply x by itself or square x ; 2 is an exponent of x
x^n	multiply x by itself as many times as is indicated in the exponent, for example, x^4 is $x \cdot x \cdot x \cdot x$
$\sqrt{\;}$	square root

are verbs or action words. Needless to add, students must not only learn the symbols but also their verbal equivalents and their synonyms.

Another set of terms comes from the *metalanguage* of mathematics, the technical words used to talk about the symbolic or object language (Brunner, 1977). Using metalanguage, we can say that the symbols $x + 3 = y$ represent an *equation* in which x is a *variable* to which a *constant* is *added* to obtain *values* indicated by the variable y. The underlined words are vocabulary items in the metalinguistic statement.

A third category of vocabulary that occurs in mathematics is made up of vocabulary terms which have special meaning in mathematics (Aaron, 1965; Collier and Redmond, 1974; Shepherd, 1978). Compare the meanings of the terms in table 14.3.

A fourth category consists of general vocabulary terms which occur frequently in mathematical problems, such as *distance* (measurement between two points), *each* (every, as each day for a week), *difference* (result of subtraction), *total* (whole or sum), and *obtain* (find the result).

The math teacher must not assume that students know the meanings of terms in any of these four categories of vocabulary, especially in the technical, precise, and abstract way in which they are used in math textbooks. They have to be taught explicitly. We think that instruction in math vocabulary should be an intrinsic part of a math lesson so that it is more likely to be applied in problem-solving. Hence, in our five strategies for meeting the wide range of individual differences in ability to learn mathematics, we consciously and deliberately include instruction in the language of mathematics.

TABLE 14.3. General and Technical Meanings of Terms Used in Mathematics

Term	Meaning Alternate	Mathematical
1. arc	luminous discharge of electricity across a gap in a circuit	any unbroken part of the circumference of a circle
2. base	one of the four stations in a baseball infield	the number with reference to which a set of numbers is constructed, e.g., base 10, base 2
3. exponent	an advocate for our side	a superscript indicating the power to which a number is raised (multiplied times itself, less one, e.g., $x^3 = x \cdot x \cdot x$)
4. expression	a vivid depiction of mood on a person's face	a meaningful combination of symbols, frequently enclosed in parentheses
5. power	control, authority, influence over others	the number of times (as indicated by an exponent) a number is to be multiplied by itself
6. prime	best, first	a number divisible only by itself or 1 (1, 2, 3, 5, 7 . . .)
7. principal	the head of a school	a capital sum of money placed at interest or due as a debt or used as a fund
8. product	result of work	the number resulting from multiplying together two or more numbers or expressions
9. radical	person associated with policies of extreme change	root part; number which has been raised by an exponent
10. set	a group of at least six games of tennis	a collection of objects with identifiable common characteristics
11. square	a person with unsophisticated or conservative tastes	a quadrilateral whose sides are equal and whose angles are right angles
12. times	*The New York Times* (a newspaper)	multiplied by (2 times 2 = 2 multiplied by 2)

STRATEGIES FOR TEACHING MATHEMATICS USING EXAMPLES FROM ALGEBRA

Directed Reading Activity (DRA)

Reading with comprehension involves identifying words, symbols, and signs, determining their meaning and the processes called for, and utilizing the reasoning abilities of analysis, inference, and interpretation. However, not all the information that is necessary for comprehending and solving problems is in the printed materials. Knowledge stored within the individual's memory must be retrieved and brought to bear upon the written material at the appropriate time. The DRA, a procedure for covering all these aspects of the reading-comprehension process, consists of this sequence of six steps:

1. *Readiness for reading.* The teacher determines whether students have the prerequisite store of knowledge for the particular lesson. The teacher may do so through (a) a review, (b) a formal pretest, (c) an informal pretest. Content for readiness consists of vocabulary, previously learned rules and processes, and general information, including knowledge of measurement.

2. *Vocabulary.* The teacher presents new vocabulary terms and their synonyms; clarifies general terms, technical words, symbols, and signs. These can be taught through directed study, including writing them on the board, listing them with their synonyms, pronouncing and defining them, and showing how they fit into the context of a problem. Then provision should be made for students to practice identifying the new vocabulary by locating it in problem sets and defining what a vocabulary item means either by verbal definition or by carrying out an operation; for example, the meaning of *minus* is demonstrated by simplifying the sentence $3x - (- 2x) - 10 = 0$.

3. *Purpose.* The teacher establishes the purpose of the lesson, for example, to learn the commutative axiom of addition, $A + B = B + A$. This purpose also states the objective. Consequently, students will be able to test themselves to determine whether they have satisfied the purpose of the lesson.

4. *Presentation.* The teacher does the following: (a) explain a concept or a process; for example, demonstrate a procedure for solving an equation, including transformation of an equation to show how to solve for each variable ($I = Prt$, $P = I/rt$); (b) apply to problems: analyze a problem (draw a picture to represent the problem whenever possible). Then divide the problem into its unknown (what is asked for) and its knowns (what is given). Show how to solve the problem by letting x = the unknown (y and z = other unknowns); then state the knowns in terms of x. Set up the equation as a sentence with terms in the sentence that correspond to the unknown and the knowns in the problem. Finally, show how to solve the equation to find what x is equal to and how to check by substituting the solution; (c) vary ways of stating the same problem: show syntactic transformations and synonyms that may occur.

5. *Practice under teacher guidance.* The teacher assists students, either in their seats or at the board in applying new knowledge (equation, concept) to problems by asking questions such as:

"What is known?" "What is unknown?" Teacher-posed questions direct students' processes of thinking in logical and precise ways. As these processes become internalized, students will use them to guide their own thinking.

6. *Phase out/Phase in.* This process shifts students from dependence on the teacher (Step 5) to independence. When many students can do the problems or exercises, the teacher organizes the class into groups to do similar problems or exercises *as groups.* The group process allows cross-ability teaching and discussion to occur. When the teacher is satisfield that most students comprehend the new lesson, then homework (individual) assignments can be given with a high probability that students will do it with understanding and ease, demonstrating their comprehension by successfully solving the set of homework problems. Those students who are still having difficulty after the group process may get some individual help from the teacher.

In box 14.10 is a DRA constructed by Ms. Stewart, a math teacher at Monroe High.

BOX 14.10. Class: Algebra (DRA)

"USING EQUATIONS"

1. Readiness (Ms. Stewart checks to be sure that prerequisites for the lesson are met.)
   a. Students can simplify by collecting like terms.
      Test: $5m + 10 - 4m - 4 - 3 = 0$.
   b. Students can add a number to each side of an equation. Test: $3t - 5 = 17$.
   c. Student can solve for an unknown by dividing each side of an equation. Test: $4m = 12$.

2. Vocabulary (Ms. Stewart reviews with the class key technical terms to be used in lesson.)
   Identify vocabulary terms and give their quantitative meaning. Although these terms are explained earlier in the text and are in the glossary, they need to be reviewed again in the context of the lesson.
   a. *longer than* means a length greater than a given length.
   b. *shorter than* means subtract the difference from the length being compared.
   c. *Overall length* means add the lengths together to get the total length.
   d. *Symbol:* something used to represent something else. In algebra, letters at the end of the alphabet, such as x, y, z, are used to represent unknown quantities or variables. If only one unknown is in an equation, it is represented by x.
   e. *Replacement set:* the members of a specified set; in this case, the number that can replace the unknown variable, x, in the equation.
   f. *Open sentence:* an equation which contains one or more variables.
   g. *Equation:* a statement of equality, i.e., where the variable(s) and quantities on one side equal those on the other side of the sentence.

h. *Positive real numbers:* 1, 2, 3 . . . n.

i. *Root of the equation:* the solution of the equation.

j. *Solve:* to determine the solution set of an open sentence over a given domain.

3. Purpose (Ms. Stewart clarifies the lesson's purpose.)

   To translate the numerical relationships of a word problem which contains an unknown quantity into an equation and then solve the equation for the unknown quantity.

   Problem: The length of the service module containing the engines of the *Apollo II* spacecraft was 4 feet shorter than twice the length of the command module housing the crew. Also, one lunar module was one foot longer than the command module. If the overall length of *Apollo II* was 45 feet, how long was the command module?

4. Explanation (Ms. Stewart explains how to solve the problem step by step, working with the class.)

   a. The first step in solving this problem dealing with length, as well as other problems whose information can be depicted, is to draw a diagram. (Note: A diagram is shown in the text, but is not listed as the first step in solving the problem.) If necessary, supply knowledge of relationships among service, command, and landing modules. Draw the diagram and indicate lengths as given in the problem.

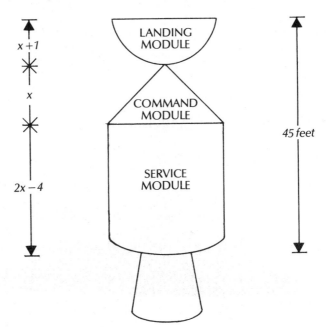

   b. Information in the problem can be divided into two categories:

   (1) What the problem asks for or what is unknown. This problem asks: how long is the command module? We let a symbol, x, represent this unknown quantity and place it on our diagram to indicate the length of the command module.

   (2) What information is given in the problem: (a) Length of the service mod-

ule is twice (two times) the length of the command module *(x)* less (minus) four feet or 2x − 4. Place this length on diagram. (b) The landing module is one foot longer (+1) than the command module *(x)* or x + 1. Place this length on diagram.

c. Now, an equation may be written by indicating how the sum of the parts (the length of each component) is equal to the overall length of the spacecraft.

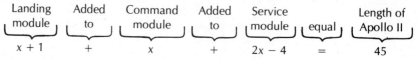

Landing module	Added to	Command module	Added to	Service module	equal	Length of Apollo II
x + 1	+	x	+	2x − 4	=	45

d. Now *solve* the equation, that is, find what the unknown, x, is.
   (1) Simplify the equation by collecting like terms:
       4x − 3 = 45
   (2) Add 3 to each side of the equation:
       $$4x − 3 = 45$$
       $$\underline{+ 3 \quad + 3}$$
       $$4x \quad = 48$$
   (3) Divide each side of the equation by 4:
       $$\frac{4x}{4} = \frac{48}{4}$$
       $$x = 12$$

∴ the unknown x, the length of the command module, is 12 ft.

e. Check results by substituting 12 for each x in the equation:

Landing Module		*Command Module*		*Service Module*		
x + 1	+	x	+	2x − 4	=	45
12 + 1		12	+	2(12) − 4	=	45

f. Now remove parentheses by multiplying 2 times 12:

| 12 + 1 | + | 12 | + | 24 − 4 | = | 45 |

g. Now add:

| 13 | + | 12 | + | 20 | = | 45 |
| | | | | 45 | = | 45 |

h. Therefore:
   Landing Module = 13 feet
   Command Module = 12 feet
   Service Module = 20 feet

   Length of Apollo = 45 feet

5. Practice Under Guidance (Now Ms. Stewart gives students additional, but similar, examples to work on in class. She directs them to (a) draw diagram, if at all possible, (b) state what is known, and (c) let x represent the unknown.)

   Example: As you walk past a school, you can see it is divided into a central part and two wings of equal length. The total length of the school is 500 feet. The central part is three times as long as a wing. How long is the central part?

6. Phase In/Phase Out (Ms. Stewart begins to withdraw guidance as students show signs of being able to work independently.)

a. When Ms. Stewart observes that some students know how to do the practice problem, she divides the class into groups to work together on additional problems which are representative of the homework problems: (a) finding perimeter, (b) determining area of a rectangle, (c) buying and selling, (d) time problems, (e) traveling problems, (e) money problems. She circulates among the groups, giving help to those students who are not benefitting from peer group work.

b. After Ms. Stewart sees that almost all students can now do the problems, she realizes that the class is ready for individual work, and so she assigns homework.

N.B. Steps 1 and 2 are in texts, but the presumption that students are able to recall the processes and meaning of the terms is frequently not warranted. Steps 5 and 6 are not in textbooks; these steps are left to the teacher to do.

Quoted material in this box is from Mary P. Dolciani and William Wooton, *Modern Algebra: Structure and Method*, Book I, revised edition. Copyright © 1973 by Houghton Mifflin Company. Used by permission.

Marginal Gloss

Another way to supplement a textbook is through a marginal gloss. These marginal notes in a textbook can define vocabulary or symbols, remind students of previously learned processes, provide knowledge or information that students are expected to have in their mental repertoire and that is necessary for making inferences or interpretations, or suggest strategies for solving problems.

Of course, a teacher cannot actually write marginal glosses in a text, but can either provide dittoed glosses keyed to text pages or else have students construct glosses from classroom comments. Students can use the glosses when doing their homework. In box 14.11 is Ms. Stewart's marginal gloss for homework problems.

BOX 14.11. A Marginal Gloss for Homework
Problems in Algebra

Gloss	Homework Problem
Given: Two numbers (b) Let x = smaller number (a) Then $3x$ = larger number (c) *Given:* Their sum is −16. 　　Then: $3x + x = -16$.	1. (a) One number is three times (b) another number, and (c) their sum is −16.

What to find? What are the smaller and larger numbers? (Note: The problem does not explicitly ask this question.)

Solution: Solve the equation.

(1) First collect like terms.

(2) Then solve for x by dividing both sides of the equation by the co-efficient of x.

(3) What does $x = ?$

(4) What does $3x = ?$

(5) Check by substitution of $3x$ and x in your equation. Simplify.

(6) When you do, does the left of the equation equal the right?

Draw a sketch to help solve problems. In this case, draw a soccer field.

Given: width $= y$, length $= y + 40$ yds. and a perimeter $= 380$ yds.

y

$y + 40$

(1) Remember that a soccer field is a rectangle; in a rectangle, widths and lengths are equal. Therefore, the other width is y yards and the other length is $y + 40$ yards.

(2) Remember: Perimeter is equal to the sum of its sides. Therefore:
$y + y + 40 + y + y + 40 = 380$ yds.

(3) What is asked for? Implicitly the problem asks you to find the width and length in yards. Therefore, solve for y.

What is given?

_____ oxygen

_____ hydrogen

_____ grams of water

What is asked for?

What will equal x in your equation?

What will be 8 times x? What do their totals equal?

Now, set up equation and solve for x. Check.

Givens:

What will $x = ?$

2. A soccer field has a perimeter of 380 yds, a width of y yds and a length that is 40 yds more than its width.

3. Water is a compound made up of 8 parts by weight of oxygen and 1 part by weight of hydrogen. How many grams of hydrogen are there in 225 grams of water?

4. Ken had 8 coins in his pocket. If he had 2 fewer dimes than nickels and

What does problem ask for?

(Note: This problem is a two-step problem. It first asks, what is *x*? After solving for *x*, you have to substitute in the equation the monetary equivalents of the coins to answer the second question.)

one more penny than nickels, how much money did Ken have?

Problems in this box are from Mary P. Dolciani and William Wooton, *Modern Algebra: Structure and Method,* Book I, revised edition, pp. 134–137. Copyright © 1973 by Houghton Mifflin Company. Used by permission.

Next the teacher can phase out and phase in students through this three-stage plan:

1. The teacher or the text demonstrates some homework problems.
2. The gloss, which decreases in degree of explicit instruction on representative homework problems, is used by groups of students working together in class. Cross-ability instruction thus operates under teacher consultation. That is, the teacher moves about the room helping wherever needed.
3. Students who demonstrate they can do problems on their own are allowed to start on their homework. The rest of the students get additional teacher aid and glosses to help them do their homework. The glosses should have decreasing degrees of teacher direction and questioning.

Reading and Learning-from-Text Guide (RLT)

The reading and learning-from-text Guide (RLT) helps the student (1) identify meaning of vocabulary and symbols used in explanations of equations or in problems, (2) processes used in solving equations, and (3) applications. Again, a phase-out/phase-in procedure is used with (1) teacher taking students as a class through a guide, then (2) having students work on guides in groups, and (3) using guides on individual assignments. In Box 14.12 is an RLT Ms. Stewart prepared.

BOX 14.12. RLT Guide for Equations Having a Variable in Both Members

RLT Guide	Text
Identify vocabulary and symbols (Note: check your responses against the glossary at the end of the text.)	In the equation $2p = 63 - 5p$ the variable appears in both members. Are you allowed to add "5p" to each member?

1. *Variable* in the problem refers to
   (a) 2p, (b) 5p, (c) p, (d) 7p.
2. Both *members of the equation* are:
   (a) 2p, (b) 63 − 5p, (c) 2p and 63 − 5p.
3. *Equation* refers to:
   (a) 2p, (b) =, (c) 63 − 5pm, (d) 2p = 63 − 5p.
4. *Real numbers* are:
   (a) 2, (b) 63, (c) −5, (d) p, (e) a, b, c, and d.
5. The symbol $\overset{?}{=}$ means:
   (a) is unequal, (b) is equal, (c) is this statement or equation true, (d) is unknown.
6. This symbol { } means:
   (a) multiply, (b) perform operations inside brackets first, (c) identifies set, (d) contains answers to problems.

For every real number p, "5p" denotes a product of real numbers, and therefore, it represents a real number. Because you are permitted to add a real number to each member of the equation, you are also allowed to add "5p" to each member without changing the solution set of the equation. Thus, you may solve the equation as follows:

$$2p = 63 - 5p$$
$$2p + 5p = 63 - 5p + 5p$$
$$7p = 63$$
$$\frac{7p}{7} = \frac{63}{7}$$
$$p = 9$$

check: $2p = 63 - 5p$
$2 \cdot 9 = 63 - 5 \cdot 9$
$18 = 63 - 45$
$18 = 18$
∴ The solution set is {9} Answer.

True or False

Indicate whether the statement is true (t) or false (f) by writing the appropriate letter in the parentheses.
1. ( ) You can add 5p to each side of the equation without changing the answer or answers for which the equation is true.
2. ( ) You can add 2p to 5p to get 7p.
3. ( ) You divide each side of the equation to find what p equals.

Processes

1. When +5p is added to −5p the result is:
   (a) 0   (b) p
2. The process of eliminating + 5p by adding − 5p to it is called:
   (a) additive inverse   (b) negative inverse
3. After 7p is divided by 7 the result is really:
   (a) 1p   (b) 0p   (c) 1
4. When any real number, except 0, is divided by itself, (a ÷ a) or multiplied by its reciprocal (a · 1/a) the result is always:
   (a) 1   (b) 0   (c) the original number

Problem

1. A salesman offered to give a storekeeper 10 pints of an expensive liquid if the storekeeper would buy four of them for $126. After the salesman left, the storekeeper wanted to know how much each bottle would have cost if he had paid $126 for all the bottles. Was he correct when he constructed this equation?
   4p = $126 − 10p
   What would each bottle then have cost him?
2. Can you make up a problem that would fit this equation?
   2p = 63 − 5p

Text passages in this box are from Mary P. Dolciani and William Wooton, *Modern Algebra: Structure and Method,* Book I, revised edition. Copyright © 1973 by Houghton Mifflin Company. Used by permission.

Another type of guide divides the information of a problem into literal (directly stated), interpretive and inferential, and applied levels (Feeman, 1973). But this type of division does not lend itself to the diagnostic categories of vocabulary, information, processes, and applications that are in the RLT guide.

Riley and Patchman (1978) help students solve problems by asking them to divide the problem into three categories: (1) facts of the problem, (2) mathematical ideas and interpretations, and (3) mathematical computations for solving the problem. This division is useful. However, the RLT guide gives much more help initially and then phases out from a maximum to a minimum.

SQ3R

This formula, originally used as a study procedure, guides the student to (1) *S*urvey the assigned reading, (2) formulate *Q*uestions to answer, (3) *R*ead to answer the questions, (4) *R*ecite the answers, and (5) finally *R*eview to check the answers. This formula could be stretched to adapt it to problem-solving in math. After *surveying* the problem, the student would ask such *questions* as "What is given?" "What is asked?" "What do the unknown or unknowns equal?" "What equation do I need to set up to fit the problem?" Next, the student would *read* the problem again to see whether the equation fits. Then the student would do the equivalent of *reciting* by solving the equation. Last, he would *review* by checking the answer in the equation and by rereading the problem to see if the answer to the equation fit the requirements of the problem.

Leo Fay (1965) set up an alternative formula: *S*urvey (read rapidly to determine purpose), *Q*uestion (find out what is asked), *R*ead (read for the facts), *Q*uestion (what process is required), *C*ompute (do computation), *Q*uestion (ask: Is the answer correct?). After going through these steps, the student would check the answer by substituting in the equation and checking. Also, check solution against the requirements of the problem.

Neither SQ3R nor Fay's formula seems to fit the problem-solving situation. We think the following formula is more appropriate.

1. *Read* the problem carefully. If necessary, to determine meaning of symbols, consult table of symbols and glossary. Also, if necessary, reread explanatory material on processes.
2. *Question$_1$:* What facts are given?
3. *Question$_2$:* What do I have to find out?
4. *Question$_3$:* What shall I let x equal?
5. Question$_4$: How shall I represent the other information given in the problem?
6. *Set up* the equation by translating the words of the problem using

the answers to 2, 3, 4, and 5, for the left and right members of the equation.
7. *Solve* the equation.
8. *Test* answer(s) or solution set for the equation by substituting the answer(s) in the equation and by checking answer(s) against the problem.

The acronym for this procedure is RQ_4S_2T. Let's apply it to a problem in box 14.13 to see how it works.

BOX 14.13. Application of the RQ_4S_2T Formula to a Problem

RQ_4S_2T	Problem
1. *R: Read* carefully. Note that all quantities are in the same unit, milligrams.	A cup of (1) *coffee contains 20 more milligrams of caffeine than a cup of tea* and
2. Q_1: What facts are given? These are numbered and underlined in the problem.	(2) *85 more milligrams of caffeine than the average cola drink.* (3) *If one cup of tea and four cola drinks contain the*
3. Q_2: What do I have to find out? See the last part of the last sentence.	*same amount of caffeine as one cup of coffee,* how many milligrams of caffeine
4. Q_3: What shall I let x equal?	are there in one cup of coffee?
(x = milligrams in a cup of coffee)	

5. Q_4: How shall I represent other information in the problem?
(x − 20 = milligrams in tea)
(x − 85 = milligrams in cola)
6. S_1: Set up the equation. See sentence three:

1 cup of tea	and	4 cola drinks	contains the same amount of caffeine as	one cup of coffee
x − 20	+	4 (x − 85)	=	x

7. S_2: Solve the equation:
  x − 20 + 4x − 340 = x
      4x   = 360
       x   = 90
8. *T:* Test answers:
  90 − 20 + 4 (90 − 85) = 90
    70 +   20 = 90
           90 = 90
∴ 1 cup of coffee contains 90 milligrams of caffeine.

As in the preceding strategies, the teacher again handles the range of individual differences by first phasing in the strategy (taking the class through the RQ_4S_2T procedure), then dividing the class into groups to work on assigned problems with this formula as a guide, and finally having individual students use the RQ_4S_2T procedure on homework problems. Eventually, the procedure will become internalized and used automatically.

Of course, the acronym RQ_4S_2T is only a way of reminding students to apply what they have learned from explanatory material and previous classroom instruction. Since math is extremely cumulative, it is imperative that teachers pace students so that their learning can be cumulative. To do so, math teachers have to adhere closely to a teach-test-reteach instructional procedure, probably on a text section-by-text section basis or at least once a week.

We believe that our strategies for handling the wide range of individual differences will help in this process. We have organized the strategies so that their effects will be cumulative and lead towards independence in reading and learning from text. Hence, we think that students who have gone through the prior strategies will now be ready to use the project method in mathematics.

Project Method

The project method places the student in a position of even greater independence. The strategy first begins with the teacher asking students to read the explanation for a new section. Then the teacher asks: "What do you want to know about this explanation?" The questions may cover a range of concerns from vocabulary to process to application. Students may then go ahead to find and try out answers to questions under teacher direction. When the class's questions have been answered and the teacher is satisfied that at least some students are able to apply their new knowledge to the solution of problems, then the class can be divided into groups which can try their ability on the next explanatory section in the text. More students are likely to demonstrate independence under this peer group cross-teaching and be able to go on to work individually on problems or even the next explanatory section.

Of course, not all students will be able to attain this stage of development. The instructor may not be able to use this strategy with all students.

Or, use of the strategy may have to terminate at the group level for most students.

Another way in which the project method can be applied to mathematics is to find out what students would like to know about mathematics in general. Some questions that may arise are: Who invented algebra? In what ways has algebra been used to solve problems? In what fields do people use algebra? Is it useful in programming computers? Questions of this kind can then be investigated through use of the library, interviews of engineers or computer scientists. The information obtained in such ways can be organized and reported upon by the group. The teacher should direct the first project for the whole class before going on to group and individual projects.

Other projects may come to mind: searching through various texts to find out different ways of explaining the same process; investigating the lives of famous mathematicians; constructing models for various equations; or, the student may use the project method to tackle extra problems listed in textbooks.

SUMMARY

Mathematics is a hierarchically organized system which starts with numbering of objects and progresses to higher order abstractions consisting of symbols. In a meaningful curriculum, this progression is developed systematically so that the student can relate the concrete to the abstract, and *vice versa*. In addition to the development of this quantitative hierarchy, the student also learns grouping operations such as addition, subtraction, division, and multiplication. Additional symbols are used to represent these operations.

Supplementing the symbols are technical terms, the language of mathematics, and metalanguage (the language about mathematics). Some of these terms are also part of general, everyday vocabulary. For example, the word *radical* has a political meaning and a medical meaning as well as a technical meaning in mathematics. Hence, instruction in symbols and terminology, and differentiation of technical meanings is an important part of math instruction, particularly when students get into algebra.

Not only must mathematical terms be taught, but they must be remembered. The best way to remember something is (1) understand or learn well what is to be remembered by studying a variety of examples, specifying the features of each term, and indicating its related concepts; (2) use what was learned; use, of course, constitutes review. Hence, to help students learn and remember terms and symbols, introduce them in an appropriate context; then use them in a cumulative way (Pearson and Johnson, 1978; Guthrie, 1978).

In addition to remembering technical terms and symbols, students must also know synonyms and syntactic transformations. We think that math texts and math instructors tend to teach formulas with only one set of technical and general terms and with one syntactic arrangement. If synonyms and syntactic transformations are taught in class, students would be more likely to have greater success with their homework and mathematics because they would know not only how to *read* the problem but also how to use syntactic and semantic knowledge to *comprehend* the problem.

A major difficulty in mathematics, particularly algebra, is having no set of procedures for systematically solving a problem. For this purpose, we believe the procedure, named by the acronym RQ_4S_2T, is appropriate. The validity of this procedure is demonstrated by applying it to several problems.

We concluded this chapter by demonstrating how our five strategies for handling individual differences in the classroom can be applied to mathematics instruction, using algebra as our example. Although the use of these strategies is time-consuming initially, each prepares for a phase out of the teacher and a phase in of the student. In short, through this phase out/phase in, students learn from the teacher, then each other, and finally they internalize how to learn to read *and* learn from their math texts.

ACTIVITIES

1. Analyze a math textbook. See whether it contains formulas with problems following them that (a) require syntactic transformations of the formulas and (b) use synonyms for the terms in the formulas. Explain how you would teach students to use syntactic transformations and synonym substitutions. Hint: You can construct a plan for a directed reading activity, for a marginal gloss, or for a reading and learning-from-text guide. Perhaps you would prefer to create your own teaching plans.
2. Interview your students to determine whether they have developed a quantitative hierarchy that extends from arithmetic through algebra. Start with an algebraic equation, such as $a \times b = c$. Ask students to supply an example in arithmetic for this algebraic equation ($3 \times 5 = 15$). Then ask them if five 3s are the same as three 5s (no; 3, 3, 3, 3, 3 is not 5, 5, 5). Ask next how three 5s would be shown on paper (substitute five 1s for each 5). If you want to take this interview a step farther, have students substitute objects for the 1s. See the sections related to boxes 14.2 and 14.3 for more explanation of a quantitative hierarchy.
3. Take a paragraph from a literature text. Try to express sentences, phrases, and words in mathematical language. (See box 14.8 for examples.)

15 | The Present: Centers for Reading

CHAPTER OVERVIEW

This book began with a discussion of instructional problems that affect an entire school. It is appropriate, then, that the concluding chapters provide a description of how an entire school can deal with the vast differences in students' abilities to read and learn from text. This chapter explains how to use the results of reading achievement survey test to classify all students in a school into four categories. The rest of the chapter describes specific centers on the current scene. We will describe each center and evaluate its strengths and weaknesses. The eight centers include (1) tracking center, (2) clinical center, (3) reading laboratory, (4) functional reading program, (5) individual reading class, (6) multi-faceted reading instruction, (7) the three-stage program, and (8) the schoolwide reading program. In addition to the eight centers, this chapter will discuss reading proficiency tests and the possible development of a new center — to teach students the curriculum for the proficiency tests. The next chapter will deal with the future scene, an "ideal" schoolwide program for reading and learning from text.

TECHNICAL VOCABULARY

developmental reading program
tracking
clinical centers
reading laboratory
functional reading program
individual reading "class"
multi-faceted reading instruction
three-stage program
schoolwide reading program
functional reading tests
proficiency test
reading specialist

power of reading
individual diagnosis
reluctant readers
affectively alienated readers
linguistically different readers
content area deficient readers
educationally underdeveloped readers
instructionally mismatched readers
word recognition deficient readers
narrow background readers
reading expectancy

AT MONROE HIGH SCHOOL

The picture at Monroe High School was beginning to look brighter, quite a contrast to that stormy faculty meeting of February 8, 1977, the one you read about in chapter 2. The principal's schoolwide committee that directed the in-depth study of the school's many problems continued on as his permanent advisory committee. The committee consisted of Ms. Jones of the social studies department, Mr. Inglish from the English department, Mr. Phelps from science, Ms. Stewart from mathematics, Ms. Jorgensen from home economics, Mr. Carter from industrial education, Ms. Williams the vice principal, and Mr. Umeki, head of the counseling department. One of the committee's recommendations was to hire a reading specialist to help solve the students' reading problems. Subsequently, the principal had the committee serve as an interviewing team to screen and recommend for hiring a new reading specialist.

The committee, chaired by Ms. Jones, screened forty applications and interviewed ten applicants. After much deliberation, the committee agreed to recommend Ms. Valdes for the job. She had exactly the kind of background and experience that the school needed. First of all, Ms. Valdes had taught in the science department of a senior high school for five years, so she was familiar with the curriculum problems of a specific content area. Second, the committee liked the fact that she had been an excellent but unusual teacher: she had enrolled in a university program so she could learn how to do something for "all those kids who had problems learning from their science textbooks." Third, her subsequent university training focused not merely upon teaching students how to read, but also on how to learn from their textbooks. The committee realized Ms. Valdes could work with the entire range of reading problems of their high school, from working with students who have severe reading problems to assisting content area teachers in making their textbooks more readable and their students more able to read and learn from them. Particularly impressive to the committee was Ms. Valdes' practical explanation of what a reading and learning-from-text specialist could do. Last of all, the committee thought Valdes was realistic about what one specialist for an entire high school could accomplish.

Here is a summary of Ms. Valdes's responses in answer to the question "How can a reading specialist serve the entire school?"

ROLE OF THE READING AND LEARNING-FROM-TEXT SPECIALIST

How a Specialist Can Serve the Entire School

Ms. Valdes began by explaining the role of a *reading specialist* in the elementary school, and then discussed the specialist's role in the secondary school.

Elementary school reading specialists could operate a schoolwide program, serving all students, with emphasis in these areas: (1) diagnosis followed up with reading improvement plans and instruction for individuals and small groups; (2) demonstration of reading and learning-from-text strategies for students in all content areas, (3) consultation with faculty on problems in reading and learning from text, (4) in-service education of faculty and (5) leadership on instruction, curriculum, and evaluation in reading and learning from text. However, in the past, most reading specialists focused on reading acquisition; they gave little emphasis to comprehension or to learning from text in the content areas. Consequently, even though the reading specialists at the elementary level have provided service to all students, they could expand the scope of the service to include more emphasis on comprehension and on teaching students to learn from texts in social studies, science, arithmetic, and literature. When they do so, elementary students will have better preparation for entry into middle school or junior high school instruction (Spache and Spache, 1977).

Typically, Ms. Valdes continued, junior and senior high school reading specialists have also had a narrow role, limited primarily to students still at the acquisition level of reading or to students whose reading achievement is two or more years below grade level. Hence, the reading specialists at junior and senior high school levels have not been providing service to all students; in general, the school has not used their expertise appropriately. If they are well-trained in reading, have majored at the undergraduate level in some academic subject, and hold a junior or senior high school credential, they are also qualified to teach in a content area and to be members of an academic department. This dual role for the reading specialist is desirable because teaching at least one academic class per semester would provide the reading specialist with credibility among the faculty and would enable the specialist to demonstrate that strategies for reading and learning from text can be combined with content area instruction over an entire semester or year. When some reading specialists did serve in this way in junior high schools, they had gained so much credibility at the end of one year that other content area teachers were willing to consult with them and invite them into their classrooms for demonstration teaching and inservice training (Singer, 1975). Thus, they were able to carry out all the functions of reading and learning-from-text specialists. However, since many specialists do not have extensive academic background in one field, they will need to rely on the expertise of all the content area teachers while carrying out these functions.

Ms. Valdes pointed out that the functions of reading and learning-from-text specialists at the junior and senior high schools are somewhat different from those of elementary reading specialists. These functions are: (1) diagnose students with reading difficulties, (2) direct or teach classes in reading acquisition in the content areas and functional reading programs, (3) demonstrate lessons in teaching reading and learning from texts in the content areas and perhaps teach at least a unit or an entire semester in a content area class, (4) advise teachers of introductory classes on strategies for teaching incoming students to learn from texts in content areas and (5) provide inservice education and serve on a school-wide committee for developing a program for teaching all students how to read and learn from text. These five functions are time-consuming, but all of them can be conducted in a school if the school has the proper ratio of reading specialists to students.

Ms. Valdes explained how to determine the proper ratio by structuring the schedule of a reading specialist: (1) Allocate one of the five periods per day to demonstration teaching of reading and learning from text in a content area with the same number of students as any other teacher (approximately 25 to 30 students). (2) Assign two of the five periods to teaching acquisition or functional reading classes for about 20 students per class. The specialist can provide ongoing observation and diagnosis, both individual and group, within the acquisition and functional reading classes. (3) Allot one period per day for advising teachers in content areas who are offering introductory courses in reading and learning from text to incoming freshmen. (This course can be a six-week minicourse for a group of 25–30 students enrolled in content area classes such as science, math, social studies, English, auto shop, and so forth. If these mini-courses are staggered during the year, then, working together, the reading specialist and the content area teachers combine to teach students how to read and learn from texts in specific content areas. Initially, the reading specialist will do most of the instruction and demonstrate to the content area specialist; gradually the content area teacher will learn and assume sole responsibility for instruction. Eventually, if a school does not have much faculty turnover, the content area specialists will be doing their introductory minicourses on their own.) (4) Allot the last of the five pe-riods in the teaching day for the specialist to direct inservice training, to consult with parents, or to chair a schoolwide committee on reading and learning from text.

Recognizing that one reading specialist could not provide all these services for an entire school, Ms. Valdes went on to explain to the com-mittee that the proper ratio of reading specialists to students could be determined by estimating the number of students who need acquisition or functional reading classes. In general, about five percent of the students in an average high school will need these classes. If the school has 3200 students, then five percent of 3200 would be 160 students. The school would need at least 4 reading specialists, each responsible for 40 of these students.

If a school had only one specialist, that specialist could concentrate on the freshman class; over a four-year period, the specialist would have served all the students and faculty in the school. In this way, one trained reading specialist could realistically carry out all five functions.

Using the Reading and Learning-from-Text Specialist

The principal accepted the committee's recommendation and hired Ms. Valdes in midsummer. By early fall, Ms. Valdes began work on her first problem, one that Ms. Jones brought to her. In looking over the scores on a reading survey test, Ms. Jones was surprised at the large number of her students who were reading well below grade level. In the past, Ms. Jones, occupied with other instructional problems, had only glanced at the scores. But now, as chairperson of the schoolwide committee, she believed she should consult Ms. Valdes because she wanted to know why these students had scored so low.

Classification and Educational Diagnosis

Procedures for diagnosis, whether at the school, classroom, or individual level, are the same. Initially, a survey test ascertains the students' current reading achievement. Current reading status consists of two major components: speed and power of reading. *Speed of reading* is the rate of processing printed materials. A speed of reading test, such as the Gates-MacGinitie,[1] consists of relatively easy passages with time for reading them drastically limited.

Power of reading is the ability of students to comprehend passages of increasing difficulty when given unlimited time to do so. Comprehension tests are "power" tests only when their paragraphs are arrayed from easy to difficult and students have unlimited time to work on them.[2] When students reach the limits of their power of reading, they usually stop; but if they continue on, their answers become merely guesses. A correction for guessing eliminates credit for any guesses that tend to be correct by chance. Typically, the initial paragraphs on graduated tests of comprehension are relatively easy while the final paragraphs are relatively difficult. Further discussion and examples of the speed and comprehension of reading items can be found in chapter 3.

A multiplicity of reasons can be given to explain why a student can be a fast or slow reader and a powerful or nonpowerful reader (Holmes and Singer, 1966). The task of the content reading specialist is to (1) determine

---

[1] We are not advocating use of the Gates-MacGinitie as a school's survey test. We are merely employing the Gates-MacGinitie as *one example* of how to use survey test results for classifying readers. We could have used other standardized survey tests that assess speed and comprehension of reading equally well for classifying readers. See chapter 3 for a list of some other survey tests and *Buros Yearbook of Mental Measurements*, Volume 8 (Highland Park, New Jersey: Gryphon Press, 1978) for critical review of survey tests of reading achievement.

[2] When time is limited, students who are slow in speed of reading are penalized. The Gates-MacGinitie manual estimates that 20 percent of students who take the 45 minute Gates-MacGinitie test are penalized by slowness in speed of reading.

the student's current reading status, (2) the cause(s) or reason(s) for this status, and (3) plan how to reduce the student's weakness and improve the student's strengths.

The initial step then is to administer survey tests. The typical survey test consists of three subtests: speed, comprehension or power of reading, and vocabulary. After the specialist administers the test to all students in a particular grade, to students in one classroom, or even to individuals, he or she can classify each student's score into one of four categories. To do so, the specialist scores the tests and finds the percentile equivalent for the score of each subtest from the manual's table of norms. The dividing line for the four categories is at the fiftieth percentile level for each grade. Thus, results from a speed of reading test place a student with a score below the fiftieth percentile into the slow category and a student with a score at or above the fiftieth percentile into the fast category.

Results from comprehension tests categorize students in the same way. If a student's score is below the fiftieth percentile, he or she belongs in the nonpowerful category; if it is at or above the fiftieth percentile, the student belongs in the powerful reader category. The result of this fourfold classification scheme is shown in table 15.1.

Procedures for Classification and Educational Diagnosis

Students in each quadrant of the fourfold classification scheme can be given additional tests to arrive at a more differentiated educational diagnosis. Generalizations about the kinds of students in the four quadrants and further tests for diagnosing them are given below.

FAST-POWERFUL READERS. These students read rapidly and with relatively high comprehension. A specialist should scan test results to determine whether any students have "broken the top of the test," that is, responded correctly to all or almost all the items. These students should take a test at a more advanced level to determine their actual reading levels, as well as specific content area tests to determine their reading levels in each content area (the *Iowa Test of Educational Development*, for example) or even informal reading inventories in each content area. While their general reading ability is in the top quarter of the class, their ability to read and learn from texts in specific content areas is likely to reveal strengths and weaknesses related to their interests and curricula.

FAST-NONPOWERFUL READERS. These students are relatively rapid, but not powerful readers. They often enjoy reading, but tend not to adjust their speed of reading to rates appropriate for difficult materials; or they have some deficiency that interferes with their comprehension of rela-

TABLE 15.1. Classification of Readers into Four Major Categories

	Power of Reading	
	Above the 50th Percentile	*Below the 50th Percentile*
Above the 50th Percentile	A. Fast–powerful readers Above the 50th percentile in both speed and power of reading.	B. Fast–nonpowerful readers Above the 50th percentile in speed but below the 50th percentile in power of reading.

Below the 50th Percentile	C. Slow–powerful readers
	Above the 50th percentile in power of reading but below the 50th percentile in speed of reading.
		D. Slow–nonpowerful readers
		Below the 50th percentile in both speed and power of reading.
		1. Linguistically different readers
		  a. Bilingual
		  b. Dialectal
		2. Low IQ reader
		3. Content area deficient reader
		4. Reluctant reader
		  a. Attitude
		  b. Ability
		5. Affectively alienated reader
		6. Physiologically handicapped reader
		7. Educationally underdeveloped reader
		8. Instructionally mismatched reader
		9. Word recognition deficient reader
		10. Narrow background reader

(Speed of Reading on vertical axis; 50th percentile marked.)

Source: Adapted from Harry Singer and Alan Rhodes, ''Problems, Prescriptions, and Possibilities,'' in *Problems in Reading: A Multidisciplinary Perspective,* edited by Wayne Otto, Charles W. Peters, and Nathaniel Peters. Reading, Massachusetts: Addison-Wesley, 1977, p. 311. Reprinted by permission.

tively difficult material. While they have probably mastered basic word recognition skills, they are likely to have a deficiency in vocabulary. Sometimes these students are referred to as ''word-callers'' because they can pronounce all the words but they do not attend to meaning. They may think of reading as pronouncing words rapidly. To test this hypothesis, examine their vocabulary scores on the survey test. If these scores are low and their general intelligence is at least average, they need vocabulary training.

An alternate hypothesis might be that some of the fast-nonpowerful readers are not flexible. To determine whether they lack flexibility, these students should be given an equivalent test, reading it slowly and doing the items more carefully. A significant improvement on scores would confirm the hypothesis.

Occasionally some students may have emotional disruptions on the day of the test. On a retest, their comprehension scores are likely to be higher, particularly if the emotional disruptions are no longer present.

SLOW–POWERFUL READERS. These students comprehend well what they read, if given adequate time. However, they tend to process all their reading in a time-consuming fashion. The specialist can test the following hypotheses to determine why the students are slow:

1. They have not mastered basic word recognition skills. An appropriate and quick test for evaluating this hypothesis is to administer the reading subtest of the *Wide Range Achievement Test* (WRAT).[3]
2. They prefer to read and analyze materials in depth — as though they were studying for an important exam. Test this hypothesis by having them read equivalent material to answer a few specific questions given to them before they read. Ask them to read only to answer these questions. If they maintain the same slow rate, interview them to find out how they read the material and how they feel when they are expected to read rapidly. (See box 15.1 for an interview schedule.)

SLOW–NONPOWERFUL READERS. These students are slow and nonpowerful readers for a variety of reasons. The group can be divided into ten common types. These types are not mutually exclusive, but tend to overlap. Some students may have characteristics that make them members of two or more categories.

1. *Linguistically different readers.*
   a. *Bilingual readers.* Upon entering school, bilingual readers may have been able to speak only their native language. Consequently, they could not benefit from reading instruction in their second language. Subsequently, they may have become proficient in their second language, but were then in grade levels where initial reading instruction was no longer given. If an interview using the questions in box 15.1 reveals this pattern of development, then, with reading acquisition instruction, they are likely to improve dramatically.
   b. *Dialectally different readers.* On the basis of oral reading tests,

---

[3] J. F. Jastak and J. R. Jastak, *Wide Range Achievement Test (WRAT)*. Austin, Texas: Guidance Testing Associates, 1965.

these students are judged to be deficient merely because their speech patterns are different. Care must be taken to determine whether their pronunciations of words are true reading errors or only dialectally different oral responses. To differentiate, put their incorrectly pronounced words into sentence context. If the context makes a difference in their pronunciations or if their pronunciations are still incorrect (but they answer questions correctly, indicating they have understood the meaning of the sentence), they are giving dialectally different responses, not making reading errors.

Another clue to dialectally different readers is a higher percentile score on a silent reading test (such as the *Gates-MacGinitie Silent Reading Tests*) than on an oral reading test (such as the *Gates-McKillop Oral Diagnostic Tests*[4]).

Dialectally different readers may also be in this category because of (a) word recognition difficulties, (b) lack of wide reading experience, (c) low intelligence, or (d) some combination of these factors. To diagnose, the specialist administers the *Gates-McKillop Reading Diagnostic Tests,* interviews students on their reading history and has a certified school psychologist administer an individual intelligence test, such as the *Wechsler Adult Intelligence Scale* (WAIS) or *Stanford-Binet Intelligence Scale* (S-B).

2. *Readers with low IQ.* Low scores in general reading achievement may be due to low mental ability, particularly if English is the native language. The specialist has an individually administered intelligence scale given to these students. Even if they do have low intelligence, some yearly improvement in reading is possible because their mental ages still increase from year to year. It is important to adjust the difficulty of reading material to the reading level of these students so that they can comprehend better.

3. *Content area deficient readers.* A student may have good general reading, but still have difficulty in reading material in a specific subject. The specialist can test this hypothesis by comparing the student's percentile or equivalent scores on a survey test and on specific content area tests (science, history, and so forth) that had been given to the same norm group. If the difference between the equivalent scores on the two tests is significant, then the student needs to learn the technical vocabulary, information background, and processes of reading appropriate to the specific content area. A selected list of standardized tests for assessing content area reading ability is in box 15.3.

---

[4] All tests referred to in chapters 15 and 16 are listed, with appropriate credits to authors and publishers, in Appendix C.

4. *Reluctant readers.* Reluctance may be due to negative attitudes or to low ability.

   a. *Attitudes.* Although at, or slightly below, grade level in reading ability when retested on the reading test under encouraging conditions, these students still refuse to read. Further confirmation comes from interviews and attitude inventory results. The interview is likely to show that although they have the ability, they have not done much independent reading. Hence, they did not develop fluency or automaticity in word recognition processes; they have a shallower and narrower knowledge of the world; and they have a less adequate vocabulary than they could have.

   b. *Ability.* These students may refuse to read because they want to hide a lack of ability. The specialist can test their word recognition skills and word attack processes through use of *Gates-McKillop Reading Tests* or *Reading Miscue Inventory.* Given high-interest, low difficulty materials, they may respond more favorably to reading assignments.

5. *Affectively alienated readers.* These students are openly hostile to reading, and perhaps have been for many years. Interviews are likely to reveal the duration of this negative attitude. They must have their curiosity rekindled and aroused and their interest in reading stimulated. The specialist should introduce short passages of high-interest, low-difficulty materials with considerable prior discussion of information and presentation of vocabulary contained in the materials. Perhaps using filmstrip stories that feature pictures with captions may awaken interest in reading. Then the specialist can progress gradually towards longer passages in which the content is more closely related to the content of the courses in which these readers are currently enrolled.

6. *Physiologically handicapped readers.* Readers in this category experience visual problems (crossed eyes, squinting or watery eyes when reading, books held too close or too far from eyes), and auditory problems. To detect hearing problems, the specialist can administer a whisper test by having a student stand 20 feet away with back to the examiner, and then having the examiner whisper, "Turn around." A correct response to this direction will indicate that the student is not likely to have an auditory acuity deficiency. Students with either of these problems or those suspected of having other physiological problems should be referred to the appropriate specialist, perhaps starting with the school nurse.

7. *Educationally underdeveloped readers.* These students have not learned one or more important components of the reading process (use of affixes, context, inference, and so forth). Tests of prefixes and suffixes are helpful here. Also, the *Reading Miscue Inventory.* Analysis of responses to comprehension tests may reveal deficiency

in inferential ability. Instruction can improve these abilities and processes.

8. *Instructionally mismatched readers.* These students are not making progress because their reading materials may be too difficult relative to their abilities. Their attitudes and desire to learn may be strong, but they are frustrated by difficult textbooks. Use of strategies for meeting the wide range of individual differences advocated in this text will tend to alleviate this problem. (See chapters 4, 9, 11, 12, 13, and 14.)

Some students may not have the prerequisite background for courses and consequently they flounder in them. The specialist can check by administering entry level tests. If the entry level tests indicate that these students do have an inadequate background, they could benefit from counseling and program changes.

9. *Word recognition deficient readers.* The *Gates-McKillop Reading Diagnostic Tests* and/or the *Reading Miscue Inventory* can determine which students have not mastered basic word recognition techniques. The *Dolch Basic Sight Word Test* (220 basic words which are usually mastered by 95 percent of students at the third grade or earlier) also assesses word recognition ability. These words account for 75 percent of all primary words and 50 percent of all words in reading materials from fourth grade up.[5] The Dolch words should have priority in reading instruction, followed by development of technical vocabulary in content areas. Together, this combination of word recognition and technical vocabulary development would improve comprehension in content areas significantly.

Most of the students in the slow-nonpowerful category are likely to lack word recognition mastery. These students need intensive instruction in content area reading acquisition.

10. *Narrow background reader.* Students who have not done much reading outside school or much collateral reading in school are likely to be slower and less powerful than they should be relative to their general aptitudes. The performance of one of these students is analogous to someone who has learned to swim but never practiced swimming. Narrow background readers did not develop automaticity in word recognition processes, nor did they acquire an adequate informational background. Observation of their oral reading and an interview would reveal their awkward processing of print and their narrow background. A guided reading program would help these students.[6]

---

[5] The Dolch Basic Sight Word Test and reading materials for teaching the Dolch words can be obtained from Garrard Press, Champaign, Illinois. The word list can also be found in Tinker and McCullough (1975).

[6] For concrete illustrations and case study vignettes of these readers and ways of working with them, see Singer and Rhodes (1977).

Principles for Individual Diagnosis

A survey test classifies students into four broad categories. To arrive at an *individual diagnosis* of the strengths and weaknesses of students in each category, the reading and learning-from-text specialist can follow the principles described under the next six headings.

INTERVIEW DATA

The specialist collects information from teachers, parents, and from students themselves about behavior in class, about attitudes towards reading[7] and towards studying in a particular content area, and about procedures used in reading their texts. To obtain this information, the specialist asks teachers and parents to tell or write down what they know about the students' reading in class or at home. More detailed information can be collected from the students. Often a specialist will interview them to bring out their past reading history, their present use of time, and their interests. A specialist might use the interview schedule in box 15.1.

BOX 15.1. Interview Schedule

1. Start by reviewing the survey test and results with students. The purpose is to find out why students made particular responses to the test. Balance correct with incorrect items. Have students redo some items aloud so that you can listen and infer what processes may have been used.
2. Have students go through their textbooks and explain how they read and study them. Ask students to read and explain sample passages from their texts.
3. Ask students about materials read at home: newspapers, magazines, books, and about current reading and type of reading done in the past.
4. Ask students to recall initial and early experiences in learning to read and in reading during elementary school, in class, and at home.
5. Ask students to tell what they would like to learn about reading and what they would like to learn from texts.
6. Discuss with students their past and future interests and their vocational plans.

Note: The interview should be informal, with the interviewer volunteering some information so that the atmosphere is conversational. Pursue additional questions and issues as they arise.

See Ruth Strang, Constance McCullough, and Arthur Traxler (1967), pp. 171, 458–472, for a thorough and revealing interview schedule and technique. See also Lou Burmeister (1974), pp. 61, 63, for a more detailed interest inventory.

---

[7] Although the interview schedule shown in box 15.1 is adequate, a standardized scale for assessing attitudes towards reading is available (Estes, 1971).

OBSERVATIONAL DATA

While interviewing students, a specialist should observe clues to possible physical and physiological causes of disabilities, such as visual and auditory deficiencies. The specialist should also listen for hints of affective alienation to school, teachers, home, and particular content areas.

A PLAN FOR DIAGNOSTIC TESTING

Knowledge gleaned from observing students reading their texts and from allowing students to give their own explanations for their difficulties, attitudes, techniques, and processes used in reading will give the reading specialist sufficient information for developing reading improvement plans for students. However, some additional diagnostic tests may be necessary, especially for quantifying difficulties in reading and for determining reading expectancy levels (how well students should read). We have compiled a list of selected diagnostic tests in boxes 15.2 and 15.3. See also the material under the heading ''Reading Expectancy'' in this chapter.

BOX 15.2. Diagnostic Standardized Tests
and Inventories

These batteries of tests can help determine the underlying skills and capacities of readers, particularly their difficulties in word identification. The tests are appropriate for normal readers in grades 1–8 and for students at grade levels 9–12 whose oral reading abilities are in the grade range from 1–8. It requires about an hour to administer these individual tests and from one to three hours to score and analyze the results.

1. *Gates-McKillop Reading Diagnostic Tests,* Grades 1–8 (New York: Bureau of Publications, Columbia University, 1962). These tests measure oral reading, word and phrase recognition, syllabication, letter names and sounds, visual and auditory blending, and spelling. Test time: 60 minutes. Comprehensive diagnostic test, well constructed. The oral-reading vocabulary subtest can be used as an estimate of reading expectancy. The assumption is that the reading ability of a student should equal performance in oral vocabulary.

2. *Spache Diagnostic Reading Scales,* Grades 1–8 (Monterey: California Test Bureau/McGraw-Hill, 1963). These measure oral and silent reading, phonics, and sight-word recognition. Test time: 30 minutes. Directions for administering the tests and test-construction information are inadequate. The listening subtest provides an estimate of expectancy in comprehension. The assumption is that the students should comprehend as well through reading as they do through listening. Each measure of expectancy, however, has its own limitations (Singer, 1965).

3. *New Developmental Reading Tests: Silent Reading Diagnostic Tests,* Grades 1–

3; 4–6 (Chicago: Lyons and Carnahan, 1968). These tests measure recognition of words in isolation and in context, reversible words in context, syllabication, root words, beginning and ending sounds, word synthesis. Time: 90 minutes. This battery of silent-reading diagnostic tests can be administered to an individual or to an entire group.

4. *Reading Miscue Inventory*, Grades 1–12 (New York: Macmillan, 1972). The inventory assesses miscues and discrepancies between print and responses to a 1500-word selection and categorizes miscues as graphemic, phonemic, and semantic. The inventory measures comprehension by having the reader retell a story (selected by the tester) approximately one grade level above the reader's ability. This inventory is not a standardized test with norms. Instead, it is a type of informal reading inventory determining processes of reading in word identification, particularly use of syntax, semantics, and graphophonemics in word recognition in context.

BOX 15.3. Selected List of Standardized Tests for the Content Areas

California Achievement Tests: Reading, Levels 6–9, 10–12 (Monterey: California Test Bureau/McGraw-Hill, 1970). Vocabulary in English, social studies, science, and mathematics. Comprehension of different types of materials. Study skills assessed.

Iowa Every-Pupil Tests of Basic Skills, Grades 3–9 (Boston: Houghton Mifflin, 1947). Map reading, use of references, use of index, use of dictionary, graphing.

Iowa Test of Educational Development, Grades 9–12 (Chicago: Science Research Associates, 1947). Test 5: Interpret Reading Materials in the Social Studies. Test 6: Interpret Reading Materials in the Natural Sciences.

Robinson-Hall Reading Tests, Grades 3–6 (Columbus: Ohio State University Press, 1949). Reading in art, geology, history, and fiction. Measures rate and comprehension.

Tests of Educational Development, Grades 9–16 (Washington, D.C.: American Council on Education, 1970). Test 2: Interpretation of Reading Materials in the Natural Sciences. Test 3: Interpretation of Reading Materials in the Social Studies. Test 4: Interpretation of Literary Materials.

CONSULTING A PROFESSIONAL LIBRARY

The reading specialist should have a professional library to consult on problems in reading and learning from text. Use of tables of contents and indexes of professional books will be helpful. A selected list of professional books can be found in box 15.4.

BOX 15.4. Selected List of Professional Books

Elementary

Burron, Arnold and Amos L. Claybaugh. *Basic Concepts in Reading Instruction: A Programmed Approach.* Second edition. Columbus, Ohio: Charles E. Merrill, 1977.

Carnine, Douglas and Jerry Silbert. *Direct Instruction Reading.* Columbus, Ohio: Charles E. Merrill/A Bell and Howell Company, 1979.

Cunningham, Patricia M., Sharon V. Arthur, and James W. Cunningham. *Classroom Reading Instruction, K–5: Alternative Approaches.* Lexington, Mass.: D. C. Heath, 1977.

Dallman, Martha, Roger L. Rouch, Lynette Y. C. Char, and John J. Deboer. *The Teaching of Reading.* 5th edition. New York: Holt, Rinehart and Winston, 1978.

Duffy, Gerald G., George B. Sherman, and Laura Roehler. *How to Teach Reading Systematically.* Second edition. New York: Harper & Row, 1977.

Durkin, Dolores. *Teaching Them to Read.* Boston, Mass.: Allyn and Bacon, 1978.

Harris, Albert J. and Edward R. Sipay. *How to Increase Reading Ability.* 6th edition. New York: David McKay, 1975.

Heilman, Arthur. *Principles and Practices of Teaching Reading.* 4th edition. Columbus, Ohio: Merrill, 1977.

Hittleman, Daniel R. *Developmental Reading: A Psycholinguistic Perspective.* Chicago, Ill.: Rand McNally College Publishing Co., 1978.

Otto, Wayne, Robert Rude, and Dixie Lee Spiegel. *How to Teach Reading.* Reading, Mass.: Addison-Wesley, 1979.

Quandt, Ivan J. *Teaching Reading: A Human Process.* Chicago, Ill.: Rand McNally, 1977.

Ransom, Grayce A. *Preparing to Teach Reading.* Boston: Little, Brown and Company, 1978.

Ruddell, Robert B. *Reading-Language Instruction: Innovative Practices.* Englewood Cliffs, N.J.: Prentice-Hall, 1974.

Spache, George D. and Evelyn B. Spache. *Reading in the Elementary School.* 4th edition. Boston: Allyn and Bacon, 1977.

Zintz, Miles. *The Reading Process: The Teacher and The Learner.* 2nd edition. Dubuque, Iowa: Wm. C. Brown, 1977.

Secondary

Burmeister, Lou E. *Reading Strategies for Secondary School Teachers.* Reading, Mass.: Addison-Wesley, 1974.

Dillner, Martha H. and Joanne P. Olson. *Personalizing Reading Instruction in Middle, Junior and Senior High Schools: Utilizing a Competency Based Instructional System.* New York: Macmillan, 1977.

Hafner, Lawrence E. *Developmental Reading in Middle and Secondary Schools: Foundations, Strategies, and Skills for Teaching.* New York: Macmillan, 1977.

Herber, Harold. *Teaching Reading in Content Areas.* Englewood Cliffs, N.J.: Prentice-Hall, 1978.

McIntrye, Virgie M. *Reading Strategies and Enrichment Activities for Grades 4–9.* Columbus, Ohio: Charles E. Merrill, 1977.

Piercey, Dorothy. *Reading Activities in Content Areas: An Ideabook for Middle and Secondary Schools.* Abridged Edition. Boston: Allyn and Bacon, 1976.

Robinson, H. Alan. *Teaching Reading and Study Strategies: The Content Areas.* Boston: Allyn and Bacon, 1975.

Robinson, H. Alan and Ellen L. Thomas. *Fusing Reading Skills and Content.* Newark, Delaware: International Reading Association, 1969.

Shepherd, David L. *Comprehensive High School Reading Methods.* Columbus, Ohio: Merrill, 1973.

Smith, Carl B., Sharon L. Smith, and Larry Mikulecky. *Teaching Reading in Secondary School Content Subjects: A Bookthink Process.* New York: Holt, Rinehart and Winston, 1978.

Strang, Ruth, Constance McCullough, and Arthur Traxler. *The Improvement of Reading.* 4th edition. New York: McGraw-Hill, 1967.

Diagnosis and Improvement of Reading

Eckwall, Eldon E. *Locating and Correcting Reading Difficulties.* 2nd edition. Columbus, Ohio: Charles E. Merrill, 1977.

Rupley, William H. and Timothy R. Blair. *Reading Diagnosis and Remediation.* Chicago, Ill.: Rand McNally College Publishing Co., 1979.

Spache, George. *Diagnosing and Correcting Reading Disabilities.* Boston: Allyn and Bacon, 1976.

Strang, Ruth. *Diagnostic Teaching of Reading.* New York: McGraw-Hill, 1964.

USING A MODEL OR MODELS OF READING

Models of reading are useful for directing the diagnostician's attention to the systems underlying speed or power of reading that may not be functioning properly or may not have been adequately developed. Psycholinguistic, affective, and developmental models are available. See Singer and Ruddell (1976).

READING EXPECTANCY

How well should a student be able to read and learn from texts? This question cannot be answered conclusively. Any criterion used for answering it is likely to be fallible for one or more reasons. Intelligence tests, for example, are not likely to be fair measuring instruments for linguistically different students or for students who were unable or lacked the motivation to learn general culturally determined information. Nevertheless, expectancy criteria will provide at least a qualified approximation of current performance expectations. One criterion is general intelligence, as determined by an individual intelligence test administered by a school psychologist. The assumption is that students' reading ages should equal their mental ages. One formula that is based upon this assumption is that of Harris and Sipay[8]:

Reading grade level expectancy = Mental Age − 5

Thus, a student with a mental age of 15 should have a general reading level of 15 − 5 or a grade equivalent of 10.[9]

Another criterion for determining expectancy is a listening test. The assumption underlying the use of such a test is that students should be able to read and comprehend as well as they listen (Sticht *et al.*, 1974).

A specialist can use an orally administered vocabulary test to assess expectancy. The underlying assumption is that *part* of the systems underlying comprehension (semantics) can be used to estimate the whole of comprehension. The oral vocabulary subtest of the *Gates-McKillop Reading Diagnostic Tests* can be used for this purpose. For an informal estimate, a specialist can readminister the oral vocabulary scale of a survey test, only reading the words and choices to students while they follow along reading silently. Although the norms were not designed for interpreting the results of this informal estimate, they can nevertheless be used as a rule of thumb for this purpose; however, the norms used this way are not precise and probably represent an overestimate of expectancy.

Much of the additional diagnostic testing may be done in Reading Content Area Acquisition Classes or in Reading and Learning from Text Centers taught or administered under the direction of the specialist.

The Specialist Provides Historical Background

Ms. Jones was glad to get the information on classification and educational diagnosis. She felt even more definitely that Monroe could use a program in reading acquisition. However, before instituting such a program at Monroe High, Ms. Valdes thought it would be a good idea to visit some neighboring schools that offered various programs for students with problems in reading and learning from text. After doing a little investigation, Ms. Jones and Ms. Valdes located eight nearby schools offering such programs. In released time, both teachers visited the schools to observe their programs. Ms. Valdes agreed to observe each program

---

[8] Albert J. Harris and Edward R. Sipay, *How to Increase Reading Ability*, 6th edition. New York: David McKay, 1975.

[9] Both the reading and the expectancy tests, however, have errors of measurement. That is, a difference between the two tests may be only a chance difference. You can use a statistical procedure to determine whether the difference between the two test scores is attributable to chance. Consult a measurement text, such as Thorndike and Hagen (1969) or Chase (1978) for further explanation on determining the reliability of the difference between two test scores.

intensively and provide thorough evaluations of each program's strengths and weaknesses. In the car enroute to the first of the eight school sites, Ms. Valdes filled Ms. Jones in on some historical background related to the teaching of reading.

High schools have been operating reading clinics, classes, and centers for over 50 years (Smith, 1965; Singer, 1970). During World War I, the country had been shocked to learn that a large number of draftees were rejected because they were deficient in reading ability. In reaction, the country called for high schools to improve the reading performance of its graduates.

But perceiving a problem and calling for its solution were not enough to produce effective high school programs. School districts lacked tests, techniques, teaching materials; they had to design, try out, and evaluate reading programs. The educational concepts and tools were not long in being produced. Thorndike (1917) started the field in the direction of teaching students to learn from text when he pointed out that, in the mature reader, reading is reasoning, analogous to solving a mathematics problem. A few years later, Gates (1921) began to develop reading tests which differentiated students' levels of abilities in reading and learning from text; and in 1927, he established the first reading clinic for diagnosis and improvement of reading. Judd and Buswell (1922) found that the reading process is not unitary, but varies according to the reader's purposes and the kinds and difficulty of the reading material. Consistent with Judd and Buswell's implications, McCallister (1932) published a book on teaching reading in the content areas at the high school level. Bond (1938) provided specific evidence that the students' comprehension varies from one subject area to another. A student may comprehend better, for example, in literature than in science. Only recently have relevant materials for teaching reading in content areas become available (Herber, 1970a, 1976) perhaps because the demand for them has become greater.

Although the need for post-elementary reading instruction was apparent, and materials, methods, and measuring devices had been or were being developed, junior and senior high schools were still slow to establish reading programs. Indeed, the concept of a developmental reading program that would provide instruction continuously from elementary grades through high school did not take hold until the 1950s (Smith, 1965a). Playing a prominent role in the establishment of this concept were Strang's research, writing, and reading demonstrations at the high school level (Strang, 1938, 1942; Strang, McCullough, and Traxler, 1946). She found that *individual* patterns of reading vary at the high school level. Other research provided further understanding of reading. Robinson and Hall (1941) discovered that reading skills for prose and nonprose are different. Later, Holmes (1954) presented evidence that a hierarchically organized set of subsystems underlies speed and power of reading. Then

Holmes and Singer (1961, 1966) reported that high school readers must not only mobilize strengths and minimize weaknesses; they must also draw upon certain essential subsystems to attain speed and power of reading.

Research on high school and mature readers has continued to expand knowlege of reading. On the instructional side, Ausubel (1964) theorized that advance organizers facilitate comprehension. Similarly, some researchers found that reading guides and structured vocabulary overviews facilitate comprehension (Herber and Sanders, 1969; Herber and Barron, 1973), while other researchers discovered that teacher-posed questions before and after reading helped students comprehend. More recently, Anderson (1976) explained that abstract concepts generate concrete scenarios which enable individuals to comprehend, that is, to assimilate, store, and retrieve information; for example, an abstract concept, such as making a sandwich, can generate a sequence of events or knowledge structures in a person's mind that can be used to assimilate a story about a person making a sandwich.

Adding impetus to the movement to improve developmental reading was the United States Army's formation of reading centers in universities during World War II. The purpose of these centers was to speed up the war effort by teaching high school and college graduates enrolled in officer training programs to improve their comprehension and speed of reading. After the war, university and college reading centers survived to serve students enrolled in regular college programs. In the 1960s and 1970s the centers were also upgrading reading achievement of minority students whose reading potential had not been fully realized. Consequently an anomalous condition existed: during the 1940s and continuing in some places even today, reading was taught in the elementary grades and in colleges and universities, but not at the levels between. Over the past thirty years, junior and senior high schools have been filling in this gap.

Pressure to eliminate the gap has also come from changes in the composition of high school enrollment. Instead of dropping out of high school for jobs in agriculture, business, and industry, high school students (especially those with low academic achievement and ability) began to remain in high school until graduation. From 1930 to 1960, enrollment of the 14- to 17-year-old age group in secondary school increased from 51.3 to 83.2 percent (Tyack, 1976). A more recent analysis of school holding power revealed that 85 percent of students enrolled in ninth grade were still attending school in the twelfth grade (Jencks, 1975). Among the determinants of this holding power was the initiation of the 100 percent promotion policy in which students were promoted regardless of their achievement levels (Caswell and Foshay, 1950). Concomitant with this policy was the development of a more differentiated and appropriate high school curriculum that could accommodate the diverse abilities, aptitudes, and aspirations of this more heterogeneous group of students as they progressed through school. Also, pressure on students to remain in school and for schools to expand their curricula to accommodate them came from civil rights groups, buttressed by the 1954 Supreme Court decision that separate schools were inherently unequal. In the 1960s, civil rights groups not only urged integration of minority students into the schools (Singer and Hendrick, 1967), but also counseled minority students to remain in school and make schools adapt instruction and curricula to their needs and interests. The goal was to have schools provide minority students with appropriate training for development of their abilities so that they could go on to college and to jobs that required a higher level of academic education.

Thus, high schools today no longer have the highly selected group of students they had some 75 years ago when the Committee of Ten had advocated a college preparatory program as *the* high school curriculum (Tyack, 1976). High schools now have not only a more heterogeneous group of students but also a more varied curriculum with numerous electives, minicourses, and programs. Indeed, the educational system has made considerable progress towards attainment of the comprehensive type of high school advocated by Conant (1959) and the "12 year common school" curriculum proposed by some educators (Caswell and Foshay, 1950).

You can view the establishment of reading programs in junior and senior high schools as a concomitant of the social, economic, legal, and educational forces that have led to the curriculum of the 12 year common school. These reading programs are helping post-elementary schools provide equality of educational opportunity to their heterogeneous student bodies and to low-achieving students who are remaining in school longer to pursue elevated academic aspirations. But in solving the problem of how to provide equality of educational opportunity for students whose reading grade equivalents range from grade 0 to 12 and higher, schools have created reading programs that vary considerably.

Since Ms. Jones and Ms. Valdes were the only two staff members from Monroe High visiting the eight sites they took careful and detailed notes for a report they would give to the Monroe faculty when they returned. During their visits they noticed that, while each of the eight schools had its own basic *type* of program, a given program often shared two or more features with another program and did not quite fit into the traditional categories of developmental, corrective, clinical or remedial, content, and enrichment classes.

As Ms. Jones was led to believe, these programs represented the best current attempts of some schools to solve the reading problems of junior and senior high school students whose reading grade equivalents range from 0 to 12 or higher. Some of these programs were specific answers to the question often posed by high school content area teachers: "What do I do with the student who can't read or learn from text?"

NINE TYPES OF PROGRAMS ON THE CURRENT SCENE

1. The Tracking System

DESCRIPTION

A familiar type of solution to the range of reading levels in a school is placement of low-achieving readers into a separate track in which curriculum and texts can be adapted to their levels of reading ability and reading instruction can be given to all the students in the track. An example of high school *tracking* appears in box 15.5.

BOX 15.5. Tracking System

I. Intake
   A. Five Instructional Tracks
      1. Honors
         a. Gifted students (IQ above 132)
         b. "Very able" high achievers
      2. X section
         a. College preparatory (IQ 110 to 131)
         b. Students reading above grade level
      3. Y section
         a. College preparatory, community-college-bound (IQ 95–109)
         b. Students reading at or slightly below grade level
      4. Z section
         a. Community college, terminal (IQ 75–94)
         b. Students reading two or more years below grade level
      5. "Correlated" (IQ below 75)
         a. Mentally retarded

II. Testing
   A. *CMM: California Test of Mental Maturity/Stanford-Binet* (special request)
   B. *Otis Quick Scoring Mental Abilities Tests* (for transfer students)
   C. *Gray's Standardized Oral Reading Test/Iowa Test/Sequential Tests of Educational Progress (STEP)*

III. Description of Students
   A. Honors and X students tended to come from professional families, small business owners, and farmer-ranchers. Noted sense of humor. Lively. Vol-

atile. Articulate. Critical, often openly. Easy access to administrative offices and counselors.

B. Y students. Tend to come from small farms and ranches, children of blue collar workers and clerks. Difficult to motivate. Frequent discipline problems. Unparticipatory in student activities.

C. Z students. Tend to come from parents that are in unskilled labor and unemployed. Fewer discipline problems than Y students. Easy to get into routine. Regarded any change with uncertainty.

IV. Typical Program and Materials
   A. Honors-X Program. Difficult and varied reading materials. Heavy involvement in discussion and dramatic activities. Creative projects. Essay examinations. Presentation of "college" objectives — "You'll need to know this when you get to college."
   B. Y program. Used some of the same texts as X students, often different texts. Academic material "watered down." Fewer opportunities for discussion, more "seat work."
   C. Z program. Used simpler texts than Y students. Unlike other sections, had almost no homework, seldom took any books home. Materials kept in classroom. Programmed instruction, drill, worksheets, low-level activities. Virtually no discussion or dramatics. Heavy use of films.

V. Grading
   Different viewpoints existed at the school. In general, grading standards were the province of individual teachers. Some teachers allowed Z students the opportunity to make the same number of As and Bs as X or Honors students. Other teachers felt that Z students should receive nothing higher than Bs and Cs. Some teachers felt that since Y students were going to college, they should be graded on the same standard as X and Honors students. Some teachers felt that X and Honors students should be graded most stringently since they would be attending university. In general, Honors students tended to have more As than X, Y, and Z students.

VI. Staffing
   Sectioning occurred in ninth-, tenth-, and eleventh-grade English and social studies and ninth-grade Science. Other courses (chemistry, typing, bookkeeping, masterpieces of Literature) tended to section themselves. Although certain teachers were selected to teach one class of Honors students, most teachers taught a mixture of sections. In other words, faculty weren't identified as X teachers and Y teachers.

VII. Moving Up and Down Sections
   For the most part, students stayed in sections throughout high school. However, certain students were resectioned on the basis of teacher request, parent request, or new testing data (one prominent example was a young Black student who scored 86 on the *Otis Quick Scoring* and *Mental Ability Tests* and later 119 on the *Stanford-Binet*). Occasionally, students were resectioned for disciplinary reasons: a disruptive X student could be perceived as not profiting from classroom instruction and would be resectioned. Also, students who were

nonachievers were frequently resectioned lower: some Honors classes contained a majority of high-achieving, nongifted students, while the X sections would have low-achieving gifted students.

CRITIQUE OF TRACKING SYSTEM

A tracking system is not appropriate for the differentiated abilities of students.[10] Moreover, the downward adaptation of curriculum for students placed in the lower track tends to increase the achievement gap between lower and higher tracks (Balow, 1964). Although research evidence on the issue is not clear (Macmillan, Jones, and Aloia, 1974), it is possible that the lower track and special classes may stigmatize at least some students and consequently be counterproductive to effective teaching and learning.

However, some specialized instruction is required for students at the high school level, especially those students still in the acquisition phase of reading development. Although grouping students into specialized classes for specific instructional need is defensible, tracking students is not. The three-level program described in box 15.5 groups students in a junior high school for specific reading instruction; these students are not tracked because they can and do progress from basic to more advanced levels of instruction. Other programs have ways of providing for specific educational needs *without tracking students.*

2. Clinical Centers

DESCRIPTION

Clinical centers tend to exist in elementary schools or in universities where they also serve as laboratories for training reading specialists. Students referred to these centers are diagnosed by reading specialists trained to use a battery of individually administered diagnostic tests. Drawing upon the diagnosis, a specialist plans a reading improvement program and then applies it to the individual, either on a one-to-one basis or in small groups. Box 15.6 contains a more detailed description of how a reading clinic operates in a school setting.

---

[10] The system of tracking students, that is, assigning them to sections for all of their course work on the basis of an aptitude test, is rapidly disappearing from American high schools. Even the high school used as an example for table 1 no longer tracks its students. The reason for the elimination of tracking is that the court in the case of Hobson *vs.* Hansen (1967) declared that tracking or ability grouping is illegal when it is based on tests which 26may be biased and when it results in placing students against whom it may be biased in an may be biased and when it results in placing students against whom it may be biased in an inferior educational program.

BOX 15.6. Reading Clinic

A Schoolwide Center Emphasizing
a Diagnostic and Prescriptive Program
for Reading Achievement and Self-Concept

Description: This Junior High is located in an agricultural area in transition to a suburban neighborhood with medium-priced, single-family homes. A high percentage of students come from Spanish-speaking homes. The center, located in the school's former library, is carpeted and air-conditioned, has a receptionist-secretary, couches in one corner in a living room arrangement, round tables seating about four or five students, and walls lined with books and materials.

The reading facility was established for a demonstration program by an annual competitive grant of $150,000 from the State of California under Assembly Bill 938, passed in 1969. Each year the least cost-effective of the fifteen demonstration programs established under the Assembly Bill is eliminated from grant support. Since the program maintains a student-to-teacher ratio of 5 to 1 with a staff of 10, including a Project Director, a full-time, on-site, bilingual (Spanish and English) counselor, three reading teachers with M.A. degrees, four instructional aides, and a full-time secretary, the program can be categorized as fitting the criteria of a school-based reading clinic.

Intake: All seventh graders, except educable mentally retarded students, are programmed into the center from their English classes. During the first year of the center's operation, English teachers accompanied their classes to the center and participated in its activities. Now, half the students from two English classes are scheduled each period; after three weeks, the other half of the students rotate into the center. This alternation procedure continues every three weeks throughout the year. Thus the center has a full-sized class of some 30 students each period while the English teachers have reduced classes of about 15 students.

Testing: All students take (in October and again in May) the *California Test of Basic Skills* which provides grade equivalents on comprehension. Those below grade equivalent 4.5 take the *Durrell Analysis of Reading Difficulty.* The *Stanford Diagnostic Test,* Levels I or II, is administered to students at grade equivalent 4.5 or above. The *Classroom Reading Inventory* by Nicholas Silvaroli is given to students entering the program later in the year for quick assessment before the diagnostic tests are given. Students take progress tests in instructional materials used at the center (*Clues to Reading Progress* for students reading at grade levels 2.0 to 4.0 and criterion-referenced testing in the Audio Reading-Progress Laboratory for students at reading levels 4.0 to 10.0). Students also take placement tests for Systems 80, controlled readers, and other programs. They take informal tests to pinpoint specific difficulties such as lack of familiarity with words on the Dolch list, consonants, vowels, blends, syllabication, affixes, and roots. Students also have auditory and visual screening and take the *Slosson Intelligence Test* and the *San Diego Interest Inventory* (Patrick Groff). Each student's test results are diagnosed and an individual prescription is written by the reading teacher. Table 1 shows the gain in achievement for a group of students after one academic year.

TABLE 1. Average Gain in Vocabulary and Comprehension
from October to May for 318 Students

Test Results CTBS, Level 3	Mean Grade Scores		
	Pretest	Posttest	Gain
Vocabulary	6.4	8.3	1.9
Comprehension	5.8	7.7	1.9

Counseling: Students initially took pretests and posttests on a "Self-concept Semantic Differential" administered on a group basis. They rated themselves through the degree of agreement or disagreement on these dimensions: I am (good *vs.* bad, useful *vs.* useless, superior *vs.* inferior, important *vs.* unimportant, failure *vs.* success, good reader *vs.* poor reader, like school *vs.* hate school, like myself *vs.* hate myself, and like to read *vs.* hate to read). But the median changes, although in a positive direction, were slight; so, the center decided to drop the test. Every student has the opportunity to participate in group counseling sessions.

Typical Program: Each student has a Student Profile Sheet which contains a list of tests taken and their results, including an estimated informal reading inventory level (Silvaroli) and a diagnostic check list of difficulties in oral communication (knowledge of English, dialect, low verbal ability), listening comprehension, visual perception (memory for words), word analysis, oral reading (processes, error types, and rate), and comprehension (vocabulary, main ideas sequence, recalling details, drawing conclusions, cause-effect relationships, inference, understanding author's purpose, silent reading (rate and comprehension), study skills (following directions, critical reading, use of reference materials, skimming and scanning), and general reading habits (insecurity, low effort, easily distracted).

A prescription/instructional plan in each area (visual perception, word attack, vocabulary, study skills, comprehension/rate, and motivation) is drawn up. Students then have a contract plan based on their instructional plan with 5 to 10 points per lesson. Under each instructional category is a list of materials in the center for instructing the student. The contract in box 15.7 contains a partial listing: Students keep a daily record for each three-week period of points earned, and at the end of the three weeks evaluate the three things learned on their contract, the lessons found to be most helpful, the skills that still need to be worked on, and their comments on the program.

How Plan Works: Each class has 18 days to complete work. Students are to earn an average of 20 points per day and minimum of 20 points for outside reading. During the first week, orientation is given on how to use the contract, responsibility for behavior, and procedures for using equipment and materials. At first, students operate in heterogeneous groups, but after orientation period, they have individual choices.

Motivation
1. Points earned. The one hundred persons who earn most points go on field trips (zoo, superior court, county museum).
2. Prize day at end of each rotation (prizes: choice of paperbacks and posters).
3. Film at end of year.
4. Immediate feedback to students.

Relation to Other Content Areas
1. Indirect: resource center; order materials.
2. Provide training for English teachers.
3. Available to work with each department.

Grades: None, but this Evaluation Sheet is filled out in a conference between teacher and student:

Learning Objectives	Most of time	Often	Sometimes	Seldom
Completes assignment				
Shows progress				
Understands what he/she reads				
Shows growth in ability to evaluate own work				
Behavioral Objectives				
Tries hard to do his/her best				
Makes good use of time				
Works well independently				
Shows consideration for others				

Conferences with Parents: Although all are invited, only about 10 percent come to conferences.

Staff Credentials: Director, M.A. in Reading; 3 teachers with M.A. One is a reading specialist.

Evaluation: Outside evaluator provides annual evaluation: analyzes pretest and post-test results; interviews random sample of students; interviews staff of center and faculty of school at beginning of year on objectives (program and personnel) and end of year on their degree of attainment; and makes suggestions for the following year.

BOX 15.7. Individual Contract

Cover page: Identification, dates, contracted points

Second page:

	Points per lesson	Date lesson completed	Points earned
Visual Perception			
EDL Tach-X	5		
Word Attack			
EDL Aud-X	5		
System 80	5		
Vocabulary			
Word Clues Series	5/7		
Language Master	5		
Study Skills			
Study Skills Library	7		
Aud-X Dictionary Skills	10		
Countdown (Scope/study skills)			
Comprehension/Rate			
Controlled Reader	10		
Go Magazine	5		
Specific Skills Series	5		
Action Units	5		
Sports Action/Skill Kit	5		
Recreational Reading			
Scope Plays	5		

Total
Contracted total:

All equipment and materials mentioned in this box, and throughout chapters 15 and 16, will be credited by publisher or manufacturer in Appendixes A and B, respectively.

CRITIQUE OF CLINICAL CENTERS

Two assumptions underlie reading improvement programs: (1) a majority of students will make significant gains in these programs — more than one year gain for each year of instruction, and (2) gains made in these programs will transfer to produce improved performance in regular classrooms and in all content areas (Evans, 1972). Skilled diagnosis and intensive treatment can result in significant reading acquisition (Balow, 1965), since the task of learning to read can be mastered by all students in the normal range of intelligence, given adequate instructional time (Carroll, 1963; Bloom, 1971; Singer, 1977). But improvement in ability to gain information from texts through concentrated instruction is more difficult to attain. When it does occur, it is exceptional, as it is in the example given in box 15.6, because there is no short cut to attainment of the concepts, vocabulary, and particularly information or world knowledge (Winograd, 1972) that readers must draw upon to learn from texts or to comprehend in various content areas. Even under the specially favorable experimental conditions of performance contracting instruction, students did not improve significantly in reading achievement (Kelley, 1973). Moreover, when students who have been successful in the clinic are returned to regular classrooms, the disparity between their "hothouse" clinic instruction and the competitive classroom environment with its demanding textbooks and assumptive instruction (Herber, 1970) overwhelms the improved readers; they become frustrated, withdraw from reading tasks, and tend to return to the clinic and the ranks of the reading disabled (Balow, 1965).

Even students who have finally mastered the closed-ended objectives of reading acquisition in laboratory or clinic reading programs are not likely to overcome deficiencies in the open-ended objectives of vocabulary development, conceptual ability, world knowledge, values, and attitudes related to reading comprehension. Indeed, if a two- to three-year achievement gap or more exists between such students and others in their peer group, they will not be able to compete successfully with their peers who have been developing in the open-ended objectives steadily throughout their school careers. Hence, it is essential to intervene, and hopefully prevent, disabilities in reading and learning from text as early as the primary grades. Although the outlook for significant gains in learning from text for disabled readers at the high school level is pessimistic, the possibility of significant gains in reading acquisition is enough to justify clinic centers (Lovell, Johnson, and Platts, 1963).

3. Reading Laboratory

DESCRIPTION

A *reading laboratory* is usually stocked with a variety of self-instructional materials. See box 15.8 for a description of some self-instructional materials that are frequently used in reading laboratories. Students are either programmed into the laboratory as a result of low reading test scores or, more rarely, as a part of a schoolwide program.

In the laboratory, students sometimes take diagnostic tests. Usually, they take a test which indicates placement level in a particular set of instructional materials. The materials consist of short stories or expository paragraphs, followed by comprehension questions and perhaps some word meaning or word recognition exercises. Students read the passages, answer the questions, check their answers against the scoring key, and graph the results in a progress booklet. Occasionally, students receive help from a teacher or a teacher's aide who may be circling the room offering help. When students complete one program of self-instructional materials, they may go on to another program. Some laboratories accept students referred by content area teachers who notice the text is too difficult for them. These students may return to class after they have completed work on one set of materials. See box 15.8 for a more detailed description of one of these programs.

BOX 15.8. A Reading Laboratory:
Developmental Reading with Motivational Emphasis

Intake: Students are referred by teachers, and evaluated by counselors and reading lab staff at weekly Friday meetings at 7 A.M. If students are reading two or more years below grade level on the *Stanford Achievement Test* administered at the ends of grades 6, 7, and 8, they are taken out of English class, unless they are enrolled in Basic Skills in English. Then they are taken out of history. Some students are kept in reading lab until openings occur in other programs (Educationally Handicapped, Learning Disability Group) — usually low IQ students.

Testing: Use *Gates-McKillop Reading Tests* (oral reading paragraphs, blending vowels, consonants, and syllabication). Then assign 20–30 students/class period to work in centers to develop these subskills. Also administer placement test for *SRA Reading Laboratory Kit.*

Description of Students: Grade equivalent range 2–6. Heavy turn-over of 50 percent of students per year because of nearby Air Force base.

Typical Programs
1. Fill out card on each student, one for file and one for referring teacher. Card is progress report on tested Gates-McKillop subtests and comprehension *(SRA Reading Laboratory Kit* Progress Chart).
2. Each student gets work contract for Monday through Thursdays at centers located in various places in the room. Centers have task card, game, or worksheet on materials related to Gates-McKillop subtests. Each center has a "Help Sign" — a Peanuts character on card students raise when they want help. Students earn points for tasks completed.
3. Students in three groups on Friday for active comprehension instruction — learning to formulate their own questions and reading to answer them. Use Scholastic Action Books or Sports Close-Up Book or SRA Pilot Library for this instruction on active comprehension.

Materials Used Frequently
1. SRA Reading Laboratory Kit
2. SRA Pilot Library — high-interest, low-difficulty paperback tradebooks.
3. *Clue Magazine*
4. Scholastic Book Services *Action Books*
5. Sports Illustrated — The Sports Illustrated Learning Program: An Interdisciplinary Approach to Education.
6. Webster Word Wheels — use for blending exercises.
7. Teacher-made task cards for syllables, vowels, consonants, affixes. Bingo games for sight words, crossword puzzles for new vocabulary. "Vocabulary Word Center" (Have list of vocabulary ranging from grades 2–7 for each step in Scholastic's Individualized Reading Program), "Word Search": Puzzle that requires students to identify words in various spatial arrays.
8. Classic Comics Illustrated.

Motivation
1. Any holiday — have contests or prizes (free books).
2. Essay Contest — "What if you couldn't read?" Schoolwide contest.
3. Read-A-Thon — two-week contest for Mental Health Association; sponsors contribute to Mental Health Association for number of books read.
4. Once-a-Month Fun Day— No contracts that day. Unannounced surprise. Usually around a holiday. Examples:
Magic show: Each student reads and performs magic tricks in group — had five different magic tricks.
Valentine's Day: Origami — made animal valentine — had to read and follow directions.
Party for graduates from lab: Receive diploma, cookies. Graduates are those students whose reading scores come up to or near grade level. Had 25 out of 200 who achieved this goal over period from September to March.
5. Earn points for each skill task, for each 10–20 pages in book chosen for free reading, complete SRA story (1 point for doing task, 2 points for 80 percent comprehension, 3 points for 100 percent comprehension).

Relation to Content Area Courses in School
1. Doesn't tie in — strictly developmental reading now, but moving to tie in with history and science. Relevant materials:
   a. Harper & Row Design for Reading: *How to Read Social Studies:* "From Falcons to Forests," "Lions to Legends," "Mysteries to Microbes," "Pyramids to Princes." Paperbacks. Teacher's Edition. Grades 2–5.
   b. *Lending Library for Teachers*
   SRA Reading Laboratory Kit
   SRA Map and Globe Skills
   Countries and Cultures (SRA Dimensions Series)
   SRA Literature Sampler
   EDL Study Skills Library: Social Studies
   SRA Reading for Understanding

Grade
1. Grade, based on effort, as assessed by progress reports in folder, goes to teacher

of class from which student came and grade is prorated for semester grade in content area course according to fraction of week spent in reading lab.
2. Retested on *Gates-McKillop Reading Diagnostic* subtests and progress report sent to content area teacher.

Assistance
1. Student aides correct papers and exercises, and determine number of points earned.
2. Aide from government-sponsored aide-training program. (Train aide for six months who then is employed in other programs.)

Staff for Lab: Two certificated teachers, one with elementary teaching credential and M.A. degree in reading and the other with a secondary credential, an M.A. in reading, and a reading specialist credential.

Budget: $1,100 for materials per year.

CRITIQUE OF THE READING LABORATORY

Packaged reading programs used in reading laboratories, such as the Science Research Associate's (SRA) *Reading Laboratory Kit,* are based on excellent principles of instruction. They start students at appropriate levels of difficulty where they can successfully comprehend, allow students to progress in small increments of difficulty at their own rates of progress, provide for immediate feedback of results on exercises and tests, have students plot results for graphed evidence of progress. Moreover, the content of the reading selections are short and highly interesting.

The limitations of this approach are the following: (1) reading lab instructors do not initiate input instruction on reading acquisition and learning from text; (2) teacher diagnosis and prescription are not continuous; (3) students must determine their own difficulties and find ways to overcome them, or at least know when and on what to ask for teacher assistance; (4) the content may be useful for reading acquisition, but is not the content the students must learn to read for their content area subjects; and (5) students are not taught, and consequently do not learn, principles or processes of reading acquisition and learning from text that they can apply to their content area courses.

4. Functional Reading Programs

DESCRIPTION

Functional reading programs use tests, materials, and objectives based upon an analysis of what adults actually have to read at home or at work. Students are trained to read these materials. They are taught to identify the particular words, understand their meanings, and do the related comprehension exercises, frequently the type that requires the reader to follow directions (reading and following a recipe), carrying out the directions of an instructional manual for repairing a car, or looking up prices and ordering supply items for a store (Sticht *et al.*, 1975). A more detailed description of two of these programs is provided in box 15.9.

BOX 15.9. Two Functional Reading Programs

A. A Functional and Developmental
Reading Class

School: High School, 1250 students — 39.4% Chicano, 7.6% Black, 52.5% Anglo, 0.5% Asian.

Testing: Entering ninth graders tested in grade 8 on the *Nelson Reading Test*. Those scoring at grade 6.5 and below then take *Spache Diagnostic Reading Scales.* (Some students score low on Nelson because they don't want to take the test, but can read well, grade 8.0 or better.) Counselors screen transfer students on mini-*WRAT*. All students take criterion-referenced test consisting of all objectives in Title I.

Description of Class: Mostly bilingual, range in reading from grade 2.5 to 8.0. Class size: 20. Two Title I ESEA bilingual aides hired from local community (score and record exercises, keep charts and attendance, salary about $4 per hour, about $4,000 per academic year). Federal programs require records and check-off of objectives.

Time Period: 50 minute classes, five days per week. All students continue in class as long as they remain below reading grade equivalent 7.0, or until they become juniors when they have option of remaining in class.

Room Arrangement: Teacher's desk, six or seven round tables and chairs, library rack for paperback books, four carrels with EDL *Aud-X* headsets and tape recorders.

Functional Reading Exercises
1. Practice in writing numbers.
2. Fill out checks.
3. Complete short form of income tax.
4. Read a map.
5. Compute wages based on hourly salary and hours worked. Read and check on wage statement.
6. Cut out want ads. Answer questions: Where to go? Whom to call?
7. Read newspaper.
8. Use telephone directory.
9. Learn to use reference materials: dictionaries, encyclopedias.

Teaching Materials for Developmental Reading
1. Scholastic Action Library.
2. Barnell-Loft "Specific Skills Series."
3. Grolier's Reading Attainment Systems.
4. Science Research Associate's (SRA) Reading for Understanding, Junior Edition (grades 3–8).
5. Scholastic Action Units.
6. Random House's Hip-Pocket Series.
7. Education Development Laboratory's Aud-X Kit.
8. Learning Trends (Globe Book) *World of Vocabulary* by Sidney J. Rauch and Zacharie J. Clements, 1974.

Typical Class Period
1. Folders for each student with objectives based on criterion-referenced test.
2. Initially, spend entire class period teaching students how to do exercises in each set of materials.
3. Occasionally, entire class works on a skill together with teacher input and instruction.
4. After initial orientation, students get three individually prescribed exercises per class period.

Relationship with Content Area Classes: Provides some support for English teacher by providing reading students with help on assignments such as capitalization.

Retesting
1. Spache in middle of year for those with reading grade equivalent 5.5 and up.
2. Year-end test: Nelson.

Grades
1. Based on point system: 10 points for daily activity, 10 points for homework turned in.
2. Letter grades: A = 90% of all points that should have been earned, B = 80–89%, C = 70–79%.

Budget
1. Aides from Title I.
2. $150/year for maintenance of kits and supplies.
3. Thermofaxing provided by central office.

Teacher's Background: B.A. at Western Michigan University, year at University of Chicago in history of religion, substitute teacher, aide at juvenile delinquent institution, teaching credential at University of California, Irvine. Set up reading program at high school as Title I teacher three years ago; now certificated teacher employed by district.

B. Functional Reading with Emphasis on Comprehension

Testing: Retest on *The Nelson Reading Test* in grade 9, administer Gray Standardized Oral Reading Tests.

Class Description: 15 students, reading grade equivalents 3–6. One teaching aide paid from Title I funds.

Materials
1. *Scope* magazine.
2. Newspapers, *Los Angeles Times;* rewrite stories daily to fourth grade level, test with one question.
3. Combine math with reading — use supermarket ads to compute bill for shopping.
4. Read want ads.
5. Skill development: laminated Science Research Associates Reading Laboratory (3A) cards. Listen to story on tapes made by teacher and answer comprehension questions. Scored by teacher's aide.

Class Organization and Period
1. Monday–Thursday, half go to library; other half get SRA cards.
2. Class activities:
   a. Vocabulary exercises or homework: Half the students bring in homework (3 words on ditto sheet — make up sentences using them).
   b. SRA Story Progress: Comprehension 0–1 errors, move up to more difficult level; 2–3 errors, remain at same level; 4 or more, move down a level.
   c. Functional activities: work in groups. Entire group completes activity on want ads, supermarket shopping, and so forth.

Gains: Some gains on specific materials, but not on standardized tests; not enough time. Students would have to read 2–3 hours per day to complete enough to gain on test.

Teacher Background
B.A. New School for Social Research.
M.A. in Psychology.
M.A. in Teaching Reading, University of New Falls.

CRITIQUE OF FUNCTIONAL READING PROGRAMS

Although the objectives of functional reading programs are laudable, they must be recognized as (1) only minimal requirements for operating in society, (2) the consequence of a decision to give up on trying to prepare some students for content area courses and the general academic objectives of school, and (3) relevant only to some specific adult reading requirements that are susceptible to change or modification. Although application questions, for example, have some common elements (name, age, address) which can be specifically taught, they also have variable elements that call for general, not specific, word identification abilities. However, because different words may refer to the same information, audio-taped directions are beginning to accompany application forms in various places such as government offices, reducing the necessity for reading application forms.

While some functional reading requirements can be specified (Harris, 1970), there is no consensus on what constitutes functional literacy (Bormuth, 1975). Vocational reading instruction is one answer, but this instruction may be as difficult or even more challenging than other content area instruction. (See chapter 8 for levels of difficulty of vocational materials.) Specific occupational reading instruction can be done on the job (Sticht and McFann, 1975), but such training can come only when people are employed or know what specific jobs they will have.

What may be most desirable in high school functional literacy classes is to use the motivational effects of adult and occupational reading materials for teaching general reading acquisition and processes of learning from text. To do so, abstract the vocabulary from these materials for teaching word identification and word meaning techniques, use the content in varying syntactic arrangements and prose organizations, and teach students to interact with printed materials, drawing upon their knowledge and experiences, particularly for making inferences and evaluations. This broader goal is likely to help students become more adaptable to changes in content and enable them to function better in diverse reading situations.

5. Individual Reading Class

DESCRIPTION

Students, usually low in "reading" achievement, are programmed into an *individual reading "class"*; frequently these classes replace regular English courses. Some teachers of individual reading classes may administer a diagnostic test and provide some individual diagnosis and instruction (Singer and Rhodes, 1977), but in many of these classes, students simply self-select and read high-interest paperback books. The paperbacks range in difficulty, but among them are many high-interest, low-difficulty materials. See box 15.10 for a more detailed description of this type of class.

BOX 15.10. Individual Reading Class

Intake: The English department at the high school has an informal tracking system. Students are rated on basis of Nelson-Denny Reading Test, given at the end of junior high school and/or counselor recommendations. Students missed through this process are referred by classroom teachers. The class is a depository for students with behavior problems, learning disabilities, and bilingual students ranging from high- to low-intelligence. Students reading at 6.0 grade level or below are urged, but not mandated, into a reading class. Those above 6.0, but still below grade level, get developmental reading which is actually an English literature program with less difficult materials, high-interest, low-difficulty adolescent fiction. Those at grade level or above take the regular English curriculum. Those whose Stanford-Binet IQs are 134 or above are placed in an English honors program.

Testing in Reading Class: Individual testing on appropriate subsections of the *Gates-McKillop Reading Diagnostic Tests* or the *Gilmore Oral Reading Test* and the *Gates-MacGinitie Reading Test.*

Class Size: Maximum of 10–15 students. No aides.

Program
1. Each student gets an individual program and a file is kept (two for each student; one for student use and the other for the teacher's records).
2. Individual program stressing oral reading. While other students silently read self-selected paperbacks, one student at a time is called to the teacher's desk where he or she reads orally for 10 minutes; students thus see the teacher once every four days.
3. Treatment:
   a. Individual, choice of a wide variety of material, including some kits, but SRA is used sparingly.
   b. Much free reading. Usually, students browse or get the instructor's advice on selection of paperbacks.
   c. Typically, little is done in the way of instruction.

A Weekly Schedule
Monday: Student selects new book and reads to teacher. They discuss the passage. Teacher evaluates appropriateness of book for student. The student starts graph or chart on pages read during session.
Tuesday: Student discusses with teacher or relates what he/she read. They go over list of difficult words or new terms.
Wednesday: Student may have a writing assignment.
Thursday: Word recognition exercises, individual or group.
Friday: Reading games.

Relationship to Content Areas: Use content area textbooks based on content area teacher's message that student needs help in reading the assigned textbook; the reading teacher gives individual student instruction on reading in the particular content area.

Materials: Primarily paperbacks.

Gains: Some students showed gains but floundered when put back in regular English classes; some students did whatever they could to stay in the reading lab. Many low IQ pupils showed no gains during four years in the lab.

Teacher Background: Five English teachers; initially, none had experience in teaching reading. Each teacher has two sections of reading and three English classes. New teachers are usually assigned to reading lab duty.

Evaluation: Teachers work hard but feel frustrated. They have limited success with a few students. They want to change the program but no one involved seems to know what to do.

For individual counseling and instruction on problems in reading in the content areas, see Harry Singer and Alan Rhodes, "Problems, Possibilities, and Programs at the High School Level," in Wayne Otto, *et al.* (eds.), *Reading Problems: A Multidisciplinary Perspective.* (Reading, Mass.: Addison-Wesley, 1976).

CRITIQUE OF THE INDIVIDUAL READING CLASS

The individual reading class is a form of tracking because students are divided up according to levels of reading achievement and provided with differentiated instruction. That is, some low-achieving students enrolled in English classes are programmed into reading classes while the higher-achieving students get regular or accelerated English instruction (analysis of literature, composition, and grammar instruction). Regardless of the label assigned to the lower track — the individual reading class — it soon stigmatizes the students involved. The negative label tends to demoralize students with high levels of aspiration and overprotects less ambitious students who may perceive the class as a refuge from regular English classes (Singer and Rhodes, 1977). However, research has not definitely established that "stigmatized" labels alone affect students in general (Macmillan, Jones, and Aloia, 1974). What may have a detrimental effect is the lowered expectations on the part of teachers with these effects: input instruction is reduced; students do not have as many assignments or classroom questions to respond to; tests may not be administered with the result that neither students nor teachers have knowledge of progress. In short, students do not obtain any of the essentials of instruction. Hence, it is not surprising to find little or no gain in reading achievement in this type of class.

Low teacher expectations of student achievement can have serious effects. Beez (1968) found that prospective teachers serving as tutors, when told their students were dull, administered only half as many words during instruction as tutors who were told their students were bright. The students were actually equal in ability. The result was an immediate gap created in words learned by the two groups.

Even if lowered expectations do not lead to differences in achievement, the change in curriculum from English to reading instruction leads to an increased gap in knowledge of English content. The gap can be avoided or at least reduced if the reading class has the same objectives and instruction as the other English classes.

Another assumption underlying the individual reading class is that the average and above average readers do not need further instruction in reading. Although they do not need reading acquisition instruction, they do need to learn how to learn from texts in the content area of literature. Some of the instruction in English classes accomplishes this purpose, particularly if it involves teaching such aspects of literature as structure in a novel or short story, characterization, literary devices (such as irony, satire, and metaphors), paragraph and chapter organization, styles of writing, and the genres. Such instruction may even be more effective for teaching students to learn from text if it were done to help students learn from text. Furthermore, such instruction is necessary and appropriate not only for the average or better student but also for lower-than-average achievers. Otherwise, tracking would merely widen the knowledge gap (Balow, 1964) between the two groups.

6. Multi-faceted Reading Instruction

DESCRIPTION

Multi-faceted *reading instruction* has a variety of exercises for students to do each class period. Most of the exercises are short and interesting. Frequently they are teacher-made learning packets or dittoed sheets of exercises or games. They may be done individually or in groups. Occasionally, the teacher may provide some input instruction, using magazine materials written for junior and senior high school students (Singer, 1973b). See box 15.11 for a more detailed description of this type of program.

BOX 15.11. Multi-faceted Program for
Reading Acquisition

Test: The Nelson Reading Test plus teacher-made criterion-referenced test, administered in English or Spanish.

Class Description: Size: 15–20, reading grade equivalents 0–4. Two Title I aides (salary $4300 per academic year).

Materials
1. Thematic units for criterion-referenced items — used on contractual basis; 20 contracts over school year
2. Scholastic Units
3. *Scope* magazine
4. Action Library Series
5. Paperbacks
6. Games
7. Language Master
8. Controlled readers — used minimally.

Class Period and Organization
1. Three or four assigned activities. Points earned for grade, arbitrary division of points.
2. Monday, Tuesday, Thursday: Activities on contracts, prescribed over 2–3 week period. Work on contracts, individually or small groups (3–4 students).
3. Wednesday, Friday: Students work on skills in sociometrically chosen groups; groups compete for prizes.

Posttest: The Nelson Reading Test; gains of 1.6 to 2 years over 9 months.

Teacher Background
1. B.A. in English and teaching credential, Bradwell University; speaks Spanish well enough to conduct class in Spanish.
2. Four years of teaching experience.

CRITIQUE OF MULTI-FACETED INSTRUCTION

Although multi-faceted instruction could be focused, coherent, and cumulative, often it is not. Students may work on word recognition exercises using words that are unrelated to those employed in word meaning assignments, and both the word recognition and word meaning tasks may be unrelated to any story or expository content occurring in the class. Although a variety of exercises is motivating and stimulating to students, the exercises can also be related — not only to each other but also to content area courses students are enrolled in. Moreover, the exercises can be organized into a sequence to promote cumulative learning and generalizations that transfer to the content area classes. Even the use of technical terms from content area courses in word recognition and word meaning exercises would provide some application from multi-faceted reading instruction to content area classes. For a more detailed presentation of this approach, see the section headed ''Reading Acquisition in the Content Areas,'' chapter 16.

7. Three-Stage Program

DESCRIPTION

Some schools have reading programs not only for low and average but also for high-achieving readers. These classes are often referred to as remedial, corrective, and accelerated classes, or by some other triad of terms. The remedial class may resemble the clinic or reading class and the corrective class may resemble the reading laboratory. The low achievers are given the remedial reading program, while readers closer to grade level are assigned to a reading laboratory. Students reading above grade level have an accelerated reading and study skills program designed to speed up their reading and sharpen their study skills in preparation for college aptitude tests, scholarship exams, and college-level work. The accelerated reading programs may resemble those that were developed for the Army at universities and are now offered to college students. A detailed description of a three-stage program is given in box 15.12.

BOX 15.12. Three-Stage Program

A Junior High School Program
for All Levels of Reading

Intake: All seventh graders take reading: students are placed according to their reading grade equivalents on the *Gates Reading Survey:* Reading Lab = 0–5.5; Developmental Reading = 5.5–7.5; and Exploratory Reading = 7.5 and up. Students can progress through all three stages.

Tests
1. *Gates Reading Survey* (Grades 3–10): Levels of comprehension and vocabulary.
2. Test is given three times a year — September, December, and May — to accommodate students who transfer into the school (about one-third of the students trickle in and out during a year).
3. No additional testing in Reading Lab. December testing on Gates is used for determining promotion from one reading class to another.

READING LAB CLASS

Objectives
1. Recognize and reproduce letters of alphabet
2. Sound-symbol correspondence and blending
3. Meaning of simple and long words
4. Recognize affixes — syllabication
5. Use sentences to find answers to questions
6. Find main idea in a paragraph
7. Read story and understand it

Materials
EDL Aud. X: Phonics for beginning level readers
EDL Tach. X: Word recognition and vocabulary study
The Sullivan Reading Program: Word recognition in sentence contexts (individual)
Kottmeyer: Conquests in Reading (beginner)
Readers' Digest New Advanced Reading Skill/Builders: On audio tape — students follow along; may reread. Educationally handicapped referrals use these tapes one period per day. A few are at second-grade level of reading, but majority read at grade equivalents 3–5.
Barnell and Loft's Specific Skills Series (Richard Boning, author): Comprehension exercises: Drawing Conclusions, Getting Main Ideas, Working with Sounds,

Using the Context, Following Directions, Detecting the Sequence. Graded materials, some in programmed instruction format and others in multiple-choice format.

EDL Controlled Reading Program: Lessons built to reinforce word recognition and vocabulary

Go Magazine

Typical Period in Lab: Assignments made at beginning of period. Teacher keeps folder with charts for each student. Individual written assignments and materials on sheet stapled into folder — lasts for semester. Students correct own papers in skills series; turn them in weekly. Class is mostly individualized.

Motivation: Celebrate holidays.

DEVELOPMENTAL READING CLASS

Objectives
1. Use word attack through structural analysis.
2. Increase vocabulary up to grade level.
3. Use context to understand unfamiliar use of word.
4. Increase comprehension through class discussion and answering questions about material read.
5. Locate the main idea and relate it to supporting details in nonfiction.
6. Follow written directions.
7. Use subject-matter textbooks (social studies and science) effectively.
8. Separate fact from opinion.
9. Recognize tone or slant in an article.

Organization of Class
1. More like regular class than individualized Reading Lab. Partly taught as class; group instruction for class; partly as small group work and individualized instruction.
2. Students usually have a choice of assignment based on their assignment sheets which lists book and unit to do in Barnell Loft (Richard Boning), Specific Skills Series, Magazines, Graph and Picture Skills Kit, SRA, Be a Better Reader.

Materials
1. SRA Labs and Vocabulary Kit.
2. Reading for Understanding.
3. Specific Skills Series.
4. Magazines: *Scope, You and Your World, Read.*
5. Selection of paperbacks.
6. Be a Better Reader Series A, B, C, or I, II.
7. Graph and Picture Study Skills.

Typical Assignment
1. Be a Better Reader "B," p. 67, "Pioneer Flights for Cape Kennedy." Do activity 1, 2, pp. 8–9.
2. Working with social studies words, p. 70.

3. *Scope* magazine: Read "Born Free."
4. Library research report due next Monday.

Typical Period
Individual: Make choice from assignments in folder. Self-selected reading.
Group: Vocabulary instruction.

Motivation
1. Keep track of progress.
2. Weekly grade of A to F on assignments; record on report card.

EXPLORATORY READING (Accelerated Reading Class)

Objectives
1. Read a whole book.
2. Read many different kinds of books on a variety of subjects.
3. Broaden understanding of history, geography, and social problems through reading.
4. Learn to read critically; be able to argue a point of disagreement with printed material.
5. Learn to read creatively: students should be able to apply what is read to situations in their own lives.

Organization of Class: Taught partly as class, but often individualized, depending on students.

Materials
1. Different kinds and levels of books.
2. *Success in Reading,* Bk. I and II by Robert E. Shafer, Arthur S. McDonald, and Karen Hess, California State Series, 1967.
3. Unit on using library.
4. Teacher-prepared reading guides on skimming, recognizing similes, use of graphs and maps, remembering what is read.

Grade: Based primarily on effort. Students can get As or Bs by doing work at level placed in. If work done, may get A or B. If not done, get D or F.

Assistance (In reading lab and in developmental reading)
1. One full time aide (paid $3/hour).
2. Teaching Assistant: 8th or 9th grade students assist with grading; help with new children. TA is graduate of class. Works with students individually in class.

Relationship to Content Area Teachers
1. In-service training on use of kits in social studies.
2. Students in each class have different teachers — grouped not by grade but by reading levels.
3. In other subjects students are also sectioned: three sections in each content area.

Sections based on reading scores and recommendations of 6th grade teacher. Lowest 9th grade has 5th grade social studies materials; but lowest 7th and 8th grade has few materials in anything — teachers are working to develop their own materials.

Consultation with Parents: Only ad hoc consultation on problems.

Budget: $500 per year.

Staff: Three reading specialists, two with M.A. degrees and reading specialist with credentials from Bullock University. One teacher converted from English to teaching developmental reading, but has had no formal instruction in reading.

CRITIQUE OF THREE-STAGE PROGRAMS

The assumption underlying the three-stage programs is that the students in the programs have qualitatively, as well as quantitatively, different instructional needs. While the quantitative assumption is likely to be true according to the criterion used in differentiating the students, it is not likely to be true on all the other skills and abilities that enter into reading and learning from texts (Balow, 1962).

The qualitative assumption is not true. Students at all stages need instruction in word recognition, word meaning, and learning from text, although students in the lower groups need a heavier emphasis on word identification. Indeed, the lower achievers are likely to include more sub-categories of learners who need individual treatment. (See chapter 16 for a reading program for acquisition in content areas for these low achievers.) All of the tracks can use relevant content from the various content areas so that the students not only can improve in the reading classes but also can transfer what they learn and consequently improve in reading and learning from texts in various content areas.

8. Schoolwide Reading Programs

DESCRIPTION

A *schoolwide reading program* may vary from one organized and administered by a reading specialist on an informal request basis (Thomas, 1969) to a program that involves the entire faculty in intensive in-service training. Although rare in the past, schoolwide in-service training is occurring now with greater frequency as faculties become less mobile and fewer new teachers are hired. Even more rare are the schools which in a concentrated attack on reading improvement use a particular technique, such as marginal glossing, on a schoolwide basis (Dillner, 1971).

CRITIQUE OF SCHOOLWIDE READING PROGRAMS

A reading consultant or specialist on a school faculty serving only on a request or informal basis is likely to have some helpful effects on faculty and students. However, beneficial results are more likely to follow from defined objectives and systematic development of faculty for teaching reading and learning from text to students in each content area. Then, students are likely to get instruction in reading and learning from text in all their content areas. The reinforcement in processes of reading and learning from text and instruction in various content areas for all students will be reflected as gains on standardized reading tests if improvement has occurred in each content area sampled by a general reading achievement test (Singer and Rhodes, 1976). Hence, a comprehensive inservice course and instruction in all facets of reading and learning from texts are preferable to the schoolwide use of a single instructional technique. However, the single instructional technique may be a necessary strategy for starting a faculty towards the goal of a comprehensive program.

9. Proficiency Examinations and Related Curriculum for a High School Diploma

DESCRIPTION

Before returning to Monroe High School, Ms. Valdes mentioned another type of program that they hadn't observed: a program that develops students for passing *functional* or *proficiency tests* mandated for high school graduation. She provided Ms. Jones with the following information:

In 1977, the Educational Testing Service reported[11] that state legislatures were mandating mastery of essential skills as a condition for high school graduation. Seven states (California, Colorado, Florida, Maryland, Virginia, New Jersey, and Washington) had already enacted such legislation, while the state boards or departments of education in nine states took action to establish proficiency testing. Other states were in the process of establishing minimal competency requirements. California enacted legislation in September 1976 (Assembly Bill 3408) that was superseded by another bill (AB65) in September 1977. The second bill requires school districts in California to assess reading proficiency by

[11] *An ETS Information Report: Basic Skills Around the Nation, February, 1977.* Princeton, N.J.: Educational Testing Service, 1977.

administering a district adopted test first at the elementary level, then again at the junior high school, and twice at the high school level. Once students have passed the test they will not have to take it again. For those students who do not pass the test, the district must provide a diagnostic and prescriptive remedial instruction conference or alternative ways of satisfying the district's course of study. After June 1980, a student who does not meet the proficiency standard will be denied a diploma.

In response to the legislation, the Los Angeles School District developed its own *Senior High Assessment of Reading Proficiency* (SHARP Test) and a curriculum in the form of miniunits directly related to the reading tasks for those students who do not pass the test. As of June 1979, only those Los Angeles high school seniors who have passed the test will receive a diploma. When the test was first administered, 24 percent of the district's high school students did not pass the test, which had a cutting score of 81 (67 per cent of the items correct). Since each of the three parts of the test is worth 40 points, the cutting score requires students who want to pass to take all three parts of the test. Since the administration of the SHARP Test and the remedial curriculum accompanying it will probably be the responsibility of reading specialists, the test and curriculum is a new type of reading program on the current scene. (See the description in box 15.13.)

BOX 15.13. Senior High Assessment of Reading Proficiency (SHARP) and Related Curriculum

Purpose: Objectively assess reading skills at the high school levels that relate to the understanding of and/or appropriate responses to printed materials. These materials represent forms and documents which adults must read and/or complete continuously.

Categories: The forms and documents adults must read and/or complete continuously fit into three categories in SHARP.
1. *Can You Follow Directions?* This category includes directions for voting, driver's tests, library cards, job and rental applications, unemployment insurance claims, letter writing, social security documents, and change of address forms.

   Sample item:

   Below is a SAMPLE EXERCISE. Please read silently as the material is read aloud.

   Beverly Clinton agreed to rent an apartment from Ellen Bertoni. The apartment rents for $235.00 per month. Beverly paid one month's rent in advance. She will move into apartment #16 on March 1. The blank receipt for the first month's rent is shown below.

Study the rent receipt. Use the information to help you answer the questions for Sample Items 1 and 2.

```
┌─────────────────────────────────────────────────────────────────────┐
│                                                                       │
│   RENT RECEIPT                                                        │
│                          No._____   _____ 19_____  │
│                                                                       │
│   RECEIVED FROM _____ │
│                                                                       │
│                 _____ DOLLARS     │
│   FOR RENT OF _____  │
│                                                                       │
│   FROM _____ TO _____ 19_____            │
│                                    _____  │
│                                                                       │
└─────────────────────────────────────────────────────────────────────┘
```

THE QUESTION FOR SAMPLE ITEM 1 IS:

1. What should be written on the line "Received from?"

   a. rent   b. apartment   c. Ellen Bertoni   d. Beverly Clinton

The correct answer is choice d. Mark it in the appropriate space on the answer sheet, now. In the shaded box, darken bubble d on the line marked S1.

THE QUESTION FOR SAMPLE ITEM 2 IS:

2. The line that reads "from_____ to_____ 19_____ " requires
   which of the dates below?

   a. March 1st to March 31st   c. March 15th to April 1st
   b. February 1st to March 1st   d. March 15th to April 15th

The correct answer is choice a. Mark it in the appropriate space on the answer sheet, now. In the shaded box, darken bubble a on the line marked S2.

2. *What's In It?* This section deals with reading and comprehension of signs, labels, and want ads, Yellow Pages, dictionaries, newspapers, warranties, bank accounts, signature cards, credit applications, and check writing.
   Sample item:

DRIVER'S LICENSE TEST-SIGNALS

Use the information on this DISPLAY to answer questions 1, 2, 3 and 4.

Mark your answers in **spaces** 1-4 of Section I on the Answer Sheet.

```
┌───────────────────────────────────────────────────────────────────────────────┐
│ ACCORDING TO ONE STATE'S VEHICLE CODE:                                          │
│                                                                                 │
│ It is necessary to signal to other drivers before making a right or left turn,  │
│ to slow down, or to stop. Hand-and-arm signals or signal lights on the car      │
│ may be used. If your vehicle is built so that hand-and-arm signals are not      │
│ clearly visible, signal lights must be used.                                    │
│                                                                                 │
│ If bright sunlight makes signal lights hard to see, the driver must use         │
│ hand-and-arm signals.                                                           │
│                                                                                 │
│ Right or left turn signals should be given during the last 100 feet before      │
│ reaching the turning point. It is not necessary to continue making the          │
│ hand-and-arm signal while making the turn.                                      │
│                                                                                 │
│ HOW TO MAKE A HAND-AND-ARM SIGNAL                                               │
│                                                                                 │
│   22111.  All required signals given by hand and arm shall be given from the    │
│           left side of a vehicle in the following manner.                       │
│                                                                                 │
│     (a)  Left turn—hand and arm extended horizontally beyond the side of the    │
│          vehicle.                                                               │
│                                                                                 │
│     (b)  Right turn—hand and arm extended upward beyond the side of the         │
│          vehicle.                                                               │
│                                                                                 │
│     (c)  Stop or sudden decrease of speed signal—hand and arm extended          │
│          downward beyond the side of the vehicle.                               │
└───────────────────────────────────────────────────────────────────────────────┘
```

1. The driver in Car #1 is going to _____.

   a. make a left turn
   b. make a right turn
   c. make a U turn
   d. continue ahead

2. The dirver in Car #2 is going to_____.

   a. make a left turn
   b. make a right turn
   c. make a U turn
   d. park his car

3. The driver in Car #1 would correctly signal to other drivers by _____.

   a. making the signal on the right side of the car blink.
   b. extending his left hand and arm upward beyond the side of the car.
   c. extending his left hand and arm horizontally beyond the side of the car.
   d. extending his left hand and arm downward beyond the side of the car.

4. The driver in Car #2 would correctly signal to other drivers by _____.

   a. making the signal on the left side of the car blink.
   b. extending her left hand and arm upward beyond the side of the car.
   c. extending her left hand and arm horizontally beyond the side of the car.
   d. extending her left and and arm downward beyond the side of the car.

Use the information on this DISPLAY. Answer question 5, 6, 7 and 8.

Mark your answers in spaces 5-8 of Section I on the Answer Sheet.

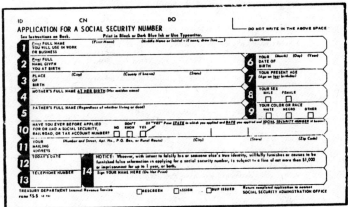

5. Giving false information on this application may result in _____.

   a. a $2,000 fine.
   b. a $5,000 fine.
   c. a $1000 fine and 5 years of imprisonment
   d. a $1,000 fine and/or 1 year of imprisonment

6. The two spaces in which information must be printed are_____.

   a. 1 and 2
   b. 4 and 5
   c. 10 and 11
   d. 13 and 14

7. The names in spaces 1 and 2 _____.

    a. must always be exactly the same
    b. must always be different
    c. can never be the same
    d. may be the same, or may differ

8. When filling in your mother's name you will _____.

    a. give her birth date
    b. give her birth place
    c. give her maiden name
    d. give her place of employment.

3. *What Does It Mean?* This part covers reading skills involved in the use of maps, area codes, cash register tapes, bank statements, TV guides, income tax forms, utility bill codes, and job resumés.
Sample item:

Use the information on this DISPLAY to answer questions 9, 10, 11 and 12.

Mark your answers in spaces 9–12 of Section I on the Answer Sheet.

TO: Tenants of Air View Apartments   March 10, 1976

FROM: James R. Stevens, Owner

SUBJECT: RENT INCREASE
             ELECTRICITY PAYMENT-POLICY CHANGE

This memo is being sent to all tenants of Air View Apartments, 445 N. Ginger Rd., Norwood, California to inform you that it has become necessary to increase the cost of rentals; also of a change in policy regarding payment for use of electricity.

Effective May 1, 1976 rents will be increased according to the following schedule:

Rental for one bedroom apartments will be increased from $125 to $140 per month.
Rental for two bedroom apartments will be increased from $150 to $170 per month.
Rental for three bedroom apartments will be increased from $175 to $200 per month.

This increase has become necessary due to increased taxes, insurance and maintenance costs. I am unable to continue renting at the former rate.

Because of the extravagant use of electricity by some tenants, electricity will no longer be included in the rental fee. Electrical costs will become the responsibility of each tenant.

It will be necessary for each renter to make arrangements with the Electric Power Company located at 112 First Street, Norwood, California, for your billing to begin and to be charged to you as of May 1, 1976. Individual meters will be installed for each apartment unit prior to that time.

It is with regret that I have to make these necessary changes and I sincerely hope that all tenants will understand my position and wish to continue living at Air View Apartments.

                                    (signed)   James R. Stevens
                                                  (owner)

---

9. The <u>memorandum</u> is a notice by a landlord of his intention to _____.

    a. add more apartments to his building
    b. remove tenants who have not paid rent
    c. remove noisy tenants
    d. increase the cost of rent

10. The memo further states that he will _____.

    a. charge tenants for use of water
    b. no longer include electricity in rental fee
    c. install individual gas meters
    d. no longer rent apartments to new tenants

11. The cost of rentals will be increased for _____.

    a. one, two, and three bedroom apartments
    b. only one bedroom apartments
    c. apartments that have a garage
    d. only two and three bedroom apartments

12. The increase in rent is necessary because of _____.
    a. increased maintenance only
    b. increased taxes only
    c. increased costs in owning this property
    d. increased insurance only

CRITIQUE OF PROFICIENCY EXAMINATIONS FOR THE HIGH SCHOOL DIPLOMA

The SHARP Test is an impressive device for assessing its specific domains. However, it includes content that is not specifically taught in the school (though perhaps it should be) and omits academic content which is stressed by the school. Hence, the test measures literacy in survival types of reading materials, not academic types of content.

A comparable proficiency test that also uses "real-life" situations for its content (but may be more closely attuned to the levels of reading ability stressed in the school) is the Educational Testing Service's Basic Skills Assessment Reading Test. Fifty percent of its items stress literal comprehension, 40 percent inference, and 10 percent evaluation (ability to distinguish fact and opinion, predict outcomes, and determine sequence, style, and tone). Even so, ETS states that the test is "easy for the high school population as a whole." (Harlstorne, 1977, p. 4.)

However, the ETS test is also not designed to test academic content. Presumably schools that want to assess this type of content can use one of the standardized achievement survey tests, such as ETS's Sequential Test of Educational Progress or the Stanford Achievement Test Battery. Another limitation of ETS's Basic Skills Assessment Test is that, in contrast to SHARP, it does not have a set of curricular materials accompanying it. Presumably ETS tries to key its items to existing curricular materials. An advantage of ETS's testing program is that ETS promises to revise its test every six months and maintain tight security over it. Hence, it is unlikely that students will have access to it before their reading proficiency is tested.

Either SHARP or the ETS test assesses basic proficiency of survival-type literacy. Presumably they will both have high reliability and adequate norms. Although the alternative curriculum is less academic than the school's standard curriculum defined by the tests and embodied in SHARP's minicourses, at least it insures that students who pass these or similar tests and receive a high school diploma will have a minimal level of competency.

If other states follow California's lead and allow local districts to set their own standards for passing the test, it is likely that the standards will be set low. Moreover, the standards are likely to vary from district to district in California and from one state to another. The public, which has clamored for a meaningful high school diploma, will still have difficulty in determining what a high school diploma means.

What reading proficiency assessment does mean is that high schools throughout the country will at least be filling the educational gap by hiring reading specialists and initiating a reading curriculum. Initiation of this program may be only a beginning. Eventually, high schools may expand the program into a schoolwide operation for reading and learning from texts in all content areas.

SUMMARY

In this chapter, we discussed how a reading and learning from text specialist can serve the entire school. The high school specialist functions in much the same way as does the elementary specialist. The high school specialist (1) diagnoses students with reading difficulties; (2) directs or teaches classes in reading acquisition in the content areas and functional reading programs; (3) demonstrates lessons on teaching reading and learning from texts in the content areas; (4) advises teachers of introductory classes on strategies for teaching incoming students how to learn from texts in the content areas, and (5) provides inservice education and participates on a schoolwide committee for developing a program to teach all students how to read and learn from text.

We also described in detail nine types of reading programs on the current scene and mentioned a potential program that teaches students to pass proficiency exams for high school graduation. Reading programs at the junior high school level tend to teach all students in the school and emphasize developmental reading. Typically an individualized approach is used: students are diagnosed; a prescription is made, and file folders for assignments and progress records are kept. At the high school level, programs are also individualized, but the emphasis is more on functional reading with a survival type of content. Hardly any instruction is given on learning from text or content area reading at the junior or senior high levels. Moreover, relationships with the content area faculty tend to be minimal.

Although the individualized programs usually supply students with materials appropriate to their reading levels, teaching practices in the programs often do not satisfy the criteria of instruction. These criteria are:

1. Diagnosing students, formulating objectives consistent with the diagnosis, and organizing materials that are appropriate for achievement of objectives and providing for feedback and evidence of progress. Most reading programs and many package programs on the current scene, such as those of the SRA Reading Laboratories, meet these criteria.

2. Input instruction, including explaining, clarifying, test trials, and additional practice to strengthen learning and to provide for individual differences in rate of learning. Some of the programs provide input instruction. The reading lab (box 15.8) provides instruction on active comprehension in small groups once a week. But, most of the time, students have to lift themselves up by their own bootstraps as they follow their assignments in packaged programs with the directions serving as the teacher. The packaged materials, however, do not diagnose student errors. Usually, students score their own exercises and fill out their own progress charts with little teacher analysis and correction of errors.

3. Coherence is minimal in all the programs. To explain coherence, consider any paragraph. What knowledge, abilities, and processes would a reader have to mobilize to comprehend the paragraph? The following is a list of major variables or subsystems underlying comprehension:
   a. Word identification skills
   b. Word meaning (vocabulary)
   c. Morphemics (knowledge of roots and affixes)
   d. Knowledge of syntax (ability to recognize intrasentence, inter-sentence, inter-paragraph relationships and relationships among larger units of organization, such as problems and solutions or parts of story structure
   e. General knowledge (knowledge supplied by the reader for filling in information a writer assumes readers know; for supplying evaluative criteria; for generating major premises; for interpretation; or for understanding literary devices such as metaphors, similes, and allusions)
   f. Attitudes and values that determine how a reader processes and reacts to the material
   g. Reasoning processes, such as inference, interpretation, concept formation, and conceptual ability, and evaluation.

   Some materials used in reading programs on the current scene have internal coherence because they do teach some word identification skills and vocabulary that occur in passages or comprehension exercises. However, most of the assignments in the programs are not coherent. Students may have one set of materials for word recognition, another for vocabulary development, and still another for comprehension without any specific relationship among them. Apparently the programs operate on the assumption that students will develop *general* abilities in each subsystem and mobilize these abilities to solve their reading problems as they need them. This is a long-range goal that must await some relatively high level of development in each subsystem before it can be achieved. Either in the long or the short run, current programs also rely on transfer of training for application of subsystems to the attainment of reading comprehension. But the evidence from research on learning is that transfer is more likely to occur when teachers teach for it; to teach for transfer, teachers should give students instruction in those specific contents and processes immediately required for a comprehension task, demonstrated in the directed reading activities (DRA) in chapters 11 to 14. Using the DRA strategy, teachers are likely to be successful in teaching students to apply the subsystems, and students are more likely to gain satisfaction from successful comprehension.

4. Psychosynchromeshing facility occurs when students not only attain the necessary content and processes but can mobilize them appropriately for attaining comprehension. This facility is more likely to be attained if students can try out newly learned content and processes in literature or expository materials. An analogy can be drawn from swimming instruction: after a skill such as an arm-stroke is taught on land, the students jump into the pool to try out the stroke in the total act of swimming. Likewise, if word recognition, word meaning, and reasoning in reading process are taught, students should have an immediate opportunity to use them in the total act of reading.

5. Isolation *vs.* Group Interaction. Most reading programs have students do their assignments in isolation. Hardly any time is allocated to group instruction or discussion. Yet students can and do benefit from group discussions. Consequently, whenever possible, reading programs should group students whose reading levels are close and have them read the same material as is done in Steps 1 and 2 of Scholastic Units. (See chapter 11 for a description of how these units work and chapter 6 for instructional procedures on discussion.)

6. Integration of reading programs with reading and learning from texts in the content areas. Students are referred to reading programs because they usually have difficulty in comprehending the assigned texts. Classroom teachers could adopt levels of texts to students. Frequently they do not, but they do expect the reading program to do so. (See single- and multiple-text strategies throughout this text but particularly in chapters 4, 5, 9, 11, 12, 13, and 14.) Yet, most reading programs do not teach students to read and learn from texts. The next chapter, about the future scene, explains how a school can

teach all students to read and learn from texts in reading programs and in courses in each content area.

ACTIVITY

Visit a nearby junior or senior high school that has a center for reading and learning from text. The program used might be similar to one described in this chapter. Interview the director of the center to find answers to these questions:

1. How does the faculty refer students, and how does the center select students for the program? What are the characteristics of these students?
2. What tests does the center use (a) to screen students, (b) to diagnose students' difficulties and to evaluate their progress during the program? What progress do students make in the center?
3. What student activities does the center have?
4. What materials does the center frequently use to improve students' performance?
5. How does the center grade students? Motivate them?
6. Who staffs the center?
7. What amount of money has the principal budgeted for running the center? What is the cost per student?

When you have compiled the information from the interview, compare it with the data other students have gathered from their interviews.

16 | The Future: A Schoolwide Program

CHAPTER OVERVIEW

Now that you have read about some of the current attempts to solve the problem of handling individual differences in reading and learning from text within a single school, you are prepared to deal with the future scene, a program that incorporates the viewpoint inherent in this book. The topics in this chapter include: (1) an outline of a reading content acquisition course that is based upon an explanation of (a) word identification (b) comprehension or interaction between the reader and the text; and (2) inservice education that involves (a) a sequence for acquiring and learning to use single- and multiple-text strategies, (b) an introductory course for reading and learning from text in the content areas, and (c) a committee on reading and learning from text.

TECHNICAL VOCABULARY

comprehension
automaticity
bottom-up and top-down processing
accommodation
psychosynchromeshing facility

We began this text by pointing out that the high school population has changed dramatically over the last 75 years. One of the major changes has been that some 87 percent of high school students now remain to graduate. However, reading achievement in this group ranges from about grade equivalent 5.0 in grade 10 to 24.0 (second year graduate school level) in grade 12. This range is normal; that is, we expect to have this range in reading achievement if all students are achieving to the best of their mental capabilities.

We have three possibilities for solving the problem of trying to educate students who vary so widely in ability: (1) We could invoke grade level standards; that is, we could insist that students who are not reading up to grade level repeat their present grade until they meet the entrance standard for the next grade. Our proficiency reading tests are a step in this direction. If we returned to invoking grade level standards which we more or less did prior to 1950, we would have an even wider range of achievement in each grade and would discourage low-achieving students from continuing in school. (2) We could have different curricula or tracks for students according to their levels of reading achievement. However, schools have officially dropped tracking students because they have had difficulty in justifying this practice to our courts. Consequently, high schools no longer assign students to classes; instead, students can select and sign up for any classes regardless of their own achievement levels. Of course, students with low reading achievement tend to avoid classes with heavy reading assignments such as English, science, social studies, and math, in favor of vocational classes, such as auto shop, sewing, and home economics. Also, some school counselors advise students to select courses that they think will match their ability levels. Hence, we have some *self-selective* and some *guided* tracking. Nevertheless, we still have a wide range of individual differences in reading achievement in all classes, even vocational classes. (3) We could adopt teaching strategies that enable teachers to provide equality of educational opportunity for all students without stigmatizing any. This text stresses the third possible solution.

The major part of the text (chapters 4–14, explains single- and multiple-text strategies for teaching content to students who differ widely in the ability to read and learn from text. This "difference" group consists of the largest numbers of students in a school. In chapter 15, we showed how schools are currently teaching students in the other three of the four reading difficulty categories (the 4 Ds) we defined in chapter 1. These are students with defects, deficiencies, and disruptions, and students who are at the low end of the difference curve. They are attending reading labs or classes in centers where they undergo further screening, take diagnostic tests, and receive instruction based on individual or group reading improvement plans.

These two types of programs fit the four types of reading difficulties and the range of individual differences in reading achievement in high school. However, high schools do not yet use single- and multiple-text strategies in any systematic way. That is, we do not know of any school where we could find teachers throughout the school using single- and multiple-text strategies in a phase-out/phase-in sequence. We could, and did, identify some schools where teachers were using one or more of these strategies.

Most schools that have reading labs or centers do not consciously employ content area materials in teaching high school students how to read; that is, these schools do not use the kind of content that appears in courses in the high school. Hence, they do not maximize transfer of learning in the content areas.[1]

We recognize that the strategies we have advocated for reading and learning from text in the content areas are not part of the current scene. Hopefully, they will become part of the future scene. This chapter suggests how a high school could develop its own program to bring about this future scene: a schoolwide program for reading and learning from text.

To begin, the school would have to have a reading and learning-from-text specialist or a reading specialist who would develop the necessary knowledge and skills for teaching a content reading acquisition course and strategies for reading and learning from text. We suggest in this chapter what this specialist would have to do to convert existing reading labs or centers to content reading acquisition labs or centers. Most centers currently do teach students how to learn to read, and they do include instruction in comprehension in their reading acquisition programs. What they would have to do to become content reading acquisition labs is to substitute content area materials for their current instructional materials and exercises. We think that with this change they would probably meet the criteria for a competency-based course we outline in this chapter.

The use of single- and multiple-text strategies throughout the school would require an inservice education program planned and implemented by a schoolwide committee. To help this committee to plan its inservice education program, we have outlined the questions committee members would probably formulate and the answers they might generate for decision-making and planning. The committee would, of course, need strong administrative support for this undertaking and a time table of about five years.

We describe four models of inservice training that have worked successfully. The schoolwide planning committee would want to consider them. We also suggest a sequence for teaching and disseminating to the

---

[1] Schools would have to construct their own materials to fit their own texts. However, some commercially prepared materials are available that will at least provide ideas on how to prepare these materials. For this purpose, see "Workbook Type Materials" listed in the appendix.

faculty strategies for reading and learning from text that would maximize its learning and minimize its resistance.

We anticipate that some teachers would cooperate and readily support the inservice program. These teachers could then teach introductory courses in reading and learning from text in their own content areas. The courses could serve as regular classes for freshmen students and as demonstration classes for other teachers.

To communicate how this future scene may come about, we employ the schoolwide committee of Monroe High School. You will eavesdrop on meetings of this committee via five dramatic scenes presented in this chapter. In the first scene (beginning below), the committee learns about a content reading acquisition class. In the second, they get a review of inservice education models. The third scene is a continuation of the second scene. It focuses on the idea of an introductory course in reading and learning from text. A week later, in the fourth scene, the schoolwide committee finds out the questions it will have to investigate in devising an inservice education program for the faculty and decides on tentative answers to them. The fifth and final scene is a meeting with the school principal. With this background, we are ready for Scene 1.

It is 4:30 in the afternoon. Monroe High students have been out of class for one hour. The schoolwide committee is meeting in a classroom with Ms. Valdes, the newly hired reading and learning specialist, to hear the results of the visits made by Ms. Valdes and Ms. Jones to neighboring schools' reading centers. Ms. Jones has described the centers and Ms. Valdes has just finished giving her evaluations of the programs. Committee members start to react.

Mr. Inglish: I sure like the sound of the individual reading class. I think that's the one we should adopt.

Mr. Phelps: Of course you do. That's the one most like a remedial English course. How's that going to help my kids with science?

Ms. Stewart: Or with math? We need something a little more imaginative.

Ms. Jorgensen: I like the functional reading program. It's practical and task oriented.

Ms. Stewart: That has its drawbacks. It tends to focus on low-level activities. And, by the way, as Ms. Valdes has said, how do we really know what it will take for these kids to function when they get through school? The way society's changing, entire vocational areas can be made obsolete overnight. Jeb, can you vouch for that?

Mr. Carter: That's true. Sometimes I feel kind of guilty teaching shop with outdated tools that the kids may never encounter and textbooks that writers, for some reason, make too damned difficult!

Ms. Jorgensen: You know what it looks like — none of these places you visited have the answer. They don't seem right for our needs.

Mr. Inglish: I still like the individual reading class.

Ms. Stewart: (good-naturedly) Who asked you? Why'd they ever let you on this committee? You've been reading T. S. Eliot too long!

Ms. Jones: O.K. Enough clowning around! Both Ms. Valdes and I have said the same things all of you are saying. We are of the opinion that none of these stituations are right for us. So, why not build our own program?

Mr. Phelps: That's going to take a lot of work.

Ms. Jones: It might be worth the work.

Ms. Valdes: You see, learning to read and learning to learn from text are different processes. Reading acquisition includes a set of skills that the majority of students master by the fourth to sixth grades, but some students are still learning how to read when they reach high school. That applies to a small percentage of students at Monroe. Most of the students we've been talking about know *how* to read; they just can't understand their textbooks.

Ms. Jorgensen: We still have to deal with those nonreaders.

Ms. Valdes: True, most of the programs that we visited handle the non-reader, but the problem with these programs is that they don't use content from the courses the students are taking, and they don't do much with comprehension of text material.

Ms. Stewart: Well, as Latrice just mentioned, since we still have this group of students that are still in reading acquisition, couldn't these kids be learning to read from the same materials that elementary kids use?

Ms. Valdes: No, to keep their interest and to help them with the words in the textbooks you are using, our students need content drawn from high school texts. Let's take a few minutes here for you to read something I wrote about reading acquisition in the content areas as well as comprehension strategies.

READING ACQUISITION IN THE CONTENT AREAS

Word Recognition

Although mastery of the acquisition stage of reading development is approached by most students by grade six, some students are still in this stage of development during junior and senior high school. Students who are slow in speed of reading and low in general reading achievement are likely to still be in the acquisition stage of development; that is, they are still learning how to read the language they use in their everyday speech. However, it would not be appropriate to have them use the same materials elementary pupils use, even though they have to learn the same words, syllables, digraphs, consonant clusters, letter-sounds, and blending processes (Singer, 1971). Moreover, junior and senior high school students also have to learn to identify technical words that occur in their content area instruction. The solution to teaching both basic word identification skills and technical word recognition skills is simply to use technical words for teaching the students word identification skills. Suppose you are teaching students the relationship between the initial consonant *p* (the *symbol*) and the *sound* it represents. You could select some words from physics *(power, piston, pulley, pressure)* and list them in a column to make the initial consonant *p* apparent, as follows:

*p*ower
*p*iston
*p*ulley
*p*ressure

Then begin teaching students as suggested below.

1. "What consonant letter do all these words begin with?" *(p)*
2. "Listen to the beginning sound of each word." (Then pronounce the words or have students do so.)
3. "Give me other words beginning with the same sound." (A student says *pump*, and passes the transfer test. Other students may add *population, peroxide, pendulum.)*
4. The words students volunteer are then written in the column.
5. At the elementary level, you would also have students look at the beginning letter and learn its features (Gibson, 1976). This step is probably unnecessary at the higher grade levels.

Thus, students could learn sound-symbol correspondences and other word identification processes (responses to digraphs, syllabication, recognizing affixes, and blending word components) *using content area words from their own texts* (Samuels, 1968; Resnick and Beck, 1974). They would not only learn word identification responses and processes but they would also be able to recognize content area words when they came to them in their texts. Furthermore, this type of content for word identification instruction is less likely to embarrass junior or senior high school students enrolled in acquisition classes. Although the processes and procedures for learning to read are the same for all students, regardless of age, reading acquisition classes can and should use instructional techniques, tests, and topical materials suitable to more mature students.[2]

FUNCTIONAL WORDS COMMON TO ALL TEXTS

Some words, particularly functional words, are common to all texts. Dolch's 220 basic words account for 50 percent of all words in a text, so it would be helpful to have a list of these words (Tinker and McCullough, 1975). The list consists of such words as noun determiners *(a, the, this, these, those, that, some, and)*; prepositions or locative words *(to, for, from, beyond, beneath, above)*; conjunctions or combining words *(and, but, nor)*; and subordinating words *(while, since, although)*. These functional words tie the contentives (nouns, adjectives, adverbs, verbs) together.

[2] You will find descriptions of materials that are useful for these classes in chapter 15 and in the appendix. You can locate additional materials elsewhere (Devine, 1969; Rupley, 1975).

By the end of grade three, 95 percent of all students have learned all the functional words. Therefore, these words should have priority in the reading acquisition program for junior and senior high school students who still cannot quickly identify functional words.

TEACHING WORDS IN CONTEXT

Do not teach functional words in isolation. Teach them in the context of content area phrases and sentences because the context is necessary for signalling the semantic and syntactical properties of functional words. You should also teach content area words in context, especially in sentences and paragraphs drawn from content area texts. Context makes the syntactic properties of the words apparent and helps the reader select the appropriate meaning of a word. The context helps identify the meaning of the word *constitution* in this sentence from a social studies text: "The people voted to change the *constitution*." In this sentence from a medical text, constitution has a very different meaning which the context helps to make clear: "The man had a healthy *constitution*." A list of some content words for use in various word identification tasks is given in table 16.1. You can locate additional words for word identification and word meaning instruction in glossaries or indices of content area texts.

TEACHING FOR TRANSFER TO THE PROCESS OF READING

Students in acquisition classes should also practice their newly learned words in content area paragraphs. You can locate paragraphs that contain these words in students' textbooks or in texts listed in the school catalogs. (See ch. 11 for school catalog information.)

WORD STRUCTURE AND MEANING

Also use content area words for teaching prefixes, suffixes, and roots. Scientific terms in particular draw heavily upon these word components. A list of affixes and roots that occur frequently in content area texts is in table 16.2.

PSYCHOSYNCHROMESHING FACILITY

Transfer all word recognition skills to the process of reading. This transfer process is analogous to first teaching a skill in swimming on shore and then having the student try out the new skill in the pool. The swimming pool for reading is a text or book in a content area that has passages which elicit the word identification response you just taught. If you want to teach a student to identify the sound of the initial consonant *p*, do not end the lesson until the student dives into a passage in the text and consciously responds with the correct sound (phoneme) each time the

TABLE 16.1. Major Functional Spelling Units (Letters and Letter Combinations Which Stand for Single Sounds) in Content Area Terms

Consonants and Consonant Combinations

*b*iology		*k*inship	*s*emicolon	*sh*ares	do*ck*
*c*ongruent	*ch*annel	*l*egislative	*t*eleplay	*th*eocracy	*th*in ju*dg*e
*d*emocracy		*m*ultiplier	*u*ltraviolet		ba*tch*
*f*actor		*n*onconductor	*v*ocal		*s*ix
*g*as	*gh*ost	*p*antomime	*w*altz	*wh*ether	
*h*umanity		*ph*ase	*y*oke		
*j*unction		*q*uartile	*z*ipper		
		*r*etrorocket			
		*rh*eostat			

Vowels and Vowel Combinations

*a*ntebellum	*ai*m/r*ay*	b*oa*st
*e*pidemic	astron*au*t/l*aw*	carg*oe*s
*i*nterplanetary	*ea*st/*ee*l	*oi*l/Tr*oy*
*o*ptical	d*ew*/d*eu*ce	m*oo*n
*u*pright	p*ie*ce	*ou*ter-space
*cy*cle		d*ue*/sl*ui*ce

Source: After Venezky (1970). Note: Simple consonants, which appear here in initial position, can occur in any position. So can most of the other units.

initial consonant *p* (grapheme) appears in a word. The student may accompany the response by tapping a finger or foot. The purpose of this transfer process is to develop *psychosynchromeshing facility,* the ability to mobilize appropriate phonemic responses to graphemes at the appropriate time and in the appropriate sequence.

Another technique for having students learn to use words or word parts in sentence context is the Singer Sentence Generator (Singer and Beasley, 1970). This sentence generator consists of the four basic sentence patterns[3] shown in box 16.1 on page 448.

Indeed, to guide students to the stage of reading acquisition where they are automatic in their responses to printed words and can consequently devote their attention to thinking or reasoning about meaning (Laberge and Samuels, 1976), there is no substitute for an abundance of easy, interesting materials in which recently acquired skills appear frequently.

[3] See Ruth Strang, Constance McCullough, and Arthur Traxler, *The Improvement of Reading,* 4th edition. New York: McGraw-Hill, 1967, pp. 309–310.

TABLE 16.2. List of Prefixes, Suffixes, and Roots in Content Area Words

Prefix	Meaning	Word	Meaning
a-	not, without	asexual reproduction	reproduction without eggs or sperm
ad-	to	adhesion	form of attraction between unlike molecules
ambi-	both	ambivalent	simultaneous attraction toward and repulsion from a person or object
ante-	before	antebellum	before the war
anti-	against	antibody	immune substance in the blood
apo-	away from	apogee	the highest point (as of a satellite) moves away from the earth
archae-	ancient, primitive	archaeology	study of early human life
auto-	self	autoregulation	self-regulation
bene-	well, good	benefactor	one who does good, makes a gift
bi-	two	binary fission	division of cells into two approximately equal parts
biblio-	book	bibliography	list of works referred to in a text
bio-	life	biology	study of life
capt-	take, seize	capture	seize
cent-	one hundred	century	one hundred years
circum-	around	circumference	perimeter of a circle; a line enclosing a circle
co-, com-	together	cohesion	stick together
con-, contra-	against	contradiction	say the opposite
de-	down	degenerative	tending to cause a lowering of vitality to a worsened state
deci-	one-tenth	decimeter	one-tenth of a meter
di-	two	diode	two-terminal radio tube
dia-	across, through	diameter	a measure across
endo-	within	endoskeleton	hard outer covering of certain animals
epi-	on, upon, over	epidermis	outer tissue

Prefix	Meaning	Word	Meaning
eu-	well, good	euthanasia	mercy killing
ex-	out	exothermic	give out heat
hemi-	half	hemianopsia	half vision
hetero-	other, different	heterodyne	mixing two frequencies to get a different frequency
hyper-	over	hypertonic solution	contains a higher concentration of solutes and lower concentration of water than another solution
hypo-	under	hypotonic solution	contains a lower concentration of solutes and higher concentration of water than another solution
il-	not	illegal	not legal
inter-	among	internode	the space between two nodes
intro-	inside	introvert	turned inward, one who is withdrawn
iso-	same	isomers	two substances having the same molecular but different structural formulas
mal-	bad	malodorous	having an offensive odor
mono-	one	monoplane	plane with one wing
multi-	much, many	multiphase	having many phases
non-	not	nonviable	not capable of living
ob-	in front of	obstetrician	literally, one who stands in front of, a physician who delivers babies
pan-	all, every	panacea	a remedy for all ills
para-	beside	parathyroid	glands adjacent to thyroid gland
poly-	many	polymer	a large molecule made up of a monomer repeated many times in a sequence
post-	after	postnatal	after birth
photo-	light	photon	a quantum of light energy
pre-	before	preamble	an introductory statement indicating what is to follow
pro-	for	pronoun	standing for a noun

Prefix	Meaning	Word	Meaning
pseudo-	false	pseudopodium	a ''false foot'' of the amoeba
retro-	backward	retrorocket	rocket producing thrust in opposite direction
semi-	half, partly	semiconductor	a solid whose electrical conductivity is nearly metallic at high temperatures and nearly absent at low temperatures
sub-	under, below	sublingual	salivary gland lying under the tongue
super-	over, beyond	supersaturation	beyond saturation
syn-	together	synergic	working together
tele-	far off, distant	telephone	instrument for producing sound at a distance
trans-	across	transgress	to go over a boundary or limit
ultra-	beyond	ultrasonic	vibrations in matter beyond 20,000 vibrations/second
uni-	one	univalent	capacity of an atom to form only one bond

Suffix	Meaning	Word	Meaning
-able	fit for	workable	practicable, feasible
-age	rate of	dosage	regulation of doses
-al	relating to	mental	relating to the mind
-an	characteristic of	median	in the middle
-ance	quality or state	hindrance	something that delays action
-ant	personal or impersonal agent	tenant	one who rents or leases land or a house
-ary	place of or for	library	a place in which literary or artistic materials are kept
-ate	action in a specified way	insulate	separate from conducting bodies
-ence	action or process	emergence	action of coming out into view
-ent	personal or impersonal agent	dependent	a person who relies on another for support

Suffix	Meaning	Word	Meaning
-er	one who performs a specified action	worker	a person who works
-ive	tending toward an indicated action	motive	something that causes a person to act
-less	not having	fearless	not having fear; brave
-ment	concrete result; object or agent of a specified action	entanglement	state of being entangled, confused, or in a complicated situation
-ness	state, quality, condition or degree	kindness	quality of wanting to help or be sympathetic
-or	one who does a specified thing	actor	one who acts a part
-ous	full	famous	widely known
-y	like that of	homey	homelike

Root	Meaning	Word	Meaning
anim	life, mind	animate	give life to
anthrop	man, human	anthropology	the science of humans
chrom	color	chromatophore	a pigment-bearing cell capable of changing skin color by expanding or contracting
chron	time	chronometer	instrument for measuring time
cycle	circle	cyclone	a storm that rotates about a center of low atmospheric pressure
dem	people	democracy	a government by the people
dic, dict	speak	dictate	to speak domineeringly
duc, duct	to lead	ductile	capable of being drawn out; easily led or influenced
fac	make	facsimile	an exact copy
fin	end	finite	having definite limits
flex	bend	reflect	bend back, as a mirror reflects light
flux	flow	fluctuate	to ebb and flow in waves

Root	Meaning	Word	Meaning
gamy	marriage	polygamous	having more than one mate at a time
gen	produce	androgen	producer
gnos	knowledge	agnostic	belief that existence of ultimate reality is unknown
loq, loqy	speech	loquacious	given to excessive talking
meter	measure	ohmmeter	instrument for measuring resistance
mov, mot	move	automotive	self-propelled
ped	foot	pedestrian	performed on foot
ped	boy	pediatrics	branch of medicine dealing with the child
phil	love	philanthropy	love of mankind; active effort to promote human welfare
phon	sound	telephone	transmit sound over a distance
rupt	break	rupture	tearing apart of tissue
scrib	write	inscription	wording on a coin, medal, or seal
spect	look	spectator	one who looks on or watches
stat	stable	static	at rest or in equilibrium
tang, tact	touch	tangent	straight meeting, a curve at one point only
vert, vers	to turn	reverse	to cause to go in opposite direction
voc	to call	vocation	a divine call to the religious life; work in which a person is regularly engaged

This table includes prefixes (Stauffer, 1942), suffixes (Thorndike, 1941), and roots (Durrell, 1940) that occur most frequently in basic reading materials. Some have more than one meaning, but we have only listed the most common.

For this purpose, content acquisition instructors should stock their classroom libraries with content area texts at various levels of difficulty. (Use the school catalogs described in chapter 9 for selecting content area texts at various levels of difficulty.) Thus, the procedure for developing effective and efficient skills alternates between learning skills accurately and then learning to apply them rapidly until students can mobilize their skills and use them effortlessly or automatically (Singer, 1966).

BOX 16.1. *Singer Sentence Generator*

USING THE FOUR BASIC SENTENCE PATTERNS

Directions: Substitute recently learned words, one at a time, for successive word slots (noun or pronoun, verb, adjective, noun determiner, noun) to generate novel sentences.

Sentence Generator 1

Sentence Pattern: Noun (or Pronoun)–Verb (NV)

Motors	run
noun or pronoun	*verb* .

Sentence Generator 2

Sentence Pattern: Noun (or Pronoun)–Verb–Adjective (NVA)

Motors	are	powerful
noun or pronoun	*verb*	*adjective* .

Sentence Generator 3

Sentence Pattern: Noun (or Pronoun)–Verb–Noun Determiner–Noun (NVN_DN)

Electricians	threw	the	switch
noun or pronoun	*verb*	*noun determiner*	*noun* .

Sentence Generator 4

Sentence Pattern: Noun (or Pronoun)–Verb–Noun–Noun Determiner–Noun ($NVNN_DN$)

Electricity	gives	condensers	a	charge
noun or pronoun	*verb*	*noun or pronoun*	*noun deter-miner*	*noun* .

Motivating Students by Putting Learning Under Their Control

THE CUMULATIVE GRAPH METHOD

In all aspects of content acquisition, and indeed in any instruction, knowledge of results motivates students to learn. A technique for motivating students and for putting achievement under a student's control (Singer

FIGURE 16.1. Cumulative pages read over a number of sessions.

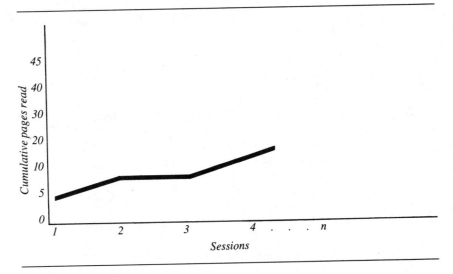

and Beasley, 1970; Singer, 1971) is to graph results that are cumulative. Figure 16.1 shows a graph of the cumulative number of pages one student read during successive sessions. The graph contains a line which shows a student has read at least the same number of pages (horizontal step) or a greater number of pages (vertical step) with each successive session. The cumulative graph cannot go down; it can only remain at the same level or go up. Thus, the graph indicates that the student read four pages the first session and an additional four pages the next day for a cumulative total of eight pages. During the third session, the student did not read any pages; so the line on the graph remained at eight pages. At the fourth session, the student read ten pages, which made the graph line go up to 18. The rate at which the line went up was under the student's control because the *student* decided how many pages to read each session. When we used this type of motivational procedure with a boy who was a severely disabled reader, he progressed from not reading at all to reading for a full 45-minute period in just eight weeks (Singer and Beasley, 1970). We used similar charts for a cumulative number of words learned, for a cumulative number of grapheme-phoneme relationships acquired, and so forth, with similar results: the line went up dramatically in each graph. We call the type of instruction where the learner decides upon his or her rate of progress "learning under the student's control."

STUDENT'S OBJECTIVES

Not only knowledge of progress but also setting of goals helps to motivate students. A useful way to provide motivation is to construct a diagnostic and prescriptive index for each student. To construct this index, place survey and diagnostic test variables on the side of a chart using whatever variables are in the tests you administered to the student. Place next to each test variable the specific materials which are relevant for developing the variables that need improvement. (See the appendix for a list of materials.) The students' beginning level of achievement on each variable should be indicated along with student-set goals. Observe progress towards these goals via charts of achievement on the specific classroom materials; retest students on the standardized test variables after you have taught the students in enough areas of a particular domain for some generalized achievement to have occurred. Table 16.3 contains a chart of a student's objectives. The reading specialist and the student in conference set up these objectives after they had reviewed the student's scores on the Gates Survey, Gates-McKillop, California Reading Achievement Tests, and Informal Reading Inventory in Content Areas.

Also place on the chart the specific skills that the student can master and materials for developing each skill. Check off the skills as soon as the student masters them. Most of the skills that a student can master are in the word recognition area (consonants, blends, vowels, digraphs, syllabication), but you can also construct a mastery list for word meanings and morphemes by specifying particular words, affixes, and roots. Students can also master some study skill techniques, such as SQ3R and the reading of charts, tables, and graphs.[4] Check off these skills as the students master them. The chart will give students knowledge of their pretest results, set their objectives, and show progress towards their goals.

Teachers and students alike should know that significant gains can occur from specific instruction. Students can learn some specific skills or a specific list of vocabulary items in a short time. But to achieve significant gains on standardized tests, students require more instructional time because these tests assess general achievement or performance over an entire domain, even if the test variable seems to be specific. The timed word subtest of the Gates-McKillop Reading Diagnostic Tests, for example, assesses automaticity for sight words. But the words on the list are only a sample of words at successive frequency levels of the Thorndike word *frequency* list.[5] To improve by at least one frequency level on this subtest, a student would have to learn to recognize quickly not just the words on the Gates-McKillop subtest, but most of the words on the next level of the word frequency list. Hence, it is important to assess both

---

[4] Teachers could, of course, construct a master reference list of variables, tests, and materials for developing these skills. See the appendix for a starter set of reference materials.

[5] Edward L. Thorndike, *The Teacher's Word Book of 30,000 Words.* New York: Teachers College Press, Columbia University, 1931.

TABLE 16.3. Student Chart

Student's name _____ Date tested _____ Retested _____				
	Pretest scores	Objectives	Materials	Dates assigned and completed	Posttest scores

Gates-McGinitie Silent Reading Tests
Comprehension
Vocabulary
Speed

Gates-McKillop Reading Diagnostic Tests
Words (timed)
Words (untimed)
Syllabication
Blending
Oral Vocabulary

California Reading Achievement Test
Vocabulary
English
Math
Science
Social Studies

Comprehension
Following directions

Informal Reading Inventory
Social Studies
Literature
Science

Study Skills
SQ3R
Graphic Aids

This form is a prototype. If you use other tests, insert them on the left. List pretest scores; inform students of test results; have students in conference with the teacher decide upon objectives and enter objectives on the chart. List materials for teaching students and dates when you assigned and students completed them. Posttest students upon completion of assignment(s) and enter scores on the chart. Use this chart for individual tests, objectives, and assignments throughout the course.

whether students have learned what was taught (specific achievement) as assessed by teacher-made tests or on informal reading inventories and whether they improved in general achievement as measured by standardized tests. The chart in table 16.3 is likely to show improvement on acquisition of *specific contents or processes* over a short term of instruction.

By using the charts, students and teachers will see that students have made specific gains. They should realize that specific gains become noticeable on standardized tests only when they have accumulated to become gains in general achievement. Thus, students can make specific gains, but they are not likely to make any gain in general achievement over a short period of instruction. If teachers administer standardized tests over this short period of instruction, they might rightfully protest that they know the students have learned but that the tests did not show it. The remedy is simple: assess students for both types of gains — specific gains over a short period of instruction (a day, week, or month) and general gains over a longer period of time (a semester or a year). Thus, the reading content acquisition class should develop, assess, and chart development for the competencies shown in box 16.2.

BOX 16.2. Word Recognition Competencies
for an Acquisition Class

1. *Objective*
Students should be able to respond accurately and quickly to graphemes in varying combinations (single consonants and vowels in beginning, middle, and final positions; digraphs, such as *ch, th* as functional units (Venezky, 1970); consonant clusters, such as *str;* syllables; roots and affixes.
Test
Given artificial words consisting of various combinations of graphemes and approximating English words, students should be able to identify 95 percent of them accurately in half a second per word. Repeat this process with content-area words.
2. *Objective*
Students will be able to utilize contextual clues (syntactic and semantic) to identify missing words that have been taught in the acquisition class.
Test
Given sentences or passages at the student's level of general reading ability in which every tenth word is omitted, students will accurately supply 85 percent of the missing words.
3. *Objective*
Student will attain automaticity for high-frequency words, such as the 220 Dolch words and 95 common nouns.
Test ·
Given relatively easy sentences in which the words are deleted, students will supply them within half a second each.
4. *Objective*
Students will be able to use affixes and roots to identify and analyze the meaning of content area technical terms taught in the acquisition class.

Test

Given a representative sample of technical terms taught in the acquisition class, students will correctly identify and explain the meanings of 85 percent of them by defining their constituent affixes and roots.

5. *Objective*

Students will develop fluency and automaticity in oral reading of passages that contain Dolch words, common nouns, and technical terms taught in the acquisition class.

Test

Given passages containing the above words, students will read 95 percent of them accurately at a speed of one-quarter of a second per word.

6. *Objective*

Students will be motivated to spend increasingly more time in reading.

Test

Cumulative charts kept of student's reading time during the acquisition class will indicate an upward slope for 85 percent of the students.

7. *Objective*

Students will transfer what they learn in acquisition classes to their content area texts.

Test

Students will keep weekly logs of the number of words from their acquisition class that occur in their content area classes and/or texts. In addition, interviews of content area teachers will indicate that at least 90 percent of the teachers of students enrolled in acquisition classes will note that these students correctly identified and used content area terms more than previously.

8. *Objective*

Teachers in content area classes will teach their classes technical terms as they occur in assignments in the text.

Test

Observation of a random sample of content area classes will reveal that teachers teach the meanings of new technical terms, either through reading guides, glosses, oral instruction, or by writing terms on the board whenever new topics are introduced. If so, then students in acquisition classes will get additional instruction in content area classes that will supplement their instruction in reading acquisition classes.

9. *Objective*

Students will have knowledge of their goals in comprehension, vocabulary, word identification, and study skills, and will progress toward these goals.

Test

Each student will have an individual chart showing the pretest levels in general and specific content area comprehension, general and specific content area vocabulary levels, word identification skills, and specified study skills. Their objectives will be shown on these charts along with the materials specified for enabling the student to reach the objectives. Students will also have progress charts of specific achievement for each objective. At least weekly entries will have been made in the specific progress charts and at least two entries per semester will have been made in the student's general chart.

Thus, the acquisition classes will use content area words for teaching word recognition, employ these words in context, and transfer their use to actual reading situations. Since acquisition students will find these words in their content area texts, they will get not only additional reinforcement but also heightened motivation. Consequently, reading acquisition classes based upon content drawn from texts used in the content areas will probably accelerate students' development toward mastery of reading acquisition.

But acquisition of word identification skills is not enough. Students in acquisition classes also need instruction in how to comprehend and learn from texts.

Comprehension: Interaction Between the Reader and Text

THE PROCESS OF COMPREHENSION

The systems involved in comprehension differ from acquisition only in a shift towards greater emphasis on the contents and processes of thinking. Russell (1958) included in contents of thinking these components: *sensations, percepts, memories, images,* and *concepts* that an individual has acquired through direct or vicarious experience, including reading. Russell might also have listed *range of information* (Holmes, 1954) or *world knowledge* (Winograd, 1972). However, we think that *range of information* or *world knowledge* are included under *memories* in Russell's list. Russell's processes of thinking are listed in box 16.3.

BOX 16.3. Russell's Processes of Thinking

1. *Concept formation* includes discrimination, abstraction, generalization, and organization of attributes and their values. *Example:* An apple has attributes of color, texture, size, taste. Each of these attributes varies in value; for example, the color of an apple varies from green to purple.
2. *Problem solving* is defined as thinking directed to a goal or a solution. *Example:* Mystery stories direct thinking to the goal of determining who committed the crime.
3. *Inference* is drawing conclusions from major and minor premises. *Example:* (Major Premise) The closing of a country's frontier necessitates conservation. (Minor Premise) The United States frontier closed in 1890. (Conclusion) Therefore, after 1890 the country became more conservative.
4. *Interpretation* involves construction of major premises and then use of a stated minor premise to infer a conclusion. *Example:* (Minor Premise Stated) Columbus left his son, Diego, behind when he set sail for the New World. (Major Premise constructed by reader) When a father goes off on an adventurous trip and leaves

his son behind, his son is sad. (Conclusion) Diego was sad when Columbus set sail for the New World.

5. *Evaluative thinking* requires (a) use of standards or criteria for judging truth or falsity of propositions or (b) employment of values for making affective responses to situations. *Example:* (Statement) Creation of the Glen Powell Dam flooded a scenic area in order to provide power for electricity. (Evaluation) The dam was undesirable. (Value) Scenic areas should be protected and not sacrificed to economic motives.

6. *Creative thinking* stresses use of imagination or cognition, particularly suppositional thinking, to devise novel ideas. *Example:* (Statement) Some people do not appreciate basic elements of life: suppose the sun shone only one hour a year. Ray Bradbury wrote a short story based on this supposition.

This list of processes of thinking provides for a more comprehensive definition of reading than does Thorndike's (1917) definition that "reading is reasoning." Indeed Russell's contents and processes categories indicate the subsystems that readers mobilize at the cognitive level when they interact with text.

Box 16.4 shows seven systems that can be used for interacting with print. At any one moment during the process of reading an individual can mobilize each system by itself or in combination with other systems (Holmes, 1954, 1965; Singer 1976a). At one moment, a reader may mobilize systems for identifying a word, at the next moment retrieve a meaning, and at the next, infer, interpret, conceptualize, or solve a problem, and store or retrieve ideas from memory.

COMPREHENSION SYSTEMS

Reading and learning from text include more system than those included among Russell's contents and processes of thinking. In box 16.4 we have listed all the major systems with which a reader can interact with printed stimuli, such as content area texts, to produce comprehension.

BOX 16.4. Systems Underlying Speed and Comprehension

1. *Cognitive Systems*
   Reasoning Processes (abstraction and generalization, concept formation, inference, interpretation, evaluation, and problem-solving)
   Morphemics (minimal units of meaning, incuding inflections, affixes, and roots)
   Semantics (word meanings, concepts, denotative and connotative meanings)
   Syntactics (grammatical structures and relationships, including relationships in and among sentences, paragraphs, and larger units of discourse)

2. *General Information or World Knowledge* (fulfilling presuppositions of writers; generating major premises for interpretations, minor premises for inferences; explicating elliptical passages)
3. *Word Identification*
 Graphophonemics (symbol-sound correspondences)
 Graphomorphophonemics (division of words into morphemes, enabling graphophonemics to be used: *shep-herd, sheep · herd · er*
4. *Perceptual Processes* (processing and differentiation of print at the letter and higher units; sampling print to reduce uncertainty)
5. *Visual and Auditory Abilities* (development of functional oculomotor efficiency and speed of processing stimuli)
6. *Attention* (automaticity in processing print which enables individual to maximize attention on comprehension)
7. *Affective and Conative Systems*
 Attitudes (criticalness)
 Values (desire to know, desire to read rapidly)
 Self-concept (confidence, independence)

See H. Singer and R. B. Ruddell, eds., *Theoretical Models and Processes of Reading* (Newark, Delaware: International Reading Association, 1976) for information on each of the systems listed in this box. See especially Irene Athey, "Reading Research in the Affective Domain," for information on affective and conative systems. David H. Russell, *Children's Thinking* (Boston: Ginn and Company, 1958), gives a definition and review of the various reasoning processes listed under cognitive systems.

SUBSYSTEMS

A reader can shift not only from one system to another, but also from one level *within* a system to another. If a reader cannot identify a whole word, then he or she might mobilize subsystems for identifying each letter and blending the letters together under the influence of other systems, such as syntax and semantics. Then the reader can give a whole-word response to the printed symbol. We depict this process in figure 16.2.
Likewise, within the systems of semantics, syntactics, and perceptual oculomotor control, a reader can shift from one level to another level of response. The purpose of instruction in reading is to develop this hierarchical structure of systems and subsystems until they function automatically (Singer, 1976; LaBerge and Samuels, 1976).

AUTOMATICITY

Individuals first learn to be accurate in performing any skill; then, with more practice, they can perform the skill without thinking about it. At this point, they have gone beyond accuracy to *automaticity* in the skill (Samuels, 1977). In learning to identify a word, an individual might process a word letter-by-letter, then "chunk" the word, that is, respond to

FIGURE 16.2. Shifting from a Holistic to an Analytic Level

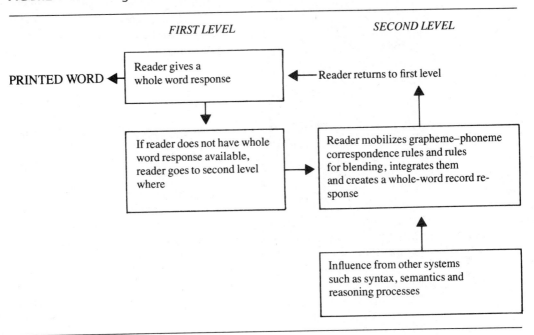

the printed word with a whole-word response without going through any intermediate processes. With continued practice, the response can become so automatic that the individual is almost oblivious of the printed word, as such, and concentrates attention upon meaning or comprehension (LaBerge and Samuels, 1976). In short, the individual has become a lexical reader who does not have to sound out the words, but can go directly from print to meaning (Chomsky, 1970).

Students can use the method of repeated reading of a story to progress at each reading from (1) identifying printed words to (2) getting the meaning of the words to (3) comprehending the story. The method is simply to have poor readers do what some good readers did as children: read and reread the same story many times. The method of repeated reading assumes that the repetitions will result in automatic processing of words so that the reader can focus attention on comprehension (Samuels, 1979; Chomsky, 1976).

Students can develop automaticity in other ways. They can read materials which are interesting but repetitious, particularly in vocabulary. For example, series books (such as the ones about the Hardy Boys, Nancy Drew, Tom Swift, and so forth) which are prevalent in the "culture of children" (Stone and Church, 1973) help readers develop automaticity because only the plots vary slightly within each series. Automatic recognition of words, particularly functional words (conjunctions and prepositions which tie together the content words — nouns, adjectives, verbs, adverbs), is most likely to develop from repeated reading, from reading series books, or from a large amount of reading of relatively easy books.

CONCEPTS, MORPHEMES, AND SEMANTICS

As individuals read and learn from text, they acquire meanings for words. When these meanings organize themselves about a word, the word becomes a label for a concept. Each concept has four general relationships of meaning associated with it: (1) class membership, that is, a concept can belong to a superordinate (a concept at a more abstract level), (2) properties or attributes, which describe what properties a concept has, (3) exemplification, lower-order concepts that are examples of the concept, and (4) relationships with other concepts at the same level of abstraction. To develop a concept, explain or provide experiences that bring out its four types of relationships. Figure 16.3 depicts a concept with its four general relationships (Pearson and Johnson, 1978).

Concepts, morphemes, and semantics are generally grouped under vocabulary. Throughout grades 1–12, vocabulary is the single most important predictor of comprehension (Singer, 1976a; Holmes and Singer, 1966). Consequently, content area teachers should stress vocabulary, especially technical terms as they use them. They should teach students what the technical terms mean, how to use them in a sentence, how to pronounce them, and what morphemes they contain. For example,

FIGURE 16.3. The Concept "City" Embedded in Four Types of Relationships

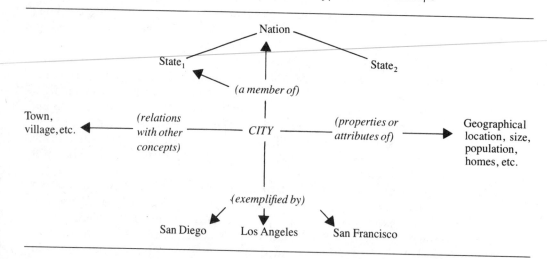

motor, motion, and *motile* contain the root *mot*, which means "to move." Teaching morphemes will reduce the complexity and magnitude of the vocabulary load in content areas. (See table 16.2 for a list of some morphemes.)

Concepts are also organized into a semantic hierarchy. Figure 16.3 shows part of one semantic hierarchy for one state. But the hierarchy contains other states and can contain other nations. When readers interact with text, they mobilize their semantic hierarchies and categorize information under the appropriate conceptual structures in their hierarchies (Anderson *et al.*, 1977).

SENTENCE RELATIONSHIPS

Each sentence contains a verb and one or more noun phrases to depict an event. In the sentence "A steam turbine produces electrical power," we have two noun phrases, "A steam turbine" and "electrical power." The noun phrases have certain relationships to verbs within sentences (Fillmore, 1968). These relationships are listed in box 16.5.

BOX 16.5. Role Relationships
Within a Sentence or Event

Actor or Agent	The doer or instigator of the action. (Who did it?) *Water pressure* (agent) causes the blades to rotate.
Instrument	Object instrumentally involved in the action. (What was the action done with?) Galileo saw the distant stars *with a telescope* (instrument).
Action	Word that conveys an action that affects the recipient. (What is happening to something or someone?) Or word that indicates a certain state exists. He *divided* (action verb) nine into three equal groups. Water *is* (stative verb) a molecule.
Objective	Whatever the verb acts upon directly. (What did the action do to something?) Water pressure causes *the blades* (objective) to rotate.
Recipient	Person or animal that verb action indirectly affects. He gave his vote *to Lincoln* (recipient).
Location	Place. (Where is it? Where did it occur?) The kinetic energy is *in the water of the dam* (location).
Time	When action or state occurred. (When did something exist or take place?) Halley's comet will return *in 1986* (time).

RELATIONSHIPS BETWEEN EVENTS

Knowledge of role relationships within sentences helps you comprehend simple sentences or events. For comprehension of complex sentences, you have to know *relationships between events*. Conjunctions express these relationships. A list of some conjunctions and the relationships between events that they express is in box 16.6.

BOX 16.6. Conjunctions: Implicit and Explicit
Relationships Between Events

Cause   Event A has an effect upon event B.
                  (A)
Implicit   The spark exploded the gas in the chamber, increasing the pressure.
                  (B)
                  The piston went down.

Explicit   The spark exploded the gas in the chamber, causing the pressure to increase and the piston to go down.

Concession   Event A grants a point in event B.
                          (A)   (B)
                  Although Jefferson was busy, he still kept very precise accounts of his money.

Conditional   Event A states a condition under which event B will occur.
                      (A)   (B)
                  If you mix sodium and chlorine together, you will get simple table salt.

Intention   Event B identifies the purpose of event A.
                          (A)   (B)
Implicit   He transferred the terms of the equation on the left side. He solved the problem.

Explicit   He transferred the terms of the equation on the left side in order to solve the problem.

Modifier   An adjective is an event (B) that describes the quality of another event (A).
                          (A)   (B)
                  He saw the precipitate. It was white.
                          (B)   (A)
                  He saw the white precipitate.

Negative   The word *not* in the sentence negates the event.
                  He did *not* see the white precipitate.

Conclusion	States a conclusion in event B that follows one or more preceding events (A).

$$\text{(A)} \qquad\qquad\qquad\qquad\qquad \text{(B)}$$

He had eliminated all other possibilities. Therefore, the white precipitate must be barium chloride.

Summary	Event B summarizes one or more preceding events ($A_1, A_2, A_3, \ldots A_n$)

$$\text{(A_1)} \qquad\qquad\qquad \text{(A_2)} \qquad\qquad\qquad \text{(A_3)}$$

He grabbed the basketball, faked to the right, then spun around to

$$\text{(B)}$$

drill in his shot. Thus, he made his eighth hook shot.

A larger organization exists in discourse or communication of thoughts in words. The organization consists of a structure or relationships among the parts of the passages.

STRUCTURE AND ORGANIZATION OF DISCOURSE

Knowledge of the structure of content areas facilitates comprehension because it provides readers with schemas, which are concepts or ideas for assimilating or categorizing information (Inhelder and Piaget, 1958; Ausubel, 1964; Anderson, 1976). Thus, if readers know the structure of a story, they can more readily organize and store incoming information and ideas (Rumelhart, 1977). However, this knowledge structure, like all knowledge structures, has a developmental gradient. During preschool years, young children who listen to parents reading to them are likely to develop at least this simple conception of the structure of a story: a story has a beginning, middle, and end. This knowledge of structure enables these children when they enter school to read and categorize information under these three aspects of a story. Subsequently, they can use knowledge of these three parts of a story as self-directing cues in response to a request to retell the story; that is, they remind themselves to give the beginning, then the middle, and finally the end of the story. Later, children may encounter more differentiated story structure in a story that has these constituents: plot events, setting, characters, theme, conflict, and resolution (Thorndyke, 1975). Children can then use these constituents of a story for assimilating and regenerating a story in greater detail. Still later, through instruction in high school and college English courses, students get an even more differentiated structure of a story, including knowledge of genres (fables, fantasies, science fiction), symbols (purity represented by the Mississippi River in *Huckleberry Finn*), and literary devices (satire, irony, flashback). Students can then use these more abstract structures for interacting with texts and for assimilating, interpreting, constructing, storing, and retrieving the resulting knowledge.

Each content area develops its own structure and ways of thinking about its content. In chapters 11–14, we outlined the structure, modes of inquiry, and major concepts in four major content areas. These contents and processes of thinking, along with other systems of reading (such as syntactic and word perception systems), can operate simultaneously or in a processing sequence from bottom-up to top-down.

BOTTOM-UP VS. TOP-DOWN PROCESSING

In general, the systems for reading, comprehending, and learning from text are dynamic. Readers can mobilize these systems in varying combinations as they interact with the text according to their changing purposes and the changing demands of the text. They may mobilize systems simultaneously or in a "bottom-up" or "top-down" mode (Fredericksen, 1976; Rumelhart, 1976). In the bottom-up mode, the reader's systems operate in a sequence — from the level of sensations of print upon the retina of the eyes to detection and unitization of these sensations into words, syntactic organization of words into phrases and sentences, association of meaning to the sentences through use of concepts and abstract structures or schemas for assimilating the incoming information, and finally, reasoning in reading processes and storage of meaning.

In the top-down mode, a reader can use abstract knowledge structures to direct attention to printed stimuli in a selective manner, and these stimuli can then confirm or disconfirm the reader's expectations. For example, a reader may use the abstract structure: "Vehicles locomote across space" which contains semantic slots and a syntactic structure for assimilating the words or ideas in such sentences as:

> The cars   raced   down the hill.
> (Vehicles) (locomote) (across space.)

Also, as individuals read, they may allocate attention back and forth between top-down and bottom-up modes, frequently even within the same sentence. In the incomplete sentence, "The car raced down the h_____," a shift from a bottom-up to a top-down mode may occur as the reader progresses across the sentence. At the beginning of the sentence, the reader takes in stimuli (words) and identifies them; as the reader takes in and processes more words, he or she inductively generates a semantic and syntactic expectancy and then may shift to a top-down process. In the top-down process, the reader uses abstract structures to predict or anticipate the final word (at least its meaning or idea) and confirms this prediction through perception of the initial consonant, or through perceptually sampling the letters of the last word. Or the reader may even skip the last word and get confirmation in subsequent sentences because the inserted word or meaning is consistent with meanings in the following sentences.

Teaching Comprehension

In teaching comprehension, the teacher's task is to develop in readers all the systems that are necessary for interacting with text and to teach the readers to use them in varying combinations for different purposes and requirements in reading. Through the acquisition stage of reading, teachers stress the word identification systems of graphophonemics in conjunction with syntax and semantics. However, some development of systems for comprehension or learning from text also occurs from the beginning of reading instruction concomitantly with reading acquisition. Gradually, with progress through the grades, a shift-over takes place towards emphasis on comprehension and learning from text; but even after the shift, teachers must still give some attention to word recognition, particularly to identification of technical words, idioms, foreign words, and expressions that have only recently become part of the language. We have already presented ways of developing word identification skills. Now, how can we develop comprehension? Some of the ways are suggested under the following headings.

WIDE READING

Individuals learn through reading, and, as they read, they acquire contents of thinking. Indeed, the broader the range and depth of their reading materials, the more individuals can acquire, store, and subsequently retrieve contents of thinking for top-down processing. Moreover, as individuals acquire more information, the less they have to acquire from any new reading task. Consequently, a wide scope to the curriculum, even though not necessarily focusing on reading comprehension *per se*, will develop systems employed in comprehension, and consequently, will improve comprehension. Hence, the strategies we have described throughout this text for teaching students to read and learn from texts in the content areas, such as inquiry, are also ways of improving comprehension for the entire range of students.

PROCESSES OF INQUIRY

Processes of inquiry in content areas are more likely to facilitate comprehension if teachers explicitly teach them. Literature teachers, for example, may teach students to formulate hypotheses for explaining a character in a novel by noting consistencies in the character's actions, statements, inward reflections, and the reactions of other characters in the story to the character under examination. Then the teacher can have students test their hypotheses by making predictions about what the character will subsequently do. Finally, the students can gain more information (read further) to test the validity of their predictions. Of course, the predictions will have to state how the character will or will not react in contrasting situations in order to have a controlled condition. This process of inquiry in literature is analogous to use of the scientific method in science. (See chapter 12 for steps in the scientific method.)

IMAGERY

Imagery facilitates comprehension (Levin, 1976; Bransford and Franks, 1972) because recall of images is superior to recall of words. The reason students may remember pictures better than words is because pictures tend to be unique, whereas words are quite similar. Therefore, have students transform words into images as they read. As a way of teaching the use of imagery, give them exercises to transform text into pictures and into pictorial sequences of events. In one such exercise, readers could construct a diagram of the relationships among the characters in Charles Dickens's *Tale of Two Cities*. This diagram would help readers comprehend the story better, just as Mendeleev's Periodic Table helps chemistry students better perceive relationships among chemical elements. Finally, advise students to draw their own visual aids when the text omits them. Use of visual aids is one way to make thought concrete. You can make thought more concrete in other ways, too.

CONCRETE LEVELS OF THOUGHT

Concretizing abstract ideas facilitates comprehension because it enables individuals to image ideas. It also lessens the level of abstraction of the ideas and hence the difficulty of comprehending them. Anderson (1976a) found that when he added adjectives to sentences he made the sentences more memorable, observing that students recalled the second of these two sentences significantly better than the first:

1. The regulations annoyed the salesman.
2. The strict parking regulations annoyed the salesman.[6]

The addition of the adjective *parking* makes the statement more particular and more imageable. Anderson *et al.* (1977) believe that individuals comprehend not just by imaging but by thinking of exemplars or instances for ideas and that these exemplars or instances are stored and help recall the ideas. The sentence, "The woman was outstanding in the theater" elicits in readers' minds the instance of *actress* for *woman*. When the same individuals subsequently see *actress*, the word helps them recall the sentence. The implication is to teach comprehension by having students

[6] Richard C. Anderson, "Concretization and Sentence Learning," in H. Singer and R. B. Ruddell, eds., *Theoretical Models and Processes of Reading*, second edition. Newark, Delaware: International Reading Association, 1976, p. 588.

"instantiate," or think of concrete examples, as they read; that is, simply instruct students to think of examples or generate instances whenever text writers omit them.

PURPOSE IN READING

Students do have varying purposes in reading a text, and their purposes will lead them to selectively attend to and store in memory certain parts of the story. When asked to recall the story, they can only retrieve the information they stored. When asked to read a story about two boys going through a house, those readers who had the perspective of a house buyer recalled information that differed from those readers who had the perspective of a burglar (Pichert and Anderson, 1977). Hence, it is important for teachers to establish purposes in reading any assignment.

Intent to understand and remember enhances comprehension, perhaps because it leads the reader to generate responses (Marks, Doctorow, and Wittrock, 1974), or to answer independently formulated questions (Singer, 1976b). These active comprehension procedures which put the motive for learning within the learner's control, have been described in more detail in chapter 4. However, students need instruction in content and processes of inquiry in content areas to help them form relevant questions (Herber and Nelson, 1977). Therefore, have individuals determine why they are reading a passage, formulate questions to answer as they read, and state their answers and reactions to the passage while they are reading. Then, they are more likely to store relevant information in their long-term memories, and consequently to be able to retrieve it when needed.

Textbooks have not been teaching students to be purposeful in reading. They have been emphasizing teacher control and direction over student thinking by having teachers ask students to answer teacher-posed questions. Both textbooks and teachers tend to emphasize development of comprehension products, not comprehension processes or potentials.

COMPREHENSION PRODUCTS, PROCESSES, AND POTENTIALITIES

A dictionary has three definitions of comprehension:

1. A product: "the knowledge gained by comprehending"
2. A process: "the act or action of grasping with the intellect"
3. A potential: "the capacity for understanding"[7]

Spache and Spache, in teaching comprehension, ask questions that elicit products of thinking, such as:

1. "Who, What, Where, When, How."

[7] *Webster's Seventh New Collegiate Dictionary,* Springfield, Mass.: G. and C. Merriam Company, 1963.

2. "What conclusions can you draw?" or "Why did this happen?"
3. "Do you approve of this action?"[8]

However, Ruddell (1974) stresses instruction in processes of comprehension by using these types of questions:

1. *focusing,* which initiates or refocuses a discussion ("What did you like best about the story?")
2. *extending,* which obtains more information at a given level ("What other information do we need about the hero?")
3. *clarifying,* which obtains a more adequate explanation or draws out a student ("Would you explain what you mean?")
4. *raising,* which moves a discussion from a factual to an interpretive, inferential, abstraction or generalization level ("We now have enough examples. What do they have in common?") [9]

Thus, Ruddell uses discussion, as we do, to lead to various levels of thought. (See chapter 13 for further explanation of these discussion procedures.)

However, both Spache and Ruddell assume that the role of the teacher is to ask questions while the student's role is to answer them. This type of instructional relationship is not only recommended in textbooks on teaching reading, but is also prevalent in practice. From the viewpoint of learning, it assumes that the teacher is modeling behavior that students will imitate. Instead of hoping this kind of transfer of training will occur, we think teachers should *directly* develop this transfer by teaching a self-questioning process of attaining comprehension which we call "active comprehension." In this mode of reading, students search for answers to questions they themselves formulate as they read.

In teaching active comprehension, teachers first model a process of comprehension by taking a class of students through a discussion strategy to arrive at products of comprehension. (See strategies for teaching reading and learning from text, single- and multiple-text strategies, chapters 4 and 9.) Next, teachers go on from this modeling of behavior to having students formulate their own processing questions, use these questions to guide their own thinking, learn through these self-directing questions to transfer relevant information to long-term memory, and arrive at their own comprehension products. In one technique to attain this transfer, a teacher divided a class into groups and had individuals take turns serving as the teacher or discussion leader for the groups as they processed a passage or a chapter in a text. Eventually, each student had an opportunity to use the questioning strategies modeled by the teacher and conse-

---

[8] *Reading in the Elementary School,* second edition. Boston: Allyn and Bacon, 1969, pp. 475–478.

[9] Robert B. Ruddell, *Reading-Language Instruction: Innovative Practices.* Englewood Cliffs, N.J.: Prentice-Hall, 1974, pp. 400–402.

quently learn to formulate questions. Then students were advised to use the questioning process on their own while reading. Thus, through phase out of the teacher and a phase in of the student, teachers can help students develop a *process of reading* which we call "active comprehension" (Singer, 1978a).

Cognitive abilities and processes, purposeful reading, and curiosity are not enough to explain performance in reading and learning from text. Students also have to have favorable attitudes, appropriate values, and self-confidence to be effective in reading and learning from text.

ATTITUDES, VALUES, AND SELF-CONCEPT IN READING

Students need confidence that they can learn and understand texts (Athey, 1976). When only counseled that they could achieve, some students who had believed otherwise improved significantly in comprehension (deCharms, 1972). This counseling strategy when used with low-achieving students, especially low-achieving minority students, may have worked because it led them to mobilize the necessary abilities and stay with difficult tasks until they comprehended them. Thus, not only instruction, but also the teacher's attitude can induce students to work up to the best of their capabilities and help them to develop confidence in their reading ability.

Developing Confident Learners

Teachers must first adapt materials to students so they can be successful in the attainment of comprehension and thus get the positive feedback necessary for reinforcing learning. But, as students learn, teachers should also gradually increase the difficulty level of the materials and teach the students how to comprehend these more difficult materials.

If you make materials in any content area easy enough, most students in a class can comprehend them. Indeed, Bruner (1963) stated that any idea can be taught to anyone at any age provided it is put into a thought form appropriate to the learner. How can you make materials easier? Here are some ways:

VOCABULARY

Substitute common synonyms for rare words. When Marks, Doctorow, and Wittrock (1974) substituted such words as *boy* for *lad,* fourth-grade students were better able to comprehend a passage. Why? Samuels (1968) explained that high-frequency words have more associations to them than do low-frequency words. Consequently, when high-frequency words appear in sentences, they are more likely to elicit associations of relevant experience. This associational process, in part, explains how students "put meaning into words."

Two books are useful for constructing easier materials: *Roget's International Thesaurus*[10] lists synonyms, and the *American Heritage Word Frequency Book*[11] contains frequencies and association values for 80,000 words. Teachers who want to prepare graded materials could use these books to substitute words that will make texts more comprehensible.

WORD IDENTIFICATION

Even students who have mastered general word identification skills still need help in pronunciation of technical terms (for example: *genre, isosceles, caveat emptor, pterodactyl, deuterium*). In general, content area teachers should not assume that students, even high-achieving readers, know how to pronounce content area terms. As a rule of thumb, teachers should model pronunciation of any terms that appear in the index to a text as they introduce these terms in class (especially terms with irregular spellings and foreign terms and phrases). Then they should use the terms in sentences, break them down into their constituent parts (prefix, affixes, roots), and explain their meanings.

SYNTAX

Comprehension of complex sentences is more difficult than simple sentences, not only because they have more ideas in them but also because they are longer and put a greater strain upon memory, particularly sentences which have left-embedded clauses in them. A left-embedded, or left-branching, sentence is one in which a clause comes before the main verb. Here is an example: "The man *who came to dinner* had a mustache and beard." A right-embedded, or right-branching, sentence is: "The man had a mustache and beard *which was white and long.*" Left-branching sentences put a greater strain on memory because readers or listeners have to keep all the information in short-term memory until they reach the main clause. In right-branching sentences, the main clause comes first. Readers or listeners can treat right-embedded clauses as separate sentences when they come to them and store each sentence in long-term memory (Gough, 1976). In general, to give students sentences that are easier to comprehend, (1) select texts that have simple syntax, (2) rewrite with right-embedded sentences, or (3) reduce complex sentences to simple sentences. Here is a long sentence with two embedded clauses: "A hydrogen atom has one electron, which has a negative charge, and one proton, which has a positive charge." You can turn this complex sentence into these three simple sentences: "A hydrogen atom

---

[10] Third edition. New York: Thomas Y. Crowell Company, 1962.
[11] By John B. Carroll, Peter Davies, and Barry Richman. Boston: Houghton Mifflin, 1971.

has one electron and one proton." "The electron has a negative charge. The proton has a positive charge."

Some sentences, however, are not easier to comprehend when split into two sentences (Pearson, 1974–75). For example, divide this sentence into two sentences: "John used a lever to move the heavy rock." You get these two sentences: "John used a lever." "He moved the heavy rock." It now requires more mental ability to comprehend the two sentences because the causal relationship between "using the lever" and "moving the rock" is no longer explicit; the reader has to infer the causal connection between the two.

EXPLICATION

Elliptical sentences are sentences that omit significant information. Readers must draw upon their own experiences and imagination in order to comprehend these sentences. Consider this sentence: "The cigarette caused the forest fire." It does not fully explain how the cigarette caused the fire (Kintsch, 1974). The reader must fill in from experience and imagination events like the following: "The cigarette was lit. It was dropped on dry tinder which smouldered and finally caught fire. Then the fire grew larger and spread to the trees, perhaps with the wind fanning the flames." Most readers could supply the necessary information and relationships from their experience and imagination to make the sentence comprehensible. When readers cannot do so, supplying it for them will enhance their comprehension for a particular passage (Marshall, 1976). This procedure will not, of course, make them generally better readers. Sometimes illustrations or diagrams also explicate what the text only implies.

The implications for content area teachers are: (1) inspect texts to determine what will have to be made more explicit, either through explanation, through addition of illustrations, diagrams, and examples, or through rewriting of material; and (2) evaluate students to determine whether they have the background information, knowledge structures, and conceptual abilities for effective interaction with the text as written.

INSTRUCTIONAL DEVICES

Teachers can facilitate comprehension through use of such instructional devices as overview and reading guides (Herber, 1970a), preposed and postposed questions (Rothkopf, 1976), use of chapter and subheadings (Smith, 1973), or acronymic formulas such as SQ3R — Survey, Question, Read, Recite, and Review (Robinson, 1961). See chapters 4 and 11–14 for explanations of these devices.

ORGANIZATION

The way in which the writer of a text organizes ideas may make the ideas more or less comprehensible. If the text states all the attributes of one car together (color, style, accessories), then the attributes of another car, and so forth, this organization is easier to comprehend than if the text first stated one attribute of each car, then another attribute, and so forth (Frase, 1969a).

All these strategies are ways for *teachers* to make texts more comprehensible. However, these comprehension-improvement procedures involve downward adaptation of materials. Teachers should phase out such materials as students improve and can comprehend more difficult materials. Thus, procedures for making texts more comprehensible are only a means of enabling students to comprehend and learn from texts until they can develop their abilities to learn from texts that have more abstract vocabulary, complex syntax, elliptical statements, and complicated sentence structures.

The reading and learning-from-text specialist can use all these procedures for improving comprehension and for making texts more comprehensible in acquisition classes. In these classes, students have to learn not only to identify words but how to use their language background to comprehend text. In box 16.7 are the competency criteria and assessment procedures for teaching comprehension in content area acquisition classes.

BOX 16.7. Comprehension Competencies
and Assessment Criteria

Objectives
1. Students in acquisition classes will attain at least 50 percent comprehension on reading tasks with materials that have been adapted to their levels of ability.
   Test
   Using the informal inventory of the cloze technique, teachers in acquisition classes will have selected content materials, perhaps through use of the *school catalogs,* that meet the 50 percent criterion for comprehension. Questioning of students in the classes will reveal that 85 percent of them state they can comprehend the materials they are reading.
2. Teachers will systematically develop each of the students' systems for comprehending and learning from texts.
   Test
   Analysis of lesson plans will indicate that students have had input instruction at least once a week in one or more of the systems related to comprehension: vocabulary; sentence, paragraph, or larger units of prose structure (macrostructures); morphemic analysis; interpretation, inference, concept formation, problem solving, critical and creative reasoning; a study skill, such as SQ3R and interpretation of graphs, charts, and maps; or a comprehension technique, such as use of imagery, concretizing abstractions, knowledge of content structure, and modes of inquiry.

3. Students will be motivated to read.
   Test
   Analysis of teachers' lessons will indicate that teachers have had students establish purposes for reading connected discourse at least once a week.
4. Students will have control over their progress in reading.
   Test
   Students will have kept cumulative charts of pages read and words learned.
5. Students will be using content area words in their acquisition instruction.
   Test
   Analysis of contentives (nouns, adjectives, adverbs, verbs) used in word identification lessons will reveal that 85 percent of them are words that are in the students' content area texts.
6. Teachers in acquisition classes will teach for psychosynchromeshing facility.
   Test
   Analysis of lessons in word identification, word meaning, concept formation, and morphemic analysis will indicate that 85 percent or more of them terminate with instructions to apply the skills taught to connected discourse or to content area texts. Provision will have been made for students to do so in class, either through specially prepared sentences, paragraphs, passages longer than a paragraph, or reading assignments in students' texts.
7. As students become able to comprehend and learn from more difficult materials, they will be assigned to these materials.
   Test
   Inspection of charts or graphs of individual students will reveal that when students approached 85 percent comprehension on a particular level of difficulty, they were given more difficult reading tasks.

Thus, acquisition classes will teach word identification, improvement in comprehension, and learning how to learn from texts. The classes will emphasize content drawn from subject matter areas and stress transfer applications in students' content area texts.

Upward Adaptation: Improvement in General Comprehension

Upward adaptation of learners to attain comprehension of more difficult material is the longer-range objective. This longer range objective requires general improvement in each system necessary for reading and learning from texts, such as contents and processes of thinking plus self-confidence and desire to know and understand. Consequently, improvement in general comprehension is not rapidly attainable, unless the student already has the necessary contents and processes of thinking in his or her repertoire of cognitive capabilities and desires to know and understand, but only needs to learn the acquisition aspects of reading. Some people — such as immigrants who can speak the language of their new country but need to learn to read it or who need to learn to both speak and write it and who read and comprehend well in their native language — can make dramatic improvements in comprehension after they learn the new language and the acquisition aspects of reading.

What is needed for improvement in general comprehension of students in addition to time to learn? Instruction in vocabulary, information, and reasoning in each content area. In short, a broad, liberal arts curriculum contributes to the development of systems necessary for improvement in general comprehension, particularly the knowledge structures, semantic hierarchies, and modes of inquiry in the various content areas. (See chapters 11–14.) Therefore, what counselors can do for students who want to improve in comprehension is to guide them into those courses where they can read and learn from texts in the content areas.

A reading and learning-from-text specialist can also guide acquisition level students towards improvement in comprehension by gradually phasing out materials that have been adapted downward and phasing in more difficult materials, including the students' own content area texts. Students in acquisition classes could then more easily make the transition back to regular course instruction in learning from texts in content areas. After students have returned to regular classes, the role of the reading and learning specialist would be to advise or instruct content areas teachers on strategies for teaching students to read and learn from texts.

INSERVICE EDUCATION

Specialists alone cannot solve the problem of teaching strategies for reading and learning from text in all content areas. The entire faculty has to acquire and use these strategies in all their courses. They can learn to do so through an inservice education program. Some schools have conducted inservice programs in an ongoing school situation to teach teachers how to use reading-from-text strategies. The way for a reading and learning specialist to bring this inservice training about is through the support of a schoolwide committee. Scene 2 of Monroe High's schoolwide committee meeting is an ideal scenario for this step.

One week after the last meeting, just after lunch. Monroe High is on minimum day. The schoolwide committee has decided to meet again with Ms. Valdes to review what they had discussed the previous week.

Ms. Jones: Ms. Valdes, I've been talking with the members of this committee and with other faculty members. The types of strategies you described last week would work well for below-grade-level students and nonreaders. But most of us are more concerned with the rest of the students, the ones that fill most of the seats in the classroom.

Mr. Umeki: It's like counseling. I tend to see the kids with problems quite frequently. But I always wonder about the majority of students that I never see.

Mr. Phelps: Ms. Valdes, as you've pointed out, the school's so large that we can't expect you to work directly with all these students.

Mr. Inglish: Maybe you should be teaching us — the teachers.

Ms. Stewart: You mean, kind of like inservice education.

Ms. Valdes: That's an excellent suggestion.

Ms. Jones: What are some of the ways teachers could be trained to do some of this work?

Ms. Valdes: There are a number of ways we could proceed. One way is to include the whole faculty in a large inservice project. This would, of course, mean bringing a number of consultants to the school to focus on areas of specialization I couldn't handle. Another way is what I call the one-to-one method, that is, my working intensively with one faculty member. Why don't we take time now, and I'll explain some alternative models of inservice education.

Models

AN "OPEN-ENDED" MODEL

This model, which Herber (1970b) devised, provides knowledge and skills for teaching reading in content areas that teachers can try out and evaluate immediately. A total of thirty-five teachers, five teachers from each of seven schools, representing four different content areas received released time for an inservice training course. The course emphasized instruction in vocabulary and preparation of reading and reasoning guides for students reading content materials. Also, the teachers prepared materials in a summer session practicum on how to integrate content with reading instruction, tested the materials with summer session students in the morning, and consulted with their summer session teachers in the afternoon. In the fall, they adopted the role of content reading specialists for their departmental colleagues and continued with their inservice seminars.

COURSE MODELS

Schleich's (1971) ten-lesson course model begins with a diagnostic reading test administered to all the students in the school. Students scoring in the lowest decile take the Wide Range Achievement Test (Reading)[12] to determine their basic word-recognition ability. The teacher interprets the test results for other teachers and department heads who enroll in the course. The topics in the course are: general reading development, readability, informal reading inventories, directed reading activities, SQ3R,

[12] J. F. Jastak and J. R. Jastak, *Wide Range Achievement Test (WRAT)*. Austin, Texas: Guidance Testing Associates, 1965.

interpretation of test results, and reading skills in content areas. Then the department heads and teachers instruct students in their content areas, even students in remedial reading classes. Individual department heads and teachers receive follow-up lessons during their free periods.

Askov, Dupuis, and Lee (1978) constructed another course model, a competency based course, that used a diagnostic-prescriptive approach, with computer printouts showing objectives that teachers in the course had mastered at three levels (cognitive, simulation, application). They taught this course over a year-long period of fifteen monthly sessions, each lasting three hours, for volunteer teachers who received 3 to 6 hours of university credit. They used videotapes of lessons in actual courses, such as the teaching of vocabulary in social studies, to illustrate how to teach reading in content areas. Askov, Dupuis, and Lee found improvements for teachers on their attitude scale, knowledge of reading, and ratings on the use of reading skills in the classroom, but they did not assess whether the teachers' students had improved in achievement.

COMBINATION MODEL

An inservice training and consultation program (Singer, 1973b) emphasized (1) strategies for teaching for a wide range of individual differences in reading achievement; (2) patterns of writing and processes of inquiry in content areas; (3) models of reading and learning from text (chapters 11–14); (4) an instructional framework for learning from text; and (5) procedures for teaching expression (writing and discussion), and ways of assessing reading, reading difficulties, and readability of materials (all of the components of this combined program are contained in this text). The inservice training program featured at each session a workshop in applying a strategy or process to a content area; and individual consultations helped classroom teachers on specific content area problems and on adaptation of the strategies and instructional frameworks to their own classes.

ONE-TO-ONE MODEL

All of the models that we have reviewed so far try to reach the entire faculty at the same time. But we know that teachers on a faculty vary in their attitudes towards reading and learning from text and in the time they have for acquiring new teaching skills (Ruddell and Williams, 1972). What we propose is to start working with teachers who want to acquire these strategies, and then gradually spread their effects to the rest of the teachers in a school. If the initial contingent of teachers then teach incoming freshmen over a four-year period, all students in the school will at least have had an introductory class in reading and learning from text. For this inservice education, the reading specialist can use one of the inservice models we have just reviewed, if the school can provide released time or summer-session support for teachers to participate in inservice education. If not, the reading specialist has to opt for a much slower form of inservice education: working with one content area teacher at a time during the regular school day.

The reading specialist works in a one-to-one relationship with a content area teacher in the following way. First, the reading specialist constructs a lesson plan using one of the reading and learning-from-text strategies that fits the class textbook. The content area teacher explains what content and objectives should go into the lesson plan. Then the reading specialist demonstrates by teaching from the lesson plan. Next, the reading specialist and content area teacher plan another lesson with the same teaching strategy, only this time the content area teacher uses it to instruct the class. Next, the content area teacher, using the same teaching strategy, prepares a plan alone. In this way, the reading specialist phases out while the content area teacher phases in for using the particular strategy. The process repeats until the content area teacher has acquired all the strategies for teaching students to read and learn from text.

Thus, in a one-to-one inservice education plan, a reading specialist can teach a content area teacher how to teach at least one introductory course in reading and learning from text in a particular content area. Then, the reading specialist can repeat the process with another content area teacher. This is a slow process for training an entire faculty and it is more expensive than the other models, but it is likely to end up with a content area teacher who knows *how* to teach and *is* teaching students how to read and learn from text. This teacher can then offer an introductory course for students and faculty.

The introductory course in reading and learning from text has two purposes: (1) to teach incoming freshmen how to read and learn from texts in their content area and (2) to serve as a demonstration course for other content area teachers who want to acquire strategies for teaching their own students. To find out how the schoolwide committee at Monroe High felt about this introductory course, read Scene 3, below.

Same setting as the previous scene. The schoolwide committee is reviewing what Ms. Valdes has just said about models of inservice education.

Mr. Umeki: I really like what you said about the one-to-one approach.

Ms. Williams: Yes, I like that too, but we might also want to look at something a little more far-reaching.

Ms. Jones: Do you think that we could take on the reeducation of our entire faculty?

Ms. Phelps: I wouldn't even want to take on the reeducation of my own department.

Ms. Valdes: Let me speak briefly about a couple of possibilities. If we instituted an introductory course in reading and learning from text for incoming freshmen, within four years, most of our students could be

reached. Monroe faculty could participate in the teaching of these introductory courses. Also, we might want to have Monroe High teachers
focus on one learning-from-text strategy at a time. Too much too soon
can be devastating.

Ms. Jorgensen: I'd like to hear more about both of these options.

Ms. Valdes: When I'm through speaking, if there are no pressing questions,
why don't we go home and think about how we want to proceed with
inservice education of the faculty. But for now, let me outline an introductory course in reading and learning from text and the sequence by
which students might learn single- and multiple-text strategies — as well
as a step-by-step process by which the faculty could learn to use the
strategies in the classroom.

In box 16.8 is Ms. Valdes's brief outline for a course in reading and
learning from text.

BOX 16.8. Introductory Course
in Reading and Learning from Text

Objectives of Introductory Classes

Content area teachers will teach regular content area classes how to comprehend
and learn from text, demonstrate to teachers of these classes strategies for handling
individual differences in reading and learning from text, and use a phase-out/phase-
in procedure so that content area teachers can learn to incorporate strategies and
techniques for teaching their own students to comprehend and learn from texts in
the content areas.

Tests

1. Observe classes utilizing strategies in reading and learning from texts in a content
   area.
2. Observe that faculty members in the content areas plan a lesson after observing
   an introductory course in reading and learning from text.
3. Time sampling of the introductory classes will indicate that the content area
   teachers will change from observing to taking charge of the introductory courses.

Sequence for Acquiring and Learning to Use Strategies

For initiating reading and learning-from-text strategies in a content area
class or for inservice education, a school can follow a sequence that
progresses from easy to difficult. We can view the understanding and
adoption of the strategies described in this text within a Piaget-like frame-

work. Assimilation and *accommodation* are the two concepts Piaget has formulated for explaining how an individual takes in and organizes information. Assimilation involves information that an individual can subsume under a schema or concept already within her or his conceptual system. Accommodation occurs when an individual has to form a new schema or concept for subsuming information that concepts within his or her conceptual hierarchy cannot assimilate. For example, teachers know how to use a single textbook with a class. Consequently, a change from using one textbook to another requires only a process of assimilation. Teachers simply use the same instructional strategy with the new text, making minor modifications to adapt the text to their usual teaching procedures. But when teachers have to modify their teaching practices, as they do when they switch from single to multiple texts, they go through a cognitive process of accommodation; that is, they must acquire concepts or schemas that will enable them to organize and subsume information that is new to them. The concepts or schemas in turn help teachers generate the necessary instructions for directing the activities of the class.

Since teachers already have a procedure for teaching with a single text, they can more readily learn alternate strategies that also employ a single text than they can acquire strategies that require use of multiple texts. Consequently, teachers (who want to expand their repertoire of teaching strategies) and reading specialists, consultants, or college instructors (who give inservice training) can ease the process of learning and facilitate transfer of what has been learned to classroom practice by starting with strategies that can be readily assimilated. Then they can progress towards strategies which require teachers to go through an accommodation process in order to acquire the new strategies.

We also recognize that knowledge alone is not enough to get teachers to try new strategies. Although teachers are willing to take risks in teaching, they would like to reduce the risks and increase their confidence that a new strategy will work for them when they try it. To increase teacher confidence, we suggest that as a teacher learns a strategy he or she should apply or test out the strategy under the inservice instructor's supervision. Starting with single-text and going on to multiple-text strategies, the instructor can increase teachers' knowledge and confidence by progressing through the strategies a step at a time. The reading specialist should spread out this process (which includes teaching not only the teacher but also the teacher's class to use the strategies) in a phase-out/phase-in procedure over an academic year. Or, if there is a college course in these strategies combined with a lab consisting of classroom experience, the instructor should spread out the strategies over the entire course. To explain how this training process can occur in a step-by-step procedure, we shall start with single-text strategies and then proceed to multiple-text strategies.

SINGLE-TEXT STRATEGIES

Teachers frequently use only a single text, and their procedure often consists of merely assigning chapters for homework. Rarely do they teach students how to read and learn from the assigned chapters. Teachers assume that instructions, discussions, and demonstrations during class will automatically transfer to students' thinking and learning processes as they read the assignment. But the evidence from experiments on the psychology of transfer is that transfer is more likely to occur if teachers teach for it by having students make the necessary applications while they are still in the classroom.

The directed reading activity (DRA), is a step towards teaching students how to read and learn from texts and consequently increases the number of students who are likely to comprehend the contents of an assigned chapter. Essentially, this strategy has the teacher explain to the class how the teacher reads and learns from the assigned chapter.[13] This process takes place as the teacher explains technical vocabulary before, or while, students take turns reading the chapter. The teacher may emphasize or clarify a process that is characteristic of the content, such as the role of allusions in literature, or the close and explicit relations between generalizations and supporting evidence in science. At another time, the teacher may point out the organization of the chapter, or the author's style of writing, or the sequence of types of paragraphs in the text. (See chapter 7 for discussion of paragraph types.) Throughout, the teacher guides the reading and discussion of the chapter by using pre-posed and postposed questions. Students thus acquire not only processes of reading and learning from text, but also knowledge of what the teacher sees as valuable to learn from the chapter.

After a few chapters, the teacher can phase out DRA and phase in the marginal gloss strategy which consists of marginal notes that students can use as they read the text. These notes are essentially what the teacher communicated orally when using the DRA strategy. An assumption underlying use of the marginal gloss strategy is that students will be able to read the notes. Hence, teachers need to write notes that students can readily understand. (See chapters 7 and 8 for information on writing and readability.)

Whenever teachers use a new strategy, they should teach it to the class through a phase-in/phase-out process. They can accomplish the phase-in/phase-out process in three steps: (1) they can use the strategy with the entire class until they are reasonably certain that a majority of students understand the strategy; (2) they can then divide the class into heterogeneous groups and again use the strategy, only now knowledgeable mem-

---

[13] All the strategies described in this section are also presented in greater detail in chapters 4, 5, and 11–14.

bers in each group may engage in cross-ability teaching to other members of the group who have not yet acquired the strategy; and (3) when the teachers who have been circulating among the groups as consultants, are satisfied that most of the class understands and can use the strategy, they can have individuals use the strategy alone. Those members of the class who still need help can get it through one-to-one instruction from the teacher while the rest of the class is employing the strategy. A chemistry teacher wanted to help her class by giving them programmed instruction lessons (worksheets). The assignment did not work because the teacher skipped from an explanation for the entire class of how to use the programmed worksheets to individual assignments. When the teacher went back and started over with the three-step process, first taking the class as a group through one worksheet, then having the class divide into groups to use the next worksheet, and finally having individuals do the third worksheet on their own, the students were then able to learn from programmed instruction worksheets.

Teachers who are familiar with a strategy may assume that a class will readily understand the same strategy. Such is not usually the case. Teachers may frequently jump from simply giving directions on how to do an assignment to use of cross-ability teaching as a way of handling individual differences. But note that cross-ability teaching is not the first, but the *second* step in the three-step procedure for phasing in the use of a new strategy. The first step is the one in which the teacher teaches a new strategy to the entire class, including those students who will be doing the cross-ability teaching. In other words, the teacher first teaches the student-teachers to understand the strategy. This understanding is prerequisite to cross-ability teaching.

SQ3R (survey, question, read, recite, and review) is another strategy that comes after students have learned — via a DRA strategy — how to read and learn from text, particularly a DRA strategy which emphasizes and teaches active comprehension, that is, students formulating and then reading to answer their own questions. After students have learned how to learn in a content area, particularly when they have learned to ask the kinds of questions that are relevant, they can then make better use of SQ3R. A variety of strategies for teaching self-questioning processes have been developed (Singer, 1978a; Hunkins, 1976).

The only strategy up to this point in our discussion that has required teachers to prepare teaching materials is the marginal gloss. Another single-text strategy that requires preparation of materials is the use of learning guides. The teacher begins writing the guide in a backward direction by first answering this question: ''What generalization(s) do I want students to acquire or construct from this chapter?'' The teacher states these generalizations explicitly. Sometimes the teacher can subsume them under controversial beliefs which the class can then debate. Next, the teacher asks: ''What relationships, interpretations, or concepts are necessary for comprehending these generalizations?'' The teacher also writes these statements down and then notes on a key the passages in the text from which students can make these interpretations or form concepts. Last, the teacher asks: ''What details or facts support these interpretations?'' The teacher then writes down the facts and prepares a key which identifies the page and line in the text where students can locate these facts. Now, the teacher can prepare a learning-from-text guide for the assigned reading, but the presentation in the learning-from-text guide is in the reverse order; the details or facts come first, interpretations next, and generalizations last. The students' task is to identify where the facts are in the text, and which interpretations, inferences, or concepts support which generalization(s).

In teaching students to use a learning guide, teachers must use a phase-in procedure. The teacher takes the entire class through the first guide, then uses groups for a subsequent guide, and finally brings students to the point where they can use guides for their own individual reading assignments. (See chapter 4 for how to expand guides for teaching students how to read and evaluate what they read.)

Next, teachers employ a phase-out procedure in which they teach students to internalize the steps in learning guides so that they can read and learn from texts without the use of guides. In this phase-out strategy, the whole class first participates as a class in constructing a guide, then the teacher forms heterogeneous groups of students to construct guides on different chapters of a text, next individual students construct their own guides, and finally the teacher has students practice reading the text for facts, interpretations, and generalizations without the use of guides. Thus, teachers can help students progress towards the goal of learning how to learn and become independent of teachers in reading and learning from text.

MULTIPLE-TEXT STRATEGIES

A strategy that provides for a transition from single to multiple texts is the *inquiry strategy*. This strategy starts with a single text. The class, under teacher direction, questions the validity of statements of ''fact'' made in the text. To help the students learn ways to check on the validity of the fact(s), the teacher first teaches the class how to locate information that is especially relevent in library reference books, such as the *Reader's Guide to Periodical Literature, The New York Times Index,* almanacs, and so forth. Next, the class learns how to abstract and file relevant material on index cards. The process of teaching students how to judge relevancy may consist of the teacher preparing transparencies for the overhead projector and then having the class as a group read passages. Students then identify and justify which sections or sentences contain information that helps answer a preposed question. The class can quote or paraphrase the information on cards, noting the source of the information. Subsequently, the class can learn to put the cards together to form a report. The process of writing this report is the reverse of outlining — here the class starts with information and groups the information into sections, then formulates subheadings, and finally selects a title. The teacher can phase in this process with a skeleton outline of main ideas in which students fill in the details. Gradually, in subsequent inquiry operations, as the students learn to identify, state, and organize main ideas, the teacher can phase out the outline.

The issue of the validity of "facts" in the inquiry strategy leads to additional information, some pro and some con. The teacher has to teach the class to weigh and evaluate the information. The teacher informs students that information which nonbiased observers have directly observed and which other observers independently corroborate has greater weight and credence than information that is indirect or second-hand, or that comes from observers with vested interests in the information. Students then learn to judge issues on the basis of what reasonable persons would do, say, or believe in similar situations. In short, the class acts as a jury to evaluate the information and arrive at a verdict.

Thus, the inquiry strategy teaches a class to read critically and to verify and evaluate information independently. Of course, the teacher employs a phase-in procedure for teaching the class, then groups, and finally individuals, how to use the inquiry strategy. In the process, the class learns how to use a library, judge relevant information, abstract and file information, debate and evaluate information, and finally write reports. The class can also use and apply all of these processes in the project method.

The project method starts with the arousal of the class's curiosity. Room environment (posters, newspapers, bulletin boards), a slide presentation, a movie, or a combination of these techniques serve this purpose well. In presenting these curiosity-arousing techniques, or commenting during the presentation, the teacher can ask questions that get questions, not answers, in return: *What questions would you like to ask about this event? What other questions would you like to ask about this issue, or event, or person?* Student monitors can list the questions on the board as their classmates formulate them. Then the teacher can take the class through a process of finding answers to their questions in library reference books. In the next phase, students can group questions with common categories; and students who posed these questions can form a group to answer the questions *as a group*. Eventually, individuals can be led to carry out individual projects to answer their own questions.

The concept strategy is similar in operation to the project method, and may even precede its use in the sequence of teaching strategies. An English teacher may start with an anthology that deals with a particular concept such as *courage*. After going through various works that involve the concept, the teacher subdivides the class into groups according to students' interests. Then each group reads, discusses, analyses, and engages in various writing activities on a particular aspect of the concept — political courage *(Profiles in Courage)* or personal courage *(The Red Badge of Courage)*. Each group can contribute to class discussions from its enriched perspective.

Next, students can use self-selection for individual projects. A commercial example of this approach is *Scholastic Magazine Units* in literature. Such materials are not readily available in other content areas, but teachers can construct their own units with the help of school catalogs. These units can include materials at different levels of difficulty, but all related to the same concept. Another example in the series of textbooks, *Concepts in Science,* edited by Brandwein *et al.* (1972), demonstrates that a clock or wind-up toy running down is a concrete instance of the concept of entropy. The series subsequently presents this concept at succeeding levels of difficulty and abstractness.

The multilevel text strategy is similar to the concept strategy except that the multilevel text strategy deals with a variety of information, concepts, and generalizations at different levels of difficulty. The teacher can use multilevel texts in various ways. He or she can introduce students to ideas in a text at a low level of difficulty and then have the class deal with particular concepts at higher levels of difficulty, progressing from easy to more difficult texts. Teachers can also use single-text strategies, such as DRA, SQ3R, and learning guides with multilevel texts.

Thus, over a year's time a teacher and a class can learn to use a wide range of strategies that involve the use of both single and multiple texts. In the process, the teacher will not only enhance students' abilities to read and learn from text, but will also (contrary to popular belief) increase the range of individual differences through this excellent instruction. (See chapter 3, pp. 39–41.)

A reading and learning-from-text specialist can teach students and faculties this sequence of strategies best. The ideal reading specialist for a high school can carry out five major functions: diagnosis at the individual, classroom, and school level; instruction of acquisition classes; education of teachers on how to teach incoming students to read and learn from texts in content areas; demonstration teaching and inservice training for the faculty; teaching a content area course as a member of a department in the school. To coordinate all five functions this specialist must also serve as chairperson of a schoolwide committee on reading and learning from text, as Ms. Valdes does in Scene 4, below.

One week later. It is 3:30 in the afternoon. The schoolwide committee is meeting in a small conference room at the rear of the library, since the counseling department is using Ms. Valdes's room for testing.

Mr. Phelps: I want you to know, Ms. Valdes, that you're responsible for my not getting any sleep — two nights last week.

Ms. Valdes: How's that?

Mr. Phelps: All that talk about reeducating the faculty got me thinking. I started worrying about whether we'd ever begin to accomplish it.

Mr. Inglish: You realize, don't you, that taking on Monroe's faculty is like taking on a band of guerrillas.

Ms. Stewart: Are you saying they're apes?

Mr. Inglish: No, Stewart, the other kind.

Ms. Jorgensen: I can just see me telling Bedilia Furgueson that she's got to teach reading. She'll say, "I'm lucky if the kids don't sew their arms to their aprons. How can I teach them to read?"

Mr. Phelps: I've got a couple of hotshots in my department who might want to take this all on — you know the type, masochists.

Ms. Jones: I think what we're saying, Ms. Valdes, is that some teachers won't want to cooperate, but that some might want to.

Ms. Valdes: That's human nature. One of the factors that makes a high school a fascinating place to work is the tremendous differences that exist among the faculty members.

Ms. Stewart: Maybe we could start with the ones that want to learn and gradually work our way down to the others. Maybe we could even entice Bedilia.

Ms. Valdes: You've got a good start already. The fact that we have a functioning schoolwide committee on reading and learning from text is a major plus. Let me take some time here to talk about the problems other schools face and bring up a few questions we might want to consider.

Schoolwide Committee on Reading and Learning from Text

Although schools may want to act ideally in developing a reading program, they usually have to act expeditiously, frequently because of lack of funds, time, and available personnel. Consequently, the board or administration has often employed one of three solutions to solve the problem of the wide range of individual differences in reading achievement in a school: (1) it imports or buys a commercial reading program, (2) it sends teachers to observe an outstanding reading program at another school for a day or two, bring back the ideas, and try to install the same program in their own school — without going through the process of staff and program development followed by the outstanding school, or (3) it hires a consultant to draw up a prescription for a reading program and has teachers in the school, usually English teachers, apply the prescription without providing them with any additional training. None of these solutions works very well because usually none of them fit the specific needs of the school. Moreover, they do not contain provisions for training the faculty in how to develop and implement the program nor do they take the faculty through a process of analysis of the problem, consideration of strategies for solving the problem, and finally selection or construction of an appropriate program for the school.

An ideal approach is to have the principal form a schoolwide committee of department heads, reading and learning from text specialists, and
the vice-principal. The function of the schoolwide committee is to advise
the reading content area specialist, provide linkages between the administration and faculty, and make and implement decisions on the school's
program for teaching students to read and learn from texts. In doing so,
the committee will have to generate a series of questions and answers to
prepare for meeting with the faculty. We have posed a large number of
questions in box 16.9, among them some that we anticipate any faculty
might ask.

BOX 16.9. Questions About a School's Program
in Reading and Learning from Texts

Testing Reading Achievement and Reporting Results

1. What is the range of individual differences in general reading achievement
   (speed and comprehension) and in reading in the content areas?
2. Describe the school's testing program. Is it adequate: (a) Are all students diagnosed in speed and comprehension? (b) Is further diagnostic testing given to
   students beyond a survey test of speed and comprehension? (c) Are students
   assessed on reading in each content area?
3. What is done with test results? Are teachers, students, and parents informed of
   test results? Do they have opportunities to consult on the results with specialists
   and obtain recommendations for improvement? Are the test results used for
   making classroom, curricular, and administrative decisions?

Attitudes of Faculty and Students

4. What are the attitudes of the faculty towards teaching students to read and learn
   from texts?
5. What is the attitude of students towards their texts and tests?

Classroom Materials, Strategies, and Purposes

6. What types of materials must students read in each content area (texts, library
   assignments, other materials)?
7. What techniques or strategies do teachers use which seem to be helpful in
   improving reading and learning-from-text skills in each content area?
8. What classwide strategies do teachers use for handling the range of individual
   differences in reading achievement? (Note: even when tracking or homogeneous grouping is used, students still vary in achievement.)
9. What is the relationship between reading improvement classes and instruction
   in content areas?
10. What problem(s) do individual teachers have with students' reading and learn-
    ing in content areas? What suggestions do these teachers have for resolving
    these problems?

Role of the Reading and Learning from Text Specialist

11. Does the school's reading specialist(s) conduct inservice training for the faculty? Consult with content area teachers on instructional problems in teaching students to learn from texts? In general, what help does the reading specialist(s) provide for content area teachers?

12. How does the school prepare incoming students for reading and learning from texts in each content area? And for learning to study (taking examinations, learning and using library skills, writing reports, planning and organizing use of time)?

13. What should be the role of the consultant in reading and learning from texts? What questions does the faculty have for the consultant? What problems should the consultant focus on and try to solve? How should the consultant's time best be used to the advantage of the entire school?

Library Facilities and Resources

14. What is the current status of the library in relation to the content areas? Does the library have books in each content area that will cover the range of individual differences in each content area? What does the library need to adequately serve the needs of content area teachers?

15. How does the librarian coordinate with content area teachers on students' reference reading and research reporting in content areas? Does the library have a set of school catalogs?

Administration and Plans for Improving Reading and Learning from Texts

16. What plan(s) does the administration have for improving instruction in reading and learning in the content areas?

17. Does the school have a schoolwide program and committee for improving reading and learning in the content areas? How does the committee operate? What is its scope? Is the committee representative (content area teachers, reading specialists, administrators)? What has the committee done about determining and solving needs? Have individual faculty members had opportunities to state their problems and suggest solutions?

18. What provision does the school have for inservice training? How are policies on inservice training formulated? (Decisions on what training is required, who is to conduct the training, whether faculty is to get released time, whether training should be for the faculty as a whole or for departments, and whether the faculty is to get salary schedule credit for participating in inservice training.)

19. How is instruction in reading and learning from texts budgeted? Are funds distributed in many budget categories or is there a specific program budget?

Although each school has its own specific factors (such as training and interests of the faculty, characteristics of the student body, and schedule of priorities of administration) which it would have to take into account in designing and developing any program, we can give some tentative general answers, directions, or procedures to the items in box 16.9.

ITEMS 1–3. Review the school's testing program. If survey test results are not available, then administer a general survey test to the entire school. Follow up the survey test with individual diagnostic tests, according to our outline in chapter 15. Note that some students may perform only perfunctorily on the survey test and consequently score low, but on the individually administered test, if you properly motivate them, they will score higher. The committee is likely to discover from the results of the testing program that they can group students in three programs: (1) those students who need instruction in learning to read — they are candidates for the acquisition classes; the committee may have to subdivide some of these students further as we explained in chapter 15; (2) the same is true for the students in category two — those students who are beyond the elementary or acquisition state of reading development, but who have comprehension levels one to three years below grade level and below the readability levels of their texts — they and their teachers are candidates for demonstration classes in comprehension and strategies for meeting the range of individual differences; and (3) those students, almost all students in the school, who need instruction in learning from texts in the content areas — their teachers are candidates for demonstration, inservice training, and for consulting on problems of teaching students to read and learn from texts in content areas.

A survey test, while closely related to a test for reading in content areas, is not sufficient for defining the students for category 3 above. Although some content area survey tests are standardized and published (see the list in chapter 15, box 15.3), they do not have specific curricular validity for a particular school and their subtest reliabilities are not adequate. Consequently, teachers should construct an informal reading inventory for assessing comprehension in their own content areas. We explained the procedure for constructing such an inventory in chapter 8.

Communicate the results of testing not only to teachers but also to parents and students. If students are to improve, they need to know what their current performance is; then they need counseling on setting their goals and procedures for improvement. Furthermore, a school should use test results in decisions on classroom instruction, curricular modification, and administrative plans.

ITEMS 4, 18. Teachers in the school can react to the attitude inventory in chapter 2. The committee can present the results of this survey to the faculty with the consequence that faculty members might then become interested in an inservice education program especially if they get released time. Following the program, they can take the attitude scale to see if their attitudes towards teaching students to read and learn from text have changed.

ITEM 10. The committee should interview teachers for their problems in teaching students to learn from texts and for suggestions on how to ameliorate the problems. The committee can act on faculty suggestions, particularly in areas of consensus, and can make special arrangements for unique problems.

ITEM 5. The committee can interview a sample of students in various content areas to assess their attitudes towards their texts and to discuss their problems in reading and learning from them in class and at home. Ask students to read passages aloud and silently and then answer informal inventory type questions about them. The reading specialist who would conduct the interviews and observe students' reading and analyze inventory responses would then compile a list of problems.

Note: Some teachers at the high school level do not use texts — they use only the lecture method. The reading specialist could record some of the lectures and class discussions, then construct an informal inventory to administer to the class to get at problems in listening comprehension.

The problems in listening parallel those in reading, and in some ways learning is more difficult through listening because students must rely more on memory and their notes. Moreover, such oral instruction does not prepare them for the next level of instruction in which texts are used.

The committee should also interview students on their attitudes towards tests and test results. The committee may find that some students do not take tests seriously because they do not receive test results. Hence, their scores are not reliable. Consequently, when referred to clinics or labs they have to be retested.

ITEMS 6–8. Conduct a survey to determine what types of materials and reading assignments students have, what techniques and strategies students use to help with their assigned reading, and what strategies teachers employ for handling the range of individual differences for the entire class.

The results of the survey will form a baseline for evaluating the effectiveness of subsequent demonstrations, inservice training, and consultation programs. Moreover, the survey may identify teachers' strategies and practices that the committee can disseminate in the program.

ITEM 9. Make an analysis of the materials and curriculum in reading improvement classes. Describe the nature of the classes. (See chapter 15 for categories of current reading improvement classes.) A key question is whether the classes use content area materials (see section on content area acquisition classes in this chapter) for instruction in reading and learning from texts. Or, do the classes teach strictly functional reading (chapter 15)? These classes have an alternative objective to content area instruction — they simply teach survival skills in reading.

ITEMS 11, 13. Assess the role of reading specialists in the school. Is the school using the specialist to best advantage for the entire school? Does the specialist carry out the major functions of a specialist as outlined in this chapter? Or is the reading specialist's scope of activities focused only on teaching reading in acquisition classes? If so, what provisions can the school make for expanding the specialist's activities?

ITEM 12. Does the school have a program for introducing students to reading and learning from texts? Are students learning how to study and prepare for examinations, use the library, write reports, participate in discussions, and learn to organize and budget time?

Some schools require all incoming students to take a class in reading and learning from texts in a content area. Perhaps what is preferable is to integrate reading and learning from text instruction in each content area class, instead of relying upon transfer from a special class.

ITEMS 14–15. Make an inventory of the school's library to determine whether the library has a range of books in each content area to meet the range of reading abilities of students. Librarians should have school catalogs (chapter 4) as references for themselves and content area teachers. A possible solution to the financial problem of developing an adequate library in each school is a central library from which teachers can borrow books for units of study.

An important function of a school librarian is coordination with content area teachers. Does the librarian get course syllabi from content area teachers? Do teachers ask the librarian to arrange, borrow, or purchase books for reference reading for the particular units, or even apprise the librarian of student assignments? Does the librarian conduct orientation sessions in how to use the library? In general, how adequate is the collection of titles and reference materials for the school's program? What can the school or librarian do to improve the library services and collection?

ITEMS 16, 17, 19. Review the plan(s) of the school for improving instruction in reading and learning from text. Does the school have a plan for such improvement? What are its goals and procedures? What is the timeline for reaching the goal? What does the school consider an adequate ratio of reading specialist to students and faculty? What are its plans and budget for inservice training of faculty? What leadership is the principal providing for the program? If the principal has appointed a committee, what charge and scope of authority has he given to the committee?

Programs need time for development. As a rule of thumb, it takes about five years to develop an adequate program. The first year is for assessment, review, and planning. The second year is for employing reading specialists, initiating plans, courses, and inservice training. The third year is for application of the results of an inservice training program and spreading its effects to students and other faculty. The fourth year is for continued inservice training (particularly for those teachers who did not participate in the first inservice program and for faculty new to the school). The fifth year is for full-scale operation of the program and review of progress made towards the school's goal.

Although schools or consultants can devise strategies for economizing on costs and teachers' time, such as demonstration teaching in content area classes, in all probability teachers will have to have some released time for inservice training and for selection or preparation of lessons, units, and plans for implementation of new teaching strategies. If the administration has a budget specifically for the reading and learning-from-text program, then the school is likely to implement the program. In general, a specific budget item is more likely to produce results than a diffused budget for a program (Carlson, 1972).

If the school has reading specialists, the administration should decide how to use them. Interview the faculty to determine the questions and problems for the reading specialist when functioning as a consultant to the faculty. What problems does the faculty want the specialist to work on and solve? Often faculties might want to simply turn their instructional problems over to specialists. While students in the acquisition stage of development need concentrated instruction in special classes, content area teachers can also help them by teaching the technical vocabulary in their content areas. The content area teachers can provide even more help if they acquire and use strategies for teaching students in all content areas how to read and learn from texts.

In addition to answering these questions, the committee has to present some feasible solutions to the principal and gain his or her support for the project. To do so, the committee would invite the principal to its next meeting, as the committee at Monroe High does in Scene 5.

The office of Mr. Towne, the principal. The schoolwide committee has decided to approach Mr. Towne with some suggestions for effecting the future scene at Monroe High School.

Ms. Jones: Mr. Towne, as you know, the schoolwide committee has been spending a great deal of time studying the problems at Monroe High, particularly, with the help of Ms. Valdes, the problems the students are experiencing in reading their textbooks.

Ms. Phelps: Some of us are already experimenting with some of the single- and multiple-text strategies in our own classes.

Ms. Jorgensen: But we think that we're going to have to do something more far reaching than that.

Ms. Stewart: I think what we're asking is, how can we best reeducate the faculty to the needs of the students at Monroe High?

Mr. Towne: What do you propose?

Ms. Jones: Ms. Valdes has come up with a couple of good suggestions about involving faculty members in the teaching of an introductory course in reading and learning from text for our freshmen.

Ms. Stewart: Also ways of working with groups of faculty on the use of single- and multiple-text strategies, perhaps on a one-at-a-time basis.

NMr. Phelps: This may amount to some extra money. Ms. Valdes has suggested bringing in outside consultants to work with teachers in areas she feels inadequate in.

Ms. Jones: Most crucial, of course, is released time during the school year, and money for summer institutes, which would allow teachers time and support for developing classroom materials in implementing these strategies.

Mr. Umeki: Ms. Valdes seems to think that within four or five years we could have a most effective all-school program in reading and learning from text.

Mr. Towne: I would like to say that I'm most impressed with what you all have been doing. I will speak to the superintendent about funding what you propose — maybe an outside grant, or extra money in his contingency fund.

Ms. Valdes: Mr. Towne, we don't want to mislead you into thinking this is a panacea. You know Monroe's students and the nature of the faculty. It could be a long haul.

Mr. Towne: I'm willing to take the risk and I'm planning to be here for at least the next five years. I hope you are too. Why don't we set up a meeting for next week at this time. By that time, I'll know whether the superintendent has money. If he can't come up with money, we'll proceed as best as we can without funding. This is too important a project to let go by the wayside.

Ms. Valdes: Well, if Superintendent Ray doesn't have funds to support our inservice program, we'll still be able to go ahead at a slower rate with our one-to-one inservice model.

Mr. Towne: I'm glad you have that alternative. No matter what the superintendent does, we need to make a start on teaching all our teachers and students strategies on how to read and learn from text.

SUMMARY

To teach all the students in a school to read and learn from text, a school has to have three programs: (1) a class in reading acquisition in the content areas that includes instruction not only in word recognition but also in comprehension; (2) an inservice education program for content area teachers and (3) an introductory course in reading and learning from text. Teachers and students alike can acquire strategies for reading and learning from text in a sequence that progresses from single- to multiple-text strategies. This sequence fits the adaptive mechanisms of assimilations and accommodation. Students and teachers are more likely to accept single-text strategies more readily than multiple-text strategies because single-text strategies are closer to familiar concepts and methods of instruction. Single-text strategies also ease the acquisition of multiple-text strategies because they teach teachers and students alike some processes that also occur in multiple-text strategies.

But having an entire school faculty learn how to teach students to read and learn from texts is a complex operation. To administer the operation and to secure the cooperation of the faculty, the principal has to appoint a representative schoolwide committee. This committee will have a full agenda of nineteen questions and will supply tentative answers to them. Even under the best of conditions, we think it will take five years for the development of a schoolwide program for teaching all students to read and learn from text.

ACTIVITIES

1. Attend a high school class in reading instruction. Compare the course with this text's description of a reading acquisition class. Specifically, does the class use content from texts in the school's content areas?
2. Use the set of nineteen questions in box 16.9 on a survey of a nearby high school. How many of the issues in these questions has the school resolved?

Epilogue

We started this text by reviewing changes that have occurred in the high school over the past several years. These changes have led to two related problems:

1. How do you teach academic and vocational courses to high school students who have a reading achievement range of about 10 to 12 years: that is, the lowest reading achievement in this range is about grade levels 2 to 5 and the highest about equivalent to sixth-year college?
2. We know that teachers in general have ambivalent attitudes towards teaching students how to read. They know that their students have to learn how to read their texts, but they do not agree that it is their job, nor that they know how to teach their students to read and learn from text. The question then is how to teach these teachers, and have them adopt strategies in their instruction that will enable all their students to read and learn from texts.

In chapters 4 through 14, we explained how single- and multiple-text strategies provide a solution to the first problem. But we recognize that some low-achieving students have to learn not only how to comprehend high school texts; they also have to learn how to read. These students need more concentrated instruction than they can get in content area classes, even if teachers of these classes have learned and are using single- and multiple-text strategies to teach students to read and learn from text. These students whom teachers refer to as "nonreaders," usually can read, but only at about the second to fourth grade levels. What can the school do about these low-achieving readers? Chapter 15 provides examples of how some schools currently answer this question: they enroll low reading achievers in reading centers for instruction in reading acquisition.

Although the reading centers help low achieving students learn to read, they can become more relevant to the students' content area courses by including materials that occur in high school texts as content for teaching reading acquisition. In chapter 3, we also point out that instruction in learning to read includes development in word recognition *and* comprehension. If reading acquisition centers did include content drawn from texts actually used in the school, they would then merit the title of *content reading acquisition centers*.[1] To help in the construction of such centers, we included in chapter 16 an outline for a competency-based content reading acquisition class.

The second problem has two solutions. The first consists of differentiating the concept of reading into two components: (1) learning to read and (2) learning to learn from text. We found high school teachers reacted much more favorably to the concept of teaching students how to *learn from text* than they did to teaching students how to *read*. Hence, our first solution for the second problem is to avoid the negative term *reading* and use the positive phrase *learning from text* whenever we teach junior and senior high school teachers how to use single- and multiple-text strategies in content area classes. We use the term *reading* only in its narrow sense to mean, "how to read." Hence, teaching students reading or how to read is an objective of reading acquisition classes.

The second solution to the problem is through inservice education, that is, teaching teachers the strategies we have explained in chapters 4–14 with emphasis on teaching students how to learn from text. We think that this emphasis will make inservice education more acceptable to teachers and influence their attitudes towards teaching students to learn from text in an even more positive direction.

We then review models for inservice education and a sequence of instruction for teaching teachers and students single- and multiple-text strategies. This inservice education should produce at least some teachers who will offer introductory courses in their content areas with emphasis upon strategies for reading and learning from text.

Thus, a high school will have at least two types of classes: (1) content reading acquisition classes for low reading achievers and (2) introductory classes that will teach students how to read and learn from texts. If inservice education for the entire faculty is successful, then the school would also have emphasis on reading and learning from text in all courses. To plan and guide the inservice program, we suggest that the principal appoint a schoolwide committee that will investigate a series of questions. Any school should ask and answer these questions if it wants to develop an inservice program that fits its unique characteristics. We not only

---

[1] Some commercially prepared materials that integrate subject matter content with instruction and exercises in reading acquisition classes are available. See the appendix for a list of these materials.

outline the questions for this committee but we also provide possible answers.

Throughout our last two chapters, we try to provide a sense of how a schoolwide committee develops a program for teaching students how to read and learn from text. We do so by letting you "eavesdrop" (in five scenes) on meetings of Monroe High's Schoolwide Committee on Reading and Learning from Text. We recognize that no schoolwide committee is likely to achieve success unless it has the support of its principal and district superintendent. Therefore, we recommend that a representative of the school administration be a member of the schoolwide committee and that the committee inform the principal of its decisions. Consequently, in the final scene in the text, the schoolwide committee reports its inservice education plans to the principal of Monroe High School, Mr. Towne.

We hope that eavesdropping on the Monroe schoolwide committee gives you a sense of participation, and that this sense of participation will lead you to provide equality of educational opportunity to your students by putting into practice the single- and multiple-text strategies we have developed in this book. However, it will take some time to change a high school. Even under the best of conditions, we think it will take five years for the development of a schoolwide program for teaching students in all content area courses how to read and learn from text.

Appendix A
Equipment

EDL is the acronym for Educational Developmental Laboratories, Western Regional Distribution Center, 8171 Redwood Highway, Novato, California 94947.

EDL Aud X. A filmstrip projector synchronized with an audio cassette. A jackbox attached to the cassette provides for multiple listening headsets. Hence, equipment can be used by an individual or by small groups.

Materials available for Aud X are:

1. Aud X. programs, Levels AA–CA for reading levels 1, 2, 3, respectively. Purpose: To introduce basic vocabulary and word attack skills to older students still at the beginning stage of reading development. New vocabulary and comprehension skills are introduced in high-interest story lessons. Word study lessons teach phonetic and structural analysis. Aud X Study Guide accompanies word recognition and sentence completion lessons. Narrator corrects most exercises. A teacher's manual provides story synopses, vocabulary lists, discussion questions and answer keys. A complete description of Aud X programs is found in "Learning 100 Instructor's Manual," available from EDL.
2. Aud X Sampler, reading levels 2 to 6. Purpose: To develop critical comprehension skills, including cause and effect, fact *vs.* opinion, interpreting diagrams, and recognizing author's purposes in various content materials. Materials consist of 25 softcover books of increasing difficulty covering a wide range of high-interest content materials, including science, math, history, humor, and literature. Filmstrips and cassettes guide the reading of the sampler books. Students are expected to respond in Sampler Lesson Books. Narrator provides for correction of responses.
3. Aud X Word Attack Review, Level DEFA. Purpose: To review word attack skills from initial consonants through vowels, blends, digraphs, syllables, prefixes and suffixes.
4. Aud X Dictionary Skills. Purpose: To teach students how to use the dictionary; 15 lessons, with lesson book and ditto masters.

EDL Controlled Reader. This equipment is essentially a filmstrip projector with a device attached that advances the story a line at a time and has a moving slot of light that makes the print visible in a left-to-right sequence. The rate of presentation can be controlled from 60 to 1000 words per minute. The machine purports to teach reading rate, visual coordination, left-to-right reading, and to correct for vocalization and word-by-word reading.

Critique: Rate of reading varies from individual to individual according to change in purposes and difficulty of the material. Furthermore, eye-movement behavior is unique. Therefore, use equipment primarily for motivational and demonstrational purposes.

Materials available for the Controlled Reader are:

1. Learning 100 Programs, grade levels 1–8; Skill Development Series, grade levels 2–9; Learning 300 Programs, grade levels 8–14.
2. Teacher's Guide, Study Guides, Filmstrip Sets, and Controlled Reader Juniors are materials needed with the Controlled Reader.
3. Supplemental materials on Biography and Sports, Mystery and Adventure, Science and Science Fiction, Sports and Biography for grades 5–6 are available from Instructional Communications, Technology Inc., Huntington, New York 11143.

SRA is the acronym for Science Research Associates, 259 East Erie Street, Chicago, Illinois 60611.

Reading Accelerator. This equipment which can be used with any book consists of a moving shutter which moves down the page at a varying rate of speed, preset by a dial. It purports to improve rate of reading.

Critique: Although students find the accelerator fascinating, have them use the accelerator for only brief periods of time because the constant, shutter-rate-per-page does not allow students to vary their rate according to their purposes on each page!

Borg-Warner Educational Systems
7450 North Natchez
Niles, Illinois 60648

System 80. A self-pacing audiovisual unit which synchronizes presentation of 80 pictures with 80 recorded messages and provides immediate feedback on test for word recognition, context clues, and applied phonics. Earphones provided for individual listening. Students are pre- and post-tested for each kit of 9–12 lessons to pinpoint weaknesses in word recognition skills. Teacher's manual provides overview of program, behavioral objectives, and suggestions for conducting the program.

Materials available are:

1. Learning Letter Sounds Primer.
2. Reading Words in Context, Grade 4.0.
3. Improving Reading Skills — Adult Basic Readers (basic survival vocabulary with adult interest level material).

Bell and Howell Language Master
Photo and Sound Company
870 Monterey Pass Road
Monterey Park, California 91754

Language Master. Essentially this equipment is a specialized tape recorder for developing vocabulary, word recognition, word analysis, and English-as-a-second-language training. A card with strip of tape passes recording head providing sound to accompany picture on card. Other track on card records student response. Student inserts card, watches picture, records response, then compares own response with instructor's response on other track. Repeat key permits relistening. Earphones provided. Color-coded controls facilitate use of machine.

Materials available are: Vocabulary Mastery, grades 4.1–12.0.

Appendix B
Materials

While commercial materials for teaching reading are attractive and interesting, they are usually not integrated into a learning sequence. For example, words taught in a word recognition program are not then used in follow-up stories. Likewise, specific skills for comprehension are not applied to content reading materials. However, some of the graded materials do introduce new words, teach their syllabication and other clues to their recognition, explain their meanings, and provide purposes for reading before students read a selection or story, and then have follow-up questions. But rarely are the vocabulary and content cumulative, as they are in basal readers.

Although some content parallels texts used in content area classes, usually only teacher-made materials designed for content area classes can integrate laboratory reading instruction with reading and learning from texts in students' content area courses. However, some basal readers for junior high school, such as the *Ginn Junior High School Series* (David Russell, ed., Boston: Ginn, 1967), do have sequential skills instruction integrated with story content.

Perhaps awareness of these limitations will help teachers overcome them by the way in which they select, modify, construct, and use materials.[1]

Learning-to-Read Materials, Grades 1 to 3[2]

1. See materials under "Equipment," above.
2. *The SRA Reading Laboratory.* (Grades 1 to 9)
   a. Lab 1 — Word Games to accompany 1A, 1B, 1C
   b. Lab lA: Range 1.2 to 3.0 (c) Lab 1B: Range 1.4 to 4.0
   c. Lab lC: Range 1.4 to 5.0 (d) Elementary Lab: Range 2.0 to 9.0
   Publisher: Science Research Associates, 259 East Erie Street, Chicago, Illinois 60611.
3. *The Sullivan Reading Program.* (Grades 1 to 3)
   Series contains 8 programed textbooks; 8 correlated readers (titles, such as *Spy in the Sky* with cartoon character illustrations); 2 teacher's manuals; 2 progress test booklets;

[1] For permission to abstract and reproduce information on some of these materials, we are grateful to Ann Glaser, Project Director, et al., "DeAnza Designs: Resources in Reading," Project Futureprint, 1976 Edition, Demonstration Reading Program, DeAnza Junior High School, 1450 South Sultana Ave., Ontario, California 91761.

[2] Grades refer to reading levels of students, not their actual grade levels.

and one placement test. Range from teaching initial consonants to words selected for context.

Publisher: Behavioral Research Laboratories, Palo Alto, California.

4. *Breakthrough.*

Paperbacks. Specific titles: "On the Level" (Grade 1) to "Making the Scene" (Grade 6). Content: sport stories, science fiction, biographies. Teacher's manual for synopsis of stories, introduction of concepts, key vocabulary, comprehension questions.

Publisher: Allyn and Bacon, Western Division, Ralston Park, Belmont, California 94002.

5. *Eye and Ear Fun, Book 4.*

A complete sequence of word recognition exercises from letter names and sounds to word meaning analysis. Use of prefixes, suffixes, and roots. By Clarence R. Stone.

Publisher: Webster Publishing Company, St. Louis, Missouri.

6. *Go Magazines.* (Grades 1 — AA to 6 — FA

Each workbook contains 30 lessons followed by skill development exercises. Brief stories and illustrations are about teenagers and adults in contemporary situations, social activities, and occupations.

Publisher: Educational Development Laboratories, Western Regional Distribution Center, 8171 Redwood Highway, Novato, California 94947.

7. *Phonics and Word Power.* My Weekly Reader Practice Books. (Grades 1–3)

Workbook type materials, ranges from initial consonants to syllabication.

Publisher: Weekly Reader, Columbus, Ohio 43216.

8. *Action Libraries.* (Grades 2.0 to 3.9)

Four paperback novels written for mature students from various ethnic backgrounds. Teacher's manual contains synopses of stories, word lists, answer keys, and discussion questions.

Publisher: Scholastic Book Services, 904 Sylvan Avenue, Englewood Cliffs, New Jersey 07632.

9. *Specific Skills Series.*

Each skill graded from grade level 1 to 6, except advanced skills are for grades 7 and 8. Each paperback booklet teaches one skill through brief explanation followed by varied and interesting exercises with appealing and amusing illustrations. Titles include: *Using Context, Locating the Answer, Getting the Facts, Drawing Conclusions, Getting the Main Idea, Detecting the Sequence* (Beginning and Advanced), *Working with Sounds* (Beginning and Advanced). Popular with students.

Publisher: Barnell Loft, Ltd., 958 Church Street, Baldwin, NY 11510.

10. *Supportive Reading Skills.*

Various skills progressive in difficulty, graded from 2.0 to 6.0, advanced 7 to 9; includes syllabication, understanding word groups (meaning of words in context).

Publisher: Dexter and Westbrook, Ltd., 958 Church Street, Baldwin, New York 11510.

11. *Plays for Reading.* (Reading levels 2 to 8)

Plays develop oral reading skills, particularly intonation, phrasing, and interrelationships among characters, plot, goal, and resolution of conflict. Box contains 22 plays, starting with miniplays and progressing to full-length plays. Parts for each play require different reading levels. Teacher's manual contains overview of program, plot summaries, reading levels for characters, suggestions for discussion, glossary of vocabulary words, follow-up activities.

Publisher: Educational Progress Corporation, P.O. Box 45663, Tulsa, Oklahoma 74145.

12. *Hip Pocket Stories.* (Grades 2.5 to 3.5)

High-interest, low readability. Five titles: *Diana Ross, Geraldo Rivera, Shirley Chisholm, Bill Cosby, Johnny Bench.* Cassette tape accompanies each biography. Teacher's manual contains word study, vocabulary, and comprehension skills.

Publisher: Random House, School Division, 400 Hahn Road, Westminster, Maryland 21157.

13. *Action Units*. (Grades 2 to 4)
Unit books with short narratives with before reading and after reading activities. Workbooks. Two anthologies: plays and stories. Word attack skills supplement.
Publisher: Scholastic Book Services, 904 Sylvan Avenue, Englewood Cliffs, New Jersey 07632.

Development of Comprehension, Grades 4 to 9

1. *Sport Action Skill Kits*. (Grades 4.5 to 5.5)
Paperbacks with read-along cassette and filmstrips on baseball, basketball, football, auto racing, boxing, tennis, swimming, gymnastics, and ice skating. Teacher's manual contains program information and answer keys for activity cards.
Publisher: Troll Associates, 320 Route 17, Mahwak, New Jersey 07430.

2. *Sports Superstars*. (Grades 5 to 6)
Paperbacks containing 52 biographies of famous male and female sports heroes with read-along tapes.
Publisher: Creative Education, 123 South Broad Street, P.O. Box 227, Mankato, Minnesota 56001.

3. *Reader's Digest Reading Skill Builders/Reader's Digest Science Reader*. (Levels range from Grades 2 to 8)
Stories and articles adapted from *Reader's Digest*. Following each story is a set of comprehension and word meaning exercises. Word count for each story facilitates timed tests for measuring speed of reading.
Publisher: Reader's Digest Services, Inc., Reading Skillbuilder, Pleasantville, New York 10570 (1959)

4. *Reading for Meaning*. (Grades 4 to 12)
A series of workbooks. Each unit contains a paragraph, usually of science information; a glossary; and test exercises (based on the paragraph) for getting word meanings, choosing the best title, selecting the main idea, identifying facts, organizing ideas into an outline, and drawing conclusions. Pupil charts progress according to grade level equivalents. By W. S. Guiler and J. H. Coleman.
Publisher: J. B. Lippincott, New York (1945)

5. *The Macmillan Reading Spectrum*. (Grades 2 to 6)
Consists of teacher guides and pupil booklets for word analysis skills, vocabulary development, and reading comprehension. Also has a teaching guide to 90 annotated books. The teaching guide contains the cast of characters, the setting, a synopsis, questions for each paragraph, related activities, and references for further reading. The package also contains paperback editions of annotated books in the teacher's guide.
Publisher: Macmillan Co., New York (1964)

6. *Kaleidoscope*. (Grades 2 to 9)
Series of eight books with high appeal and relevant content. Includes word attack, vocabulary, comprehension, and study skills. Henry Bamman (Director).
Publisher: Field Education Publications, San Francisco, California (1970)

7. *Scope Magazine*. (Grades 4 to 8)
Periodical with curriculum-related articles, stories, and exercises. High-interest topics on youth, contemporary issues. Excellent teacher guides accompany classroom orders.
Publisher: Scholastic Magazines, Inc., 902 Sylvan Ave., Englewood Cliffs, New Jersey 07632.

8. *Be a Better Reader*. (Grades 2 to 4; 4 to 8)
Basic skills practice in word recognition. Comprehension exercises in content fields of science, mathematics, social science, and literature. By Nila Banton Smith.
Publisher: Prentice-Hall, Englewood Cliffs, New Jersey (1968)

9. *Read.* (Grades 4 to 8)
   A periodical magazine; contains short stories and plays on contemporary issues.
   Publisher: American Education Publications, Columbus, Ohio.

10. *Impact.* (Reading levels 4 to 6)
    Four paperbound anthologies (*Conflict, Search for America, Sight Lines, Unknown World*). Series is accompanied by recordings of stories and supplementary filmstrips. Charlotte K. Brooks (Editor).
    Publisher: Holt, Rinehart, and Winston, New York (1967)

11. *Tactics I.* (About grades 4 to 8)[3]
    Contains these exercises: (1) attacking words by using context, structure, and sound clues; (2) reacting to imagery; (3) following sequence; (4) understanding sentences; (5) drawing inferences; (6) understanding paragraphs; (7) analysis of affixed words which have common foreign roots. By Olive Niles et al.
    Publisher: Scott, Foresman, and Co., Palo Alto, California (1961)

12. *Countdown (Scope/Study Skills).* (Grades 4 to 6)
    Skills workbooks. Each lesson focuses on one skill and uses high interest materials.
    Publisher: Scholastic Book Services, 904 Sylvan Avenue, Englewood Cliffs, New Jersey 07632

13. *Countries and Cultures (Dimensions Series).* (Grades 4 to 9.5)
    A kit with 120 3-page selections, each with its own skill card. Sentence completion questions can be used for discussion. Stories set in various parts of the world.
    Publisher: Science Research Associates, 259 East Erie Street, Chicago, Illinois 60611

14. *Word Clues Series.* (Grades 7 to 10)
    Programed workbooks, each with thirty lessons of ten words each. Used with a tachistoscope.
    Publisher: Educational Developmental Laboratories, Western Regional Distribution Center, 8171 Redwood Highway, Novato, California 94947

15. *Reading for Understanding.* (Grades 2 to 14)
    A series of kits, each containing 400 lesson cards, sequenced in 100 steps of reading difficulty with a lesson card at each level. Questions for critical thinking are included on each card. Placement tests and student record books are included.
    Publisher: Science Research Associates, 259 East Erie Street, Chicago, Illinois 60611

16. *Conquests in Reading,* by William A. Kottemeyer and Kay Ware.
    Publisher: McGraw-Hill, 1121 Avenue of the Americas, New York 10020

17. *Design for Reading: How to Read Social Studies.* (Grades 2 to 5)
    Publisher: Harper and Row, 10 East 53rd Street, New York 10022

18. *World of Vocabulary,* by Sidney J. Rauch and Zacharie J. Clements.
    Publisher: Globe Book Company, 175 Fifth Avenue, New York 10010

19. *Webster Word Wheels.*
    Publisher: Webster Division of McGraw-Hill Book Co., 1221 Avenue of the Americas, New York 10020

20. *SRA Pilot Library.*
    Publisher: Science Research Associates, 259 East Erie Street, Chicago, Illinois 60611

21. *SRA Map and Globe Skills.*
    Publisher: Science Research Associates, 259 East Erie Street, Chicago, Illinois 60611

22. *SRA Literature Sampler.*
    Publisher: Science Research Associates, 259 East Erie Street, Chicago, Illinois 60611

23. *Scope Plays.*
    Publisher: Scholastic Magazine and Book Services, 50 West 44th Street, New York 10036

---

[3] For other materials, see Thomas G. Devine, "About Materials for Teaching Reading," *English Journal,* Sept. 1969, 58, No. 6, pp. 842–852.

24. *Scope Magazine.*
    Publisher: Scholastic Magazine and Book Services, 50 West 44th Street, New York 10036
25. *Scope/Skills Books.*
    Publisher: Scope, 904 Sylvan Avenue, Englewood Cliffs, New Jersey 07632
26. *Scholastic Units.*
    Publisher: Scholastic Magazine and Book Services, 50 West 44th Street, New York 10036
27. *Scholastic Individualized Reading Program.*
    Publisher: Scholastic Magazine and Book Services, 50 West 44th Street, New York 10036
28. *Reading Attainment Systems.*
    Publisher: Grolier Educational Corporation, 845 Third Avenue, New York 10022
29. *SRA Graph and Picture Study Skills.*
    Publisher: Science Research Associates, 259 East Erie Street, Chicago, Illinois 60611
30. *The Sports Illustrated Learning Program: An Interdisciplinary Approach to Education.*
    Publisher: Sports Illustrated-J. P. Lippincott Co, East Washington Square, Philadelphia, Pennsylvania 19105.
31. *Success in Reading, Books I and II,* by Robert E. Shafer and Arthur S. McConald.
    Publisher: California Department of Education, California State Series, Sacramento, California
32. *Clue Magazine.*
    Publisher: Education Progress Corporation, P.O. Box 45663, Tulsa, Oklahoma 74145
33. *You and Your World,* by Willets R. Bolinger.
    Publisher: Fearon Publishers, 6 Davis Drive, Belmont, California 94002

Study Skills

Study Skills Library. (Grades 3.0 to 9.0)
A series of three kits at grade levels 3 to 9 that have graded and sequential material in the areas of science, social studies, and reference skills. Teacher's Guide contains information on teaching study skills, has a chart of skills taught in the program at various grade levels, and procedures for teaching the program.
Publisher: Educational Developmental Laboratories, 8171 Redwood Highway, Novato, California 94947

Content Area Related Materials [4]

ART

1. *Pictoral History of Western Art,* by Erwin O. Christensen.
   Publisher: American Library (World Publishing Co.), 110 East 59th Street, New York 10002 (1964)
2. *Photography,* by Herbert S. Zim, et al.
   Publisher: Golden Press (Western Publishing Co.), 1220 Mound Avenue, Racine, Wisconsin 53404 (1964)

[4] The books listed in this section were selected by Content Area Reading Specialists. For a more complete listing, see Harry Singer, *Preparation of Reading Content Specialists for the Junior High School.* Final Report, U.S. Office of Education, 1973. Available from ERIC.

ENGLISH

1. *Troubleshooter: A Program in Basic English Skills.*
   Seven booklets programmed for individual progress, beginning with sounds of letters, word attack skills, vocabulary building, sentence construction, and paragraph development. By Patricia Ann Benner.
   Publisher: Houghton Mifflin, Palo Alto, California (1969)
2. *Enrichment Paperback Classroom Library.* (Reading levels 5 to 7)
   Contains multiple copies of 107 illustrated novels, stories, and pamphlets on contemporary themes, including 20 adapted classic novels, short stories, and poems; 12 original novels and short stories on contemporary life; 5 anthologies on modern life styles; 18 short stories on earning a living; 50 pamphlets on interpersonal relationships in the working world. Editor: James T. Olsen.
   Publisher: McGraw-Hill Book Co., New York
3. *Macmillan Gateway English.*
   A three-year developmental literature and language arts program for educationally disadvantaged and reluctant readers. The four softback anthologies in the program contains short stories, articles, plays, folk tales, songs, and poems drawn from contemporary and traditional sources, such as *Negro Digest,* television scripts, *Life* magazine, ballads, and mythology. Reproduction of art and photographs are integrated with the text. Project Director: Marjorie B. Smiley.
   Publisher: The Macmillan Co., New York (1970)

HOME ECONOMICS

1. *Molly Goldberg Jewish Cookbook,* by Gertrude Berg and Myra Waldo.
   Publisher: Doubleday, New York (1970)
2. *Pocket Book of Etiquette,* by Emily Post.
   Publisher: Pocket Books, Inc., Simon and Schuster, 1 West 39th Street, New York 10018

INDUSTRIAL ARTS

1. *How and Why Wonder Book of Building.* Wonder-Treasure Books, Inc.
2. *How and Why Wonder Book of Electricity.* Wonder-Treasure Books, Inc. Grades 4 to 6.
3. *How and Why Wonder Book of Robots and Electronic Brains.* Wonder-Treasure Books, Inc. Grades 4 to 6.
   Publisher: Grosset and Dunlap, 51 Madison Avenue, New York 10010

MATHEMATICS

1. *Magic House of Numbers.* Irving Adler.
   Publisher: New American Library (World Publishing Co.), 110 East 59th Street, New York 10002 (1957)
2. *One, Two, Three . . . Infinity.* George Gamow.
   Publisher: Bantam Books, Inc., 666 Fifth Avenue, New York 10019 (1961)
3. *Mathematics for Pleasure.* Oswald Jacoby.
   Publisher: Fawcett World Library, 67 West 44th Street, New York 10036 (1970)
4. *Fun with Mathematics.* Jerome S. Meyer
   Publisher: Fawcett World Library, 67 West 44th Street, New York 10036 (1967)
5. *Fun with the New Math.* Jerome S. Meyer and Stuart Hanlon.
   Publisher: Fawcett World Library, 67 West 44th Street, New York 10036 (1966)

6. *Understanding the New Mathematics.* Evelyn B. Rosenthal.
   Publisher: Fawcett World Library, 67 West 44th Street, New York 10036 (1965)

MUSIC

1. *Folksongs for Fun.* Oscard Brand, editor.
   Publisher: Berkeley Publishing Corp., 200 Madison Avenue, New York 10016 (1961)
2. *What to Listen for in Music.*
   Publisher: New American Library (World Publishing Co.), 110 East 59th Street, New York 10002 (1964)

PHYSICAL EDUCATION

1. *Champion Sports Stories.* Charles I. Coombs, ed. (Grades 5 to 9)
   Publisher: Pocket Books, Inc. (Simon and Schuster), 1230 Avenue of the Americas, New York 10020
2. *Baseball's All Time Greats: The Top Fifty Players,* by Mac Davis.
   Publisher: Bantam Books, Inc., 666 Fifth Avenue, New York 10019 (1970)

SCIENCE

1. *Pathways in Science: Chemistry, Physics, Biology, Earth Science.* (Reading level: Grade 5)
   Purpose: Teach concepts in four major disciplines, use of simple lab equipment and home materials, develop word study skills in science. Excellent outline in teaching guide for "Hints on Good Science Teaching." Authors: Joseph M. Oxenhorn, Michael N. Idelson, and Peter Greenleaf.
   Publisher: Globe Book Co., New York (1968)

WORKBOOK MATERIALS IN THE CONTENT AREAS

1. *How to Read the Humanities.*
   For advanced high school and college level readers. Author: Royce Adams.
   Publisher: Scott, Foresman, Palo Alto, California (1969)
2. *How to Read the Social Sciences.*
   (A companion volume for *How to Read the Humanities.*) Authors: Charles M. Brown and W. Royce Adams.
   Publisher: Scott, Foresman, Palo Alto, California (1968)
3. *Go: Reading in the Content Areas.*
   Content for the exercises comes from all the academic content areas. About a junior high school level in reading difficulty. Authors: Harold Herber and Mary Lee Johansen.
   Publisher: Scholastic Book Services, New York (1973)
4. *Why They Can't Read It?*
   Materials for an inservice education program on teaching reading in the content areas. High school level. Author: Irene M. Reiter. Consultant: George D. Spache.
   Publisher: Polaski Company, Box 7466, Philadelphia, Pennsylvania 19101

Appendix C
Tests Currently in Use

Some of these tests, and others not listed here, are discussed in table 3.2, box 15.2, and box 15.3.

I. Survey Tests
   A. General (group tests)

   Comprehensive Tests of Basic Skills: Reading
   Grades 1–12, 60–65 minutes. Vocabulary and comprehension. Monterey, Calif.: California Test Bureau/McGraw-Hill, 1970.

   Dvorak-Van Wagenen Diagnostic Examination of Silent Reading Abilities
   Grades 4–16. Time 140–150 minutes. Assesses rate of comprehension, perception of relations, vocabulary, information, details, central thought, influences, interpretation, reading for ideas. Minneapolis: Van Wagenen Psychoeducational Laboratories, 1954.

   Gates Reading Survey
   Grades 3–10. Assesses vocabulary, level of comprehension, speed and accuracy of reading, New York: Bureau of Publications, Columbia University, 1935 (out of print).

   Gates-MacGinitie Reading Tests
   Grades 1–9. Assesses vocabulary and comprehension. Speed and accuracy in reading measured in grades 2.5–9. New York: Teachers College Press, Columbia University, 1970.

   Metropolitan Achievement Test
   Roger Farr, George A. Prescott, Irving H. Balow, and Thomas P. Hogan. K–12. A two-component system yielding norm-referenced and criterion-referenced information: I. The *Survey* test battery contains subtests on Reading, Mathematics, Language, Science, and Social Studies. II. The *Reading Instructional* test battery contains diagnostic tests on visual discrimination; letter recognition; auditory discrimination; phoneme/grapheme: consonants; phoneme/grapheme: vowels; vocabulary in context; word part clues; rate of comprehension; skimming and scanning; and reading comprehension. The battery also contains Mathematics and Language Instructional Tests. New York: The Psychological Corporation/Harcourt, Brace, Jovanovich, 1978.

   Nelson Reading Test
   Grades 3–9. 30 minutes. Vocabulary and Comprehension. Boston: Houghton Mifflin, 1962.

Nelson-Denny Reading Test, 1973 ed.

Grades 9–16. 40 minutes. Vocabulary, Comprehension, and Rate. Boston: Houghton Mifflin, 1973.

B. Specific content areas (group tests)

California Achievement Tests: Reading

Ernest W. Tiegs and Willis W. Clark. Elementary, junior, and senior high school. 50–75 minutes. Assesses vocabulary, study skills, comprehension in English, math, social studies, and science. Monterey, Calif.: California Test Bureau. McGraw-Hill, 1970.

Iowa Every-Pupil Test of Basic Skills

Tests of basic skills, grades 3–9. Time 55–90 minutes. Group tests of map reading; use of references, index, dictionary, and graphing. Boston: Houghton Mifflin, 1947.

Iowa Tests of Educational Development, 1971 ed.

Grades 9–12. 70 minutes. Ability to interpret reading materials in the social studies (test 5), natural sciences (test 6), literature (test 7), and uses of source of information (test 8). Chicago: Science Research Associates, 1961.

Metropolitan Achievement Test

(See Survey Tests, General.)

Robinson-Hall Reading Tests

Group test. Grades 13–16. Assesses reading abilities for art, geology, history, fiction, rate, and comprehension. Columbus, Ohio: Ohio State University Press, 1949.

Stanford Achievement Test

(See Diagnostic section.)

C. Inventory (individual tests)

Classroom Reading Inventory

Nicholas Silvaroli. Grades 2–8. Individual test in three parts: (1) graded word lists; (2) graded oral paragraphs; scored for independence, instructional, and frustration levels; and (3) hearing capacity level. Also contains a spelling survey which can be adminstered to a group. Dubuque, Iowa: Brown, 1979.

II. Diagnostic Tests

A. Silent (group tests)

Metropolitan Achievement Test

(See Survey section.)

Silent Reading Diagnostic Tests

Guy Bond, Bruce Balow, and Cyril Hoyt. Grades 2–6. 90 minutes. Words in isolation and context, visual structural analysis, syllabication, word synthesis, beginning and ending sounds, vowel and consonant sounds. Chicago: Lyons and Carnahan, 1970.

Stanford Diagnostic Reading Test

Grades 1.5–9.5. 90–110 minutes. Subtests cover auditory vocabulary, auditory discrimination, phonetic analysis, word reading, reading comprehension, and rate. New York: Harcourt Brace Jovanovich, 1976.

New Developmental Reading Tests

Guy Bond, Bruce Balow, and Cyril Hoyt. Assesses vocabulary, reading for information, relationships, interpretation, and appreciation. Chicago: Lyons and Carnahan, 1968.

Sequential Tests of Educational Progress (STEP)

Grades 4–14. 45 minutes. Measures comprehension. Princeton, N.J.: Educational Testing Service, 1969.

Stanford Achievement Test, Grades 1.5–12

Grades 1.5–2.4: vocabulary, comprehension, word study, math concepts, math computation, math applications listening comprehension, and spelling.

Grades 2.5–3.9: also includes social science and science subtest.

Grades 4.0–6.9: includes additional subtest: language.

Grades 7–12: battery includes advanced paragraph meaning and high school reading (assesses only literal and factual comprehension).

New York: Harcourt Brace Jovanovich, 1973.

B. Oral (individual tests)

Durrell Analysis of Reading Difficulty

Grades 1–6. About 60–90 minutes. Oral and silent reading tests; listening; word recognition and analysis; naming, identifying, and matching letters; visual memory of words; sounds of words and letters; spelling; handwriting. New York: Harcourt Brace Jovanovich, 1955.

Gates-McKillop Reading Diagnostic Tests

Arthur I. Gates and Anne S. McKillop. Grades 1–8. Subtests include oral reading, word recognition, phrase recognition, syllabication, letter names and sounds, visual and auditory blending, spelling. New York: Bureau of Publications, Teachers College, Columbia University, 1962.

Gilmore Oral Reading Test, new ed.

Grades 1–8. 20 minutes. Word accuracy, comprehension, and rate of oral reading. New York: Harcourt Brace Jovanovich, 1968.

Gray Oral Reading Test

Grades 1–16. Assesses reading on passages that range from preprimer to adult. Passages at each grade level have four literal questions to assess comprehension. Grade equivalent scores are based on (a) errors and (b) time to read passages. Indianapolis: Bobbs-Merrill, 1963.

Reading Miscue Inventory

Yetta Goodman and Carolyn Burke. Grades 1–12. Time varies. Qualitative and quantitative analyses of miscues, that is, of oral reading responses that depart from the expected (printed) responses on materials that are one grade level beyond the reader's level. Analysis of miscues according to sound, graphic, syntactic, and semantic similarity. Comprehension (immediate retelling) score for expository and narrative materials. Manual provides valuable suggestions for diagnosis and improvement. New York: Macmillan, 1972.

Spache Diagnostic Reading Scales, rev. ed.

Grades 1–8. Disabled readers, grades 9–12. 20–30 minutes. Word recognition-phonics. Oral and silent reading. Determines listening expectancy level. Monterey, Calif.: California Test Bureau/McGraw-Hill, 1963.

III. Criterion-Referenced Tests

Metropolitan Achievement Test

(See Survey Tests.)

Wisconsin Design for Reading Skill Development

Individual or group administered criterion-referenced tests for grades K–6. Six subtests: word attack, comprehension, study skills, self-directed reading, interpretive reading, and creative reading. Minneapolis: National Computer Systems, 1972.

IV. Subskill Tests

A. Group

Dolch Basic Sight Words Test

E. W. Dolch. The 220 Dolch Basic Sight Words consist mostly of high frequency words, accounting for 75 percent of words in primary grades and 50% of all words in adult reading materials, arranged in multiple choice form for group testing. Champaign, Ill.: Garrard, 1936.

B. Individual

Wide Range Achievement Test

J. F. Jastak and J. R. Jastak. Reading is individually administered; other subtests can be group administered. Level I, ages 5–11; Level II, ages 12–adult. About

15–30 minutes. Three subtests: (1) Reading: recognizing and naming letters; identifying words. (2) Spelling: copying; writing names, printing or writing from dictation. (3) Arithmetic: counting; reading numerals; oral and written computation. Austin, Texas: Guidance Testing Associates, 1978.

Clues to Reading Progress
In *Clue* magazine. Grades 2–6. Diagnostic and evaluative tests appear in the center of the magazine. The tests correlate with a criterion test score chart. Brief lessons that correlate with the tests and with cassette tapes are in the magazines. Tulsa, Okla.: Educational Progress Corp., P.O. Box 45663.

V. Proficiency or Functional Reading Tests (group tests)

Basic Skills Assessment Program (BSA)
High school level. This program assesses three areas entitled "reading," "a writer's skills," and "mathematics." The tasks in reading are categorized into roles of reading as a consumer (telephone directory), learner (newspaper, magazine, dictionary), citizen (tax forms, driver's license, law propaganda), and so forth, and the responses to the tasks are grouped into three types of comprehension: literal, inferential, and evaluative. A total score and item results are reported. The writer's skills are also grouped into roles similar to those in reading, such as writing a check and writing a letter to a bank; the results are classified into two categories: mechanics and effectiveness. Mathematics consists of two categories: computation and problem solving. Princeton, N.J.: Educational Testing Service, 1977.

Senior High Assessment of Reading Proficiency
Assesses ability to read to follow directions and to perform everyday reading tasks, such as reading a T.V. Guide, rent receipts, and utility bills. Monterey, Calif.: California Test Bureau/McGraw-Hill, 1975.

VI. Interest Tests (group tests)

San Diego Interest Inventory
Patrick Groff. San Diego, Calif.: Department of Education, San Diego County, 1961.

VII. Intelligence Tests
   A. Group
      California Test of Mental Maturity
      A 60–90 minute group intelligence test, grades K–16, yielding scores in logical reasoning, spatial relationships, numerical reasoning, verbal concepts, memory, language total, and nonlanguage total. Norms are in IQ, MA, and grade placement. Monterey, Calif.: California Test Bureau/McGraw-Hill.

      Otis Quick Scoring Mental Ability Tests
      Grades 1–16. Scores reported as MA and IQ. New York: Harcourt, Brace, Jovanovich, 1954.

   B. Individual
      Slosson Intelligence Test
      Individual test, ages 4–adult. 10–20 minutes. Hand scored. Aurora, N.Y.: Slosson Educational Publications, 1974.

      Stanford Binet Intelligence Scales (S-B)
      Administered and scored by a trained examiner. Ages 2–adult. Tests, such as vocabulary, memory, perception, problem solving, and inductive reasoning are grouped into age levels. Results reported as MA and IQ scores. Boston: Houghton Mifflin, 1973.

      Wechsler Adult Intelligence Scale (WAIS)
      Scored by a trained examiner. Ages 16–75. About 40–60 minutes. Performance, verbal, and total MA and IQ scores are derived. Verbal scores are based on subtests of information, comprehension, arithmetic, similarities, digit span, and vocabulary. Performance subtests are digit symbol, picture completion, block design, picture arrangement, and object assembly. New York: Psychological Corporation, 1935.

Wechsler Intelligence Scale for Children (WISC)
Scored by a trained examiner. Ages 5–15. 40–60 minutes. Performance, verbal, and total MA and IQ scores are derived. Verbal scale includes subtests of information, comprehension, arithmetic, similarities, vocabulary, digit span. Performance scale consists of subtests of picture completion, picture arrangement, block design, object assembly, mazes, and coding. New York: Psychological Corporation.

Glossary

Academic discipline: the formal and scholarly study of an area of content. For example, in social studies, some theorists believe that history and geography should be taught as separate entitites or disciplines. (ch. 12)

Accommodation: the process of adjusting to a new situation by changing behavior. In inservice education, teachers accommodate new teaching strategies by trying them out in class and eventually incorporating them into their general teaching style. (ch. 16)

Active comprehension: the process of students reading to find answers to their own questions. (ch. 4)

Adjunct questions: questions inserted within a text. (ch. 4)

Aesthetic criticism: the method of analyzing and evaluating literature that focuses on the literary work's structure and craft. (ch. 11)

Affectively alienated readers. Students who dislike reading. (ch. 15)

Alliteration: the repetition of initial consonants in a closely related sequence of words: e.g., sister Suzie spoke slowly and softly. (ch. 11)

Argumentation: the process of persuading the reader to accept a particular attitude or point of view, e.g., defending a social ideology, taking a stand on a current event, attacking or defending an individual. (ch. 7)

Assimilation: the process of relating a new situation to one's own current behavior patterns. In inservice education, teachers assimilate suggested teaching behaviors that are close to their own current behaviors. Therefore, in reeducating teachers, it is advisable to begin with introducing initially those teaching strategies that come closest to strategies the teachers may already be using. (ch. 16)

Associative law: When adding or multiplying numbers, you obtain the same result, regardless of the order of addition of the numbers or multiplication of the factors: e.g.
$$2 + (4+3) = (2+4) + 3,$$
$$2 \cdot (4 \cdot 3) = (2 \cdot 4) \cdot 3;$$
$$a + (b+c) = (a+b) + c,$$
$$a \cdot (b \cdot c) = (a \cdot b) \cdot c. \text{ (ch. 14)}$$

Assumptive teaching: teacher presumes students already have the knowledge that the teacher is supposed to provide. (ch. 2)

Attitude: a way of feeling, acting, or thinking. Teachers' attitudes vary on whether or not they should be teaching students reading or learning from text. (ch. 2)

Automaticity: the shift in processing a word from letter-by-letter to "chunking" the word or responding to the printed word with a whole-word response without going through any intermediate phonological processing and without conscious attention to the word. (ch. 16)

Behavioral objectives: statements of what the teacher would like the students to know and

and do as a result of a unit of instruction. (ch. 5)

Bottom-up and top-down processing: In bottom-up processing, the reader initiates operations from the level of sensations and progresses up to a conceptual system where the printed stimuli that have been processed are organized into concepts that interact with the reader's knowledge system and reasoning processes. In top-down processing, the reader uses knowledge and reasoning processes to direct attention to printed stimuli in a selective manner and to confirm the reader's expectations. (ch. 16)

Characterization: The author develops characters with dialogue and action. In studying literature, students learn to draw their own conclusions about a character by examining what the character thinks, says, does, and how the characters react to events. (ch. 11)

Clinical centers: centers operated by reading specialists who diagnose and teach readers (frequently severely retarded readers) on a one-to-one basis or in small groups. Emphasis is on complete, continual diagnosis. Clinical centers also frequently train reading specialists. (ch. 15)

Cloze technique: a procedure for determining the difficulty of a piece of text, relative to the reading ability level of the individual or group of students who are actually going to read the material. A passage of 250 words is taken from the text with each fifth word deleted. The student supplies the missing words. The percentage of correct words supplied indicates how difficult the passage is for the student. (ch. 8)

Colloquy: a discussion technique, whereby students supplement a symposium, a panel discussion, or a debate with a panel of outside experts who make themselves available for further information, clarification, or dilemma settlement. (ch. 9)

Commutative law: Addition or multiplication of two quantities can be in either order, e.g., $a + b = b + a, 2 + 3 = 3 + 2; a \times b = b \times a, 2 \times 3 = 3 \times 2$. (ch. 14)

Composing *vs.* copying: composing is the process of students using their own words to create a piece of writing, rather than copying, using the words of others. (ch. 7)

Comprehension: refers to a potential, a process, or product. In current usage, comprehension represents an interaction between the reader and the text. The reader brings to the text knowledge of the world, and the text provides information. The reader then can add knowlege to the text and, through processes of reasoning, arrive at products of thought, such as interpretations, generalizations and evaluations that go beyond those that are made in the text. (ch. 16)

Concept: an idea of something formed by mentally combining all its particular characteristics. A concept also has relationships with other concepts that are superordinate, co-equal, or subordinate (exemplars) in a mental hierarchy. (ch. 12; ch. 13; ch 16)

Concept technique: a multiple-text strategy in which students can choose materials to read from a large variety of texts related to a particular concept, topic, or theme. (ch. 9)

Content area deficient readers: readers whose weak background in the subject causes low speed and power of reading in a particular content area. (ch. 15)

Controlled discussion: discussion that occurs when students contribute information in a carefully planned, articulated and sequenced hierarchy, generally starting with lower order information and going on to higher order concept formation. (ch. 6)

Convoy method: the practice of operating the classroom according to the level and rate of progress of the slowest students who are frequently nonreaders. (ch. 1)

Creation in literature: that process whereby a student responds to text by developing an art-media project, a musical medley, original prose or poetry, pantomime, or dance. (ch. 11)

Cross-ability teaching: an able person teaching a less able one. (ch. 4)

Debate: a discussion technique whereby two teams of speakers present opposing views on a controversial issue. (ch. 9)

Defect: physical or physiological difficulty, such as a visual difficulty—astigmatism. (ch. 1)

Deficiency: inadequacy in skill development, such as the inability to identify printed words. (ch. 1)

Description: the process whereby students picture an event or situation in words, either spoken or written. (ch. 11)

Developmental reading program: a program that provides instruction in reading and learning from text to students of all abilities throughout the grades. (ch. 15)

Difference: mismatch between instruction and student capability or mode of learning. For example, some textbooks in certain content areas may be too difficult for some of the students. (ch. 1)

Directed Reading Activity (DRA): a single text strategy that uses an instructional dialogue between teacher and students as they read a selection together. It consists of five steps: (1) surveying the students' background, (2) building the students' background, (3) directing the students to read a text, (4) discussing the text with the students, and (5) engaging the students in follow-up activities that make use of the information they have read. (ch. 4)

Discrimination: the process of determining the unique features of a piece of literature or a type of literature. (ch. 11)

Discussion: the process of a group of individuals presenting different points of view and trying to solve the problem. (ch. 6)

Discussion clusters: small groups of students discussing, simultaneously, the same teacher-posed problem or different aspects of the teacher-posed problem. (ch. 6)

Disruption: emotional interference in reading and learning, such as anxiety over inability to achieve in school. (ch. 1)

Distributive law: Multiplication is distributive over addition. That is, when multiplying one factor by a sum of numbers you can multiply the factor by each number in the sum in any order:
$2 \cdot (3+4) = 2 \cdot 3 + 2 \cdot 4$, and $(3+4) \cdot 2 = 3 \cdot 2 + 4 \cdot 2$; or $a \cdot (b+c) = ab + ac$, $(b+c) \cdot a = ba + ca$. (ch. 14)

Drill theory: the theory of teaching mathematics, developed by Thorndike, in which students work repeated problems and are continually reinforced by their teachers with correct answers. (ch. 14)

Educationally underdeveloped readers: readers whose generally weak educational background causes low speed and power of reading in all content areas. (chapter 15)

Elliptical: characterized by the omission of key words, phrases, or information which the student supplies to gain meaning from text: e.g., "John paid attention, but his brother did not." or, "The cigarette . . . caused . . . the forest fire." (ch. 16)

Entry level test: a teacher-made instrument that assesses what information students have retained from prior coursework or experience that will be useful in forthcoming reading. (ch. 5)

Evaluation of literature: the process whereby a student determines the worth of a piece of literature by using preposed criteria. (ch. 11)

Expected reading range: A teacher can *expect* a range of ability to read and learn from text equal to two-thirds the average chronological age of the students within the teacher's classroom, if the students are a representative sample of their peer group. For example, a teacher of a tenth-grade history class can expect a ten-year range of ability if the class's average chronological age is fifteen years. However, the range may actually be wider or narrower, depending upon the representativeness of the individual class. (Ch. 3)

Exposition: explaining (in writing) a process, a point of view, an idea, or a philosophy. (ch. 7)

Extensive writing: a piece of lengthy writing that students do in response to long-term classroom activities, e.g., library reports, essay examinations. (ch. 7)

Fact: a statement that can be proved by the presence of observable evidence. (ch. 12)

Fluency level: the grade level of a passage in an informal reading inventory at which the reader can correctly answer 90 percent or more of the comprehension questions. (ch. 8)

Foreshadowing: a literary device whereby an author plants clues or hints about a major event which will occur later. For instance, an author may foreshadow a character's death from pneumonia by having the character say, early in the selection, "This cold will probably kill me!" (ch. 11)

Free discussion: discussion that is relatively unstructured and demands a minimum of teacher control, e.g., students speaking randomly on a controversial issue. (ch. 6)

Frustration level: the teacher-constructed test for a text or the grade level on an informal reading inventory at which the reader's comprehension drops below 70 percent. (ch. 8)

Functional reading level: the reading level a person needs in order to function on the job or in life. The term has no precise meaning, since no two individuals "function" in the same manner: college students *function* by having to read 16,000 pages of reference material a semester; a television repairman has to comprehend manuals written at the 14th grade level. (ch. 8)

Functional reading program: a reading center that teaches students how to read those materials that will affect their adult lives: prescription labels, job applications, insurance forms, drivers' manuals. (ch. 15)

Functional reading test: a comprehension test based on reading tasks that adults must do at home or work, such as, read and fill out rent receipts, tax forms, and job applications, or comprehend maps, cash register tapes, bank statements, TV guides, and utility bills. (ch. 15)

Generalization: a relationship between or among concepts. (ch. 13)

Generalization, in literature: the process whereby students apply what they have learned about one work of literature to the reading of another work. (ch. 11)

Generalization, in social studies: a cluster of related concepts. Generalizations provide a structure for analyzing and interpreting data: "During the renaissance, European rulers sought to extend their influence by exploring new continents." (ch. 12)

Gestalt: the practice of showing students the "whole" before teaching about the "parts." In arithmetic, students would be shown the entire multiplication tables before learning the individual combinations. (ch. 14)

Glosses: also referred to as *marginal glosses*. A single-text strategy in which the teacher supplements the text with explanatory marginal notes. (ch. 4)

Guides: The use of guides is a single-text strategy. Guides take the form of mimeographed or otherwise duplicated sheets that engage the students in discussion and writing activities aimed at helping them comprehend the text. (ch. 4)

Historical/biographical criticism: the method of analyzing and evaluating literature that focuses on the author's personal life and the contemporary world that may have influenced the writing. (ch. 11)

Holistic evaluation techniques: strategies for evaluating a piece of writing in its entirety. Two types of holistic strategies are popular: (1) general impression method and (2) analytical scale method. (ch. 7)

Humanistic criticism: the method of analyzing and evaluating literature that focuses on human values as they exist in the literature. (ch. 11)

Hypothesis: a tentative explanation, formed from limited observation of data, but proved or disproved by additional observation under controlled conditions that eliminate alternative explanations. (ch. 13)

Hypothesizing from data: forming explanations for given observations made under controlled conditions. (ch. 13)

Individual diagnosis: the process of determining an individual student's strengths and weaknesses in reading and learning from text and their causes. Formal diagnosis includes use of standardized, criterion-referenced, and individually administered tests. Informal diagnosis includes use of interviews and observation techniques; it supplements formal diagnosis. (ch. 15)

Individual differences: variations in ability among a group of students, e.g. the range of ability to read and learn from text within a school or classroom or any group of individuals. (ch. 3)

Individual reading "class": a reading acquisition class that low-ability students sometimes take in place of English. The materials are mostly from literature programs, with books of easy reading and high interest. Since the program enrolls low-ability students, it has the potential of stigmatizing the students in the same way as does the tracking system. (ch. 15)

Informal Reading Inventory: a teacher-constructed instrument that includes graded passages with comprehension questions after each to assess the reading level of the students. (ch. 8)

Inquiry: the technique of solving problems by careful examination, interpretation, and evaluation of evidence. (ch. 9)

Instructional level: those texts or teacher-constructed tests or passages on an informal reading inventory at which the reader attains 70 to 90 percent comprehension. (ch. 8)

Instructionally mismatched readers: readers whose low speed and low power can be attributed to an inability to comprehend the level of texts used in a given content area class: e.g., the student with a fifth-grade reading level enrolled in an English class that studies Shakespeare's plays. (ch. 15)

Interpretation: the process whereby students construct major premises and then use information in the text as minor premises to infer the meaning of the passage or text. (ch. 11)

Issue: a controversial event or idea. For example, some theorists believe that the various academic fields (history, geography, economics, etc.) in social studies shoud be integrated to focus on issues of current interest and importance: the role of government in our private lives. (ch. 12)

Language of mathematics: sounds, syntax, and semantics whose meaning is shared among members of a speech community, which are mobilized by mathematicians in response to mathematical symbols, operations, and problems. (ch. 14)

Layer-by-layer curriculum: Sometimes referred to as the "old math curriculum," the layer curriculum consisted of topics organized by grade levels: first grade, addition; fifth grade, fractions; etc. (ch. 14)

Learning from text: the ability to comprehend information in a text by using general infor-

mation, semantic and conceptual abilities, and reasoning processes in interaction with the text, and storing the resulting knowledge in long-term memory. (ch. 3)

Learning-from-text guide: a guide that directs the student to process information from the text using four levels of comprehension: (1) factual, (2) inferential, (3) generalized, and (4) evaluative. (ch. 4)

Learning to read: See *reading acquisition.*

Linguistically different readers: readers whose low speed and low power can be traced to language problems, specifically those students whose first language is not English and those students whose dialect varies from "standard" English. (ch. 15)

Literary criticism: writings of scholars that analyze and evaluate literature. (ch. 11)

Literary genres: literary types: the short story, poetry, novel, drama, nonfiction (ch. 11)

Logograph: the symbolic representation, in writing, of a number: e.g., 5, 3, 2, 8. (ch. 14)

LTD method: LTD stands for "learning through discussion." LTD is a nine-step plan that guides students through a close and careful examination of a text. (ch. 6)

Mainstreaming: refers to enrollment of handicapped children into regular classes for most of their school day. Technically stated: placing child into least restrictive educational environment. (ch. 2)

Mastery level: the point at which a student has acquired the skills necessary to perform a task. By sixth, seventh, and eight grade, most students have mastered reading acquisition skills. (Ch. 3)

Meaningful arithmetic: the technique of teaching students in such a way that they develop a quantitative hierarchy and an understanding of the relationships among numbers and arithmetic processes, rather than teaching students on the basis of teacher authority and rote memorization. (ch. 14)

Metalanguage: in mathematics, the *technical words* that are used to talk about the symbolic or object language: e.g., a + 4 = b can be described as an *equation* in which *a* is a *variable* to which a *constant* is *added* to obtain *values* indicated by *variable* b. (ch. 14)

Motivation: in literature, that which causes a character to act and feel in a certain way. (ch. 11)

Multi-faceted reading instruction: reading instruction given in a center that uses a variety of methods and media to instruct students, generally of low ability, to read and learn from text. Among the materials are games, puzzles, controlled readers, kits, self-instructional materials, listening booths. (ch. 15)

Narration: storytelling. Written forms of narration include jokes, anecdotes, tall tales, vignettes, and short stories. (ch. 7)

Narrow background readers: readers whose low speed and low power can be attributed primarily to having done little or no reading outside the classroom. (ch. 15)

Nonfiction: prose that is generally non-narrative, organized according to the development of ideas rather than a story line: e.g., essays, articles. (ch. 11)

Observation: the process of experiencing through the senses, and noting the resulting impressions. (ch. 13)

Overview guide: a reading guide that previews for the student the content of a particular text. It may take the form of a précis, a summary, an outline, or graphic aid, such as a diagram or chart. (ch. 4)

Panel discussion: a discussion technique whereby a group of three or more students stage a problem-solving situation before the class. The group members, working from a common outline of main points, interact with one another under the guidance of a chairperson who regulates the discussion. (ch. 9)

Paraphrasing: the process of translating a text into one's own words. (ch. 7)

Personal Reading Inventory: See Informal Reading Inventory. (ch. 8)

Physiologically handicapped readers: readers whose low speed and low power can be attributed to a physical defect: e.g., deafness, blindness. (ch. 15)

Postposed questions: questions given to a student at the end of a text passage. (ch. 4)

Power of reading: the performance level in comprehension a student attains when given a survey test that has comprehension items graduated in difficulty and that provides students with unlimted time to complete the text. (ch. 15)

Preposed questions: questions given to a student to guide the student's comprehension of a text before the student begins to read it. (ch. 4)

Prescriptive teaching: teacher explains instructional procedure in a step-by-step manner. (ch. 2)

Problem demonstration sequence: a method that textbook writers, especially in science and mathematics, use to show students how to do a problem in a step-by-step fashion. However, the sequence usually does not explicitly show the student how to manipulate the formulas, how to deal with synonyms in word problems, or how to transform grammatical syntax so that sequence in the word problem conforms to the sequence of symbols in the formula. (ch. 13)

Processes of literature: ways students respond to text, e.g., describing their feelings, or expressing a value preference for one story over another. (ch. 11)

Processes-of-reading guide: a reading guide that teaches the student, in a step-by-step manner, a specific reading or thinking skill. Processes-of-reading guides might emphasize such skills as cause and effect, chronological sequence, differentiating between fact and opinion, or locating main ideas. (ch. 4)

Proficiency reading test: a functional reading test, except that the proficiency test has a criterion score that a student must achieve in order to pass into a higher grade or to receive a graduation document, such as a high school diploma. (ch. 15)

Project method: a multiple text strategy whereby students generate questions for which they find the answers by engaging in reference reading. (ch. 9)

Psychosynchromeshing facility: the ability to mobilize the necessary content and processes to printed materials at the appropriate time and in the appropriate sequence. (ch. 15; ch. 16)

Quantitative hierarchy: sequence of mathematical operations, moving from most specific and concrete to most general and abstract: e.g., counting fifteen oranges, to adding fifteen 1's, to adding 5 plus 5 plus 5, to multiplying 5 by 3, to 3X equals 15, to ax = y. (ch. 14)

Quest: a sequence of questions, moving from lower order thinking to higher order thinking. In science, this instructional procedure is used to guide students from observation to conceptualization to generalization. (ch. 13)

Readability: the grade level difficulty of a particular text; the reading grade level a student would need to read and comprehend a particular text. (ch. 8)

Readability formula: a computational procedure for determining the grade level difficulty of a piece of text. (ch. 8)

Reading acquisition: the process of learning to read. It consists of integrating the use of language abilities to anticipate words with the application of acquired print-to-sound relationships. (ch. 3)

Reading age: a student's level of comprehension, as measured against a normative population. For example, a seven-year-old can be reading as well as an average ten-year-old, according to results on a standardized reading test. This student, then, would have a reading age of ten years. (ch. 3)

Reading Ease Formula: Flesch's mathematical procedure for computing the readability of a text by using the number of syllables per hundred words and the average number of words per sentence in a formula and computing the results. (ch. 8)

Reading Expectancy: a general term that refers to how well or to what level of achievement a student *should* perform on the basis of specific criteria; e.g., mental age, listening age, etc. (ch. 15)

Reading frequency: the amount of time an individual spends reading each day. (ch. 8)

Reading guides: materials that focus on teaching students skills necessary for them to read text. Reading guides consist of three types: overview guides, vocabulary guides, and processes-of-reading guides. (ch. 4)

Reading laboratory: a reading acquisition center, staffed by a reading teacher or reading specialist, which is equipped with all sorts of tests, kits, programed materials, booklets, exercises, apparatus, and self-instructional materials. Students work independently of

one another. The teacher functions as a consultant, helping individual students when they need it. (ch. 15)

Reading range: the distribution of abilities in reading and learning from text from the lowest to the highest performing student, within a school, a classroom, a school district, etc. (ch. 3)

Reading specialist: a specially trained teacher who functions in a school by (1) administering survey tests and classifying students in achievement categories in reading and learning from text, (2) diagnosing students, (3) teaching classes in content reading acquisition, (4) working with parents and teachers on an individual and group basis, (5) directing inservice education programs, (6) doing demonstration teaching. (ch. 15)

Reading to learn: See *learning from text.*

Recreational reading level: the reading level a person needs to comprehend leisure time reading materials, such as comic books, popular magazines, newspapers, etc. (ch. 8)

Reflexive writing: the writing that students do in response to their own thoughts and feelings, e.g., a poem, a diary entry, a social letter. (ch. 7)

Relation: the process of perceiving how elements within a single work of literature function together. (ch. 11)

Reliable: In education, a testing instrument is reliable when a group of individuals achieve similar or highly correlated scores on split-halves of a test or successive trials of the same test or equivalent tests. (ch. 2)

Reluctant readers: readers whose low speed and low power can be attributed to either (a) a poor attitude toward reading or (b) inadequate experience in reading and (c) lack of ability in reading which they might want to conceal. (ch. 15)

Reporting: oral or written communication of information in response to a question or longer assignment. (ch. 7)

Rhyme: a word or line whose last parts sound alike: e.g., *cat* and *bat;* My cousin Willy/Is very silly. (ch. 11)

Schools of criticism: ways of analyzing and evaluating literature. When a group of critics agree about how to analyze and evaluate literature, their views form a "school" of criticsm. (ch. 11)

Schoolwide reading program: instruction in reading and learning from text in three types of courses: (1) content reading acquisition classes, (2) introductory classes in reading and learning from text in content areas, and (3) classes throughout the school that teach students to read and learn from text in each content area. (ch. 15)

Scientific method: the experimental method, consisting of six steps: observation, hypothesis formation, establishing controlled conditions, testing the hypothesis, interpretation of data, and conclusion. (ch. 13)

SEER technique: an acronym for "Singer Eyeball Estimate of Readability." The technique involves matching a passage of unknown readability with a paragraph from a set of scaled paragraphs of known readability levels. (ch. 8)

Semicontrolled discussion: discussion that occurs when students exchange and integrate information for some future instructional purpose, e.g., discussing material from differing, but related, textbook assignments. (ch. 6)

SMSG: School Mathematics Group, a group of educational leaders and mathematicians who, with a large grant from the National Science Foundation, revised the traditional mathematics curriculum around "new" principles. (ch. 14)

Social promotion policy: custom of promoting one hundred percent of the students from one grade level to the next, regardless of their achievement levels. (ch. 1)

Spiral curriculum: the organization of course content around basic concepts and principles, taught at various nonsuccessive grade levels, but at increasing depth and difficulty, e.g., American history may be taught in grades 5, 8, and 11. (ch. 14)

SQ3R: a single-text strategy that directs students to *survey* a text, pose *questions*, *read* to find answers to their questions, *recite* answers to their questions, and then *review* the text to check their recitations. (ch. 4)

Standardized test: any test whose content is a sample drawn for a defined universe of content and whose table of norms is based on administration of the test with the same set of directions to a representative norm group, a sample of subjects drawn from a defined population. A student's performance on the test can then be interpreted by comparison with the results of the norm group. (ch. 3)

Story problems: mathematics problems stated in short narrative passages containing the numbers to substitute in the variables of a formula that can solve the stated problem: e.g., John brought 3 sandwiches, 6 cookies, and 9 carrot sticks to school in his lunch box. His friends, Fred and Tom, brought no lunch; so John divided his lunch equally among the boys. How much was John left with? Formula: $a/n = x$ where x = anyone's share, n = number of persons, and a = item to be divided. (ch. 14)

Strategy: (1) a method of modifying or supplementing a text or teaching students ways of processing information that will enable them to read and learn from a particular textbook. (2) a particular process or procedure for reaching a given goal. For example, a marginal gloss facilitates a student's reading and learning from text. (ch. 4)

Symbol: a literary device whereby an author has a concrete object represent an abstract idea. For example, in Paul Dunbar's poem, "We Wear the Mask," the mask represents the false front that black people have had to assume in order to survive. (ch. 11)

Symposium: a discussion technique that involves a group of two or more students reporting together to the class, each on separate aspects of the same problem. (ch. 9)

Taba's levels of thinking: a method of controlled discussion that proceeds in nine sequential levels. The levels are subdivided into four categories: (1) stating the facts or knowns or observations; (2) abstracting from information to form concepts; (3) interpreting, inferring from given information, forming generalizations among concepts; and (4) applying generalizations to new situations. (ch. 6)

Table of specifications: an evaluation grid indicating units of content (vertically arranged) and the process needed to achieve the content of a course (horizontally arranged). This grid is useful in evaluating a course's or an individual student's performance on a test against the table of specifications for the test. (ch. 13)

Task analysis: a description of the contents, processes, and sequence of acquisition that students must go through to attain the behavioral objectives the teacher has set. (ch. 5)

Text: printed material of any length. (ch. 1)

Texts: textbooks, books that students use in school. (ch. 1)

Theory: an explanation that usually involves a set of interrelated generalizations: e.g., "When a country engages in war, it begins to destroy its economy." (ch. 12)

Three-stage program: a program that provides instruction in reading and learning from text for three types of students: (1) students in the reading acquisition stage, (2) students who are reading only slightly below grade level, and (3) students reading at grade level who want to perform even better. All three types need instruction in how to interact with and learn from text. (ch. 15)

Topics and themes: methods of organizing literary works into units of study. *Topics* are ideas common among a group of literary works: *survival, courage,* and so forth. *Themes* are predicated statements: "The sur-

vival of the human race depends upon its knowledge of scientific law." (ch. 11)

Tracking: the practice of grouping students according to a single criterion, such as general intelligence or reading achievement, and keeping each group together for all its education, regardless of specific aptitudes or achievement of members of the group. (ch. 15)

Unstructured assignment: assignment that does not include suggestion(s) on how to do the task. (ch. 4)

Valuing in literature: explicating the importance of literature to one's own life. (ch. 11)

Valuing in social studies: expressing likes, dislikes; stressing, ignoring; treasuring or discarding ideas, attitudes, and beliefs. (ch. 12)

Vocabulary guide: materials containing technical or otherwise difficult words a student will encounter when reading a particular text. The guide teaches the students how to pronounce the words, where the words can be found in the text, and the contexts in which the words occur. The vocabulary guide is given to the students before the students read the text. (ch. 4)

Word-recognition deficient readers: readers whose low speed and low power can be attributed to inadequate knowledge and use of (a) print-to-sound relationships and/or (b) integration of these relationships with semantic and syntactic abilities. (ch. 15)

References

Aaron, Ira E. Reading in mathematics. *Journal of Reading*, 1965, *9*, 391–401.

Aiken, Lewis R., Jr. Language factors in mathematics. *Review of Educational Research*, 1972, *42*, No. 3, 359–385.

Algren, Nelson. He swung and he missed. In Robert C. Pooley, et al., eds., *Accent: U.S.A*. New York: Scott, Foresman and Company, 1965.

Allen, R. V. Grouping through learning centers. *Childhood Education*, 1968, *45*, 200–203.

Anderson, Richard C. Concretization and sentence learning. In H. Singer and R. B. Ruddell, eds., *Theoretical Models and Processes of Reading*. Newark, Del.: International Reading Association, 1976a.

Anderson, Richard C. Context, knowledge of the world, and language comprehension. Unpublished paper presented at the National Reading Conference, Georgia, December 1976b.

Anderson, Richard, Rand Spiro, and W. E. Montague, eds. *Schooling and the Acquisition of Knowledge*. Hillsdale, N.J.: Lawrence Erlbaum Associates, 1977.

Amstrong, Hugh. The relationship of the auditory and visual vocabularies of children. *Dissertation Abstracts*, 1953, *13*, 716.

Askov, Eunice N., Mary M. Dupuis, and Joyce W. Lee. Content Area Reading Project. Final Report, Project 09-6905, Division of Adult and Community Education, Pennsylvania Department of Education. University Park, Pa.: The Pennsylvania State University, 1977.

Athey, Irene. Research in the affective domain. In H. Singer and R. B. Ruddell, eds., *Theoretical Models and Processes of Reading*. Newark, Del.: International Reading Association, 1976.

Ausubel, David. The use of advance organizers in the learning and retention of meaningful verbal material. *Journal of Educational Psychology*, 1960, *51*, 267–272.

Ausubel, David. Some psychological aspects of the structure of knowledge. In S. Elam, ed., *Education and the Structure of Knowledge*. New York: Rand McNally, 1964.

Babbitt, Irving. *Literature and the American College*. Los Angeles: Gateway, 1956.

Balow, Bruce. The long term effects of remedial instruction. *The Reading Teacher*, 1965, *18*, 581–586.

Balow, Irving H. Does homogeneous grouping give homogeneous groups? *Elementary School Journal*, 1962, *63*, 28–32.

Balow, Irving H. The effects of homogeneous grouping on seventh grade arithmetic. *The Arithmetic Teacher*, 1964, *11* (3), 186–191.

Barrett, Thomas C. The Barrett taxonomy: Cognitive and affective dimensions of reading comprehension. In H. M. Robinson (ed.), *Sixty-Seventh Yearbook of the National Society for the Study of Education, Part II*. Chicago: University of Chicago Press, 1968.

Barrilleaux, Louis E. An experiment on multiple library sources as compared to the use of a basic textbook in junior high school science. *Journal of Experimental Education*, 1967, *35*, 27–35.

Barrington, Kaye and Irving Rogers. *Group Work in Secondary Schools and the Training of Teachers in Its Methods*. Gateshead: Oxford University Press, 1968.

Barron, Richard F. The use of vocabulary as an advance organizer. In Harold Herber and Peter Sanders, eds., *Research in Reading in the Content Areas: First Year Report.* Syracuse, New York: Syracuse University Press, 1969.

Bartecki, Jan. Activating the teaching process by group work. *International Review of Education,* 1965, *11,* 109–111.

Beez, W. V. Influence of biased psychological reports on teacher behavior and pupil performance. Unpublished doctoral dissertation, summarized in Samuel L. Guskin and Howard H. Specker, Education research in mental retardation. In Norman Ellis, ed., *International Review of Research on Mental Retardation,* Vol. 3. New York: Academic Press, 1968.

Belden, Bernard B. and Wayne D. Lee. Readability of biology textbooks and the reading ability of biology students. *School Sciences and Mathematics,* 1961, *61,* 689–693.

Berget, Ellsworth. Two methods of guiding the learning of a short story. In Harold L. Herber and Richard F. Barron, eds., *Research in Reading in the Content Areas: Second Year Report.* Syracuse University: Reading and Language Arts Center, 1973.

Bierce, Ambrose. An occurrence at Owl Creek Bridge. In Jay Cline, Ken Williams, Barbara Mahoney, and Kay Dziuk, eds., *Voices in Literature, Language, and Composition,* 4. Boston: Ginn and Company, 1969.

Blank, Joseph P. Sport's worst tragedy. In Jay Cline, Ken Williams, and Dan Donlan, eds., *Voices in Literature, Language, and Composition,* 2. Boston: Ginn and Company, 1969.

Bleich, David. *Readings and feelings: An introduction to subjective criticism.* Urbana, Ill.: National Council of Teachers of English, 1975.

Bloom, Benjamin S., et al. *Taxonomy of Educational Objectives: Handbook 1, Cognitive Domain.* New York: Longmans, Green and Co., 1956.

Bloom, Benjamin S. Mastery learning and its implications for curriculum development. In Elliot W. Eisner, ed., *Confronting Curriculum Reform.* Boston: Little, Brown, 1971.

Bond, Eva. *Reading and Ninth Grade Achievement.* New York: Bureau of Publications, Teachers College, Columbia University, 1938.

Bormuth, John R. Readability: A new approach. *Reading Research Quarterly,* 1966, *1,* 79–132.

Bormuth, John R. The cloze readability procedure. *Elementary English,* 1968, *45,* No. 4, 429–436.

Bormuth, John R., Julian Carr, John Manning, and David Pearson. Children's comprehension of between and within sentence syntactic structures. *Journal of Educational Psychology,* 1970, *61,* 349–351.

Bormuth, John R. Reading Literacy: Its definition and assessment. In John B. Carroll and Jeanne S. Chall, eds., *Toward a Literate Society.* New York: McGraw-Hill, 1975.

Boylan, Paul J., revisor. *Elements of Physics.* (Original authors: D. Lee Baker, Raymond B. Brownlee, Robert W. Fuller.) Boston: Allyn and Bacon, 1962.

Bradbury, Ray. *Fahrenheit 451.* New York: Ballantine, 1953.

Braddock, Richard, Richard Lloyd-Jones, and Lowell Schoer. *Research in Written Composition.* Urbana, Ill.: National Council of Teachers of English, 1963.

Brandwein, Paul, Elizabeth K. Cooper, Paul E. Blackwood, Elizabeth B. Hone, and Thomas P. Fraser. *Concepts in Science,* Third Edition. New York: Harcourt Brace Jovanovich, 1972.

Bransford, J. D. and J. J. Franks. Memory for syntactic form as a function of semantic context. *Journal of Experimental Psychology,* 1974, *103,* 1037–1039.

Bransford, John D. and Marcia Johnson. Contextual prerequisites for understanding: Some investigations of comprehension and recall. *Journal of Verbal Learning and Verbal Behavior,* 1972, *11,* 717–726.

Britton, James, Tony Burgess, Nancy Martin, Alex McLeod, and Harold Rosen. *The Development of Writing Abilities (11–18).* London: Macmillan, 1975.

Brownell, William A., et al. *Meaningful vs. Mechanical Learning: A Study in Grade III Subtraction.* Duke University Research Studies in Education, No. 3. Durham, N.C.: Duke University Press, 1949.

Brownell, William A. Rate, accuracy, and process in learning. In T. L. Harris and W. E. Schwahn, eds., *Selected Readings in the Learning Process.* New York: Oxford University Press, 1961.

Bruner, Jerome. *The Process of Education.* New York: Vintage, 1963.

Brunner, Regina Baron. Reading mathematical exposition. *Educational Research,* 1977, *18,* No. 1, 208–213.

Burmeister, Lou E. *Reading Strategies for Secondary School Teachers.* Reading, Mass.: Addison-Wesley, 1974.

Buros, Oscar K. *The Eighth Mental Measurements Yearbook.* Highland Park, N.J.: Gryphon Press, 1978.

Buswell, Guy T. Educational theory and the psychology of learning. *Journal of Educational Psychology*, 1956, *47*, 175–184.

Call, Russell and Real A. Wiggin, Reading and mathematics. Eugene D. Nichols, ed. *Mathematics Teacher*, 1966, *59*, 149–157.

Capps, L. R. Teaching mathematical concepts using language arts analogies. *Arithmetic Teacher*, 1970, *17*, 329–331.

Carlsen, G. Robert. *Books and the Teen-age Reader*. New York: Bantam, 1967.

Carlson, Thorsten R., ed. *Administrators and Reading*. New York: Harcourt Brace Jovanovich, 1972.

Carroll, John B. A model of school learning. *Teachers College Record*, 1963, *64*, 723–733.

Carroll, John B., Peter Davies, and Barry Richman. *American Heritage Word Frequency Book*. Boston: Houghton Mifflin, 1971.

Carter, Glenda S. and Ronald Simpson. Science and reading: A basic duo. *The Science Teacher*, 1978, *40*, 13–21.

Carver, Ronald. Improving Reading Comprehension, Final report. Washington, D.C.: American Institute for Research, 1974.

Caswell, Hollis S. and A. Wellesley Foshay. *Education in the Elementary School*, Second Edition. New York: American Book, 1950.

Chapin, Jone R., Raymond J. McHugh, and Richard E. Gross. *Quest for Liberty*. Palo Alto, Calif.: Field Educational Enterprises, 1971.

Chase, Clinton I. The position of certain variables in the prediction of problem solving in arithmetic. *Journal of Educational Research*, 1960, *54*, 9–14.

Chase, Clinton I. *Measurement for Educational Evaluation*, Second Edition. Reading, Mass.: Addison-Wesley, 1978.

Chomsky, Carolyn. Reading, writing, and phonology. *Harvard Educational Review*, 1970, *40*, 287–309, 314.

Chomsky, Carolyn. After decoding: What? *Language Arts*, 1976, *53*, 3, 288–297.

Ciardi, John and Miller Williams. *How Does a Poem Mean?* Boston: Houghton Mifflin, 1975.

Clark, Leonard H. *Teaching Social Studies in Secondary Schools: A Handbook*. New York: Macmillan, 1973.

Clark, Leonard H. and Irving S. Starr. *Secondary School Teaching Methods*. New York: Macmillan, 1976.

Coleman, James. The concept of equality of educational opportunity. *Harvard Educational Review*, 1968, *38*, 7–22.

Collier, Calhoun C. and Lois A. Redmond. Are you teaching kids to read mathematics? *The Reading Teacher*, 1974, *27*, 804–808.

Conant, James B. *The American High School Today*. New York: McGraw-Hill, 1959.

Connell, Richard. The most dangerous game. In Inglis, et al, eds., *Adventures in American Literature*. New York: Harcourt Brace and World, 1953.

Cook, Walter W. The functions of measurement in the facilitation of learning. In E. F. Lindquist, ed., *Educational Measurement*. Washington, D.C.: American Council on Education, 1951.

Cooper, Charles R. and Alan C. Purves. *A Guide to Evaluation*. Lexington, Mass.: Ginn and Company, 1973.

Cooper, Charles R. and Lee Odell. *Evaluating writing: describing, measuring, judging*. Urbana, Ill.: National Council of Teachers of English, 1977.

Corey, Noble B. The use of rewritten science materials in ninth grade biology. *Journal of Research in Science Teaching*, 1977, *14*, No. 2, 97–103.

Cronbach, Lee J. Comments on mastery learning and its implications for curricular development. In E. Eisner, ed., *Confronting Curriculum Reform*. Boston: Little, Brown, 1971.

Dale, Edgar and Jeanne Chall. A formula for predicting readability. *Educational Research Bulletin*, February 18, 1948, *27*, 37–54.

Davis, Frederick B. Research in comprehension in reading. *Reading Research Quarterly*, 1968, *3*, 499–545.

deCharms, R. Personal causation training in the schools. *Journal of Applied Social Psychology*, 1972, *2*, 95–113.

DeMott, Benjamin. The math wars. In Robert W. Heath, ed., *New Curricula*. New York: Harper & Row, 1964.

Denburg, Susan. The interaction of picture and print in reading instruction. Unpublished doctoral dissertation, University of Toronto, 1975.

Devine, Thomas. What does research in reading reveal about materials for teaching reading? *English Journal*, 1969, *58*, 847–857.

Dillner, Harriet. The effectiveness of a cross-age tutoring design in teaching remedial reading in the secondary schools. *Dissertation Abstracts*, 1971, 6075.

Dolciani, Mary P. and William Wooton. *Book One: Modern Algebra: Structure and Method*, Revised Edition. Boston: Houghton Mifflin, 1973.

Donlan, Dan. The negative image of women in children's literature. *Elementary English*, 1972, *50*, 604–611.

Donlan, Dan. Implications of elementary school practice on small group instruction. *Arizona English Bulletin*, 1973, *15*, 82–86.

Donlan, Dan. In the classroom: Nonverbal responses. *California English*, 1974, *10*, 14.

Donlan, Dan. Multiple text programs in literature. *Journal of Reading*. 1976, *19*, 312–319.

Dunbar, Paul Laurence. We wear the mask. In Arna Bontemps, ed., *Anthology of American Negro Poetry*. New York: Hill and Wang, 1963.

Durkin, Dolores. *Children Who Read Early*. Columbia University: Teachers College Press, 1964.

Durrell, Donald D. *Improvement of Basic Reading Abilities*. New York: World Book, 1940.

Earle, Richard A. Use of the structured overview in mathematics classes. In Harold L. Herber and Peter L. Sanders, eds., *Research in Reading in the Content Areas: First Year Report*. Syracuse University: Reading and Language Arts Center, 1969a.

Earle, Richard A. Developing and using study guides. In Harold L. Herber and Peter L. Sanders, eds., *Research in Reading in the Content Areas: First Year Report*. Syracuse University: Reading and Language Arts Center, 1969b.

Earle, Richard A. *Teaching Reading and Mathematics*. Reading Aids Series. Newark, Del.: International Reading Association, 1976.

Early, Margaret. What does research in reading reveal about successful reading programs? *English Journal*, 1969, *58*, 368–85.

Earp, N. Wesley. Procedures for teaching reading in mathematics. *The Arithmetic Teacher*, 1970, *17*, 575–579.

Educational Testing Service. *An ETS Information Report: Basic Skills Around the Nation*. February 1977.

Ehman, Lee, Howard Mehlinger and John Patrick. *Toward Effective Instruction in Secondary Social Studies*. Boston: Houghton Mifflin, 1974.

Emig, Janet. *The Composing Processes of Twelfth Graders*. Urbana, Ill.: National Council of Teachers of English, 1971.

Estes, Thomas H. A scale to measure attitudes toward reading. *Journal of Reading*, 1971, *15*, 135–138.

Estes, Thomas H. Guiding reading in social studies. In Harold L. Herber and Richard F. Barron, eds., *Research in Reading in the Content Areas: Second Year Report*. Syracuse University: Reading and Language Arts Center, 1973.

Estes, Thomas H., Daniel C. Mills, and Richard F. Barron. Three methods of introducing students to a reading-learning task in two content subjects. In Harold L. Herber and Peter L. Sanders, eds., *Research in Reading in the Content Areas: First Year Report*. Syracuse University: Reading and Language Arts Center, 1969.

Estes, Thomas H. and Dorothy Piercey. Secondary reading requirements: A report on the states. *Journal of Reading*, 1973, *17*, 20–24.

Evans, Howard M. Remedial reading in secondary schools — still a matter of faith. *Journal of Reading*, 1972, *16*, 111–114.

Evans, K. M. Group methods. *Education Research*, 1966, *9*, 44–50.

Fader, Daniel. *The New Hooked on Books*. Berkeley: Berkeley Publishing Co., 1976.

Fay, Leo. Reading study skills: Math and science. In J. A. Figurel, ed., *Reading and Inquiry*. Newark, Del.: International Reading Association, 1965.

Feeman, George F. Reading and mathematics. *The Arithmetic Teacher*, 1973, *20*, 523–529.

Fidel, Estelle A. and Toby M. Berger, eds. *Senior High School Library Catalog*, Tenth Edition. New York: H. W. Wilson Co., 1972. Annual Supplements.

Fidel, Estelle A. and Gary L. Bogart, eds. *Junior High School Library Catalog*, Second Edition. New York: H. W. Wilson Co., 1970. Annual Supplements.

Fillmore, Charles J. The case for case. In E. Back and R. G. Harms, eds., *Universals in Linguistic Theory*. New York: Holt, Rinehart & Winston, 1968.

Flanders, Ned. *Teaching with Groups*. Minneapolis: Burgess Publishing Co., 1954.

Flesch, Rudolph F. *The Art of Readable Writing*. New York: Harper & Row, 1949.

Forester, Jean. Group work in colleges. *English Language Teaching*, 1969, *21*, 19–24.

Fraenkel, Jack R. *Helping Students Think and Value*. Englewood Cliffs, N.J.: Prentice-Hall, Inc. 1973.

Frase, Lawrence T. Learning from prose material: Length of passage, knowledge of results, and position of questions. *Journal of Educational Psychology*, 1967, *58*, 266–272.

Frase, Lawrence T. Effect of question location, pacing, and mode on retention of prose material. *Journal of Educational Psychology*, 1968a, *59*, 244–249.

Frase, Lawrence T. Some data concerning the mathemagenic hypothesis. *American Educational Research Journal*, 1968b, *5*, 181–189.

Frase, Lawrence T. Paragraph organization of written materials: The influence of conceptual clustering upon the level and organization of recall. *Journal of Educational Psychology*, 1969a, *60*, 394–401.

Frase, Lawrence T. Structural analysis of the knowledge that results from thinking about text. *Journal* of *Educational Psychology Monograph*, 1969b, *60*, (6).

Fredericksen, Carl H. Effect of talk-induced cognitive operations on comprehension and memory processes. In John B. Carroll and Roy O. Freedle, eds., *Language Comprehension and the Acquisition of Knowledge*. Washington, D.C.: V. H. Winston, 1972.

Fredericksen, Carl H. Discourse comprehension and early reading. In Lauren Resnick and Phyllis Weaver, eds., Pittsburgh Conference on Reading, May 12–14, 1976. Proceedings to be published in 1980.

Freed, Barbara. Secondary reading — state of the art. *Journal of Reading*, 1973, *17*, 195–201.

Fry, Edward. A readability formula that saves time. *Journal of Reading*, 1968, *11*, 513–16, 575–78.

Fry, Edward B. Fry's readability graph: Clarifications, validity, and extension to level 17. *Journal of Reading*, 1977, *21*, 242–252.

Gagné, Robert M. The acquisition of knowledge. *Psychological Review*. 1962, *69*, 355–65.

Gans, Roma. A study of critical reading comprehension in the intermediate grades. *Teachers College Contributions to Education*, No. 811, 1940.

Gates, Arthur I. An experimental and statistical study of reading and reading tests. *Journal of Educational Psychology*, 1921, *12*, 303–314.

Gates, Arthur I. Vocabulary control in basal reading material. *Reading Teacher*, 1961, *15*, 81–85.

Gates, Arthur I. and Guy L. Bond. Reading readiness: a study of factors determining success and failure in beginning reading. *Teachers College Record*, 1936, *37*, 679–685.

Gibson, Eleanor. Learning to read. In H. Singer and R. B. Ruddell, eds., *Theoretical Models and Processes of Reading*. Newark, Del.: International Reading Association, 1976.

Gibson, Eleanor J. and Harry Levin. *The Psychology of Reading*. Cambridge, Mass.: MIT Press, 1975.

Gilbert, Doris Wilcox. How well do you READ? *California Monthly*, Alumni magazine of the University of California, Berkeley, October 1955.

Gilbert, Doris. *Power and Speed in Reading*. Englewood Cliffs, N.J.: Prentice-Hall, 1956.

Glaser, Robert. Psychology and instructional technology. In R. Glasser, ed., *Training Research and Education*. Pittsburgh: Pittsburgh Press, 1962.

Gleason, H. A., Jr. *An Introduction to Descriptive Linguistics*, rev. ed. New York: Holt, Rinehart & Winston, 1961.

Goodman, Kenneth S. Behind the eye: What happens in reading. In H. Singer and R. B. Ruddell, eds.,

Theoretical Models and Processes of Reading. Newark, Del.: International Reading Association, 1976.

Guest, Anna. Beauty is truth. In Jay Cline and Ken Williams, eds., *Voices in Literature, Language, and Composition, 3*. Boston: Ginn and Company, 1969.

Gundlach, Bernard H. *The Laidlaw Glossary of Arithmetical-Mathematical Terms*. River Forest, Ill.: Laidlaw, 1961.

Guszak, Frank J. Teacher questioning and reading. *Reading Teacher*, 1967, *21*, 227–234.

Guthrie, John T. Models of reading and reading disability. *Journal of Educational Psychology*, 1973, *65*, 9–18.

Guthrie, John T. Research: Context and memory. *Journal of Reading*, 1978, *22*, 266–268.

Hafner, Lawrence E. *Developmental Reading in Middle and Secondary Schools: Foundations, Strategies, and Skills for Teaching*. New York: Macmillan, 1977.

Harlstorne, Nathaniel, ed. News of the basic skills assessment program. *Educational Testing Service*. Princeton, N.J.: 1977, *1*, No. 2.

Harris, Albert J. *How to Increase Reading Ability*, 5th ed. New York: McKay, 1970.

Harris, Albert J. and Edward R. Sipay. *How to Increase Reading Ability*, 6th ed. New York: McKay, 1975.

Harris, Louis, and Associates. Survival literacy study. *Congressional Record*, 1970, November 18, E9719-9723.

Hater, Mary Ann, Robert B. Kane, and Mary Ann Byrne. Building reading skills in the mathematics class. *The Arithmetic Teacher*, 1974, *21*, 663–668.

Heath, Robert W., ed. *New Curricula*. New York: Harper & Row, 1964.

Heller, Jack H. Learning from prose text: Effects of readability level, inserted question difficulty, and individual differences. *Journal of Educational Psychology*, 1974, *66*, 202–211.

Herber, Harold L. *Teaching Reading in Content Areas*. Englewood Cliffs, N.J.: Prentice-Hall, 1970a.

Herber, Harold. Reading in content areas: A district develops its own personnel. *Journal of Reading*, 1970b, *13*, 587–592.

Herber, Harold, consultant. *Scholastic's GO: Reading in the Content Areas*. Englewood Cliffs, N.J.: Scholastic Book Services, 1976.

Herber, Harold. *Teaching Reading in Content Areas*, Second Edition. Englewood Cliffs, N.J.: Prentice-Hall, 1978.

Herber, Harold and Richard F. Barron, eds. *Research in Reading in the Content Areas: Second Year Report.* Syracuse University: Reading and Language Arts Center, 1973.

Herber, Harold and P. L. Sanders, eds. *Research in Reading in the Content Areas: First Year Report.* Syracuse University: Reading and Language Arts Center, 1969.

Hersey, John. *Hiroshima.* New York: Knopf, 1946.

Hilgard, Ernest and Gordon Bower. *Theories of Learning,* 4th ed. New York: Appleton-Century-Crofts, 1975.

Hill, Walter. Characteristics of secondary reading: 1940-1970. In Frank P. Greene, ed., *Twentieth Yearbook of the National Reading Conference,* 1971.

Hill, William. *Learning through Discussion.* Beverly Hills, Calif.: Sage Publications, 1969.

Hobson *v.* Hansen, 269 F. Supp. 401 (DDC 1967).

Holmes, Jack A. Factors underlying major reading disabilities at the college level. *Genetic Psychology Monographs,* 1954, *49,* 3–95.

Holmes, Jack A. Basic assumptions underlying the substrata-factor theory. *Reading Research Quarterly,* 1965, *1,* 5–27.

Holmes, Jack A. and Harry Singer. *The Substrata-Factor Theory: Substrata-Factor Differences Underlying Reading Ability in Known Groups.* U.S. Office of Education, Final Report No. 538, 1961.

Holmes, Jack A. and Harry Singer. *Speed and Power of Reading in High School.* U.S. Government Printing Office, Cooperative Research Monograph No. 14, Superintendent of Documents Catalog No. FS 5.230:30016, 1966.

Hunkins, Francis P. *Involving Students in Questioning.* Boston: Allyn and Bacon, 1976.

Inhelder, B. and Jean Piaget. *The Growth of Logical Thinking from Childhood to Adolescence.* New York: Basic Books, 1958.

James, Glenn and Robert C. James. *Mathematics Dictionary.* Princeton, N.J.: D. Van Nostrand, 1959.

Jastak, J. F. and J. R. Jastak. *Wide Range Achievement Test (WRAT).* Austin, Texas: Guidance Testing Associates, 1965.

Jencks, Christopher S. Effects of high schools on their students. *Harvard Educational Review,* 1975, *45,* 273–324.

Johnson, Harry C. The effect of instruction in mathematical vocabulary upon problem solving in arithmetic. *Journal of Educational Research,* 1944, *38,* 2, 97–110.

Johnson, Osa. Filming a cannibal chief. In Guy Wagner, Gladys Person, and Lillian Wilcox, eds.,

Reading Skill Builder, Level VI, Part I, Pleasantville, N.Y.: Reader's Digest, 1950.

Judd, Charles and Guy T. Buswell. *Silent Reading: A Study of the Various Types.* Supplementary Educational Monographs, No. 23. Chicago: University of Chicago Press, 1922.

Kelley, J. Effectiveness of a performance contracting program on reading and mathematics relative to educationally deprived secondary students. *Dissertation Abstracts,* 1973, 4567a.

Kenworthy, Leonard S. *Social Studies for the 70's.* Lexington, Mass.: Xerox Publishing Company, 1973.

Keyes, Daniel. Flowers for Algernon. In Jay Cline, Ken Williams, Barbara Mahoney, and Kay Dziuk, eds., *Voices in Literature, Language, and Composition, 4.* Boston: Ginn and Company, 1969.

Kirby, Dan and Tom Liner. *Inside Out: Developmental Strategies for Teaching Writing.* Rochelle Park, N.J.: Hayden Book Co., 1980.

Kintsch, Walter. *The Representation of Meaning in Memory.* Hillsdale, N.J.: Laurence Erlbaum Associates, 1974.

Kintsch, Walter and Teun A. van Dijk. Toward a model of text comprehension and production. *Psychological Review,* 1978, *85,* 363–394.

Klare, George R. *The Measurement of Readability.* Ames, Iowa: The Iowa State University Press, 1963.

Klare, George R. Assessing readability. *Reading Research Quarterly,* 1974–1975, *10,* 1, 62–102.

Knight, Lester N. and Charles H. Hargis. Math language ability and its relationship to reading in math. *Language Arts,* 1977, *54,* 4, 423–428.

Knowles, John. *A Separate Peace.* New York: Bantam, 1959.

Kohlberg, Laurence. The child as moral philosopher. *Psychology Today,* 1968, *2,* 25–30.

Krug, Edward A. *The Secondary School Curriculum.* New York: Harper & Row, 1960.

LaBerge, David and S. Jay Samuels. Toward a theory of automatic information processing in reading. In H. Singer and R. B. Ruddell, eds., *Theoretical Models and Processes of Reading.* Newark, Del.: International Reading Association, 1976.

Lee, Dorris M. Do we group in an individualized program? *Childhood Education,* 1968, 45, 197–199.

Lees, Fred. Mathematics and reading. *Journal of Reading,* 1976, *19,* 621–626.

Levin, Joel R. Comprehending what we read: An outsider looks in. In H. Singer and R. B. Ruddell, eds., *Theoretical Models and Processes of Reading.* Newark, Del.: International Reading Association, 1976.

Lindille, W. J. The Effects of Syntax and Vocabulary upon the Difficulty of Verbal Arithmetic Problems with Fourth Grade Students. Doctoral dissertation, Indiana University. Ann Arbor, Mich.: University Microfilms, 1970, No. 70-7957 (*DA* 30A:4310, April 1970).

Litsey, David M. Small-group training and the English classroom. *English Journal*, 1968, *58*, 920–927.

Lovell, K., E. Johnson, and D. Platts. A further study of the educational progress of children who had remedial instruction. *British Journal of Educational Psychology*, 1963, *33*, 3–9.

McCallister, James M. *Remedial and Corrective Instruction in Reading*. New York: Appleton, 1936.

McCullough, Constance M. What teachers should know about language and thought. In R. Hodges and R. Rudorf, eds., *Learning to Read*. New York: Houghton Mifflin, 1971, 202–215.

McLaughlin, G. Harry. SMOG grading — A new readability formula. *Journal of Reading*, 1969, *12*, 639–646.

McLean, Harvard W. Models for effective groupwork. *Elementary School Journal*, 1967, *67*, 271–275.

MacMillan, Donald, Reginald Jones, and Greg Aloia. The mentally retarded label: A theoretical analysis and review of research. *American Journal of Mental Deficiency*, 1974, *79*, 241–261.

Mager, Robert F. *Preparing Instructional Objectives for Programmed Instruction*. Palo Alto, Calif.: Fearon Publishers, Inc., 1962.

Mallinson, George G., Harold E. Sturm, and Lois M. Mallinson. The reading difficulty of textbooks for high school physics. *Science Education*, 1952, *36*, 19–23.

Marks, C. B., M. J. Doctorow, and M. C. Wittrock. Word frequency and reading comprehension. *Journal of Educational Psychology*, 1974, *67*, 259–262.

Marshall, Nancy. The Structure of Semantic Memory for Text. Unpublished dissertation, Cornell University, 1976.

Mauldin, Bill. *Up Front*. New York: Norton, 1968.

Merriam-Webster. *Webster's Seventh New Collegiate Dictionary*. Springfield, Mass.: G. & C. Merriam Company, 1963.

Moffett, James. *A Student-Centered Language Arts Curriculum, Grades K–13: A Handbook for Teachers*. Boston: Houghton Mifflin, 1968.

Montague, William E. and John F. Carter. Vividness of imagery in reading connected discourse. *Journal of Educational Psychology*, 1973, *58*, 707–718.

Moore, Walter. About reading in the content fields. *English Journal*, 1969, *58*, 707–718.

Morgan, Ashley, Stanley Rachelson, and Baird Lloyd. Science activities as contributors to development of reading skills in first grade students. *Science Education*, 1977, *61*, 2, 135–144.

Moss, John. *Patterns of Isolation in English Canadian Fiction*. Toronto: McClelland and Stewart, 1974.

Murphy, Helen and Donald D. Durrell. *Reading Readiness Analysis*. New York: Harcourt Brace Jovanovich, 1965.

National Council for the Social Studies. *Guide to reading for social studies teachers*. Jonathan C. McLendon, ed. Bulletin 46. Washington, D.C.: National Council for the Social Studies, 1973.

Norwin, William W. Some practices in grouping. *Childhood Education*, 1968, *45*, 189–196.

Nyquist, Jody L. Grouping other than ability. *English Journal*, 1968, *57*, 340–344.

O'Donnell, Mabel and J. Louis Cooper. *The Harper & Row Basic Reading Program: How to Read in the Subject Matter Areas, Strand II*. New York: Harper & Row, 1963.

O'Hare, Frank. *Sentence Combining: Improving Student Writing Without Formal Grammar Instruction*. Urbana, Ill.: National Council of Teachers of English, 1972.

Otto, Wayne and Richard Smith. Junior and senior high school teachers' attitudes toward teaching reading in the content areas. In George B. Schick and Merrill M. May, eds., *The Psychology of Reading Behavior*. National Reading Conference Yearbook, 1969, 10, 49–54.

Paivio, A. Mental imagery in associative learning and memory. *Psychological Review*, 1969, *76*, 241–263.

Pearson, P. David. The effects of grammatical complexity on children's comprehension, recall, and conception of certain semantic relations. *Reading Research Quarterly*, 1974–1975, *10* (2), 155–192.

Pearson, P. David and Dale Johnson. *Teaching Reading Comprehension*. New York: Holt, Rinehart & Winston, 1978.

Petracca, Joseph. Four eyes. In Jay Cline, Ken Williams, and Dan Donlan, eds., *Voices in Literature, Language, and Composition, 3*. Boston: Ginn and Company, 1969.

Pichert, J. W. and R. C. Anderson. Taking different perspectives on a story. Technical Report No. 14. University of Illinois at Urbana–Champaign: Center for the Study of Reading, 1976.

Pooley, Robert C., Lillian Z. White, Edmund J. Farrell, and Joseph Mersand. *Exploring Life through Literature*. Glenview, Ill.: Scott, Foresman and Company, 1968.

Powell, William R. Validity of the IRI reading levels. *Elementary English*, 1971, *48* (6), 637–642.

Pribnow, Jack R. Why Johnny can't read word problems. *School Science and Mathematics,* 1969, *69,* 591–598.

Pyle, Ernie, *Brave Men.* New York: Holt, Rinehart & Winston, 1943.

Rand, John M. and Franklyn O. Taylor. Why group? *Childhood Education,* 1968, *45,* 187–188.

Rasco, Ronald W., Robert D. Tennyson, and Richard C. Boutwell. Imagery instructions and drawings in learning prose. *Journal of Educational Psychology,* 1975, *67,* 188–192.

Resnick, Lauren B. and Isabelle L. Beck. Designing instruction in reading: Interaction of theory and practice. In John T. Guthrie, ed., *Aspects of Reading Acquisition.* Baltimore: The Johns Hopkins University Press, 1974.

Riley, James D. and Andrew B. Patchman. Reading mathematical word problems: Telling them how to do it. *Journal of Reading,* 1978, *21,* 531–534.

Robinson, Francis P. Study skills for superior students in secondary school. *The Reading Teacher,* 1961, *15,* 29–33.

Robinson, Francis P. and Prudence Hall. Studies of higher-level reading abilities. *Journal of Educational Psychology,* 1941, *32,* 445–451.

Robinson, H. Alan. *Teaching Reading and Study Strategies: Content Areas.* Boston: Allyn and Bacon, 1975.

Rosenthal, Ted L., Barry J. Zimmerman, and Kathleen Durning. Observationally induced changes in children's interrogative classes. *Journal of Educational Psychology,* 1970, *16,* 681–688.

Rosten, Leo. Mr. KAPLAN, the comparative, and the superlative. In Cline, et al., eds., *Voices in Literature, Language and Composition, 2.* Boston: Ginn and Company 1969.

Rothkopf, Ernest Z. Learning from written instructive materials: An exploration of the control of inspection behavior by test-like events. *American Educational Research Journal,* 1966, *3,* 241–249.

Rothkopf, Ernest Z. Writing to teach and reading to learn: A perspective on the psychology of written instruction. In N. L. Gage (ed.), *The Psychology of Teaching Methods,* The Seventy-Fifth Yearbook of the National Society for the Study of Education, Part I. Chicago: University of Chicago Press, 1976.

Rothkopf, Ernest Z. and E. E. Bisbicos. Selective facilitative effects of interspersed questions on learning from written materials. *Journal of Educational Psychology,* 1967, *58,* 56–61.

Ruddell, Robert B. Effect of the similarity of oral and written patterns of language structure on reading comprehension. *Elementary English,* 1965, *42,* 403–410.

Ruddell, Robert B. *Reading-Language Instruction: Innovative Practices.* Englewood Cliffs, N.J.: Prentice-Hall, 1974.

Ruddell, Robert B. Language acquisition and the reading process. In H. Singer and R. B. Ruddell, eds., *Theoretical Models and Processes of Reading.* Newark, Del.: International Reading Association, 1976.

Ruddell, Robert B. and Arthur C. Williams. A Research Investigation of a Literary Teaching Model: Project Delta. Final Report to U.S. Department of Health, Education, and Welfare, Office of Education, EPDA Project No. 005262. Berkeley, Calif.: School of Education, 1972 (Multilith).

Rumelhart, David E. *Toward an Interactive Model of Reading.* University of California, San Diego: Center for Human Information Processing, 1976.

Rumelhart, D. E. Understanding and summarizing brief stories. In D. LaBerge and S. J. Samuels, eds., *Basic Processes in Reading: Perception and Comprehension.* Hillsdale, N.J.: Lawrence Erlbaum Associates, 1977.

Rupley, W. H. ERIC/RCS: Secondary reading materials. *Journal of Reading,* 1973, *17,* 252–254.

Russell, David. *Children's Thinking.* Boston: Ginn and Company, 1958.

Russell, David H. and Henry Fea. Research on teaching reading. In Nathan Gage, ed., *Handbook of Research on Teaching.* Chicago: Rand McNally, 1963.

Ryan, F. L. *Exemplars for the New Social Studies.* Englewood Cliffs, N.J.: Prentice-Hall, 1971.

Ryan, Frank and R. Wheeler. Using the textbook as a source of inquiry. *Instructor,* 1974.

Ryan, Margaret. *Teaching the Novel in Paperback.* New York: Macmillan, 1963.

Salinger, J. D. *The Catcher in the Rye.* Boston: Little, Brown, 1951.

Samuels, S. Jay. Attentional processes in reading: The effect of pictures on the acquisition of reading responses. *Journal of Educational Psychology,* 1967, *58,* 337–342.

Samuels, S. Jay. Effect on word associations on reading speed, recall, and guessing behavior on tests. *Journal of Educational Psychology,* 59, 1968, 12–15.

Samuels, S. Jay. Success and failure in learning to read: A critique of the research. In F. Davis, ed., *The Literature of Research in Reading with Emphasis on Models.* New Brunswick, N.J.: Rutgers University, 1971.

Samuels, S. Jay. Modes of word recognition. In H. Singer and R. B. Ruddell, eds., *Theoretical Models and Processes of Reading.* Newark, Del.: International Reading Association, 1976.

Samuels, S. Jay. Word Recognition: Letter-by-Letter or Chunk — Resolved? Paper presented at the National Reading Conference, New Orleans, December 2, 1977.

Samuels, S. Jay. The method of repeated reading. *The Reading Teacher,* 1979, *39,* 403–404.

Sax, G. and J. R. Ottina. The arithmetic achievement of pupils differing in school experience. *California Journal of Educational Research,* 1958, *9,* 15–19.

Schank, R. C. and R. P. Abelson. *Scripts, Plans, Goals and Understanding.* Hillsdale, N.J.: Lawrence Erlbaum Associates, 1977.

Schleich, Miriam. Groundwork for better reading in the content areas. *Journal of Reading,* 1971, *15,* 119–126.

Schnabel, Ernst. *Anne Frank, A Portrait in Courage.* New York: Harcourt Brace, 1958.

Scholastic Literature Units. Series 5100. New York: Scholastic Book Services, 1970.

Selman, Elsie M. The school that discovered silence is not golden. *Instructor,* 1968, *78,* 117, and 140.

Sharon, Amiel T. What do adults read? *Reading Research Quarterly,* 1973–74, *9* (1), 148–169.

Shavelson, Richard J., David C. Berliner, Michael M. Ravitch, and David Loeding. Effects of position and type of question on learning from prose material: Interaction of treatments with individual differences. *Journal of Educational Psychology,* 1974, *66,* 40–48.

Shepherd, David L. *Comprehensive High School Methods,* Columbus, Ohio: Merrill, 1973, 1978 (2nd ed.).

Shive, R. Jerrald. *Social studies as controversy.* Pacific Palisades, Calif.: Goodyear, 1973.

Shor, Rachel and Estelle A. Fidel, eds., *The Children's Catalog.* New York: H. W. Wilson Co., 1972.

Simon, Sidney B., Leland W. Howe, and Howard Kirschenbaum. *Values Clarification: A Handbook of Practical Strategies for Teachers and Students.* New York: Hart, 1972.

Singer, Harry. Substrata factor patterns accompanying development in power of reading, elementary through college level. In Eric Thurston and Lawrence Hafner, eds., *Philosophical and Sociological Basis of Reading.* Fourteenth Yearbook of the National Reading Conference, 1964, *14,* 41–56.

Singer, Harry. Research that should have made a difference. *Elementary English, 42,* 1970, 27–34.

Singer, Harry. Teaching word recognition. In Mildred Dawson, ed., *Teaching Word Recognition Skills.* Newark, Del.: International Reading Association, 1971.

Singer, Harry. Measurement of early reading ability: Norm-referenced, standardized tests for differential assessment of progress in learning how to read and in using reading for gaining information. In Phil Nacke, ed., Proceedings of the National Reading Conference, 1973a (Abstract).

Singer, Harry. *Preparation of Reading Content Specialists for the Junior High School.* Final Report. U.S. Office of Education, 1973b. ERIC Retrieval No. ED 088 003 CS 000 924.

Singer, Harry. The SEER technique: A non-computational estimate of readability. *Journal of Reading Behavior,* 1975, *7,* 255–267.

Singer, Harry. Substrata-factor patterns accompanying development in power of reading, elementary through college level. In H. Singer and R. B. Ruddell, eds., *Theoretical Models and Processes of Reading.* Newark, Del.: International Reading Association, 1976b.

Singer, Harry. Theoretical design for teaching reading. In H. Singer and R. B. Ruddell, eds., *Theoretical Models and Processes of Reading.* Newark, Del.: International Reading Association, 1976b.

Singer, Harry. IQ is and is not related to reading. In ERIC *Document Resumes,* July 1974, ED 088 004 MF $0.75 HC $1.85. Also in Stanley Wanet (ed.), *Issues in Evaluating Reading.* Arlington, Va: Center for Applied Linguistics, 1977.

Singer, Harry. Active comprehension: From answering to asking questions. *The Reading Teacher,* 1978a, *31,* 901–908. Revised version in Constance McCullough, ed., *Inchworm, Inchworm: Persistent Questions in Reading Education.* Newark, Del.: International Reading Association, 1979.

Singer, Harry. Attitudes towards reading and learning from text. Paper presented at National Reading Conference, St. Petersburg, Fla., 1978b.

ıger, Harry and Sherrel Beasley. Motivating a disabled reader. In Malcolm P. Douglas, ed., *Claremont Reading Conference Yearbook,* 1970.

Singer, Harry and Irving G. Hendrick. Total school integration: An experiment in social reconstruction. *Phi Delta Kappan,* 1967, *49,* 143–147.

Singer, Harry and Alan Rhodes. Learning from text: A review of theories, strategies, research at the high school level. In *Reflections and Investigations of Reading,* Twenty-Fifth Yearbook of the National Reading Conference, 1976.

Singer, Harry and Alan Rhodes. Problems, prescriptions, and possibilities in high school reading instruction. In Wayne Otto, Charles W. Peters and Nathaniel Peters, eds., *Reading Problems: A Multi-disciplinary Perspective.* Reading, Mass.: Addison-Wesley, 1977.

Singer, Harry and Robert B. Ruddell, eds., *Theoretical Models and Processes of Reading,* Second Edition. Newark, Del.: International Reading Association, 1976.

Singer, Harry, Jay Samuels, and Jean Spiroff. The effect of pictures and contextual conditions on learning responses to printed words. *Reading Research Quarterly,* 1973–1974, 9, 555–567.

Skoog, Karen. Tenth Grade Literature Unit on Medieval Tales and Legends (Exploring Life Through Literature, 1968). A term paper in senior author's course in Reading in the Content Areas, University of California, Riverside, 1974.

Smith, A. E. The effectiveness of training students to generate their own questions prior to reading. In P. L. Nacke, ed., *Diversity in Mature Reading: Theory and Research,* Twenty-Second Yearbook of the National Reading Conference, 1973.

Smith, Nila Banton. Patterns of writing in different subject areas, part I. *Journal of Reading,* 1964a, 8, 31–37.

Smith, Nila Banton. Patterns of writing in different subject areas, part II. *Journal of Reading,* 1964b, 8, 97–102.

Smith, Nila Banton. *American Reading Instruction.* Newark, Del.: International Reading Association, 1965a.

Smith, Nila Banton. Reading in subject matter fields. *Educational Leadership,* 1965b, 22, 382–385.

Smith, Richard J. and Wayne Otto. Changing teacher attitudes toward teaching reading in the content areas. *Journal of Reading,* 1969, 12, 299–304.

Smith, William L. The controlled instrument procedure for studying the effect of syntactic sophistication in reading: A second study. *Journal of Reading Behavior,* 1972–1973, 5, 242–251.

Spache, George. A new readability formula for primary grade reading materials. *Elementary School Journal,* 1953, 53, 410–413.

Spache, George. *Toward Better Reading.* Champaign, Ill.: Garrard, 1963.

Spache, George D. and Evelyn B. Spache. *Reading in the Elementary School.* Boston: Allyn and Bacon, 1969 (Second Edition), 1977 (Fourth Edition).

Stauffer, Russel G. A study of prefixes: The Thorndike List to establish a list of prefixes that should be taught in the elementary school. *Journal of Educational Research,* 1942, 35, 453–458.

Stein, Jess, editor-in-chief. *The Random House Dictionary of the English Language.* New York: Random House, 1973.

Stephens, John M. *Educational Psychology,* rev. ed. New York: Holt, 1956.

Sticht, Thomas, L. J. Beck, R. N. Hauke, G. M. Kleiman, and J. H. James. *Auding and Reading: A Developmental Model.* Monterey Calif.: Human Resources Organization, 1974.

Sticht, Thomas G., John S. Caylor, and Richard P. Kern. *Project Realistic: Evaluation and Modification of Reading, Listening, and Arithmetic Requirements in Military Occupations Having Civilian Counterparts.* Presidio of Monterey, Calif.: Human Resources Research Organization, 1970.

Sticht, Thomas G. and Howard H. McFann. Reading requirements for career entry. In Duane M. Nielsen and Howard F. Hjelm, eds., *Reading and Career Education.* Newark, Del.: International Reading Association, 1975.

Stone, L. Joseph and Joseph Church. *Childhood and Adolescence,* 3rd ed. New York: Random House, 1973.

Strang, Ruth. *Problems in the Improvement of Reading in High School and College.* Lancaster, Pa.: The Science Press, 1938.

Strang, Ruth. *Explorations in Reading Patterns.* Chicago: University of Chicago Press, 1942.

Strang, Ruth, Constance McCullough, and Arthur Traxler. *The Improvement of Reading,* Fourth Edition. New York: McGraw-Hill, 1967.

Taba, Hilda. The teaching of thinking. *Elementary English,* 1965, 42, 534–542.

Taba, Hilda. *Teachers' Handbook for Elementary Social Studies.* Palo Alto, Calif.: Addison-Wesley, 1967.

Tate, Walter Jackson. *Prefaces to criticism.* New York: Doubleday Anchor, 1959.

Taylor, W. L. Cloze procedure: A new tool for measuring readability. *Journalism Quarterly,* 1953, 30, 415–433.

Thelen, Judith. *Improving Reading in Science.* Newark, Del.: International Reading Association, 1976.

Thomas, Ellen Lamar. The role of the reading consultant. In H. Alan Robinson and Ellen L. Thomas, eds., *Fusing Reading Skills and Content.* Newark, Del.: International Reading Association, 1969.

Thomas, Ellen Lamar and H. Alan Robinson. *Improving Reading in Every Class.* Boston: Allyn and Bacon, 1972.

Thorndike, Edward L. *The Teaching of English Suffixes.* Columbia University Contributions to Education, No. 847. New York: Teachers College, Columbia University, 1941.

Thorndike, Edward L. Reading as reasoning: A study of mistakes in paragraph reading. *Journal of Educational Psychology,* 1917, 8, 323–332.

Thorndike, Edward L. and Clarence L. Barnhart. *In-*

termediate Dictionary. Garden City, N.Y.: Doubleday and Company, 1971.

Thorndike, Robert L. and Elizabeth Hagen. *Measurement and Evaluation in Psychology and Education,* 3rd ed. New York: John Wiley, 1969.

Thorndyke, Perry. Cognitive structure in human story comprehension and memory. Unpublished doctoral dissertation, Stanford University, 1975.

Tiegs, Ernest W. and Willis W. Clark. *California Achievement Tests,* Complete Battery. Monterey, Calif.: California Test Bureau/McGraw-Hill, 1963.

Tinker, Miles A. and Constance McCullough. *Teaching Elementary Reading,* 4th ed. Englewood Cliffs, N.J.: Prentice-Hall, 1975.

Toffler, Alvin. *Future Shock.* New York: Bantam, 1970.

Tolleson Union High School. *The Tolleson Story.* Unpublished research report. Tolleson, Arizona, 1973.

Tyack, David B. *Turning Points in American Educational History.* Waltham, Mass.: Blaisdel/Ginn, 1967.

Vanderlinde, Louis F. Does the study of quantitative vocabulary improve problem-solving? *Elementary School Journal,* 1964, *65,* 143–152.

Van Wagenen, Marvin J. *Van Wagenen Rate of Comprehension Scale.* Minneapolis: M. J. Van Wagenen, 1953.

Venezky, Richard L. Linguistics and spelling. In A. H. Markwardt, ed., *Linguistics in School Pro-*

grams. The Sixty-Ninth Yearbook of the National Society for the Study of Education, Part II. Chicago: University of Chicago Press, 1970.

Watts, Graime and Richard C. Anderson. Effects of three types of inserted questions on learning from prose. *Journal of Educational Psychology,* 1971, *62,* 387–394.

Wesley, Edgar B. and Stanley P. Wronski. *Teaching Secondary Social Studies in a World Society.* Lexington: D. C. Heath and Company, 1973.

Wiener, M. and Ward Cromer. Reading and reading difficulty: A conceptual analysis. *Harvard Educational Review,* 1967, *37,* 620–643.

Winograd, Terry. Understanding natural language. *Cognitive Psychology,* 1972, *3* (whole issue).

Wolfe, Helen M. A structure approach to pronouncing unfamiliar words. *Journal of Reading,* 1974, *17,* 356–362.

Wooton, William. The history and status of the school mathematics study group. In R. W. Heath, ed., *New Curricula.* New York: Harper & Row, 1964.

Wright, Richard. *Native Son.* New York: Harper & Row, 1940.

Zigler, Edward. Familial mental retardation: A continuing dilemma. *Science,* 1967, *155,* 292–298.

Zimmerman, Richard. Project report. Summarized in H. Singer, *Preparation of Reading Content Specialists for the Junior High School.* Final Report, U.S. Office of Education, 1973. ERIC No. Ed 088 003 CS 000 924.

Index